Economics and Policies of an Enlarged Europe

To Alexandra, Caterina, Olga, Silvia and Victoria

Economics and Policies of an Enlarged Europe

Carlo Altomonte

Bocconi University, Milan, Italy

Mario Nava

European Commission, Brussels, Belgium

Edward Elgar

Cheltenham, UK • Northampton, MA, USA

Published by
Edward Elgar Publishing Limited
Glensanda House
Montpellier Parade
Cheltenham
Glos GL50 1UA
UK

Edward Elgar Publishing, Inc.
136 West Street
Suite 202
Northampton
Massachusetts 01060
USA

A catalogue record for this book
is available from the British Library

ISBN 1 84376 832 1 (cased)

Printed and bound in Great Britain by MPG Books Ltd, Bodmin, Cornwall

Contents

Foreword

The European Union has changed radically since its inception in 1958. Over the years, the Union has progressively enlarged from the original six (Belgium, France, Germany, Italy, Luxembourg and the Netherlands) to the current 25 member states. As a result, its population has grown from 170 million to 460 million and its land area has increased from 1.2 million to nearly 4 million square kilometres. By comparison, the population of the United States has grown from 180 million to 280 million and its land area has stood at 9.4 million square kilometres. At the same time, the Union has evolved from a mere free trade area to a Single Market, with half of its member countries currently sharing a single currency, the Euro, which is already the world's second most important reserve currency behind the US dollar.

The latest enlargement of the European Union, which took place on 1 May 2004, is far larger and more challenging than the previous enlargements, which occurred in the 1970s (Denmark, Ireland and the United Kingdom), the 1980s (Greece, Portugal and Spain) and the 1990s (Austria, Finland and Sweden).

The 2004 eastern enlargement (Czech Republic, Estonia, Hungary, Latvia, Lithuania, Poland, Slovakia and Slovenia) and southern enlargement (Cyprus and Malta) presents both similarities and differences when compared with the southern enlargement to Mediterranean countries in the 1980s. In terms of size (population, GDP) relative to the EU total of the time, the rounds are quite similar. However the income gap between the new member states and the current EU is much larger than the one between the Mediterranean countries and the then EU. The accession of ten more countries has also added a dimension of complexity and heterogeneity that was not present in the previous round. At that time, enlargement increased the number of members by one-third (from nine to 12), whereas in 2004 the EU membership increased by two-thirds (from 15 to 25).

Because of the gap in income, convergence between the new member states and the current EU members is more than ever the key to successful enlargement. Neither theory nor the experience of earlier enlargement convincingly supports a hypothesis of automatic convergence. Convergence occurs only in the presence of certain key growth factors and supporting policies. Identification of these factors and assessing the extent to which they are present in the new member states are necessary to answer the question whether they are well equipped for rapid and sustained growth. On the one hand, the new member states have relatively high levels of human capital. On the other hand, they have a legacy of old industrial investment, environmental damage and poor public administration to remedy.

The new member states are not only poorer than the old ones; they are also structurally different. Against this background, it may be assumed that their economic priorities can differ, not only from those in the old member states, but also among themselves. This poses a double challenge with respect to EU-wide macroeconomic policy: first, how to ensure the necessary degree of fiscal discipline and coordination in a grouping of 25 countries with quite diverse macroeconomic and structural characteristics; and, second, how eventually to conduct a single monetary policy in a currency area with increased economic heterogeneity.

The increasing heterogeneity of the EU poses another challenge. The model of governance of the EU was initially conceived for a Community, which was small and homogenous as regards level of economic development. Successive rounds of wider and deeper integration have made the task of economic governance more and more complex. Challenges are already apparent in a wide range of policy domains, ranging from regulatory policies to the macroeconomic field. They could trigger a hollowing out of the intermediate layers of governance based on commitment and coordination to the benefit of the two 'corner solutions' of delegation and member state autonomy, unless the EU is able to achieve significant efficiency gains in making coordination and cooperation work better.

The volume by Carlo Altomonte and Mario Nava provides an excellent and pertinent economic analysis of the many challenges that lie ahead for the conduct of economic policies within the enlarged European Union. My hope, and my conviction, is that by reading this volume the reader will also appreciate the huge economic opportunities that lie ahead for the enlarged Union as it adapts its economic policies to the new domestic and global environment.

André Sapir
Brussels

Preface

Not surprisingly for two economists, the motivations behind the writing of this book lie in our analysis of the demand and the supply of educational material on the European Union (EU). As for the demand side, the students of all ages and nationalities who attended in the last five years our graduate and post-graduate courses in EU-related subjects across several EU Universities and Institutions have been giving us two crystal-clear indications. First, over the years they showed a growing interest in EU policies and in the EU integration process. Second, however increasing this interest was, it was accompanied by a growing critical attitude towards what they perceived as unintelligible EU policy making. Such a critical attitude, in the best tradition of academia, translated into a growing will to understand the rationale (be it political or economic) behind such policies. As a consequence, our supply of educational material has been trying, over the years, to keep pace with the increasingly changing process of EU integration, trying at the same time to respond to these two clear indications. It was therefore natural, at a certain point, to gather all this material into the organic framework of a book.

The book has been written in about 18 months, between July 2003 and December 2004, building on the desire to explain the roots of the economics and policies of the European Union and the will to assess them critically in light of the deeply changed framework of the EU integration process. In particular, our enterprise has been stimulated by the fact that the EU has successfully completed three enormous projects that seemed pure wishful thinking only a few years ago: the Euro, the 2004 enlargement with ten new countries, eight of which lying on the eastern side of the now fallen Iron Curtain, and the signing of the EU Constitution in Rome on 29 October 2004. Indeed much of the energy behind the book is due to the fact that both of us have been working, with different and changing responsibilities within EU-based institutions, towards achieving these goals, since we both remain genuinely convinced of the necessity of pursuing the remarkable adventure initiated by the founding fathers of Europe.

We trust that the combination of factual explanation and of critical assessment characterising the book and capitalising on our academic background and our professional experience within the EU institutions renders the book valuable within the current panorama of publications on the same subjects. However it goes without saying that this book has been written in our personal capacity only, and, while we gratefully acknowledge the permission to publish granted by the European Commission, it does not engage whatsoever any of the institutions with which we have been interacting, solely representing our personal opinions.

Clearly, in the process of writing this book, many people have generously helped us in many and different ways. Although we feel equally indebted towards all of them, there are two persons whose continuous presence, help and encouragement have been determinant in imbuing us with the necessary skills and will for writing this book. One is Carlo Secchi, professor of European Economic Policy at Bocconi University (and Rector between 2000 and 2004): first our European affairs professor in our *alma mater*, then our mentor, supporter, professional guide and many things else. The other is André Sapir, Chief Economist of the Group of Policy Advisors of the EU Commission President (between 2001 and 2004), gentle, patient, generous and inspiring intellectual guide and human and professional example.

We are also indebted to the many people with whom we had the chance to confront, over the last ten years, many ideas and theses that now feature in this book. Some agreed with us, some did not, some convinced and charmed us, some were eventually convinced by us: at any rate, they all were extremely important in the elaboration of the ideas behind our work, and very generous in sharing their ideas with us. This list is very composite since it includes people of different positions, work, seniority and age (some are unfortunately not with us any longer). Hence we have decided to list them in strict alphabetical order: Philippe Aghion, Sergio Alessandrini, Roberto Artoni, Tassos Belessiotis, Massimo Bordignon, Renato Brunetta, Marco Buti, Angelo Cardani, Alessandra Casarico, Antonio de Lecea, Alex Ellis, Sylvie Goulard, Alexis Jacquemin, Mick Keen, Wilhelm Kohler, Jozef Konings, Richard Layard, Ricardo Levi, Erkki Liikanen, Maurice Marchand, Wim Moesen, Mario Monti, Francesco Passarelli, Lucio Pench, Jean Pisani-Ferry, Silvano Presa, Antonio Preto, Romano Prodi, Peer Ritter, Luis Romero, Riccardo Rovelli, Elena Saraceno, Michaela Schreyer, Leo Sleuwaegen, Peter Martin Smith, Alexander Stubb, Guido Tabellini, Alessandro Turrini, Johan Ureel, Reinhilde Veugelers, Helen Wallace, David Wright, Maurizio Zanardi . . . and many, many others.

A special mention goes to the undergraduate and graduate students of Bocconi University and ISPI in Milan, who regularly lived through our courses or had their dissertation supervised by us: with their intellectual brilliance, they constituted a constant and fundamental source of stimuli for us, greatly contributing to the development of many of the analyses contained in this book.

We are particularly indebted to Stefano Riela, who jointly drafted with us the chapter of this book on competition policy and, together with Silvio Contessi, read different versions of our early drafts, providing us with very valuable contributions and suggestions. Pamela Cranston greatly helped us with the final formatting of the text.

Finally, but most importantly, we must thank our parents and siblings and Alexandra, Caterina, Olga, Silvia and Victoria, the five beautiful women of our lives who, with a broad palette of words, deeds and smiles, make each and every day worth living.

NOTE TO THE INSTRUCTORS

The book constitutes the material for a typical third-year undergraduate course in the economics of EU integration. In particular, the material is broadly organised in two parts. After an introductory chapter dealing with the very basic elements and key concepts of the European Union, from the Treaty of Rome to the European Constitution, the first part, covering Chapters 2 to 5, presents the economic tools underlying the process of European integration: the theory of economic integration (Chapter 2), the economics of the Single Market (Chapter 3), the Economic and Monetary Union (Chapter 4), and the rationale of the process of structural reforms known as 'Lisbon strategy' (Chapter 5). The second part of the book, covering Chapters 6 to 10, deals instead with the main EU policies, starting with the budget (Chapter 6), then the expenditure policies of agriculture (Chapter 7) and cohesion and growth (Chapter 8), the competition policy (Chapter 9), and the EU external policy, with a particular focus on the World Trade Organisation (Chapter 10). Finally, Chapter 11 concludes with a discussion on the main challenges that lie ahead of the European Union.

In every chapter we have tried to offer a short historical perspective, the current state of evolution of the discussed instrument or policy, and the implications that the enlargement of the Union to 25 member states will have on the same instrument or policy in the years to come. To aid the reader, we have highlighted in bold new concepts or keywords every time we have discussed them for the first time. We have also tried to keep pace with the most recent evolutions of the EU integration process which are likely to shed their influence in the following years. In particular, in Chapter 1 the reader will find a schematic discussion of the innovations possibly introduced by the EU Constitution. The March 2005 reform of the Stability and Growth Pact is discussed in detail in Chapter 4, while the Commission's draft of the new EU Financial Perspectives for the period 2007–13 are presented in Chapter 6. Chapter 10 also introduces the latest evolutions in the Doha Round of negotiations at the World Trade Organisation.

On the basis of our experience, the material presented in the book can be exhaustively taught in approximately 64 hours (8 ECTS), equally shared between the economics part and the one dealing with policies. Less advanced versions of the course (6 ECTS, 48 hours) can be taught skipping the analysis of economies of scale in Chapter 2, the history and working of the European Monetary System in Chapter 3, the debates on the future of Economic and Monetary Union and its enlargement in Chapter 4, the controversy on the EU income distribution in Chapter 5, and the technical Appendixes and Boxes in Chapters 6 to 10, without compromising the general readability of the text. A very large set of accompanying slides, which can be used as teaching material, is available, on request, from the publishing house.

1. The multiple dimensions of an enlarged Europe

1.1 THE HISTORICAL DIMENSION

Looking at the geopolitical map of Europe at the beginning of the twenty-first century, many unprecedented achievements characterise in various respects the evolution of the picture. For the first time, in fact, since Charlemagne's Holy Roman Empire in the ninth century, most of the European continent, that is, nowadays around 400 millions of citizens, are again united and in peace. For the first time in the entire history of Europe, this unification has taken place peacefully, according to the democratic will of the European people. For the first time, at least since the last century, a set of countries have autonomously decided to relinquish to a supranational authority the control of one of the key symbols of a nation, the national currency, without however renouncing their political independence and their national identity.[1] And the list could continue with many other innovations.

It is then natural to wonder how all these processes could have happened in such a relatively short period of time (less than 60 years), and what have been the driving forces behind them. A good starting point is to bear in mind that in Europe, historically, every period of war has ended with one or more treaties which have deeply changed the nature of the cohabitation of the states in the continent. The Treaty of Westfalia in 1648 ended the Thirty Years' War and balanced the power between European states, establishing the principles of individual sovereign nations that continue to shape the international system today. The Congress of Vienna was called in 1814 in order to re-establish a balance of power among the countries of Europe after the rise and fall of Napoleon I. The Paris Peace Conference ended World War I in 1919 and, in many respect, created the preconditions for World War II (WWII). The end of WWII, in turn, produced a series of treaties which, among other things, laid down the founding pillars of the modern European Union.

1.1.1 The First 40 Years: 1950–89

It is acknowledged that the start of the process of European integration (a complete chronology is reported in Box 1.1) can be identified in the so-called '**Schuman Declaration**', the speech by Robert Schuman, the French foreign minister, on 9 May 1950.[2] On that occasion, he proposed that France and Germany, and any other European country wishing to join them, pool their coal and steel resources. The content of the Schuman Declaration was deeply linked to the outcome of WWII and had very strong and controversial political implications. First of all, it was an opening of credit to Germany, only five years after the last Nazi tank had left the Champs Elysées in Paris. The Declaration thus implicitly recognised the new world order, that saw France and (West) Germany allied with the United States.[3] At the same time, it was also a way to guarantee the security of France with respect to Germany (which had already been at war with France three times since 1870): coal and steel were in fact key strategic resources for any possible programme of rearming, and thus putting them under an independent common control was a vital interest for France, if the country was to safely accept an alliance with Germany. Finally the opening up of the programme to other European countries was not only augmenting the economic gains achievable through the process,[4] but it was also perfectly consistent with the evolution of European relations with respect to the United States under the NATO Treaty.

Germany, led by Chancellor Konrad Adenauer, accepted the French proposal, and so did Italy (with its prime minister Alcide De Gasperi), Belgium, Luxembourg and the Netherlands. These countries signed on 18 April 1951 the Treaty of Paris, giving birth to the **European Coal and Steel Community (ECSC)**.[5] On 1 January 1953, the ECSC levy, the first commonly agreed European tax, came into force, while a common market for coal and iron ore was set into place, with the removal of custom duties and quantitative restrictions on these raw materials among the six member states. A European Court of Justice (ECJ) was set up in 1954, in order to rule on the decisions agreed within the ECSC.

Capitalising on this success, the six member states tried to further deepen the process of integration under the two dimensions embedded in the ECSC: the political (security) and the economic dimensions. From the political point of view, an attempt was made, right after the signing of the Treaty of Paris, to create a European Defence Community. The project was, however, ultimately rejected formally because of the objection of the French Assembly in 1954. More likely, the failure was due to the scant compatibility of such an autonomous European project of defence with the new system of international alliances characterising the bipolar world of those times.

In contrast, the economic pillar of the ECSC progressed: within a few years, the same six countries decided to go one step further and integrate several sectors of their economies other than coal and steel. In 1957, they signed the Treaties of Rome, creating the European Atomic Energy Community (EURATOM) and the **European Economic Community (EEC)**. In particular, the **Treaty establishing the European Community (TEC)** signed in Rome is still today (with its subsequent amendments, normally called treaties, followed by the name of the city where they have been agreed), the main legislative basis of the European Union. With the TEC, the member states set about removing trade barriers between them and started the (long) process of forming a **single market** (or common market), where the so-called '**four fundamental freedoms**' (free circulation of people, services, capital and goods) would be guaranteed (see Chapter 3 for a detailed discussion).

During the 1960s, owing to General De Gaulle's attitude of preserving as much as possible the French national interest, the European Community made no significant progress, a situation that ended in 1966, thanks to the introduction in the treaties of a special 'safeguard clause' (the **Luxembourg Compromise**) that allowed member states to call for a unanimous vote any time they judged their vital interests to be at stake. As a result of this new impetus, the next year the institutions of the three European communities (ECSC, EEC, EURATOM) were merged. From 1967 on, there was a single **Commission**, the independent body representing the general interest of the Community, a single **Council of Ministers**, representing the member states, and a **European Parliament**, representing the European citizens.[6]

On 1 July 1968, 18 months before the deadline foreseen, the **EEC Customs Union** entered into force. Remaining customs duties in intra-Community trade were abolished and a Common External Tariff (CET) was introduced, replacing national customs duties in the trade flows with the rest of the world (see Chapter 2). In 1970, with the signing of the Treaty of Luxembourg, the gradual introduction of a system of own-resources (the financial resources accruing autonomously to the European institutions) was set up, under which the Community will receive all customs duties on products imported from non-member countries, all levies on agricultural imports and part of the financial receipts deriving from each country's value-added tax (see Chapter 6). On 1 January 1973, the Community was enlarged for the first time to admit three new member states, the United Kingdom, Ireland and Denmark.[7]

The enduring Cold War in Europe prevented any path-breaking political achievement in the integration process during the 1970s and 1980s, with the significant exceptions of the accession of Greece, in 1981, and of Portugal and Spain in 1986. The European Economic Community, whose influence was crucial in restoring democracy in these countries, now included 12 member states. The economic pillar of the Community, however, continued to progress during this period. In 1979, the **European Monetary System (EMS)**, a system of quasi-fixed exchange rates among the member states, entered into force (see Chapter 3). In 1986, the 12 signed the **Single European Act (SEA)**, modifying the TEC in order to streamline the decision-making procedures, in particular introducing for the first time the principle of qualified majority voting in the Council.[8] As a result, the adoption of the necessary laws needed to complete the single market, originally planned in Rome in 1957, received a great boost, with the single market virtually completed, at least as far as the circulation of goods was concerned, by 1 January 1993 (see below and Chapter 3 for more details). At the same time, the idea of creating an Economic and Monetary Union (EMU) started to be explored, culminating in a report presented by the Commission's president of the time, Jacques Delors, in 1989.

The political scenario, however, radically changed at the end of 1989, with the disruption of the Eastern European side of the Soviet bloc, signalled by the fall of the Berlin Wall on 9 November. The end of the Cold War in Europe paved the way for a new treaty, set to change the relations among member states, reviving the dormant political pillar originally embedded in the historic nucleus of the integration process.

1.1.2 The Integration Process of an Enlarged Europe: 1990–2004

Owing to the historic changes which took place in 1989, the **European Council** held in Dublin in June 1990 opened two parallel **Intergovernmental Conferences (IGC)**[9] with the aim of reforming the existing treaties: one on the project of **Economic and Monetary Union (EMU)** and the other on possible aspects of a political union. The successful work of the two IGCs produced[10] a new **Treaty on the European Union (TEU)**, introducing a political dimension into the integration process through procedures for cooperation among member states in the area of 'common foreign and security policy' (in a sense reviving the old idea of a European Defence Community) and in the area of 'justice and home affairs'. These two new **pillars** would be directly run by the member states through the **intergovernmental method**: with unanimity and not always with the involvement of the Commission or the European Parliament. The two new pillars were added to the existing 'Community' pillar, that is, the set of EU policies established by the TEC, run instead through the **Community method**, that is, qualified majority voting (with some exceptions) by the Council and the Parliament together, on a proposal put forward by the European Commission.

The three-pillar system, and the cohabitation of the intergovernmental and Community methods, thus created what is known today as the **European Union (EU)**.

The agreements concluded in Maastricht also led to a profound revision of the Community pillar, since they introduced in the TEC the institutional provisions leading to the creation of the single currency. What became known in everyday jargon as the **Maastricht Treaty** thus ideally completed the economic dimension of the integration process, setting the rules (the so-called Maastricht 'criteria') and the time framework for the Economic and Monetary Union, the maximum possible step in the economic process of integration among countries (see Chapter 4 for further details).

In principle, it is possible to liken the evolution of the Community towards the European Union and the single currency to the process of formation of the Coal and Steel Community: even in this case, after the end of a war ('cold', but still a war), Europe goes through a profound reshaping of the relations among states, the most notable case being the 1990 German reunification; and, as had already happened with the ECSC, France and Germany, and then all the other member states wishing to do so, put under common control the 'strategic' asset of the time, money, in order to strengthen their mutual trust.[11]

Finally negotiations started at the beginning of the 1990s for the accession of three more countries to the European Union: Austria, Finland and Sweden. Given the status of these countries, the negotiations posed no particular problem,[12] and hence these countries became member states from 1 January 1995, thus increasing the number of countries to a total of 15 (what we refer to as EU-15 in this book).

However, even before 1995, the overall political scenario had already changed. In fact, one week after the new treaties were agreed upon in Maastricht, the EU signed, on 16 December 1991, its first cooperation agreements with Poland, Hungary and Czechoslovakia, and set up a specific financial programme for aid and reconstruction, the PHARE (the acronym for 'Poland and Hungary Aid and Reconstruction') programme. In the Copenhagen European Council of June 1993, the European heads of state and government then assured all the countries of Central and Eastern Europe (CEECs)[13] that they would become full members of the EU as soon as they satisfied the requisite political and economic conditions, the so-called **Copenhagen criteria**.[14] Thus, even before the new treaties agreed in Maastricht were in force (November 1993) and with the enlargement negotiations with Austria, Finland and Sweden still going on, Europe was bound to another set of institutional reforms needed to rebalance the relationships among its 15 current members and the future ones.

In all respects, enlarging the Union to admit the countries of Central and Eastern Europe was at the beginning of the 1990s a daunting task. Comparing the potential new enlargement to the most similar one to take place in the past, the enlargement of the 1980s involving Spain, Portugal and Greece, the differences were striking.[15] First of all, if done at once, the enlargement to the CEECs, although comparable in relative terms to the one of the 1980s, would have been in absolute terms the largest enlargement in the history of the Union, involving ten countries and almost 80 million new citizens. Second, and more importantly, the enlargement would have involved countries in transition from a planned to a market economy, still with severe macroeconomic imbalances and in need of a deep restructuring of their economies. Third, Europe would have opened its doors to significantly poorer countries, thus facing severe problems in terms of regional disparities and potential labour migration.[16] Fourth, the agricultural sector of these countries would have been in direct competition with the traditional products of the Common Agricultural Policy (corn, beef, milk), while the previous enlargement to the southern countries of Greece, Spain and Portugal was involving mainly Mediterranean products, complementary to the traditional continental ones. Finally the EU institutions, originally designed for six member states, and already stretched to encompass 15 members, would have been clearly inadequate to work, if left unreformed, in a system comprising 25 or more member states.

Notwithstanding these potential problems, the enlargement of the Union to the CEECs was considered, for various reasons (see Chapter 3), non-deferrable. As a result, after 1993, the European integration process acquired a triple dimension:

1. the completion of the Community pillar of integration, completing the single market with the creation of the Economic and Monetary Union;
2. a 'new start' (after the ECSC) in the construction of a European dimension in the two political pillars of foreign policy and justice and home affairs;
3. the implementation of the largest and most complex enlargement in the history of the Union.

The first two issues were tackled by a new Treaty agreed within the EU in Amsterdam, in 1997. In terms of the Community pillar, the heads of state and government formally endorsed in Amsterdam the so-called '**Stability and Growth Pact (SGP)**', an EU regulation which ideally complemented the legal framework agreed in Maastricht for the introduction of the common currency (see the next paragraph and Chapter 4 for a detailed description). In addition, a new title related to the coordination of employment and social policies in the EU was added to the TEC. Concerning the second pillar, the Amsterdam Treaty allowed (among other things) for the establishment of common strategies in the field of foreign policy first codified in the Maastricht Treaty, and created the figure of the EU High Representative of the Common Foreign and Security Policy (CFSP). In terms of justice and home affairs (the third EU pillar), many issues initially foreseen as a matter to be dealt with within member states (thus in an intergovernmental way) were, in the EU jargon, 'communitarised' by the Amsterdam Treaty, that is, were brought under the Community method, away from the direct influence, and the vetoes, of member states. In particular the Treaty of Amsterdam stated that the visa and asylum policies of the member states and all the immigration rules had to be progressively dealt with at the European, not national, level.

However the Treaty failed to tackle adequately the last dimension of the integration process, the implementation of an adequate institutional framework able to allow Europe to cope with a possibly enlarged number of members. In fact, no agreement was reached in Amsterdam on changes in the composition and working of the EU institutions, thus leaving the way open for a new round of talks among member states and, eventually, to a new Treaty. The reasons for this 'institutional' failure of the Treaty of Amsterdam are several. First of all, in 1997, the EU member states were still involved in the process of economic adjustment that should have led some of them (once they had matched the Maastricht criteria) to participate, starting from 1999, in the common currency. Hence the institutional framework, even within the current EU members of the time, was uncertain. Second, the situation of the potential new member states in Eastern Europe was still unclear, since the time span needed for these countries to match the Copenhagen criteria, and thus join the EU, was unknown. Finally the resources eventually available for enlargement were still unknown, given the fact that the new **Financial Perspectives** of the Union (the multiannual financial framework on which the EU budget is based, see Chapter 6) were not supposed to be renegotiated before 1999.

Notwithstanding the lack of reforms of the EU institutions emerging from the Amsterdam Treaty, the enlargement process kept on progressing during the second part of the 1990s, as soon as some of the uncertainties surrounding the operation had been progressively cleared. In 1997, the Commission recognised that the reforms in the Czech Republic, Estonia, Hungary, Poland, Slovenia and Cyprus allowed these countries to match both the political and the economic criteria agreed in Copenhagen. Hence negotiations between the EU and each of these countries could start (from March 1998) for the incorporation of the *acquis communautaire* in their internal legal systems (the third Copenhagen criterion).[17] The accession would have then been granted once the process had been completed. At the Helsinki European Council in December 1999, the same process was started with the remaining CEECs (Bulgaria, Latvia, Lithuania, Romania, Slovak Republic) and Malta. Turkey also gained the status of country candidate for membership, although no formal negotiations were started at the time, given the non-fulfilment by Turkey of the political and economic criteria (the first two Copenhagen criteria).

Still in 1999, a special meeting of the European Council in Berlin (in March) agreed the new Financial Perspectives of the Union for the period 2000–2006, creating a specific multiannual line of budget dedicated to the financing of the enlargement process.[18] Finally the common currency, the Euro, was also launched, from 1 January 1999, with 11 member states participating (Austria, Belgium, Finland, France, Germany, Ireland, Italy, Luxembourg, Netherlands, Portugal and Spain). Greece joined the EMU in 2001.

Following these achievements, and thus with a concrete perspective of an EU with 25 or more member states in the close future, a new Intergovernmental Conference was launched in January 2000, with the aim of reforming at least four fundamental items of the EU institutions and decision-making mechanisms.[19]

First, the **working and composition of the EU Commission** had to be dealt with. With 25 or more member states, a collegial body such as the Commission, where the 'large' member states (France, Germany, Italy, Spain and the UK) appointed two Commissioners and the 'small' member states one Commissioner each, was clearly inefficient. Therefore either the number of Commissioners must be reduced, or the agenda-setting powers of the President increased, or both.

Second, the **weighting of votes of member states at the Council** posed relevant problems since, in the decision-making procedures that did not require unanimity (see below), the Council used to decide with a qualified majority (around 70 per cent of votes), with each member state having a weight more or less proportional to the square root of its population; as a result, the system was naturally biased towards small member states. With the enlargement to the CEECs, however, most of the new members would have been small ones, and therefore the 'natural' bias of the system would have become unacceptable,[20] thus requiring a re-weighting of the votes.

Third, the enlargement also required a revision of the **number of topics agreed by unanimity or by qualified majority**. With the increase in the number of member states, it was in fact obvious that the more topics were left to be agreed on unanimously, the more the system would have lost in efficiency, risking being paralysed by cross-vetoes of the different countries (as had happened before the adoption of the Single European Act, when unanimity was the rule). However an equilibrium had to be found between two contrasting arguments. From one point of view, it would have been optimal to decide every topic, including foreign policy and internal affairs, by qualified majority (essentially, bringing it under the first 'Community' pillar, that is, under the control of the EU institutions) rather than unanimously in an intergovernmental way. However, looking at the question purely from an efficiency point of view, a similar gain in efficiency could have been obtained by simply bringing back each topic from a commonly agreed EU framework to the individual decisions of the single countries, thus depriving the EU institutions of some of the competences they acquired over time. Clearly the more topics are run at the Community level and under a qualified majority rule, the more the European Union tends towards a federal system, with member states progressively renouncing their national sovereignty over the different policy issues.

Finally the **composition of the European Parliament** had to be modified. The Treaty of Amsterdam had ruled that, in order to guarantee the democracy and efficiency of the institution, the total number of members of the European Parliament, that is, the sum of the members allocated to each member state in proportion to their population, could not exceed a maximum threshold of 700. Since the Parliament of the EU-15 already comprised 626 members, new national quotas had to be agreed for both the current and the forthcoming member states.

The **Nice Treaty**, agreed in December 2000 by the heads of state and government at the end of the IGC, and signed in February 2001, somehow managed to provide the answers to the questions raised above. First of all, from 2005, the composition of the EU Commission is limited to one Commissioner per member state. Once the Union numbers 27 countries, the number of Commissioners will be limited to a number lower than 27, with nationalities decided according to a rotating mechanism. The President is indicated (not appointed) by the European Council by qualified majority, and then he has to win, as presidential candidate, a 'confidence vote' by the European Parliament. Only then can he form his team, deciding the allocation of Directorates (portfolios) to each Commissioner proposed by the member states. The entire team is then subject to a confidence vote by the European Parliament. The President is however able to change over time each Commissioner's competences and can ask a single Commissioner to resign, thus overcoming what was in the past a joint responsibility of the Commission when faced with a lack of confidence by the European Parliament.[21]

In terms of the working of the Council, each country's weight in the voting system has been re-weighted owing to the entry of the new member states (see Table 1.1). The qualified majority is now subject to a double

Table 1.1 The current weighting of votes at the Council and seats at the EP in EU-25

Old member state	Votes	New member state	Votes
Austria	10 (4)	Bulgaria*	10
Belgium	12 (5)	Cyprus	4
Denmark	7 (3)	Czech Republic	12
Finland	7 (3)	Estonia	4
France	29 (10)	Hungary	12
Germany	29 (10)	Latvia	4
Greece	12 (5)	Lithuania	7
Ireland	7 (3)	Malta	3
Italy	29 (10)	Poland	27
Luxembourg	4 (2)	Romania*	14
Netherlands	13 (5)	Slovakia	7
Portugal	12 (5)	Slovenia	4
Spain	27 (8)		
Sweden	10 (4)		
United Kingdom	29 (10)		
Total	**237 (87)**	**Total**	**108**

Old member state	EP seats	New member state	EP seats
Austria	17 (21)	Bulgaria	17
Belgium	22 (25)	Cyprus	6
Denmark	13 (16)	Czech Republic	20
Finland	13 (16)	Hungary	20
France	72 (87)	Estonia	6
Germany	99 (99)	Latvia	8
Greece	22 (25)	Lithuania	12
Ireland	12 (15)	Malta	5
Italy	72 (87)	Poland	50
Luxembourg	6 (6)	Romania	33
Netherlands	25 (31)	Slovakia	13
Portugal	22 (25)	Slovenia	7
Spain	50 (64)		
Sweden	18 (22)		
United Kingdom	72 (87)		
Total	**535 (626)**	**Total**	**197**

Note: * Romania and Bulgaria will join in 2007; figures in brackets indicate the number of votes or seats before the Nice Treaty.

rule: first, the decision has to obtain a minimum number of votes agreed upon and changed as new accessions take place (comprising between 71.3 per cent for an EU with 15 countries and up to 74.8 per cent of votes for an EU with 27 countries); second, the decision has to obtain the vote of the majority of member states (for example, at least 13 countries have to agree upon a proposal, independent from their weight, in the current Union of 25 members).

Every member state can however ask for verification that the qualified majority so obtained includes the votes of countries making up at least 62 per cent of total EU population. The lack of such a threshold will impair the decision.[22]

In terms of unanimity versus qualified majority, around 30 EU competences up to the Nice Treaty requiring unanimity have been moved to a qualified majority decision-making procedure, among them judiciary and civil cooperation, multilateral agreements on services and appointment of the President of the EU Commission.

Finally the composition of the European Parliament has been changed, fixing 732 members as a new, maximum threshold, with a re-weighting of seats of each member state, as indicated in Table 1.1.

The Treaty of Nice entered into force on 1 February 2003. It is the legal framework on which the EU is currently built and, thanks to the agreed changes in the working of the EU institutions, it constitutes the necessary juridical base for the enlarged European Union. The new member states of Eastern Europe (including Malta and Cyprus) in fact completed, with the exception of Bulgaria and Romania, their process of adoption of the Community *acquis* by December 2002 and, therefore, satisfying all three Copenhagen criteria, have joined the European Union since 1 May 2004, thus making up what we refer to as the current EU-25. Bulgaria and Romania are expected to join by 2007 at the earliest, while negotiations have been going on with Turkey. Some countries of the Balkans (with Croatia at the forefront) are also currently negotiating their accession to the enlarged European Union.

1.1.3 Towards a European Constitution? 2005 and Beyond

After the signing of the Treaty of Nice, and the different compromises it needed in order to be finalised, the heads of state and government annexed to the draft treaty a Declaration (the 'Declaration N. 23 on the Future of the Union') in which they stated that, having opened the way to the enlargement of the Union by the changes agreed in the new treaty, it was however necessary to start 'a deeper and wider debate about the future of the European Union', in terms of better defining its nature, its institutions and its role in the world. In particular, it was already agreed that, following a report to be drawn up for the European Council in Gothenburg in June 2001, the European Council, at its meeting in Laeken/Brussels in December 2001, would have produced a declaration containing appropriate initiatives in this sense.

The following **Laeken Declaration**, approved on 15 December 2001, stated that, after 50 years of its integration process,

> the Union stands at a crossroad, a defining moment in its existence. The unification of Europe is near. The Union is about to expand to bring in more than ten new member states, predominantly Central and Eastern European, thereby finally closing one of the darkest chapters in European history: the Second World War and the ensuing artificial division of Europe. [. . .] What is Europe's role in this changed world? Does Europe not, now that it is finally unified, have a leading role to play in a new world order; that of a power able both to play a stabilising role worldwide and to point the way ahead for many countries and peoples?

In order to explore these issues further, and to start deriving some institutional answers, as a follow-up to the Laeken Declaration the European Council decided to convene a **Convention**, a discussion forum composed of the main parties involved in the debate on the future of the Union. As a result, one representative of the governments of the 15 member states and the 13 (including Turkey) candidate countries at the time, representatives of their national Parliaments, representatives of the European Parliament and of the European Commission, 13 observers from the Committee of the Regions and the Economic and Social Committee, plus representatives of the European social partners were invited to participate in the Convention, which started in Brussels on 28 February 2002.

The same Laeken Declaration established the mandate of the 105 members of the Convention and their alternates, under the chairmanship of Giscard d'Estaing, former French president. The aim was to examine the essential questions raised by the future development of the Union, and to seek responses to be presented in a document which would have been used as the starting point for the negotiations of a future IGC on institutional developments. In particular, following the Nice agenda previously discussed, the institutional issues under scrutiny by the Convention were related to a better distribution of the Union's powers, a simplification of the instruments whereby the Union takes action, better guarantees of democracy, transparency and effectiveness in the Union, a simplification of the current treaties, and their transformation into a veritable European Constitution.

BOX 1.1 THE EU CHRONOLOGY

- 9 May 1950: In a speech inspired by Jean Monnet, Robert Schuman, the French foreign minister, proposes that France and Germany, and any other European country wishing to join, pool their coal and steel resources ('Schuman Declaration').
- 18 April 1951: The Six (Belgium, France, Germany, Italy, Luxembourg, Netherlands) sign the Treaty of Paris establishing the European Coal and Steel Community (ECSC).
- 25 March 1957: The treaties establishing the European Economic Community (EEC) and the European Atomic Energy Community (EURATOM) are signed by the Six in Rome; thereafter they will be referred to as the Treaties of Rome.
- 1 July 1967: The Merger Treaty, fusing the Executives of the European Communities (ECSC, EEC, EURATOM), enters into force. A single Commission and a single Council are established.
- 1 July 1968: the Common External Tariff of the EU Customs Union enters into force.
- 1 January 1973: Denmark, Ireland and the United Kingdom join the EEC.
- 13 March 1979: The Paris European Council creates the European Monetary System (EMS).
- 7–10 June 1979: First elections to the European Parliament by direct universal suffrage.
- 1 January 1981: Greece joins the EEC.
- 17 February 1986: The Single European Act modifying the Treaty of Rome is signed, paving the way for the completion of the single market. It enters into force on 1 July 1987.
- 1 July 1986: Portugal and Spain join the EEC.
- 1 July 1990: The first phase of the Economic and Monetary Union (EMU) comes into force, with free capital mobility established in the single market.
- 10–11 December 1991: The Maastricht European Council sets up the Treaty on the European Union (TEU), introducing the two 'pillars' of common foreign and security policy and justice and home affairs; it also amends the Treaty of the European Community (TEC) with the provisions related to the monetary union. One week after, Europe

Agreements are signed with Poland, Hungary and Czechoslovakia.

- 1 January 1993: The completion of the Single Market Programme removes all the obstacles to the free circulation of goods in the single market, still to be completed as far as services and people are concerned.
- 22 June 1993: The Copenhagen European Council grants membership to the countries of Central and Eastern Europe as soon as they satisfy the required political and economic criteria.
- 1 January 1994: Stage II of economic and monetary union begins.
- 1 January 1995: Austria, Finland and Sweden join the European Union.
- 17 June 1997: The European Council meets in Amsterdam and stipulates a draft treaty.
- 30 March 1998: A ministerial meeting launches the accession process for five Central and Eastern European applicant countries (Czech Republic, Estonia, Hungary, Poland, Slovenia) and Cyprus.
- 3 May 1998: A special European Council decides that 11 member states satisfy the conditions for adopting the single currency on 1 January 1999. The President of the European Central Bank (ECB) is appointed. The ECB takes up its functions on 1 July.
- 1 January 1999: The Euro is officially launched. Austria, Belgium, Finland, France, Germany, Ireland, Italy, Luxembourg, The Netherlands, Portugal and Spain adopt it. Greece joins in 2001.
- 12 December 1999: The Helsinki European Council launches the accession process with the remaining applicant countries of Eastern Europe (Bulgaria, Latvia, Lithuania, Romania, Slovakia) and Malta. Turkey gains the status of candidate country but no negotiations are started.
- 7–8 December 2000: A new treaty is signed in Nice, amending the working of the EU institutions in light of the enlargement of the Union.
- 15 December 2001: The Laeken Declaration launches the constitutional process of reform.
- 28 February 2002: The national currencies cease to have legal value in the EMU. Euro banknotes and coins enter

circulation. The Convention for institutional reforms starts its work in Brussels.

- 12–13 December 2002: The Copenhagen European Council officially close the accession negotiations with ten applicant countries; a financial package is agreed for each of the years 2004, 2005, 2006.
- 1 February 2003: The Treaty of Nice, the current EU juridical base, enters into force.
- 16 April 2003: The accession treaties for the ten new member states are signed in Athens.
- 20 June 2003: The Convention presents the text of a draft Constitution to the heads of state and government in Salonika. The IGC conference for the constitutional round of reforms starts in Rome in October.
- 1 May 2004: Following the ratification of the accession treaties, ten new member states join the European Union: Cyprus, Czech Republic, Estonia, Hungary, Latvia, Lithuania, Malta, Poland, Slovakia and Slovenia.
- 8–13 June 2004: a reunified Europe elects in 25 member states the new members of the European Parliament for the 2004–9 legislature.
- 18 June 2004: the text establishing the EU Constitution is agreed in Brussels by the European Council.
- 29 October 2004: the Constitution is officially signed in Rome; the process of ratification starts in each of the 25 member states.
- 22 November 2004: the new European Commission starts its works. It will stay in office until 2009.
- 17 December 2004: the EU decides to open accession negotiations with Turkey.

The Convention met over a period of 15 months in plenary sessions lasting two or three days, and involving one or two monthly meetings in the premises of the European Parliament in Brussels. In parallel with the Convention's plenary sessions, work was also organised within working groups, focusing on a series of specific topics. At the end of this work, the Convention reached a consensus on a draft **Constitution for the European Union**, submitted to the Salonika European Council on 20 June 2003.[23]

More specifically, the draft Constitution reorganises in a single text all the existing treaties, adding some significant improvements. It consists of four parts. Part I contains the provisions which define the Union, its objectives, its powers, its decision-making procedures and its institutions. The Charter of Fundamental Rights of the European Union, solemnly proclaimed at the beginning of the Nice European Council in December 2000, has been incorporated into the draft European Constitution as Part II. Part III of the draft Constitution focuses on the Union's policies and actions and incorporates many of the provisions of the current treaties. Part IV contains the final clauses, including the procedures for adopting and reviewing the Constitution. Box 1.2 presents in some detail the major innovations put forward by the European Constitution.

The text submitted by the Convention served as the basis for the work of the Intergovernmental Conference, still legally needed to ratify all the proposed institutional changes and write a new Treaty. The IGC started in October 2003 in Rome, failed to reach an agreement at its first scheduled meeting of December 2003, but was then successfully concluded on 18 June 2004, in Brussels. On that occasion, the 25 heads of state and government politically approved the **Treaty establishing a Constitution for Europe**, which was then formally signed in Rome on 29 October of the same year, as a sign of continuity with the Treaties of Rome which originally gave birth to the European Community in 1957. In fact, for the first time, the EU members did not approve amendments to an existing treaty (TEC or TEU), but set up an entirely new comprehensive treaty to act as the reformed legal basis of the European Union.

At the time of printing, the text has started the uncertain process of ratification by the 25 member states, discussed in the last chapter of the book.

BOX 1.2 THE MAIN INSTITUTIONAL CHANGES CONTAINED IN THE EUROPEAN CONSTITUTION*

The Constitutional Treaty establishes only one European Union endowed with juridical personality, thus replacing the present 'European Communities' (TEC) and the 'European Union' (TEU) with the 'Treaty establishing a Constitution for Europe'. The three 'pillars' of the EU policy will be merged, even though special procedures in the fields of foreign policy, security and defence are maintained. The integration of the Charter for Fundamental Rights into the text, the clear acknowledgment of the Union's values and objectives as well as the principles underlying the relationship between the Union and its member states allow us to attribute to this basic text the status of 'Constitution'. In legal terms, however, the Constitution remains a treaty. Therefore it will enter into force only when all member states have ratified it (see the concluding chapter of the book). It should also be noted that any modification of the Constitution at a later stage will require the unanimous agreement of the member states and, in principle, ratification by all. For some modifications, however – for example with regard to the extension of the scope of qualified majority voting (see below) – a unanimous decision by the European Council will suffice.

Like other constitutional charters, this text also contains a clearer presentation of the distribution of competences between the EU and the member states and a hierarchy of acts. In particular, distinctions are drawn between three categories of Union powers: areas of exclusive competence, where only the EU Institutions can act (common commercial policy and customs union, competition policy, monetary policy), areas of shared competence (where member states can act provided that the Union has not already done so: for example most of the EU policies) and areas where the Union may only take supporting actions to those undertaken by the member states (for example in the fields of education or health care). Particular cases that do not fit into the general classification are dealt with separately: for example, the coordination of economic and employment policies and common foreign and security policy. In terms of a hierarchy of acts, the Constitution abolishes all the previous categories of acts produced by the EU institutions (directives, regulations, decisions, opinions and so on) and establishes a distinction between legally binding acts (defined as laws, framework laws, regulations and decisions) and non-binding acts (opinions and recommendations); within the legally binding acts, a further distinction is made between legislative acts (laws and framework laws) and non-legislative acts (regulations and decisions).

As far as the legislative acts are concerned, the Constitution restates that the power of legislative initiative lies with the Commission, although this is shared with at least a quarter of member states as regards certain aspects of the area of freedom, security and justice. The draft Constitution also states that, as a general rule, laws and framework laws are to be adopted by codecision of the EP and the Council, the latter with a qualified majority, a procedure to be known as the 'ordinary legislative procedure', which is practically an extended version of the current procedure. As a result, 95 per cent of all European laws will be adopted jointly by the Parliament and the Council once the Constitution enters into force.

In particular, the definition of qualified majority for the co-decision making in the Council has been changed with respect to the Nice Treaty: a qualified majority will require the support of 55 per cent of the member states representing 65 per cent of the population, thus abolishing the vote-weighting system traditionally characterising the decision making at the Council. However, two further elements of guarantee have been introduced. First, in order to avoid the situation where, in an extreme case, only three (large) member states would be able to block a Council decision thanks to an increase in the population threshold, a blocking minority needs to comprise at least four member states. Moreover a number of Council members representing at least three-quarters of a blocking minority, whether at the level of member states or at the level of population, can demand that a vote be postponed and that discussions continue for a reasonable time in order to reach a broader basis of consensus within the Council.

In terms of institutional changes, the main innovation is the creation of the post of Union minister of foreign affairs, who will be responsible for the representation of the Union on the international scene. This function will merge the present tasks of the High Representative for the Common Foreign and Security Policy with those of the Commissioner for external relations. The minister of foreign affairs will thus be mandated by the Council for common foreign and security policy, while being a full member of the Commission and as such in charge of the Commission's responsibilities in the field of external relations as well as of the coordination of the other aspects of the Union's external action; in addition, he will chair the External Relations Council. The Union's newly acquired single legal personality will also enable it to play a more visible role in world affairs.

The Constitution also establishes the European Council as an institution, distinct from the Council. The European Council will be chaired by a president, with limited powers, appointed for a period of two and a half years. On the other hand, and in contrast to what had been proposed by the Convention, the system of twice-yearly rotation among the member states of the presidency of the different Council formations (with the exception of the External Relations Council) will be maintained, although within a 'team presidency' of three countries. This system will be able to evolve in the future since it can be altered by the European Council acting by qualified majority.

As to the composition of the institutions, the IGC finally decided to raise the maximum number of seats in the European Parliament to 750. These seats will be allocated to the member states according to the principle of 'degressive proportionality', with a minimum of six and a maximum of 96 seats. The precise number of seats attributed to each member state will be decided before the European elections in 2009. It was also decided to maintain the current composition of the Commission (one Commissioner per member State) until 2014. From then on, the Commission will comprise a number of Commissioners corresponding to two-thirds of the number of member states. The members of the Commission will be chosen according to a system based on equal rotation among the member states, which had already been decided by the Nice Treaty.

The Constitution also significantly updates provisions in the field of justice and home affairs, in order to facilitate and improve the establishment of the area of freedom, security and justice. In fact, the standard community method will from now on apply to all the areas in question, thus falling to a large extent within the scope of qualified majority voting. Nevertheless the Constitution retains or introduces some special features in these areas, namely judicial cooperation in criminal matters and police cooperation.

The provisions regarding external relations have been rewritten, but, in essence, the distinction between common foreign and security policy and the other aspects of EU external action still determines the respective roles of the institutions and the procedures that apply. Nevertheless the possibility now admitted of providing more ways for the member states to cooperate more closely in the field of defence will underpin the credibility of the Union's foreign policy.

For some other policies, the essential changes are limited to a further extension of the scope of qualified majority and a near generalisation of the codecision procedure. It should be noted that, in addition to some specific provisions, unanimity is however retained in the field of taxation, on the EU budget (both on the expenditures and the revenues side) and, partially, in the field of social policy and common foreign and security policy. Although 'passerelles' allow, via a unanimous decision, that henceforth qualified majority will apply in a given area without modifying the treaty, it remains to be seen whether the existence of such clauses will be sufficient to maintain the Union's capacity to act.

Note: * We report here extracts from a summary text prepared by the European Commission. The document has no legal status or ambition; therefore our synthesis is only meant to provide prompt information on the European Constitution. The experienced reader might thus want to refer directly to the draft text of the Constitution (available at http://www.europa.eu.int/constitution/index_en.htm).

1.2 THE ECONOMIC AND SOCIAL DIMENSION

In the historical events so far analysed we have presented a series of tools of economic policy (customs union, single market, common currency). Their development by the EU policy makers can then be used as a pathway to assess the route the EU has decided to follow in order to attain its ultimate economic and social goals. Indeed, once the goals became progressively clearer over the last 50 years of European integration, the EU tools grew in number and importance. Hence we start by first introducing the objectives of the EU economic and social policy and then the tools available to achieve those objectives. Since the analysis of the different tools available to the different actors of the EU economic system (EU institutions, member states and regions) is the focus of this book, by introducing them we are also able to detail the structure of the book.

1.2.1 The Objectives of the EU Economic and Social Policy

Over the last 50 years the European Union has agreed to pursue three main objectives of economic policy: **growth, stability** and **cohesion**.[24] These three goals are not only objectives of economic policy, but also the defining cornerstones of the EU economic and social model, since the EU considers, with a deliberate political attitude, that the three objectives have to be pursued jointly, thus reinforcing one another. In other words, the EU does not pursue economic growth per se, but together with stability (mainly defined in terms of low inflation rates) and cohesion (a low level of disparities both within and across countries).

It is of course not surprising that the EU pursues **economic growth**, a standard objective of almost any economic policy. In this respect, Europe has traditionally had a very good record of growth since World War II. At the end of the war, per capita income of the EU stood at only 45 per cent of the US figure. By 1975, however, after 30 years of sustained growth only interrupted by the first oil shock, the per capita income of the EU reached 70 per cent of the US level. During these 30 years, known as '*les Trente* *glorieuses*', Europe displayed higher growth rates than the USA and was therefore able to achieve a convergence in per capita income towards the US values. After 1975, however, growth in Europe slowed down and per capita income convergence stopped – this notwithstanding the fact that, since the 1970s, US demographic growth has been greater than the European: therefore, in recent decades European aggregate income has grown less than US income. It is only natural, then, that since 2000 the EU has set reviving growth as a top priority for the next decade.

However, for all the emphasis the EU places on growth, Europeans have rejected growth as a single and only objective. The EU in fact believes that a model of economic development aiming uniquely at achieving the highest possible growth rates, without consideration of its distribution and of its environmental impact, is not sustainable in the long run. The goal of the EU therefore is to achieve **sustainable growth**, which respects the environment, which is robust over time (that is, it does not lead to inflationary pressures) and which is equitably distributed across its citizens.

Stability, within the EU economic model, then means essentially two things: stable prices (low inflation rates) and sound finances. The evolution of stability over the last 50 years is very different from the evolution of growth. The EU had relatively high stability until 1973, then followed by a period of prolonged instability that lasted until the Maastricht Treaty (1993), which marks a decisive turning point in this respect. Through this treaty, in fact, the member states, in order to join the European and Monetary Union, had to set and abide by quantitative limits in terms of deficit, debt, interest rates and inflation (the 'Maastricht criteria'). Such behaviour allowed, during the second half of the 1990s, a spectacular recovery of stability: public deficits and inflation have since then been brought down to historically very low levels (see Chapter 4 for more details).

Cohesion is not always quoted as an explicitly declared objective in the economic policy agenda of non-European countries.[25] A high level of cohesion means essentially a low level of total inequality in the distribution of income. As will be discussed throughout the book, total income inequality can itself be decomposed as the sum of 'across-countries inequality' and 'within-country inequality'. The first refers to the difference in the level of richness across countries (for example, the German per capita income is higher than the Greek one). The latter refers to the distribution of richness within countries, that is, how great is the distinction between levels of income of rich and poor people, however defined, within a country. The EU has historically enjoyed a very high level of cohesion: total income inequality somewhat decreased over the last 30 years (and reached its minimum in the 1980s) being some 30 to 40 per cent lower than in the USA (see Chapters 5 and 8 for more details). However, when this result is decomposed in 'within-country inequality' and 'across-countries inequality', the picture is totally different. While inequality within countries first fell from 1970 to 1980, and subsequently rose back to the 1970s levels by the late 1990s, inequality across countries fell by half between 1970 and 2000, with a particularly sharp decrease starting in the 1980s.

On the one hand, one can thus see that the ability to reduce within-country inequality seems to be in direct proportion to growth: the reduction was high in periods of high growth (such as the 1960s to the 1980s) and much smaller or non-existent in periods of moderate growth (such as the 1980s to 2000). On the other hand, the ability to reduce across-countries inequality seems to be linked to specific policies of European integration and cohesion, which were substantially implemented only after the mid-1980s. Thus higher growth rates might decrease within-country inequalities but not necessarily across-countries inequalities, with an ambiguous impact on total inequality. At the same time, wrong cohesion policies can negatively interfere with growth. If the two policies are instead coordinated, higher growth for the poor regions translates into higher cohesion, and higher cohesion, reducing countries' heterogeneity of preferences, allows a more efficient decision-making process towards common policies stimulating growth. It is precisely because of this reason that the EU economic policy focuses simultaneously on cohesion and growth.

In sum, we can therefore state that the particularity of the EU social and economic model, often referred to as a **'social market economy'**, consists not only in its choice of these three goals, but also in its declared will to pursue these three goals simultaneously.

1.2.2 The Tools for the EU Economic and Social Policy

This book is organised around the policy tools necessary to achieve the EU goals detailed above. Two main categories of tools can be identified: (a) those managed in a decentralised way at the national level, but subject to commonly agreed targets and constraints; (b) those managed in a centralised way at the EU level, but subject to decentralised targets and constraints. To this purpose, it is worth mentioning here two key juridical principles on which the Union is based, and which dictate the limits of its competences.

Under the **principle of conferral**, the Union can act only 'within the limits of the powers conferred upon it' by the member states (TEC, art. 5, para. 1), that is, for a competence to be exercised at the EU level, the member states have to attribute it explicitly to the EU institutions, considering that this is the best way of achieving the goals previously described.

Under the **principle of subsidiarity**, the Union can act 'only if and insofar as the objectives of the intended action cannot be sufficiently achieved by the member states and can therefore, by reason of the scale or effects of the proposed action, be better achieved' by the Union (TEC, art. 5, para. 2). This means, for example, that it does not make sense for the EU institutions to set the hour of turning on street lights across the whole of Europe, since local authorities can more efficiently deal with the issue; however, owing to relevant externalities, it is maybe more efficient to have the EU institutions decide the environmental policy for the Union, rather than leave it to each member state.

By and large, the first part of this book (Chapters 2 to 5) deals with those tools which, consistently with the two principles discussed above, have a decentralised management but are subject to EU-decided targets and constraints. The second part (Chapters 6 to 10) deals instead with specific policies that, under the principle of subsidiarity, are better suited to a centralised management and therefore have been conferred upon the EU institutions, subject to decentralised national constraints.[26]

Historically the EU toolbox evolved along with the process of integration, from a set of unrelated tools with few objectives to an organic web of related objectives to be pursued via different tools. In other words, nowadays not only does each objective have in principle its own tools, but also each tool very often has more than one objective. In particular, the evolution has had five key moments:

1. the implementation of a **Customs Union (CU)** and of a **Common External Tariff (CET)**, since 1968;
2. the implementation of the **Single Market Programme** as a strategic objective for the period 1986 to 1992;
3. the adoption of the **Financial Perspectives** in 1988, which were meant to structure, within a single instrument (the EU budget), the *multi-annual* economic policy at the EU level;
4. the progressive establishment of the **Economic and Monetary Union (EMU)** from 1993 and its related rules (namely, the Maastricht criteria and the Stability and Growth Pact);
5. the adoption of the so-called '**Lisbon Agenda**' in March 2000.

Though these projects could and should still be improved in many respects,[27] they have constituted the driving forces for a coherent economic policy in the EU. In fact, by relying on the Custom Union, on the Single Market Programme, on the Financial Perspectives, on the EMU and on the Lisbon Agenda, the Union endeavours to achieve an economic space wherein growth, stability and cohesion are jointly obtained and self-reinforcing. We shall look at these five defining moments in turn, and we shall explore how these will be affected by the enlargement of the Union to admit the new Central and Eastern European members. This, in essence, identifies the plan of the book.

First, as previously mentioned, the EU successfully implemented a Customs Union from 1968, before the deadline foreseen in the Treaties of Rome. Under a single CU every government levies EU custom duties instead of national custom duties. Goods entering and paying duties in a country gain free circulation in all of the EU, while the revenues from the CET accrue to the EU budget (after deduction of a collection fee for the collecting member state). In general a Customs Union is a precondition to achieve growth in an economic integrated area. It is also generally the first step (and sometimes remains the only one) of any attempt at forming political unions. Chapter 2 deals with this issue, while Chapter 10 will explore the external implications of the EU common commercial policy.

Second, the Single Market Programme is a complex network of legislative proposals launched by the Commission back in 1985 with the aim of boosting growth by eliminating barriers in the circulation not only of goods, but also of services, capital and people across countries, thus fostering competition and increasing productivity levels. More competition and greater productivity facilitate the reallocation of resources, which in turn leads to higher growth. It is in general acknowledged that, by 1 January 1993, the single market for goods was a reality. The single market for capital, persons and services has made great improvements with respect to the pre-1992 situation;[28] however, nowadays, it cannot be judged as complete. In some cases, in fact, the geographical dimension of the internal market does not coincide with the EU (as regards, for example, the free circulation of persons); in other cases, the free circulation does not concern all the items of each category (namely capital and services). Competition policy also plays a central part in enhancing the performance of the single market by enforcing at the EU level both the antitrust and state aid policy. Chapter 3 deals with the single market issue in greater detail, especially in terms of its enlargement to the new member states, while Chapter 9 deals with the contribution of competition policy to EU growth.

Third, Jacques Delors, late president of the European Commission, was the architect of the Financial Perspectives (FP) in the 1980s. The FP are rightly celebrated as a turning point in EU public finances, since they transform the EU budget from a set of annual ad hoc measures into an instrument of multiannual programming to deliver cohesion and growth in the EU. The financial perspectives are intimately connected with the single market since they meant to be the 'federal' financial tool to help decentralised national governments to adopt the measures necessary for the removal of the obstacles of the single market. The first FP had the great merit of forcing the EU budget to move progressively away from the Common Agriculture Policy. As a result, the EU budget started to pursue directly two of the EU objectives previously mentioned: cohesion (across regions and across countries via the so-called structural policy) and growth (by financing research and education programmes). The Delors Commission understood that the financial perspectives could be a way to balance the opening up of all EU markets and their integration into a single market. In fact, the single market was in the first place mainly beneficial for the richest countries: the Financial Perspectives, by introducing a structural programme of support to the poorest areas of the EU, corrected this imbalance, in favour of the poorest countries. In particular, the aim was to foster the poorest countries' income convergence towards the rest of the Union, making sure that, in due time, these countries could also benefit from the single market. Chapter 6 deals with these budgetary issues in greater detail, while Chapter 7 (agricultural policy) and 8 (cohesion and growth) show the evolution of the single policies within the financial perspectives over time, again with a particular focus on the implications brought by the latest enlargement of the Union.

Fourth, the establishment of an Economic and Monetary Union (EMU) has been above all a political step towards an ever-closer Union consciously taken by member states. Few things bond countries together more than their currency, since a currency is as intimately part of a country as its flag or its anthem.[29] However political the decision is, its implementation and the related rules have nevertheless a very well grounded economic nature, aiming at promoting growth and stability in the EU. On the one hand, to guarantee the full success of the EMU, the member states have adopted a number of rules and regulations aimed at fixing objectives and constraints to their national fiscal policies. The Maastricht criteria, for example, fix annual limits to each country's debt, deficit, inflation and interest rates. The Stability and Growth Pact (SGP), adopted by the EU Council in 1997, fixes annual and long-term objectives for the national budget deficits. On the other hand, in order to guarantee price stability, the heads of state and governments created an independent authority, the European Central Bank, and entrusted it with the primary objective of maintaining price stability. As a result the policy stance in the context of the EMU is the result of the use of two very different tools: national fiscal policies, decentralised but subject to a centralised constraint (essentially the Stability and Growth Pact) and a single monetary policy, centrally driven with homogeneous targets across the EU. Chapter 4 deals in greater details with these issues.

Fifth, the heads of state and government met in Lisbon in March 2000 with the intention of sketching the EU economic objectives for the next decade. The lower than expected growth performance in the 1990s and the need to maintain and update the European economic and social model are the driving forces behind the ambitious agenda agreed in Lisbon, which does not introduce any new tools to the picture (as in the four previous cases), but rather aims at setting up a strategy able to improve the performance of the existing economic system. The resulting Lisbon Agenda in fact sets out a roadmap for the EU's economic and social renewal in the medium to long term, revisiting the traditional EU objectives and setting a new strategic goal for the EU: 'to become the most competitive and dynamic knowledge-based economy in the world capable of sustainable economic growth with more and better jobs and greater social cohesion' (EU Council, 2000). The greatest potential of the Lisbon Agenda lies, in our opinion, in the coordinated nature of the reforms it proposes. Goods and labour markets, social protection system, taxation, investment in knowledge and education are all part of this same strategy of reforms.[30] The greatest weakness of such a strategy lies probably in its enforcement. The Lisbon Agenda is not endowed, in fact, with a binding instrument such as the Stability and Growth Pact for the Economic and Monetary Union; rather it relies on the so-called '**open method of coordination**', which is essentially a forum for benchmarking and exchange of best practices among Governments. Chapter 5 deals in greater detail with the implementation of the Lisbon Agenda.

Figure 1.1 summarises the goals and tools for the conduct of the EU economic policy. Goals are indicated in italic, while tools are in small bold caps. Tools positioned between two goals indicate that they pursue not only the

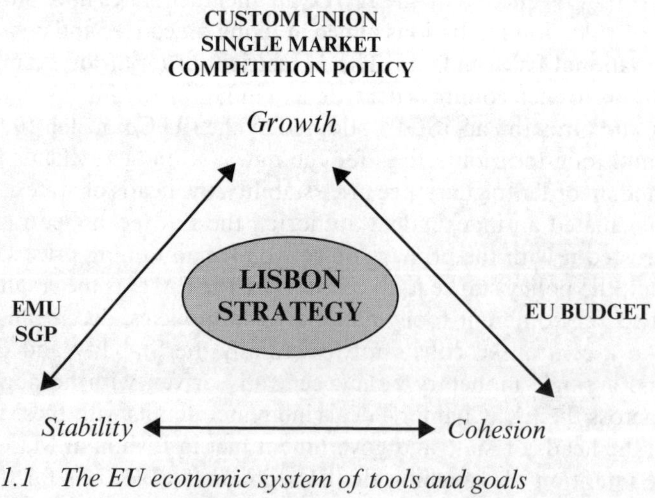

Figure 1.1 The EU economic system of tools and goals

more immediate target, but also growth. Two-headed arrows indicate the mutually reinforcing element of these three goals. The Lisbon strategy sits at the centre of this system.

1.3 THE EXTERNAL DIMENSION

The European Union, thanks to its integration process, has progressively become the world's leading trade power, with its external trade (excluding intra-EU transactions) accounting for more than 20 per cent of the world's trade in both manufacturing and services.[31] The corollary of this prominent economic role is the will to acquire a similar worldwide role at the political level, a struggle often summarised in the consideration that the EU as an institution is a global economic giant but a political dwarf.

From the economic point of view, the approach advocated by the founding fathers has gone a long way towards establishing a European identity on the international scene: we have already discussed how, in 1968, the Community introduced a common customs tariff, an external corollary to the internal abolition of customs duties and quotas which gave birth to the EU Customs Union. In addition, since Europe's economy is based primarily on the conversion of imported raw materials into manufactured goods and services with a high added value, the Union has worked to promote an open trading system worldwide. Within the **General Agreement on Tariffs and Trade (GATT)**, the EU has played a leading role, emphasising liberalisation in the major rounds of trade negotiations. As a result, the weighted average rate of customs duty applied to industrial goods imported into the Union is now less than 5 per cent, from more than 40 per cent in 1948. In 1994, the Union and its partners in the GATT concluded negotiations for new rules on trade in services and agricultural products, and created the **World Trade Organisation (WTO)** which provides a permanent framework for settling multilateral trade disputes and further liberalising the world's trade flows.[32]

Clearly the drive towards trade liberalisation has not been undertaken by the EU without several controversies. In particular, the debate around the Union's trade policy has evolved between two extremes: whether the single market will turn the Union into a protectionist fortress or whether the EU will become an open dumping ground, exposed to competition from all sides and unable to protect its own manufacturers. The prospect of a market of more than 400 million consumers, in which income levels are high and standards harmonised, in fact makes the Union particularly attractive to the world's exporters. On the contrary, EU firms often press their national governments for more protection. As a result, the trade policy of the Union creates worldwide disputes that often have strong political implications.

In addition to trade policy, the Maastricht and Amsterdam treaties created two new tools that the Union can use to fulfil its political role in the world: the single currency and an embryo of common foreign and security policy. It remains to be seen, however, how far the member states, having pooled sovereignty in trade and then the monetary area, are willing to progress also on the foreign affairs policy.

Meanwhile, the Union has already started to use its available, yet limited, tools in order to pursue a political role in the global context. The decisions to impose sanctions on Argentina during the Falklands War, and again on Iraq in the lead-up to the first Gulf War, for example, were taken and implemented in the Community framework. The Union enjoys observer status at the United Nations and is represented by a permanent Commission delegation and the presidency of the Council. It has signed some 50 UN conventions and agreements in its own right and attended numerous international conferences, such as the World Food Summit and that on global warming in Kyoto in December 1997.

The European Union has now the potential to become a political power too, if it is prepared to exploit all the opportunities created by its institutional developments, especially the ones foreseen in its Constitution. Chapter 10 and the concluding chapter of the book will analyse these issues in depth.

NOTES

1. Technically, one can consider the monetary union between Belgium and Luxembourg, which took place in 1927, as the natural precursor of the current European one, although on a much smaller scale. See Bordo and Jonung (1999) for further references on the history of monetary unions.
2. Robert Schuman was himself a perfect European: he was born in Luxembourg, he spoke fluent German and he became a French foreign minister.
3. The Treaty founding the North Atlantic Treaty Organisation (NATO) had been signed in 1949.
4. In the following chapters, we will explore in detail the gains achievable through a process of removal of trade restrictions.
5. The ECSC is the first historic nucleus of countries in the process of European integration. Therefore France, Germany, Italy and the Benelux are considered the six 'founding members' of the European Community (as it was known at the time).
6. Originally, the members of the European Parliament were chosen by the national parliaments and only had consultative powers, but in 1979 the first European, supranational elections with universal suffrage were held, allowing every citizen of the member states to vote for the candidates of their choice. Since then, direct elections have been held every five years, and the powers of the EP substantially increased.
7. The European Union is in principle open to any European state wishing to join, provided that it satisfies specific accession criteria. The issue is discussed later on in this paragraph and more thoroughly at the end of Chapter 3.

8. With the original procedure agreed in Rome, all the Community legal acts had to be unanimously approved by member states. Clearly this led to some difficulties, evidenced by the series of French vetoes in the 1960s. The Single European Act, instead, introduced (with art. 100A of the Treaty, as it was numbered at the time) the principle of qualified majority voting for most of the decisions related to the creation of the single market. Since then, the weighting of votes has been subject to various changes, as well as the competences and powers of the European institutions involved in the process. In this book we present the current version in force, as agreed in the Treaty of Nice, although the EU Constitution, once in force, will again change it (see Box 1.2).
9. The European Council is a special meeting of the Council of Ministers held at the level of heads of state or government; the Intergovernmental Conference is a temporary body made up of High Representatives of the member states set up with the aim of negotiating changes (unanimously agreed) to the existing Treaties.
10. In Maastricht it was agreed to set up an entirely new treaty, the Treaty on the European Union (TEU), and to modify the existing Treaty establishing the European Community (TEC), originally drafted in Rome and then modified by the Single European Act. Technically the two treaties were negotiated in Maastricht during the Maastricht European Council of 10–11 December 1991, and then signed in February 1992, after the legal revisions. The treaties then entered into force on 1 November 1993. At this point, it is worth recalling that a European Treaty enters into force once it has been ratified by all the member states, in accordance with their respective constitutional rules.
11. Although we do not have objective evidence of such a scenario, some witnesses of the dialogue taking place in 1990 between the French President of the time, François Mitterrand, and the German Chancellor Helmut Kohl have put forward the idea of the assent of France to German reunification being given in exchange for the assent of Germany to the common control of the national currencies. The chronology of events supporting this hypothesis (uncertain opening of the IGC on monetary union in June 1990, German reunification in October, successful closure of the IGC and signature of the Maastricht Treaty in the following year) is explored in detail in Chapter 4.
12. All these countries had already been participating in the European Free Trade Area (EFTA) for at least a decade, already sharing many features of the single market.
13. Bulgaria, Czech Republic, Estonia, Hungary, Latvia, Lithuania, Poland, Romania, Slovakia, Slovenia. The Mediterranean countries of Malta and Cyprus have been added to the list of potential entrants since 1997, as well as Turkey since 1999.
14. See Chapter 3 for a thorough discussion of the Copenhagen criteria and their implications for the EU single market, and for a more detailed presentation of the enlargement process. In synthesis, the Copenhagen criteria require (1) a political system based on democratic institutions, the rule of law and the respect of human rights and minorities; (2) a functioning market economy able to withstand competitive pressures; (3) the integration of the EU body of law into the national one.
15. See European Commission (2001a) for a full description of these data.
16. In the mid-1990s, the average GDP per capita of the CEECs stood at around one-third of the EU average, compared to 65 per cent in the case of Spain, Portugal and Greece at the time of their accession to the EU.
17. With the French word *acquis* (acquired) it is meant the entire body of EU laws underpinning the single market.
18. The 2000–2006 Financial Perspectives, as well as the proposal for the 2007–13 financial framework, are discussed in detail in Chapter 6.
19. This set of reforms has been unofficially referred to as the 'fourth' Copenhagen criterion, that is, the one the EU imposes on itself to judge its readiness to admit new members.
20. Keeping unaltered the weighting of votes as from the Treaty of Amsterdam, for example, in a Union of 25 members, Germany, with its 80 million inhabitants, would have had 10 votes at the Council. The sum of the 17 smallest member states, also accounting for 80 million inhabitants in total, would, however, have counted for 57 votes at the Council.

21. The rule establishing the joint responsibility of the Commission led, in March 1999, the entire Commission, at the time led by Jacques Santer, to resign as a consequence of some financial scandals involving Edith Cresson, one of the French Commissioners.
22. See Baldwin *et al.* (2001) and, more recently, Barr and Passarelli (2004) for a critical discussion of this rather complex institutional framework.
23. A detailed report of all the work of the Convention, as well as the debate of the IGC then leading to the draft constitutional text, can be downloaded (http://www.europa.eu.int/futurum/index_en.htm).
24. Growth, stability and cohesion were first identified as key EU objectives by Padoa-Schioppa *et al.* (1987). Sapir *et al.* (2004) also regard these three objectives as the three main targets of EU economic policy. Art. 2 of both the TEC and the TEU mentions the three of them.
25. For example the USA Council of Economic Advisers, in its paper of December 2002, 'An agenda for a global growth', does not seem to consider cohesion as one of the elements necessary to achieve sustainable global growth. See Hubbard (2002) for a more detailed discussion.
26. One could also identify two more categories of tools: those totally decentralised at the national level and those totally centralised. Totally decentralised policies are the counterpart of the application of the principles of conferral and subsidiarity: these are policies that, as regards their characteristics, retain a predominant national character, with hardly any externality on the EU system as a whole, and thus remain under national competences (for example, personal income taxation). For this reason they are not dealt with in this book. The only totally centralised EU policy, the monetary policy, because of its characteristics is managed by the European Central Bank, an independent and centralised authority. For reasons of consistency it is dealt with in the first part of the book, in Chapter 4, where the provisions of the Economic and Monetary Union are discussed.
27. With the possible exception of the Customs Union, given the fact that the Nice Treaty (art. 133, para. 5) has finally established the principle of qualified majority voting also for any decision related to the negotiation and conclusion of agreements in the fields of trade in services and the commercial aspects of intellectual property (although unanimity still holds for a series of issues, as will be discussed in Chapter 10).
28. In particular, capital can now freely circulate in the EU, and the Schengen agreement has ensured the free circulation of persons (but not of workers!) among the member states signatories to the agreement.
29. The campaign for the Swedish consultative referendum of September 2003 and the present discussion in the United Kingdom show that the arguments against or in favour of the adoption of the Euro are of more a political than an economic nature.
30. In the words of the Presidency Conclusion of the Lisbon's summit: 'Achieving this goal requires an overall strategy aimed at: – preparing the transition to a knowledge-based economy and society by better policies for the information society and R&D, as well as by stepping up the process of structural reform for competitiveness and innovation and by completing the internal market; – modernising the European social model, investing in people and combating social exclusion; – sustaining the healthy economic outlook and favourable growth prospects by applying an appropriate macro-economic policy mix.'
31. The United States displays similar figures, albeit some percentage points lower, followed by Japan, below 10 per cent, and then all other countries.
32. Under the Treaty of Rome, the Union's institutions have sole responsibility for negotiating customs duties, implementing safeguards and anti-dumping measures and drawing up rules on public procurement. See Chapter 10 for further details.

2. The classic theory of economic integration

2.1 INTRODUCTION

It is not unusual to hear the argument that, among the causes behind the start of World War II (WWII), there was the 'protectionist' attitude of many countries, and the 'commercial wars' that this attitude generated. Nowadays protectionism and its opposite, free trade, are two concepts often making the headlines in the current debate on the so-called 'globalisation' of economic activities, a phenomenon ultimately based on the progressive liberalisation of trade flows across the world.[1]

The **theory of economic integration** studies how and at what cost countries can pass from a situation of total **protectionism**, that is, a closure of a country's borders to the international flows of goods, services and factors of production, to a situation of **free trade**, an institutional set-up in which goods, services and (eventually) factors of production can freely circulate across countries. Clearly a comprehensive answer to this question implies considering at least four different dimensions.

1. The **degree** to which free trade is achieved: restrictions to trade can be totally or only partially abolished.
2. The geographical **coverage**: a country can **bilaterally** agree to have free trade with one/more other countries or groupings of countries, or it can **multilaterally** open up its borders with respect to the rest of the world, in general through an agreement signed within an international organisation.
3. The **extent** of free trade: restrictions on trade flows can be removed only for certain goods and/or services and/or factors of production.
4. The **range** of effects considered: economic integration can affect, within a country and internationally, the allocation of resources, the eventual exploitation of economies of scale, the terms of trade, the productivity of factors, the profit margins of firms, and in general the rate of economic growth and the distribution of income.[2]

The **orthodox theory** of economic integration (Viner, 1950; Corden, 1971) limits itself to considering only part of the above aspects, studying the effects of the progressive removal of trade restrictions on goods (thus excluding services and factors of production) among a limited set of countries (hence dismissing general equilibrium considerations) and disregarding by and large issues such as technological progress, economic growth or income distribution. Essentially it is a comparative static analysis resting on the following **assumptions**: (a) perfect competition in (homogeneous) goods and factor markets, (b) factors of production are mobile within countries but not across them, (c) transport costs are ignored, (d) prices reflect the opportunity cost of production, (e) trade is balanced (exports equal imports) and (f) resources are fully employed. Although these hypotheses might seem very restrictive, essentially they are the same as standard models of international trade, and as such can be used to derive some insights on the different modalities of economic integration among countries.

For a first assessment of the dynamics of integration, let us consider a single country *H* (country 'Home') and a second, residual country *RoW* which represents the 'Rest of the World'. In country *H*, the preferences of the representative consumer and the production function for a given (homogeneous) good are such that a downward-sloping linear demand curve D_H and an upward-sloping linear supply curve S_H can be drawn,[3] as reported in Figure 2.1. The two curves cross at the equilibrium price and quantity, denoted p_H and Q_H, respectively. In addition, country *H* is considered to be small with respect to the rest of the world (**small country**

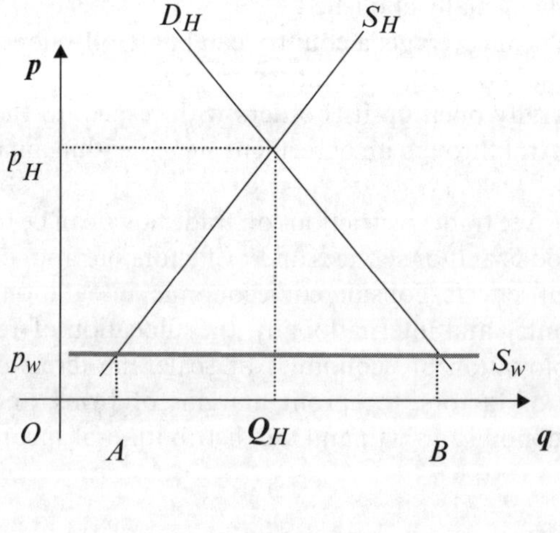

Figure 2.1

hypothesis), so that any change in the quantity of the good produced or demanded in *H* is not able to affect world prices and the production of the same good worldwide. As a result, the supply curve of the rest of the world faced by country *H*, S_w, can be considered perfectly elastic; that is, the rest of the world is able to supply any quantity of the good to country *H* at a given price p_w. Moreover it is assumed that the RoW is more efficient than country *H*; that is, that $p_w < p_H$.

If no restrictions to trade are in place, consumers in *H* have access to the *RoW* supply at a price p_w, and hence they will demand the quantity *OB* for consumption. Of this quantity, *OA* will be domestically produced, while *AB* will be imported from the rest of the world. Now country *H* may consider that the local amount of production *OA* is too small,[4] and hence decide to restrain the quantity imported from the rest of the world, thus **protecting** partially or totally its market in order to stimulate local production. There are several ways in which this protection can be achieved. The most widely used method is to impose a **tariff** on the imported goods: customs officials block the imported good at the border of country *H* and apply a surcharge to its original price, p_w. Such a surcharge can be expressed in percentage terms (in this case we will have an *ad valorem* tariff) or can be specific, consisting of a given amount of money to be summed to the original price p_w. Other measures include **quotas**, that is, quantitative restrictions on the total volume of imports that are allowed to enter a given market, and **non-tariff barriers** (NTBs), that is, rules and regulations on the product characteristics (for example, in respect of given production standards or the presence or absence of specific components) without which the good or service cannot be legally imported.[5]

Considering the case of a specific tariff *T*, the ultimate outcome of the imposition of the tariff is to increase the price of the imported good at a level $T_H = p_w + T$, so that the total demand will shrink to the quantity *OB*′ while local production will increase to *OA*′, with lower imports *A*′*B*′ (see Box 2.1 and Figure 2.2). By applying a tariff, or a quota, or an NTB, which are all equivalent in this respect, country *H* has thus become more protectionist, in the sense that it has 'protected' part of its local production (which increases to *OA*′ in our example) from the external competition (imports decrease from *AB* to *A*′*B*′). If the imposed tariff *T* equals the difference between the world price p_w and the internal equilibrium price p_H, that is, $T_H = p_w + T = p_H$, then the entire market will be served by domestic production OQ_H which will also equal domestic demand, with no imports entering the country. In this case, we will have a **prohibitive tariff**, a tariff whose outcome is to close completely the market of country *H* to imports from the rest of the world.[6] Country *H* thus enters into a situation of **autarky**.

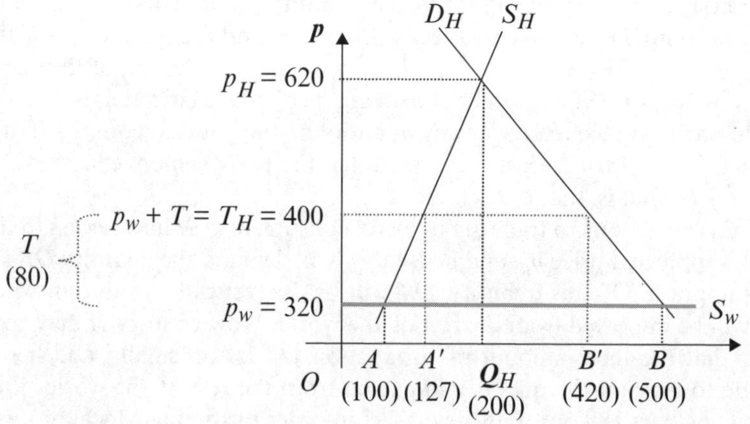

Figure 2.2

Clearly, in this partial equilibrium analysis, the protectionist policy adopted by country *H* works to the detriment of local consumers, who see the price of the imported good increase (from p_w to T_H) and the total demand shrink (for example, from *OB* to *OB*′ in the case considered in Figure 2.2). Two considerations, however, mitigate this result: first of all, we observe an increasing liberalising trend in the international policies of countries, which, rather than increasing their level of protection, have more and more liberalised over time their trade policies.[7] Second, as will be made clear in the last part of the chapter, the negative link between increased protection and consumers' welfare is not always true: if the country considered has, for example, an economic size large enough to influence the world supply of a given good (that is, if we remove the small-country hypothesis), some degree of protection might then be preferred to a perfectly free trade policy.

2.2 FREE TRADE AREAS AND CUSTOMS UNIONS

We have just learned that, since the end of WWII, countries have passed from protectionist equilibria to relatively free trade policies. Such an outcome, however, has been achieved gradually and not in a multilateral context; historically countries have started to liberalise part of their trade (for example in goods but not in services or factors of production) with some partner countries (thus not with the entire rest of the world), creating what are known as **Regional Integration Agreements**, or RIAs.

BOX 2.1 A NUMERICAL EXAMPLE OF A PROTECTIONIST POLICY

Suppose that the demand curve in country H, D_H, is $Q=820-p$, while the supply curve S_H is $p=20+3Q$. Equilibrium quantity and prices in H in this case would be, respectively, $Q_H=200$ and $p_H=620$. If the world price of the considered good is $p_w=320$ and country H adopts a free trade policy, then the total demand of consumers in country H will increase to $OB=500$ (by solving $Q=820-p$, with $p=320$), with a domestic production of $OA=100$ (by solving $p=20+3Q$) and imports $AB=400$, the difference between total demand and domestic supply. Suppose now that country H, in order to stimulate local production, decides to apply an *ad valorem* tariff t of, say, 25 per cent, or, alternatively, a specific tariff $T=80$. In both cases, we will find that the final price of the imported good faced by the consumers in H will increase, and notably we will have $T_H=p_w+T$ (or $p_w\,t$ for the *ad valorem* tariff) $=400$. The higher price of the imported good will reduce total demand to $Q=820-400=420$ (OB'), of which approximately 127 (by solving $400=20+3Q$) will be produced locally (OA') while 293 ($A'B'$) will be imported (see Figure 2.2).

If a specific tariff $T=300$ is set, then $T_H=p_w+T=620=p_H$ and hence all the resulting total demand of 200 will be served by domestic production, with no imports from the rest of the world: $T=300$ would thus be a prohibitive tariff.

Following Venables (2000), regional integration agreements can be defined as groupings of countries formed with the objective of reducing barriers to trade between members of the group. Historically they are not a product of recent times (the most famous example being the 'Zollverein' of nineteenth-century Germany), although it was in the post- WWII period that the major developments were undertaken. One of the first, and certainly the foremost example of an RIA is the European Union (EU), which originally started in 1957 as the European Economic Community (see Chapter 1). In terms of relevance of the phenomenon, of the total 250 regional agreements notified to the World Trade Organisation (WTO) up to December 2002, 130 were notified after January 1995. As a result, over 170 RIAs are currently in force and an additional 70 are estimated to be operational although not yet notified. Within the next year, the total number of RIAs in force might well approach 300;[8] in other words, almost all countries are nowadays members of at least one RIA, and more than one-third of world trade takes place within such agreements.

But what are the modalities through which countries reduce their trade barriers with partners? Essentially, two main type of agreements have been employed: **Free Trade Areas** (FTA) and **Customs Unions** (CU). In free trade areas, countries abolish their barriers to trade with partners, but maintain independent barriers with the rest of the world. For example, within the North American Free Trade Area (NAFTA), which since 1994 comprises Canada, the United States and Mexico, all barriers to trade are removed among the three participating countries; however the United States maintains independent tariffs with respect to other countries in the world, different from the Mexican or Canadian ones. For example, while in the year 2000 Mexico signed with the European Union a free trade agreement, several tariff barriers are still in place between the United States and the EU.

The independence of each country member of an FTA to decide its own tariffs with respect to non-member countries is instead relinquished in customs unions: in this case, not only do participating countries abolish their barriers to trade with partners, but they also establish a **common external tariff** (CET) to be applied by each one of them with respect to the rest of the world. In a sense, it can be said that a CU is a free trade area to which the harmonisation of the participating countries' trade policies is added. The most notable example of CU is the European Economic Community: as we have seen in Chapter 1, as early as 1957, in fact, the Treaty establishing the European Community (TEC) laid down the provisions which created a common commercial policy and allowed the six founding member states to agree on the common external tariff, which entered into force on 1 July 1968.

In order to understand the pros and cons of FTAs and CUs we have to extend our original two-country framework to a third country, partner of country H in the regional integration agreement, therefore denoted country P. We also assume country P to have linear demand and supply curves, D_P and S_P, respectively, and to be more efficient than country H: its internal equilibrium price p_P on a given good is lower than p_H, although higher than the price of the rest of the world, p_w. We maintain our assumptions as far as the supply of the rest of the world S_w is concerned; that is, P is also a 'small' country (see Figure 2.3).

2.2.1 The Working of Free Trade Areas

In order to analyse the economics of FTAs, we have first to solve what might seem an apparent paradox: how it is possible that countries maintain

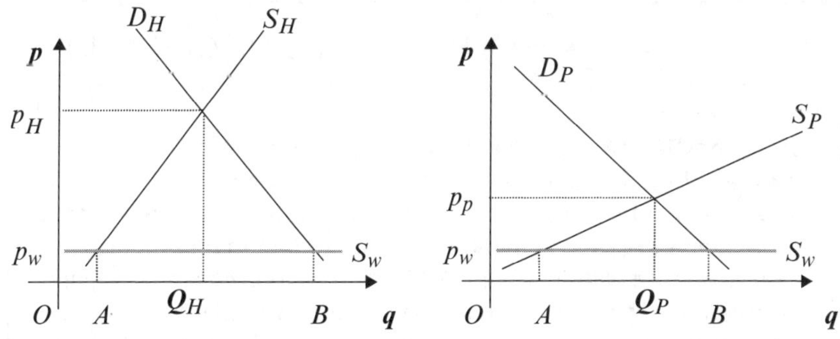

Figure 2.3

independent and different tariffs with respect to the rest of the world, liberalising at the same time the trade flows with partner countries. Going back to the NAFTA example, in other words, we have to clarify how it is possible that the United States maintains positive tariffs towards the imports of goods coming from the European Union, while at the same time they participate in an FTA with Mexico which, in turn, established in the year 2000 a free trade agreement with the European Union. Cannot the EU goods be imported freely in Mexico, thanks to the 2000 free trade agreement, and then, via the provisions of NAFTA, enter through the US–Mexican border the United States free of tariff, thus circumventing the US–EU tariff structures? This phenomenon is known to economists as '**trade deflection**', a name indicating the fact that trade flows, rather than taking the most straightforward direction (US–EU), are 'deflected' (deviated) through a given country (in this case Mexico) in order to take advantage of specific provisions (in this case the set of existing free trade agreements).

Clearly countries have organised themselves in order to prevent the emergence of trade deflection, and therefore the establishment of any FTA is characterised by the enforcement of complicated **rules of origin**, rules that, for every product, specify the conditions according to which a product is considered to be originating in a partner country (and therefore can enter the market of another member of the FTA free of tariff) or not (and therefore a tariff has to be applied, even if the product enters a given market via a partner country).[9] Box 2.2 discusses in more detail the provisions behind the setting up of rules of origin.

Having assessed this, it is convenient to start our analysis from a situation in which, before the regional integration agreement, both countries *H* and *P* were applying a prohibitive tariff with respect to the rest of the world, so that $T_H = p_H$ and $T_P = p_P$, with no imports entering the two

BOX 2.2 AN EXAMPLE OF RULES OF ORIGIN IN FTAS

Using the NAFTA example, suppose Mexico imports a European car free of tariff, thanks to the 2000 EU–Mexico FTA. The car is registered in Mexico, so it has a Mexican plate, and then it is sold to the United States. Is this a Mexican product that can enter the US market free of tariff, via the NAFTA provisions? Clearly not, and the rules of origin specify this. The situation would have been different if instead, the components of the car had been imported free of tariff in Mexico from the EU, and then the car assembled in Mexico. In this case, most of the value-added of the car would be created in Mexico, so it is likely that the rules of origin could qualify the product as a Mexican one, therefore entitling it to enter the US market free of tariff.

countries. Since country *P* is more efficient than country *H*, we also find that $T_P = p_P < T_H = p_H$.

If a free trade area is formed between country *H* and country *P*, consumers in *H* will have access free of tariff to the entire production of country *P*. Therefore the relevant supply curve for country *H* becomes $S_H + S_P$, the horizontal sum of the two supplies. Depending on the shape of *H*'s demand curve, the intersection of D_H with $S_H + S_P$ will determine a new price of the good in *H*, denoted as p_{FTA}, that is, the price resulting from the free trade agreement. Clearly p_{FTA} will be comprised between p_H and p_P. In turn, this new price will affect the equilibrium quantity demanded in *H*. Two situations can be envisaged for this purpose.

First, the extra quantity of the good demanded by consumers in *H* at the new price p_{FTA} can be entirely provided by production in country *P*. In this case $p_{FTA} = T_P = p_P$. As a result, consumers in *H* will see the price of the good decrease, from T_H to p_{FTA}, and hence increase their consumption from the quantity OQ_H to the quantity *OD*. Of this total quantity consumed, *OC* will be produced locally, while *CD* will be imported at the price p_{FTA} from country *P* (see Figure 2.4a). In terms of welfare, consumers in *H* now have access to greater quantities (from OQ_H to *OD*) at lower prices (from T_H to p_{FTA}) and hence experience a positive surplus, while producers in *H* sell lower quantities (from OQ_H to *OC*) at lower prices (from T_H to p_{FTA}) and hence experience a negative surplus. The net effect (the difference between consumers' and producers' surplus) is, however, positive, represented by the

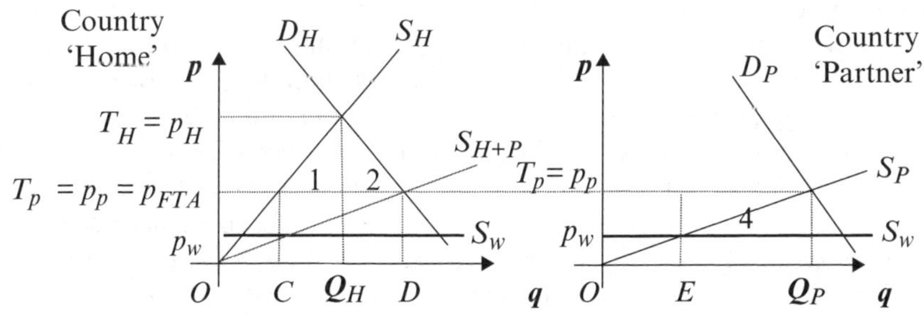

Figure 2.4a

triangle $T_H CD$. This net positive welfare effect is named **trade creation**, the creation of welfare deriving from trade, which allows shifting from the consumption of higher-cost domestic products in favour of lower-cost products of the partner country. In particular, trade creation can be decomposed into two triangles: the first one (indicated by the number 1 in Figure 2.4a) represents a **production effect**; that is, the fact that a certain quantity produced (in country *P*) at lower prices is now available, while the second (indicated by the number 2) is a **consumption effect**; that is, the increase in the consumption possibilities induced by the lower price.

One point remains to be clarified: if country *H* imports the quantity *CD* from country *P* at price T_P, what happens to consumers in country *P*? Can they still consume the original quantity OQ_P at the original price T_P? The answer lies in the fact that, thanks to the independence of the tariffs each country can set towards the *RoW*, country *P* can compensate for the goods it has exported to country *H* by importing them from the rest of the world. In the case depicted in Figure 2.4a, country *P* would then be exporting the quantity *CD* to country *H* and importing the quantity $EQ_P = CD$ from the rest of the world. In doing so, country *P* experiences a positive gain, since it now sources the quantity EQ_P at world prices p_w, but it then sells it internally at price *Tp* (the world price plus the tariff), therefore gaining a tariff revenue equal to the product of the tariff ($T = T_P - p_w$) times the quantity imported EQ_P. The induced change in trade flows (imports from the rest of the world are now entering the FTA in country *P*), and the subsequent positive welfare gains it generates (indicated in the figure by the rectangle-shaped area numbered 4), is known as **indirect trade deflection**. Thanks to this effect, the rest of the world also benefits from the FTA, since it passes from a situation of no exports to the two considered countries (they were both applying prohibitive tariffs before the free trade was established) to exporting the quantity EQ_P to country *P*. The phenomenon of indirect trade deflection is a feature typical of free trade areas, and cannot be eliminated by the rules of origin.

Another situation might however arise in which, at price p_{FTA}, the extra quantity of the good demanded by consumers in H is larger than the one it can be supplied by the internal production in country P at price p_P. This case emerges, for example, if the demand curve of country H in Figure 2.4a becomes more elastic, thus giving rise to higher imports from the partner's country once the FTA has been created (see Figure 2.4b). Because of this higher demand, in this case $p_{FTA} > T_P = p_P$. As a result, consumers in H will see the price of the good decrease, though less than in the previous case, and hence increase their consumption from the quantity OQ_H to the quantity OD'. Of this total quantity consumed, OC' will be produced locally, while $C'D'$ will be imported at the price p_{FTA} from country P (see Figure 2.4b). In terms of welfare, consumers in H now have access as before to greater quantities (from OQ_H to OD') at lower prices (from T_H to p_{FTA}), and hence experience a positive surplus, while producers in H sell lower quantities (from OQ_H to OC') at lower prices (from T_H to p_{FTA}), and hence experience a negative surplus. Again the triangle $T_HC'D'$ displays the trade creation resulting from the free trade area, always decomposed into the two production and consumption triangles (indicated by the numbers 1 and 2 in Figure 2.4b). However trade creation is now smaller than in the previous case, since p_{FTA} is set at a higher level.

Country P this time exports its entire production OQ_P to country H, and again it compensates for the goods it has exported by importing them from the rest of the world. In doing so, country P experiences the **maximum** possible level of **indirect trade deflection** (indicated in Figure 2.4b by the area numbered 4), since it has switched its entire production with cheaper imports from the rest of the world, then sold internally at the price T_P. However two differences characterise this situation with respect to the

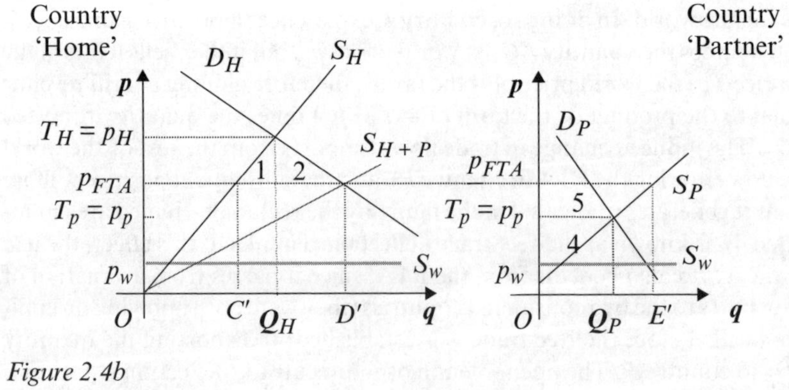

Figure 2.4b

previous one: first of all, the quantity OQ_P is sold to country H at price p_{FTA}, now higher than T_P; second, the total local production is not enough to satisfy the demand of imports $C'D'$ of country H, since $OQ_P < C'D'$. However, since $p_{FTA} > T_P$, producers in country P will experience an extra production of the quantity Q_PE' in order to satisfy consumers in H ($C'D' = OE'$), selling it at the price p_{FTA}. The two combined effects (production OQ_P sold at the higher price p_{FTA} and extra production Q_PE') will generate an extra revenue (producers' surplus) for country *P*, indicated by the area numbered 5 in Figure 2.4b. Nothing changes for consumers in country P, which will continue to consume the quantity OQ_P at price T_P. Thus a **price discrimination** will arise in country P, with one price (T_P) faced by domestic consumers and another, higher price (p_{FTA}) relevant for the producers in P and the consumers in country H.[10]

So far, we have assumed that both countries were adopting a prohibitive tariff before the formation of the free trade area. Although this is a convenient simplifying assumption, it is not very realistic. In what follows we will therefore assume that at least one country (say country H) was not adopting a prohibitive tariff before joining the FTA; that is, $T_H < p_H$, with some imports from the rest of the world entering country *H*'s market. We develop the analysis for the case in which country P is capable of satisfying entirely the new demand arising in country H after the formation of the free trade area; that is, the case in which $p_{FTA} = T_P = p_P$ with $p_{FTA} < T_H$. We leave all other cases, in which the nature of the effects is the same (only the magnitude changes) as useful exercises.

Before the formation of the FTA, country H was imposing a tariff $T_H < p_H$ generating a total demand of *OB*, local production of *OA* and imports of *AB* from the rest of the world, as can be seen in Figure 2.5. When the FTA is formed, country H can now access the entire supply of country P at a price $p_{FTA} = T_P < T_H$. As a result, consumers in H will see the price of the good decrease from T_H to p_{FTA} and hence increase their consumption from the quantity *OB* to the quantity *OD*. Of this total quantity consumed, *OC* will be produced locally, while *CD* will be imported at the price p_{FTA} from country P (see Figure 2.5), thus displacing imports from the rest of the world. In terms of welfare, consumers in H have now access to greater quantities (from *OB* to *OD*) at lower prices (from T_H to p_{FTA}), and hence experience a positive surplus, while producers in H sell lower quantities (from *OA* to *OC*) at lower prices (from p_H to p_{FTA}), and hence experience a negative surplus. The difference between the positive consumers' surplus and the negative producers' one is the area indicated by the two triangles 1 and 2 and the rectangle 6 in Figure 2.5. However, before calculating the net surplus accruing to country H from the FTA, we have to consider the fact that country H is switching the source

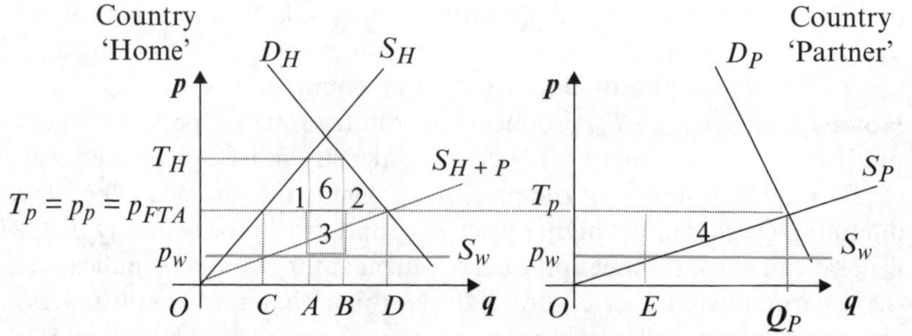

Figure 2.5

of its imports from the most efficient producer (the rest of the world, at price p_w) to a less efficient producer (country *P*, at price $p_{FTA} = T_p > p_w$), albeit more efficient than country *H* itself. This effect, called **trade diversion** (because trade flows are 'diverted' from the most efficient producer to another, less efficient, country) generates a welfare loss for country *H*. In particular, country *H* loses the tariff revenues it was making from its imports from the rest of the world, equal to the tariff $(T_H - p_w)$ times the quantity imported (*AB*), the area indicated by the two rectangles 3 and 6 in Figure 2.5. In terms of net effects, thus, the areas 1, 2 and 6 are positive and the areas 3 and 6 are negative, so the area 6 cancels out; hence we have the result that the FTA generates in country *H* a positive welfare effect of trade creation (the two triangles 1 and 2) and a negative welfare effect of trade diversion (the rectangle 3). Insofar as trade creation is larger than trade diversion, country *H* will find it convenient to enter the free trade agreement.

The effects in *P* are unchanged with respect to the situation previously depicted in Figure 2.4a, with the country experiencing positive indirect trade deflection, again indicated by the rectangle-shaped area 4. Also the rest of the world experiments a net gain since, while it sees its exports *AB* to country *H* vanish, it now exports the quantity $EQ_P \geq AB$ to country *P*.[11]

2.2.2 The Working of Customs Unions

As already stated, the typical feature of customs unions is that participating countries, apart from abolishing all restrictions to trade among themselves, also relinquish their ability of independently fixing their tariffs toward the rest of the world in favour of a common external tariff (CET). As a result, countries have to find an agreement in order to fix the CET at a level which is convenient for each member of the customs union, and in order to share proportionately the revenues accruing from the application of the tariff to the imports from the rest of the world.

In terms of economic analysis, the main difference between FTAs and CUs is found in the mechanism of formation of the price after the CU has been created. (See Box 2.3 for an analysis of the EU Customs Union.) Once the CET has been decided, in fact, country *P* cannot any longer freely supply its production to country *H*, then replacing it with imports from the rest of the world, because country *P* is no longer free to decide its own tariff independently. As a result, after the CU has been created, country *P* will be able to supply to country *H* only its (eventual) excess of supply, indicated as M_P. This excess of supply is clearly a function of the chosen level of the CET: it will be positive as long as CET $> p_P$.

BOX 2.3 THE WORKING OF THE CU IN THE EUROPEAN UNION

TEC art. 133 states that '*the Commission shall submit proposals to the Council for implementing the common commercial policy*', therefore setting the level of the CET on goods. The Council, acting by a qualified majority, approves the Commission's proposal. Before the Treaty of Nice was implemented, all decisions related to a CET relative to trade in services were instead taken by the Council acting unanimously, on a proposal from the Commission and after consulting the European Parliament. Since the entry into force of the Nice Treaty (February 2003), these decisions are also taken by qualified majority, with the exception of a few issues (such as cultural products), in which the unanimity principle still applies (see Chapter 10). As far as the agreement on the apportionment of the revenues generated by the CET is concerned, in the EU Customs Union these revenues are part of the Union's annual budget.

In terms of results, it can be stated that the process of EU integration has worked well, meaning that trade creation has been apparently greater than trade diversion, even though the increase in trade concerned much more intra- than extra-EU trade. As a consequence, while before 1957 the six founding member countries obtained more than two-thirds of their imports from RoW, already in 1990 the same percentage was generated from within the customs union. For an average EU country, approximately three-quarters of its total trade takes place within the wider European area.

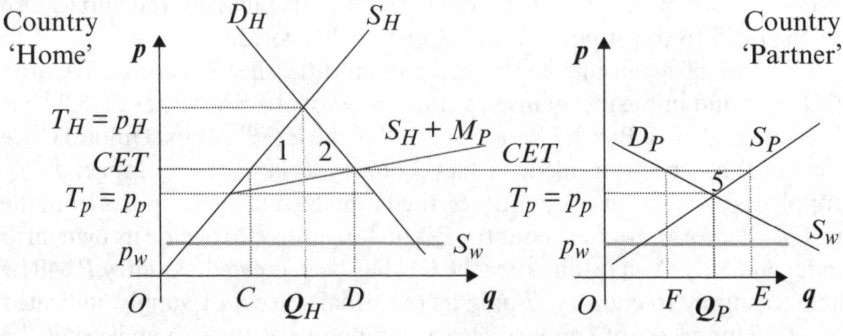

Figure 2.6

As for the case of free trade areas, we start our analysis from a situation in which both countries apply a prohibitive tariff; that is, $T_H = p_H$ and $T_P = p_P$, and thus no imports from the rest of the world enter the two countries before the formation of the CU. As before, since country *P* is more efficient than country *H*, we also have that $T_P = p_P < T_H = p_H$. However here we are dealing only with excesses of supply from country *P*, determined by the chosen level of the CET; hence it is pointless to determine, as we did for the case of free trade areas, whether country *P* is capable or not of satisfying country *H*'s demand at its original price p_P: the only relevant equilibrium price in the CU is in fact the CET.

Suppose that a CET which lies in between T_H and T_P is agreed upon (a 'tariff-averaging' customs union).[12] Once the CU is formed, therefore, country *H*'s consumers will see the price of the good decrease (from T_H to *CET*), and hence increase their consumption from the quantity OQ_H to the quantity *OD*. Of this total quantity consumed, *OC* will be produced locally, while *CD* will be imported at the price *CET* from country *P* (see Figure 2.6) via its excess of supply M_P (note how the excess of supply of country *P* starts to become available only as long as $CET > T_P$). In terms of welfare, consumers in *H* now have access to greater quantities (from OQ_H to *OD*) at lower prices (from T_H to *CET*), and hence experience a positive surplus, while producers in *H* sell lower quantities (from OQ_H to *OC*) at lower prices (from T_H to *CET*), and hence experience a negative surplus. As in the case of the FTA, the triangle T_HCD displays the **trade creation** resulting this time from the customs union, always decomposed into the two production and consumption triangles (indicated with the numbers 1 and 2 in Figure 2.6).

The effects of the CU are different for country *P* with respect to the free trade area situation. Since country *P* can no longer source its imports from the rest of the world at its own tariff, the internal equilibrium price of country *P* changes, increasing from T_P to *CET*. This affects negatively

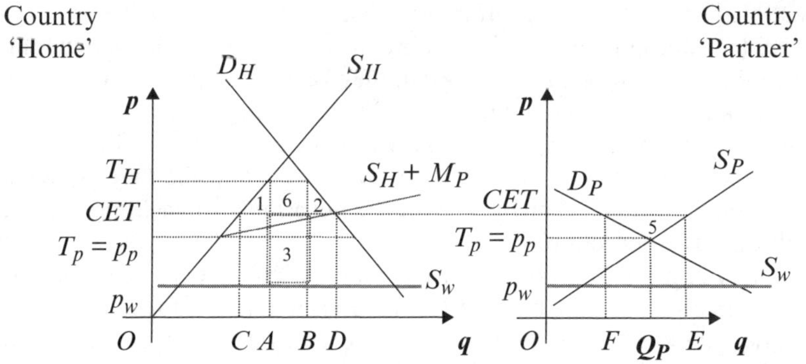

Figure 2.7

consumers in P, which experience a loss in income (they now consume less, from OQ_P to OF, at a higher price); however it benefits country P's producers, which now sell more (OE rather than OQ_P) at a higher price, exporting to country H their excess of production ($FE = CD$). The net difference in welfare is however positive for country P, which sees its total welfare increase[13] by the reversed triangular area numbered 5 in Figure 2.6.

The case of one country (say country H) not adopting a prohibitive tariff before joining the CU is represented in Figure 2.7, which is essentially a mix of Figure 2.5 and 2.6. Country H will experience trade creation and trade diversion, as in the FTA case depicted in Figure 2.5, while country P will see its producers gain from the excess of supply sold to country H, as we have just seen in Figure 2.6.

In terms of net welfare, it can be shown (Robson, 1998) that trade creation in a CU is larger the larger is the economic area of the customs union and the more numerous are the countries of which it is composed; the lower is the post-union average tariff, the more competitive are the economies of the member states and the greater are the differences in unit costs of the same industries across the member countries, since in this case low-cost producers of the same product are relatively easier to find in the partner countries. A comparison of the net welfare will then determine whether or not a CU will be created among the potential participants.

2.3 AN ASSESSMENT OF CUSTOMS UNIONS AND FREE TRADE AREAS

In the previous section we have developed the orthodox theory of free trade areas and customs unions. Comparing under standard assumptions the case of the FTAs and the tariff-averaging CUs, it is clear how the latter tend to be less efficient: since CU are more likely to lead to a higher common price for the good ($CET > p_{FTA} = p_P$), they generate smaller trade creation effects and, on average, larger trade diversions in country *H*. As far as country *P* is concerned, consumers will be worse off in a tariff-averaging CU, since their internal price will increase to *CET*, while they experience no change in price in an FTA, with the government benefiting from the indirect trade deflection.

And yet, notwithstanding this theoretical argument, we observe in the world the formation of both customs unions and free trade areas, indicating that, in some cases, a CU must be more efficient than an FTA. In the rest of this section we will analyse in detail the cases in which such an event is going to happen.

More generally, consider that the rationale under which we can show an FTA or a CU to be superior to a protectionist tariff policy is the same as that leading us to conclude that any regional integration agreement is inferior, in terms of welfare gains, to free trade. In other words, under the restrictive assumptions of the basic model, in any case the first best solution for a given country would be represented by a free trade situation, since CUs and FTAs, although welfare-improving with respect to a protectionist tariff, are selective forms of protectionism, yielding an equilibrium price (in our examples, *CET* or p_{FTA}) higher than the world price p_w.

However this argument is not necessarily true once the most unrealistic assumptions of the basic model are removed. As will be made clear in the following sections, issues like imperfect information, transaction costs or the presence of economies of scale might provide a rationale for the formation of regional integration agreements even from a welfare point of view.

2.3.1 The Role of the Small Country Hypothesis

In order to analyse the optimality of a free trade situation with respect to regional integration agreements, we have to discuss critically some of the hypotheses underlying the standard model of protectionism introduced in section 2.1.

First of all, when looking at the process of economic integration taking place in the real world, it is clear that CUs and FTAs arise among countries that cannot always be considered as 'small' with respect to the rest of the world. The EU Customs Union, for example, accounts for 26 per cent of world GDP and some 20–22 per cent of the world trade flows,[14] while the corresponding figures for the North American Free Trade Area (NAFTA) are 36 and 18–20 per cent, respectively (2003 data). As a result, it is unrealistic to assume that the rest of the world is able to supply any quantity of the good to these countries at a given price: when analysing RIAs such as the EU or NAFTA, the supply curve of the rest of the world, S_w, can no longer be considered as perfectly elastic; rather it will be positively sloped. To our purpose, a good analytical framework to assess our model of economic integration when the small country hypothesis has been removed is to use a diagram known as an **'offer curve'**, originally developed by the British economists Marshall and Edgeworth at the beginning of the twentieth century.[15]

Imagine a world made up of two countries, one (large) country *H* and a country *P*, making up the rest of the world. The left-hand side of Figure 2.8 shows the production possibility frontier *TT* of our country Home, given any two goods, say food and textiles. Denoting the prices of food as P_F and of textiles as P_T, we can draw a number of **isovalue lines** *VV* on the same graph, lines along which the value of output *V* is constant for the different quantities Q_F and Q_T of food and textiles produced.[16] We can also draw standard indifference curves of the representative consumer in country *H*. Combining this information, the economy will produce at point *Q*, which is on the highest possible isovalue line, but will decide to consume at *C*, where the isovalue line is tangent to the highest possible indifference curve. Comparing the baskets of goods *C* and *Q*, it can be seen that country *H* produces more textiles than it wishes to consume; that is $(Q_T - C_T)>0$, so it exports textiles; in contrast, the ideal consumption of food C_F is higher than the level produced internally, Q_F, and hence the difference $(C_F - Q_F)$ will be imported from the rest of the world. We can summarise this information on the right-hand side of Figure 2.8, where we measure the trade flows directly on the axes. In particular, the horizontal axis measures the exports of country *H*, and hence, in this case, the difference between the production and the consumption of textiles $(Q_T - C_T)$, while the vertical

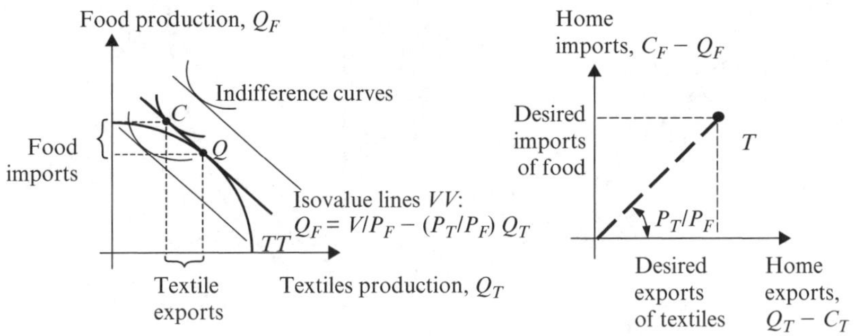

Figure 2.8

axis measures the imports of this economy, and hence the difference between the consumption and the production of food ($C_F - Q_F$). Point T in the right-hand side of Figure 2.8 therefore summarises the information contained comparing the baskets C and Q on the left-hand graph.

Let us now change the relative prices, assuming, for example, that the price of textiles increases to P_T' with respect to the price of food, so that $P_T' / P_F > P_T / P_F$. This entails a change in the slope of the isovalue line, as depicted in Figure 2.9, which becomes steeper (from VV to VV^1).[17] As a result, the production of the economy shifts from the basket Q to the basket Q^1, while consumption shifts from the basket of goods C to C^1. Trade flows change accordingly, with the economy now exporting more textiles and importing more food, since the production of textiles relative to food has increased (from Q to Q^1).[18] The offer curve depicted on the right-hand side of Figure 2.9 summarises this change in trade flows, from T to T^1, as a consequence of the change in relative prices. In general, the offer curve shows how the country's 'offer' (what it exports in exchange for what it imports) varies as the relative prices of the goods change. As can be seen, the offer curve is not linear: its slope is increasing with the increase in exports; that is to say, in order to induce country H to export more textiles, a progressively higher relative price of textiles is required, because (a) country H incurs increasing opportunity costs in specialising in the production of textiles and (b) the more food and the fewer textiles (in relative terms) available for internal consumption (since textiles are exported), the more valuable to country H's consumers becomes, at the margin, one unit of the exported good.

One can clearly see that each point on the offer curve is associated with a particular level of relative prices: this value is often referred to as the **terms**

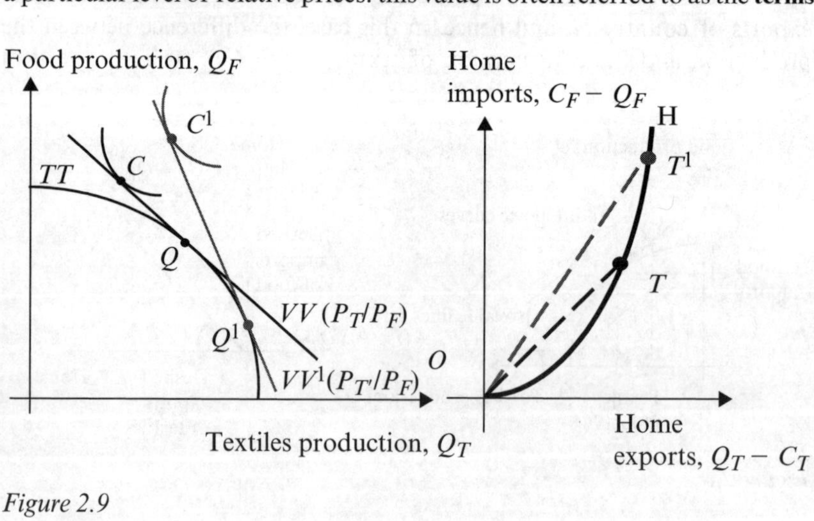

Figure 2.9

of trade. More formally, the terms of trade of a nation are defined as the ratio of the price of the good it exports to the price of the good it imports. In our example, since country *H* is exporting textiles, its terms of trade would be P_T/P_F. It goes undisputed, then, that a rise in the terms of trade (that is, an increase in the price of the good the country exports, in this case P_T) raises a country's welfare (the price that a country receives for its exports rises relative to the price it pays for its imports), while a decline in the terms of trade reduces its welfare.

Given the case of a two countries world, whatever country *H* exports (in our example, textiles for the quantity $Q_T - C_T$) will then be imported by its trade partner (country *P* summarising the Rest of the World, or RoW), and vice versa for country *H*'s imports (in our example, food for the quantity $C_F - Q_F$). Therefore, country *P* will export food and import textiles, and its terms of trade will be defined by P_F / P_T. It is worth noting that, because country *H* is large, the rest of the world's (that is, country *P*'s) offer curve is influenced by country *H*, and so it also has some curvature rather than being a straight line.

BOX 2.4 MEASURING THE TERMS OF TRADE

In a world of many (rather than two) countries and goods, the terms of trade of a country are given by the ratio of the price index of its exports to the price index of its imports. The following table presents the evolution of the terms of trade for selected countries in the world, taking 1995 as the base year (1995=100).

	1972	1980	1986	1990	1996	2000	2001
United States	123	87	104	98	100	97	99
Japan	95	52	77	73	92	96	97
Germany	109	89	100	102	100	93	95
France	95	85	94	94	99	95	95
United Kingdom	107	91	94	101	101	103	104
Italy	110	93	97	98	104	100	102
Canada	115	111	95	100	101	103	103
Industrial countries	105	85	93	95	99	97	98
Developing countries	60	105	90	101	101	108	—

Source: Salvatore (2003) elaborated from data in IMF, *International Financial Statistics*, various years.

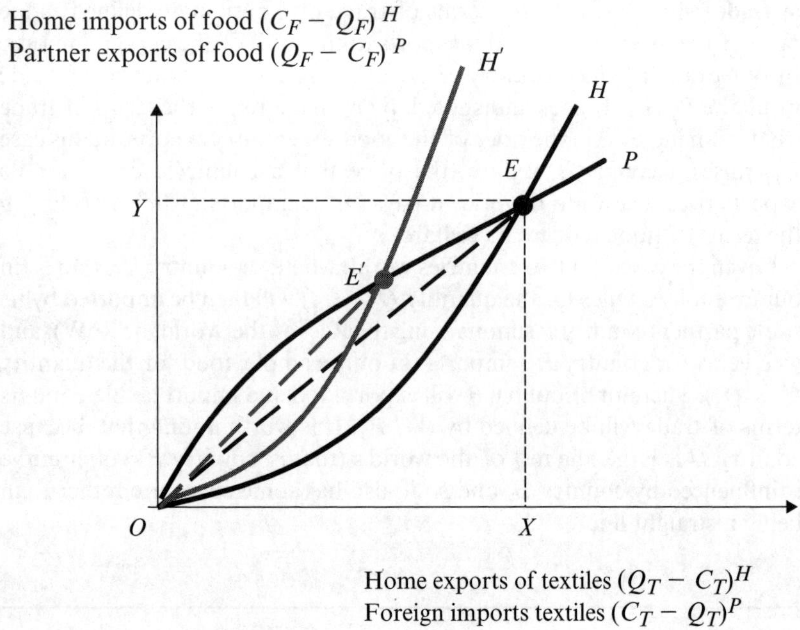

Figure 2.10

More precisely, the curvature of the RoW's offer curve is due to the fact that, the more the relative price of textiles increases, the more country *H* will decide to export textiles and import food; however, since the demand for food coming from country *H* is not negligible to country *P* (*H* is large), the good that country *P* exports to *H* (food) will become scarcer in relative terms to *P*, and hence also country *P* will start asking for a progressively higher relative price for exporting food.

Figure 2.10 shows both countries' offer curves. The world equilibrium is where the two offer curves intersect:[19] the world's demand for food arising from country *H*'s imports, denoted as $(C_F - Q_F)^H$ on the axis, will be satisfied by the exports of country *P*, denoted as $(Q_F - C_F)^P$ on the same axis, and vice versa for the textiles. At the equilibrium point *E*, the relative price of textiles with respect to food, P_T / P_F (the terms of trade of country *H*), is equal to the slope of the segment *OE*. The quantity *OX* indicates country *H*'s exports of textiles, which equal country *P*'s imports, while the quantity *OY* indicates country *H*'s imports of food, which equal at equilibrium country *P*'s exports. It can be seen that *E* is a **general equilibrium**; that is, demand and supply are equalised for both products in both markets at the same time.

If now country H imposes a tariff on its imports (food) from the rest of the world, a price differential arises between the internal price of food in H (where a tariff has been levied) and the world price of food (the price registered in P). Imports become in country H more expensive and thus less attractive. Hence people in H will be willing to exchange fewer exports for the same amount of imports. This will lead to a reduction in the quantity of textiles exported (that is, supplied to the world) and thus (country H is large) an increase in P_T.[20] As a result, the terms of trade of country H, defined as P_T / P_F, will have to improve in order to be consistent with the new general equilibrium, moving from OE to OE'. The offer curve of country H will therefore shift in H' towards the axis measuring the good on which the tariff has been imposed (the imports of food), and the general trade equilibrium moves from E to E'. Here we recover the standard result that a protectionist policy reduces trade flows (both imports and exports are reduced in E'); however, contrary to the small country case, here the welfare of one country, country H, increases after the protectionist policy, owing to the positive change in its terms of trade (which instead remain constant in the small country hypothesis). Given this, it might then be convenient for large countries to adopt an 'optimal' degree of protectionism (that is, to impose tariffs) in order to maximise their welfare.[21]

Actually, to try to impose an optimum tariff is not that easy, since the gains of a country would come at the expense of other countries. As a result, as country H uses a tariff in order to try to improve its welfare, the rest of the world is likely to retaliate, imposing tariffs as well. The final effect on the new general equilibrium attained is uncertain, apart from the (certain) negative impact that this attitude will have on the total volume of trade flows. The final effect will depend on the **bargaining power** of a given country, that is on the ability of, say, country H to move in its favour the terms of trade after the imposition of a tariff, without suffering too much from the eventual retaliation from the rest of the world.

This theoretical finding provides a rationale for the formation of customs unions, especially the ones among relatively large countries (where the small country hypothesis does not hold). Since in a CU the trade policy of every partner country is common, the effects of a CET on the terms of trade are a function of the bargaining power of the entire set of countries, rather than the single countries (as it would be in an FTA). Hence, by creating a CU, it is more likely that, by changing the CET, the terms of trade of all the partner countries can improve, leading to a more favourable general equilibrium.

2.3.2 The Role of Transaction Costs

We have seen in the previous section the reasons why customs unions can be preferred to FTAs when the textbook hypothesis of small countries is removed (or, more precisely, when the sum of the market shares of the countries participating in the CU is large enough to affect significantly their terms of trade). The theory of offer curves and general equilibrium considerations can in fact explain very well the reason for a CU being created among countries which, otherwise, would have a very limited bargaining power on the world scene. The rationale fits perfectly the European Union case: without a Customs Union and a CET, it is very unlikely that Germany or France, not to mention the smaller EU countries, could negotiate on an equal footing with countries like the United States or China in international trade fora, something that instead currently happens thanks to the joint bargaining power of the European Union.

According to a similar logic, MercoSur, the regional integration agreement signed in the 1990s between Argentina, Brasil, Paraguay and Uruguay, is also developing as a Customs Union. Following the same rationale, we would therefore expect CUs to include medium to large countries, and FTAs formed among small or non-numerous countries. And yet, in the real world it is possible to observe free trade areas created among 'large' countries. The most notable case is the already discussed NAFTA regional integration agreement, where three countries the size of the United States, Canada and Mexico decided to opt for an FTA rather than a Customs Union, thus renouncing the extra bargaining power that the adoption of a common external tariff might have yielded them.

The rationale for such a decision lies in the consideration that any 'union' of countries, whether political or economic, is essentially an equilibrium between two opposite forces: the economies of scale that can be achieved by implementing policies together, and the heterogeneity of preferences among the countries which participate in the union.[22] The presence of economies of scale fosters the creation of larger and larger unions, while the political costs of mediation among different exigencies generally prevent unions from growing too large, or too differentiated in terms of policy objectives.

In the case of trade policy, the economies of scale are represented by the increased bargaining power achievable when a larger set of countries enforces a common external tariff. However, since the common external tariff has to be decided by a political agreement, its fixing conveys a **transaction cost**. Now the larger the number or the more different (heterogeneous) the countries' preferences, the more likely it is that the political costs of mediation outweigh the benefits achievable through the common external tariff, and thus the more likely that a free trade agreement is preferred to a CU. In the case of NAFTA, clearly the political costs of defining a CET in a hypothetical Customs Union would be very high, given the very different trade structures of the countries involved, while the benefits achievable in terms of extra bargaining power would be definitely limited, with one country (the USA, in our example) already significantly larger than the other two. As a result, an FTA was preferred. In turn, in the EU case, the similar trade structures of the countries involved, together with the political will of deepening even further the integration process to include some key policy areas, made the transaction costs of negotiating a CET fairly small with respect to the gains achievable by each partner country.

2.4 ECONOMIES OF SCALE IN CUSTOMS UNIONS

We have seen that, removing the small country hypothesis and moving to a general equilibrium framework, it is possible to overturn the standard result of CUs being less efficient than free trade areas. Transaction costs considerations in turn can again change the balance between the two forms of economic integration studied. A third possible option is to study the problem of efficiency of customs unions within our traditional analytical framework, thus maintaining the small country hypothesis, but changing the hypothesis on the production technology, and hence the shape of the domestic supply curves. In particular we will assume in this section that the production technology is subject to **increasing returns to scale**; that is, the greater the quantities supplied, the lower are the average costs that firms face for the production of each unit, a concept also called '**economies of scale**'.[23]

With this hypothesis on the production technology, firms now have to cover their fixed costs of production, not only their marginal costs, and thus the supply curves in our two countries, S_H and S_P, coincide with the average costs (denoted AC_H and AC_P) and are downward sloping in quantities, as depicted in Figure 2.11. Equilibrium prices p_H and p_P are then determined

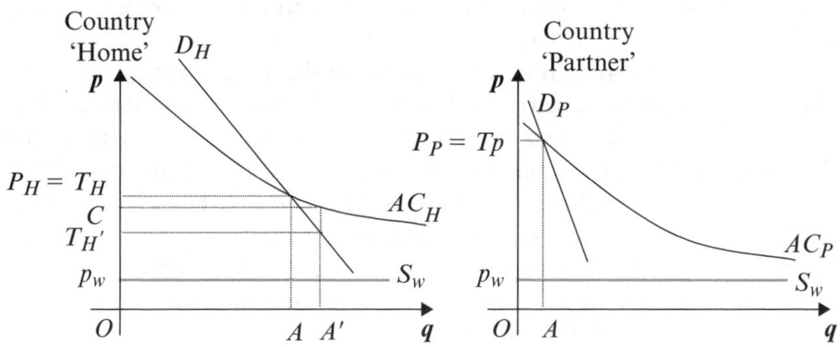

Figure 2.11

at the intersection between these new supply curves and the (linear) demand curves D_H and D_P. We maintain all the other assumptions listed in section 2.1.[24] In particular, using the small countries hypothesis, the supply curve of the rest of the world S_w can be considered perfectly elastic: the rest of the world is able to supply any quantity of the good to country *H* and *P* at a given price p_w. Moreover it is assumed as before that the RoW is more efficient than country *H* and country *P*; that is, $p_w < p_P$ and p_H.

With respect to the standard analysis of customs unions, two caveats need specific attention when dealing with the hypothesis of economies of scale, both shown in Figure 2.11. First of all, note that the minimum tariff allowing for internal production is the prohibitive one. Given the world price p_w, the prohibitive tariff in, say, country *H* is $T_H = p_w + T = p_H$, with domestic demand equal to the domestic production *OA*, and no imports entering from the rest of the world. Should the tariff be set at $T_{H'} < p_H$, then the quantity demanded would be *OA′*, but the average unit costs of producing domestically such a quantity (the price *C*, read on the supply curve with respect to the quantity *OA′*) would be higher than the price obtained for the same quantity ($T_{H'}$) and thus no local production would take place, with the world supplying the entire quantity *OA′* at the price p_w, and the government getting the resulting tariff revenue.[25]

The second consideration relates to the identification of the level of technological efficiency of each country considered. So far, we have assumed that country *P* is more efficient than country *H*: in particular, we have expressed this hypothesis assuming that the equilibrium price (or prohibitive tariff) of country *P*, $T_P = p_P$, was lower than the corresponding tariff/price in country *H*, $T_H = p_H$. However, when economies of scale are at stake, it can happen that the dimension of the market affects the equilibrium prices in such a way that the price alone is not able any more to reveal information on the technological efficiency of a country. Consider the case depicted in Figure 2.11. Clearly country *P* is technically more efficient than country *H*, since its average cost (supply) curve AC_P always lies below the corresponding curve for country *H*, AC_H, for any given quantity. However, since country *H* has a significantly larger market than country *P* (country *H*'s demand is larger than *P*′s, that is, D_H is farther from the origin than D_P), the economies of scale achievable in *H* are higher than in *P*, and thus the equilibrium price p_H is lower than p_P. Thus, looking only at the information conveyed by prices, one would erroneously assume country *H* to be more efficient. As a result, in order to correctly identify efficiency in the case of economies of scale, information on the production technology has also to be available.

Having clarified these two important differences with respect to the traditional analysis, we can start looking at the formation of a Customs Union

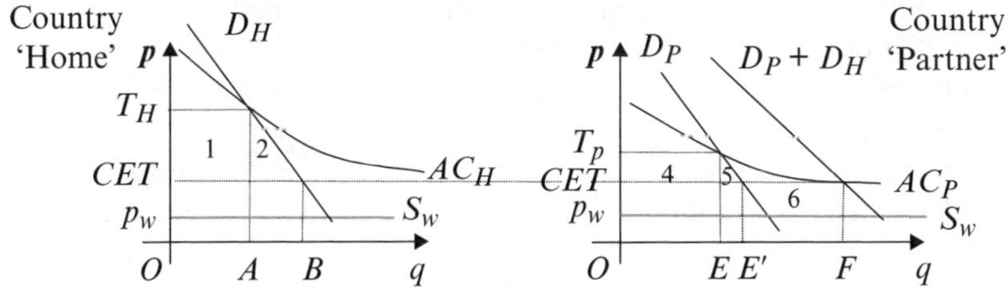

Figure 2.12

between two small countries where economies of scale are present. In order to allow for domestic production in both *H* and *P* before the formation of the CU, we assume prohibitive tariffs T_H and T_P in both countries. As usual, country *P* is more efficient than country *H*: assuming country *H* not to be significantly larger than country *P*, this hypothesis safely translates into a prohibitive tariff in *P* lower than the one in *H*; thus $T_P < T_H$, as shown in Figure 2.12.

When the CU is formed, a CET is agreed upon and country *H* starts to import the excess of supply from country *P*, the latter being more efficient, as in the standard case. However, contrary to the standard 'tariff-averaging' Customs Union, as soon as the excess of supply is produced in country *P* in order to serve the needs of country *H*, the increase in the quantity produced in *P* further stimulates economies of scale, and hence the equilibrium price in *P* (of which *H* also takes advantage) drops.[26] As a result, for both countries it is optimal to let *P* produce as much as possible, in order to maximise the exploitation of economies of scale. Hence country *P* will produce in order to serve the demand of both country *H* and country *P*, and the CET will be fixed at the intersection between the combined requirement of the market, that is, the sum of the two demand curves $D_H + D_P$, and the average costs curve of *P*, that is, AC_P.

Once the CET is fixed and the CU established, country *H*'s consumers will see the price of the good first decrease from T_H to T_P, as soon as the restrictions to trade are removed, and then to $CET < T_P$, when economies of scale start to display their effects in country *P*. Hence they will increase their consumption from the quantity *OA* consumed in autarky to the quantity *OB* consumed within the Customs Union. In terms of welfare, consumers in *H* now have access to greater quantities (from *OA* to *OB*) at lower prices (from T_H to *CET*) and hence experience a positive surplus, or **trade creation**, as we have learned to call it, always decomposed into the two production and consumption areas. In particular, the rectangular area indicated by the number 1 in Figure 2.12 is the production effect, resulting from the replacement of more expensive domestic production with cheaper imports produced in country *P*; the triangular area indicated by number 2 results instead from the increased consumption induced by the lower domestic price.

The effects of the CU are different for country *P* with respect to the standard analysis. Country *P* in fact now obtains its domestic supplies at a lower cost of production, since it exploits economies of scale deriving from its producers also serving the demand of country *H*. As a result, its consumers face lower internal prices (from T_P to *CET*) and thus can consume greater quantities (from *OE* to *OE'*), therefore benefiting from a positive surplus, always decomposed into the two production and consumption areas (indicated by the numbers 4 and 5 in Figure 2.12). Although this surplus is a consequence of the trade undertaken with country *H*, it is not an orthodox trade creation effect, since it does not result from the access to an external supply, but from the greater efficiency of domestic producers. As a result, it is more correct to name this positive welfare effect accruing to country *P*'s consumers **cost reduction** rather than trade creation (Corden, 1971). Finally country *P*'s producers also benefit from a positive welfare effect, since they sell extra production to country *H* (in particular the quantity $E'F = OB$, by construction) at a price higher than the world price ($CET > p_w$). This is indicated by the rectangular area numbered 6 in Figure 2.12.

Looking at the welfare results of customs unions with economies of scale we can see that these tend to be greater with respect to the traditional analysis. Comparing Figure 2.6 with Figure 2.12, in fact, in the former case the increasing costs in the supply curves generate a CET at levels above T_P, with negative effects for the consumers in *P* and less positive effects for those in country *H*. In Figure 2.12, instead, the presence of economies of scale is such that the CET is even lower than T_P, and thus positive welfare effects are maximised. We therefore find here another rationale for the formation of customs unions rather than FTAs.

However a CU characterised by economies of scale, though theoretically perfectly viable, suffers from some difficulties when it comes to its concrete application. In particular, suppose a case in which there is production only in one country, say the most efficient one, country *P*, with country *H* importing from the rest of the world.[27] When the CU is formed, *P* gains, as in the case analysed above, but country *H* will suffer from trade diversion, a more expensive source of imports ($CET > p_w$) having replaced the world one. If instead the producing country is the less efficient one (country *H*), the formation of a Customs Union will give rise to a reversal of production, with *P* starting to produce for both countries and *H* terminating its production. Consumers in *H* will benefit from the trade creation analysed in the standard case, but in *P* the imports from the rest of the world will be terminated in favour of the local production (for both countries). Although producers in *P* will gain from this situation, its consumers will experience a negative welfare effect ($CET > p_w$) similar to the trade diversion and known as **trade suppression**, the replacement of the more convenient imports from the rest of the world by the more expensive domestic production.

Finally, if no country was producing the good before the formation of the CU, it might well be the case that the pattern of trade resulting from the establishment of the CET leads to a **perverse specialisation** (Grubel, 1967), as analysed in Figure 2.11: in the absence of information on the actual shape of the average cost curves, the larger country (say, country *H*) will capture the entire production of the CU thanks to the exploitation of larger economies of scale, without its necessarily being the more efficient one. As a result, in equilibrium, country *H* will produce the combined quantities of the market at higher unit cost than that achievable had the production taken place in country *P*.

The possibility of perverse specialisation led Grubel to argue that trade liberalisation does not necessarily produce an optimal pattern of location of economic activities, and hence some forms of economic planning might be required in order to achieve a first-best solution. However, though appealing, this solution implies that the planner should have perfect information on the cost functions in the countries considered, in order to identify the most efficient producer and locate there the production for the entire area. In addition, an eventual planner, more than the market, might be subject to a lobby's pressure resisting the relocation of production activities, ultimately leading to second-best outcomes.

2.4.1 The Production of Public Goods

Another reason according to which a preferential trade agreement might be preferred to a free trade policy is linked to the provision of goods characterised by the fact that the benefit of consuming them does not only accrue to the purchaser but enters the social welfare function of a country. Given these characteristics, such goods are known as **public goods**. Now there might be cases in which the internal production of these goods, desirable from a welfare point of view, cannot take place owing to the existing competition from the rest of the world. As a result, on the basis of these social grounds, governments might decide to protect the local, weaker firms from foreign competition via the imposition of tariffs, and thus permit the local production of public goods and the collection of the social benefits deriving from their production.

A typical example is a good which is technology-intensive; that is, its local production requires the performance of research and development activities; these activities, being not entirely appropriable, then spill over into the entire economy, generating a higher rate of innovation and growth. That might not be entirely the case if the good in question was produced in the rest of the world and only imported in the country.[28]

Often, however, such a rationale for protectionism is based on arguments relying more on 'social' externalities (such as local production that creates employment) rather than strictly on the 'public good' characteristics of the product in question. These latter arguments, in particular, are known as the **infant industry argument**: a government introduces some sort of protectionism for a local industry in order to protect its initial stages of development and allow it to achieve social objectives, exposing it only later to competition from the rest of the world. Although the infant industry argument has been extensively used by policy makers to justify protectionism in the past, many authors (Corden, 1997, among others) have found that infant industry protection ultimately does not correct market distortions, therefore concluding that the optimal policy is to address these distortions directly at their source (that is, to try to achieve a local production more competitive with respect to the rest of the world) rather than indirectly through the trade policy. Accordingly an economic rationale for selective forms of protectionism on the basis of the public goods argument might be viable only if political pressures or other constraints rule out in the short run the direct redressing of such market distortions.

If, in addition to its public good nature, a product is also subject to economies of scale, then clearly the formation of customs unions is more efficient than unilateral tariff protection, since a CU ultimately allows a lower tariff in the country considered through the cost reduction effects (Robson,1998). However, if the entire production of the public good is produced at lower costs only in the partner country after the formation of the Customs Union, the home country does not achieve through the CU its objective of local production, although benefiting from the gains of integration. As a result, some protection within the Customs Union might be necessary. This rationale justifies the inter-union protective devices known as **transition periods** that, for example, the European Union negotiates with its prospective members. In general, in order to protect the local production and ensure a smooth accession to the EU, acceding countries are not exposed immediately to the internal free circulation of goods and services. Rather some sectors within the CU retain a certain degree of internal protection, which is then progressively dismantled.

All these problems ultimately result from an issue which has been overlooked so far, namely the fact that the analysis of a CU with economies of scale does not measure the welfare losses arising in a country when production is terminated in favour of another country. Consider the standard case depicted in Figure 2.12, where every agent seems to be better off: we have seen that consumers in P benefit from a cost reduction effect, while producers sell their extra output to H at a price in excess of world market prices; consumers in H, in turn, benefit from trade creation. But what about producers in H, which lose their entire production? The answer might be that they will specialise in the production of another good (only one homogeneous good at a time is considered in the analysis), but this might entail huge transaction costs in the form of reconversion of their production lines and in the learning process associated with it.

Furthermore, having insofar supposed perfect competition in the market, we avoided to investigate what happens to the market structure when economic integration takes place. However, in order to precisely assess the relevance of these arguments, other, deeper forms of economic integration which go beyond the simple use of tariff policies have to be considered. This will be done in the next chapter.

NOTES

1. A famous book by a Norwegian economist, Ragnar Nurske (1944), *International Currency Experience: Lessons from the Inter-War Period*, points out the effects of flexible exchange rates and commercial wars. In a more recent, controversial paper on 'feasible' globalisations, Rodrik (2002) points out that 'During the first four decades following the close of the Second World War, international policy makers had kept their ambitions in check. They pursued a limited form of internationalisation of their economies, leaving lots of room for national economic management. . . . This strategy changed drastically during the last two decades. Global policy is now driven by an aggressive agenda of "deep" integration – elimination of all barriers to trade and capital flows wherever those barriers may be found' (Rodrik, 2002, p. 2).
2. Robson (1998), ch. 2.
3. Essentially it is assumed that individuals have a constant rate of substitution in preferences, while firms face costs increasing with quantities.
4. For example, because of the pressures of the local producers on the government.
5. See Salvatore (2003, pp. 273–95) for a good survey on the different tariff and non-tariff barriers to trade.
6. Technically it is always possible to assume a tariff T_H which is higher than p_H, what is known as a 'more than prohibitive' tariff. In this case, we would be generating an extra surplus for the local producers.
7. The World Trade Organisation reports, for example, that the average (*ad valorem*) world tariff on manufactured goods declined from 46 per cent at the end of World War II to levels close to 3 per cent at the end of the 1990s. Chisik (2003) provides a theoretical rationale for the gradual, rather than immediate, removal of trade barriers among countries.
8. The World Trade Organisation provides on its website a constant update of the situation of Regional Integration Agreements worldwide (see http://www.wto.org/english/ tratop_e/region_e/region_e.htm).

9. The EU free trade agreement with Poland had 81 pages of small print in its rules of origin section, and NAFTA some 200, which can turn the bargaining over rules of origin into a very costly exercise (Krueger, 1997).
10. A price discrimination is not unexpected, since two 'different' goods are now present in *H* and in *P*: consumers in *P* consume only the goods imported from the Rest of the World, while consumers in *H* consume only the (entire) production of country *P*.
11. This result cannot be generalised, however, since if country *H* is significantly larger than country *P* (that is, the previously discussed case in which country *P* is not able to fully satisfy the extra demand of country *H* with its own production at price p_P), then it might well be that the loss in exports the rest of the world experiences in country *H* (*AB*) is larger than the new exports (EQ_P) arising in country *P* due to the effect of indirect trade deflection.
12. When a WTO member enters into a regional integration agreement such as an FTA or a CU, through which it grants more favourable conditions to its partners in the agreement than to other WTO members, it departs from the guiding principles of non-discrimination as the basis of the WTO regulation (see Chapter 10). WTO members are however permitted to enter into such arrangements under specific conditions which are spelled out, among others, in paras 4 to 10 of art. XXIV of GATT (the original agreement on which the WTO is based). In this article it is said that, if a free trade area or customs union is created, duties and other trade barriers should be reduced or removed on substantially all sectors of trade in the group. In any case, non-members should not find trade with the group any more restrictive than before the group was set up. Hence the opportunity of a so-called 'tariff averaging' customs union, where the CET is set as the (weighted) average of the previous tariffs of the members, thus satisfying the requirements of art. XXIV.
13. We abstain here from considerations on the potentially perverse redistributive effects of such a gain in welfare in country *P*, since the welfare shifts from consumers to producers.
14. Excluding, of course, the trade flows taking place within the EU.
15. We draw here upon Krugman and Obstfeld (2003, ch.5), to which the reader should refer for a more comprehensive analysis.
16. Analytically, we can write $V = P_F Q_F + P_T Q_T$. A given isovalue line expresses the different combinations of textiles and food that (i) can be produced within the production possibility frontier and (ii) once considered together, yield a constant value.
17. Given the analytical expression of the isovalue line, we can in fact write $Q_F = V/P_F - (P_T/P_F)Q_T$.
18. This makes perfect economic sense: the economy has experienced an increase in the price of the good in which it was already a net exporter. To know exactly what happens to the trade flows, however, that is where C^1 lies with respect to *C*, one should investigate the standard income and substitution effects associated with such a change. The discussion is very well summarised in Krugman and Obstfeld (2003, ch. 5, pp. 97–8).
19. At any other relative price, the desired quantities of imports and exports of the two goods would in fact not be equal, and this would put pressure on the relative price to move towards its equilibrium level.
20. One can also see this by looking at the effects of an increase in P_F on the isovalue lines of country *H*.
21. See Salvatore (2003), ch 8, pp. 254–6 for a useful discussion on this point.
22. See Alesina *et al.* (2001a) for a formal, political economy theory of international unions of countries.
23. This normally arises when the production technology is characterised by high fixed costs (for example, design of a product or setting up of production chains) and low variable costs. Typical cases are car production or the software industry. In this case the total cost of production *C* will be $C(q) = F + cq$, where *c* is the marginal cost, *q* is the quantity supplied and *F* are the fixed costs. It can then be seen that in this case average costs (AC) are given by $C/q = F/q + c$ and thus are decreasing with quantities.

24. Actually, assuming fixed costs of production and increasing returns, we depart from a perfectly competitive set-up, since, for a given price, the number of firms in equilibrium cannot be infinite (firms will not be atomistic, but rather will have some market power). This is due to the fact that, for a given equilibrium price, the entry of a new firm would reduce the quantities sold by all firms, and thus raise the average costs faced by each firm above the price. Hence only a finite number of firms can operate in a given market. For the time being, we will ignore this point, which will be discussed in Chapter 3.
25. As in the previous cases, it is always possible to also assume a more than prohibitive tariff T_H higher than p_H, generating an extra surplus for the local producers.
26. In the traditional analysis, instead, the increasing costs characteristics of the supply curve are such that any excess of supply in *P* comes at higher prices than the equilibrium price, as shown in Figures 2.6 and 2.7.
27. This and the following examples have been proposed by Robson (1998).
28. There is, however, some evidence that trade is one of the main channels through which technology transfers might take place. See Keller (2004) for a general survey of this issue.

3. The theory of market integration and the EU Single Market

3.1 INTRODUCTION

In Chapter 2 we have shown that, within the framework of the orthodox analysis of economic integration, selective forms of protectionism such as customs unions (CU) or free trade areas (FTA) are in general not superior, on welfare grounds, to free trade situations. We have also learned that the picture changes when we move away from canonical hypotheses and introduce in the analysis issues like imperfect information, transaction costs, economies of scale and large countries. In the latter case, CU might be superior to FTA, contrary to the standard findings (Krueger, 1997). Customs unions, to a certain extent, might even be superior to a free trade situation if, through these agreements, a given set of countries achieved enough bargaining power with respect to the rest of the world.[1] On these arguments, the European Union (EU) thus pursued its regional integration agreement (RIA), setting up in 1968, as we have seen, its Customs Union.

But what have been the effects of the EU Customs Union in terms of economic growth? Limiting our analysis to the effects forecast by the orthodox theory of market integration (that is, excluding the case of economies of scale), we find that the CU in its early years did not create a large trade diversion, but at the same time it added only 0.5 per cent to the GDP of its six founding members (Balassa, 1975). The reason lies in the fact that 'classical' forms of integration can generate gains for the member countries essentially in accordance with the law of comparative advantages: by liberalising the free circulation of goods, countries can have access to the most efficient producer in the area, rationalising their production and improving the allocation of resources. The magnitude of these effects, as seen in the previous chapter, will, however, depend on the extent of the change in imports and the level of the tariff. Now, as pointed out by Baldwin and Wyplosz (2003), in the 1960s the Six had an import-to-GDP ratio of around 20 per cent, and *ad valorem* average tariffs already below 25 per cent. Taking into account the import demand elasticity (how much imports respond to changes in price, estimated at around 2.0 per cent), the gains obtained in Europe through a pure trade integration effect could not be very high.

In a sense, the latter result was also recognised by policy makers. In Chapter 1 we have seen in fact that, as early as 1957, with the Rome Treaty, the member states not only decided to remove trade barriers between them, but also started the process of forming a **single market** (or common market), where the so-called **four fundamental freedoms** (free circulation of people, services, capital and goods) would be guaranteed. The general idea was precisely to go beyond the static (and limited) gains analysed by the orthodox theory of economic integration, trying to achieve gains which would have also a 'dynamic' component. Essentially the **theory of market integration** classifies these gains as deriving from different sources: (a) static gains deriving from the increase in market size resulting from the reduction in trade barriers, which allow for higher economies of scale and a change in the market structure; (b) dynamic gains deriving from increased rates in the accumulation of the factors of production (capital and labour); (c) dynamic gains from the wider range of varieties of differentiated products brought onto the market, increasing the general welfare of consumers (when 'love of variety' is assumed).

In what follows we will leave aside the welfare effects brought to consumers by the provision of differentiated products, an analysis which goes beyond the scope of this book.[2] We will instead concentrate our attention on the changes in market structure induced by a process of economic integration, and on the gains deriving from factor mobility.

3.2 THEORETICAL GAINS FROM A SINGLE MARKET

We have already explored in the previous chapter the overall effects of economies of scale on trade integration. On that occasion we mentioned that, with increasing returns, the underlying market structure is not perfectly competitive any more, but rather a finite number of firms exist on the market, each with the ability to charge positive mark-ups (the difference between price and marginal costs) in order to cover their fixed costs. It is now time to explore this issue in greater detail, trying to assess what happens in the background of the economies of scale model we have analysed in Chapter 2.

This is important, since in general situations where firms are not atomistic and enjoy some market power (or even monopoly positions) more closely represent the reality of the Union. In such a set-up, trade integration can lead to gains beyond the ones identified by the orthodox analysis, since, provided that certain conditions are met, it induces changes in the underlying market structure, leading to fewer, bigger and more efficient firms, with lower mark-ups and thus lower prices for consumers.

The chain of events is as follows:[3] suppose that, before the process of economic integration, the market is fragmented along national dimensions, with firms enjoying some market power in their own market and zero power in the others. In the short run, once products can freely circulate, firms start to compete for market shares also in the other national markets. Provided that these firms do not collude, the new equilibrium price will be characterised by a lower mark-up, induced by the greater competition each firm faces in its national market, with each firm selling individually less than before, but with a total quantity now available in equilibrium on the single market greater than before, thanks to the lower mark-ups and thus prices.[4] However, because of the lower quantities produced by each firm, the average cost of each firm will increase. This will determine the long-term dynamics of the market structure. If in fact the resulting price turns out to be below the average cost now faced by each firm, each firm will start making losses.[5] Hence a process of industrial restructuring will take place, with some firms leaving the market, mark-ups (and prices) slightly increasing and firms increasing their sales level (and reducing their average costs) to the long-run equilibrium level.[6] At the end of the process, prices in the single market will have decreased with respect to the pre-integration situation, and quantities will have increased. Consumers will therefore experience an increase in their welfare, as shown with the trade creation and cost reduction effects analysed in the economies of scale model of Chapter 2. At the same time, however, the total number of firms will be less than the sum of firms previously operating in each national market, with each firm now bigger and more efficient, charging lower mark-ups but selling greater quantities and thus facing lower costs.

In a nutshell, the process of economic integration leads, in the following order, to a reduction in market segmentation, greater competition, lower oligopolistic mark-ups and thus prices, higher quantities produced, and industrial restructuring leading to fewer, bigger firms. The resulting gains, as we shall see in the next paragraphs, can be substantially higher than the ones measurable through the standard orthodox theory of market integration.

However the nature of these gains remains a static, allocative one. They arise once and for all when the policy change (free circulation of goods) is implemented, leading to a reallocation of resources generating a new market structure. But the growth rate of the economy is not permanently affected, unless new liberalisation policies are implemented (such as the free circulation also of services). The goal of the policy makers is instead to implement policies allowing the economy to grow at permanently higher growth rates, that is, to achieve what we have called **dynamic gains**. Factor mobility (free circulation of capital and people) plays for this purpose a very important role.

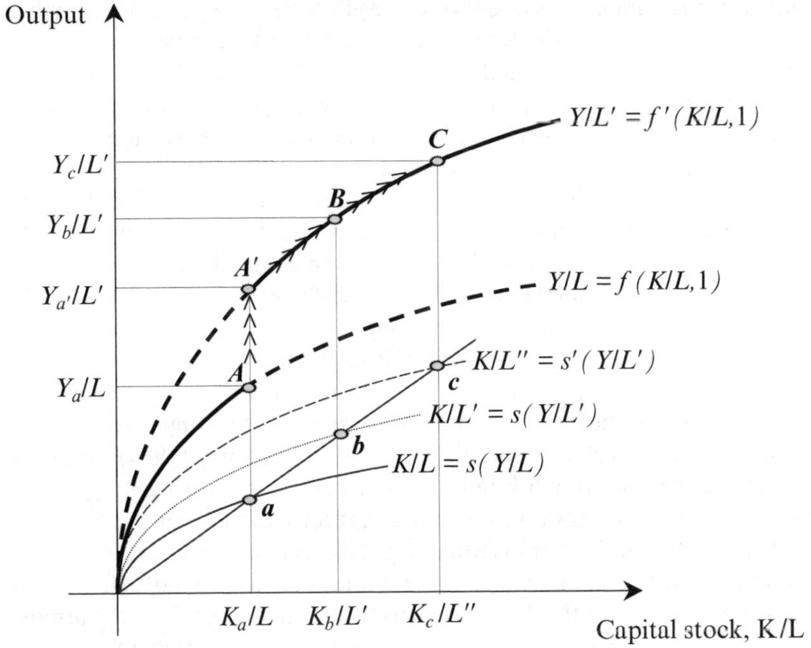

Figure 3.1 Theoretical gains from a common market

The gist of the latter argument can be found in Figure 3.1, which employs a standard neoclassical growth model *à la* Solow to make the point.[7] Essentially the static, once and for all efficiency gains of market integration previously analysed can be summarised as a higher productivity of the capital/labour ratio K_a/L, that is an upward shift in the production function (from Y/L, depending on f, to Y/L', depending on f' in the figure). This leads to a higher output (from A to A' in the figure) and thus an increase in the EU GDP ($Y_{a'}/L' > Y_a/L$).

However, owing to the shift in the production function, K_a/L is no longer the equilibrium capital/labour ratio, which is now determined by the K/L' curve (recall that $K/L = sY/L$). In other words, with an output level of $Y_{a'}/L'$, and given the constant depreciation of capital (the constantly sloped line starting from the origin), the marginal productivity of capital has risen, and thus point a does not denote any more an equilibrium between capital accumulation and capital depreciation. As a consequence, if the single market allows for a greater availability of capital through its free circulation, more capital will be invested until the higher marginal productivity of capital will again be equal to its cost (the point *b* in the figure, associated to the level of capital K_b/L'). This further increases the output at the level Y_b/L' (point *B* in the figure).

If, in addition, the integrated market increases the overall efficiency of all industries, including the financial sector, it is even possible also for the cost of each unit of capital to become lower, and hence for more investment to be brought to the market. In our diagram, this results in an increase in the saving rate, from s to s'. This further magnifies the growth effect because the equilibrium capital/labour ratio will now be determined by the K/L'' curve, obtained starting from K/L' with the new rate of savings s', in turn leading to the new equilibrium levels of capital and output K_c/L'' and Y_c/L' (points *c* and *C* in the figure), respectively.

The increased growth rates of GDP experienced while the economy moves from point A' to *B* and then to *C* thus represent the dynamic gains that free factor mobility (of capital, in our simplified setting) can generate on the common market. Using this framework, Baldwin (1989) estimates this 'medium-term growth bonus' to be equal, in total, to the aggregate static gains (the shift from *A* to A', in our figure) achievable on the common market via the simple liberalisation of goods/services.

Two considerations arise from the above arguments. First of all, in order for both the static and the dynamic gains to be generated, it is of the utmost importance that markets be thoroughly integrated, that is that all obstacles (tariffs and non-tariff barriers) to the free circulation of goods, services, capital and people are removed. This is much easier said than done, owing to the resistance that the process of market restructuring normally generates among the economic agents, since some firms end up exiting from the market. Competition rules have also to be set up and enforced, to prevent firms from colluding and maintaining higher than normal mark-ups and entry barriers. The second consideration relates to the fact that the higher stock of (more productive) capital does not necessarily modify the growth rate of the EU economy in a permanent way. In the proposed framework, in fact, once the output has reached the equilibrium level Y_c/L' (point *C* in the figure), growth stops, and only a new shock perturbing the underlying equilibrium of the capital/labour ratio with respect to the savings rate will be able to restore it.

The latter point will be extensively dealt with in Chapter 5 of the book, where we will discuss the appropriate strategies (the so-called 'Lisbon Agenda') set up by the EU to foster permanently higher growth rates across the member states. The issue of market integration, and the process of removal of all obstacles (tariffs and non-tariff barriers) to the free circulation of goods, services, capital and people will be discussed in the following sections. Finally, competition issues will be the subject of Chapter 9.

3.3 CREATING A SINGLE MARKET

In order to maximise the gains previously analysed, markets should be perfectly integrated. In particular, we can define **market integration** as a situation such that the flows of products, services and factors between countries are on the same terms and conditions as within countries. It implies that products can be traded between distinct markets or countries just as they are within a country, and thus the resulting common area can be referred to as the '**single market**'. Hence, in the single market, price differences eventually arising among countries should be no more than the cost of transportation plus related transaction costs. As already recalled, the EU tries to guarantee such a set-up, advocating the establishment in the single market of the **four fundamental freedoms**, that is, the free circulation of people, services, capital and goods across the member states.[8]

In order to achieve such a result, and thus maximise the gains from market integration, at least two dimensions of potential costs/distortions have to be eliminated, namely the issues of **market fragmentation** and the associated **regulatory framework**. Fragmented markets derive essentially from the presence of the **non-tariff barriers (NTBs)** we have analysed in Chapter 2. As we have already argued, these restrictions on trade, different from tariffs, originate from the existence of production standards or licensing regimes, and are often put in place in order to protect local market niches and thus resist the restructuring costs (the exit of firms) imposed by the process of market integration. Since these barriers prevent the free circulation of goods, capital, services and people, they have to be dismantled in order for us to grasp all the potential benefits of the integrated market.

However, in certain sectors, especially in services, it is not enough to remove NTBs to ensure smooth trade flows, never mind the fact that most services are non-tradable.[9] An adequate regulatory framework, in fact, has to be in place in order to guarantee also the **right of establishment**: the possibility for every national of a member state to exercise his own economic activity in another member state, in a level playing field equal for all the economic agents operating within the Union.[10] In order to foster such an attitude, which stimulates competition and economic restructuring, the same set of generic principles and rules has to be applicable throughout the single market. The further countries are from such a common regulatory framework, the higher are the costs and missed opportunities arising from the integrated market, as we have seen in the previous paragraph.

Finally, a third dimension of potential costs has to be considered, namely the negative **macroeconomic spillovers** that can arise for countries participating in an integrated market, where the four fundamental freedoms are guaranteed but no coordination of economic policies is ensured. In order to clarify this point, it is useful to exploit the features of a standard IS–LM model in an open economy context (*à la* Mundell and Fleming). Let us consider two countries, *A* and *B*, which operate within an integrated market, that is with perfect circulation of goods, capital and services (we can abstract from people's mobility here) and do not coordinate their macroeconomic policies. As a result, the two countries have a flexible exchange rate between their currencies determined by the uncovered interest parity (UIP).[11]

Hence

$$E_{A/B} = \frac{\bar{E}}{1 + i_A - i_B} \qquad \text{(UIP)}$$

where $E_{A/B}$ is the exchange rate of currency *A* versus currency *B*, $\bar{E}$ are the (fixed) expectations on the same exchange rate, i_A and i_B are the equilibrium interest rates in the two countries.

In equilibrium, country *A* produces Y_A^* at an interest rate i_A^*, so does country *B*, and the exchange rate is set at $E_{A/B}^*$. This situation is depicted in Figure 3.2a.

Let us now consider an autonomous fiscal expansion in country *A*. The *IS* curve moves to the right at *IS*′, and country *A* produces more ($Y_A' > Y_A^*$) at higher interest rates ($i_A' > i_A^*$). However, as can be seen, as soon as the interest rate in *A* increases, its exchange rate appreciates (fewer units of currency *A* are needed for a unit of currency *B*) because of the UIP, which holds thanks to the free circulation of capital. The lower value of the exchange rate $E_{A/B}'$ is such that the goods of country *A* become less competitive, and hence the shift to the right of its *IS* curve is partly hindered by the loss of exports (only the net effect is shown in Figure 3.2a). What is interesting, however, is what happens in country *B*. Since currency *A* appreciates, currency *B* depreciates (recall that $E_{B/A}$ is the reciprocal of $E_{A/B}$) and the competitiveness of country *B* increases. As a result, also the *IS* curve of country *B* moves to the right at *IS*′ thanks to the boost of exports (we have free circulation of goods) and the income of *B* increases to $Y_B' > Y_B^*$. Thus, owing to the existence of the common market, which guarantees free circulation of goods, capitals and services, country *B* benefits, without any policy intervention, from a positive spillover.[12]

However, a very different picture emerges if *A* tries to boost its competitiveness via a **competitive devaluation**, that is a depreciation of its currency via a reduction in its interest rates, leading to an increase in its exports. In such a scenario, depicted in Figure 3.2b, country *A* adopts an

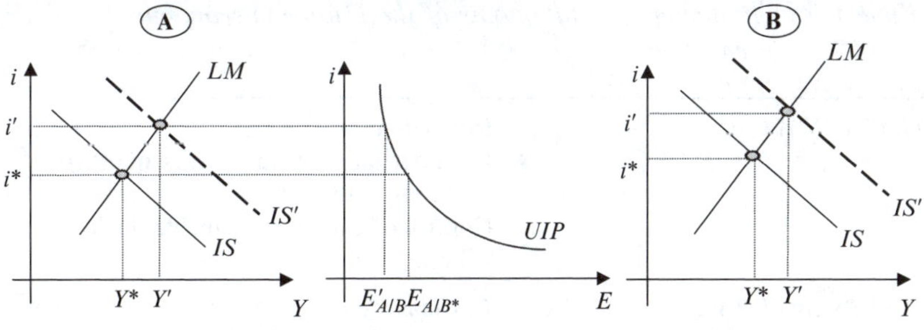

Figure 3.2a The effects of a fiscal expansion in A

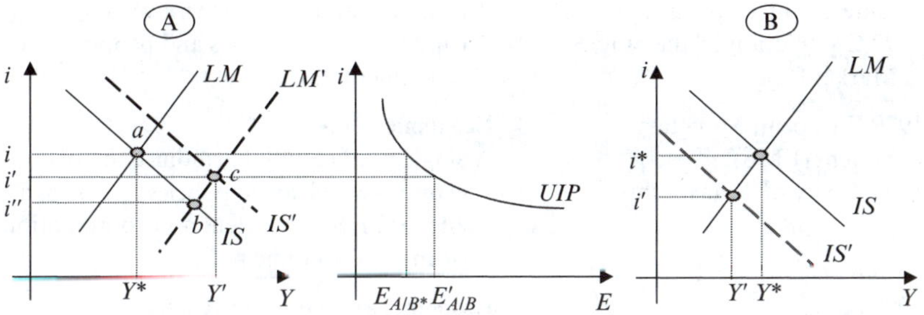

Figure 3.2b The effects of a monetary expansion in A

expansionary monetary policy (*LM* shifts in *LM'*), initially leading to an equilibrium at point *b* characterised by lower interest rates, and then, via the associated effect of the exchange rate depreciation (there is perfect capital mobility), to the equilibrium *c*, in which exports increase and hence the *IS* curve of country *A* shifts in *IS'* (we show here all the effects). The depreciation of currency *A* corresponds to an appreciation of currency B. Hence country *B*, without any change taking place in its economic policy, experiences a decline in competitiveness, a drop in exports (there is free movement of goods and services) and, ultimately, lower income levels, with its IS curve moving to the left at *IS'*. In this latter case, the existence of an integrated market (free circulation of goods, services and capital) together with flexible exchange rates opens the way, in the short run, to negative spillovers arising in one country owing to the uncoordinated macroeconomic policy taking place in a neighbouring partner.[13] As a result, in order to prevent these kinds of '**beggar-thy-neighbour**' policies (as they are also known) arising, member states have an incentive to set up some forms of macroeconomic coordination.

Table 3.1 Chronology and taxonomy of the European economic integration

Until WW II	**Protectionism** High barriers to trade (tariffs, quotas) among countries Control of capital movements. Tight immigration rules
1957 Treaty of Rome 1968 Entry into force of CET	**Customs Union** A free trade area with a common external tariff (CET) towards the rest of the world
1985 Single European Act (entered into force in 1987) 1992 Completion of the Single Market Programme	**Single Market** A customs union plus free movement of capital, goods, services and people (four fundamental freedoms)
1979 European Monetary System (EMS) 1993 Treaty of Maastricht	**Economic Union** A single market with harmonisation of economic and social policies to ensure an effective free movement and coordination of macroeconomic policies
1999 onwards	**Economic and Monetary Union** An economic union with a common monetary policy
Other forms of economic integration pursued by the EU with third countries	
2000 EU–Mexico 2002 EU–Chile 2010 (possibly): EU–south Mediterranean countries	**Free Trade Area (FTA)** All barriers to trade among integrating members are removed. Existing barriers to trade of each member towards the rest of the world are in place

Some authors claim that macroeconomic coordination transforms a single market (an area where the four fundamental freedoms are guaranteed) in a different, deeper form of economic integration known as **economic union**, as summarised in the taxonomy presented in Table 3.1. The question is mainly a semantic one, and thus we will use the definition of a single (or common) market to encompass both concepts.

In particular, in the next section we analyse in detail the evolution of the European Single Market, showing the institutional changes undertaken in order to minimise the costs previously analysed and to maximise the gains associated with its creation.

3.4 THE EU SINGLE MARKET

3.4.1 The Institutional Design

As we have already seen in Chapter 1, from its very beginning the EU, with the Treaty of Rome, was established not only as an area in which the free circulation of goods was guaranteed (the Customs Union), but also as a single market, that is, an area based on the four fundamental freedoms plus some degree of macroeconomic coordination.[14] Essentially all the developments in the integration process that occurred from 1968 to the early 1990s are related to ensuring the effective implementation of these freedoms, as can be seen in the taxonomy of Table 3.1.

In fact, in Rome, the six founding states agreed to create, besides the Customs Union, a programme for the approximation of their national legislation. Nevertheless, in this field, the developments proceeded at a very slow pace, owing to the willingness of member states to keep some markets segmented, in order to retain some form of market power and prevent the restructuring of local industries considered as 'strategic' (such as public utilities).[15]

Nevertheless, between the 1970s and the mid-1980s, a growing conviction emerged among the major industrial powers in Europe that the fragmentation of the internal market was an obstacle to European competitiveness, since it was preventing the dynamic gains typically associated with common markets (previously analysed) being fully exploited. Such a political consensus led the European Institutions to start eliminating some of the potential costs/distortions still existing in the Community (as the Union was known at the time).

In particular, in 1979, a judgment of the Court of Justice, known as the 'Cassis de Dijon' case (see Box 3.1), established the **principle of mutual recognition** of national rules, claiming that the legislation of another member state is equivalent in its effects to domestic legislation. More specifically the principle states that, in those sectors which have not been subject to harmonisation measures at the Community level, or which are covered by minimal or optional harmonisation measures, every member state is obliged to accept on its territory products which are legally produced and marketed in another member state. Member states may only challenge the application of the principle in cases where, in particular, public safety, health or the protection of the environment are at stake. However, in these cases, any measures taken must be compatible with the principles of necessity (member states have to prove the need for a given measure) and proportionality (the measure has to be proportional to its goal; that is, it has to achieve the goal minimising as much as possible distortions to the free movement of goods).

BOX 3.1 THE CASSIS DE DIJON CASE (CASE 120/78 RULED ON 20 FEBRUARY 1979)

The case was related to the import of a consignment of a fruit liqueur, '*Cassis de Dijon*', originating in France for the purpose of marketing it in Germany. The German monopoly administration denied the authorisation to import the product in question as an alcoholic beverage, on the grounds of its insufficient alcoholic strength (15–20 per cent versus a minimum German standard of 25 per cent). Such a standard resulted in the product not being marketable in Germany as a beverage, while it was freely sold in France. The European Court of Justice ruled that the fixing by the German authorities of a minimum alcohol content leads to the result that well-known spirits products from other member states of the Community cannot be sold in the Federal Republic of Germany; as a result, since the provision constitutes a restriction on the free movement of goods between member states, it has to be removed.

The three principles of mutual recognition, together with the **principle of non-discrimination** laid down in TEC, art. 12[16] as well as the already mentioned right of establishment foreseen by TEC, art. 43, have been crucial for the creation of the single market. In fact, the extension of these principles to the free circulation of services and factors of production clearly helped to reduce drastically the typical obstacles to market integration previously analysed.[17]

Against this background, work also started on the second dimension of costs/distortions, namely the one related to the completion of the regulatory framework. In fact, in addition to the direct provisions of the Treaty (the application of the right of establishment and the principle of non-discrimination) and the ones deriving from case law (the principle of mutual recognition), it should be noted that TEC, art. 3 provides for 'the approximation of the laws of member states to the extent required for the functioning of the common market'. In other words, as already considered in the previous paragraph, the three principles of non-discrimination, right of establishment and mutual recognition are not sufficient to guarantee the complete removal of all NTBs operating in the common market, and thus to ensure the free circulation of goods, services, capital and people. Rather a common set of rules (in EU terms, **directives** or **regulations**[18]) have to be agreed by member states in order to harmonise national rules, create a level playing field for every economic agent in Europe and generate mutual confidence in the regulatory frameworks.

To this purpose, in 1985 the Commission published a White Paper on the completion of the internal market (European Commission, 1985), and identified 282 legislative measures needed to remove obstacles to trade within the Community, putting forward a schedule for the creation of the Single European Market on 31 December 1992. In particular, the White Paper identified and proposed to dismantle two main categories of obstacles to the completion of the internal market: (a) **cost-increasing barriers**: all measures causing delays at borders due to border controls and customs administration, or the need to comply with different national technical regulation and standards; (b) **market entry restrictions**: all measures preventing the right of establishment or trading across frontiers in certain service industries (such as insurance or electricity) or professions, or entry to some regulated markets (such as civil aviation or public procurement[19]).

At the same time, a Council Resolution of 1985 implemented a new system for technical **harmonisation** and standardisation (the so-called 'new approach') according to which the harmonisation directives would, from then on, focus on the essential demands of health, safety and environmental protection at the European level, avoiding the overconcentration on details which unnecessarily prolonged the process of drafting and negotiating legislation. Defining technical standards has been left since then to specialised bodies such as CEN (European Committee for Standardisation), CENELEC (European Committee for Electrotechnical Standardisation) and ETSI (European Telecommunications Standards Institute), and other specialised committees eventually set up for this purpose.[20]

Notwithstanding these developments, achieving the 1992 single market objective would have required not only the technical instruments proposed by the European Commission, but also the political will of the member states. In fact, it would have been impossible to meet the 1992 deadline had the decision-making process still required unanimity. As a result, the 1985 Milan European Council which endorsed the Commission's White Paper on the completion of the internal market also came to political agreement on the **Single European Act** (SEA), which was signed in 1986 and came into force on 1 July 1987. As already recalled in Chapter 1, the SEA changed the decision process originally foreseen in the treaty agreed in Rome, making it possible for certain decisions to be taken by a majority vote in the Council of Ministers. In particular, the SEA inserted a new article into the EC Treaty, Article 100a (Article 95 under the Treaty of Nice numbering), stating that all the decisions on the measures aiming to establish the internal market, that is, related to the abolishment of the previously mentioned categories of obstacles, had to be agreed by qualified

BOX 3.2 MONITORING THE APPLICATION OF RULES ON THE SINGLE MARKET

The task of monitoring the ongoing application of the EU legislation on the single market falls in the first instance to national authorities, which must verify that all European directives are correctly applied following their transposition into national law. The Commission and the European Court of Justice, however, check that the EU-agreed law is adhered to over time, and that directives are actually transposed in the national legislation. In order to track this dynamic process, the Commission publishes an annual report on the application of Community law in the member states and, since 1996, a 'Single Market Scoreboard', (http://europa.eu.int/comm/internal_market/en/update/score/index. htm), a document which contains information on progress in member states' adherence to Community rules on the single market.

The Commission's monitoring methods are based on complaints lodged by private individuals, businesses or member states. If the Commission notes an infringement, it begins an infringement procedure addressed to a member state, demanding information and possibly issuing a recommendation to eliminate the infringement. In the few cases in which the member state in question does not comply with the Commission's recommendations, the Commission may begin an action before the Court of Justice, which gives a ruling as a last resort. Since the Treaty on European Union came into force in 1993, the court has been able to impose sanctions in the form of penalty payments on the infringing member states.

majority, in co-decision with the European Parliament (with the exception of measures relating to fiscal provisions, freedom of movement for persons and the rights and interests of workers).[21] As a result, the frequent delays inherent to the search for unanimous agreement were avoided, and the process of completion of the single market by and large managed to meet its 1 January 1993 deadline.

It is worth recalling here that the Community legislation governing the setting up of the single market is largely in the form of directives. These are juridical instruments which set equal rules across member states, and require the adaptation of the national legislation to the agreed principles

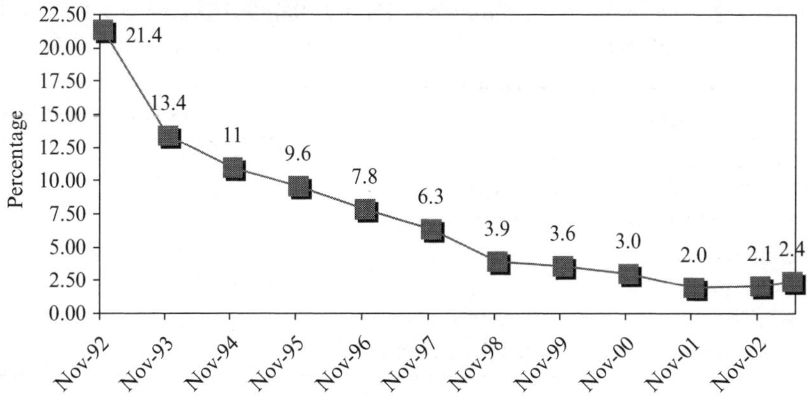

Note: Transposition deficit is the percentage of internal market directives not yet communicated as having been transposed in relation to the total number of internal market directives which should have been transposed by the deadline.

Source: European Commission, DG Internal Market.

Figure 3.3 Transposition deficit in the EU Single Market, 1992–2004

via the enactment of **transposition measures**. The transposition process has the advantage of allowing a degree of flexibility to member states in order to take into account their different legislative systems, but opens the possibility of delays and problems in such an exercise. Figure 3.3 shows the 'transposition deficit' in 2004, the percentage of single market directives not yet communicated as having been transposed by member states, in relation to the total number of single market directives which should have been transposed by the deadline.[22]

3.4.2 Consistency of the Design and Results Achieved

Once the process of completion of the single market had been set in motion, in order to give it further momentum the Commission launched in 1988 a study aiming at a comprehensive quantitative assessment of the economic gains to be achieved via the single market. The final Report (European Commission, 1988) was the synthesis of 16 volumes of studies of which the second, the 'Report on the Cost of Non-Europe', also known as the **Cecchini Report**, from the name of the economist who led the group of experts responsible for its drafting, is central. This document measured the costs associated with the lack of a single market in Europe as ranging, on various assumptions, between 4.3 and 6.4 per cent of EU GDP in 1985.

Table 3.2 The gains from completing the EU Single Market (Cecchini Report)

Category of gain	% EU GDP in 1985[a]
Elimination of trade barriers	0.3
Elimination of production barriers	2.4
Gain from reducing cost-increasing barriers	*2.7*
Economies of scale	0.5
Competition effects	1.6
Gain from reducing market-entry restrictions	*2.1*
Total gains from Single Market Programme	4.8

Note: [a] Estimates are based on partial equilibrium methods and on 1985 data at 1985 prices.

Source: European Commission (1988), Table 10.1.1.

As can be seen from Table 3.2, the reduction of cost-increasing barriers was estimated to generate the highest gains from market integration (at 2.7 per cent of the 1985 EU GDP). However these are short-term gains, achieved once and for all as soon as these types of barriers, directly bearing on firms' operative costs, are eliminated. More interesting from an economic policy point of view is the estimate of the second category of gains, those associated with a change in the underlying market structure via the process of market integration. Although these effects are estimated to account for a smaller amount of gains (2.1 per cent of 1985 EU GDP) and might take longer to happen, we have seen in the previous paragraphs that they are likely to be persistent over time, thanks to the structural change in the degree of competition taking place in the unified market. As a result their overall impact is a function of the degree of persistency of the increased market size brought in by the process of industrial restructuring. In particular, if a perfect degree of market integration is assumed to be in place after 1992 (that is, with firms charging the same price to all buyers in the EU), then the total amount of estimated gains increases from the reported 2.1 per cent (where some market segmentation is still assumed) to some 3.7 per cent of EU GDP.

The estimates provided by the EU Commission are clearly subject to some degree of criticism, in particular being essentially derived from partial equilibrium models, which disregard the welfare effects of adjustment costs (the restructuring process) and the time of adjustment. In addition the overall estimates are derived from the sum of industry-level estimates, and thus a simple algebraic sum might lead to some bias.[23] Finally the estimates are still basically static in nature, since they do not really take into account the long-term dynamic gains associated with the increased competition in the market, that is, a possible permanently higher growth rate for the EU economy.

Given these potential problems, and the overall limited amount of gains found by the Cecchini Report, especially when compared to the political cost of its implementation, one might wonder what has been the driving force behind the programme of completion of the single market. Actually policy makers tried to achieve exactly what we are less able to measure, the dynamic effects of the integrated market on innovation, productivity and investment, and hence on growth. If the single market can increase structurally, even by a modest amount, the overall growth rate of the European economy, the argument went, then this would soon translate into a large increase in the real income of citizens.[24]

The key question is then whether the latter argument holds: whether the single market programme is able to generate a structural increase in the growth rate of the European economy. In this regard, Baldwin (1989) argues that, in the medium term, such an effect is very likely to happen, and hence that the Cecchini Report substantially underestimates the overall gain associated with the single market programme, since it lacks a proper measurement of the dynamic economic gains. Hence, employing the model discussed in section 3.2, Baldwin estimates what he calls the 'medium-term growth bonus', that is, the change from the output levels A to C in Figure 3.1. He estimates this extra growth to be equal, in total, to the aggregate static gains calculated by the Cecchini Report. In addition, he finds that the resulting higher stock of capital might also permanently modify the growth rate of the EU economy, adding a permanent 0.5 per cent of extra growth a year, and thus a real increase in household's income of 5 per cent every ten years.

These ex ante evaluations of the single market programme were assessed in 1996 by an ex post exercise run by the European Commission (1996a). The study is based on a series of 38 in-depth sectoral analyses assessing the degree of implementation of the single market in the various European industries, and across them, in order to explore trade, investment and competition patterns across Europe. Although it is not easy to completely disentangle the effects of the single market from the other events that normally affect the economic cycle, the European Commission was able to conclude that, among other things, the single market seems to have generated, itself alone, an increase in output in the EU of more then 1 per cent on a permanent basis; to have created between 300 000 and 900 000 new jobs; to have decreased, thanks to the reduction in mark-ups, inflation rates in Europe by 1–1.5 per cent; and to have stimulated investment by an additional 2.7 per cent.

In addition, transport costs have decreased by €5 billions a year, thanks to the abolition of internal borders, while the new regulatory framework put in place in the telecommunications sector has decreased the price of telecom services by 7 per cent, saving the European consumers more than €1.5 billion a year.

Notwithstanding these positive results, which are in line with the ex ante expectations of the single market programme (although maybe on a lower order of magnitude), the single market is hardly ever seen as the main driving force of the business dynamics in a particular sector. Rather the integrated market should be seen as a driver of change: it helps to create the environment where businesses are more likely to pursue pan-European strategies, rather then directly dictating these strategies. Such an effect has been clearly visible in sectors such as air transport, banking, car production and telecommunications.

However two problems remain. First of all, the gains achieved by the single market, even on a permanent basis, do not seem to be enough to allow the EU to remain competitive worldwide, especially in comparison with the United States and its growth rates. As we have already discussed, the 'lack of growth' remains the crucial problem for the EU in the current decade. We will discuss this issue extensively in Chapter 5.

Second, and related to the previous point, a non-adequate working of the single market might be in part responsible for the poor growth performance of the EU. In fact, creating a genuinely integrated market is not a finite task, but rather a continual process, which requires not only the production of new legislation in order to encompass the changing needs of the EU economy, but also constant vigilance, in order to make sure that the EU legislation is then transposed and implemented at the national and local level. While the single market for goods and persons (as far as the EU competences are concerned)[25] is virtually completed, other areas remain still relatively unaffected by the single market programme, with markets still segmented along national lines. This is particularly true of some of the financial sector (including insurance), the pharmaceutical sector and energy. The lack of a truly integrated market in these industries might thus be responsible for the lower order of magnitude of the gains in growth measured by the EU Commission studies. As a result, further work needs to be done to squeeze out extra benefits from the single market,[26] allowing for a more rapid implementation of its provisions and a wider reach of its effects, extended also to small and medium firms in Europe.

These issues are analysed in detail in the next section, where we report progress in the creation of a single market for financial services, a process that started only in 1999.

3.5 FROM GOODS TO FINANCIAL SERVICES: THE FINANCIAL SERVICES ACTION PLAN

By no means did the 1992 deadline put an end to the efforts of the EU institutions in the construction of the single market, an effort further developed and strengthened in recent years. In fact, in line with the evolution in the structure of the European economy, which has seen a progressive shift from manufacturing to services,[27] the internal market had to be extended into new sectors, such as air transport, telecommunications, energy and financial services, crucial to the competitiveness of the economy as a whole. Consumer and environmental protection has also been significantly enhanced.

Indeed, due to these industrial dynamics, a programme such as the single market (for goods, persons, services and capital) typically goes through three phases: (a) the conception and the economic justification for the single market; (b) the adoption and the implementation of the legislative programme; (c) the exploitation by EU firms and citizens of these new opportunities. In a nutshell, the single market for goods and people (as far as the EU competences are concerned) can be said to be already in phase (c), while the single market for services, including public utilities and financial services, is still in phase (b).[28]

In particular, given the centrality of efficient financial services for the competitiveness of any modern economy, the European Commission started in 1999 the legislative phase for the financial services area, proposing an extremely ambitious plan known as the **Financial Services Action Plan** (FSAP), then endorsed by the heads of state and governments in June 1999 at the Cologne European Council.

The FSAP marks a landmark change in the strategy to complete the single market for financial services, and in general it establishes a new methodology for any further extension of the single market to new sectors. It is composed of 42 measures initially due for completion by mid-2004, in order to allow enough time for the transposition into national legislations. At the end of 2004, 39 of the 42 measures were adopted and the three remaining measures will likely be concluded by the end of 2005. Quite naturally, the FSAP is therefore generally considered as a success for the Commission. To understand the reason for this success, we shall analyse in detail the various aspects of the FSAP, starting with its content.

3.5.1 Content and Procedures of the FSAP

The FSAP pursues the main strategic objective of enhancing the functioning of underperforming pan-European financial markets and, by so doing, improving the prospects for sustainable, investment-driven growth and employment. Several studies have tried to quantify the benefits of financial markets integration at the EU level in terms of growth and employment. The most recent and comprehensive study (see London Economics, 2002) put benefits at some 1.1 per cent of the EU GDP (ranging from 0.3 per cent to 2 per cent across each member state, with the majority of countries in the range of 0.9 per cent to 1.2 per cent). The 1.1 per cent of GDP increase can be explained via the two usual channels of reduction in cost-increasing barriers (in this case, the reduction in the cost of credit due to increased liquidity),[29] and the increased degree of market integration.

Again the results of the study are essentially static and do not take into account any dynamic effects stemming from the increased demand for capital due to the reduced costs of credit. In fact the European financial market integration will affect the EU economies through a number of additional channels (better portfolio allocations, greater access to finance, more innovation and so on): thus the figure of 1.1 per cent of GDP can be said to be a relatively conservative estimate of the likely impact of deeper European financial market integration.

To achieve its goal, the FSAP has been divided in three sub-objectives, or areas of action: (a) to adapt the current supervisory framework to the integrated EU financial markets, by taking into account its global dimension; (b) to create an efficient internal market for customer business and remove legal obstacles so as to facilitate capital supply on an EU scale; (c) to ensure that retail financial services are both safe and competitive on an EU-wide scale. Thus, after the introduction of the single currency, the FSAP represented the single most important set of measures to reduce costs and ensure the safety of cross-border trading, both for the wholesale and for the retail market.

In our opinion, the strategic element behind the success of the FSAP lies in its **comprehensive character** (42 measures concerning retail and wholesale markets), driving expectations of economic agents towards a change in attitudes. Financial markets are in fact an area where, almost by definition, credible projects can be self-fulfilling.[30] The FSAP introduced dynamism and credibility in the whole process and favoured not only the convergence of the economic indicators (as detailed below), but also the growing presence of financial institutions on partner country markets.

To monitor the economic benefits from financial integration, the European Commission, since the year 2004, issues a regular report containing a series of indicators.[31] The first of such reports (see European Commission, 2004a) shows a marked degree of convergence over time of the main financial indicators, albeit to a varying extent, the difference depending essentially on the liquidity of the financial instrument and on the competition in the market for that instrument (see Figures 3.4 and 3.5).

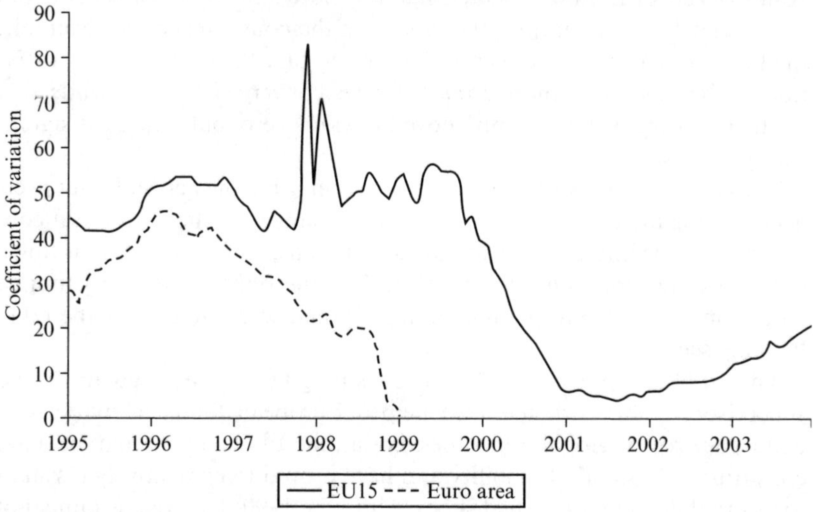

Source: ECB and Commission Services.

Figure 3.4 Convergence of the three-month money market rates

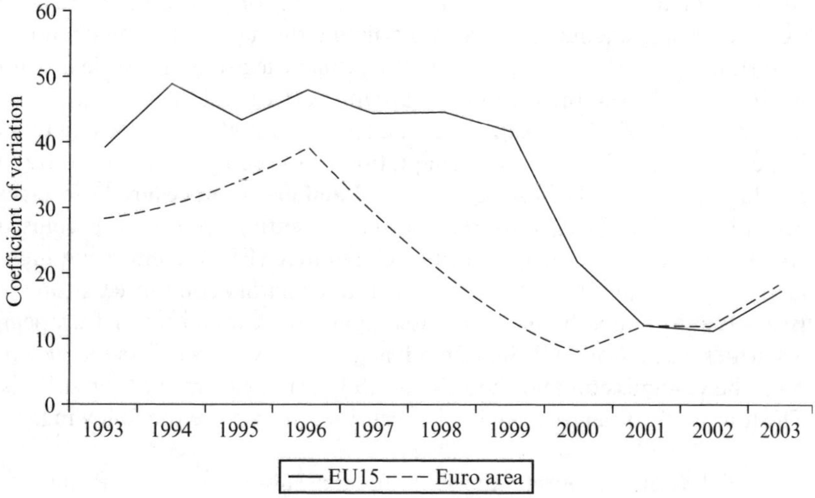

Source: ECB and Commission Services.

Figure 3.5 Convergence in bank lending rates: short-term loans to corporations

A simple rule of thumb indicates that, the more liquid the instrument, and the greater the competition, the greater is the convergence. For example, the liquidity effect can be seen by observing that the coefficient of variation in the unsecured money market rates converged to zero, while that of the government bonds only moved towards zero, but remained significantly positive.

The competition effect is visible when comparing the across-EU convergence of the interest rates for corporation loans with the across-EU convergence of the interest rates for consumer loans: while the former is down to less than half of its historical value, the latter only shows a very limited reduction, likely due to the remaining national segmentation of the retail banking sector.

The emphasis put by the FSAP on strengthening the regulatory and supervisory framework has also helped European financial markets to better face recent global difficulties. So far, the EU financial markets have constituted an island of stability and have proved to be relatively resistant to external monetary and real shock. Until the 1990s this was certainly not the case, with the reaction of EU financial markets to any external shock often being divergent across countries, thus exacerbating the initial problem and introducing asymmetries into the EU economies.

Technically speaking, most of the measures of the FSAP rely on the **extended comitology procedure**. In plain words, the FSAP extends and adapts to financial markets the standard EU comitology procedure, the one we have already encountered when discussing the harmonisation of industrial standards across the EU: there the primary legislation was dealt with by the Commission, the European Parliament (EP) and the Council, while the technical level, the so-called 'secondary legislation', was delegated to ad hoc committees of experts. The adaptation of the comitology procedure to the financial markets, also called the **Lamfalussy procedure**,[32] foresees instead a four-level legislative process and the setting up of two specialised committees: the European Securities Committee (ESC), comprising high-level member states officials and acting as a regulatory committee, sitting in Brussels and chaired by the Commission; and the Committee of European Securities Regulators (CESR), an advisory committee providing advice to both the Commission and the ESC on technical measures, sitting in Paris. The four levels of legislation for the securities market are the following.

Level 1 (**principle level**): the Commission submits to the EP and the Council, after wide consultation with both private and public stakeholders, a framework directive to be adopted under the standard co-decision procedure (qualified majority in the Council and absolute majority of votes in the EP).[33] The framework directive should contain

only general principles, while the technical aspects are delegated to the second level of legislation.
Level 2 (**technical level**): the CESR prepares the implementing measures of the proposed directive, which are then submitted by the Commission to the ESC for approval. If the ESC approves, the Commission adopts.
Level 3 (**implementation level**): the consistent implementation of the approved EU legislation across member states is strengthened by reinforced cooperation of national regulating authorities through the CESR.
Level 4 (**monitoring level**): the Commission in any case monitors the member states' transposition of the agreed legislation and, in face of any infringement of EU law, it takes the necessary legal action, as for the standard implementation of the single market's legislation.

This procedure, which may undoubtedly seem cumbersome, has at least three main advantages. First, the EP and the Council do not have to discuss technical details, which would render almost impossible a truly political debate on general principles, let alone reaching any meaningful agreement. Second, it assigns clear responsibility at the various levels of governance, and it allows informed decisions thanks to the obligation of having any proposal underpinned by an impact assessment. Third, it forcefully indicates that drafting and adopting legislation in the EP and in the Council is not the end, but rather the beginning, of the project. Indeed the Lamfalussy procedure puts emphasis on national implementation and community monitoring, being able to integrate these two fundamentally important phases into the process. The adoption of legislation at the EU level, then followed by inconsistent national implementation, would in fact be more damaging than beneficial, and would certainly not deliver the target advantages.

In particular, two recent developments stand as proof of the efficiency of the Lamfalussy procedure and its appropriateness for financial services. First, the EP attitude towards it turned from openly hostile to supportive in just a couple of years. Initially the EP felt that the Committee structure would lack a basic democratic character and could risk undermining its own authority, due to the executive powers delegated in the second level of the procedure. Indeed the EP approved only half-heartedly the Lamfalussy procedure in 2002, incorporating a revision clause. However, following an explicit commitment by the Commission in 2004 to duly involve the EP also in the technical and implementation phases of the procedure, should the EP wish to intervene, our educated guess is that, in the framework of the revision of the Lamfalussy procedure, the EP will not ask for a radical modification of its current functioning.

Second, the Lamfalussy procedure, initially foreseen only for the EU securities market, has been extended to banking, insurance and collective investment funds; equivalent committees to the ESC and CESR have been created, as detailed below.

	Securities	Banking	Insurance and Occupational Pensions
Level II adopting committee	ESC (Brussels)	EBC (Brussels)	EIOPC (Brussels)
Level III supervisory committee	CESR (Paris)	CEBS (Frankfurt)	CEIOPS (London)

Given the breadth of the FSAP, and the high stakes of the industry it aimed at reforming, its near completion within the foreseen deadline clearly puts it among the success stories of EU integration. The Commission has been unanimously supporting it and has relentlessly pushed the EP and the Council to back up the project. The Council and the EP, after the initial resistance, have been responding positively to the whole process, notwithstanding specific difficulties and national sensibilities regarding one or the other measure.

Probably part of the public commitment to respect the FSAP deadlines comes from the overall support that markets (both the 'supply' side, such as banks and insurance, and the 'demand' side, such as consumers' associations and corporations) lent to the process. Wide consultation with private and public stakeholders that translated into greater involvement, greater transparency and a speedier procedure explains why markets have been so supportive of the FSAP. Without such commitment from all parties involved, a legislative process of such a magnitude and depth would have never been accomplished in full and in time.

3.5.2 The Extra-EU Dimension

The area of financial services has been characterised by an increasing degree of integration of financial markets worldwide, with considerable spillover effects towards and from other countries. As a result, the European Commission is engaged in several regulatory dialogues with third countries, in particular the USA and Japan, dealing with problem solving or prevention, the facilitation of market opening and the reduction of the regulatory burden for businesses.

In particular, in the last few years, the US attitude towards the EU in the area of financial services has significantly changed. By and large, until the adoption of the Euro and the launch of the FSAP in 1999, issues in financial services were dealt with on a bilateral basis between the USA and the individual member states. Since then, given the continuously increasing integration of the EU and US financial markets, the adoption of the FSAP on the EU side and the regulatory reform on the US side (for example the Sarbanes–Oxley Act) have raised the interest of both parties in talking and exchanging views and projects at an early phase of the legislative process.[34]

Furthermore an integrated, deep and efficient single market also for financial services in the EU gives a major opportunity for US firms in terms of choice of investors, portfolio allocation and greater returns on investment. The larger liquidity would also facilitate the financing of EU-based US companies, thus reducing their costs of borrowing and capital. In short, it is both in the US and the EU interest that the Financial Services Action Plan and the US regulatory reform succeed. To this purpose, a formal forum called the 'Financial Market Regulatory Dialogue', meeting roughly twice a year, has been established at senior level between US regulators (SEC, Treasury, relevant Congress committees) and EU regulators (the EU Commission, namely the DG internal market and its Commissioner).

Growing in importance, albeit under different formulas, is also the regulatory dialogue on financial matters that takes place with Japan, Switzerland, Canada and Australia. The Commission has also indicated that it plans to extend the dialogue to other countries, and specifically to China, given the fast-growing trade flows and relations between the EU and China.

3.5.3 Beyond the FSAP: Implementation of Existing Legislation

By the end of 2004, with the FSAP very close to completion, the regulation of financial markets in Europe had undoubtedly progressed and it had greatly strengthened the single market 'pillar' of the Economic and Monetary Union. More efficient and coordinated financial markets are in fact the best insurance against the rise of asymmetric shocks in the EU and are one of the tools through which to grasp the full benefits in terms of growth from the single currency (see next chapter). In particular we discuss here two possible future developments related to the regulation of financial markets in Europe: new legislation to be adopted, and the evolution of the process of tax coordination in the European Union.

As far as the first issue is concerned, the Commission launched in 2004 a detailed consultation exercise with market participants to establish the market appetite for further regulation in the post-FSAP era. The consultation process gave three clear indications. First, following the intensive legislative activity generated by the FSAP, markets and national authorities need a breathing space and especially need the time to transpose efficiently into national law the EU directives. A new major legislative programme (let us call it a 'FSAP II') would not have been welcomed by the industry.

Second, without prejudice to the first finding, market participants have indicated a few areas where legislative activity would be justified and welcome: these areas are the post-trade industry (essentially clearing, settlement and safekeeping, see Box 3.3), the asset management area, and the retail services area.

Third, in any case, the new legislation must be subject to a thorough regulatory impact assessment analysis prior to the Commission proposal being put in front of the European Parliament and the Council.

The Commission has agreed with this approach, and therefore it is likely that in the future it will produce fewer single market laws (see Box 3.3), paying instead more attention to the way the same laws are implemented, a crucial issue to ensure that Europe is ready to reap all the benefits from a thorough market integration in all its different sectors.

In addition to ensuring coherent implementation, the Commission has also committed itself to ensuring a quick repression of abuses. In fact, the possibility of appealing to the European Court of Justice in order to resolve an infringement of single market rules (see Box 3.2) is certainly important as a matter of principle, but it is scarcely practical if one considers that, in the event that a case goes to the court, half of the infringement cases take more than two years to be solved, and one-third take longer than four years. Citizens and businesses need much faster and more effective solutions to their problems, especially in the financial sector. To that end a network which encourages stronger cooperation between national administrations, called SOLVIT, has been created for all the single market cases (not only financial services). Its main characteristic is the ease of access for citizens and the assurance that relevant national administrations have a framework for effective cooperation. The initial results from SOLVIT are very encouraging.

3.5.4 Beyond the FSAP: Tax Coordination

The second possible legislative development in the single market, with a particular focus on the financial sector, relates to the actions that the EU has been taking with respect to the problem of **tax coordination** across member states, as also underlined by the 'Kok Report' (Kok, 2004) on the implementation of the Lisbon Agenda (see Chapter 5). To this end a distinction has to be made between direct taxation (such as personal and business income) and indirect taxation (such as VAT). In fact, while the

BOX 3.3 THE POST-TRADE INDUSTRY

The post trade industry is that part of financial industry that operates once investors have taken their investment decisions (for example, to buy 100 shares at a given price). The main functions of the industry are clearing (fixing the terms of trade), settlement (ensuring that the passage of securities takes place against the exchange of money) and safekeeping (safeguarding the securities and ensuring that the owner can properly exercise his or her rights). This industry is therefore considered crucial for ensuring a sufficiently high volume of trade in the EU financial markets. Currently obstacles to cross-border clearing and settlement segment a potentially integrated EU market into closed national markets, and therefore deprive any of them of the necessary volume and liquidity. Since at present there is no EU common regulatory and supervisory framework for this industry, the EU Commission has put forward a work plan that may lead, by 2009, to the implementation of a directive.*

In every member state there are typically three actors: (1) investors (both retail and wholesale) that hold money and securities accounts in commercial banks; (2) commercial banks, which are also called 'custodian banks' because they safeguard the title of property of the securities with the Common Securities Depository (CSD), where the changes in the individual securities accounts are settled; (3) one CSD (CREST for the UK, Euroclear Bank for Belgium, France and the Netherlands, Montetitoli for Italy, Clearstream Bank Frankfurt for Germany and so on) where securities are issued and registered. Nowadays, owing to some market consolidation of subnational CSDs and the legislative intervention of national authorities, there is only one CSD in each country.

Clearly, such an industry constructed across national lines works in a much less efficient way for cross-border transactions. For example, when an investor of, say, country *A* goes to a bank of country *A* to buy a share issued and registered with the CSD in country *B*, the bank of country *A*, not having direct access to the CSD in country *B*, would generally need to go through another bank in country *B* to complete the transaction. More intermediation means essentially three things, all detrimental: greater costs, reduced safety and fragmented liquidity. It has been calculated that cross-border clearing and settlement within the EU costs up to 10 times as much as domestic clearing and settlement within the

EU. This is in contradiction to the single market spirit, which aims at abating costs differential between cross-border and domestic transactions within the EU.

With the expansion of cross-border trading, market forces are reacting and providing some solutions to the current unsatisfactory situation. On the one hand, market forces are leading to some significant regional integration of the post-trade industry (for example, in Ireland and the UK), accompanied by an easier system of access rights; on the other hand, within national boundaries there is also emerging some vertical integration of the post-trade industry with the trade industry, a development potentially leading to a generalised cost reduction and a safer environment. If these market forces should prove unable to deliver a satisfactory result on a European scale within a reasonable time span, the EU institutions may then consider putting forward some other legislative alternatives. One possible alternative would be to grant generalised access rights (a sort of EU passport to custodian banks and national CSDs) and enforce a common regulatory and supervisory framework across the different actors of the post-trade industry. Advocates of this possibility claim that this solution has the merit of stopping short of indicating the optimal market structure, allowing existing market forces to shape it. On the contrary, others contend that the optimal market structure for the EU economy is given by one single CSD (as is the case in the USA, for example) and therefore one should consider establishing by law a single EU CSD, possibly user-owned or public-owned. Obviously these different approaches to the problem differ in a number of respects: the final benefits, the costs and the distribution of costs. The Commission has endeavoured to produce a detailed impact assessment report on this matter, together and in parallel with the legislative proposal (if any).

Note: * The work plan of the Commission foresees the publication of the regulatory impact assessment (RIA), together with a Directive (if the case is proven by the RIA) proposed by the Commission by mid 2006, then the standard 18 months for adoption in the EP and the Council, and the standard 18 months for national implementation.

former is entirely and autonomously decided by member states, the second has to be harmonised at the EU level, in order to ensure a smooth circulation of goods and services in the single market.[35]

Border controls on VAT were therefore abolished with the introduction of the single market in 1993, and a 'transitional' VAT system was put in place.[36] Since then, traders are required to keep detailed records of purchases from, and sales to, other countries; the VAT is then paid at the final destination of the good (**destination principle**), with the system policed by administrative cooperation between member states' tax authorities. The **origin principle** generally applies instead to all sales to final consumers: that is, once VAT has been paid on goods in one country, they can be moved within the Community without further control or liability to tax.[37]

The intention was that this transitional system should apply until the end of 1996, and then move towards a new VAT system based on the generalised application of the origin principle, which however requires an agreement among the member states' tax authorities to distribute the VAT revenues so collected. Owing to the difficulties experienced in this step of the procedure, which in any case requires unanimity according to TEC, art. 93, no formal legislative proposal has appeared so far. Rather the Commission has now shifted its emphasis from a move to a 'definitive' system towards measures to improve the present 'transitional' arrangements, although we cannot exclude some legislative action in future years.[38]

In terms of direct taxation, instead, although this is not formally an area of strict EU competence, during an informal meeting of the EU Ministers of Finance (ECOFIN) in Verona (Italy) in April 1996, the Commission proposed a new and comprehensive 'global' view of direct taxation policy (European Commission, 1996a). The document pointed out that the lack of coordination of taxation policy across member states in a single market where goods and capital were freely mobile was hindering the achievement of important Union objectives, such as promoting growth and employment. In particular, some forms of unfair tax competition started to emerge in the 1990s across member states, with non-resident citizens or firms being granted a more favourable tax treatment than local undertakings. As a result, some member states experienced a reduction in their capital tax base, while at the same time they were forced to decrease the tax rate on capital in order not to further aggravate the problem. To compensate for the missing revenues, however, they increased the taxation of labour, the latter being less mobile and hence less easily attracted by forms of preferential tax treatment in other member states. Such **harmful tax competition** thus resulted in an increase of unemployment and less growth across the EU.

For the above reasons, finance ministers welcomed the Commission paper and agreed on the need to consider these issues in a high-level discussion group, thus bringing for the first time issues related to direct taxation under a (partial) EU competence. The discussion produced a 'Tax Package' of measures to tackle harmful tax competition in the EU (also known as the **Monti package**, from the name of the Commissioner responsible for the dossier at the time), which consisted of a code of conduct to eliminate harmful business tax regimes, a measure to ensure an effective minimum level of taxation of savings income, and a measure to eliminate source taxes on cross-border payments of interest and royalties between associated companies. Negotiations on the three elements of the Tax Package resulted in a political agreement on 21 January 2003, with the tax package formally adopted at the ECOFIN meeting of 3 June 2003.[39] Box 3.4 discusses in detail the new directive on the taxation of savings income, which should enter into force in 2005.

BOX 3.4 THE TAXATION OF SAVINGS DIRECTIVE

The Council Directive 2003/48/EC of 3 June 2003 on taxation of savings income in the form of interest payments will apply as soon as agreements with certain third countries (Switzerland, Andorra, Liechtenstein, Monaco and San Marino) for equivalent measures will also be in place. Without these agreements, in fact, capital might easily bypass the EU directive, and thus evade taxation, by locating in neighbouring non-EU countries. Under the provisions of the directive, member states have introduced a system of automatic provision of information on the interest payments received by a non-resident individual to the member state in which the taxpayer is resident, in order to allow for the taxation of this income. Belgium, Luxembourg and Austria, however, will introduce the system of information reporting only at the end of a transitional period, during which they will levy a withholding tax at a rate of 15 per cent for the first three years, 20 per cent for the following three years and 35 per cent thereafter. They will transfer 75 per cent of the revenue of this tax to the investor's state of residence.

The Commission's report of 27 November 2002 considered the progress of negotiations with the United States, Switzerland, Liechtenstein, Monaco, Andorra and San Marino, obtaining assurances in relation to measures that could be considered equivalent to those provided for in the draft directive on savings taxation (that is, the exchange of information or the withholding tax). On the basis of the Commission's report, the Council considered that equivalent measures were in place in the case of the United States, while they were still to be implemented in the cases of Switzerland, Liechtenstein, Monaco, Andorra and San Marino. Therefore the

Council asked the Commission to continue negotiations with Switzerland and the other third countries, and to press for the exchange of information (rather than the withholding tax) as the EU's ultimate objective, reporting back to the Council before 2007, which therefore is the ultimate date for the entry into force of the directive.

The length of the 'transitional period' for the application of the withholding tax for Belgium, Luxembourg and Austria is also linked to the date on which the above-mentioned third countries will be committed to the exchange of information (rather than to a seven-year time limit specified in the directive as originally proposed). Clearly this might never be the case for some countries which are likely to keep on imposing the withholding tax rather than disclosing information, and hence in the EU a dual system of taxation of savings income might be in place in the future.

By its very nature, comprising both legislative and non-legislative acts, the tax package is still evolving, and its final outcome is not clear yet, since it depends on the willingness of the member states to press on towards the coordination or the competition dimension in disciplining the taxation of economic activities in the single market. Some member states fear that too much competition will lead to the harmful results experienced in the past, while others fear that too much tax coordination will generate a 'tax cartel' with member states ultimately colluding to impose high tax rates across the single market, to the detriment of the EU competitiveness.

The debate is likely to continue in the future, owing to the fact that the new member states of Eastern Europe, contrary to most of the EU-15, have some of the lowest corporate tax rates in the world.

3.6 THE EUROPEAN MONETARY SYSTEM

So far we have explored the institutional way in which the EU has responded to the two dimensions of potential costs/distortions that have to be eliminated in a common market, namely the issues of market fragmentation and the associated regulatory framework. We have seen that the single market programme, in its addressing the cost-increasing barriers and market entry restrictions of the EU segmented market, has been an efficient way to deal with the problem, and has helped in generating significant benefits for the European economy.

There remains to be considered, however, the third dimension of potential costs associated with the creation of a common market, as summarised

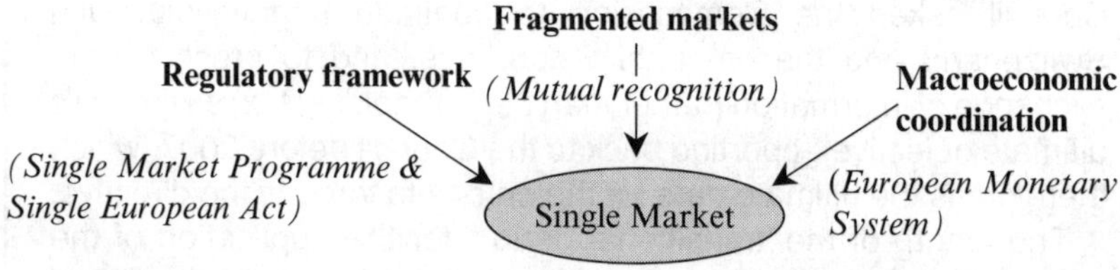

Figure 3.6 Implementing the single market

in Figure 3.6: the negative macroeconomic spillovers that can arise for countries participating in a market where the four fundamental freedoms are guaranteed but no coordination of economic policies is ensured. In particular, using a simple Mundell–Fleming model, we have seen in section 3.3 that these negative spillovers essentially derive from a set-up where exchange rates are perfectly flexible. Hence the incentive for the European countries to design schemes to try to fix their exchange rates.

Given the above, the careful reader might then wonder why the Treaty of Rome, which was already advocating the implementation of the four fundamental freedoms in Europe, did not consider these types of costs. The reason is that, at the time the Treaty was written, the international financial markets were already operating in a system of quasi-fixed exchange rates known as the **Bretton Woods system**. The latter was in fact the international monetary regime that prevailed worldwide from the end of World War II until the early 1970s. Essentially the Bretton Woods system was a **target zone** system of exchange rates, where the currencies had central parities pegged to the US dollar and the central banks were bound to maintain their currencies within narrow (1 per cent) bands of fluctuations, with the possibility of realignments over time of the central parities, following negotiations among members. The system was technically designed to be anchored to a pool of gold and national currencies reserves (with the IMF acting as the depository institution); however, given the scarcity of gold held as a reserve outside the United States, in the Bretton Woods system the USA became in practice the only source of global liquidity. In other words, the USA guaranteed the convertibility of US dollars into gold at a fixed price, thus making the dollar a near-perfect substitute for gold. The system worked fairly well until the mid-1960s, assuring a degree of financial stability unseen since the 1920s on the international financial markets. Therefore, in 1957, the Treaty of Rome could tackle the issue of the creation of the common market without having to deal with the problems of macroeconomic coordination and exchange rates.

After 1965, however, the US economic policy became increasingly destabilising for the Bretton Woods system, mostly as a result of increased government spending on social programmes at home and the escalating costs of the war in Vietnam. Inflation began to rise in America, together with balance of payments deficits, thus putting some strain on the gold–dollar convertibility. Yet the US policy makers, mainly concerned with their internal problems, declined to undertake any actions with respect to the exchange rate system, under a calculated policy of 'benign neglect'. Since the pegged-rate system was incapable of coping with widening balance of payments imbalances, a confidence problem arose, as speculators were encouraged to speculate on devaluation of the dollar or revaluations of the currencies of Europe or Japan.

Finally, concerned about America's rapidly deteriorating situation, as well as a rising protectionist sentiment in the US Congress, President Richard Nixon on 15 August 1971 suspended the convertibility of the dollar into gold, letting the dollar value float in currency markets. Eighteen months later, in February 1973, after new waves of speculation against a realigned structure of central parities negotiated in late 1971 (the so-called 'Smithsonian agreement'), the currencies of all the industrial countries became completely flexible.

As a result, in the mid-1970s, the EU member states were continuing the process of creation of a common market lacking any form of coordination of their exchange rates, a situation potentially very harmful for the process of economic integration. Hence, after a few years of great economic turbulence and great stress for the free circulation of goods within the common market, the EC endorsed in 1978 a proposal to form a 'zone of monetary stability' in Europe by establishing the **European Monetary System** (EMS), which started to become operational in 1979.[40]

The EMS worked remarkably well throughout most of the 1980s (see Box 3.5), in spite of major shocks to the European economy, and ensured across member states that degree of macroeconomic coordination which eliminated the possible negative spillovers deriving from a common market. In fact, in order to keep each currency within the agreed band of fluctuation, every member state had to prevent its inflation rate being too distant from the European average, otherwise, as time went by, the (nominal) fixed exchange rate would not have reflected the real purchasing parity of the currency, thus causing pressures for devaluation or revaluation of the central parity. Essentially, in the EMS, the problem translated into having an inflation rate not too distant from the one set by the Bundesbank for the Deutschmark, which, like the US dollar in the Bretton Woods system, became the anchor of the EMS. Although it was always possible to renegotiate the central parities, this required the unanimity of all the participating countries, and therefore the renegotiation was not granted, thus exposing any inflationary country to periods of real appreciation of its currency which were deleterious to its competitiveness.[41]

BOX 3.5 THE WORKING OF THE EMS

The EMS was nothing short of a mini-Bretton Woods system, limited to the European member states: the French franc, the Italian lira, the German Deutschmark and other European currencies in the system were fixed to a virtual currency, known as the European Currency Unit (or ECU), made of fixed quotas of all the EU currencies participating in the system, roughly in proportion to each country's economic weight. The fixing of the central parity of each currency to the ECU then determined the cross-rates for all the currencies. As in Bretton Woods, bands of fluctuations around the central parities were foreseen (countries could opt for a narrow band of +/− 2.5 per cent or a wider band of +/− 6 per cent), as well as the possibility of renegotiating the central parity, after a unanimous agreement of all the participating members.

The key to the viability of the system was the 'Very Short Term Financing Facility' (VSTFF), a financial instrument available to the central banks participating in the system through which each central bank could borrow overnight foreign currencies from the other central banks, in order to intervene on the market and defend the parity of its national currency without having to use its reserves. For example, if the French franc was being devalued against, say, the Deutschmark, thus hitting the top margin of the agreed band of fluctuation, the Banque de France could sell marks on the market (buying francs in order to sustain its fixing) borrowing via the VSTFF the same marks from the Bundesbank rather than using its (limited) foreign exchange reserves.

As a result, there was a strong incentive for countries to align their national inflation rate with the EU average, and this basically implied an implicit coordination of each member state's monetary policy to the policy set by the Bundesbank. Thus, via the EMS, the potential source of negative spillovers arising from uncoordinated macroeconomic policies (see section 3.3) was de facto eliminated.

In Chapter 4 we will try to understand what has led member states to replace the macroeconomic coordination framework provided by the EMS with the single currency. In the remainder of the present chapter, we will analyse the institutional framework that has led the single market to be enlarged to 25 member states, and the problems that might eventually derive from this decision.

3.7 THE EU ENLARGEMENT AND THE SINGLE MARKET

3.7.1 The Institutional Framework of the Enlargement

We have already seen in the first chapter of the book that, in June 1993, the Copenhagen European Council assured the countries of Central and Eastern Europe (CEECs) that they would become full members of the EU as soon as they satisfied the requisite political and economic conditions. Now we also realise that such a process started only a few months after the EU had (partially) met the 1992 deadline relating to the completion of the Single Market Programme,[42] during a very delicate phase of transition from the European Monetary System to the single currency (the Maastricht Treaty had been signed in February 1992). Comparing the new enlargement to the others which took place in Europe in the past, we also know that the enlargement to embrace the CEECs was a daunting task, being in absolute terms the largest in the history of the Union, involving ten countries and almost 80 million inhabitants.

An obvious question is why the EU at the beginning of the 1990s decided to face the political and financial challenge of combining at the same time its **deepening**, that is, a further progress in the integration process of the incumbent 15 member states through the setting up of a single market and a single currency, with its **widening**, an extension of the EU membership to new countries. Three main entwined factors can be identified in this regard.

The first factor is related to **history and geography.** The countries of Central and Eastern Europe historically have always been part of the 'traditional' European states, even from a religious point of view. By and large, Hungary, Slovenia, the Czech and Slovak Republics and part of Romania were for centuries part of the Habsburg Empire; Poland was first independent and then, together with Lithuania, it became Prussia, and so on. In terms of geography, the notion of 'Eastern' countries is itself biased,[43] since both Helsinki and Athens, two European capitals, are further east than most of the CEECs, and likewise Vienna is located to the east of, say, Prague. Such a historical and geographical proximity also brought about firm cultural ties between the two sides of Europe.[44] In sum, the last 50 years of divisions caused by the Cold War were but a very limited, though dramatic, interruption in what had otherwise been a history of shared experiences and culture across the Continent.

The second factor concerns **politics and security.** Such proximity of the CEECs, although in principle a factor of union across Europe, in the short term immediately posed a political problem for the current member states.

After the fall of the Berlin Wall in 1989, the CEECs, in views of the historic ties, immediately looked to the European Union, and the outstanding level of prosperity it had reached, as the natural scenario within which to take their first steps as independent countries. To deny those countries the membership they sought would have been anti-historic, for the reasons outlined above, and contrary to the spirit of the EU treaties, which set up the Union as a means of creating peace and prosperity. In addition, and most importantly, it would have also posed a clear problem of security for the incumbent member states, with mounting pressures from the CEECs to have access to EU markets and institutions, and of potential widespread political instability in the area.

Economics is the last, and probably overwhelming, factor that caused the EU institutions to quickly offer membership to the CEECs, driven by the behaviour of European firms, which, from 1989, started to invest heavily in the area, pre-empting the new markets. By 1993, the year in which the Copenhagen summit took its historic decision, the amount of foreign direct investment in the area totalled more than €11 billion, of which more than 70 per cent (or €8 billion) was capital invested by the top European firms, with estimates predicting a continuously growing trend in the years to come.[45] Clearly the EU institutions had to provide a consistent policy framework to back up and guarantee the increasing European business interests in the area.

For the above reasons, between 1991 and 1995 the Central and Eastern European countries all signed Association Agreements[46] with the European Union (the so-called **Europe agreements**) and then applied for EU membership, as reported in Table 3.3. However, in 1993, at the Copenhagen European Council, the EU institutions made membership conditional on the fulfilment of three criteria (the so-called **Copenhagen criteria**) by the acceding states:[47]

1. **Political criterion**: the acceding countries have to have stable institutions guaranteeing democracy, the rule of law, human rights and respect for minorities;
2. **Economic criterion**: the acceding countries have to prove themselves to be functioning market economies, able to face without disruption the competitive pressures existing in the single market;
3. ***Acquis communautaire***: the acceding countries have to incorporate in their own legislation the entire European body of law related to the various political, economic and monetary aims of the Union.

These accession criteria were confirmed in December 1995 by the Madrid European Council, which also stressed the importance of adapting the

Table 3.3 The timing of the CEECs' accession (as of December 2004)

Country	Signature of association agreement	Accession application date	Closed chapters (tot. 31)
Bulgaria	1-3-1993	14-12-1995	28
Cyprus	19-12-1972	3-7-1990	31
Czech Rep.	6-10-1993	17-1-1996	31
Estonia	12-6-1995	24-11-1995	31
Hungary	16-12-1991	31-3-1994	31
Latvia	12-6-1995	13-10-1995	31
Lithuania	12-6-1995	8-12-1995	31
Malta	5-12-1970	3-7-1990	31
Poland	16-12-1991	5-4-1994	31
Romania	8-2-1993	22-6-1995	28
Slovakia	6-10-1993	27-6-1995	31
Slovenia	10-6-1996	10-6-1996	31
Turkey	12-9-1973	14-4-1987	—

applicant countries' administrative structures to create the conditions for a gradual, harmonious integration of the CEECs in the EU. A special Directorate General of the Commission was set up in order to monitor the progress of the candidate countries with respect to these criteria, and financial resources were allocated accordingly.

It is beyond the scope of this book to explore how during the 1990s, the CEECs managed to meet the first two criteria, a process which by itself has created a new branch of research in economics known as **transition economics**.[48] Suffice it here to say that the bulk of the adjustment took place after several crises in the early 1990s, with serious macroeconomic imbalances arising in the CEECs as a result of a 'cold shower' approach to the transition from planned to market economies: markets were suddenly liberalised and the privatisation of economic activities was attempted. This approach generated phenomena of widespread unemployment, hyperinflation and a generalised fall in output. Only after 1994–5 did these countries realise that the imposition of discipline through the application of market rules in their economies was an essential prerequisite to allow a market economy to operate smoothly, and hence the situation quickly improved, as shown in Table 3.4. Clearly the perspective of adhesion of these countries to the European Union, and thus the need to fulfil the Copenhagen criteria, acted as a powerful incentive to consistently impose the 'right' set of policies over time, notwithstanding the changes in government that took place in these countries over the years.

Table 3.4 The evolution of transition in the CEECs

	Number of consecutive years of real GDP decline	Maximum negative percentage of variation of real output before the recovery
Central Europe	**3.2**	**−16.2**
Poland	3	−19
Hungary	4	−18
Czech Rep.	3	−13
Slovenia	2	−14
Slovak Rep.	4	−17
Baltic Countries	**4**	**−41**
Estonia	3	−29
Lithuania	4	−44
Latvia	5	−50
CIS	**4.7**	**−35.1**
Russia	5	−39
Ukraine	7	−50
Kazakhstan	4	−27
Kyrgyz Rep.	3	−36
Moldova	7	−37
Tajikistan	4	−49
Uzbekistan	3	−8

Source: Authors' elaborations based on World Bank–WDI data.

As a result of these dramatic improvements, in December 1997 the Luxembourg European Council called for the opening of bilateral negotiations (i.e. the implementation of the third Copenhagen criterion) between the EU and those countries which the Commission judged to be fulfilling the first two criteria. It also stated that the enlargement process affected not only all the ten CEECs but also Malta and Cyprus.

It is worth noting here that the Copenhagen criteria are in themselves rather different. The first two criteria, in fact, represent the basic preconditions imposed by the EU on any country that is a candidate for membership. Since they are mainly related to the internal working of the political and economic system of the country considered, the **direct role** of the Union is very limited, with a minimum amount of money allocated to aid the candidate, in order to avoid interfering with the free determinations of what remains an independent state. However, as considered above, the EU plays a fundamental **indirect role** with respect to the fulfilment of the political and economic criteria, since the offer by the EU of a credible prospect of membership imposes a sort of external constraint on the economic policies of the candidate country, therefore ensuring their consistency over time notwithstanding changes in government or varying economic conditions.

Once a candidate country fulfils the first two criteria, the shape of its relationship with the EU changes, since the prospect of its membership is far more concrete. As a result, in order to meet the third Copenhagen criterion, the adoption of the *acquis*, the EU and the acceding state embark on a bilateral series of negotiations, in which the EU Commission (a) monitors on a yearly basis the transposition and implementation in the national legislation of the considered state of all the legal provisions which form the single market, and (b) provides to this end substantial financial support during the process.

Such an exercise is fundamental in order to guarantee that the enlarged market will not result in a change of the basic rules adopted by the economic agents already operating in the European Union. The process is known as **reinforced pre-accession strategy**, and it is based on political documents (**Accession Partnerships**) agreed by the administration of each candidate state and the EU Commission, in which the priorities for the candidates as they prepare themselves to become members of the EU are set out, and all the different forms of support offered by the EU to this end are brought within a single framework. Yearly national programmes for the adoption of the *acquis* are agreed, highlighting the priorities for each country and the main instruments and financial resources available to meet the identified objectives effectively.

Operationally the entire legislation of the EU Single Market has been divided into 31 chapters, one for each policy area (industrial policy, competition, environment and so on), with bilateral negotiations tackling each individual chapter. The bilateral negotiations started on 30 March 1998, with the five CEECs which the Commission considered as fulfilling the first two Copenhagen criteria: Estonia, Czech Republic, Hungary, Poland and Slovenia, plus Cyprus, the so-called **Luxembourg Group**. In December 1999, the formal accession process was then extended by the Helsinki European Council to the remaining CEECs (Bulgaria, Latvia, Lithuania, Romania and Slovakia) and Malta. On that occasion, Turkey gained the status of candidate country; that is, the Commission started to evaluate the fulfillment by Turkey of the first two Copenhagen criteria, but no negotiations were started at that time.

For those candidate countries who were able to fulfil the first two Copenhagen criteria, the EU increased the funds available for the implementation of the Community *acquis*. In particular, while the EU had committed for the CEECs less than €10 billion for the period 1990–98, following the developments of 1999 the three financial funds[49] available for accession assistance were endowed with a yearly allotment of €3120 million to be divided proportionally (on the basis of the population) among each of the CEECs.

Thanks to this new impetus, and to the continuing efforts in the candidate countries, in October 2002 the Commission stated that eight CEECs (the Luxembourg group plus Lithuania, Latvia, Slovakia and Malta) would have met all the three Copenhagen criteria by the end of 2002, thus formally recommending to the European Council the closure of the accession negotiations and the subsequent signing of the accession treaties. On 12–13 December 2002, the European Council, again held in Copenhagen, officially closed the accession negotiations with the eight CEECs plus Malta and Cyprus, agreeing an extra financial package worth €41 billion for each of the years 2004–2005–2006 (see Chapter 6 for further details). On 16 April 2003, the Accession treaties for the ten new member states were signed in Athens, and in May 2004 the ten new member states joined the European Union.

Bulgaria and Romania did not complete the bilateral negotiations for the implementation of the Community *acquis*, as shown in the last column of Table 3.3, by 2002 and hence are expected to join the Union in 2007 at the earliest. In the meantime, Croatia also applied for membership in March 2003, and received the status of candidate country in June 2004, with negotiations starting in 2005.

Finally, following positive political and economic developments in the country, in October 2004 the Commission recommended the start of accession negotiations also with Turkey. However, in the case of Turkey the Commission also made it clear that the accession negotiation is by its nature an open-ended process: while the objective, accession to the EU, is clear, it cannot be guaranteed beforehand.

3.7.2 The Impact of the Enlargement on the EU Policies

In order to assess the impact that the last EU enlargement will have on the various Union policies and the single market, it is useful to recall the comparison we made in the first chapter between the current accession of the CEECs and the most similar other enlargement of what was at the time the European Community (EC), namely the enlargement of the 1980s involving Spain, Portugal and Greece. There are in fact a number of similarities in the two enlargements: the population of Spain, Portugal and Greece was at the time around 22 per cent of that of the nine incumbent member states, while the combined population of the CEECs was 28 per cent of the EU-15 (1999 data); the weight of the acceding countries in terms of the Union's GDP was 10 per cent in the case of Spain, Portugal and Greece and 6 per cent for the

CEECs. The largest state entering the EC in the 1980s, Spain, accounted for roughly 14 per cent of the EC population, a figure similar to that of Poland, the largest of the CEECs, accounting for 10 per cent of the population of the EU-15.

On the basis of these figures, and knowing that the enlargement of the EC to Spain, Portugal and Greece did not create major drawbacks for the process of European integration, one could reassuringly state that, given the previously mentioned similarities, the current enlargement will not pose major problems for the EU either. However, looking behind the general picture, a series of significant differences emerge between the two considered enlargement processes.[50]

First of all, the current enlargement has involved countries in transition from a planned to a market economy, and therefore possible macroeconomic imbalances might still be present, due to the need for restructuring of these economies. Second, Europe has opened itself to potential new countries which are significantly poorer, with an unprecedented gap in terms of richness between the new and the incumbent member states. While Spain, Portugal and Greece were significantly poorer than the EC-9, their per capita GDP (measured in Purchasing Power Standards, or PPS) was still 66 per cent of the EC-9 average at the time, while the similar measure for the CEECs stood at 38 per cent of the EU-15 average.[51] Such a huge disparity opens up two potential problems: once the free movement of persons is guaranteed via the provisions of the single market in an enlarged Europe, significant flows of labour migration might arise within Europe, disrupting the employment rate of incumbent member states; in addition, economic and social cohesion (that is, the reduction of regional imbalances) being one of the key objectives of the EU treaties, such disparities call for a reform of the EU cohesion policy, again to the possible detriment of the incumbent member states.

Another problem of the current enlargement is related to the agricultural sector. The agricultural production of the CEECs is in fact in direct competition with the traditional products of the Common Agricultural Policy (corn, beef, milk), while the previous enlargement to the southern countries of Greece, Spain and Portugal mainly involved Mediterranean products complementary to the traditional continental ones. In addition, the production structure of the CEECs is still heavily imbalanced in favour of agriculture, rather than manufacturing or services, and therefore an extension of the Common Agricultural Policy to such a great number of farmers would pose an unbearable burden on EU finances.

Finally the EU institutions, originally designed for six member states, and already stretched to encompass 15 countries, would be clearly inadequate to work, if left unreformed, in a system comprising 25 or more member states. Such a problem, which we referred to as the 'fourth' Copenhagen criterion, has only been partially solved by the institutional innovations introduced by the Nice Treaty.

The first two potential problems (the degree to which the CEECs have managed to overcome the shortcomings of their transition process and the potential for labour migration within the EU) will be discussed in the present section, since they are more directly related to the working of the EU Single Market. The implications of the enlargement for the two most relevant expenditure policies of the Union, that is, the Common Agricultural Policy and the regional policy, will be the subject of Chapters 6 to 8 of the book. Because of the continuing nature of the debate, the institutional changes brought forward by the enlargement of the Union and going beyond the Nice Treaty, that is, the debate around the EU Constitution, will be analysed in the concluding chapter of the book.

More generally, a number of studies already exist on the possible economic implications of enlargement (for example, Boeri *et al.*, 2002; Baldwin *et al.*, 1997; Breuss, 2001). The main findings emerging from this literature point to the fact that enlargement is likely to produce economic benefits, to both current members and the accession countries, provided adequate and coherent accompanying national policies are pursued. Depending on the methodology used, estimates of economic gains from enlargement in terms of cumulative increases of GDP vary between 0.5 per cent and 0.7 per cent for the EU-15 as a whole and between 6 per cent and 19 per cent for the new member states for the period 2000–2010. These gains include both static and dynamic effects of integration, as with those considered in the first part of this chapter. The difference in the order of magnitude is clearly dependent on the different sizes of the countries considered: the new member states represent around 5 per cent of the EU-15 GDP and some 12 per cent of their exports. As a result, while they will greatly benefit from their membership of the EU, the overall impact for the incumbent member states will be limited.

Though these estimates are obviously sensitive to the underlying assumptions concerning, inter alia, the level of actual financial transfers to new members and the degree of labour market flexibility, the general finding of significant direct economic gains from the enlargement is quite robust. Some authors (for example, Nava, 2004) also point to the asymmetric impact that the enlargement will have on the EU-15. The countries with which the new member states are closest or have the strictest economic ties are in fact likely to benefit more from the enlargement with respect to other EU members. In particular, for Germany, Austria, Finland and Italy, the positive impact of enlargement can be calculated as 0.5 per cent of extra GDP growth each year. This leads in turn to 'indirect gains' from enlargement: in the context of the single market and the single currency, the extra growth in some member states easily spills over to the other member states, therefore ensuring a proper distribution of the gains from the enlargement. Recent estimates, in particular, find the indirect effects as having the same order of magnitude as the direct effects.

3.7.3 The Enlargement and the EU Single Market: Open Issues

The fear that the single market might be endangered by the enlargement of the Union contrasts sharply with the spirit of the second and third Copenhagen criteria: only the countries that enjoy a stable macroeconomic picture and that have transposed and implemented in their national legislation the Community *acquis* can become members, thus preserving the integrity and continuity of the EU Single Market, even in its enlarged form.

In terms of macroeconomic data, the CEECs are performing relatively well: in the years immediately preceding their accession (2000–2002) all countries experienced positive GDP growth rates, ranging between 1.5 per cent (Romania) and 6 per cent (Estonia). On average for the ten CEECs, the cumulative GDP growth rate for the period 1995–2000 has been more than 20 per cent, against a bare 12 per cent for the EU-15. The main problem here is related to the contribution of labour to the growth rate. As shown in Table 3.5, the latter is in fact negative, contrary to the positive contributions of capital accumulation and the technological progress. Such a result clearly indicates a further need for reform of the labour markets in these countries, ensuring their smoother functioning.

In terms of public finances, during transition some deterioration of the state budget was inevitable, due to the upward pressures on public

Table 3.5 The contribution of factors of production to growth in the CEECs (1991–9)

	Cumulative GDP growth	TFP growth	Contribution of employment	Contribution of capital
Czech Rep.	9.1	4.6	−4.3	9.0
Hungary	16.6	20.2	−11.1	9.2
Poland	47.9	20.9	−1.6	24.3
Slovakia	21.8	2.0	6.2	12.4
Slovenia	25.6	21.0	−6.4	10.9

Source: Economic Policy Committee (2003), 'Key structural challenges in the acceding countries: the integration of the acceding countries into the Community's economic policy co-ordination processes', Occasional paper no. 4, June.

expenditure coming from the needs of restructuring the productive sector of the economy, and problems in the tax collection system (characterised by a narrow tax base and significant degrees of tax evasion). However, by the end of transition, these phenomena had not dramatically impaired the state of public finances in the CEECs, which are now close to meeting the EMU criteria, as will be made clear in the next chapter. Some imbalances are, however, present in terms of demographic dynamics, which will lead the CEECs, as well as the EU-15, to a significant increase in the public expenditures related to retirement systems if no reforms are undertaken. At the microeconomic level, some problems still exist in terms of level of state aid,[52] currently above the EU average, and the pervasiveness of administered (rather than market) prices, a leftover from the traditional planned economic system.

Notwithstanding the overall positive indications coming from the CEECs, the EU-15 have decided to adopt a series of **safeguard clauses** related to the working of the single market, in order to guarantee themselves against eventual possible disruptions. In particular, the Brussels European Council of October 2002 decided to include in the accession treaties a general economic safeguard clause and two specific safeguard clauses concerning the operation of the internal market and the area of justice and home affairs. In other words, for a period of up to three years after accession (that is, up to 2007), a safeguard clause may be invoked upon a motivated request by any member state or at the Commission's initiative: measures under the general economic safeguard clause concern any member state, while measures under the two specific safeguard clauses can be eventually addressed only to the new member states that have failed to implement commitments undertaken in the context of their accession negotiations.

The second potential problem for the working of the enlarged single market is related to the free circulation of workers. There were in Europe fears of a risk of mass migration after the opening up of borders with the new member states, with subsequent pressures on national labour markets and national welfare systems. As already mentioned, migration pressures are feared because it is assumed that higher wages and greater levels of social protection would induce workers from the new members to migrate to the EU-15.[53] While it is true that, not surprisingly, employment fell notably at the start of transition, with unemployment reaching an average rate in the CEECs of 12.5 per cent in 2000, the internal social disparities of the CEECs are, in relative terms, not dissimilar from the EU-15, as will be made clear in Chapter 5. Such a similar distribution of income within countries, together with the existence of relevant social and cultural barriers to mobility, is likely to reduce significantly the number of workers that will move from the East to the West in Europe. In particular, the Commission estimates that no more than 200 000 workers will move every year from the CEECs to the EU-15, and this for a period up to 2009 (European Commission, 2001a). As a result, the overall impact of these migration flows will be in total less than 0.5 per cent of the EU working-age population. However the impact will be different for each member state, with Austria and Germany likely to bear most of the burden. As a result, special transition periods have been negotiated between the CEECs and the EU-15. These provisions limit up to 2009 the free circulation of people between Eastern and Western Europe, with a possible extension of two extra years granted to Austria and Germany in light of their peculiar situation.

In conclusion, it can be stated that most of the fears related to a possible negative impact of the enlargement on the EU Single Market are exaggerated. Problems have been largely solved by the thorough application of the Copenhagen criteria and, in the areas in which some difficulties might persist, special derogations have been undertaken. It is, however, important to realise that, in order to cope effectively with the various risks and challenges of enlargement, it is essential to address first and foremost their primary cause, the income gap between Eastern and Western Europe. This means that policies (such as the EU regional policy) aimed at ensuring an income convergence as rapidly as possible for the new members towards the EU-15 income levels should become a key priority of the post-enlargement economic strategy.

NOTES

1. As we have seen in Chapter 2, the latter result holds as long as the rest of the world does not retaliate, in which case the free trade situation remains the preferred set-up.
2. See Thisse *et al.* (1992) for a comprehensive treatment of these issues.
3. We follow here Baldwin and Wyplosz (2003), to which we refer the reader for a more comprehensive analysis.
4. If you are unfamiliar with these concepts, the intuition is that a firm in a duopoly will have less market power than if it is acting under a monopoly, and the more so every time a new firm enters the market; in other words, as the number of firms in the market increases, the firm will be forced to charge lower prices, and hence its mark-up (the difference between price and marginal cost) will be lower. Baldwin and Wyplosz (2003, ch. 6) provide an exhaustive, yet simple, analytical treatment of these arguments.
5. Assuming firms are not heterogeneous, if prices are below the average cost then $p < c + F/q$, that is, $pq < cq + F$: the total revenue of the firm is lower than the firm's total costs, and hence negative profits (losses) are generated.
6. If prices were above the average costs, that is, with too few firms operating in the market, the positive profits will induce the entry of new firms, and similar dynamics will be generated until the long-run market structure is reached.
7. We follow here Baldwin (1989). We recall that in the Solow model the equilibrium output per worker (Y/L) depends on the amount of capital per worker (K/L) invested, itself a constant fraction of output determined via the saving rate s, that is $K/L = s(Y/L)$ and the

depreciation of the *K*/*L* ratio, itself a constant fraction δ of capital. Decreasing returns are assumed on capital and thus on output.

8. Clearly the free circulation of goods is already guaranteed by the provisions of the EU Customs Union.
9. Non-tradable services are characterised by the fact that the physical location of their production cannot be disentangled from their consumption (for example, transport or tourism or personal services, such as the barber shop).
10. TEC, art. 43 states that 'restrictions on the freedom of establishment of nationals of a member State in the territory of another member state shall be prohibited. Such prohibition shall also apply to restrictions on the setting up of agencies, branches or subsidiaries by nationals of any member state established in the territory of any member state. Freedom of establishment shall include the right to take up and pursue activities as self-employed persons and to set up and manage undertakings . . . under the conditions laid down for its own nationals by the law of the country where such establishment is effected'.
11. We recall that the uncovered interest parity is an arbitrage condition followed by international financial markets under the assumption of perfect circulation of capitals. It links the current exchange rate of a given country to its level of interest rates, to the level of interest rates of a second country (or the Rest of the World) and to the expectations on the future variations in the exchange rate.
12. Note that the shifting of the *IS* curve increases the interest rate also in country *B*, with a slight appreciation of its exchange rate. Again, we show here only the net effects.
13. In the long run, one can expect inflationary pressures to arise in country *A* owing to the higher cost of its imports eroding its initial competitive advantage, with the resulting inflation compensating the initial depreciation of its real exchange rate.
14. The exact wording of the Treaty is (TEC, art. 14.2): 'The internal market shall comprise an area without internal frontiers in which the free movement of goods, persons, services and capital is ensured in accordance with the provisions of this Treaty.' The European Monetary System was set up in 1979, anticipating de facto the full implementation of the single market (the Single European Act entered into force in 1987).
15. The 1966 Luxembourg Compromise discussed in Chapter 1, through which member states could invoke the national interest and thus call for unanimity in some of the key decisions related to the single market, contributed to this attitude of member states.
16. Article 12 of the EC Treaty prohibits 'any discrimination on grounds of nationality'. Discrimination is understood as meaning different treatment, on the basis of nationality, under the same circumstances.
17. For example, most NTBs cannot be opposed against the principle of mutual recognition. For the operational application of the principle, see http://europa.eu.int/comm/internal_market/en/goods/mutrec.htm.
18. We recall that directives are EU framework laws requiring a transposition into the national legislation of each member state, while EU regulations are directly applicable.
19. Only 2 per cent of government contracts were awarded to other EU nationals in the mid-1980s, when imports in general reached well over 20 per cent.
20. Depending on the case in hand, these committees have an advisory role or are required to give their imperative opinions (most often this is the case with the so-called 'regulatory' committees) based on proposals from the Commission. The measures adopted have the same legal status as the primary act which has been amended and must, where appropriate, be transposed into the national legislation of the member states. These institutional developments have given birth to a branch of EU law named 'comitology', that is, the law and proceedings deriving from these various Committees in which technical standards are discussed and decisions are taken.
21. Unanimity in these sectors has been partially eliminated by the entry into force of the Treaty of Nice in 2003.
22. Today it is estimated that on average around 50 per cent of the legislation produced in any given year by each member state is actually the transposition (in the case of directives) or the direct reception (in the case of regulations) of a legal act agreed at the EU level.

23. A later study (Smith *et al.*, 1992) undertaken within a general equilibrium framework broadly confirms the previous estimates but questions their overall magnitude.
24. The latter argument, with which we fully agree, has been made by Robson (1998).
25. Not all the provisions related to the free circulation of workers are directly dealt with at the EU level. Rather a good deal of autonomy is still left to the national legislation of member states.
26. For example, the European Commission (1996a) estimates that the liberalisation of the electricity sector could generate further gains of €4–6 billion a year.
27. In the EU, the industrial sector, which used to represent more than 50 per cent of the economy, is now down to less than 25 per cent; the services sector, which used to be the smallest component of the economy, is now up to about 70 per cent.
28. As far as goods, capital and services are concerned, within the European Commission the Directorate General (DG) for Economic Affairs and the DG Internal Market take care of phase (a). The DG Internal Market takes care of phase (b) and DG Enterprise takes care of phase (c). As a signal of the different stages of advancement in the goods and in the services area, President Barroso in January 2005 has reorganised the Commission services by moving out the area of 'free movement of capital' from the DG Economic and Financial Affairs towards the DG Internal Market (to ensure complete implementation and adoption of the legislative programme), and by moving out the area of 'free movement of goods' from the DG Internal Market to DG Enterprise (since the legislative programme is nearly completed, and the EU enterprise system needs to exploit it to increase its competitiveness).
29. In particular, the study shows that the greatest impact comes from the reduction in the cost of equity finance, then from the reduction in the cost of bank finance and finally from the reduction in the cost of bond finance.
30. For example, if banks of country *A* believe that banks of country *B* will reduce their underwriting fees for Euro bonds issues due to the FSAP, banks of country *A* will feel compelled to compete and do the same ex ante, which in turn leads to a generalized cost reduction.
31. The reports can be found at http://www.europa.eu.int/comm/internal_market/en/finances/actionplan/index.htm.
32. In July 2000, the EU finance ministers called upon Alexandre Lamfalussy, former president of the European Monetary Institute, the predecessor of the European Central Bank, to chair a 'Committee of Wise Men' with the task of improving the EU's securities regulatory process. In February 2001, this Committee presented its report recommending the extension and adaptation of the comitology procedure to financial markets.
33. The Commission is also committed to producing a detailed Regulatory Impact Assessment (RIA) before submitting any proposal to the EP and the Council.
34. The business cycle literature that looks at the synchronisation across countries of GDP components has found that, contrary to what theory would suggest, consumption is generally less synchronised across countries than GDP. However, recent empirical research has shown that the co-movement of private consumption has increased within the Euro zone and, interestingly, also between the Euro zone and the USA, likely owing to the presence of more integrated financial markets.
35. As a matter of fact, VAT receipts have constituted one of the sources of revenue for the EU budget. See Chapter 6 for more details.
36. Directives 91/680/EEC of 16 December 1991 and 92/111/EEC of 14 December 1992.
37. There are three 'special regimes' where this principle does not apply: (1) distance sales, over a certain threshold, have to be taxed at the rate applied in the country where the goods are delivered (destination principle); (2) tax-exempt legal persons (hospitals, banks, public authorities and so on); (3) new means of transport (boats, aircraft and cars under six months old), which are taxable in the purchaser's country, even if acquired in another member state.
38. See http://www.europa.eu.int/comm/taxation_customs/taxation/vatindex_en.htm for an update on the VAT legislation.

39. See http://europa.eu.int/comm/taxation_customs/taxation/information_notes/taxation_package/taxpack.htm.
40. The proposal originated with the German Chancellor Schmidt and French President Giscard d'Estaing, and was based on an initiative of the European Commission President Roy Jenkins. See Box 3.5 for details on the working of the EMS.
41. An example might be useful to clarify this point: suppose the Italian lira has an inflation of 10 per cent a year, while the DM has inflation of 2 per cent a year, and the central parity is fixed at 750Lit/DM. Suppose also that a sandwich costs 750Lit in Italy and 1DM in Germany, so the nominal agreed exchange rate also reflects the real one. After one year, the sandwich in Italy would cost (750 + 10%) = 825Lit while in Germany it would cost (1 + 2%) = 1.02DM. The inflation differential would thus imply a real exchange rate of 808.8 Lit/DM and hence, keeping the nominal exchange rate of 750 Lit/DM agreed within the EMS, implies an appreciation of the Italian currency (and hence a loss of competitiveness) of around 8 per cent a year.
42. We have already considered that the Single Market Programme is a dynamic venture, with continuous efforts required in terms both of the transposition of the EU directives into national laws, and of the production of new regulatory frameworks as a result of the changing economic structure of the member states.
43. The new member states in fact should be referred to, with good reason, as 'Central European' states.
44. To name but a few examples, Immanuel Kant, one of the greatest European philosophers, taught and died in Königsberg, currently Kaliningrad, a Russian enclave between Poland and Lithuania; Fredric Chopin, one of the greatest European musicians, operated in Paris but was Polish-born; and Franz Kafka, one of the most influential European writers, was Czech.
45. Publications on the dynamics of foreign direct investment in the CEECs include Alessandrini (2000) and Altomonte and Guagliano (2003).
46. The Association Agreements are the closest form of cooperation offered by the European Union to external states, involving free trade agreements and financial aid. See Chapter 10 for a detailed discussion.
47. A fourth criterion, which we mentioned in the first chapter, relates to the ability of the EU institutions to work efficiently when enlarged to 25 member states. As we have seen, these considerations led to the adoption of the Nice Treaty, the current legal framework on which the EU is based, and then to the project of the EU Constitution.
48. For a general policy reference, see World Bank (2002); Roland (2001) is a rich source on theories of transition.
49. PHARE, a fund financing institution building measures accross all sectors and investment (except agriculture and the environment), including integrated regional development programmes, with an annual budget of €1560 million; ISPA, which finances major environmental and transport infrastructure projects, with an annual budget of €1040 million; SAPARD, financing agricultural and rural development, with an annual budget of €520 million.
50. See European Commission (2001a) for a more detailed analysis.
51. 1999 data. The figure is however continuously, albeit slowly, increasing because of higher growth rates of the new member states with respect to the EU-15.
52. The issue of state aid and competition policy in the enlarged Europe will be explored in Chapter 9.
53. Nominal wages in EU-15 in year 2000 were on average four times higher than in the CEECs, while in real terms the difference is much smaller, although still in favour of the EU-15.

4. The Economic and Monetary Union

4.1 INTRODUCTION

The idea of a common currency is well rooted in the process of European economic integration. As early as 1970, in fact, two years after the creation of the European Customs Union, the **Werner Report** proposed to parallel the current construction of the single market with the creation of a single currency. The timing was not accidental. In Chapter 3 we have in fact analysed the progressive inability of the Bretton Woods system of exchange rates to maintain the European currencies anchored to the US dollar, and thus fixed among themselves. Such instability of exchange rates within member countries, we have learned, seriously hampers the smooth working of the Customs Union and the single market, owing to the negative spillovers that might arise among countries. The initiative for a 'European' currency therefore originated in this context.

However, the time not being ripe for such a step forward in the integration process, the idea was set aside, and the European Monetary System (EMS) was instead created in 1979 (see Chapter 3). In parallel with the entry into force of the Single European Act and the process of completion of the single market, the Commission nevertheless revamped the idea of a common currency. Capitalising on a series of debates on the issue among economists and politicians, the Hanover European Council of June 1988 decided in fact to entrust to a committee, chaired by the (newly reappointed) President of the European Commission, Jacques Delors, the task of studying and proposing concrete stages leading towards the monetary union. The committee was asked to complete its work sufficiently well ahead of the meeting of the European Council scheduled in Madrid in June 1989.[1]

Interestingly, notwithstanding the short span of time during which it worked (eight meetings were held), the **Delors Committee** managed to submit to the Madrid European Council a report which *in nuce* contained the main features (mandatory guidelines on national budget deficits, irrevocably fixed exchange rates, the European System of Central Banks and so on) then actually retained by the institutional framework of the single currency, and analysed later in this chapter. Most importantly, the Delors Committee proposed to approach the creation of the single currency in stages, with the first stage supposed to start in parallel with the full liberalisation of capital movements in the single market, a decision already agreed within the Single Market Programme analysed in the previous chapter, and scheduled for adoption on 1 July 1990.

The European Council in Madrid agreed to start the first stage of the Economic and Monetary Union (EMU) officially on 1 July 1990 and to convene an Intergovernmental Conference (IGC), with the aim of considering the Treaty changes necessary for moving beyond the first stage. Interestingly the European Council did not set a date for the start of the IGC, stating that 'full and adequate preparations' had to be put in place first. In reality, as already considered in Chapter 1, the problem was mainly a political one, given that a common currency would have changed the balance of power across the Union. It is not surprising, therefore, that the IGC started its work in Rome in December 1990, two months after the 'green light' given by the member states to the German reunification (3 October 1990). The IGC work was virtually concluded on 10 December 1991, with the agreement reached during the Maastricht European Council, giving birth to what is commonly known as the **Maastricht Treaty**.[2]

The Maastricht Treaty retained the institutional set-up originally proposed by the Delors Committee and stated that EMU was to be achieved in three stages:

1. First stage (starting retroactively from 1 July 1990): free movement of capital between member states (with transitory periods granted to Greece, Ireland, Portugal and Spain), closer coordination of economic policies and closer cooperation between central banks (in part already achieved via the European Monetary System);
2. Second stage (starting from 1 January 1994): convergence of the economic and monetary policies of the member states (to ensure stability of prices and sound public finances) via meeting of some criteria; creation of the European Monetary Institute (EMI);
3. Third stage (starting as soon as the second stage was complete, and in any case no later than 1 January 1999): irrevocable fixing of exchange rates and introduction of the single currency on the foreign exchange markets and for electronic payments; replacement of the EMI with the European Central Bank (ECB) and creation of the European System of Central Banks (ESCB); introduction of Euro notes and coins, replacing the national legal currencies after a transition period.

The third stage of EMU was finally launched by an extraordinary European Council held in Brussels on 2–3 May 1998. There it was decided that, by 1 January 1999, 11 member states would have adopted the European single currency, named the **Euro** (€).[3] Greece joined two years later. Three member states have not adopted the single currency: the United Kingdom and Denmark, both of which negotiated an **opt-out clause** in Maastricht, and Sweden. The latter country, according to the Treaty, has an obligation to join, but officially it does not at present meet all the criteria regarding the independence of its central bank.[4] On 1 January 2002, Euro notes and coins were introduced in the member states, gradually replacing the national currencies (see Box 4.1 for a complete chronology).

BOX 4.1 A BRIEF HISTORY OF THE SINGLE CURRENCY

1970	The Commission submits for the first time to the Council a memorandum on the preparation of a plan for the establishment of the Economic and Monetary Union (EMU). The Council assigns the task to a committee of experts presided over by Pierre Werner (Werner Report).
1971–9	In 1971, the Council adopts the Werner Report aimed at strengthening the coordination of economic policies. Member states have to take measures to harmonise their budgetary policies and to reduce the margins of fluctuation between their currencies. In 1979, an agreement is reached setting up the European Monetary System (EMS) based on a European currency unit (the ECU).
1988	The European Council held in Hanover asks the president of the Commission, Jacques Delors, to monitor, jointly with central bank governors of member states, the progressive implementation of the EMU. At the European Council held in Madrid in 1989, the Delors Committee presents a report proposing the introduction of economic and monetary union in three stages.
1990	EMU first stage: full liberalization of capital movements by 1 July 1990. Four member states

	(Spain, Portugal, Greece and Ireland) are granted an exceptional regime given their insufficient progress towards financial integration.
1992–3	The Treaty on the European Union is signed in Maastricht in 1992, together with the amendments agreed to the Treaty of the European Communities. The latter lays down the criteria to participate in the single currency. On 1 November 1993, the Treaties of Maastricht enter into force.
1994	EMU second stage: setting up of the European Monetary Institute (EMI), whose task is to strengthen cooperation among the national central banks and to carry out the necessary preparations for the introduction of the Euro.
3 May 1998	A special European Council decides that 11 member states (Austria, Belgium, Finland, France, Germany, Ireland, Italy, Luxembourg, Netherlands, Portugal and Spain) fulfil the criteria for the adoption of the single currency, starting from 1 January 1999.
1 July 1998	The European Central Bank (ECB) is set up. A single monetary policy is introduced and entrusted to the European System of Central Banks (ESCB), which includes the central banks of member states and the ECB, which replaces the EMI.
1 January 1999	The Euro is officially launched. Austria, Belgium, Finland, France, Germany, Ireland, Italy, Luxembourg, The Netherlands, Portugal and Spain adopt the Euro as their official currency. The common monetary policy starts and the irrevocable conversion rates between the national currencies and the Euro are set. On the financial markets the Euro is used as virtual currency.
1 January 2001	Greece becomes the twelfth member of the Euro zone.
1 January 2002	The Euro coins and notes start gradually to replace the national currencies. The changeover is formally completed by 28 February.

The physical replacement of the national currencies with the common one is not strictly necessary for the working of the EMU, once exchange rates have been irrevocably fixed and the centralised monetary authority has been created. However this move was deemed necessary for a number of reasons: in economic terms, a physically unique currency allows a better functioning of the single market (see the next paragraph). From a political point of view, the elimination of the national currencies gives a sense of irreversibility to the creation of the EMU, thus fostering a sense of political unity across the participating countries.

4.2 THE RATIONALE FOR A SINGLE CURRENCY

When looking at the road to Economic and Monetary Union from a historical point of view, one reckons that, at a given point in their integration process, some member states engaged in a complex series of actions and political decisions, voluntarily swapping one powerful symbol of the state, the national currency, for a 'European' symbol, the Euro. The latter, however, did not have behind it a political centralised authority (at least in the traditional sense).[5] In addition, from an economic point of view, the same member states handed over to an independent, supranational authority the control of two key instruments of economic policy, namely the monetary policy and the exchange rate, keeping for themselves only the use (albeit partial, as will be made clear) of the fiscal policy instrument.[6] Given the scope and extent of the changes undertaken, one therefore wonders what was the rationale behind the introduction of the single currency.

A first, partial answer can be found in the quite obvious consideration that a single market works better with a single currency.[7] With the Euro, the European market becomes in fact much more integrated, with no **exchange rate risks** (and the associated hedging costs for firms) or **transaction costs** for the conversion of one national currency to the other. In addition, the single currency greatly lowers the exposure of the single market to international financial crisis, since it dramatically reduces the **degree of openness** of each member state, with the Euro acting as a 'buffer' for both the real and the financial side of the economy.[8]

However the undoubted benefits achievable for the single market through these effects are probably not enough to justify the endeavour of renouncing the national currency, since the same European Commission (1990) estimated these benefits to be a mere 0.5 per cent of the EU GDP in the mid-1980s, while other authors put this figure at 1 per cent, if the gains from reduced volatility on the financial markets are also considered.

A second argument is related to the already discussed advantages of **pegging the exchange rates** within a single market in which independent monetary and fiscal policies are run.[9] Although the provisions of the EMS were adequate to ensure a correct working of the common market in the 1980s and the early 1990s, quasi-fixed exchange rates (target zones) are possible only if central banks cooperate strictly among themselves. In the EMS, as we have seen in Chapter 3, the cooperation was achieved through the lending instrument called 'Very Short Term Financing Facility' (VSTFF). Nevertheless, if asymmetries start to emerge in the objectives of central banks in terms of desired inflation and interest rates, the system becomes unstable, since one central bank might become unable, or unwilling, to increase its monetary base by lending money to the other central banks (through the VSTFF) in order to realign the exchange rates. Such an event took place in September 1992: the Bundesbank, because of the restrictive monetary policy it had to pursue as a consequence of the German reunification,[10] did not allow the Bank of Italy and the Bank of England to borrow Deutschmarks (DM) via the VSTFF in order to support their currencies. Hence, once these banks run short of their reserves in DM, both the Italian lira and the British pound exited the EMS.[11]

After 1992, it had therefore become clear that, in order to attain the objective of quasi-fixed exchange rates, either restrictions on the capital mobility within the single market were necessary (thus removing the integration issue altogether) or the independence of monetary policies had to be eliminated.[12] Clearly these lines of argument became significant only after the EMS crisis, that is, after the signing of the Maastricht Treaty (but before its ratification by all member states), and hence they might have been responsible for accelerating the process of adoption of the single currency, rather than for constituting its original rationale. And in fact, it is worth noting that the politically controversial ratification of the Maastricht Treaty by France took place in 1992 only after the crisis of the European Monetary System.

The most important rationale behind the adoption of the single currency is however related to the residual margin of sovereignty that individual European countries were retaining after the completion of the single market. Already at the beginning of the 1990s, in fact, the implementation of the four fundamental freedoms, together with the worldwide ongoing process of economic and financial integration, had significantly reduced the ability of individual member states to manage effectively their own independent monetary and exchange rates policies.[13] In addition the individual member states, with their very generous welfare systems but an ageing population, were less and less able to face the increasing competitive pressures coming from more dynamic areas of the world. As a result, a 'shock therapy' had to be designed in order to stimulate competition and investment in Europe and generate again those growth rates that the member states had experienced in the first 30 years after World War II. Rather than a goal in itself, the Euro was therefore seen as an extra tool to preserve the viability of the desired **European social model**, and its joint objectives of sustainable growth, stability and cohesion.[14]

In terms of stimulus to the EU performance, a consensus emerged on the fact that the Euro could facilitate achieving higher rates of economic growth over the medium term and help to reduce the cyclical fluctuations of the economy, thus achieving two (growth and stability) of the three key objectives of the EU social model.[15] In fact the introduction of a single currency, by eliminating the periodical adjustments of the exchange rates negotiated within the EMS, fosters a direct and more immediate comparison of prices denominated in the same currency across Europe. As a result, temporary nominal gains in competitiveness through exchange rate devaluations (the sort of 'beggar-thy-neighbour' policies analysed in the previous chapter) are impossible to obtain. On the contrary, competition increases on the single market, stimulating firms to invest in order to achieve real gains in efficiency and remain profitable. In addition, if an adequate monetary and fiscal policy mix is enforced, leading to low inflation and low interest rates, the microeconomic stimulus to private investments induced by the increase in competition takes place under ideal macroeconomic conditions, thus leading to capital accumulation, higher employment, increases in productivity and, ultimately, growth.

In terms of prima facie evidence on the policy mix, Figure 4.1 shows a comparison of inflation and unemployment data in Europe and the United States. In the second half of the 1990s, both the United States and Europe were able to reduce inflation dramatically and thus achieve price stability. However, as discussed by Sapir *et al.* (2004), while the USA was able to reduce unemployment and inflation jointly to levels close to those of the 1960s, the reduction in European inflation took place with broadly constant, historically high rates of unemployment, which pushed the natural rate of unemployment to levels four times higher than in the 1960s.

Starting from the 1970s, as already stated in Chapter 1, the United States also experienced higher growth rates than in Europe, and the gap seems to be widening. This chapter and the next will therefore analyse in detail how and under what conditions the setting up of a single currency and a better working of the single market are able to stimulate investments and employment, thus bringing the Union back to its historic growth rates.

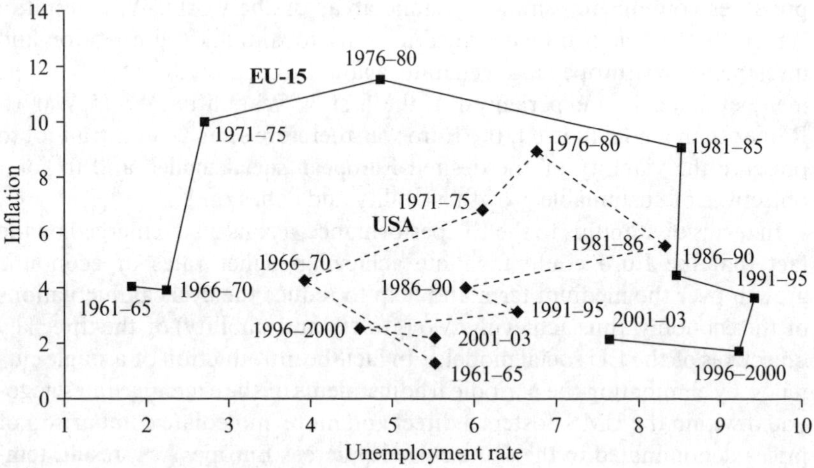

Source: Sapir *et al.* (2004).

Figure 4.1 Inflation and unemployment in Europe and the United States, 1960–2000

4.3 POLITICAL AND ECONOMIC ISSUES ON EMU

The Economic and Monetary Union is, in many respects, a unique and original process if compared to past experiences of integration. First of all, it is not surprising that, in Europe, the continent which has seen the birth of the concept of nation, the process of economic and monetary integration is not formally or explicitly linked to a goal of political union. Thanks to the principle of conferral through which the EU works (see Chapter 1), member states retain their political specificity, maintaining their prerogatives of autonomous subjects of international law.[16] Because of this distinctive institutional feature, the process of economic and monetary integration takes place without the formal creation of a centralised fiscal authority: member states formally retain control over their budget balances and the redistributive effects of their fiscal policies, with national budgets several times bigger than the EU central budget.[17]

In principle, such an attitude of nation states towards monetary unions is not a novelty: several examples exist of cases in which it has been easier to surrender monetary sovereignty than fiscal sovereignty to a central authority.[18] As discussed by Jonung (2002), within the existing examples of monetary unions accompanied by fiscal decentralisation, however, several possible patterns are present. At one extreme, one can put federal states like the United States or Canada, in which the monetary union is coupled with a central government which retains a significant role in the management of the fiscal policy. At the other extreme, one can put 'dollarised' countries, that is countries whose exchange rate is linked to a foreign currency through, in general, a currency board agreement (for example, Estonia or Bulgaria recently linked to the Euro, or Argentina, linked to the dollar during the 1990s): the monetary policy of these countries depends *in toto* on the monetary policy behind the foreign currency they have adopted, but no formal fiscal coordination is foreseen.[19] Such a misalignment between a completely exogenous monetary policy and an independent fiscal policy often leads to the instability of the framework, with Argentina in 2001 being the most notable example. The Economic and Monetary Union in Europe is somehow in between these extreme cases, with a centralised (federal) monetary policy, and decentralised (national) fiscal policies, however subject to a certain degree of coordination. It remains to be seen whether such an institutional framework, centralised monetary policy coupled with rules ensuring an enhanced coordination among the independent fiscal authorities, will be enough to guarantee the stability of the system over time.

The design of the EMU thus results from a mixture of the European political peculiarities with the theoretical features of currency unions pointed out by several strands of macroeconomic theories. We now turn to analyse the main contributions of these theories, limiting our attention to those then retained by the European policy maker.

First of all, since the seminal work of Mundell (1961), it is well understood that a region engaging in a process of economic and monetary integration can be considered an **Optimal Currency Area (OCA)** if four conditions are met:

1. the **business cycles** are perfectly **synchronised**, in order to ensure an optimal conduct of the centralised monetary policy;
2. fiscal policies are able to cope with **asymmetric shocks** which may affect the area;
3. **prices** and **wages** are perfectly **flexible** across the area;
4. **product** and **labour markets** are **integrated**.

A second, important strand of macroeconomic literature critically influencing the setting up of the EMU are the theories on inflation and the **time-inconsistency problem** of monetary policy.[20] The general idea is that any economic environment conducive to growth has to guarantee **price stability**, especially minimising unexpected inflation, since it is widely recognised both theoretically and empirically that inflation imposes a cost on society.[21] The latter can in fact turn out to be particularly detrimental to growth, since it leads to arbitrary redistribution of income and wealth, a shrinking of financial markets, excessive risk premia on interest rates to compensate for the higher volatility of prices, slower adjustments of the economic cycle towards its long-term equilibrium, and so on.[22] Given this consensus, it was therefore necessary to design centralised monetary institutions able to outperform significantly the poor record of inflation achieved in Europe after the 1970s and reported in Figure 4.1.

The economic literature on the matter long since recognised that, if central banks care about unemployment (for example, because they are influenced by the government), there is an incentive for them, once wages have been fixed, to deviate upwards from the 'announced' rate of inflation, in order to achieve lower unemployment rates. Thanks to the recognition of this fact by rational economic agents, a central bank free to deviate from the announced inflation rate inherently generates higher expectations of inflation, with a final equilibrium therefore characterised by the same rate of unemployment but higher inflation.[23] As a result, in order to reduce expected (and thus actual) inflation, no incentive has to exist for central banks to deviate from the announced inflation rate. This is possible if **central banks** have to care only about inflation, not unemployment, that is, if they are completely **independent** from the national government and the political cycle. Figure 4.2

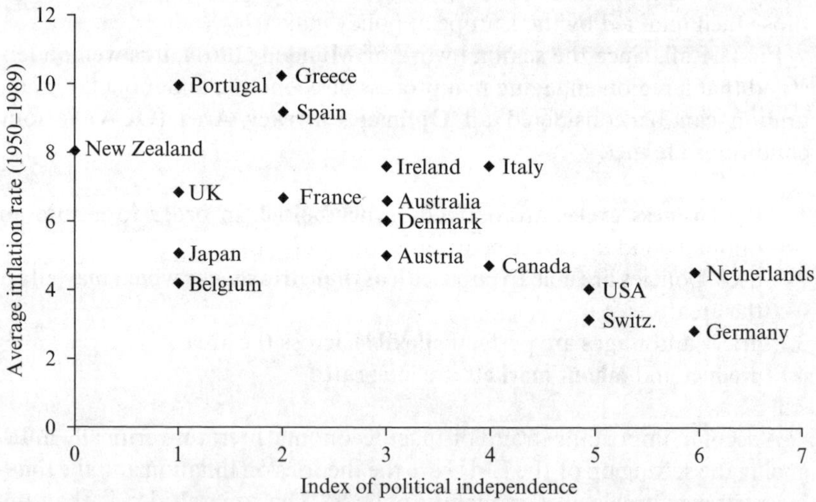

Source: Author's elaboration on the basis of data contained in V. Grilli, D. Masciandaro and G. Tabellini (1991) 'Political and monetary institutions and public financial policies in the industrial countries', *Economic Policy*, October, 341–92.

Figure 4.2 Central bank independence and inflation

relates the degree of independence (measured according to various institutional indicators) of several central banks in the world to the historic rate of inflation they have managed to achieve, clearly showing that a higher degree of independence from the government tends to be associated with a lower inflation record.

Macroeconomic theories on fiscal policies also heavily enter into the design of the European EMU. In direct relation to the previous considerations, in fact, fiscal and monetary policies are linked through the **intertemporal budget constraint**; in the long run, the discounted sum of a government's expected expenditures cannot exceed the discounted sum of its expected revenues: sooner or later, governments' public debts have to be repaid (Sargent and Wallace, 1981). However, among the expected revenues for a government there are not only taxes, but also seignorage, the ability of a government to finance its deficits through the creation of money.[24] As soon as there are public deficits to be closed, therefore, there is an incentive for governments to try to increase money growth and generate inflation: recognising this, rational agents raise their expectations of inflation. Therefore, in an economy which experiences significant budget deficits, inflation rates tend to be relatively higher. As a result, in order to ensure price stability, **public finances** need to be **balanced** in the medium run. Sound public finances are also necessary since high public deficits tend to crowd out resources to the detriment of private investments, thus hampering growth. Low public deficits and debt, instead, contribute to growth, since they contribute to keeping both interest rates and the tax burden under control.

The previously discussed effects are all strong cases for budgetary discipline in any context, in particular from a national point of view. In a context of monetary union with decentralised fiscal policies, however, there are two other **additional channels** which call for a stricter joint control of public finances. Suppose that a government, once a single currency has been created, starts to increase its public spending: in this case it will experience a greater internal demand, associated with higher interest rates. However, since monetary policy is common, part of the increase in the interest rates spreads out to other countries, generating a **negative spillover** for everyone. There is therefore an incentive to agree on common rules that discipline public finance. A second channel is related to the possible **moral hazard** a single government faces as soon as it is part of the EMU: once the monetary policy is common and the financial markets become progressively integrated, it is in the ultimate interest of the central bank not to let any single country go bankrupt, since an insolvency would negatively affect all the member states. Anticipating this result, governments, if left free to set their public deficits, will opt for looser attitudes in the running of their public finances. Lacking explicit rules that prevent such behaviour, as soon as the budgetary positions deteriorate the central bank will be expected either to set lower than needed interest rates, in order not to worsen the budgetary position of governments, or to monetise the public debt. In all cases, the lack of an explicit deficit rule will hinder price stability.[25]

But why would governments ex ante run a budget deficit, given these drawbacks? The standard explanation lies in the so-called **tax-smoothing** optimal rule of public finance: since it is not optimal to change the tax rate continuously in order to balance the budget, deteriorations and improvements in budget balances are used as a buffer to accommodate the effect of cyclical fluctuations of economic activity. However Figure 4.3, originally proposed by Buti and Sapir (1998), shows that, in the period 1970–90, budgetary policies in Europe were asymmetric over the cycle, thus violating the tax-smoothing rule: deficits increased during recessions, but never reverted to a position of surplus during expansionary phases. As a result, governments have experienced an upward trend in the national public debt as a share of GDP.

Various economic theories have been put forward to explain this apparently myopic behaviour:[26] the existence of 'fiscal illusion', according to which voters typically overestimate the benefits of current government spending and underestimate the costs of future taxation, leading to a political business cycle (governments tend to adopt expansionary policies during

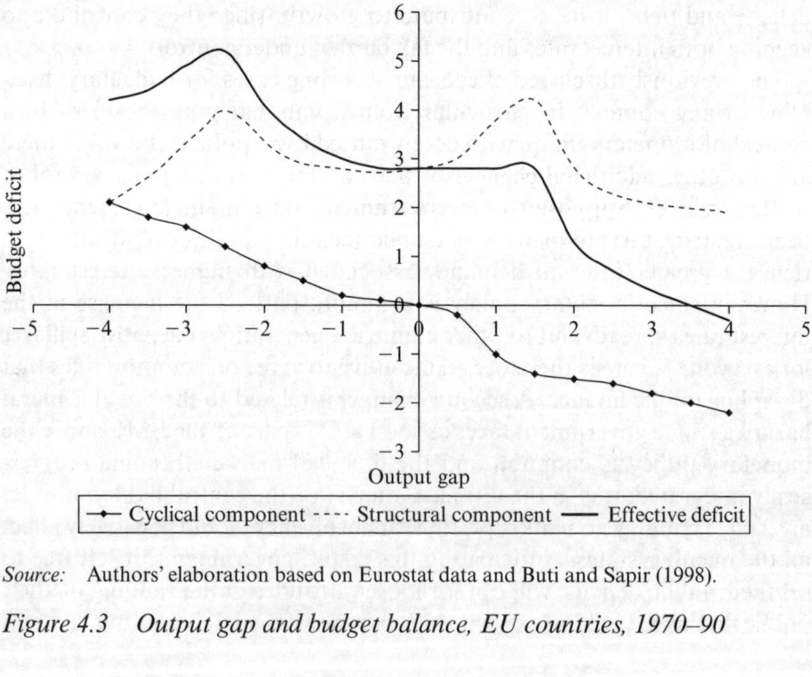

Source: Authors' elaboration based on Eurostat data and Buti and Sapir (1998).

Figure 4.3 Output gap and budget balance, EU countries, 1970–90

election years); the incentive for a government in power, with scant chances of being re-elected, to accumulate debt in order to limit the budgetary options available to its successor; the underlying features of political institutions, with weak coalition governments and parliamentary systems normally associated with a tendency to debt accumulation. Considering the presence across Europe of many such features, it is not surprising to observe a general deterioration of public finances in the 1970–90 period.

Given all the previous discussion, it is now possible to identify the key optimal 'ingredients' of an Economic and Monetary Union: the design has to achieve its benefits (growth and stability) satisfying both the specific political constraints typical of the European experience and the prescriptions of the various economic theories dealing with it. In particular, the latter can be summarised in a design in which (a) the four costs predicted by the OCA theory are minimised; (b) monetary policy is able to achieve price stability, with the relative implications in terms of independence of the central bank and its statutory objective; (c) fiscal policies, though decentralised, concur with the objective of price stability and growth, being balanced in the medium run.

Now, while the first feature of an optimal EMU is straightforward, the other two are subject to various degrees of political compromise in their set-up. Therefore, in what follows, we will try to understand whether and how an optimal balance has been reached between these normative predictions and the peculiarities of the process of European integration.

4.4 MONETARY POLICY IN EMU

4.4.1 Institutional Design

The extraordinary European Council held on 2–3 May 1998, in addition to the launch of the single currency for the first 11 member states, also determined the first composition of the Executive Board of the European Central Bank, one of the bodies of the **European System of Central Banks (ESCB)**, the institution which manages the monetary policy of the Euro area. In particular, the Treaty establishing the European Community states that the basic tasks to be carried out through the ESCB are as follows (TEC, art. 105, para. 2):

(a) to define and implement the monetary policy of the Community;
(b) to conduct foreign exchange operations (following the instructions eventually given by the Council, according to TEC, art. 111 of the Treaty);

(c) to hold and manage the official foreign reserves of member states (though the governments are still able to hold foreign exchange working balances);
(d) to promote the smooth operation of payment systems (the so-called 'TARGET' system).

Moreover the ESCB participates in the definition of the policies implemented by the single member states relating to the prudential supervision of credit institutions and the stability of the financial system.

In order to comply with all these goals, the Treaty has provided the ESCB with several managing bodies: the Executive Board of the European Central Bank, the Governing Council and the General Council. The **Executive Board** comprises the ECB president, the vice-president and four executive members appointed by the European Council at the level of heads of state or government. Their mandate lasts up to eight years (they can be appointed for a shorter time span) and it is not renewable. The Executive Board manages the European Central Bank and thus it is entrusted with the **implementation** of the monetary policy, also providing directions to this extent to the national central banks. The president of the ECB is accountable to the European Parliament through periodical auditions (TEC, art. 113).

The **Governing Council** of the ESCB is composed of the six members of the ECB Executive Board and the 12 (at the moment) governors of the national central banks participating in the EMU. The main task of the Council is the **definition** of the monetary policy of the Union through appropriate decisions on the use of standard tools of monetary policy (monetary policy targets, interest rates levels and the amount of monetary reserves for the EMU system).[27] Furthermore the Council sets the guidelines for the operational implementation by the ECB of the agreed monetary policy. The Council decides by majority, according to the principle of 'one head–one vote'. Assuming that the Executive Board always votes together, such a voting rule implies that, with the current 12 members, the Board only needs the vote of three other governors of the participating members to win (the president's vote is decisive in this case). Such a balance of power may swing significantly in favour of national states once the new members from Central and Eastern Europe participate in the EMU, with implications in terms of credibility for the monetary policy decided by such a body. The last section of this chapter describes the new rules that have been designed to this extent, in order to ensure a smooth enlargement of the ESCB.

Finally the **General Council** of the ESBC comprises the president and the vice-president of the ECB and the governors of national central banks of all member states (both participating and not participating in the EMU). The General Council is responsible for the definition of the rules necessary for the **harmonisation** of national central banks' systems of book-keeping and reporting; moreover it has to write every four months and each year the reports of the ECB, and to fulfil a consulting function.

As already mentioned, because of the uniqueness of the single currency experiment, the ESCB has been organised around the model of the most credible and stable continental monetary institute which preceded it, the German Bundesbank. The reasons behind such a decision are twofold. First of all, a clear attempt has been made to create an institution which could inherit the credibility and reputation the Bundesbank has enjoyed on the financial markets. Second, the statute of the latter seemed to fit well the EMU needs, given that also in the case of the Bundesbank we are dealing with a monetary policy enforced in an economic area characterised by a strong fiscal federalism (with the obvious differences, member states can be considered for the ESBC as German Länder are for the Bundesbank). As a result, the ESCB goals mimic the Bundesbank's, with its **primary objective** explicitly defined: to **maintain price stability** (TEC, art. 105). Such a strict rule is further stressed in para. 2 of art. 105, in which is envisaged the possibility for the ESCB to support the general economic policies in the Union in accordance with the principle of an open market economy, but always 'without prejudice to the objective of price stability'.

Consistently with the German experience, the Treaty also endows the ESCB with a very high degree of **independence**, stating that 'neither the ECB nor a national central bank nor any member of their decision making bodies shall seek or take instructions from Community Institutions or bodies, from any Government of a member State or from any other body' (TEC, art. 108). Furthermore, to prevent any possibility of moral hazard by member states, TEC art. 101 states explicitly that 'overdraft facilities or any type of credit facility with the ECB or with the central banks of the member states in favour of Community institutions or bodies, central governments, regional, local or other public authorities, other bodies governed by public law, or public undertakings of member states shall be prohibited, as shall the purchase directly from them by the ECB or national central banks', a rule known as **'no bail-out' clause**.

4.4.2 Consistency of the Design and Results Achieved

From the characteristics of the institutional design defining the common monetary policy, it is evident that the ECB possesses all the necessary features to be credibly considered independent and strongly committed to price stability. Actually the whole framework of the Treaty implies that the degree of independence of the ECB is probably the highest of any central bank in the world (Buti and Sapir, 1998, p. 5). Why is this so? Essentially the reason derives from the political peculiarities of the European EMU, in which countries retain a very strong degree of fiscal independence.

Lacking a centralised management of fiscal policies, we have seen that in the EMU the temptations for a government to generate higher than normal budget deficits are strong, with the resulting implications in terms of lower price stability. In this case, the degree of commitment of the 'new' central bank to price stability has to be particularly strong if the bank wants immediately to generate low expectations of inflation and establish for itself a good reputation as a guardian of stability. In a sense, the ECB was in the same position as those newly hired sports players, who have to convince the trainer and the fans (the market, in this case) that they are particularly good (that is, really committed to price stability): in the beginning, every mistake will count as double, and double efforts will be needed to establish a firm reputation.

Obviously, in parallel with the institutional design of the bank, a high degree of macroeconomic coordination among the member states is complementary to the smooth working of the EMU. Two dangers in particular can arise for the centralised monetary policy from the behaviour of member states. First, as already discussed, even a very robust institutional design, ex ante strongly independent and committed to price stability, might fail to generate low expectations of inflation if the public finances of member states are not sufficiently close to balancing. Second, as recalled from the OCA theory, a centralised monetary policy is efficient if the economic policies of the member states are not too diverging, that is, their business cycles are sufficiently synchronised.

Let us have a look at this last point. Assume that country *A* before entering the EMU has a rate of inflation equal to 2 per cent, while country *B* has a rate of inflation equal to 7 per cent, with interest rates set accordingly. What is the optimal monetary policy once the EMU is created in this case? The ECB is likely to react to the resulting average inflation of the monetary union with a restrictive monetary policy, if it judges inflation to be too high, or vice versa if according to the bank the average inflation rate is too low. Clearly the more countries are distant from the average inflation (the higher the dispersion of inflation rates around the average), the higher will be the costs of adjustment of each country to the monetary policy set by the bank. In this case, one monetary policy would not fit perfectly the needs of all countries.[28] On the contrary, if all countries have inflation rates very close to each other, the average inflation on which the ECB bases its decisions would not be too distant from the individual inflation rates. Hence, whatever direction the bank decides to take, in this case the resulting monetary policy will not be too distant from the monetary policy that each individual member state would have chosen independently.

In order to avoid the problems outlined above, the Maastricht Treaty, which laid down the foundations of the Economic and Monetary Union, elaborated some **convergence criteria** (since then known as the 'Maastricht criteria') to be fulfilled by member states before joining the monetary union. In particular, the Maastricht criteria state that, in member states willing to participate in the single currency, the following apply:

1. the ratio of government deficit to gross domestic product must not exceed 3 per cent;
2. the ratio of government debt to gross domestic product must not exceed 60 per cent;[29]
3. there must be a sustainable degree of price stability and an average inflation rate (observed over a period of one year before the examination for joining the EMU) which does not exceed by more than 1.5 percentage points that of the three best performing member states in terms of price stability;
4. there must be a long-term nominal interest rate which does not exceed by more than 2 percentage points that of the three best performing member states in terms of price stability;
5. the normal fluctuation margins provided for by the exchange rate mechanism of the European Monetary System (in its post-1992 version) must have been respected without severe tensions for at least the last two years before joining the EMU.

Criterions 5 (exchange rate) and 3 (inflation), when combined, ensure that the national currency is able to withstand the agreed (and irrevocably fixed) exchange rate with the Euro without too much variation of its real exchange rate.[30] Criterions 3 (inflation) and 4 (long-term interest rates) are in place in order to ensure the synchronisation of the business cycles (at least as far as the monetary component is concerned) and hence minimise the costs of running a centralised monetary policy. Criterions 1 (deficit/GDP ratio) and 2 (debt/GDP ratio) complement the institutional design of monetary policy, guaranteeing that the drive towards stability of the ECB is not put in danger by public finances of member states which are off-balance. Incidentally, as already mentioned, these criteria also ensure that private investments, and ultimately growth, are not crowded out by negative public savings.

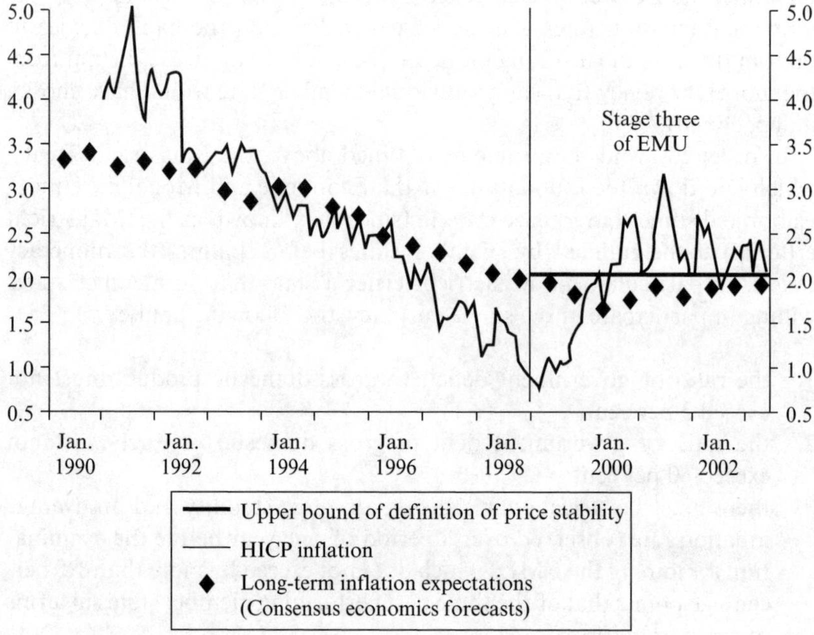

Source: European Central Bank, *Monthly Bulletin*, June 2003.

Figure 4.4 Actual and expected inflation in EMU, 1990–2003 (annual percentage changes)

In terms of results, Figure 4.4 and Table 4.1 show how the Maastricht criteria were successfully met by the 11 member states that in 1999 joined the economic and monetary Union, with the EMU achieving a spectacular and unprecedented degree of convergence of its economies. The respecting of the criteria, together with the institutional design of the ECB, allowed the bank to score well immediately in terms of inflation record, with an average EMU inflation rate always below 3 per cent since its creation, and expected inflation set at even lower levels (see Figure 4.4). Most importantly, this inflation record has been consistently obtained, setting a relatively low level of interest rates, with real interest rates across the EMU 1 per cent lower in the period 1999–2001 with respect to the pre-Euro triennium 1996–8.

Considering the extent of the experiment of monetary unification, involving three out of the seven largest economies in the world, its peculiar characteristics and the scepticism with which some observers had prematurely judged the process of monetary unification, such a performance has to be considered positively.

Table 4.1 The convergence criteria of public finances in EMU

Deficit/GDP											
	Belgium	Germany	Spain	France	Ireland	Italy	Lux.	Neth.	Austria	Portugal	Finland
1991	−6.3	−3.1	−4.4	−2	−2.3	−10.1	1.9	−2.9	−3	−6	−1
1992	−7	−2.6	−4	−3.8	−2.5	−9.6	0.7	−3.9	−2	−3	−5.9
1993	−7.3	−3.2	−6.8	−5.7	−2.2	−9.5	1.6	−3.2	−4.2	−6.1	−7.1
1994	−4.9	−2.4	−6.2	−5.8	−1.7	−9.2	2.7	−3.8	−5	−6	−6.4
1995	−3.8	−3.3	−7.1	−4.9	−2.1	−7.7	1.8	−4.1	−5.1	−5.7	−4.6
1996	−3.1	−3.4	−4.5	−4.1	−0.2	−6.6	2.8	−1.8	−3.7	−3.3	−3.1
1997	−1.6	−2.7	−2.5	−3	1	−2.7	3.8	−1	−1.8	−2.5	−1.2
1998	−0.9	−2	−1.7	−2.9	2.4	−2.7	2.5	−0.7	−2.2	−2.2	0.9

Public Debt/GDP											
	Belgium	Germany	Spain	France	Ireland	Italy	Lux.	Neth.	Austria	Portugal	Finland
1991	128.5	41.4	44.6	35.7	94.3	101.5	4	79	57.9	62.9	23.1
1992	130.1	44	47.1	39.6	91.1	108.7	4.9	80	57.9	56.3	41.3
1993	136.8	48	59	45.7	92.6	119.1	5.9	81.2	62.7	61	57.6
1994	135.1	50.2	61.3	48.5	86.1	124.9	5.5	77.9	65.4	63.8	59.3
1995	132	58.3	64.2	52.8	78.4	125.3	5.8	77.9	69.4	65.9	58.1
1996	128.8	60.8	68.5	55.7	68.6	124.6	6.3	76.1	69.8	64.9	57.6
1997	123.4	61.5	67.1	53.1	59.9	122.4	6.4	70.8	64.1	61.7	55
1998	118.2	61.1	65.1	53.8	49.5	118.7	6.9	67.5	63	57.8	49.7

Source: Authors' elaboration on Eurostat data.

4.4.3 Open Issues: how much Inflation in EMU?

Notwithstanding these comforting results, however, the management of monetary policy by the European Central Bank has not been devoid of criticism. Essentially, two main issues are raised: the first criticism is related to the 'communication skills' of the Bank, that is the degree to which it is able to influence the behaviour of financial markets, especially if compared to the reference role that the Federal Reserve of the United States has gained in the matter. The second criticism deals with the monetary strategy itself, in that most commentators judge it as unnecessarily restrictive, with interest rates set at too high levels with respect to the needs of the European economy. We shall begin by dealing with the latter argument.

The ECB, some months after its establishment, announced the foundations of its monetary policy, which consist of a 'double pillar' strategy.[31]

Under **direct inflation targeting**, in line with the most recent experiences of other central banks in the world (for example, the Reserve Bank of New Zealand or the Bank of England), the bank commits itself to controlling the inflation rate in the medium run, publicly announcing its inflation target. Such an announcement, in turn, provides a quantitative benchmark for the general public to form inflation expectations, and for the setting of prices and wages.[32] As a result, the ECB will intervene every time that, on the basis of the real economic activity and the financial conditions, it estimates that a discrepancy is likely to arise between the target inflation rate and the one foreseen. The ECB announced as its original target an inflation rate between zero and 2 per cent.

Direct inflation targeting is considered by the ECB to be a good instrument in the short to medium run for controlling price stability. However such a strategy is considered less able to track the mechanisms by which monetary factors influence inflation, since in any case it remains the case that long-term variations in inflation are closely associated with long-term movements in money.[33] As a result, according to the ECB, there is a need for monetary policy to extract information more explicitly from monetary developments, which otherwise risk being overlooked or underestimated, thus paralleling the direct inflation targeting with a strategy known as **monetary targeting**. Hence, while the ECB responds to changes in inflation induced by economic developments as they arise, the fundamental factor driving prices over extended horizons – the rate of money growth – also remains consistently under observation. In particular, the ECB has set as a reference value for the monetary developments an annual growth of the broad monetary aggregate M3 of 4.5 per cent.[34] However the bank has always emphasised that, owing to the medium to long-term nature of the monetary perspective, its monetary policy would not react mechanically to deviations of M3 growth from the reference value but, rather, the reference value would be used as a quantitative benchmark for assessing monetary developments in the medium-term horizon set by the bank.

The reason behind this double pillar strategy is probably linked to the fact that the natural 'ancestor' of the ECB, the German Bundesbank, has consistently and successfully used a monetary targeting strategy for maintaining price stability over recent decades. Since the ECB had to build from scratch its reputation on the financial markets, probably the choice of a strategy of pure inflation targeting would have constituted an unnecessary break with respect to the 'tradition' of the German institution by which the ECB is clearly inspired, with subsequent negative implications for its credibility in the early days of the Euro.

Using the **Taylor rule**[35] calculated for the ECB, the Bundesbank and the US Federal Reserve, it is possible to compare the actual strategy of the bank (that is, the level of the interest rates it has chosen since 1999) with the theoretical interest rates that would have been chosen by the German Bundesbank or the US Federal Reserve, had they been in the place of the ECB.[36] In particular, calculating the FED and Bundesbank Taylor rules, and assuming the FED to be more prone to a strategy of direct inflation targeting and the Bundesbank to one of monetary targeting, Figure 4.5 clearly shows how the FED Taylor rule is a better fit for the current ECB strategy with respect to the Bundesbank one.[37] Combining this evidence with the historical record of M3 growth in the Euro area (always above the 4.5 per cent reference value) it can be stated that, in practice, the ECB has followed in its monetary conduct a strategy more aimed at directly targeting inflation rather than controlling monetary growth via its announced 'double pillar' approach.

As a result, Galì *et al.* (2004) then conclude that money plays an unnecessarily prominent role in the ECB's stated strategy. They examine several of the arguments provided by the ECB for maintaining in place its monetary targeting strategy, previously analysed, but find none of them convincing. Therefore, since even the ECB does not seem to follow its stated rules on money growth, they claim that inflation, not money growth rates, should be the only central focus of the ECB's analysis at present and in the future.

Considerations of this kind, together with the fact that the ECB has failed to achieve its stated key objective of avoiding inflation in excess of 2 per cent (with 'core' inflation in general always between 2 and 3 per cent in the EMU since the introduction of the Euro), lead to the criticism that the ECB has a tendency to announce and try to run a monetary policy overly restrictive with respect to the actual economic conditions prevailing in Europe.

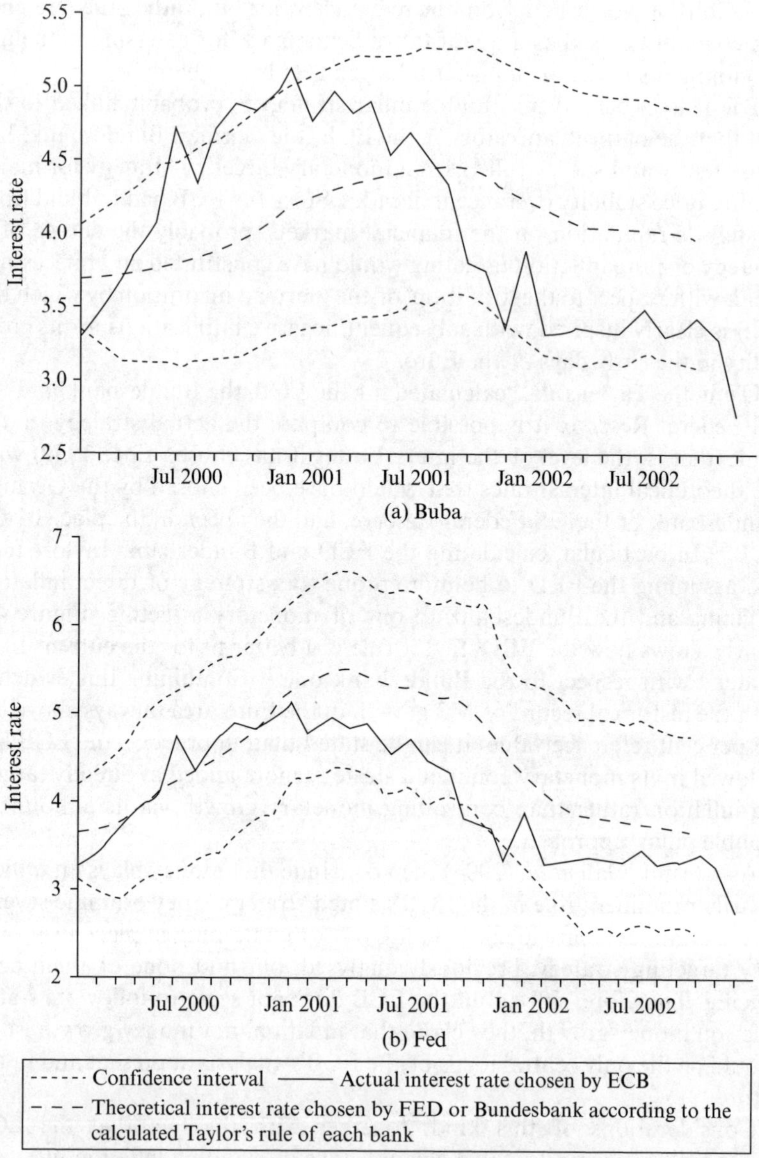

Source: Courtesy of Carlo Favero, updated from C. Favero, X. Freixas, T. Persson and C. Wyplosz (2000), *One Money, Many Countries. Monitoring the European Central Bank, No. 2*, London: CEPR.

Figure 4.5 Monitoring the ECB strategy: inflation versus monetary targeting

Essentially, three costs are associated with a lower than necessary inflation (Sapir *et al.*, 2004). First of all, if inflation, calculated as an average, is too low, it might imply an ineffective monetary policy, due to the zero lower bound for nominal interest rates. Second, it is possible that consumer price indices may be subject to measurement errors. Such errors may arise if prices are not adequately adjusted for changes in quality or if relevant transactions remain systematically outside the sample used to construct the index. In the past, these systematic errors (or bias) have usually been estimated as small but positive for some industrialised countries, suggesting that a rate of measured inflation at zero could actually imply a slight decline in the actual price level. Third, there is some (though not conclusive) evidence that prices and wages are subject to downward nominal rigidities, a resistance to accept nominal reductions in prices and wages, especially if these are already very low. Since movements of relative prices are a key element in the efficient allocation of resources in a market economy, some inflation may actually 'grease' the adjustment of relative prices and thus also the real adjustment of the economy to various shocks.

A fourth consideration, more typical of a context of monetary unions, deals with the inflation differentials that might arise in EMU. In principle, inflation differentials across regions (or countries) are and should be considered a normal feature of any monetary union, being an integral part of the adjustment mechanism resulting from demand and supply shocks. In addition, they might be due structurally to differences in income levels and a continuing process of catching up in standards of living across regions, the so-called **Balassa–Samuelson effect**.[38] As a result, monetary policy cannot and should not try to reduce inflation differentials (DeGrauwe, 2000), nor should it be too restrictive.[39] In fact, if the average inflation rate is already low and the monetary policy intervenes to reduce further an inflation differential, some regions characterised by a structurally lower-than-average inflation rate risk experiencing deflation and a worsening of their downward nominal rigidities, a situation that would magnify their financial instability and would prevent them from quickly adjusting to macroeconomic shocks.[40]

Taking into account these critiques, the ECB revised, on 8 May 2003, its monetary strategy. It confirmed that, in principle, its monetary policy decisions would continue to be based on a comprehensive analysis of the risks to price stability, organised, as in the past, on the basis of the two complementary perspectives of inflation and monetary targeting. However, in confirming the definition of price stability as an inflation rate which is 'comprised between zero and 2 per cent', the Governing Council at the same time has clarified the point that, within the definition, it aims to maintain inflation rates 'close to 2 per cent over the medium term'. With this clarification, the

ECB underlines the stronger relevance of the upper bound of the definition, an inflation rate closer to 2 rather than zero per cent, in order to 'provide a safety margin to guard against the risk of deflation'. Implicitly acknowledging some of the critiques addressed to the management of its second pillar of monetary strategy, monetary targeting, the ECB also stated that, in the future, the 'monetary analysis will take into account developments in a wide range of monetary indicators including M3, its components and counterparts, notably credit, and various measures of excess liquidity', thus broadening its perspective. In addition, it also explicitly stated that 'the monetary analysis mainly serves as a means of cross-checking, from a medium to long-term perspective, the short to medium-term indications coming from economic analysis'. As a result, the ECB decided no longer to conduct on an annual basis a review of the reference value for the money growth of M3.

In terms of the other general critique addressed to the ECB, that is, its inability to influence significantly the sentiments of financial markets, part of the issue is probably related to difference in the time horizon considered by the markets, normally shorter than the medium term on which the ECB has decided to base its monetary policy. Comparing the number of interventions on the market between the US Federal Reserve and the ECB, the more 'interventionist' attitude of the former is clear. Figure 4.6 in fact shows the number of changes in the level of interest rates undertaken by the FED and the ECB in the period 1999–2003. Starting from the year 2001, the FED has lowered its interest rates from more than 6 per cent to around 2 per cent, with almost one cut per month.[41] This more 'radical' attitude of the FED might be currently perceived by the financial markets as more suited to their needs, since it offers them a continuous signal

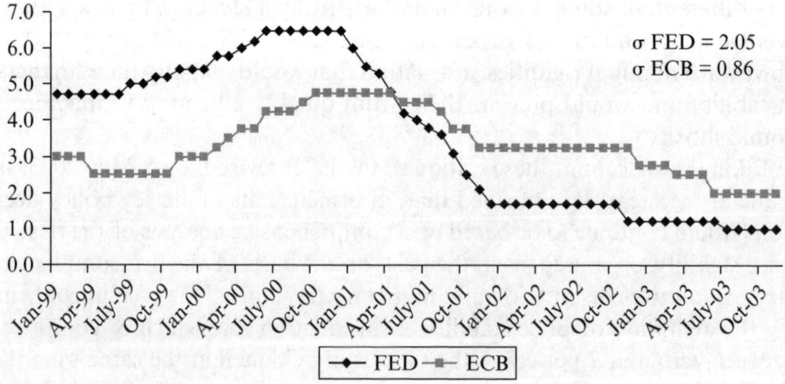

Figure 4.6 The FED versus ECB interest rates, 1999–2003

against which to update expectations. In turn, the ECB maintains a more conservative attitude, less correlated with the volatility of the financial markets, and hence perceived as less able to influence their behaviour.

Given the relatively short time horizon in which the ECB has operated on the markets, and the delicacy of its task (the building up of reputation for a newly established institution hinging upon a decentralised fiscal framework), there is clearly a need for a reciprocal learning process between the markets and the ECB. To this end, the critiques argue, a more proper definition of the monetary strategy, definitely abandoning the monetary pillar together with a slight upward revision of the inflation target, might help to avoid the mistake of 'tough rhetoric without delivery' (Galì *et al.*, 2004).

4.5 FISCAL POLICY IN EMU

4.5.1 Institutional Design

For the reasons previously outlined, at the core of the design of fiscal policies in EMU there are two requirements: (1) achieving solid budgetary discipline and maintaining it over time; and (2) achieving a strong coordination of macroeconomic policies. The latter issue, leading to the so-called Broad Economic Policy Guidelines, will be dealt extensively in the next chapter, since it is now related to the overall strategy of reforms of the Union, while we focus here on budgetary discipline.

The Treaty, in art. 104, para. 1, states that, in EMU, 'member states shall avoid excessive government deficits'. The compliance of a member state with the Treaty's requirements is assessed, inter alia, on the basis of the two fiscal criteria outlined in the Maastricht Treaty and previously discussed: a government deficit below 3 per cent of the GDP and a government debt ratio below 60 per cent of GDP. Higher values are accepted only if 'the ratio is sufficiently diminishing and approaching the reference value at a satisfactory pace' (TEC, art. 104, para. 2*b*). Box 4.2 presents in detail the **excessive deficit procedure**, through which member states commit themselves to keeping public finances under control.

However, on the eve of the introduction of the single currency, the excessive deficit procedure was deemed not completely adequate to guarantee the fiscal discipline of member states, especially in light of the dreadful records of public deficits and debt achieved in the past by some member states. As a result, in 1997, the excessive deficit procedure was complemented by the **Stability and Growth Pact** (SGP), which essentially clarifies and strengthens the provisions of TEC, art. 104.

BOX 4.2 ARTICLE 104 OF THE EC TREATY (EXTRACTS)

1. Member States shall avoid excessive government deficits.
2. The Commission shall monitor the development of the budgetary situation and of the stock of government debt in the member states with a view to identifying gross errors. In particular it shall examine compliance with budgetary discipline on the basis of the following two criteria:
   (a) whether the ratio of the planned or actual government deficit to gross domestic product exceeds a reference value, unless: either the ratio has declined substantially and continuously and reached a level that comes close to the reference value; or, alternatively, the excess over the reference value is only exceptional and temporary and the ratio remains close to the reference value;
   (b) whether the ratio of government debt to gross domestic product exceeds a reference value, unless the ratio is sufficiently diminishing and approaching the reference value at a satisfactory pace.

   [. . .]
3. If a member State does not fulfil the requirements under one or both of these criteria, the Commission shall prepare a report. The report of the Commission shall also take into account whether the government deficit exceeds government investment expenditure and take into account all other relevant factors, including the medium term economic and budgetary position of the member State. The Commission may also prepare a report if, notwithstanding the fulfilment of the requirements under the criteria, it is of the opinion that there is a risk of an excessive deficit in a member State.

   [. . .]
5. If the Commission considers that an excessive deficit in a member state exists or may occur, the Commission shall address an opinion to the Council.
6. The Council shall, acting by a qualified majority on a recommendation from the Commission, and having considered any observations which the member State concerned may wish to make, decide after an overall assessment whether an excessive deficit exists.

7. Where the existence of an excessive deficit is decided according to paragraph 6, the Council shall make recommendations to the member State concerned with a view to bringing that situation to an end within a given period. Subject to the provisions of paragraph 8, these recommendations shall not be made public.
8. Where it establishes that there has been no effective action in response to its recommendations within the period laid down, the Council may make its recommendations public.
9. If a member state persists in failing to put into practice the recommendations of the Council, the Council may decide to give notice to the member state to take, within a specified time limit, measures for the deficit reduction which is judged necessary by the Council in order to remedy the situation. In such a case, the Council may request the member State concerned to submit reports in accordance with a specific timetable in order to examine the adjustment efforts of that member State.

   [. . .]

11. As long as a member state fails to comply with a decision taken in accordance with paragraph 9, the Council may decide to apply or, as the case may be, intensify one or more of the following measures:

    – to require the member State concerned to publish additional information, to be specified by the Council, before issuing bonds and securities,
    – to invite the European Investment Bank to reconsider its lending policy towards the member state concerned;
    – to require the member state concerned to make a non interest bearing deposit of an appropriate size with the Community until the excessive deficit has, in the view of the Council, been corrected;
    – to impose fines of an appropriate size.

Historically, the first proposal for a 'stability pact' was put forward by the German finance minister Theo Weigel in November 1995. The European Council reached an agreement on the principles and the main features of the pact in Dublin in December 1996, with the SGP legally contained in two EU Regulations, EC 1466/97 and 1467/97. Following two Commission's documents (European Commission 2002c and 2004c) and an intense debate, the provisions of the Stability and Growth Pact have been ultimately modified by the member states in March 2005. We present here the original characteristics of the Pact, devoting the last part of the section to the discussion of its recent modifications.

The core elements of the SGP include a strengthening of the surveillance of budgetary positions (the so-called **preventive arm** of the pact), setting time limits by which the various steps of the excessive deficit procedure of art. 104 have to be put in place by the competent institutions. The SGP also specifies in detail the exceptions according to which a member state can exceed the deficit threshold. While TEC, art. 104, para. 2*a* states that the excess has to be 'exceptional and temporary', the SGP translates this situation into a recession in a member state of more than 2 per cent of GDP in a given year.[42] In any case, however, the excess of the deficit over 3 per cent of GDP has to be temporary. Therefore, in order to avoid sanctions, the deficit has to move back below the reference value in the year following the one during which these 'exceptional' circumstances occurred.

In addition, the Pact also contains a **dissuasive arm**, formalising the amount of the sanctions (foreseen by art. 104, para. 11) accruing to a member states failing to take appropriate actions against an excessive deficit. In the first year of application, the sanction takes the form of a non interest bearing deposit, composed of a fixed component equal to 0.2 per cent of GDP of the defaulting state and of a variable component equal to one-tenth of the difference between the deficit and the 3 per cent reference value. A ceiling of a total of 0.5 per cent of a member state's GDP is set. In each subsequent year until the excessive deficit position persists, the variable component of the sanction will be applied. The sanction will be returned if, following its imposition, the interested state takes all the steps necessary to eliminate the excessive deficit. Otherwise, the state failing to do so, the interest-bearing deposit will be transformed into a permanent fine, and the revenues distributed among the other member states.

Apart from these technical details, however, the new, substantial requirement of the SGP is that EU countries are obliged to set country-specific medium-term objectives of budgetary positions 'close to balance or in surplus'. In other words, the mere respecting of the 3 per cent ceiling of budget deficit foreseen by the Maastricht criteria is not enough. Rather member states have to achieve a **zero per cent deficit** in the medium run, or even a budget surplus. In order to obtain this result, countries have to design and undertake multiannual plans, called **stability programmes**,[43] updated each year, and evaluated by the Commission in the framework of the multilateral budgetary surveillance. Of course the exceptionality clause can be called upon if the deficit overshooting takes place in the presence of a severe economic downturn, as previously defined.

Finally, TEC, art. 104, para. 3, states that, in identifying a 'safe' budgetary position allowing the deficit to be kept below 3 per cent of GDP, two issues need to be examined: (a) 'whether the government deficit exceeds government investment expenditures', (b) 'all other relevant factors, including the medium term economic and budgetary position of the member state'.

The first issue is often referred to as the **golden rule** of public spending, and will be analysed in detail at the end of this section, having been the subject of an intense debate among policy makers. Concerning the second issue, the SGP has clarified the need to take into due consideration the influence of **cyclical fluctuations** in economic activity on the budget balance in the medium term; that is, the 'structural' budget of a country. The latter depends on the size of cyclical fluctuations in output as well as on the sensitivity of the budget to the cycle, itself a function of the degree to which **automatic stabilisers** work in any given economy. Box 4.3 discusses in detail these concepts and shows how the cyclical component can be removed from the budget balances.

BOX 4.3 AUTOMATIC STABILISERS, OUTPUT GAPS AND THE STRUCTURAL BUDGET DEFICIT

Fluctuations in economic activity significantly affect government budget receipts and expenditures. In fact, the modern systems of welfare are designed in such a way that, during recessions, the government's fiscal policy becomes slightly expansionary, in order to smooth the social negative implications of an economic downturn, while the opposite (a moderate restrictive fiscal policy) occurs during periods of sustained growth, in order to cool down inflationary pressures. Such an outcome is achieved without any discretionary intervention by the government (no specific laws have to be passed), thanks to the working of the so-called 'automatic stabilisers'. Essentially these are policy tools by and large constituted by the standard, progressive system of taxation (the system in which the marginal tax rate is higher for higher individual incomes) and by social provisions linked to the unemployment rate. In the event of a recession, a certain proportion of people will move from high to middle incomes, and therefore, on average, citizens will be taxed less than before; in turn, more people will find themselves unemployed, and therefore a higher proportion of citizens will be entitled to an unemployment subsidy. As a result, owing to the working of the automatic stabilisers (taxes are reduced, while public social expenditure is increased) the fiscal policy becomes automatically a bit more expansionary, thus smoothing the negative effects of recession. However the impact on the public budget of the working of the automatic stabilisers will be negative, because the government will see its tax provisions decrease and its expenditures increase. The opposite will happen in the case of an economic boom: the working of the automatic stabilisers is such that fiscal policy becomes moderately restrictive, while the budget balances improve.

Recessions and economic booms are defined with respect to the 'potential output' of an economy, that is, the equilibrium growth rate achievable when all the resources of a country are used without giving rise to inflationary pressures. Deviations from this equilibrium path are known as 'output gaps': these are positive in periods of economic expansions (there is a more than normal use of resources in the economy) and negative during recessions (fewer resources are used than are available, with creation of unemployment and accumulation of inventories).

As a result, to understand which is the 'real' or, better, the 'structural budget' position of a country, it is necessary to subtract from the official budget balances the effects induced by the eventual output gap incurred by each country. In practice this is easier said than done, since there are several cyclical adjustment algorithms, and no consensus has emerged so far on a prevailing methodology. The European Commission uses the Hedrick–Prescott filter to calculate trend output over the cycle, while the OECD and the IMF follow another approach and use a Cobb–Douglas production function to estimate potential output, obtaining similar but not identical results (which is crucial since, often, the policy debate is centred on decimal figures of the budget). Revenue and expenditure elasticities are then applied to the output gap in order to estimate the impact of the cycle on the government receipts and expenditures. In general, all these methodologies show that the sensitivity of the budget balances to the cycle for the European Union as a whole lies on average at around 0.5. This means that each increase in a negative output gap by 1 percentage point increases the government deficit by 0.5 percentage points of GDP in Europe, owing to the working of the automatic stabilisers. However, given the various structures of welfare provisions existing across the European countries, this coefficient might vary greatly among member states.

One could therefore summarise the logic of the Stability and Growth Pact with the following statement: countries should bring their structural budget balances towards equilibrium (zero deficit) so as to have sufficient room for manoeuvre to let automatic stabilisers play in cyclical downturns without breaching the 3 per cent deficit ceiling.

4.5.2 Consistency of the Design and Results Achieved

From the previous discussion it is clear that the design of the Stability and Growth Pact seems to be perfectly consistent with the goal foreseen by the OCA theory of creating enough 'room for manoeuvre' for the fiscal policy to cope with asymmetric shocks, without endangering at the same time price stability in EMU.

Figure 4.7 visualises how this goal can be reached. The output gap (see Box 4.3) is measured on the horizontal axis, while the total deficit is measured on the vertical axis, so budget surplus is indicated by negative values. The negative sloped lines indicate the cyclical component of the budget. They are negatively sloped because the more negative the output gap, the higher the impact of the automatic stabilisers on the budget deficit. The interception between the cyclical component line and the vertical axis

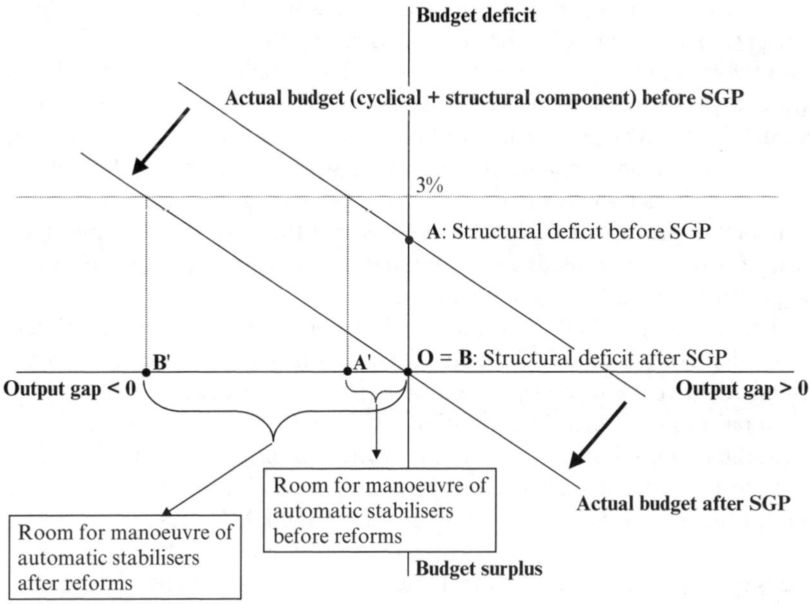

Figure 4.7 The rationale of the Stability and Growth Pact

measures the structural deficit, that is, the deficit that a country is producing when the output gap is zero (when the economy is working at its optimal potential level). As reported by Figure 4.3, virtually all European countries had a positive structural deficit (indicated by point *A* in Figure 4.7) before the adoption of the SGP, and hence they would see their total budget rapidly hitting the 3 per cent threshold in the event of downturns. In this situation, the automatic stabilisers do not have enough 'room for manoeuvre' to work or, better, if a country allows them to work fully in order to cope with the asymmetric shock, the same country quickly breaches the 3 per cent threshold, thus endangering the stability of the Euro area.

To correct this imbalance, the SGP requires the value of the structural deficit to be 'close to balance' (point *B* in Figure 4.7), or even in surplus. As can be seen, this allows for a larger margin (OB') in the use of the automatic stabilisers should a negative shock affect the system, since the worsening of the budget deficit associated with the working of the automatic stabilisers is likely to remain in any case below the 'critical' threshold of 3 per cent. At the same time, allowing only the automatic stabilisers to intervene on the working of the economic cycle, one avoids discretionary (and often distortionary) interventions by the member states in the cycle.

Looking at the quantitative aspects of the fiscal criteria, the 3 per cent ceiling of budget deficit is not a randomly chosen figure. In fact, analysing all the cases of recessions taking place across member states in Europe in the period 1961–90, it has been demonstrated (Buti and Sapir, 1998) that, had these member states experienced a close to balance structural deficit, the cyclical component of the budget activated by the automatic stabilisers would never have crossed the threshold of a 3 per cent deficit until the recession was over. Only in cases of 'large' recessions would the resulting deficit have been larger than 3 per cent: this is the reason why the institutional framework previously discussed foresees that the SGP is not applicable if 'extraordinary circumstances' (more than a 2 per cent decrease in output in a given year) befall a member state.[44]

The threshold of 60 per cent of public debt over GDP derives directly from the fixing of the 3 per cent deficit ceiling: this is in fact the level of public debt that can be sustained with a 3 per cent deficit when having a nominal growth (including inflation) of 5 per cent a year, a figure in line with the potential output of the European economy at the time.[45]

In terms of results achieved, contrary to the institutional framework set up for the monetary policy, the fiscal side of the EMU presents a series of drawbacks. In particular, looking at the record of member states in terms of budget deficits, it is evident from Table 4.2 that the goal of the SGP, to bring the EU public finances 'close to balance' has been missed, with a significant and continuous worsening of budget balances in EMU after year 2000.

Table 4.2 The budgetary position in EMU (GDP percentage)

	2000	2001	2002	2003	2004	2005
Total receipts (1)	47.2	46.5	46.1	46.2	45.7	45.4
Total expenditure (2)	47.1	48.1	48.3	49.0	48.4	48.0
Actual balance (3)=(1)−(2)	0.2	−1.6	−2.2	−2.8	−2.7	−2.7
Interest (4)	4.1	4.0	3.6	3.6	3.4	3.4
Primary balance (5) =(3)+(4)	4.2	2.3	1.4	0.7	0.7	0.8
UMTS	1.1	0.0	0.0	0.0	0.0	0.6
Cyclically adjusted balance (6)	−1.9	−2.3	−2.4	−2.3	−2.2	−2.2
Cyclically adj. prim. balance=(6)+(4)	2.2	1.6	1.3	1.2	1.3	1.2
Change in actual balance	1.5	−1.8	−0.6	−0.6	0.1	0.0
Due to • Cycle	0.6	−0.3	−0.5	−0.7	−0.1	0.1
• UMTS	1.1	−1.1	0.0	0.0	0.0	0.6
• Interest	0.2	0.1	0.4	0.0	0.2	0.0
• Cycl. adj. primary balance	−0.4	−0.6	−0.3	−0.1	0.1	−0.1
Gross debt	70.2	69.2	69.0	70.4	70.7	70.7
p.m. Actual balance EU-15	1.0	−0.9	−1.9	−2.7	−2.6	−2.4
p.m. Primary balance EU-15	4.8	2.7	1.4	0.6	0.5	0.7
p.m. Cycl. adj. prim. balance EU-15	2.6	2.0	1.3	1.1	1.1	1.2

Note: Total expenditure, actual and primary balances include UMTS, while cyclically adjusted figures exclude UMTS proceeds.

Moreover, and more worryingly, a closer look at the budgetary trends reveals that the deterioration in nominal deficits persists in several countries even after correcting for the effects of the cycle. This indicates a discretionary loosening of the fiscal stance by some member states over the period, generated by a combination of unfunded tax cuts, discretionary expenditure increases and poor budgetary execution (European Commission, 2003a). Hence it can be stated that the SGP has clearly failed to induce structural changes in the behaviour of some governments (notably those of larger countries). Most of the consolidation achieved has in fact been obtained only thanks to higher growth rates in Europe, but, as soon as growth slowed down, deficits expanded accordingly (Crockett *et al.*, 2003).

As a consequence of this misbehaviour, the European Commission has requested from the Council the activation of the excessive deficit procedure against several countries since 2002, as reported in Table 4.3. However all these steps have been accompanied by a long stream of conflicts between the Commission and the Council, and among member states.[46] For example, according to the procedures presented in Box 4.1, the Council voted for an excessive deficit procedure for Portugal and Germany, but did not agree to vote, some months before, for an official 'early warning' proposed by the Commission against the same member states. It voted for an 'early warning' against France in January 2003 and, lacking any indications of correction by the French government, the start of an excessive deficit procedure also for France later in June 2003. In November 2003, owing to what it judged an insufficient correction of the budgetary position, the Commission proposed to go on with the second step of the excessive deficit procedure (the sanctions) against France and Germany, but again its proposal was not put to vote by the Council. In July 2004, following an appeal of the Commission to the European Court of Justice, the same court ruled that the behaviour of the Council was not legal, urging it to apply all the provisions of the Pact. The struggle has led the EU institution and the member states to define new proposals for a reform of the Pact (see European Commission, 2004c, and below) as a way to exit from this juridical impasse.[47]

Clearly the overall judgment of these events in terms of economic efficiency is negative. However it is also important to bear in mind that fiscal policy in EMU is affected by extremely binding political constraints, in line with the previously discussed finding that, within economic unions, member states are more eager to renounce their monetary than their fiscal sovereignty. As a result, notwithstanding the need in EMU for an enhanced level of fiscal coordination called for by the economic theory, member states currently retain a strong degree of political control of the entire process. In other words, while the governance of monetary policy is made efficient by the presence of a central and independent authority, no similar institutions exist for the time being for the non-monetary governance of the EMU.

Actually the problem lies in the implementation, rather than the setting up of adequate rules. The Treaty and the SGP in fact explicitly charge the Commission with the task of monitoring budgetary developments in EMU, committing member states to the preparation of and adherence to the multiannual stability programmes, and empowering the Commission with a critical evaluation of the same programmes. However, in terms of enforcement, TEC, art. 104 confers on the same member states the power of ultimately judging and condemning misbehaving partners, since it is the

Table 4.3 *The application of the excessive deficit procedure*

Documents	D	PT	F	NL	UK	CZ	CY	HU	MT	PL	SK	GR
Commission report (104§3)	19.11.02	24.9.02	2.4.03	28.4.04	28.4.04	12.5.04	12.5.04	12.5.04	12.5.04	12.5.04	12.5.04	19.5.04
Comm. opinion (104§5) and recommend. for a Council decision (104§6) and recommend. (104§7)	8.1.03	16.10.02	7.5.03	19.5.04								24.6.04
Council decision (104§6)	21.1.03	5.11.02	3.6.03	2.6.04		5.7.04	5.7.04	5.7.04	5.7.04	5.7.04	5.7.04	5.7.04
Council recommend. (104§7)	21.1.03	5.11.02	3.6.03	2.6.04		5.7.04	5.7.04	5.7.04	5.7.04	5.7.04	5.7.04	5.7.04
Comm. recommend. for a Council decision (104§8)	18.11.03		8.10.03									
Comm. recommend. for a Council decision (104§ 9) to give notice	18.11.03		21.10.03									
Comm. recommend. for a Council decision (104§12) abrogating the decision on the existence of an excessive deficit		28.4.04										

Source: Authors' elaboration from European Commission sources.

Council that, on the basis of a recommendation made by the Commission, has to decide that an excessive deficit exists, with all the subsequent actions. Given the already analysed incentive that each member state has to 'free-ride' on EMU by deviating in a given year from the agreed deficit, it is clear that, in a game repeated over time, a state voting in favour of a punishment in one year will lower its chances of free-riding in a next year, owing to the higher chances of retaliation by other members. Therefore, in a dynamic decision-making process, the 'no punishment' strategy might become the optimal one for all member states. In addition, since the Council technically acts upon a recommendation, not a proposal, by the Commission, the Council can easily change the content of the Commission's recommendation by qualified majority, while it would need unanimity to change the content of a proposal put forward by the Commission.[48]

Given these drawbacks, there is a clear risk that, if member states keep on with such an attitude, the successful performance of the Economic and Monetary Union might be at risk, with the possibility of a dangerous reversal in the process of economic integration. As a result, the debate on some reforms of the fiscal policy framework for EMU, presented below, is of the utmost importance.

4.5.3 Open Issues: the Reform of the Stability and Growth Pact

Looking at the performance of the SGP in retrospect, it is clear that some adjustments have to be made to its design if the original (good) idea of the SGP is to be retained. The first criticism[49] addressed to the Pact has already been implicitly discussed: the SGP suffers from the 'original sin' of member states which have failed to achieve a structurally balanced budget position in the medium run. As a result, the SGP becomes extremely rigid, or not too 'smart', in recessionary phases of the cycle, because it reduces budgetary flexibility and ultimately forces a procyclical policy in member states. Suppose in fact that a country is in the situation indicated by point *A* in Figure 4.7, that is, it maintains a positive structural deficit. In this case, should an economic downturn strike the country, the working of its automatic stabilisers would start correcting this imbalance, at the cost of a deterioration in its budgetary position. However we have seen that, in this situation, the room for manoeuvre is very limited: the budget deficit very soon hits the 3 per cent threshold. Now, according to the SGP, this implies the immediate activation of the excessive deficit procedure foreseen in TEC, art. 104, and eventually the imposition of fines on the deflecting country. In order to avoid this procedure, the country is therefore forced to correct its budget imbalances, running a procyclical policy; that is, it has to increase taxes and/or reduce public expenditures, aggravating rather than improving its recession.

Because of these initial problems, the 'political ownership' of the SGP by member states has diminished (European Commission, 2002c, 2003a), with a divergence developing progressively between budgetary commitments and the concrete actions needed to achieve the stated commitments. In addition, as already considered, member states found no incentives to exert a collective peer pressure on countries that miss budgetary targets, owing to the drawbacks in the enforcement mechanisms of the SGP.

Another drawback of the Pact, already implicitly discussed, is related to its asymmetric functioning: in favourable cyclical periods the SGP does not restrain the procyclical attitude of governments to increasing expenditure or cutting taxes. In other words, there is no rule obliging countries to take advantage of periods of strong growth; that is, to create funds to be used in the 'rainy days' of recession. We have already discussed this evidence of a procyclical bias still affecting budgetary policies in the Euro area. In particular, looking at the fiscal consolidation achieved in the year 2000–2001, we have pointed out how, in a situation of buoyant growth (3.4 per cent for the Euro area as a whole), countries with high deficits failed to seize the opportunity to reduce structurally their fiscal imbalances. As soon as the growth conditions deteriorated, the underlying budgetary position worsened, thereby creating the budgetary problems the EMU experienced over the subsequent two years.

In addition to these evident problems, all related to the 'original sin' of the SGP, other critiques have been made of the composition of expenditures that the SGP generates (Sapir *et al.*, 2004). Maintaining budget positions 'close to balance or in surplus' in each year, in fact, implies that large capital expenditures on public investments projects, whose benefits are deferred over time, will have to be funded each year from the same (large) amount of current revenues, rather than financed by revenues raised from different generations of taxpayers. This may imply a disincentive to undertake large investment projects, with the disincentive being stronger during consolidation periods, with negative consequences for the capital accumulation and, ultimately, growth. The issue is actually controversial: while there is a widespread perception that the process of budgetary consolidation (both before and after the launch of the Euro) and the application of the SGP has contributed to excessively low levels of public investment, data analysis shows that the decline in public investment rates is a long-run tendency that started as early as in the 1970s, and affected all industrialised countries, and not just EU member states. Moreover there is evidence that roughly half of the episodes of fiscal consolidations undertaken in EU countries in the past three decades have been followed by an immediate acceleration in growth (European Commission, 2003a). Box 4.4 analyses in detail these **non-Keynesian effects** of economic policy.

BOX 4.4 CAN FISCAL CONSOLIDATION BE EXPANSIONARY?

According to standard macroeconomic models, a restrictive fiscal stance would result in a short-run negative impact on aggregate demand and then on output and employment. However, in a recent, very good survey Giudice *et al.* (2003) summarise the growing evidence that, in some cases of fiscal consolidations, the effects of fiscal policy on short-run growth may actually be positive. Cases have been documented of countries in which tax increases or expenditure cuts have in fact been followed by accelerated growth in the short run. A number of rationalisations have been provided for what are commonly called the 'non-Keynesian' effects of fiscal policy. Some of these factors concern the impact of fiscal policy on private consumption (for example, Giavazzi and Pagano, 1990; Perotti, 1999; Giavazzi *et al.*, 2000). In particular, it has been shown that the reduction of budget deficits may lead to an increase in aggregate consumption in the short run through wealth and confidence effects. In this sense, the credibility of consolidations is crucial: the fiscal adjustment should be perceived to lead to a permanent increase in future disposable income streams via reduced taxation. To this end, consolidations leading to a substantial improvement of the budget balance or starting from situations of high debt/GDP ratios, as in the case of EMU, are more likely to affect consumers' expectations and induce an immediate increase in consumption through confidence and wealth effects. Another strand of research (for example, Alesina *et al.*, 2002) focuses instead on the effects of fiscal policy on business investment and concentrates on the supply side, in particular on how profits are affected through the impact of fiscal policy on real wages in the private sector. Fiscal consolidations may lead to higher expected profits and higher investment by reducing the tax burden on firms and inducing wage moderation. Consistent with the predictions of theory, the empirical evidence reported in existing studies shows that the size and persistence of the fiscal adjustment (as measured by a sufficient degree of improvement in cyclically adjusted budget balances), the composition of adjustment (the extent to which the adjustment is achieved through tax increases or expenditure cuts) and the initial state of public finances (mainly the debt/GDP ratio) are relevant in driving episodes of expansionary consolidation.

Related to this 'myopic' attitude of the SGP, other critiques point to the fact that the Pact stimulates 'creative accounting' and one-off measures by member states, which are put in place in order to comply each year with the requirements of the SGP, at the expense of a more comprehensive programme of structural reforms. In addition, since the stock of public debt does not enter the SGP and neither do the contingent liabilities of public pension systems, de facto the Pact treats equally countries which are themselves very different in terms of medium and long-term prospects of sustainability of public finances and debt levels.[50]

Finally, always because of this short-term attitude, the Pact may prevent countries from implementing policies, such as pension reforms, which improve the sustainability of public finances over the medium and long term, but at the price of a short-term deficit worsening.

Several ideas have been proposed to correct, to various extents, the previously discussed drawbacks of the Stability and Growth Pact.[51] The same European Commission has put forward two Communications, on 27 November 2002 and 3 September 2004 (European Commission, 2002c and 2004c), in which a number of 'institutional' proposals to tackle the shortcomings of the SGP were elaborated. The European Council of 22 and 23 March 2005 capitalised on all this work, and unanimously agreed on a comprehensive reform of the Stability and Growth Pact, which we sketch here in its most important elements.[52]

First of all, as far as the general **governance** of the Pact is concerned, member states agreed that, in a Union with 25 member states, characterised by considerable heterogeneity and diversity, a stronger emphasis is needed on the economic rationale of the SGP rules, rather than their technical application, in order to better cater for differences in economic situations across the EU. In particular, the Council stated that 'the aim is not to increase the rigidity or flexibility of current rules but rather to make them more effective . . . Also, the instruments for EU economic governance need to be better interlinked in order to enhance the contribution of fiscal policy to economic growth.'

To this extent, it has been agreed that the domestic governance arrangements should complement the EU framework: member states, when preparing the first update of their stability programme after a new government has taken office, have to show continuity with respect to the budgetary targets already endorsed by the previous government, and have to set out a budgetary strategy, providing information on the means and instruments which they intend to employ, with an outlook for the whole legislature; national parliaments should be involved in the discussion of the follow-up to recommendations in the context of the early warning and the excessive deficit procedures; sanctions should be imposed on those member states which fail to provide the obligations to duly report government data and statistics.

In terms of the **preventive arm** of the Pact, the medium-term objectives of 'close to balance or in surplus' will be differentiated by member states. Moreover, these budgetary objectives will be defined in cyclically adjusted terms, net of one-off and temporary measures, thus isolating the impact of transitory factors, and in particular the effects of the economic cycle on the budget position, as previously discussed (see Box 4.2). The Council has also recognised that other transitory elements beyond the cyclical component have an impact on the budget positions, both positively and negatively (for example, the extent to which a country is engaged in structural reforms affecting its potential growth, the public debt position of a country and so on). These elements thus need to be considered when assessing the underlying budgetary position of a member state, so as to avoid rigid policy conclusions. As a result, the range for the country-specific, cyclically adjusted medium-term objectives should be between −1 per cent of GDP for low debt/high potential growth countries and balance or surplus for high debt/low potential growth countries.

In terms of the adjustment path to the medium-term objectives, whose lack has been termed by many as the 'original sin' of the Pact, member states should pursue an annual adjustment in cyclically adjusted terms, net of one-offs and other temporary measures, of 0.5 per cent of GDP.[53] However, the adjustment effort should be higher in two cases: a) in 'good times', that is, in periods where output exceeds its potential level, and b) for countries with higher debt. Moreover, structural reforms will be taken into account when defining the adjustment path to the medium-term objective for countries that have not yet reached this objective, or a temporary deviation from this objective will be allowed for countries that have already reached it.[54] In any case, a safety margin to ensure the respect of the 3 per cent of GDP reference value for the deficit has to be guaranteed, while the budgetary position is expected to return to the medium-term objective within the programme period. To this extent, the medium-term budgetary objectives could be revised when a major reform is implemented, and in any case every four years, in order to reflect developments in government debt, potential growth and fiscal sustainability. If, notwithstanding this flexibility, a member state should not follow the required adjustment path, it has to explain the reasons for the deviation in the annual update of its stability programme, and can be exposed to an early warning by the European Commission.

As far as the **golden rule** is concerned, the latter has already been operational in the European context, and notably in Germany and the UK. In both cases, the rule is designed in such a way that budget deficits should not be higher than some definition of public investment (gross for Germany, net, that is, minus the depreciation, in the UK). Although the performance of such a rule seems to have been positive in the two countries considered, applying it at the EMU level presents a series of drawbacks. First, a golden rule based on a national accounts system could lead to a bias in expenditure decisions in favour of physical capital and against spending on human capital (education, training) or other productive items (health care, R&D) which also contribute to growth and employment.[55] Second, if applied to gross investment, depending on the specific design and implementation of the reform, the adoption of a golden rule in the SGP framework may imply substantially higher deficits, thus compromising the objective of sustainability of public finances. Hence the relevant concept for the application of the golden rule should be net investment. However, it is not always possible to compute reliable, comparable and timely data on this type of investment. As a result, a solution often advocated to the difficulties in the application of the golden rule is to let the Commission decide what should be considered as investment expenditures, then to be excluded from the computation of the deficit measures. However, while the rationale of such a proposal is straightforward (after all, it is the Commission that is ultimately charged with the task of budgetary surveillance in the EMU), allowing the Commission to decide what counts as investment spending in each member state essentially means empowering the Commission with a strong degree of influence on each member state's decision on the allocation of their public expenditures.[56] Hence, the golden rule is not included among the provisions of the reformed SGP.

A much more flexible attitude has instead been adopted by the member states in their redefinition of the rules related to the **dissuasive arm** of the Pact, that is, in the application of the excessive deficit procedure foreseen in TEC, art. 104. The Council has clearly stated that the excessive deficit procedure has to be engaged when there is an overshooting of the 3 per cent deficit criterion. However, the exceptions to this rule already foreseen in the Treaty, as well as the timing of the application of the procedure, have been significantly amended in order not to hinder structural reforms of public finances and avoid a pro-cyclical behaviour of the SGP. In particular, the Council has redefined the exception foreseen in TEC, art. 104, para. 2*a*: any (temporary) excess over the reference value which results from a period of negative growth rate (thus no longer a recession of at least 2 per cent, or 0.75 per cent), or even from the accumulated loss of output during a protracted period of very low growth relative to potential growth, should be considered as exceptional, and therefore not sanctioned, thus correcting one of the major criticisms of the Pact, namely its pro-cyclical attitude.

Moreover, the Council has stated that 'all other relevant factors' foreseen by TEC, art. 104, para. 3 in assessing a 'safe' budgetary position should be better taken into account with respect to the past implementation of the Pact, without prejudice, however, to the overarching principle that, before other relevant factors are taken into account, the excess over the reference value is temporary and the deficit remains close to the reference value. In particular, to foster the implementation of structural reforms, the Council has proposed that the Commission's report under TEC, art. 104, para. 3 should 'appropriately reflect developments in the medium-term economic position (in particular potential growth, prevailing cyclical conditions, the implementation of policies in the context of the Lisbon agenda and policies to foster R&D and innovation) as well as developments in the medium-term budgetary position (in particular, fiscal consolidation efforts in 'good times', debt sustainability, public investment and the overall quality of public finances)'. Furthermore, the Council has also stated that 'due consideration has to be given to any other factors which, in the opinion of the concerned member state, are relevant in order to comprehensively assess in qualitative terms the excess over the reference value. In that context, special consideration has to be given to budgetary efforts towards increasing or maintaining at a high level financial contributions to fostering international solidarity and to achieving European policy goals, notably the unification of Europe, if those have a detrimental effect on the growth and fiscal burden of a member state'. The Council and the Commission, in all the budgetary assessments within the framework of the excessive deficit procedure, will also give due consideration to the implementation of pension reforms.

At any rate, the Council has decided that allowing for giving special consideration to different types of expenditure should not amount to a redefinition of the 3 per cent limit. In the words of the Council 'no redefinition of the Maastricht reference value for the deficit via the exclusion of particular budgetary items should be pursued'.

Finally, the deadlines for the various procedures foreseen under TEC, art. 104 have been extended. In particular, the standard deadline for correcting an excessive deficit has been maintained as the year after its identification and thus, normally, the second year after its occurrence. The Council has agreed, however, that the overall assessment of 'all other relevant factors' foreseen by TEC, art. 104, para. 3 should be taken into account in setting the initial deadline for the correction of an excessive deficit. As a result, while as a benchmark countries in excessive deficit are required to achieve within one year a minimum fiscal effort of at least 0.5 per cent of GDP in cyclically adjusted terms (net of one-off measures), in case of special circumstances resulting from the previously discussed assessment, the initial deadline for correcting an excessive deficit could be set one year later, that is, the second year after its identification and thus normally the third year after its occurrence.[57] Moreover, these deadlines for correcting the excessive deficit could be further revised and extended if unexpected adverse economic events with major unfavourable budgetary effects occur during the excessive deficit procedure.

Clearly, these new rules provide for a much greater flexibility in the application of the SGP, correcting most of its major drawbacks. As a result the reform, coupled with the repeated call for enhancing microeconomic adjustment mechanisms (improving the functioning of labour and product markets, as discussed in the following chapter), goes in the right direction. However, it remains to be seen whether, in the light of enlargement, the new rules go far enough to improve the cyclical stabilisation of public finances in the EMU.

The reform of the Stability and Growth Pact has in fact transferred a more discretionary power to the member states: it is the Council that has to ultimately evaluate whether the exceptions to the excessive deficit procedure, or to the fulfilling of the medium-term objectives, are applicable or not, since it is always possible to overrule a Commission's report by qualified majority. If member states recognise that a non-cooperative attitude, such as the one displayed in the past, risks having them lose most of the benefits of the EMU, there may be a chance of some improvements in the management of fiscal policies. Otherwise a dangerous political loop might arise: an imperfectly working EMU induced by the same loose fiscal behaviour of member states might be perceived as imposing only unnecessary binding constraints without delivering adequate results. Such a perception might become particularly strong in a context of sluggish growth, where the cycle does not compensate for the structural drawbacks in the management of the economic policies in the EMU context. Member states might react to this situation with a further increase in the degree of discretion of their fiscal policies, avoiding condemning themselves within the 'new' Stability and Growth Pact, and thus further worsening the situation, ultimately leading to an intrinsic instability in the design of economic and monetary unification.

4.6 EMU IN AN ENLARGED UNION

The enlargement of the European Union is taking place at a time when the Union is still facing the previously discussed adjustment processes induced by the management of the monetary and fiscal policies in the EMU context. In particular we have already pointed out that the ECB (correctly) does not fine-tune its monetary policy in order to meet the particular economic challenges in every specific member country, while fiscal policies, even if subject to a threshold in terms of total debt and deficit they can generate, are defective in terms of overall coordination. Hence there is the possibility of a significant asymmetry between the centrally chosen monetary policy and the inflation rates arising across member countries.

In this respect the participation in the single currency of the new member states might further exacerbate the possible asymmetries, given the heterogeneous economic structure of the Central and Eastern European Countries (CEECs) analysed in the previous chapter. Thus, at least in theory, there seems to be a rationale for the postponement of an enlargement of the EMU to admit the new member states until a greater degree of economic convergence has been reached across the EU-25.

And yet, although membership of the EU does not imply the adoption of the Euro from the very beginning,[58] the new member states are nevertheless under an obligation to adopt the *acquis* also as far as the EMU is concerned, since during the accession negotiations they have not asked for an 'opt out' clause similar to that of Denmark or the UK. Therefore all the new member states have to start respecting all the provisions of the common monetary policy immediately, adopting the single currency as soon as they fulfil the necessary criteria. Since the direction of the path is inescapable, two relevant issues therefore arise: (a) from the point of view of the new member states, the speed at which the transition to the Euro should be undertaken is under discussion; (b) from the point of view of the current 12 EMU members, the issue of how and whether the monetary policy has to change in order to encompass the needs of the new member states becomes relevant.

As far as the first point is concerned, two opposite forces are likely to play a role. First of all, there seems to be a rationale for the new member states to adopt the Euro quickly (Eichengreen and Ghironi, 2002). As shown in Figure 4.8, these economies are not very far from meeting the fiscal criteria of public debt and deficit and all have independent central banks. The current misalignments they are experiencing in their inflation[59] and interest rates with respect to the EU averages clearly put some strain on the respecting of the first two monetary criteria. However past experience of the EMU suggests that these variables tend to converge relatively quickly on the EU averages as soon as the expectations of membership arise. More generally, as discussed in more detail in Chapter 10, the CEECs are open economies which trade disproportionately with the EU-15 (around 60 per cent of their total imports and exports) and hence a more structured stability of their exchange rates via the adoption of the common currency might be desirable, as it has been for the current Euro members. To remain within the exchange rate mechanism, in fact, might be optimal in the short

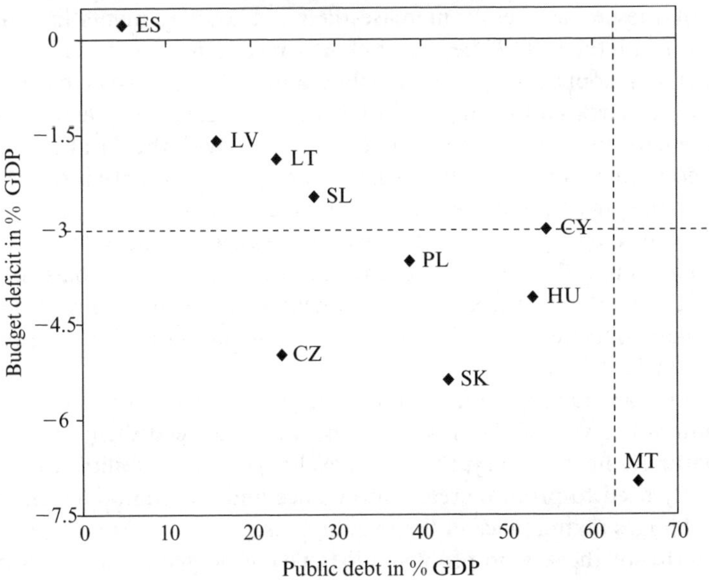

Figure 4.8 The fiscal criteria for EMU in new member states (2002)

to medium run, but in the long run not joining the Euro might expose these countries to financial crises, as already experienced by the EU in 1992. A resolute commitment to the adoption of the single currency would instead immediately improve the market's expectations on their economic fundamentals, and thus anticipate some of the benefits of participation to the Euro. In addition there is always the possibility that the fiscal consolidation required to adopt the Euro might generate also in the new member states those positive non-Keynesian effects which were experienced by some of the member states at the time of their convergence on the Maastricht criteria, as we have previously discussed.

Other issues, however, suggest some caution in a quick transition of the new member states to the EMU. First of all, in those member states where the fiscal consolidation leads to a standard effect of contraction in the economic cycle, their path of income convergence to the EU level will halt. In addition, as pointed out by Sapir *et al.* (2004), since these countries are more exposed to country-specific problems (owing to the heterogeneity of their economic structures), they will need to have a larger safety margin below the deficit ceiling set by the SGP if their fiscal policy is to be capable of coping with asymmetric shocks. In addition the attempt to reduce their structural deficits immediately after accession contrasts sharply with the need of these countries to increase their public investments in order to catch up with the rest of the Union.[60] As a result, unless the SGP for these countries is applied in a very flexible, almost country-specific way (or unless very large and positive non-Keynesian effects are foreseen), it will be very hard for the new member states to cope with the fiscal consolidation requirements of the EMU, since their political priority is clearly oriented to the provision of the necessary financing for new public investment and income convergence with the rest of the Union. Nor would a golden rule be optimal: the golden rule introduces an unnecessary bias towards material investment, while nothing indicates that material investment in candidate countries is needed more than immaterial ones (Moesen and Nava, 2004).

In sum, abstracting from country-specific considerations, a too short transition to EMU of the new member states may lead them to abandon prematurely the monetary, fiscal and exchange rate flexibility which they currently need to promote real convergence and accommodate the structural changes taking place in their economies.[61]

In terms of the second problematic issue considered in this section, the impact of the enlargement on the current monetary policy of the ECB, a first consideration is straightforward: the overall economic relevance of this effect is likely to remain limited, being the relative weight of acceding countries' economies in the enlarged Euro area below 10 per cent of EU GDP. Also, if higher inflation persists in some of these countries after they enter the Euro area, owing to Balassa–Samuelson effects, this inflation is confined to non-tradable sectors, and therefore does not significantly influence inflation in other countries of the Euro area. Hence, from the economic point of view, the actual problem of an enlarged EMU remains the choice of a target rate of inflation able to encompass a smooth process of inter-country adjustment within the Euro area.

Some preliminary evidence shows in fact that the theoretical Phillips curve of an enlarged Euro zone displays an average worsening of the inflation–unemployment trade-off (Altomonte and Depace, 2003). As a result, given the current structural conditions prevailing in the new member states, if the ECB maintains its current monetary policy stance in an enlarged EMU, the effect will be such as to increase the average level of unemployment in some of the new member states. The ECB might then consider the possibility of revising upward its current inflation target, which we have seen to be already subject to severe criticism for being too strict, in order not to depress the prospects of growth in an enlarged EMU. However the ECB is also likely to consider that, because of capacity constraints, the same enlargement risks generating structurally higher inflation levels in the EMU, and hence it might decide not to opt for a straight loosening of the monetary policy. As a result, if structural reforms expanding the supply capacity in EU-25 are delayed, the ECB will have to choose between two alternatives: it might want to respect fully the target of 2 per cent for the inflation rate, accepting a permanently higher level of unemployment in the enlarged Euro area; or, on the contrary, it might decide to abandon the 2 per cent target to serve the needs of the new member states, a rather unrealistic option. Both scenarios thus point to the fact that the EMU is not likely to be enlarged before structural reforms and the catch-up process of the new member states have progressed further.

Somewhat more complex is the institutional dimension of an enlargement of the EMU, given that, with 22 members (the current 12 plus the ten new member states) the balance between the ECB Executive Board and the national governors within the Governing Council of the ESCB radically changes in favour of the latter. As already discussed, an excessive weight of the nation-specific component within the ECB might entail rising expectations of inflation, since the resulting strategy might be biased in favour of specific national needs, which also acquire a more heterogeneous dimension.[62] In order to start solving this problem, the ECB Governing Council has proposed a reform to its composition, which has been endorsed by the European Council.[63] Under the new arrangement, the six members of the Executive Board will retain their full voting rights. On the other hand, a rotation system with three categories of members will be introduced, under which the national central bank governors from the larger member states would sit on the Council more frequently and the number of governors with voting rights in any period would be limited to 15, thus maintaining a balanced proportion between the Executive Board members and the national governors.

NOTES

1. See Gros and Thygesen (1998, ch. 10) for a detailed analysis of the history of EMU.
2. As already stated in Chapter 1, in Maastricht an agreement was reached on a revision of the 'Treaty establishing the European Community' (TEC) originally signed in Rome, containing the institutional provisions leading to the creation of the single currency. A new 'Treaty on the European Union' (TEU), containing innovations on the political issues of justice and home affairs and common foreign and security policy, was also agreed upon.
3. The participating member states were Austria, Belgium, Finland, France, Germany, Ireland, Italy, Luxembourg, Netherlands, Portugal and Spain. The 1996 Madrid European Council chose to call the new currency the 'Euro'. Technically, it replaced with a one-to-one exchange rate the European Currency Unit (ECU) calculated within the reformed EMS, the participation in which was one of the necessary criteria the countries had to satisfy to join the single currency.

4. As is well known, the real problem is the lack of political will of the Swedish citizens to move towards the Euro.
5. In a sense, the Euro can be referred to as a currency without a state but with many members behind it.
6. The TEC states that the monetary policy is managed exclusively and independently by the European System of Central Banks (art. 105 and following), while the Council might decide on the exchange rate of the Euro (art. 111) in accordance with the ECB. See the next section for further details.
7. See in this regard the European Commission (1990) strategic paper 'One market, one money'.
8. The degree of openness of an economy is calculated as the sum of its exports and imports over its GDP. Since on average more than 60 per cent of the trade flows of each member state in the Union takes place among Euro area members, the introduction of the single currency reduces the exposure of an economy to fluctuations in exchange rates. A similar effect (albeit more limited, owing to the stronger role of the US dollar) takes place on the denomination of assets in the financial markets, as discussed in Chapter 10.
9. See the application of the Mundell–Fleming model to the single market, discussed in Chapter 3.
10. On 3 October 1990, Chancellor Kohl announced the German reunification, with a 1 to 1 exchange rate between the Deutschmark and the Eastern mark, together with significant financial transfers from the federal government to the new Eastern Länder in order to finance their economic restructuring. The combination of an enlarged monetary base, not matched by similar levels of productivity across East and West Germany, and the expansionary fiscal policies of the government, was creating inflationary pressures in Germany. Following its statutory obligation of maintaining price stability, the Bundesbank reacted with a sudden restriction in the monetary policy, which significantly revalued the DM and put a lot of strain on the EMS.
11. A more detailed analysis of the EMS crisis can be found in Gros and Thygesen (1998).
12. In a famous statement, Tommaso Padoa-Schioppa, an Italian economist, mentioned the 'inconsistent quartet' that was characterising the EU macroeconomic picture at the time: free circulation of goods; free circulation of capitals; quasi-fixed exchange rates; independent monetary policies.
13. This is particularly true for countries such as the European ones, deeply integrated in the world trade and capital flows.
14. See Chapter 1 for a description of the EU social model, and Chapter 5 for an analysis of the EU pattern of economic growth.
15. Buti and Sapir (1998) first referred to it as the 'Brussels–Frankfurt' consensus. The role of the Euro in affecting the third EU objective, cohesion, will be discussed in Chapter 8.
16. The European Union was born without a juridical personality. The draft EU Constitution (art. 6) gives juridical personality to the Union; however, art. 5, para. 1 states that the Union '*shall respect the national identities of the Member States [. . .] and their essential State functions, including those for ensuring the territorial integrity of the State, and for maintaining law and order and safeguarding internal security*'; art. 9, para. 2 restates the principle of conferral, declaring that '*the Union shall act within the limits of the competences conferred upon it by the Member States [. . .] Competences not conferred upon the Union in the Constitution remain with the Member States*'.
17. Buti and Nava (2003) report that, given its small size (1.05 per cent of EU GDP in 2003 and 2 per cent of total EU public spending), the EU budget has practically no macroeconomic relevance. National budgets, measured as the average of public spending, amounted in 2002 to 48 per cent of GDP in the Euro area and 47 per cent of GDP in the EU as a whole. The US federal budget is around 30 per cent of US GDP and contributes about 75 per cent of total US public spending. See Chapter 6 for further details.

18. This is likely due to the fact that fiscal federalism is often the only available framework through which it is politically feasible to unify regions very different in terms of cultural and historical backgrounds.
19. A currency board between a local currency *A* and a foreign currency *B* (in general the Euro or the US dollar) is characterised by the commitment of the local monetary authority to back up every new issue of currency *A* with the same amount of currency *B* held as a reserve, so as always to guarantee the convertibility of the local currency.
20. The EMU is based on Nobel prize-winning pieces of macroeconomics. Owing to the concrete relevance in the process of creation of the European EMU, the OCA theory won its author, Robert Mundell, the Nobel prize in Economics in 1999. The two authors originally behind the time-inconsistency problem of economic policy, Finn Kydland and Edward Prescott, won the Nobel prize in Economics in 2004.
21. As pointed out by Sapir *et al.* (2004), if inflation is perfectly anticipated, it becomes essentially a tax on holding liquid money for consumers. In this case people will minimise the amount of cash they use daily and will only experience the 'shoe leather' cost of frequent money withdrawal, along with the cost of frequently changing the price lists ('menu' costs).
22. See Mishkin and Posen (1997) for a survey on the costs of inflation. In terms of empirical evidence, Barro (1996) finds a significant negative correlation between inflation and growth on the basis of a panel of around 100 countries in the period 1960–90. More controversial is the issue on the 'optimal' level of inflation, since the relationship between inflation and growth is more ambiguous for low (single-digit) inflation rates: economists disagree on whether, at low levels, inflation puts 'sand' or 'grease' in the wheels of the price formation mechanism. See Feldstein (1999), Andrés *et al.* (2000) or Akerlof *et al.* (2000) for contrasting views on the subject.
23. We refer here to the seminal papers by Kydland and Prescott (1977) and Barro and Gordon (1983) which were among the first to analyse a possible problem of time-inconsistency in the conduct of monetary policies.
24. When a government is able to print money (for example because it influences the central bank), it is in essence borrowing interest-free, since it receives goods today in exchange for the money, and must accept the money in return (when the consumers use the money for their transactions) only at some future time. In addition, the government gains further if, by issuing new money, it creates inflation, since the latter reduces the real value of its debts.
25. See Beetsma (2001) and Canzoneri and Diba (1996), as reported in Sapir *et al.* (2004).
26. See Alesina and Perotti (1995) and Persson and Tabellini (2004) for a more detailed discussion.
27. For an operational reference on the conduct of monetary policy by the ECB, see the document, 'The implementation of monetary policy in the euro area: general documentation on Eurosystem monetary policy instruments and procedures', a legal text in force since 8 March 2004 (available at http://www.ecb.int/pub/pdf/gendoc2004en.pdf).
28. This argument is known in the economic literature as the 'one monetary policy fits all?' problem.
29. The reference values on deficit and debt are contained in Protocol no. 5 of the Maastricht Treaty. The rationale of these figures is discussed later on in this chapter.
30. As already discussed in Chapter 3, we recall that the real exchange rate of a country is defined as its nominal exchange rate times the ratio between foreign and domestic prices.
31. The two pillars have to be considered as a reference scheme, since the ECB follows them with some flexibility, as will be made clear in the remainder of this section. See Gali (2002) for a detailed survey of the monetary strategy of the ECB.
32. The ECB is very clear in clarifying that its strategy is a medium-term one, stating that 'it would be impossible for any central bank to keep inflation at a specific point target at all times or even to bring it back to a desired level in a very short time. Monetary policy is ill-equipped to fine-tune economic developments or control prices at short horizons.

Instead, monetary policy needs to act in a forward-looking manner and can only maintain price stability over longer periods of time' (ECB, *Monthly Bulletin*, June 2003, p. 82).
33. Recalling standard macroeconomic analysis, the inflation process can be broadly decomposed into two components, one associated with the interplay between demand and supply factors in the short to medium run, and the other connected to longer-run trends. The latter component is closely associated with the medium-term trend growth of the monetary base.
34. The monetary aggregate M3 comprises currency in circulation plus certain liabilities of the financial institutions (and, in the case of deposits, of some institutions such as post offices and Treasuries) resident in the Euro area. These liabilities include overnight deposits; deposits with an agreed maturity of up to two years; deposits redeemable at notice up to three months; debt securities with maturity of up to two years; unit/shares of money market funds and money market paper (net).
35. The Taylor rule as proposed (Taylor, 1998) states that the interest rate (the federal fund rate, in the original version) should be increased or decreased according to what is happening to both real GDP and inflation. In particular, if real GDP rises 1 per cent above potential GDP, the interest rate should be raised, relative to the current inflation rate, by a given percentage. And if inflation rises by 1 per cent above its target, then the interest rate should be raised by a given coefficient relative to the inflation rate. When real GDP is equal to potential GDP and inflation is equal to its target, the interest rate should remain constant. By changing the percentages (coefficients) according to which interest rates react to GDP or inflation gaps, one can thus track the behaviour (or 'preference') of different central banks in the world.
36. See Sapir *et al.* (2004, p. 47) for an analysis of monetary policy in Europe before 1999.
37. Clearly, such a fit has to be considered over the time horizon of the ECB, which takes into account only the medium run (Alesina *et al.*, 2001b).
38. The particular feature of inflation known as the Balassa–Samuelson effect argues that, under certain conditions, sustained inflation differentials between two regions can be caused by differences in the relative rate of productivity growth of tradable and non-tradable goods sectors in each region. Since the effect is a phenomenon naturally associated with the convergence of growth rates, in principle it would not require a corrective action by economic policies.
39. Depending on the sources and causes of these differentials, regional remedies of a more 'structural' nature may be needed if too dispersed inflation levels turn out to be harmful for the regions concerned.
40. A countercriticism to this argument, however, is that such an effect is not persistent: if a single country or region in the Euro area would fall into a situation of decline in prices, this would lead to significant gains in its competitiveness. The ensuing positive effects on demand for its products would then counteract contemporaneous downward price pressures, thereby dispelling any expectations that such a situation could be sustained over time (Sapir *et al.*, 2004).
41. The standard deviation of the FED interest rate is 2.05, against 0.86 measured for the ECB.
42. Exceptions are foreseen also for recessions comprising between 0.75 and 2 per cent of GDP, although in this case no automatic exemption is granted: the Council has to expressly authorise the temporary excessive deficit.
43. These programmes are known as 'convergence programmes' for the member states not participating in the EMU, the idea being that these countries should also comply as much as possible with the fiscal provisions of the economic and monetary union.
44. See Buti and Sapir (1998) for a precise assessment of these figures. As we have seen, in the case of a downturn comprising between 0.75 and 2 per cent of GDP, the provisions of art. 104 might not be applied, although no automatic exemption is foreseen.
45. Moesen and Nava (2004) point out that these figures imply a sort of golden rule of public finance: the authorised maximum deficit was of the same order (3 per cent) of public gross capital expenditures (historical data revealed that on average public

investment accounted for some 3 per cent of GDP across Europe), thus implying that gross capital investment can also be financed by future generations of taxpayers via public debt.

46. See European Commission (2003a, Pt II) for a detailed analysis of these events.
47. In order to pave the way to a serene debate on the reform of the SGP, the Commission ultimately proposed to suspend the excessive deficit procedure against France and Germany at the end of 2004, following the commitments of the two member states concerned to correct their public deficits by the end of 2005.
48. In order to correct this drawback, the Commission had proposed a change in this rule, allowing the Council to overrule the Commission in the application of art. 104 only by unanimity; however the proposal has not been retained in the final draft of the European Constitution.
49. In what follows we mainly refer to the survey work of Buti *et al.* (2003).
50. In other words, under a strict SGP rule and given the amount of current revenues, the interest burden competes with current expenditures and with the net investment, as pointed out by Moesen and Nava (2004).
51. For a detailed discussion of the proposals of modification of the SGP and their implementation see, among others, Buti *et al.* (2003), Sapir *et al.* (2004), Crockett *et al.* (2003), Moesen and Nava (2004).
52. The proposals are contained in the Ecofin Council's report to the European Council 'Improving the implementation of the Stability and Growth Pact', adopted at the extraordinary ECOFIN meeting on 20 March 2005. The agreed recommendations form the basis of a formal juridical proposal to be prepared by the European Commission.
53. We recall that this does not imply that the nominal budget balance must improve every year by an equivalent amount, since, being the threshold defined in structural terms, there may be some scope to allow the automatic stabilisers to operate, with a deterioration in the nominal budget balance during downturns.
54. The Council clarifies that 'only major reforms which have direct long-term cost-saving effects, including raising potential growth, and therefore a verifiable positive impact on the long-term sustainability of public finances, will be taken into account'. In particular, the Council has acknowledged that special attention must be paid to pension reforms, since these reforms entail a short-term deterioration of public finances during the implementation period, but improve the long term sustainability of public finances.
55. An often quoted example is that, according to the golden rule, a government would tend to increase the number of school buildings and classrooms (capital expenditures), but not necessarily hire in the same proportion a number of teachers that will teach in these classrooms (current expenditures). See Moesen and Nava (2004) for a comparison between a 'rigid', a 'flexible' and a golden rule-style implementation of the Stability and Growth Pact.
56. In a given year, the expenditure on item *X* by a member state might or might not be undertaken, according (also) to the Commission's decision on whether the latter can be excluded or not from the computation of the budget deficit.
57. The Council has also specified that 'the initial deadline will be set without prejudice to the taking into account of systemic pension reforms and without prejudice to deadlines applying to new and future member states'.
58. Recall the last monetary criterion elaborated in Maastricht, according to which a country joining the EMU has to undertake a minimum period of two years, during which its exchange rate with respect to the Euro must be kept within the band of fluctuations of the ERM.
59. Currently the Balassa–Samuelson effect previously mentioned is particularly evident in these countries, since they have recently started their catch-up process with the rest of the Union. However, according to the empirical estimates, the size of the Balassa–Samuelson effect is likely to diminish gradually over time, given the present convergence in per capita GDP among countries.

60. Although the Union will largely finance through the Structural Funds the regional development of the new member states, in any case a significant amount of national resources has to be used to cofinance the Union's interventions. See Chapter 8 for further details.
61. The EU institutions have however implicitly recognised this necessity since, in the drafting of their stability programmes, the new member states have been allowed to set for themselves the date when they commit themselves to reaching a balanced budget position.
62. See Baldwin *et al.* (2001, Ch. 6), for an extensive and insightful discussion.
63. Regulation 2003/223/CE in *Official Journal of the European Union*, L 83/66–68, 1 April 2003.

5. Managing the EU economic policy: the Lisbon Agenda

5.1 INTRODUCTION

In the previous chapters we have seen how the EU has tried to achieve growth through the process of economic integration. We have in fact analysed the (static) growth implications of the Customs Union (Chapter 2), the gains, both static and dynamic, achievable through the single market (Chapter 3) and the contribution to growth (and stability) of the EMU (Chapter 4). We have also considered that what really matters for the EU economy is to achieve a permanent boost to growth from the process of economic integration. In this respect, the tools previously summarised represent a valid contribution, but ultimately a permanent increase in the growth rate of a given economy depends on structural changes in the long-run supply conditions that determine its potential output.

To this purpose, the so-called **Lisbon Agenda** of reforms, implemented in the Union from the year 2000, aims precisely at improving in this sense the EU economic performance. The aim of the Lisbon Agenda, or process, is in fact easily summarised in a sentence: to implement structural reforms so that Europe enjoys higher levels of sustainable growth in a stable macroeconomic framework and in a climate of social cohesion. Clearly, while the risk of pompous rhetoric is always behind declarations of principles of this kind, the difficult part of the Lisbon Agenda resides in its practical implementation, that is, how to meet this goal.

In order to better understand the Lisbon process and then evaluate its outcomes, this chapter first gives a description of what we mean by 'growth' for Europe[1] (section 5.2) and then it looks at the Lisbon targets (section 5.3) and tools (section 5.4). The recent progress across EU member states towards the Lisbon targets are assessed in section 5.5, while section 5.6 concludes with some perspectives on the implementation of the Lisbon Agenda in the enlarged Europe.

5.2 THE GROWTH RECORD OF THE EU ECONOMY

As already discussed in Chapter 1, Europe displayed an outstanding record of economic growth from World War II to 1973 (the first oil shock). At the end of WWII, per capita income of the EU stood at only 45 per cent of the US figure, while, by 1973, after 30 years of sustained growth, it reached 70 per cent of the US figure. The post-war production structure of the EU relied on large industries exploiting economies of scale and on the assimilation of technologies coupled with process innovation. Standardised production and the growth in volumes of production, all achievable via the process of economic integration analysed so far, were sufficient to put Europe on a converging income path with the USA (already one of the fastest growing economies in the world) at the amazing pace of one percentage point per year (see Figure 5.1).

The first oil shock of 1973 brought this virtuous circle to a sudden halt. The price of this crucial input increased fourfold in a few years, thus provoking the largest supply shock since WWII. While the USA quickly recovered from the shock, growth rates in Europe never recovered to the pre-1973 levels (Figure 5.2) and thus virtually no income convergence with the USA has been achieved since then (Figure 5.1).[2] The enlargement of the EU to the new member states, given the limited weight of these economies, does not seem to have changed the picture, at least so far (compare the EU-15 with the EU-25 in Figures 5.1 and 5.2).

In particular in the 1990s, the overall growth performance of Europe has been particularly disappointing. The overall growth has been equal to 2.1 per cent (to be compared with 3.6 percent in the USA), mainly owing to

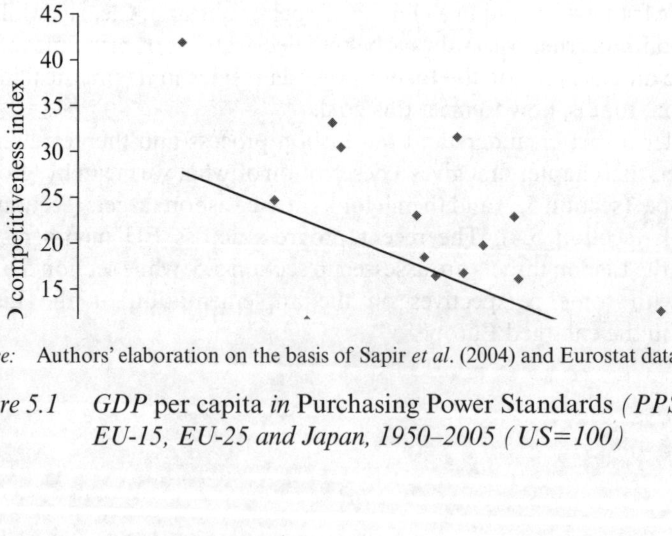

Source: Authors' elaboration on the basis of Sapir *et al.* (2004) and Eurostat data.

Figure 5.1 *GDP* per capita *in* Purchasing Power Standards *(PPS) for EU-15, EU-25 and Japan, 1950–2005 (US=100)*

sustained growth in the cohesion countries (Spain, Ireland, Portugal and Greece) and in Finland, the Netherlands and the United Kingdom, counterbalanced by slow growth in Germany and Italy (see Figure 5.3). Certainly the fact that cohesion countries grew faster is very positive for the overall cohesion of the EU (see *infra*), but their impact on the overall EU growth is necessarily limited, given their small size.

5.2.1 Decomposing Growth: Employment, Productivity and Organisational Forms

To better understand the reasons behind the slow European growth after the 1970s, we resort to a standard growth decomposition. Let us first, in equation 5.1, write the national income or output (Y) as the quantity of labour employed (L) times the average labour productivity (Y/L), measured as the output produced by one unit of labour. We can thus write the following identity:

$$Y = L^*(Y/L). \tag{5.1}$$

Growth is the first-order derivative (with respect to time) of the national income Y, and can therefore be written as the sum of two components: the

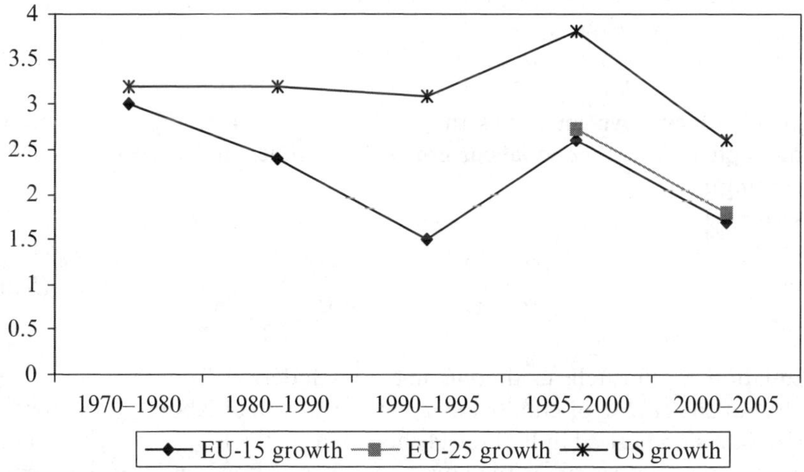

Note: Values for 2005 are forecasts.

Source: Authors' elaboration on the basis of Sapir *et al.* (2004) and Eurostat data.

Figure 5.2 EU versus USA average real growth, 1970–2005, constant prices, 1995

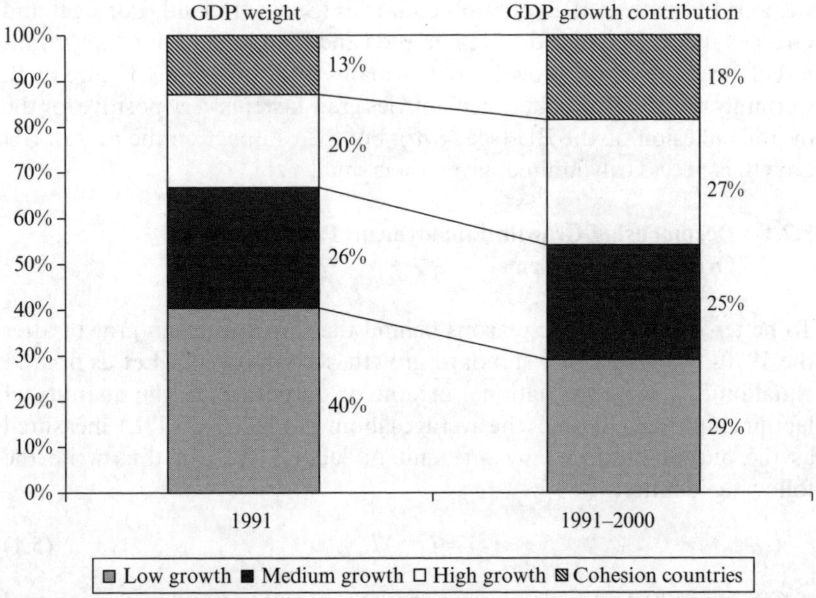

Source: Sapir *et al.* (2004).

Figure 5.3 The EU growth performance in the 1990s, by groups of countries

growth of **employment** (times the productivity of the additional labour force) plus the change in **labour productivity** (times the number of people working):[3]

$$\frac{dY}{dt} = \frac{dL}{dt} * Y/L + \frac{d(Y/L)}{dt} * L \qquad (5.2)$$

Equation 5.2 thus tells us that income growth derives from the composite effect of the growth of employment and the growth of labour productivity. The data summarised in Figure 5.4 show that, in the EU, (a) the growth of employment (measured as the annual number of hours worked) has been traditionally lower than in the USA (albeit there is a significant difference between the second and the first half of the 1990s: see below); (b) the growth of labour productivity (measured as GDP per hour worked) used to be traditionally higher than in the USA, but it became lower in the second half of the 1990s.

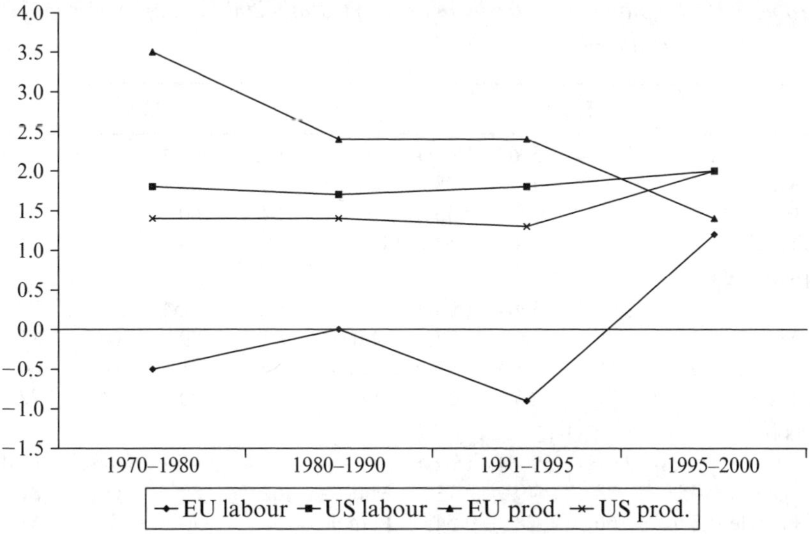

Note: Employment is measured as the annual number of hours worked and labour productivity as GDP per hour worked. Data for 1970–90 include former West Germany; data for 1991–2000 include Germany.

Source: Our elaboration on the basis of Sapir *et al.* (2004).

Figure 5.4 Employment and labour productivity growth in EU and USA, 1970–2000

The reasons behind the very low contribution of employment to growth in Europe might be related to the particular evolution of the EU labour markets. Traditionally the European labour market institutions have been characterised by a certain degree of rigidity, with tough laws and rules disciplining the hiring and firing of people, a phenomenon known in the economic literature as **Eurosclerosis**.[4] As a result, the employment rate[5] in Europe fell over time, passing from 103.6 per cent of the US figure in the 1970s to 87.6 per cent in 2000. These dynamics, together with a reduction of the working hours per person employed, which fell from 101 per cent of the US average in the 1970s to 85.6 per cent in 2000, entailed a decrease in the total number of hours worked in Europe (fewer people working for fewer hours), at least up to 1990, thus serving to generate high levels of labour productivity in Europe (the same output was produced with relatively fewer hours worked).

After the mid-1990s, some reforms of the labour markets were introduced in various member states, generating a relative increase in the employment levels, with the total employment rate in the EU rising from

Table 5.1 Employment rates by age cohort, 1980–2000 (% of working age population)

1980	EU-8					USA			
	15–24	25–54	55–64	15–64		15–24	25–54	55–64	15–64
Male	51	92	64	78	Male	64	89	70	80
Female	40	48	28	43	Female	54	60	40	55
Total	45	70	44	60	Total	59	74	54	67
1990									
	15–24	25–54	55–64	15–64		15–24	25–54	55–64	15–64
Male	45	88	49	73	Male	63	89	65	81
Female	37	55	23	46	Female	56	71	44	64
Total	41	71	36	59	Total	60	80	54	72
2000	EU-15								
	15–24	25–54	55–64	15–64		15–24	25–54	55–64	15–64
Male	45	88	49	73	Male	62	89	66	81
Female	37	66	28	54	Female	58	74	50	68
Total	41	77	39	64	Total	60	81	58	74

Source: Sapir *et al.* (2004).

59 per cent in 1990 to 64 per cent in 2000, as shown in Figure 5.4 and then reported in Table 5.1. In particular, Table 5.1 shows that, while the EU has always been on a par with the USA for the employment rates of prime-age males, it still suffers a large (though partially decreasing) gap vis-à-vis the USA for the other age groups, owing to the labour market institutions characterising the EU, whose rigidities tend to hamper the employment of less advantaged categories of workers (in particular, young people and females). Particularly worrying, considering that this age cohort is bound to increase in the next few years, is the gap still existing between the USA and the EU for the 55–64 age group, both male and female, essentially the result of generous pension systems paid in member states.[6]

However, as revealed by Figure 5.4, the slight increase in the employment level (and hence in the total number of hours worked) of the mid-1990s translated in Europe into a simultaneous decrease in labour productivity, which for the first time since the 1970s fell in terms of growth rate below that of the USA. In absolute terms, labour productivity is now around 90 per cent of the US figure, up from 65 per cent in the 1970s, as revealed by Figure 5.5, which also shows that the enlargement of the Union, if anything, is likely to worsen the performance of labour productivity in EU-25. As a result, the gap in per capita income compared with the USA is not likely to narrow unless major reforms are undertaken.

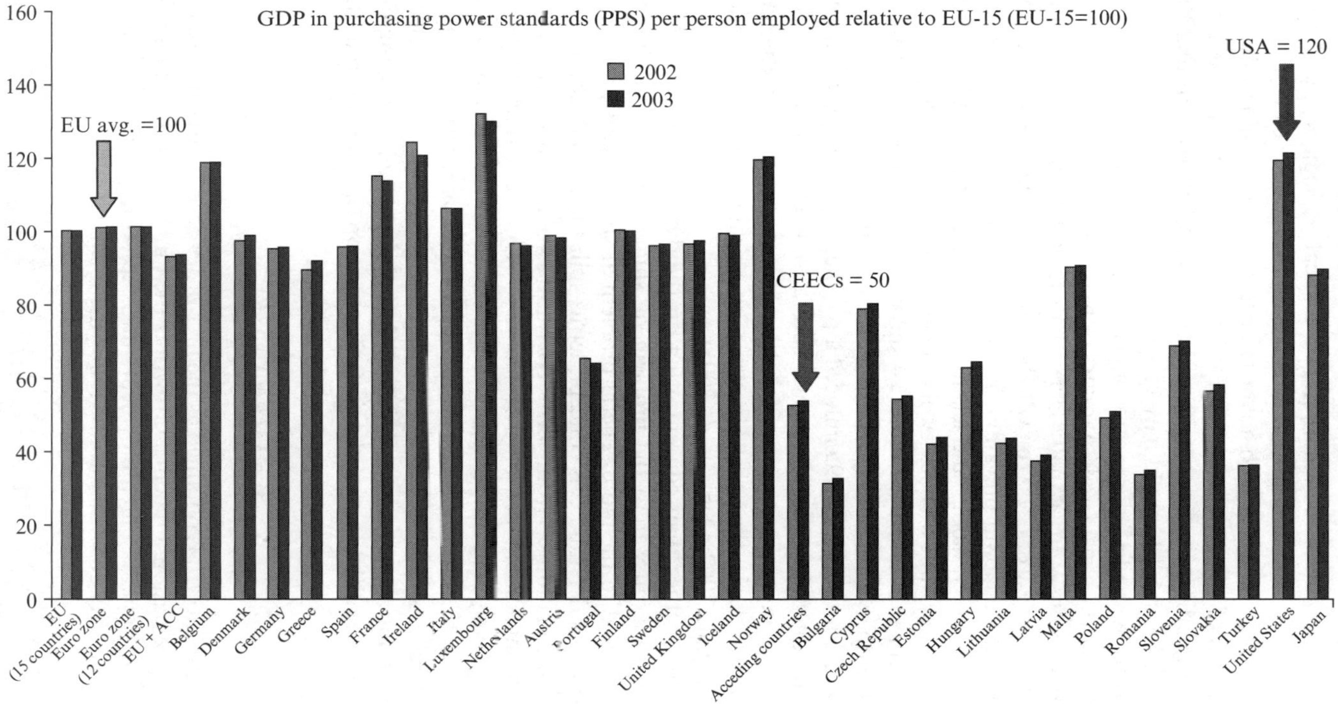

Source: Eurostat.

Figure 5.5 Labour productivity per person employed in EU-25, 2001/2002

All these data, initially summarised in the so-called **Sapir report** (2004)[7] raised a great deal of attention and discussion in the EU academic, economic and political circles, with a debate arising on the possible solutions to the problem of sluggish growth in Europe. One of the most heated discussions, originally stimulated by Blanchard (2004), revolved around the issue on whether the EU could have caught up with the USA had relative hours worked by the EU workers remained the same, rather than decreasing, in the period considered. A quite surreal debate then followed on whether Europeans were actually lazier than their US counterparts, and hence preferred to work less, or whether such a choice was induced by higher tax rates on labour prevailing in Europe, generating a higher substitution effect between labour and leisure. As a matter of fact, it is unclear how much the amount of hours worked can eventually grow at constant rates of labour productivity. Figure 5.4 shows in fact that even the slight increase in employment rates (and hence of the total hours worked) which took place in Europe after 1995 induced a parallel drop in the growth rate of labour productivity. The existence of such a trade-off indicates that the European economies are operating inside or at best along the production possibility frontier rather than growing by pushing out the frontier (Acemoglu *et al.*, 2002; Denis *et al.*, 2005).

As a result, rather than concentrating on the dynamics of the labour market only, the answer to the problem of sluggish growth in Europe should be related to the more general problem of 'total factor productivity'. To better understand this concept, let us split the overall labour productivity of equation 5.1 (our term Y/L) into two elements: (a) human and capital investment per unit of labour (K/L), often referred to as '**capital deepening**'; (b) output produced per unit of human and capital investment (Y/K), often referred to as '**total factor productivity**' **(TFP)**. The latter reflects factors such as know-how, regulatory environment, provision of infrastructures and so on. Introducing such a decomposition of the overall labour productivity in equation 5.1, we generate the equation 5.3:

$$Y = L^*(K/L)^*(Y/K). \tag{5.3}$$

Once again, growth is obtained as the first-order derivative (with respect to time) of the national income. Growth is then influenced by changes in the three components of employment rate, capital deepening and total factor productivity according to the following formula:

$$\frac{dY}{dt} = \frac{dL}{dt} * Y/L + \frac{d(K/L)}{dt} * L * \frac{Y}{K} + \frac{d(Y/K)}{dt} * K. \tag{5.4}$$

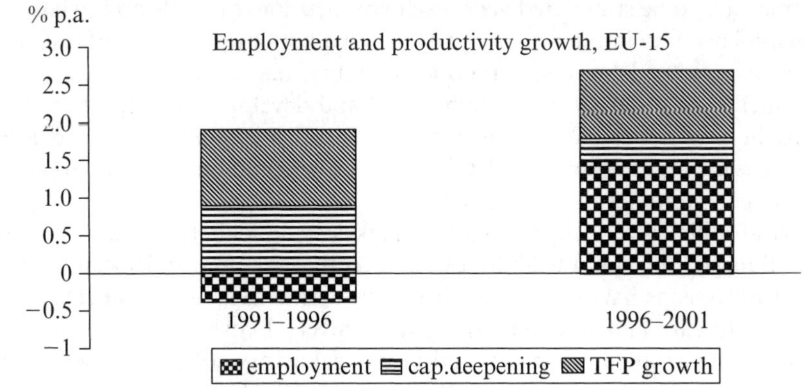

Source: European Commission (2003b).

Figure 5.6 Determinants of GDP growth

Looking at the empirical evidence behind equation 5.4 then allows us to have better insights into the problem of sluggish growth in Europe. In this regard, the European Commission (2003b) gives an interesting graphical decomposition (see Figure 5.6) of the determinants of GDP growth in the EU in the period 1991–2001. Consistently with Figure 5.4, it is not surprising to see that, in the first part of the 1990s, EU growth has been generated at the expense of jobs (there has been an overall decrease in employment levels). In the second part of the 1990s, employment growth again became positive and very supportive of overall growth, but the contribution of capital deepening and of TFP to growth was much reduced.

In this respect, the previous analysis clearly indicates that the most important determinant of the lower European TFP is probably a too low degree of innovation in Europe. Essentially, over recent decades, both production and consumption have shifted away from codified and standardised products towards more personalised and customer-tailored products. As a result, the catching up process of the EU vis-à-vis the USA can not longer rely only on volumes, accumulation and imitation but has to rely more and more on innovation on a larger scale. Failing an appropriate response on these grounds by the EU, which, by and large, is currently imitating rather than improving US-based technologies, the EU income gap with respect to the USA will tend to persist. To keep pace with the USA in Europe, in other words, the service and innovation component of each product has to become larger and larger over the years.[8]

However, as we have seen, innovation and growth cannot be induced only by a greater labour market flexibility. Rather, new organisational forms for firms have to be stimulated via greater competition, more flexibility has to be implemented in the products market via a better market integration, as well as greater labour and product mobility, and more venture capital financing, in order to stimulate research and development. The slow and non-homogeneous pace at which these reforms are being implemented in Europe is thus imposing a high toll on EU growth and on its ability to catch up in per capita terms with the USA.

And still low or sluggish growth makes it difficult to sustain, in the medium to long run, the ambitious and costly economic and social model that Europeans have chosen for themselves. An almost universal coverage of health care and pensions, an almost universal coverage against social risks (such as unemployment) and in general a very cohesive society (see *infra*) can in fact be sustained in the long run only if growth is up or close to potential.

The motivation of the Lisbon strategy therefore lies in the need to transform in such a coordinated way the European economy in response to these major challenges.[9]

5.3 A DESCRIPTION OF THE EU ECONOMIC AND SOCIAL MODEL

Before discussing to what extent the Lisbon strategy is succeeding in its goal of reviving growth in Europe, it is also important to understand into what kind of economic and social model the same strategy aims at transforming the EU economy. Actually, in order to describe an economic and social model, one could describe either its goals or its results, or both. We have chosen both, although we maintain a clear emphasis on results.[10]

As far as goals are concerned, growth is an essential element of the EU economic and social model, but is certainly not the only one. Growth, in the EU system, is both an objective and a tool to be able to sustain the ambitious and very costly EU social model. As already discussed in Chapter 1, the EU does not believe in a model of economic development aiming uniquely at achieving the highest possible economic growth, without consideration of its distribution and of its environmental impact. As a result, the EU objective declared in both the TEC and the TEU (and retained in art. 3 of the projected European Constitution) is one of sustainable and balanced growth, not simply growth. In other words, both the EU and the US economic and social agenda put a clear emphasis on growth.[11] However, with respect to the EU, the US policy agenda does not explicitly attach the same importance to considerations of income distribution.

As a result, in the following subsections, we look at income and income distribution within the EU as a proxy to describe some of the results reached by the EU economic and social model.

5.3.1 The Income Distribution in the European Union

Studies of income distribution within the EU as well as international comparisons give a fair idea of the extent to which the EU society is and has developed as a **cohesive society**. A distinct feature of a cohesive society is the ability to deliver greater growth together with lower total inequality in income distribution. Many different indicators may measure total inequality. We have chosen to discuss the three best-known ones: the ratio of the income held by the top 5 per cent (the richest 5 per cent) over the income of the bottom 20 per cent (the poorest 20 per cent),[12] the Gini coefficient[13] and the Theil index.[14] The three indicators (see Table 5.2) confirm that income inequality in Europe reached its minimum in 1980, subsequently rising again. A useful property of total inequality as measured by the Theil index is that it can be usefully decomposed into **within-country inequality** and **across-countries inequality**, as already defined in Chapter 1.

The decomposition is particularly important in policy terms, since within-country inequality concerns interpersonal redistributive policies undertaken at the level of the individual member states, while across-countries inequality is the concern of policies undertaken at the EU level. The citizens' attitude towards the 'optimal' income redistribution that exists, for example, in Sweden is in fact very different from the one that exists, say, in Italy or Hungary, which, in turn, is very different from the one that exists in the UK. By and large, Swedes expect from their welfare system a much greater correction of the market-generated income inequality than Italians do; Italians, in turn, expect more than Britons do, and so on. Thus any attempt to have some sort of EU average income distribution within the population is certainly bound to fail, owing to the extremely high heterogeneity of preferences in this matter across EU countries. For these reasons,

Table 5.2 Indicators of total inequality in EU-15, 1970–2000

Tot. inequality indicator	1970	1980	1990	1995	1998	2000
Top 5% / bottom 20%	2.01	1.73	1.77	1.73	1.86	1.86
Gini coefficient	0.32	0.299	0.301	0.303	0.309	0.308
Theil index	0.169	0.146	0.154	0.150	0.160	0.159

Source: Morrisson and Murtin (2004).

Table 5.3 Theil index 'within' and 'across' countries in EU-15, 1970–2000

Index/years	1970	1980	1990	1995	1998	2000
Within-country	0.152	0.130	0.145	0.142	0.152	0.152
Across-countries	0.017	0.016	0.009	0.008	0.008	0.007
Total inequality	0.169	0.146	0.154	0.150	0.160	0.159

Source: Morrisson and Murtin (2004).

income inequality within countries is a national matter and no EU role in this area is laid down or foreseen for the future. On the contrary, the inequalities existing across countries in the EU are affected by policies implemented at the EU level (mainly the single market) and thus require also a European, not only national, level of management (these are known as cohesion or regional policies, and will be analysed in Chapter 8).

The aggregate figures of Table 5.3 tell us that within-country inequality first fell from 1970 to 1980, and subsequently rose back to the 1970s levels by the late 1990s. Across-countries inequality remained stable in the 1970s and decreased dramatically after the 1980s. Table 5.3 also tells us that until 1995 the bulk of total inequality in the EU was within countries, not across countries.

The ability to reduce within-country inequality seems to be in direct proportion to growth: inequality decreased rapidly in the EU in periods of high growth (from 1960 to 1980) and increased again in periods of moderate growth (1980–2000). However behind this general finding there are very large differences across countries, due to the eminently national character of the systems of welfare state and interpersonal redistributive policies. The reduction of inequality across countries in the EU seems to be related to changes in each country's characteristics, and hence points to a certain success of some EU policies (the single market, but also structural expenditures, as will discussed in Chapter 8) implemented more decisively since the 1980s.

Consistently with the high growth experienced up to the 1980s, EU member states have also been particularly successful in fighting poverty. The general finding of Table 5.4 is one of a massive reduction in absolute poverty, measured as a daily income of $10 or $20 (in constant prices and purchasing power parity, PPP). In particular, the second index, which corresponds to a monthly income of about $600, that is more than the minimum wage in most member states, has fallen dramatically from about 35 per cent of the EU population in 1970 to less than 10 per cent in 1998.

Table 5.4 Percentage of EU population below poverty thresholds

% of population / years	1970	1980	1990	1995	1998
Absolute poverty ($10 a day)	10.4	2.2	1.0	1.1	1.1
Poverty ($20 a day)	34.9	20.1	13.8	12.4	9.2

Source: Morrisson and Murtin (2004).

Table 5.5 World income inequality

	USA			World		
Inequality indexes / year	1980	1986	1995	1970	1980	1992
Top 5% / bottom 20%	2.59	2.42	2.43	15.55	17.50	16.36
Gini coefficient	0.363	0.337	0.342	0.650	0.657	0.657
Theil index	0.225	0.185	0.190	0.808	0.829	0.855
Within-country inequality	n.a.	n.a	n.a	0.315	0.330	0.342
Across-countries inequality	n.a	n.a	n.a	0.493	0.499	0.513
Poverty indicators (% of population below)						
Absolute poverty[a]	4.9	4.4	3.2	35.2	31.5	23.7
Poverty[b]	14.4	12.9	9.3	60.1	55.00	51.3

Notes:
[a] $1 a day for the world and $10 a day for the USA;
[b] $2 a day for the world and $20 a day for the USA.

Source: Morrisson and Murtin (2004).

5.3.2 EU vs. the Rest of the World

The comparison of the EU results on both inequality and poverty with the same results for the rest of the world is particularly striking. Table 5.5 shows that the world inequality is incomparably higher than the inequality in the EU. It also shows that total EU inequality is, at any point in time, some 10 per cent lower than in the USA and some 50 per cent lower than in the world. Furthermore both within-country and across-countries inequality in the world has been rising in the period considered, in stark contrast to the observed data for the EU.[15] As far as poverty is concerned, the EU record is better than the US record for the absolute poverty (less than $10 a day) and comparable to that of the USA for the poverty measure (less than $20 a day). The EU therefore remains a high-income area, with the poorest Europeans being among the 20 per cent richest on a world scale,

Table 5.6 Distribution of the pre- and post-tax income in EU and USA, 1985 and 1995

Top 5% / bottom 20%	1985		1995	
	Pre-tax	Post-tax	Pre-tax	Post-tax
EU	3.49	1.51	4.14	1.66
USA	5.12	2.42	4.97	2.43
Gini coefficient	**1985**		**1995**	
	Pre-tax	Post-tax	Pre-tax	Post-tax
EU	0.381	0.279	0.408	0.294
USA	0.415	0.337	0.421	0.342

Note: EU data refer to Belgium, Denmark, Germany, France, Ireland, Italy, the Netherlands, Finland, Sweden and the United Kingdom. Unfortunately, there are no data available for the EU as a whole.

Source: Morrisson and Murtin (2004).

with a remarkably low level of income inequality (both within and across countries) and poverty in a global context of much higher inequality.

Looking at the relations between these results and the chosen EU economic and social model, it can be stated that the relative low inequality and poverty in Europe are due in part to a less unequal 'market' distribution and in part to effective policies undertaken in order to reduce them. These findings are shown in Table 5.6, which compares inequality in market income (pre-tax income) and in disposable income (post-tax income) in the EU and in the USA.[16] Results for 1985 and 1995 show that inequality in market income is higher in the USA than in the EU, and also that the redistributive effect of the tax and welfare system is lower in the USA than in the EU. In the EU, the tax and welfare system in fact reduces inequality by about 25 per cent to 30 per cent, and in the USA by at most 20 per cent. In other words, the EU system basically doubles the income share of the bottom 20 per cent of the population, while the US system increases it by about 70 per cent.

5.3.3 Income Distribution within EU Member States

The aggregate EU-wide results just presented conceal, however, many differences across the member states, since the EU countries display a very high heterogeneity of preferences for redistribution. Some countries have very high values of social spending, while others have very low ones, although most countries have tended to support greater social spending

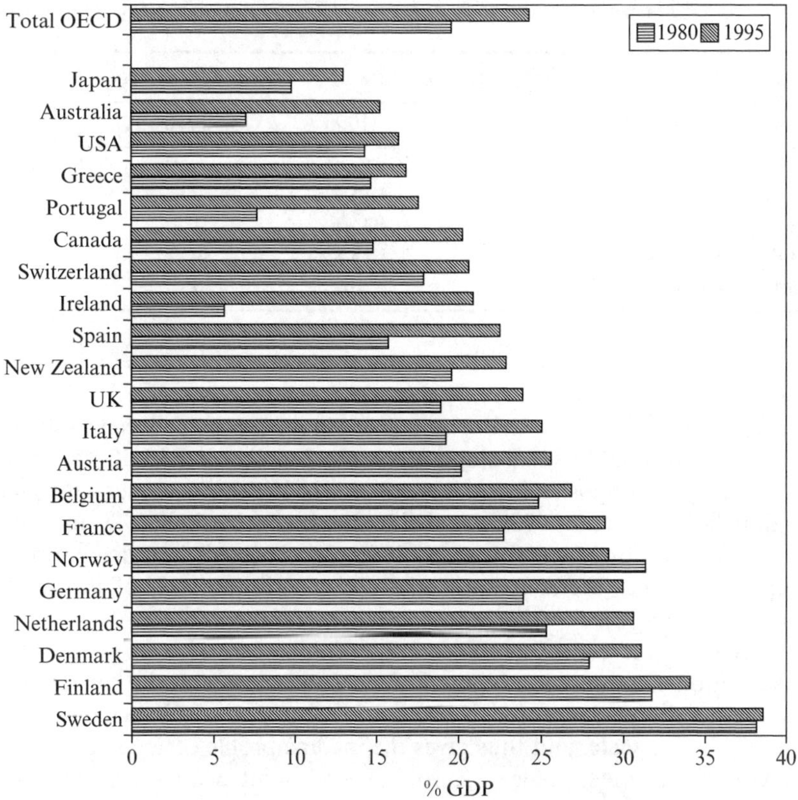

Source: De Grauwe and Polan (2003).

Figure 5.7 Social spending in OECD countries

over the last 20 years (see Figure 5.7). Given this extreme heterogeneity of preferences, no single policy of interpersonal income distribution across Europe would be justified or even feasible. Hence, as already stated in Chapter 1, the management of within-country inequalities is essentially left in the hands of the member states.

Counting therefore only on their own policies, most countries witnessed, in the period 1970–90, a reduction in their own inequality and an increase afterwards, thus generating the EU-wide trend previously analysed. As reported by Morrisson and Murtin (2004), Germany, Italy and the UK are the three main exceptions. Inequality in Germany has been roughly constant except for a steep increase at the moment of reunification and a mild reduction afterwards. Italy had a 15 per cent decrease in inequality in

Table 5.7 The distribution of population: EU income quantiles

Country/year	Bottom 20%		Top 10%	
	1970	1998	1970	1998
Spain	41.7%	34.4%	5.7%	6.5%
France	14.8%	12.3%	13.8%	12.2%
Ireland	48.8%	24.1%	3.5%	12.7%
Italy	24.9%	25.8%	9.4%	11.3%
United Kingdom	15.3%	20.9%	9.5%	12.3%

Source: Morrisson and Murtin (2004).

the 1980s and a nearly 20 per cent increase in inequality between 1990 and 1995, with inequality stabilising afterwards. Finally, in the UK, the trend was exactly the opposite: inequality rose to the highest level ever witnessed in the whole EU in the 1990s, then fell by 20 per cent between 1990 and 1995 and rose again by 5 per cent up to 1998. As expected, Nordic countries, Benelux, France, Germany and Austria display lower levels of inequality than other countries.

An even better picture of the dynamics can be derived by looking at the distribution of population by the **European income quantiles**,[17] which tells us whether the residents of a given country are poor or rich when measured on a EU-wide scale, and thus gives the income profile of a country compared to the income profile of Europe. The most interesting cases are summarised in Table 5.7. For example, in 1970, nearly 50 per cent of the residents in Ireland were among the 20 per cent poorest Europeans, while in 1998, only 24 per cent of the residents in Ireland were among the 20 per cent poorest Europeans. On the contrary, the number of Irish residents among the 10 per cent richest Europeans increased nearly threefold between 1970 and 1990. The United Kingdom saw the numbers of both the poor and the rich go up, thus giving rise to an income polarisation effect. The same phenomenon was observed, to a much lower extent, in Italy. In contrast to the development in the UK and in Italy, France saw a reduction of income polarisation, since the share of both rich and poor went down and therefore the share of 'middle class' increased.

A symmetric analysis is performed by looking at the distribution of the **income quantiles by country**, compared with the share of each country in the EU population. This tells us where rich and poor reside across the EU countries. Again the most interesting cases are summarised in Table 5.8.

For example, Spain had, in 1998, 10.5 per cent of the EU population, but about 18 per cent of the poorest and 6.8 per cent of the richest. Ireland,

Table 5.8 The distribution of population: income quantiles by country

Country/year	Bottom 20%		Top 10%		Percentage
	1970	1998	1970	1998	Share of population
Spain	21.9%	18.1%	5.9%	6.8%	10.5%
France	11.6%	9.7%	21.7%	19.1%	15.8%
Ireland	2.2%	1.2%	0.3%	1.3%	1%
Italy	20.7%	19.7%	15.7%	13.3%	15.4%
United Kingdom	13.2%	16.4%	16.4%	19.4%	15.8%

Source: Morrisson and Murtin (2004).

with 1 per cent of the EU population, had only 0.3 per cent of the richest Europeans in 1970 and more than 1.3 per cent of them in 1998, while the percentage of poorest living in Ireland nearly halved (from 2.2 per cent to 1.2 per cent). Italy has lost both very rich and very poor residents, thus increasing the size of the middle class. The United Kingdom, on the contrary, has increased both its very rich and its very poor residents, thus reducing the size of its middle class in line with the polarisation result previously obtained.

In line with the scope of this chapter, which correlates the growth performance of Europe with its underlying economic and social model, Box 5.1 discusses whether and to what extent the heterogeneity in social spending across member states has translated into heterogeneity in terms of their economic perfomance.

5.3.4 Income Distribution across EU Member States

We have already considered in Chapter 1 that, because of its cross-country nature, across-countries inequality is not dealt with by member states, as is the case for the management of within-country inequality, rather it is a concern of policies undertaken at the EU level. In this respect, the evidence reported in Table 5.4 points to decreasing values of across-countries inequality in the EU, with across-countries inequality constituting only a minor component (on average not even 10 per cent) of the total inequality in the EU income distribution. Notwithstanding the limited importance of across-countries inequality, and the prima facie evidence of its reduction over time, the issue of income distribution across the EU is one of the most disputed subjects in the economic literature of the last few years.

BOX 5.1 SOCIAL SPENDING AND ECONOMIC PERFORMANCE

Regressing the ranking of countries' competitiveness with countries' social spending may shed some light on the often-assumed existence of a trade-off between the social spending and the competitiveness of a country. It is generally claimed that excessive social spending may claim too high a toll on competitiveness and ultimately on growth. A well-known paper by De Grauwe and Polan (2003) looked at this question in some detail. They use two indices of competitiveness, which are closely correlated and therefore deliver a very similar ranking. The indices are those calculated by the IMD of Lausanne (www.imd.ch) and by the World Economic Forum (www.weforum.org). Both compute a competitiveness index and rank nations in decreasing order (a low value indicates great competitiveness).

The results of the regression of competitiveness and social spending are shown in the figure. Rather clearly, a trade-off between social spending and competitiveness cannot be found. On the contrary, a positive correlation between social spending and competitiveness can be found. The USA represents the most notable exception to this rule, being ranked first in terms of competitiveness during 1997–2001 but providing relatively little public

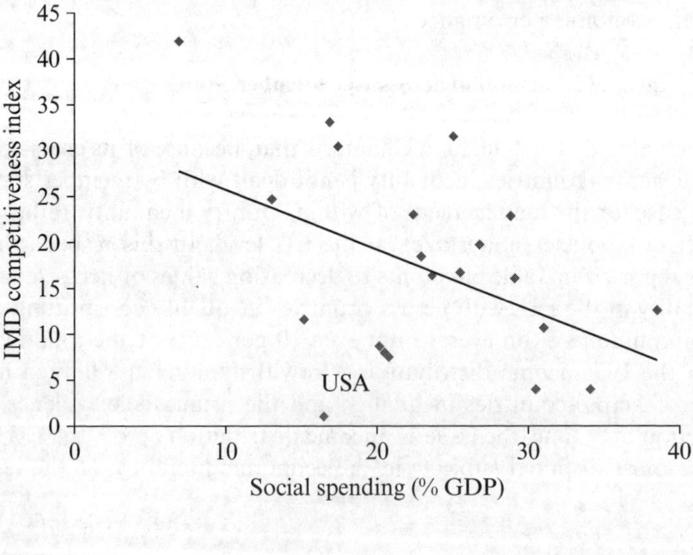

money for social expenditures: only 17 per cent of its GDP, compared to about 30 per cent in most northern European countries.

The results are somewhat surprising, given the widespread claims that globalisation and economic integration would lead to a race-to-the-bottom of social spending, because social spending harms competitiveness. De Grauwe and Polan (2003) show that neither the reduction of social spending nor a negative correlation between competitiveness and social spending can be proved. Rather their evidence shows that more competitive countries tend to provide more on social spending than less competitive countries.

Of course the direction of the causality link of this finding is far from clear. On the one hand, it could well be that more competitive (and therefore richer) countries have simply greater resources to spend for social purposes. On the other hand, there could be good reasons why social spending may improve competitiveness, since social spending improves the quality of human capital or helps to differentiate risks in the economy, thus making both workers and entrepreneurs more willing and ready to take risks and thus innovate.

The question therefore boils down to the **quality** of social spending. When public money is not used efficiently, as is the case of some European countries, this amounts to a drain on resources and thus lowers competitiveness. Other countries, especially in northern Europe, are able to combine a high level of social spending with the effective provision of goods and services which allow them to rank high in the competitiveness league.

Extreme views are common: one may find authors showing, via sophisticated econometrics, a great deal of **income convergence** within the EU, and other authors showing no sign of convergence within the EU.[18] A result by and large accepted by the profession is that one can observe a tendency of per capita income convergence at the level of member states, but not at the level of the 211 administrative regions which make up the EU-15. The gist of this finding is that low-income countries have a tendency to grow faster, on average, than high-income ones, as previously shown. However, within each high-growing country, income levels might tend to diverge across regions, thus increasing inequalities measured at this level of disaggregation.

From this to conclude that only convergence across countries and no convergence across regions took place, however, is a very large conceptual jump, that we will discuss in detail in Chapter 8 of the book. For the time being, let us anticipate that the level of 'administrative region' as identified by the national statistical offices might not be the right unit of analysis when assessing whether or not income convergence across regions is taking place. The 211 EU administrative regions so identified are in fact far too different in size and economic structure, levels of national and EU integration, endowments and infrastructure, to be ideal for economic analyses. In addition, the picture is likely to worsen when analysing the enlarged EU-25, since in some of the new member states administrative regions have been artificially created only recently, in order to respond to the need for a bureaucratic harmonisation of the EU official statistics.

5.3.5 The Enlarged European Economic and Social Model

All the results analysed so far change in terms of both their economic and political implications for the EU social model, because of the recent enlargement of the Union to include the ten new member states of Central and Eastern Europe.

In particular, as reported by Table 5.9, the recent enlargement of the Union has led to a significant increase (around 20 per cent) in the overall level of inequalities registered in the EU along all the identified inequality measures. Moreover the picture is likely to worsen further when the EU admits Romania and Bulgaria (EU-27) and then eventually Turkey, with total inequality increasing by 30 per cent and 40 per cent, respectively. Notably this new inequality dimension makes the EU, for the first time in recent history, a less egalitarian place than the USA (the Theil index of EU-25 is 0.195, and of the USA 0.190), and therefore constitutes a serious challenge for the EU economic and social model.

When looking at the political consequences of such an outcome, it is important to disentangle, as we have done for the EU-15, the measures of within- and across-countries inequalities induced by the enlargement. As shown in Table 5.10, most notably the enlargement has generated a

Table 5.9 Indicators of total inequality in the enlarged EU, 2000

Tot. inequality indicator / dimension of the EU	EU-15	EU-25	EU-27	EU-27 + Turkey
Top 5% / bottom 20%	1.86	2.38	3.01	3.88
Gini coefficient	0.308	0.342	0.367	0.397
Theil index	0.159	0.195	0.225	0.262

Source: Morrisson and Murtin (2004).

Table 5.10 Theil index 'within' and 'across' countries in the enlarged EU, 2000

Theil index/ dimension of the EU	EU-15	EU-25	EU-27	EU-27 + Turkey
Within-country	0.152	0.152	0.152	0.166
Across-countries	0.007	0.043	0.073	0.096
Total inequality	0.159	0.195	0.225	0.262

Source: Morrisson and Murtin (2004).

significant increase in the across-countries inequality, while leaving substantially unaltered the within-country inequality. The situation is likely to be the same also in the case of EU-27, changing only slightly when including Turkey in the picture.[19] Therefore the figures reveal that the new member states have a within-country income distribution relatively similar to the one of the EU-15 countries. However their average income level is considerably lower than that of the EU-15.

These findings, maybe not surprising in statistical terms, have however a profound political implication, since the new member states can influence with their voting power the future evolution of the EU policies. Now, had the difference in inequality between the EU-15 and the new member states been only attributable to within-country inequality, the solution of the problem would have remained essentially in the hands of the individual member states, since we have seen that the competence to manage this type of inequality resides only with them. Unfortunately, however, the nature of the inequalities to be corrected between the incumbent and the new member states is precisely the one (across-countries) on which the EU, and not the individual member states, has the competence to act. Therefore the chance of political attrition in the future evolution of the EU redistribution policies is very likely.

Nevertheless the (partially) good news with this respect is that both the EU institutions and the member states have been able in the past to reduce the across-countries inequality in the Union, maintaining a strong degree of internal social cohesion, with regional policies and the completion of the single market having been the two main instruments in this regard.

It is therefore of paramount importance for the enlarged EU to continue to use these two instruments if total inequality is to be reduced, especially in the across-countries dimension. While doing so, it is also necessary to update continuously the functioning of the welfare systems, including the social institutions related to the labour market, which are crucial in containing within-country inequality also in the new member states, as shown by Box 5.2.

BOX 5.2 WITHIN-COUNTY INEQUALITY AND THE LABOUR MARKET INSTITUTIONS

In EU-25 there is evidence that employment rates play a great role in reducing economic inequality within countries. The figure shows in fact that those countries with high employment rates tend to have low income inequality, while those with high income inequality tend to have low employment rates. The few exceptions are mainly driven by a large social and redistributive system (for example, Belgium has low inequality in spite of a low employment rate) and a reduced social and redistributive system (for example, the UK has high inequality in spite of a high employment rate).

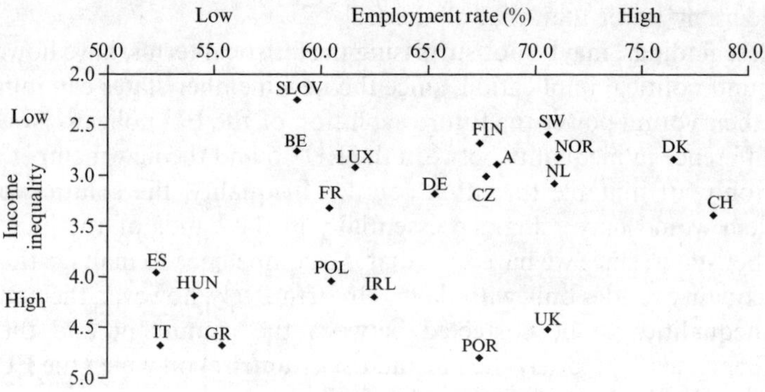

Source: Eurostat Labour Force Survey for employment rates and OECD; Eurostat for inequality.

Summing up, the EU economic and social model has been put under stress, for at least a decade, by technological changes, globalisation and increased competition on a world scale. Enlargement adds to this picture and constitutes at the same time a challenge for the economic and social model to remain sustainable, and an opportunity for growth to resume. The Lisbon Agenda previously introduced aims at reviving growth via innovation, and via a better allocation of resources across the enlarged Europe, maintaining at the same time the sustainability of the enlarged EU economic and social model, in the sense so far analysed. In order to achieve such a result, the Lisbon Agenda calls for a homogeneous and coordinated strategy of structural reforms, discussed in the rest of the chapter.

5.4 THE LISBON AGENDA: TARGETS, STRATEGY AND TOOLS

5.4.1 The Targets

The Lisbon Agenda, in spite of its name, is the result of a two-year-long decisional process and of five European councils (Lisbon in March 2000, Nice in December 2000, Stockholm in March 2001, Gothenburg in June 2001 and Barcelona in March 2002), with the process initiated by the heads of state and governments meeting in Lisbon in March 2000.

On that occasion, the EU Council intended to sketch a roadmap of the EU economic targets for the next decade. In this respect, it is important to underline that the context in which the decisions were taken was one of favourable growth prospects,[20] after the stagnation of the previous decade. The positive global outlook, with the stock markets still in frenzy at the prospects of the so-called 'new economy' generated by the developments in information and telecommunication technologies, and the achievement of healthy public finance in basically all EU countries, contributed to the optimism in which the Lisbon Council met. Essentially the EU economy was seen approaching its full potential output, which, as we have seen, was however below the US one. Building on this positive scenario, the Lisbon Agenda thus wanted to increase EU potential growth structurally, through reforms aiming at an improvement in labour market flexibility and a facilitation of the necessary investment in R&D and innovation.

Somewhat pompously, the Presidency Conclusions (point 5) of the Lisbon Council translated this target with the following statement: 'The Union has today set itself a ***new strategic goal*** for the next decade: to become the most competitive and dynamic knowledge-based economy in the world capable of sustainable economic growth with more and better jobs and greater social cohesion' (emphasis in the text). More operationally, apart from this empty rhetoric, probably influenced by the general economic climate of the time, the Lisbon Council set a number of specific targets to give momentum to this European commitment, suggesting that 'recognising their different starting points, member states should consider setting national targets for an increased employment rate. This, by enlarging the labour force, will reinforce the sustainability of social protection systems targets'. Even more specifically, the European Council also stated that 'the overall aim [should be] to raise the employment rate from an average of 61 per cent today to as close as possible to 70 per cent by 2010, and to increase the number of women in employment from an average of 51 per cent today to more than 60 per cent by 2010'.

In addition to the adoption of a new treaty for the enlarged Union, the Nice summit of December 2000 also launched the Social Policy Agenda, which sets out the necessary measures to achieve the Lisbon objectives of more and better jobs and a modern welfare state within a more inclusive society. The Social Agenda 'defines, in accordance with the Lisbon European Council conclusions, specific priorities for action for the next five years around six strategic orientations in all social policy areas [full employment, labour mobility, management of the technological progress, ageing, implications of enlargement and globalisation]. This Agenda constitutes a major step towards the reinforcement and modernisation of the European social model, which is characterised by the indissoluble link between economic performance and social progress'.

The employment targets set by the Lisbon summit were then further increased one year later at the Stockholm Council, in March 2001. The Stockholm European Council in particular agreed 'to set intermediate targets for employment rates across the Union as a whole for January 2005 of 67 per cent overall, and 57 per cent for women. It has also agreed to set an EU target for increasing the average EU employment rate among older women and men (55–64) to 50 per cent by 2010'.

Three months later, the European Council of Gothenburg (Sweden) of June 2001 added to the Lisbon Agenda the environmental dimension of sustainable growth. The environmental dimension substantially modifies the growth strategy by increasing the emphasis on long-term concerns (such as climate change issues, including the ratification of the Kyoto protocol, and renewable energy issues) and by insisting on the decoupling of production from the use of resources. The Gothenburg Council concluded that 'sustainable development – to meet the needs of the present generation without compromising those of future generations – is a fundamental objective under the Treaties'. It then agreed that 'it requires dealing with economic, social and environmental policies in a mutually reinforcing way. Failure to reverse trends that threaten future quality of life will steeply increase the costs to society or make those trends irreversible'. It also agreed on a 'strategy for sustainable development, which completes the Union's political commitment to economic and social renewal, adds a third, environmental dimension to the Lisbon strategy and establishes a new approach to policy making'.[21]

Finally, in March 2002, the Barcelona European Council identified as priority action a reinforcement of the Employment Strategy along national and EU-wide policy lines aiming at full employment. It identified three broad areas ('Active policies towards full employment, a reinforced Employment Strategy, promoting skills and mobility in the European Union') which required specific impetus from the EU member states and EU institutions in view of the pursuit of the Union's long-term objectives.

We have reported for the sake of completeness the institutional framework which has led to the creation of the Lisbon Agenda and its related **targets**. We are, however, well aware of the fact that to agree on the general targets is the easy part of the story: after 50 years of political and economic integration, and given the picture of growth of the last decade within Europe and the emphasis placed on the social dimension of the process, only a few eccentric people would disagree with them. The most difficult part of the Lisbon process, however, is the implementation of the **strategy** and the identification of the **tools** needed to reach those targets. Without this, the entire exercise translates into what some authors have called 'a myriad of meaningless pompous statements' (Alesina and Perotti, 2004). In addition, even if the strategy and the tools are identified clearly, it is still debatable whether, for example, undifferentiated, very specific, quantitative targets on various structural indicators for the EU economy as a whole are the right approach to the problem. These issues are the subject of the next two sections.

5.4.2 The Strategy

The greatest potential of the Lisbon strategy lies, in our opinion, in the coordinated and comprehensive nature of the advocated reforms, which cover microeconomic, social and macroeconomic aspects. Indeed the Presidency Conclusion of the Lisbon summit read: 'Achieving this goal [sustainable economic growth with more and better jobs and greater social cohesion] requires an ***overall strategy*** aimed at:

- preparing the transition to a knowledge-based economy and society by better policies for the information society and R&D, as well as by stepping up the process of structural reform for competitiveness and innovation and by completing the internal market;
- modernising the European social model, investing in people and combating social exclusion;
- sustaining the healthy economic outlook and favourable growth prospects by applying an appropriate macro-economic policy mix'.

Such a strategy is perfectly consistent with the previously identified need for the EU to promote a broad series of reforms able to increase the overall productivity of the Union. Moreover the last element, a healthy macroeconomic outlook, constitutes the framework within which to achieve the first and second elements: microeconomic reforms to revive growth and move the economy towards a knowledge-based society, and social reforms to preserve EU low levels of inequalities.[22]

In particular, within a healthy macro environment, the Lisbon strategy specifically focuses on eight areas of action. Three deal specifically with the completion of the single market: product market liberalisation and reduction of state aid; completion of the EU networks (telecoms, utilities, transport and so on) and completion of the EU financial markets. The remaining five dealing with other policies are improving the information society; fostering R&D and innovation; improving the business environment; maintaining and reinforcing the European social model and environment and climate change.

The Lisbon strategy is thus wide-ranging, and as such it has both positive and negative implications. On the positive side, as already stated, the multifaceted strategy of response to the problem of the lack of growth in Europe is the correct approach. In a sense, it can be viewed as a 'political equilibrium' where every country (and EU institution) finds the policy and objective best suited to its contingent needs, yet in an overall coordinated framework.

On the negative side, the Lisbon process mixes final targets (sustainable growth, social cohesion), intermediate objectives (such as employment rates, themselves divided under various categories of the workforce and undifferentiated across member states) and policy measures. Even within the latter, the Lisbon Agenda appears to be more a list than a strategy: too many priorities in fact imply no priority at all. Furthermore too many goals and structural indicators to fulfil imply a risk of complacency, as any country can find at least some dimensions in which it performs relatively well.

5.4.3 The Tools

The Lisbon Agenda also defines a method for implementing the previously discussed strategy of reforms: 'improving the existing processes, introducing a new open method of coordination at all levels, coupled with a stronger guiding and coordinating role for the European Council to ensure more coherent strategic direction and effective monitoring of progress' (Lisbon European Council, Presidency Conclusions).

Therefore the strategy underlying the Lisbon Agenda essentially relies for its implementation on a mix of the traditional **Community method** (in which the Commission proposes and the Council and the European Parliament adopt in co-decision) and a new method, the so-called **open**

method of coordination (OMC), where individual member states act directly, without the need for a Commission proposal or a Council adoption, but rather through a mechanism of peer pressure and periodical review of the progress achieved.

More specifically the traditional community method is used within the Lisbon Agenda to implement the measures related to the single market, where across-countries spillovers are greater (for example, rules related to a better working of financial markets or trans-European networks of infrastructures) and where therefore there is a rationale for an EU competence. On the other hand, the OMC is used for the other policies where across-countries spillovers are smaller (for example, promotion of labour market flexibility) and therefore where adoption at the Community level would be more difficult.

Spillovers can thus be seen as a sort of market mechanism which discriminates between benchmarking (coordinated intervention by individual member states) and EU-level decision making, thus translating economically the juridical rationale of the subsidiarity principle enshrined in the treaties (see Chapter 1). When spillovers are relevant, they allow the EU institutions to exercise peer pressure on any country to reform, because any country is affected by any other country's reform, and thus the likelihood of approval of a law at the EU level is higher. On the contrary, when spillovers are smaller, the EU institutions are less effective as a pressure tool, and each country should count on its own will to reform through the OMC.

The introduction of the open method of coordination therefore implies, at least in theory, a new governance architecture combining elements of centralisation and subsidiarity, since it involves areas of policy that are not within the competence of the Union, but that are in any case subject to a certain degree of coordination. The Commission plays an important role in it by proposing guidelines, developing indicators and monitoring results. Member states adapt these policy guidelines to national contexts and retain considerable freedom by deciding their preferred approach to implement them. The monitoring and review of the result is then done jointly by the member states and the Commission.[23]

However, although in principle very intriguing, the introduction of a very mild coordination process in these policy areas via the OMC is turning out to be rather problematic, with a dreadful record of progress achieved. Many observers point out in this regard that the OMC is essentially a forum for benchmarking and exchange of best practices among governments, with some commitments and some good intentions, but no binding instruments. In other words, the OMC is considerably weaker than the Community method, and much weaker than the coordination tools used to obtain fiscal consolidation within the EMU (for example, the Maastricht criteria and the Stability and Growth Pact discussed in the previous chapter). The OMC in fact lacks most of the elements that are necessary to foster reforms and that made the Maastricht criteria and the SGP reasonably strong policy tools: visibility, political ownership, right incentives, constraining calendar, effective monitoring and collegial culture.[24]

To circumvent this limit, some authors (such as Secchi and Altomonte, 2002) have evoked the possibility of linking structural reforms, derived from the Lisbon Agenda, to the stability programmes developed within the EMU, since the latter possess a much more powerful degree of political implementation.[25] Indeed a sluggish implementation of structural reforms translates into a greater difficulty of respecting the stability programme, since lower growth rates tend to put pressure on the maintenance of deficit targets close to balance. Such a juridical loophole could authorise the Commission to initiate the infringement procedures against those countries not implementing the structural reforms. In this sense, the proposal is consistent with the recent Commission's proposals on the SGP, which have been discussed at length in Chapter 4. To be effective, however, such a proposal implies that member states accept the Commission playing a greater role in economic policy coordination with respect to the current situation. Unfortunately, as we discussed in Chapter 4, this is an area where the consensus among academics and the current political will are particularly at odds.

Even more dangerously, the OMC, in spite of its lack of enforcing and binding instruments, can generate in the general public the expectation that something vaguely remembered as 'Europe' will take care of the problem, thus basically facilitating inaction at the national level, rather than fostering action. In other words, not only is the OMC revealing itself as ineffective, but at the same time it might also blur the responsibility for policy inaction (Micossi, 2002).

To coordinate the use of the tools, both the community method and the OMC are managed within a single framework made up of the **Broad Economic Policy Guidelines** (BEPGs) and the **Employment Guidelines** (EG).[26] This single framework is the object of the annual **Spring European Council**, which monitors, reviews and fosters the progress of the EU economy towards the Lisbon targets.

In particular, as mentioned in Chapter 4, the BEPGs were originally foreseen as a coordination tool for the EMU (their legal base is TEC, art. 99, in the part of the Treaty dealing with the monetary union), but are nowadays used as a tool for implementing the Lisbon strategy of structural reforms. The BEPGs are prepared by the Commission and are contained in a single document indicating the general economic guidelines valid for all EU countries, as well as the specific recommendations of economic policy valid for individual countries. The BEPGs moved in 2003 from an annual to a triennial focus, thus ensuring a better consistency of the measures over time and hence a stronger economic governance system.

The employment guidelines (EGs) foreseen by TEC, art. 128 follow the same logic as the BEPGs, and are meant to offer to member states general and specific guidelines for their employment policies. In particular the EGs have three interrelated and overarching objectives: full employment, quality and productivity at work, and social cohesion and inclusion. In order to pursue these objectives, member states are called upon to develop measures in many directions, such as job creation and entrepreneurship, active and preventive measures for the unemployed and inactive workers, promoting development of human capital and lifelong learning, and so on.

In recent years both the BEPG and the EG have been streamlined and synchronised to improve the consistency of this model. In any given year, they are prepared by the Commission before summer, and presented to the member states for their implementation. Before March of the following year, the Commission issues an evaluation on the status of implementation of the two documents across member states; the results of this report act as a background reference for the Spring (March) European Council of the heads of state and governments, which, since March 2000, is the annual forum for reviewing and providing guidance for economic policy coordination in the Union. In particular the Spring Council provides general orientations to the various Council formations: (a) for actions to be decided at the Union level; (b) for priorities to be fed into the next year's BEPGs and EGs, as well as recommendations for the implementation of the principal instruments for coordinating member states' structural reforms.

Clearly a consistent implementation of the EU policies (developed from Chapter 6 onwards) and of the member states' policies set out according to the BEPGs and the EGs is crucial for the success of this model of economic governance. In particular, consistency is measured at two levels: consistency between targets and tools and consistency between levels of government (the EU level, the national level and the regional level). Consistency between the defined targets and the implementing tools for actions undertaken at the EU level essentially concerns the definition of the overall budgetary envelope of resources necessary and available to meet the declared targets (for example, the development of trans-European networks of infrastructures or Community initiatives on R&D). Much too often the EU level has in fact suffered from a shortage of tools with respect to the declared goals, because the total size of the EU intervention (the EU budget) has been seen as a political issue per se, rather than an instrument to reach the declared goals (see Chapter 6 for a detailed discussion). At the national level, the problem of a consistent implementation of policies is not necessarily related to a lack of resources, since, as already considered, the nature of the tools to be managed by member states within the Lisbon Agenda is often related to regulatory interventions (such as reforms of the labour market or the pension systems), whose main difficulty is linked to the generation of the necessary level of political consensus.[27]

A second and related issue is the consistency between EU and national intervention. To prevent divergences arising, the EU common policies and their financial underpinning should be integrated in the BEPGs framework, so that the latter could steer the overall budgetary amount of both national and EU spending. Within this total envelope, allocation to one or the other level of government should be made according to the efficiency of any level in designing and implementing any given policy (the spillover mechanism previously described). Such a solution is certainly superior to fixing ex ante and somewhat arbitrarily quantitative targets and constraints for any level of action. In addition, leaving such an allocation process to a market-related mechanism makes it possible, in the steady state, to minimise the total amount of public spending (national plus EU) for a given level of output, since there might be different political national sensibilities which might impose, in certain 'sensible areas', ceiling or floors for EU intervention.[28]

5.5 HOW FAR ARE WE FROM THE LISBON TARGETS?

The 2004 Spring Report (see European Commission, 2004d) gave a graphical, very useful assessment of how far the EU is from the Lisbon targets for the two main components of growth, employment and productivity, which we discussed in equations 5.1 to 5.4 earlier in the chapter. Figure 5.8 shows quite clearly that most countries are within 10 per cent of the employment target, but still far away from the productivity level of the USA.[29]

The need for reform is clearly stronger in those countries having employment levels well below 60 per cent, being those at serious risk of not reaching either the intermediate target (67 per cent by 2005), or the final target (70 per cent by 2010) for employment. The picture shows, however, that there are as many as seven countries already above the intermediate target and four countries above the final targets. Reassuringly enough, all these countries (with the exception of Portugal) maintain a productivity very much in line with the average EU productivity, around which there is a significant cluster of countries.

The same picture in terms of growth of productivity and employment in 2001 and 2002 shows the recent progress of countries in these two dimen-

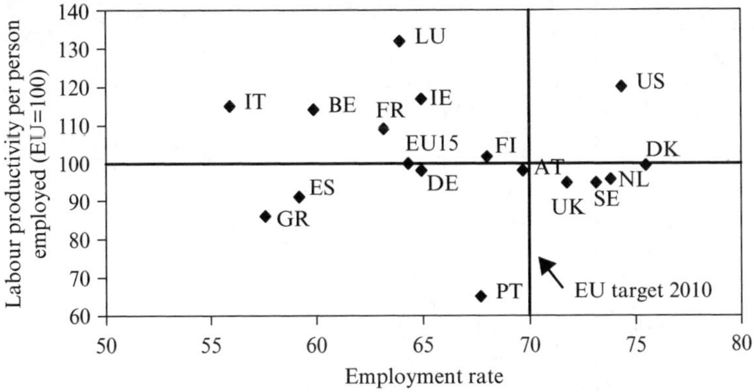

Source: European Commission (2004d).

Figure 5.8 Employment and productivity in the EU-15, 2003

sions (Figure 5.9). It also indicates that most countries have progressed both in terms of productivity and in terms of employment. Two have had mildly negative employment growth coupled with sizable productivity growth and three have had negative productivity growth coupled with a solid employment growth.

Figure 5.9 thus reveals that the first results of the reforms of labour and product markets are now becoming apparent and show their potential to raise the overall performance of the Union. Yet much has still to be done in order to increase employment and achieve higher productivity. As for the first, the persistence of long-term unemployment rates (LTU) is a particular European concern. Figure 5.10 shows that the proportion of LTU in Europe is still significant, with LTU at 3.5 per cent out of a total of 9 per cent of average EU unemployment. In other words, LTU accounts for roughly 40 per cent of the EU unemployment rate, a proportion seven times greater than in the USA. The situation is even worse for the new member states. Persistence of LTU certainly indicates a great difference in labour market regulations, but, given its heterogeneity across the Union, it also points to very different burdens for the social protection system and differences in the EU social model. The fight against the LTU is definitely one of the greatest priorities for the EU strategy to meet the Lisbon targets, also considering the role played by employment in ensuring a smaller income inequality, as shown in Box 5.2.

As for the increase in productivity, many hopes are raised by the EU comprehensive strategy of reforms fostered by the Lisbon Agenda. Only the combination of many policies (education and training, efficient financial

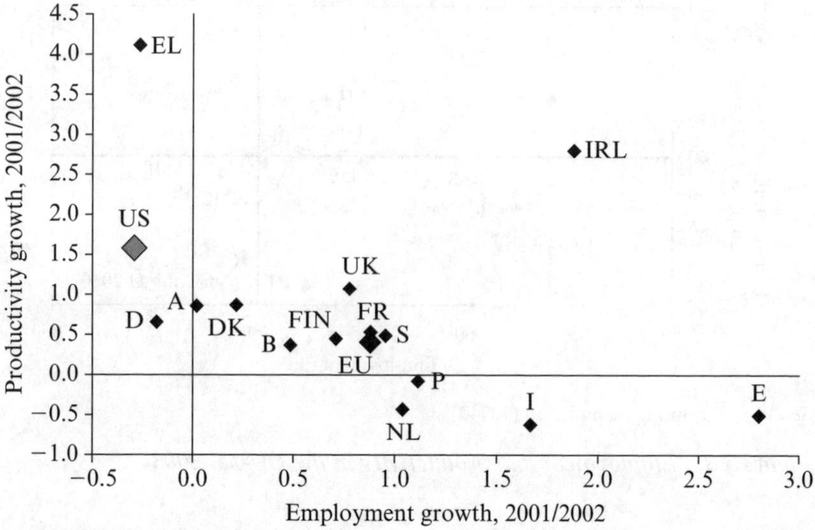

Source: European Commission (2003b).

Figure 5.9 Changes in employment and productivity in EU-15, 2001/2002

markets for innovation, competitive product markets for innovative goods) is in fact able to improve both the 'supply' and the 'demand' for innovation. In particular, to improve the supply of innovation, EU member states should be making more investment in knowledge, in R&D, education, lifelong learning, vocational training and so on. On R&D expenditure, as will be detailed in the second part of this book, the gap with the USA, and with the rhetorically declared EU intentions, is still in fact very wide. Clearly the main constraint on this type of investment is seen as financial, especially in a period of low cycles. Two considerations can be made here: first of all, the debate is still open on whether the increase in these types of expenditures should be public or private, since both sources of expenditures have in fact pros and cons.[30] However, since a first-best solution would be to increase both, it is important to try to foster at the same time public and private expenditures on innovation. In terms of public expenditures, it should be made clear in the political debate that to allow current expenditures (such as generous pension systems) to crowd out capital expenditures (R&D) is a sign of political short-sightedness, rather than an economic constraint, ultimately violating the EU goal of sustainable development and solidarity, since such a policy attitude leads to a more intensive use of resources today at the expense of future generations.[31]

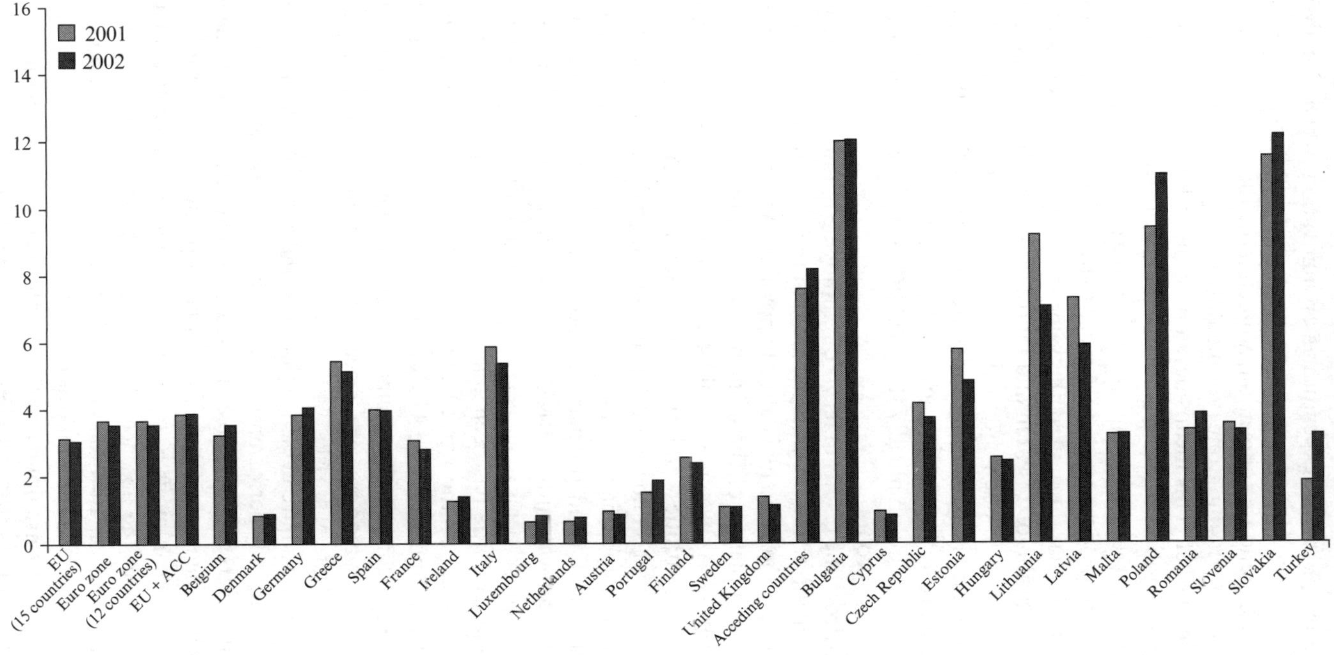

Notes: These figures report long-term (12 months and more) unemployment rates (LTU). They do not consider the relevance of the informal and grey sectors. The total official unemployment rate, currently at around 9 per cent in the EU, is the sum of the LTU plus the short-term (<12 months) unemployment rate.

Source: Eurostat.

Figure 5.10 Long-term unemployment rates in EU-25, 2001/2002

Second, in terms of private expenditures on innovation, which are also very low throughout the Union, adequate attention should instead be paid to increasing the demand for innovation, a much more difficult task, since it requires an encompassing strategy aimed at making innovation more profitable on the market. This means developing the risk capital industry and promoting integration of the EU financial markets so as to ensure a proper thickness of the capital market for innovation. It also implies removing barriers in product markets in order to force firms to innovate to remain competitive, guaranteeing at the same time legal coverage to the commercial exploitation of research and innovation and a proper respect for competition rules.[32] In one word, if the single market for products and services is efficient, and if competition rules are respected, competitiveness rises, since the end of 'protected markets' exposes every actor to competition and increases automatically the incentive to innovate in order to maintain or increase profits.

Moving away from the results in terms of employment and productivity, an overall assessment of the progress achieved in the eight areas of action identified by the Lisbon strategy is already possible. As far as the actions dealing with the completion of the single market are concerned, it appears that distinct progress has been made only in the completion of the EU networks of telecoms, utilities and transports. Some progress has been achieved in product market liberalisation and state aid reduction, as well as in the completion of the financial markets. Concerning the other actions identified, some very limited progress has been made in the information society, fostering innovation and R&D, and reforming the social model. Finally no real progress seems to have been made in improving the business environment, and too little has been achieved in the environmental area, especially with respect to the agreed objectives. The distance from the declared objectives (and from the US standards) in the innovation and R&D policy as well as in the improvement of the business environment is certainly a source of major concern, since lack of progress in these areas may put the whole strategy at risk.

Overall, therefore, we have evidence that in some areas of action some member states are already performing in line with the targets set at Lisbon. This proves that targets are reachable and suggests that there is unfulfilled potential in other member states. This rather optimist conclusion, is, however, far from unanimous.[33] It hinges crucially on the belief that member states, even in the absence of strong coordination mechanisms, will, in any case, realise how decisive and important microeconomic reforms are, especially as far as innovation policies are concerned. If the microeconomic reforms are not carried through, then also the chances of achieving the Lisbon targets will dramatically diminish.

5.6 MEETING THE LISBON AGENDA IN AN ENLARGED EUROPE

The implementation of the Lisbon goals is, if possible, even more important, given the enlargement of the Union. The challenge of the enlargement calls into question neither the usefulness nor the underlying validity of the Lisbon targets. Quite to the contrary, it opens up new possibilities. Enlargement has not only macroeconomic effects but also other – arguably even more important – microeconomic effects. Larger markets offer consumers greater choice and make R&D activity more profitable. Enlargement thus acts as a catalyst for competition among both consumers and producers in most European markets. Improved competition may be able to give a much-needed fillip to economic reforms and to foster change, and may thus lead to a better allocation of resources and therefore to larger growth. Furthermore the enlargement-related boost to investment and productivity may lead to the creation of a truly efficient pan-European industrial organisation, some examples of which are already visible.[34]

Clearly the Lisbon targets and tools will also need to be enlarged to include the new member states, some of which are still lagging behind, especially in terms of microeconomic reforms, as shown in some of the data previously presented. However the participation of these countries in the EU integration will likely speed up their convergence process. To this end, the lesson we can draw from the financial markets is particularly telling. First, over the last ten years the new member states have seen a steady improvement in their credit ratings as the prospect of enlargement has drawn closer. Second, the new member states and the remaining accession countries (that is, Bulgaria and Romania) enjoy an 'accession premium', since their bonds trade at tighter spreads than equally rated countries from other parts of the world.

In sum, Lisbon targets are now part of the Community wisdom and the political way of thinking, as much as the debate on the Economic and Monetary Union. They are certainly not any longer in question, and they are viewed by many as representing the intimate political and economic nature of Europe. Thus, in the intellectual sense, the Lisbon process is a success, since the economic and social model it supports has won the battle of ideas.

Unfortunately the Lisbon targets are also very difficult to attain, since the tools proposed to reach them are difficult to implement. Many, if not all, member states have, since March 2000, been making considerable efforts to foster growth by improving the quality and quantity of jobs and by starting (at least in their policy proposals) a widespread process of microeconomic reforms. However only a few have (partially) succeeded, and only a few more can be considered to be on the right track. Many member states have instead put in place only partial attempts at reforms (such as the labour market), completely neglecting other equally crucial areas related to the working of the product and services market (for example the financial sector, or competition policy), crucial for raising innovation and productivity and without which the targets cannot be reached. Again the Lisbon Agenda is an overall process of structural change, whose aims can be achieved only if a comprehensive package of reforms, both at the microeconomic and the macroeconomic level, is undertaken.

This limited success has raised concerns about the method itself, in particular the open method of coordination, which is applied to those areas not directly linked to the single market. A firm judgment cannot, at this stage, be made, but the discussion on whether this method should be strengthened or replaced altogether by another one is well under way. To this purpose, establishing a link between the failure in implementing structural reforms and the ability to abide by the stability programme, therefore applying the stability programme rules to those countries who are late in reforming, is a possible way to strengthen the OMC. This would require, however, a certain willingness of the member states to let the Commission have effective powers in economic policy coordination, an attitude which is yet to manifest itself.

To this extent, the mid-term review of the Lisbon Agenda, undertaken by the Commission in February 2005, concluded that the process had yet to deliver on many of its promises and that success was piecemeal in Europe rather than uniformly distributed. Essentially the mid-term review stated that, overall, the Lisbon strategy is the correct one for Europe, but its objectives need to be more specifically formulated and more focused. Also the governance tools and the policies to attain those objectives need some upgrading. Specifically, the Lisbon mid-term review called for three avenues for improvement:

- greater commitment of member states to the Lisbon Agenda and greater consistency of the policies to be pursued (member states are asked to appoint a Ms or Mr Lisbon at ministerial level);
- to renew and refocus the programme around completion of the single market, investment in knowledge, innovation and long-life training, thus fostering the demand for more and better jobs;
- to improve Lisbon governance and ensure a better link with the other EU policies, such as the EU budget and macroeconomic stability.

Clearly, the question is whether this mid-term review will be enough to re-establish the coherence between the objectives and the tools necessary to obtain the desired results. Certainly, since February 2005, goals are more focused, tools have been upgraded and the need for more synergy with other policies, namely the EU budget and the Stability and Growth Pact, has been stated. However, budget negotiations have yet to come close to the result of bringing the EU budget in line with Lisbon (see Chapter 6) and the reformed Stability and Growth Pact (see Chapter 4) has yet to undergo its first stress test. Hence, it is still unclear how much these policies can help with respect to the Lisbon objectives.

Time will tell whether the 2005 review of the Lisbon Agenda has been a big enough move, or whether the entire Lisbon objectives are too ambitious for the current EU capabilities.

NOTES

1. The stability issue and the EU achievements in terms of inflation reduction and public finance consolidation have been addressed in detail in Chapter 4. The other strategic EU goal of cohesion will be dealt with in Chapter 8.
2. The income gap in per capita terms between the EU and the USA remained constant after the 1970s, notwithstanding substantially lower growth rates of the EU, owing to the greater US demographic growth over the period.
3. Here we have simply used economic names for the terms resulting from the derivative with respect to time of equation 5.1.
4. See Saint-Paul (1996, 2004), for a discussion of the evolution of labour markets in Europe.
5. The employment rate is calculated as the share of the working population with a job in the total population of working age (between 15 and 54 years of age).
6. Indeed increasing the employment rate of workers aged 55–64 is, together with increasing the female employment rate, an explicit target of the Lisbon strategy (see sections 5.3 and 5.4).
7. The Sapir report was prepared by an Independent High-Level Study Group, established on the initiative of the president of the European Commission, to analyse the consequences of the two strategic economic goals set by the European Union for the decade ending in 2010: to implement the so-called Lisbon Agenda and to make a success of the pending enlargement by rapidly raising living standards in the new member states. The group was asked to review the entire system of EU economic policies and to propose a strategy for delivering faster growth together with stability and cohesion in the enlarged Union. The group made a series of recommendations:concerning the EU policies (microeconomic, macroeconomic and solidarity) and concerning its tools (economic governance and the EU budget). The report was released in July 2003 and then published as a book in 2004.
8. Indeed, between 1980 and 2000, the share of services in the EU economy increased by 13 percentage points, reaching 70 per cent of the GDP.
9. As pointed out by the EU Council in Lisbon in 2000: 'The EU is confronted with a quantum shift resulting from globalisation and the challenges of a new knowledge-driven economy. These changes are affecting every aspect of people's lives and require radical transformation of the European economy. The Union must shape these changes in a manner consistent with its values and concepts of society and also with a view to the forthcoming enlargement.'
10. The numerical evidence of this whole section (with the exception of subsection 5.3.4) is taken from Morrisson and Murtin (2004), which is the EU adaptation, for the period 1970–2000, of the Bourguignon and Morrisson (2002) study on income distribution. Subsection 5.3.4 borrows instead from Sapir *et al.* (2004).
11. See, for example, Hubbard (2002).

12. For example, a value of 2 means that the richest 5 per cent of the population commands twice the income of the poorest 20 per cent of the population. Since the share of the latter population is four times greater than the former, this means that, in per capita terms, the income of the richest is eight times the income of the poorest.
13. The Gini coefficient ranges from 0 to 1 and indicates the distribution of income across a population. A totally egalitarian population (where each 1 per cent of population commands 1 per cent of income) has a Gini coefficient of zero, while a totally non-egalitarian population (where one individual commands 100 per cent of income, and all the other individuals command no income at all) has a Gini coefficient of 1. Gini coefficients below 0.25 are usually regarded as 'low' (for example, Sweden with a Gini of 0.228, is regarded as a low inequality society), while coefficients around or above 0.5 are regarded as 'high' (for example, Turkey with a Gini of 0.49 is regarded as a high inequality society). Gini coefficients in the EU in 1998 ranged from 0.211 (Finland) to 0.361 (Portugal).
14. The Theil index is a much less intuitive measure of inequality than the Gini index. The fundamental idea behind the Theil index is that it provides a way to measure the discrepancy between the structure of the distribution of income across groups and the structure of the distribution of individuals across those same groups. Groups that have their 'fair share' of income contribute nothing to the Theil index. The Theil index has a potential range from zero to infinity, but it ranges generally between 0 and 1 (see Theil, 1967). A useful rule of thumb to interpret the Theil index is that, for a given distribution, when the Gini index is smaller than 0.5, the Theil index is likely to be smaller than the Gini index, while when the Gini is greater than 0.5 per cent the Theil index is likely to be greater than the Gini index. The reason why the Theil index is widely used in spite of its non-intuitive construction is that it can be decomposed in an additive way (see Conceição and Ferreira, 2000).
15. The most recent data on the world income distribution, however, reveal that, after a peak of inequality registered in the early 1990s, the trend seems to have been stabilising. See Crafts (2004) for a discussion.
16. Measuring the income distribution using the pre-tax income reveals how much inequality is generated by the market mechanism; comparing this result with a measure of income distribution which uses the post-tax income tells us how effective redistributive policies are in changing the income distribution originated by the market. The market pre-tax income includes income from labour and capital. Unemployed persons are included as persons with a zero income from the labour market. The post-tax, disposable income underestimates the actual size of redistribution, since transfers in kind are not considered.
17. The distribution of the EU population by EU income quantiles is obtained by ranking all citizens of the EU from the poorest to the richest and then looking at the ranked group: the poorest 20 per cent, those between 20 and 40 per cent, those between 40 per cent and 60 per cent and so on.
18. The convergence of income levels of a given country or region to the EU average corresponds to a reduction in across-countries (or regions) inequalities. Among several authors, European Commission (2001b) and (2004a) or Leonardi (2003) support the view of income convergence; others, such as Boldrin and Canova (2001), disagree.
19. Contrary to the entry of other new members, an eventual entry of Turkey into the enlarged EU would generate a further increase in inequality via an increase of both the within-country and the across-countries inequality, owing to the greater inequality (with respect to the EU) existing within Turkey.
20. The heads of state or government stated that an average economic growth rate of around 3 per cent in real terms should be a realistic prospect for the coming years, if the measures they had adopted in Lisbon were implemented against a sound macroeconomic background. See EU Council (2000).
21. The fiercest advocates of the Gothenburg addition to the Lisbon strategy would insist on the need to call the Lisbon strategy, the Lisbon–Gothenburg strategy and, more especially, on the need to replace the Lisbon-related concept of 'sustainable growth' with the concept

of 'sustainable development'. In their minds, the difference lies in the fact that the term 'development' is a comprehensive concept (including social and environmental aspects) enshrined in the Treaty (TEU, art. 2), while the term 'growth' is mainly an economic concept and does not reflect social or other considerations. To us, the debate is basically semantic. However, to avoid confusion, and to show our intimate conviction that raising potential growth is the largest challenge ahead of Europe and the greatest opportunity to preserve Europe's social *acquis*, we prefer to stick to the term 'sustainable growth'.

22. As an example of the need for a coordinated approach, we have seen in Chapter 4 that, in the period 2001–3, member states reacted to a sluggish economic situation with a considerable degree of budgetary easing, hoping to revive in this way private consumption, by far the main component of the GDP. And yet private consumption did not foster growth in any way. The reason lies precisely in the non-Keynesian effects analysed in the previous chapter: now that a culture of stability has been achieved and people are aware of the importance of having sound finances, budgetary easing generates a reduction in confidence, which spurs people to save rather than consume.
23. According to Radaelli (2003), the case for OMC as a new mode of supranational governance rests on six characteristics of the method in its ideal form: (1) new and more limited role of law, with no real demarcation between rule making and rule implementation; (2) new approach to problem solving which relies on iteration, cooperation and standard settings; (3) participation and power sharing which is higher than in traditional legislation; (4) inbuilt diversity and subsidiarity; (5) new ways to produce knowledge; (6) a new policy learning process. However the same Radaelli (2003) stresses that there is no guarantee that these characteristics of an ideal form of OMC are maintained in the practical implementation of the method.
24. For example, when the ECOFIN of 25 November 2003 suspended the application of the procedure of the SGP, the news made headlines in all the media for two days. An eventual suspension of the OMC would have probably gone unnoticed. See Buti and Giudice (2002) for a critical discussion of these aspects.
25. More recently, some commentators have identified this idea with the concept of 'Lisbonisation' of the Stability and Growth Pact.
26. And other related and now synchronised documents.
27. In other words, lacking mandatory enforcement mechanisms, a successful implementation of the open method of coordination requires that all member states be able to raise a political consensus adequate to pass the same kind of (controversial) reforms of their system of welfare state within a certain time horizon (2010, according to the Lisbon target). Implicitly this means that all EU governments, acting and to be elected in the next years, should have by and large the same agenda of economic reforms in their political programmes.
28. See Buti and Nava (2003) for a formal discussion of the relationships between the EU and the national budgets.
29. The extremely high productivity of Belgium and Italy is a statistical effect due to the extremely low (official) employment rate. Since productivity is measured as Y/L, the lower the (official) L, the higher Y/L appears to be.
30. Advocates of public expenditure on R&D state that it covers sectors of basic, non-immediately marketable research that the private sector might neglect, while advocates of private R&D spending point to the inefficient use of resources that public R&D expenditures might entail.
31. To ease the financial, and hence political, constraint, many have suggested adopting a sort of 'golden rule' for capital expenditures, excluding them from the balance of public finances. Its pros and cons have been discussed extensively in Chapter 4.
32. In that respect the adoption in 2003 of the European Patent Directive has been a major advance in making innovation more marketable.
33. For a more pessimist view on the ability of the EU to reach the Lisbon goals see, for example, Gros *et al.* (2003).
34. See, for example Deardorff, (2004).

6. The EU budget

6.1 INTRODUCTION

Chapters 1 to 5 of this book detailed how the different steps in the process of economic integration (Customs Union, Common Market, EMU) have contributed to the achievement of growth and stability, two of the three key goals in the EU model of economy and society. We have also clearly identified growth as the 'missing' element in the picture of the most recent years, and analysed some solutions to this problem (the Lisbon strategy).

From this chapter onwards, we shall concentrate instead on how specific EU policies foster (or hinder) the achievement of the two previously discussed objectives, together with the attainment of the third, related, EU goal, cohesion. In this regard, it is quite obvious to point out that, without its own money, the EU would have a hard time conducting any such policies.

In general, the financial flows to and from the EU and its member states, regions, private economic agents (citizens, firms, universities, local entities and so on) are varied and complex. Understanding their rationale (be it of an economic, social or political nature) and understanding the interinstitutional procedures through which these flows are authorised, is crucial to understanding any EU policy. The EU budget in particular is the tool with which money is collected and spent for EU policies.

Overall the EU budget has a very modest dimension. The maximum ceiling for the financing of the EU budget, politically agreed among member states, is 1.27 per cent of the EU GNP (which is equivalent to 1.24 per cent of the EU GNI[1]). In practice, the EU budget has always stayed well below that ceiling. In the years preceding the 2004 enlargement, it hovered at some 1 per cent of the EU GNI and then it started to increase progressively, being expected to reach some 1.15 per cent of the EU GNI by 2013.[2] Given that the sum of the EU national public expenditure is equal to about 40–45 per cent of the EU GNI, an EU budget equivalent to 1.15 per cent of the EU GNI thus translates into saying that the public expenditure implemented via the EU budget corresponds to only about 2.5 per cent of the sum of the public expenditure implemented through the national budgets.

In spite of its small size, however, the EU budget has a fundamental political importance, which is reflected in the cumbersome procedure needed for its adoption and in the interest it attracts across member states. The Council and the European Parliament, together, represent the so-called 'budgetary authority' and their agreement, following a specific Commission's proposal, is needed for budget adoption. In particular, the EU budget is subject to an **annual** adoption procedure, which fixes the actual annual authorized expenditure for the year in question for any given policy, while respecting at the same time the maximum thresholds set within a **multi-annual** budgetary framework. The multi-annual framework is a document, enshrined in legal texts, indicating over a seven-year horizon the EU budgetary guidelines for both revenues and expenditure. These legal texts are known as 'Financial Perspectives' (FP) for the expenditure and 'Own Resources Decision' (ORD) for the revenues, and their negotiation among the member states has often represented a critical point in the political life of the Union, as we shall discuss later.

In terms of revenues, the EU budget is financed either directly, from levies paid by individual taxpayers, or indirectly, via contributions paid by the member states. Either way, EU resident taxpayers are the ultimate resource for the money available to the EU budget. In terms of expenditures, most of the EU budget is spent in EU countries, with a non-negligible share (some 10–15 per cent of the total) for non-EU countries. The rationale for the EU budgetary expenditure lies in a 'double market failure'. Recalling the debate on the division of competences between the EU and the member states, analysed in Chapter 1, expenditure is (or should be) undertaken at the EU public level and financed by the EU budget when, *ceteris paribus,* both the private market (first failure) and the national public authorities via the national budgets (second failure) would provide a suboptimal amount.[3] Clearly, the looked-for outcome of such a simple economic rationale is, more often than not, entangled with political considerations, which do alter the jurisdiction level at which public expenditure is undertaken, as will be discussed in the next sections.

This chapter will analyse in turn both the annual and the multi-annual procedures of the EU budget (section 6.2), the structure of the expenditure of the EU budget (section 6.3) and the structure of its revenues (section 6.4). Finally it will look at the thorny issue of the net balances, that is, the political and economic rationale of the accounting difference between how much a country pays to and receives from the EU budget (section 6.5). Section 6.6 will then sum up and conclude with a discussion of the future prospects for the finances of an enlarged Europe.

6.2 THE EU BUDGET PROCEDURE

6.2.1 The Annual Procedure

The adoption procedure of any national public budget goes normally through five annual phases, which are the responsibility of different authorities. These five phases are present in any national public budget, and are the following:

1. budget proposal: government's responsibility;
2. budget adoption: Parliament's responsibility;
3. budget execution: government's responsibility;
4. budget technical control: responsibility of Court of Auditors (or similar national institutions);
5. budget political clearing: Parliament's responsibility.

These five phases and the division of powers across national institutions ensure both the democratic character of any expenditure (that is, any coin spent has been authorised and managed by direct citizens' representatives) and the correct functioning of the system of checks and balances, proper to any developed democracy. The translation of such a mechanism at the EU level is not immediately easy, owing to the specificity of the Commission and the Council. However, when one takes the 'standard' view that the Commission is the EU government and the European Parliament (EP) and the Council are the two parliamentary chambers,[4] the EU budget procedure resembles very closely the national procedure in terms of democratic legitimacy and power separation. This is the result of a 20-year long institutional evolution from the Treaty of Rome in 1957 to the Brussels Council of 1975.

Table 6.1 illustrates, for a typical year *N*, the five annual phases, the EU institution responsible for each phase and its timing. The budget **proposal** consists of the EU Commission making the necessary internal arbitrages across the spending bids of the different Commission departments responsible for the different EU policies. This phase usually takes the first four months of the year. According to article 272 of the TEC, the Commission should present its proposal before 1 September of the year $N-1$. However an agreement between the EU institutions lays down a more 'pragmatic' calendar according to which the EU Commission endeavours to present its proposal by 1 May of the year $N-1$.[5]

Once the proposal is ready, it is sent to the budgetary authorities (EP and Council) that proceed to its **adoption** via a mechanism of double reading, which starts from the Council and ends with the second reading of the

Table 6.1 The phases of the EU budget

Budgetary Phase	Institution responsible	Timing
Proposal	Commission	By end of April $N-1$
Adoption	EP and Council	By December $N-1$
Execution	Commission	During year N
Technical control	EU Court of Auditors	Around November $N+1$
Political clearing	EP	Around March $N+2$

Parliament, leading to the formal adoption of the EU budget. This normally happens during the December session of the European Parliament. As we argued in Chapter 1, before the establishment in 1988 of the financial perspectives it happened a few times that the EP and the Council could not reach an agreement by the end of the year, and therefore the budgetary year would start subject to the so-called 'rules of twelfth': in any month of the year N, the EU budget could not exceed a temporary limit of one-twelfth of the planned expenditure of the year $N-1$ (TEC, art. 273). Since the existence of a multi-annual framework, however, the EU budget has regularly been adopted by December of the year $N-1$, and it is very likely that this procedure will continue smoothly.

Formally speaking, budgetary expenditures are divided in two mutually exclusive sets: **compulsory expenditures** and **non-compulsory expenditures**. The former is the expenditure that originates directly from the Treaty, essentially only the Common Agricultural Policy (CAP) and the pensions for EU employees; the latter is the expenditure whose execution is a discretional act of the EU institutions (all the remaining expenditures, excluding CAP and pensions). The Council is the last authority for the compulsory expenditures, while the EP is the last authority for the non-compulsory expenditures. The rationale behind this division of responsibility lies in the fact that the expenditure originating directly from the provisions of the Treaty has already received parliamentary approval, at the national level, when the same Treaty was ratified in the national parliaments, while the remaining expenditure has not.[6] Therefore EP approval is necessary only for this second group of expenditures, while for the first group a Council approval is sufficient. Such a mechanism ensures that every single coin spent out of the EU budget has received, at a certain point of the procedure, a direct citizens' approval.

Once the budgetary authority adopts the budget, the EU Commission proceeds to its execution. According to TEC, art. 274, the 'EU Commission executes the budget under its own responsibility'. Strange as it may seem, this applies also to that expenditure which, although financed by the EU budget, is executed by member states, by regions and even by private agents.[7] This goes against both economic principles (responsibility should be at the level of the action concerned) and political principles (subsidiarity and level accountability, as discussed in Chapter 1). If expenditure is decentralised, responsibility should also follow. Authoritative voices have argued in this direction (see Sapir *et al.,* 2004), but the legislative evolution does not seem to move in this direction. Clearly the incentive for member states to assume responsibility for the expenditure they execute is very small, since they prefer the Commission to remain the sole body responsible for it, and thus respond before the EP.

The **technical control** of budgetary execution is the responsibility of the European Court of Auditors which replaced the old Control Commission in 1975. The creation of the European Court of Auditors (the only existing supranational Court of Auditors in the world) was an important step in the direction of rendering the EU budget a more communitarian rather than an intergovernmental tool.[8] To perform its controlling tasks, the EU Court of Auditors prepares every year a central document called the 'Annual Report of the Court of Auditors'. This report contains the Court's observations and the Commission's replies on virtually any item of expenditure and revenue of the EU budget. The mandate of the Court lays down that the Court should clearly indicate all cases of bad execution of expenditure or non-recovery of revenues, and that the Commission has the right to offer a written explanation for these occurrences. Once finalised, the report of the Court of Auditors is sent to the European Parliament together with the Court suggestion on whether to grant political clearing or not to the Commission for the budgetary execution.

The **political clearing**[9] of the EP to the Commission for its execution of the budget is probably one of the most significant acts of the EP during its period of activity. This means that the EP takes the political responsibility to guarantee to the EU citizens that the budget has been correctly executed according to what was agreed during the adoption phases. In order to grant political clearing, the EP bases itself on the technical control of the Court of Auditors (and on whatever other evidence it judges necessary), but it is not obliged to follow its recommendations. The EP has de facto complete freedom in assessing the political relevance of the Court's remarks. More than once, it happened that the EP had decided to grant political clearing to the Commission in spite of negative advice from the Court of Auditors. Such an outcome is possible and legitimate because the Court of Auditors' advice is of a technical nature, while the Parliament's clearing has a political meaning. In sum, by giving the EP the exclusive responsibility for granting political clearing of the EU budget, one ensures that the EU budget is entirely subject to the laws of democracy.

The EP votes the political clearing by qualified majority (50 per cent + 1 of the EP members) and, in case the political clearing is not given, it can cast, by overqualified majority (66 per cent + 1 of the EP members) a vote of non-confidence, which leads to the dismissal of the Commission. As recalled in Chapter 1, this is what almost happened in March 1999, when the Santer Commission resigned.[10]

6.2.2 The Multi-annual Procedure

The annual EU budget procedure serves to fix the annual budgetary expenditures and revenues within the boundaries set by the multi-annual framework provided by the **Financial Perspectives** (FP) on the expenditure side and the **Own Resources Decision** (ORD) on the revenue side. The FP indicates the maximum amount, per year and per type of expenditure, which the budgetary authority can allocate to any given policy. The ORD indicates the parameters that allow the EU to raise money from both citizens and governments in any given year.

Both FP and ORD are adopted by unanimity in the Council,[11] following a Commission's proposal and a unanimous political agreement reached by the European Council (heads of state and government). The unanimity rule transforms the negotiations on these multi-annual legal texts into arguably the fiercest negotiation among EU member states. However, once these texts are agreed, several years of budgetary peace are guaranteed. As recalled in Chapter 1, FP and ORD were introduced in the 1980s in response to a dire need for financial discipline and financial planning. Since then, they have been immensely successful in ensuring an orderly development of expenditures and revenues, which is a *conditio sine qua non* for any policy implementation.

However the unanimity rule in the Council for the adoption of both the FP and the ORD transfers the entire powers of the legislative process to the Council, and thus seizes the exclusive right of initiative from the Commission. Owing to the need to reach unanimity, in fact, the European Council (heads of state and government) will change whatever proposal the Commission submits into what has been unanimously agreed at the political level. Equally the EP is deprived of its role, since when the 'precious' unanimity is reached in the Council, often after hard fights and inefficient compromises among member states, there is little room for also taking the EP's advice into account. In addition, the unanimity rule does encourage a perverse focus among ministers on the net balance results of the planned expenditures ('how much of this comes to my country?'), while neglecting an evaluation in terms of EU added value ('what is the contribution of this expenditure to the EU added value?'). As we shall discuss in the next sections, the rationale of the net balance exercise is very questionable.

Such an approach, in addition, certainly does not allow estimating whether the rule of the double market failure is respected, that is, whether the expenditure at the EU level is justified or not. This leads to suboptimal decisions. On this ground, many observers share the view that the multi-annual FP should continue to be formulated as such, since they have certainly proved their worth, but the use of unanimity for their adoption should be discontinued. Unanimity for multi-annual spending decisions at the EU level is seen as the major obstacle to arriving at a genuine debate on the value added of the EU budget. This is a very significant and important drawback in the whole EU budgetary procedure, and it drives the system away from a community system. The European Convention drafting the EU Constitution immediately became aware of the issue and drafted in its original proposal a text that would have replaced unanimity with qualified majority voting for the FP from 2007 onward. Unfortunately, the ensuing intergovernmental conference watered down this disposition and thus it is likely that the unanimity rule for the voting of the Financial Perspectives will last at least until 2013.

In terms of the Own Resources Decision, the debate has become more intense in the last few years, and is centred on the issue of whether the Commission should be granted the power to levy a European tax to finance its expenditures. Some preliminary indications of the main issues under discussion will be presented in section 6.4 of this chapter.

6.2.3 Budgetary Principles

The EU budget is regulated by six budgetary principles, which are enshrined either in the Treaty or in the Financial Regulation. These budgetary principles are the principles of unity, universality, annuality, specification, unit of account and equilibrium.[12]

The principle of **unity** says that all expenditure and revenues must be found in the budget.[13] The principle of **universality**, which is the corollary of the principle of unity, states that no contraction between expenditure and revenues is possible, and that revenues should be assigned to the entire EU budget and cannot be earmarked for one or the other expenditure.[14]

The principle of **annuality** requires budget appropriations to relate to a specific financial year. In order to reconcile this requirement with the necessity of engaging in multi-annual operations, two types of expenditure are entered into the EU budget: commitment appropriations (the expenditure committed by the EU in a given year in respect to operations that can be carried out over a longer period of time) and payment appropriations (the expenditure effectively incurred by the EU in a given year in meeting the commitments of that and/or of previous years).

The principle of **specification** states that no commitment can be entered in the EU budget without a definite scope and purpose. Financial reserves constitute the only exception to this principle. Since 1999, the **unit of account** of the EU budget has been the Euro. Until 1958, the unit of account of the European Coal and Steel Community was the dollar. From 1958 to 1970, the budget was expressed in 'gold parity', in accordance with the Bretton Woods agreement (see Chapter 3). From 1970, following the demise of the Bretton Woods system, a search for a new unit of account started and from 1977 the ECU, the basket-currency acting as nominal anchor of the European Monetary System, was used.

These five budgetary principles are all rather self-explanatory: they respond to general principles of good financial management and they are common to most public budgets. However, the remaining one, the so-called 'principle of equilibrium', is neither self-evident nor common to public budgets.

The principle of **equilibrium** is enshrined in TEC, art. 268, which reads: 'the revenue and expenditure shown in the budget must be in balance'. This amounts to a total lack of intertemporal flexibility for the EU budget. The EU budget cannot be planned to run a deficit or a surplus and, during the year, any deficit or surplus should be corrected by an increase or reduction of the member states' contributions. On the one hand, it is of course understandable that, in the medium to long run, both the EU budget and the national budgets have to respect constraints in terms of deficits. On the other hand, while national budgets are subject to the medium-term target of 'close to balance or in surplus' of the Stability and Growth Pact, the EU budget is subject to a much stricter requirement. The difference between the two conditions boils down to the fact that the EU budget must always be balanced in each and every year, while national budgets have to be broadly balanced over the cycle, thus allowing for deficits (up to 3 per cent of the GDP) to appear in recession years and surpluses in boom years (Buti and Nava, 2003). Recalling our discussion in Chapter 4, it is worth noting that, in the context of the European Monetary Union, flexibility at the lower level (national budgets), and no flexibility at all at the higher level (EU budget), amounts to an institutional design atypical of a federalist setting and potentially destabilising. In the absence of enforceable constraints, the national authorities have a free-riding incentive in the management of their fiscal policy, while the budgetary rigidities at the EU level prevent the use of the budget as a form of centralised fiscal policy.

Thus an economic rationale for the very strict requirement of the budgetary equilibrium principle can hardly be found. This requirement is the result of a politically conscious choice of limiting the financial autonomy of the EU. In other words, the Council wanted to prevent the EU institutions from misusing a non-balanced budget as an additional budgetary resource (that is, the EU could borrow to spend instead of levying resources from member states). The result is an excessive and unnecessary rigidity of the EU budget, which limits the growth potential of the EU as a whole.

6.2.4 The Future of the EU Budget Procedure

The adoption procedures of the EU budget have evolved considerably since the first budget of the European Communities. In some 25 years, the EU budget transformed itself from a simple 'plan of expenditure' financed by governments (like any other international organization, such as the United Nations, IMF, the World Bank and the like) to a sort of federal budget. Now every coin spent from and received by the EU budget is first authorized and then certified by EU citizens, and power separation is enforced across the EU institutions.

However the Council's unanimity required to set the multi-annual framework, that is the upper limits of the annual expenditure and revenues, prevents full participation in the process of both the EP and the Commission. This considerably reduces the democratic character of the EU budget. Unfortunately, in spite of several calls for moving away from unanimity to qualified majority voting, and in spite of an agreement in principle at the EU level, no major advance has been made.

We feel that such a myopic attitude, in a Union of 25 members characterised by unprecedented disparities and thus different views on the role of the EU expenditures, dramatically limits the possibilities of using the EU budget in a truly European value-adding perspective.

6.3 THE STRUCTURE OF EXPENDITURES

The absence of a multi-annual programming plan seriously hampered until 1988 the development of the EU policies in domains other than the Common Agricultural Policy (CAP, for details see Chapter 7). In the 1960s to 1980s the CAP was by far the most dominant policy, accounting in some years for about 80 per cent of the EU budget. Being the only non-cofinanced expenditure (that is, financed only at the EU level without accompanying financing from the national level), the CAP could in fact be developed in the absence of multi-annual programming, albeit at the risk of losing control of its costs. Other expenditures, and in particular structural expenditures meant to reinforce investments in some regions or countries (for details see Chapter 8), needing national co-financing could only be developed under a multi-annual programming, so as to guarantee financial solidity to the national and regional counterparts.

The first Financial Perspectives (known as Delors I) were introduced for the period 1988–92. They were followed by those for the period 1993–9 (Delors II), then 2000–2006 (Agenda 2000) and finally 2007–13. One could easily read the sequence of FP as repeated attempts of the EU to reduce the share of CAP expenditure in favour of other policies. FP have been decisive in accompanying this move, but have introduced a rigidity in the EU budget which we now consider, at least in some respects, excessive. Indeed the EU budget lacks the flexibility to move money not only horizontally (that is, across different years), but also vertically (the same year across budgetary items). Hence the procedure to reallocate funds from one to the other budgetary item is basically as cumbersome as the procedure to establish the FP.

This political choice in favour of stability at the expense of flexibility is not too different from the one characterising the EMU. In Chapter 4 we have seen that, in the run up to, and in the early years of the EMU, the trade-off between stability and flexibility of national finances was clearly and firmly resolved in favour of the former. Given the difficulties that such an approach was causing, we have seen that as early as 2002, the Commission had moved in the direction of taking flexibility into account (European Commission, 2002c) by accepting that countries with sound public finances (low stock of public debt, low implicit liabilities) could run small structural deficits without violating the requirements of the Stability and Growth Pact, as discussed in Chapter 4. Many have argued that there is ground for a similar move to be undertaken in the EU public finances (for example, Buti and Nava, 2003), a form of flexibility that, as discussed above, would also be beneficial for the management of the EMU.

In spite of the need to improve the FP, it is beyond any reasonable doubt that the same FPs have been the tool by which the economic policy of the EU has developed. The so-called **Delors I Financial Perspectives** (see European Commission, 1987) agreed for the period 1988–92 are unanimously considered a masterpiece of President Delors' stewardship of the European Commission. This financial package was presented to member states as 'the means for their ambitions', leading to the establishment of the EU single market analysed in Chapter 3. Intellectually the Delors I package relied also on the very influential Padoa-Schioppa report (see Padoa-Schioppa *et al.*, 1987) that, as we have discussed, highlighted cohesion as a challenge to meet in order to achieve the completion of the single market. The Delors I package thus establishes the structural policy and endows it, from its inception, with a considerable amount of money and a significant share of the budget. In addition to that, the Delors I package doubles the funds allocated to internal policies (such as education and training, research and so on). In doing so, the Delors I package represents the very first and decisive move away from agricultural expenditure towards other policy fields. In 1988, CAP amounted to 60 per cent, structural expenditure to 17 per cent and research to 2.5 per cent of the EU budget, while in 1992 the same percentages were respectively 56 per cent, 25 per cent and 4.5 per cent.

With the Delors I FP (Table 6.2), the maximum ceiling of the budget was increased to 1.2 per cent of the EU GNP. Obviously an increase in the ceiling does not automatically entail an increase of actual expenditure by the same proportion. Any budget foresees a margin between the theoretical ceiling and the planned expenditure (payments appropriations). Furthermore the actual expenditure is always lower than the payments appropriations, because of the unspent amounts (which, generally, are uncommon in the CAP and more common under other headings).

The **Delors II Financial Perspectives** (Table 6.3; see European Commission, 1992), agreed for the period 1993–9, continued and reinforced this trend. By 1999, CAP had dropped to 47 per cent of the EU budget, structural expenditure had risen to 36 per cent, internal policy to 6 per cent and external expenditure had achieved a significant share of 7 per cent.[15] The Delors II package was the budgetary response to two major political events: the desire of the existing EU countries to achieve in the medium term the Economic and Monetary Union, and the desire of the Eastern European countries to undertake the necessary reforms of their economy and their political systems so as to be able, in the medium term, to join the EU.

As for the first issue, in a bid to compensate partially the short-term effects of fiscal discipline, imposed by the Maastricht Treaty (which entered into force in 1993), the Delors II established the Cohesion Fund in favour of the four poorest countries of the EU. At the same time, the maximum ceiling of the EU budget was raised from 1.2 per cent to 1.27 per cent of the EU GNP (or 1.24 per cent of EU GNI). However this budget ceiling was significantly lower than the 1.37 per cent originally required by Delors. As for the second issue, the Delors II package laid down substantial financial assistance to the then candidate countries of Eastern Europe in support of their efforts for joining the EU. Pre-enlargement expenditure was essentially directed at improving the administrative capacity of the candidate countries. This proved very useful for both the candidate countries and the EU-15, since it

Table 6.2 Delors I financial perspective, 1988–1992 (Euro millions, 1988 prices)

	1988	1989	1990	1991	1992
Appropriations for commitments					
1. EAGGF Guarantee Section	27 500	27 700	28 700	29 000	29 600
2. Structural Funds	7 790	9 200	10 600	12 100	13 450
3. Policies with multi-annual allocations	1 210	1 650	1 900	2 150	2 400
4. Other policies	2 103	2 385	2 500	2 700	2 800
5. Repayments and administration	5 700	4 950	4 500	4 000	3 550
6. Monetary reserve	1 000	1 000	1 000	1 000	1 000
Total	***45 303***	***46 885***	***48 900***	***50 950***	***52 800***
of which:					
– compulsory expenditure	33 698	32 607	32 810	32 980	33 400
– non-compulsory expenditure	11 605	14 278	16 090	17 970	19 400
Appropriation for payments	***43 779***	***45 300***	***46 900***	***48 600***	***50 100***
of which:					
– compulsory expenditure	33 640	32 604	32 740	32 910	33 110
– non-compulsory expenditure	10 139	12 696	14 160	15 690	16 990
Appropriations for payments as % of GNP	1.12	1.14	1.15	1.16	1.17
Own resources ceiling as % of GNP	1.15	1.17	1.18	1.19	1.20

Source: Interinstitutional Agreement (OJ C 331, 7.12.1993).

helped to forge ties with these countries, facilitating their forthcoming adoption of the *acquis communautaire*, as discussed in Chapter 3.

In 1999, at the time of negotiations for the new budgetary framework for the period 2000–2006, many had expected that, given the forthcoming eastern enlargement, a major change to the budget, if not an increase of the EU budget itself, was to be proposed. The EU priorities, needs and the same EU ability and willingness to enter into different fields of policy had significantly changed since the early and mid-1990s, and were likely to change again during the period 2000–2006. As discussed in Chapter 3, the

Table 6.3 Delors II financial perspective, 1993–9 (EUR 12), (Euro millions, 1992 prices)

	1993	1994	1995	1996	1997	1998	1999
Appropriations for commitments							
1. Common agricultural policy	35 230	35 095	35 722	36 364	37 023	37 697	39 389
2. Structural Funds	21 277	21 885	23 480	24 990	26 526	28 240	30 000
Structural fund	19 777	20 135	21 480	22 740	24 026	25 690	27 400
Cohesion fund	1 500	1 750	2 000	2 250	2 500	2 550	2 600
3. Internal policies	3 940	4 084	4 323	4 520	4 710	4 910	5 100
4. External action	3 950	4 000	4 280	4 560	4 830	5 180	5 600
5. Administrative expenditure	3 280	3 380	3 580	3 690	3 800	3 850	3 900
6. Reserve	1 500	1 500	1 100	1 100	1 100	1 100	1 100
Monetary reserve	1 000	1 000	500	500	500	500	500
External action:							
loan guarantees	300	300	300	300	300	300	300
emergency aid	200	200	300	300	300	300	300
Commitment appropriations, total	***69 177***	***69 944***	***72 485***	***75 224***	***77 989***	***80 977***	***84 089***
Payment appropriations, total	***65 908***	***67 036***	***69 150***	***71 290***	***74 491***	***77 249***	***80 114***
	1.2	1.19	1.20	1.21	1.23	1.25	1.26
Appropriations for payments as % of GNP	0	0.01	0.01	0.01	0.01	0.01	0.01
Own resources ceiling (% of GNP)	1.2	1.20	1.21	1.22	1.24	1.26	1.27

Source: Interinstitutional Agreement (OJ L 185, 15.7.1998).

eastern enlargement constituted, from a financial standpoint, a serious commitment, given the wide disparities in the level of wealth between the candidate countries and the incumbent member states.

The Santer Commission, in its document for the 2000–2006 FP known as **'Agenda 2000'**, proposed three substantial reforms (see European Commission, 1997): a CAP reform, which however was only partially undertaken, not having won the Council's approval on its fundamental element, the CAP co-financing (see Chapter 7); a substantial simplification and concentration of the structural expenditures in the poorest areas of the EU (see Chapter 8); and a strengthening of the pre-accession strategy for the pending enlargement, which was then supposed to take place in 2002 and to be limited to six countries (Estonia, Poland, Czech Republic, Hungary, Slovenia, Cyprus).[16] As for the structure of the FP, however, the Santer Commission preferred to continue in the line of the Delors packages, instead of proposing major revisions. Marginal modification of an existing structure is certainly the path of least resistance and, arguably, it has the merit of facilitating budgetary negotiations. However, as time passes, it certainly drives the EU budget away from its purposes. In fact, applying the same budgetary structure and logic for 20 years has transformed the EU budget into a stratification of different deals and side-payments, rather than a coherent set of measures aimed at pursuing EU objectives. This effect, compounded by the unanimity procedure referred to above, led to an exacerbation of the net balance logic and a complete sidelining of the EU added value logic.

By the end of this planning period, therefore, the budget was supposed (still) to spend 43 per cent on CAP, 36 per cent on structural expenditure, 5 per cent on external expenditure and 8 per cent on research, this time for the whole of EU-25. In spite of all the changes in terms of number of countries and timing of the enlargement, policies and so on, the total amount of the budget agreed for the EU-25 by the Council in June 2004 was very similar to the one agreed by the Council in March 1999, and not dramatically dissimilar, in terms of overall relevance of the different chapters of expenditure, from the first 1988 FP.

And yet, notwithstanding this slow change in the structure of the EU budget, when looking over a long period of time, one can certainly appreciate some signs of evolution. In particular the gap between the CAP and the structural expenditure to foster intra-EU convergence has been substantially reduced. Increased external expenditures for the enlargement process and more spending on research and internal policy to favour a growth agenda also marked the evolution of community expenditure over time, as appears clearly from the Table 6.5 below, which details the budgetary chapters of the main policies across the different FP.[17]

Table 6.4 Agenda 2000 Financial Perspectives, 2000–2006 (EU-25), (Euro millions, 1999 prices)

Millions Euros (1999 prices) commitment appropriations	2000
1. Agriculture	**40 920**
CAP (excluding rural development)	36 620
Rural development	4 300
2. Structural actions	**32 045**
Structural funds	29 430
Cohesion fund	2 615
3. Internal policies	**5 930**
4. External policies	**4 550**
5. Administration	**4 560**
6. Reserves	**900**
Monetary reserve	500
Emergency aid reserve	200
Guarantee reserve	200
7. Pre-accession strategy	**3 120**
Agriculture	520
Pre-accession structural instrument	1 040
PHARE (applicant countries)	1 560
8. Compensations	
Total appropriations for commitments	**91 995**
Total appropriations for payments	**89 590**
Appropriations for payments as % of GNI (ESA 95)	1.07
Margin for unforeseen expenditure (%)	0.17
Own resources ceiling as % of GNI (ESA 95)	**1.24**

Source: OJ L 147, 14.7.2003.

Table 6.5 A comparison of the Financial Perspectives over time

	Delors I (1988)	Delors I (1992)	Delors II (1999)	Agenda 2000 (2006)
CAP	60%	56%	47%	43%
Structural expenditure	17%	25%	36%	36%
Internal policy	2.5%	4.5%	6%	8%
External expenditure	3.6%	3.7%	7%	5%

2001	2002	2003	2004	2005	2006
42 800	**43 900**	**43 770**	**44 657**	**44 657**	**45 807**
38 480	39 570	39 430	38 737	39 602	39 612
4 320	4 330	4 340	5 920	6 075	6 195
31 455	**30 865**	**30 285**	**35 665**	**36 502**	**37 940**
28840	28250	27 670	30 533	31 835	32 608
2 615	2 615	2 615	5 132	4 667	5332
6 040	**6 150**	**6 260**	**7 877**	**8 098**	**8 212**
4 560	**4 570**	**4 580**	**4 590**	**4 600**	**4 610**
4 600	**4 700**	**4 800**	**5 403**	**5 558**	**5 712**
900	**650**	**400**	**400**	**400**	**400**
500	250	0	0	0	0
200	200	200	200	200	200
200	200	200	200	200	200
3.120	**3.120**	**3.120**	**3.120**	**3.120**	**3.120**
520	520	520			
1.040	1.040	1.040			
1.560	1.560	1.560			
			1 273	1173	940
93 385	**100 255**	**102 035**	**102 985**	**105 128**	**106 741**
91 070	**98 270**	**101 450**	**100 800**	**101 600**	**103 840**
1.08	1.11	1.10	1.08	1.06	1.0
0.16	0.13	0.14	0.16	0.18	0.18
1.24	**1.24**	**1.24**	**1.24**	**1.24**	**1.24**

6.3.1 Towards the 2007–13 Financial Perspectives

In the most recent years, in spite of the improvement with respect to the past, the EU budget has attracted many criticisms. The main reproach addressed to the EU budget relates to its ineffectiveness in supporting the EU agenda of reforms. The budget and the Lisbon Agenda are in fact still perceived as two parallel but disconnected projects, in spite of the potentially high contribution that the EU budget could make to growth.

On these issues, the EU Commission had initiated in February 2003 a thorough process of revision of the EU priorities and of its budgetary orientations, with a view to presenting, by February 2004, a budgetary package for the period 2007 onward. In July 2003, in the middle of that process, came the already mentioned **Sapir report** (Sapir *et al.*, 2004), which acted (also) in this debate as a powerful stimulus. The report's recommendations relating to the EU budget, in particular, started with a forceful statement: 'As it stands today, the EU budget is an historical relic.'[18] The report continued by claiming that 'if the Union is serious and determined to achieve growth and solidarity in an enlarged Europe, the EU budgetary envelope should move away from the present inertia, which allows for only minor tinkering, and be radically restructured'. In its recommendations, the same report called for 'A radical restructuring of the EU budget to support the growth agenda proposed by this Report in line with the Lisbon objectives. The budget should be organised into three funds: 1) a fund to promote growth through expenditure for R&D, education and training, and infrastructure; 2) a convergence fund to help low-income countries catch up; 3) a fund to support economic restructuring. Meeting the growth agenda implies, if the overall size of the budget remains the same, a sharp reduction in EU agricultural expenditure.'

The report also gave an illustration (not a recommendation) of what a possible budget could look like, reported in Table 6.6. It assumed that, in the post-2007 period, the budget for economic and social activities (which excludes external and administrative expenditure) could be kept at 1 per cent of the EU GDP in line with the 2000–2006 expenditure. Hence 45 per cent

Table 6.6 The Sapir report's proposal for the budget in the post-2007 financial period

Expenditure	% of EU GDP
Growth	**0.45**
of which:	
R&D	0.25
Education & Training	0.075
Infrastructure	0.125
Convergence	**0.35**
of which:	
to new member states	0.20
to old member states	0.10
phasing out for regions	0.05
Restructuring	**0.20**
of which:	
for displaced workers	0.05
for agriculture	0.05
phasing out for agriculture	0.10
Total economic and social activities	**1.00**

Source: Sapir *et al.* (2004).

of the budget would be assigned to the growth funds, 35 per cent of the budget to the convergence funds (mainly for the poorest countries and regions in Europe) and the remaining 20 per cent for a restructuring fund (half of this fund, 10 per cent of the total budget, would be devoted to the restructuring of agriculture). With respect to the present situation, the Sapir report's proposal would increase the involvement of the EU budget in enhancing growth and in solidarity expenditure, and reduce drastically its involvement in agricultural expenditure.

The Commission proposal, made public on 10 February 2004 (see European Commission, 2004e and Table 6.7), responds to a number of criticisms and, in some respects, it can be seen as having taken on board many of the suggestions of the Sapir report. First, and most importantly, the Commission moved radically away from proposing the usual set of marginal modifications to the 1988 budgetary structure. The 2004 Commission's proposal includes an altogether new structure of the EU budget, in a clear (and brave) bid finally to use the EU budget as a tool to meet the EU political goals. Indeed the new FP revolve around the three overriding EU priorities: to foster sustainable growth, to develop European citizenship and to improve the external dimension of Europe (see European Commission, 2002d).

Sustainable growth is the central concept of the Lisbon strategy. As argued in Chapter 5, it points to a model of economic growth that is sustainable, both socially and environmentally, in the long run. The financial translation of the Lisbon objective therefore calls for at least three areas of intervention:

1. pursuing the reforms instrumental to the completion of the single market, thus fostering EU competitiveness. This is dealt with under the new heading 1a, which is certainly the single largest change of the Commission's approach. Expenditure for competitiveness and growth, which includes research expenditure, education, trans-European networks and so on, should increase in monetary terms by about three times from 2006 to 2013, and as a share of the EU budget it should go from 8 per cent to 16 per cent. This reflects the Commission's strong will to transform the EU budget into an instrument for achieving the Lisbon objectives;
2. additional investment in the poorest regions or countries to support and speed up their economic convergence towards the EU average. As we have argued in Chapter 5, the across-countries inequality, measured by the standard inequality indicators, will be as large as ever in the post-enlargement EU and, for the first time in history, total EU inequality will be larger than total US inequality. Persistent and large inequalities are not part of a sustainable EU model of society: major

Table 6.7 New Financial Perspectives, 2007–13 (EU-25), (Euro millions, 2004 prices)

Commitment appropriations	2006[a]	2007	2008	2009	2010	2011	2012	2013	
1. Sustainable growth	**47.582**	**59.675**	**62.795**	**65.800**	**68.235**	**70.660**	**73.715**	**76.785**	
1a. Competitiveness for growth and employment	8.791	12.105	14.390	16.680	18.965	21.250	23.540	25.825	
1b. Cohesion for growth and employment[b]	38.791	47.570	48.405	49.120	49.270	49.410	50.175	50.960	
2. Preservation and management of natural resources	**56.015**	**57.180**	**57.900**	**58.115**	**57.980**	**57.850**	**57.825**	**57.805**	
of which: agriculture, market-related expenditure and direct payments	43.735	43.500	43.673	43.354	43.034	42.714	42.506	42.293	
3. Citizenship, freedom, security and justice	**1.381**	**1.630**	**2.015**	**2.330**	**2.645**	**2.970**	**3.295**	**3.620**	
4. The EU as a global partner[c]	**11.232**	**11.400**	**12.175**	**12.945**	**13.720**	**14.495**	**15.115**	**15.740**	
5. Administration[d]	**3.436**	**3.675**	**3.815**	**3.950**	**4.090**	**4.225**	**4.365**	**4.500**	
Compensations	1.041								
Total appropriations for commitments	***120.688***	***133.560***	***138.700***	***143.140***	***146.670***	***150.200***	***154.315***	***158.450***	
Total appropriations for payments[b c]	***114.740***	***124.600***	***136.500***	***127.700***	***126.000***	***132.400***	***138.400***	***143.100***	***Average***
Appropriations for payments as a percentage of GNI	1.09	1.15	1.23	1.12	1.08	1.11	1.14	1.15	1.14
Margin available (%)	0.15	0.09	0.01	0.12	0.16	0.13	0.10	0.09	0.10
Own resources ceiling as a percentage of GNI (%)	1.24	1.24	1.24	1.24	1.24	1.24	1.24	1.24	1.24

Notes:
[a] 2006 expenditure under the current financial perspective has been broken down according to the proposed new nomenclature for reference and to facilitate comparisons.
[b] Includes expenditure for the Solidarity Fund (€1 billion in 2004 at current prices) as from 2006. However corresponding payments are calculated only as from 2007.
[c] The integration of EDF in the EU budget is assumed to take effect in 2008. Commitments for 2006 and 2007 are included only for comparison purposes. Payments on commitments before 2008 are not taken into account in the payment figures.
[d] Includes administrative expenditure for institutions other than the Commission, pensions and European schools. Commission administrative expenditure is integrated in the first four expenditure headings.

efforts are therefore required by the EU to close these gaps. This expenditure is dealt with under the new heading 1b;

3. preserving and managing natural resources to ensure both the economic viability of agriculture and its environmentally friendly character. The Common Agricultural Policy constitutes the largest part of this area of intervention, which is covered by heading 2 of the new 2007–13 FP. The Commission's proposal for the CAP was dictated by the overall financial dimension of the CAP agreed upon by unanimity by the Council in October 2002, well in advance of the Commission's proposal of February 2004. The agreement, as we will see in Chapter 7, fixes the agricultural expenditures for the period 2007–13 at the levels agreed in Agenda 2000 (more precisely, the levels foreseen in 2006 plus a nominal adjustment). In other words, the Commission did not really have any margin to manoeuvre in the final discussion on the size of the CAP and had to accept the Council's decision as a constraint.[19] Fortunately, however, the Council's decision lays down substantial stability of the CAP expenditure in monetary terms, which translates into a significant reduction of its share in the EU budget (from about 35 per cent in 2006 to less than 27 per cent in 2013).

The development of a space for European citizenship is a recurrent demand coming from EU citizens. Through the integration of the EU Charter of Fundamental Rights, the Union will have a legal obligation to ensure that fundamental rights are not just respected, but actively promoted as well. That translates into the completion of a large EU area where fundamental freedoms are guaranteed, where justice rules, where security and safety are maintained and where access to basic public goods is preserved. In this context, the EU is also developing a common asylum policy and a common policy on immigration. Furthermore the ferocious terrorist attacks on the USA and the EU during the first part of the present decade have generated a climate of fear and uncertainty throughout the EU and in general in the Western world. Clearly these challenges require common actions on different policy areas. These objectives find their financial translation in heading 3 of the FP, which by 2013 will triple (to €3.6 billion) with respect to the Agenda 2000 FP the funds available for this purpose.

Since 1989, the EU external dimension has been closely linked to the approaching enlargement to the eastern and Mediterranean countries. Once enlargement is completed, the EU external dimension changes significantly, from an enlargement perspective to a perspective of EU relations with the rest of the world, as discussed in detail in Chapter 10 of the book. This expenditure is financed as under heading 4, and bound to increase by 40 per cent in the new FP.

Each of the four headings includes the part of the administrative expenditure that can be linked directly to the development of the policies financed under the same heading. On the contrary, the part of the administrative expenditure that cannot be directly linked to one of the headings (such as EU civil servants' pensions) is to be found under heading 5.

Table 6.8 compares the Agenda 2000 situation with the current Commission's proposal for the period 2007–13 and with the Sapir report's suggestions for the EU budget. It emerges quite evidently that the main difference between the Sapir report and the Commission's proposal lies in the size of agricultural expenditure: while the former advocated a major reduction, the Commission was forced to retain the October 2002 Council agreement, as discussed above.

At this stage, only the Commission proposal is on the table, and decisions are expected by June 2006. It is fair to say that this proposal is a step in the right direction of refocusing the EU budget to support the EU objectives and specifically the Lisbon Agenda. In addition, the Commission's proposal respects each year the maximum budgetary ceiling of 1.24 per cent of EU GNI, fixing yearly expenditures at no more than 1.15 per cent of the EU GNI. Six countries (Germany, France, Netherlands, Austria, Sweden and Great Britain) have however requested that the overall ceiling

Table 6.8 A comparison of the most recent proposals on the future FP

Commitments appropriations	Agenda 2000 (2006)	Commission proposal (2007)	Commission proposal (2013)	Sapir report (2013)
Heading 1				
Sustainable growth, of which:				
growth	0.08	0.11	0.21	0.45
cohesion	0.37	0.44	0.41	0.35
Heading 2				
Preservation and management of natural resources	0.53	0.53	0.46	0.15
Heading 3				
Citizenship, freedom, security and justice	0.01	0.02	0.03	0.05
Heading 4				
External dimension	0.09	0.09	0.1	No position

Note: Figures indicate percentage of EU GNP/GNI.

of total expenditure should not exceed 1 per cent of the GNI. The latter figure does not seem to have a magnitude able to reflect an analysis of the EU and national needs, rather it seems a statement of principle. It is clear to us that, if the EU expenditure were reduced to a figure lower than 1 per cent, the EU goals also would need to be downgraded, but the six-country proposal does not seem to have a clear answer to that problem. However, even if at this stage it is very difficult to foresee the final outcome of the negotiations, it is very unlikely that the position of these six countries will be shared by the remaining 19 countries. Given the need to find unanimity, the risk of going back to the old net balance logic is therefore very high. However the Council would be making a very big political error if it were to conduct its negotiations according to such logic. That would constitute a serious backtracking with respect to the initial Commission's proposal and the current needs and goals of the EU policies.

The formal adoption by the Council and the EP, according to the rules detailed in section 6.2.2, was initially foreseen during the first semester of 2005.[20]

The first budgetary negotiations on the new financial perspectives, in June 2005, failed in spite of the concessions being made by the new member states. Once again, this round of negotiation has been dominated by the *juste retour* logic (see section 6.5) and inserted in a strictly inter-governative environment, which has not allowed the dimension of the EU added value of the expenditure to be considered. Depending on each one's political and national allegiance, the burden of failure was put either on the UK government, for its defence of the UK rebate (see section 6.4) or on the French one, for its defence of the Common Agricultural Policy (see Chapter 7). In reality this failed round of negotiations has just proven once more the inextricable link between the CAP and UK rebate, and the need to solve both issues during the same negotiations. Neither can be solved in isolation from the other. For this purpose, recall that the Sapir report, extensively quoted by several heads of state and government, argued that neither such a large CAP at the EU level nor the UK rebate are compatible with a 'Lisbon friendly' budget (see Chapter 5), especially if a tight budget constraint (slightly more than 1 per cent of the EU GDP) has to be respected. EU politicians need to have the courage to choose which budget they want: in particular, they should realise the need for having a budget more consistent with the Lisbon objectives.

At the time of going to press, it is very difficult to forecast how and when negotiations will end. At any rate, we believe that another compromise built on marginal adjustments of the previous seven-year budgetary plan may be a politically viable option. However, it is not what Europe needs: that is, a serious rethinking of how to integrate the EU budget in its policies and objectives.

6.4 REVENUES

The history of the revenue side of the EU budget can be read as a continuous attempt to marry, in the EU budget, financial autonomy and sufficiency of resources. The first EU budgets of the European Coal and Steel Community (ECSC) contained a very modern 'communitarian' element as a reflection of the 'communitarian' nature of the ECSC itself. ECSC expenditure (divided between administrative and operative expenditure) was financed through a tax-based resource (a levy on steel production). This levy on steel production guaranteed complete financial independence to the ECSC from its underlying member states, and required no other element to close the budget.

Unfortunately financing via direct levies did not find its way into the first EC budgets which instead were financed in a totally intergovernmental way, not dissimilar from the way that other international institutions were financed. The Treaty of Rome laid down that the EU budget should be fully financed via direct contributions from member states according to fixed shares (article 200, now repealed). There was no indication of any levying capacity and therefore of any financial autonomy of the EC from its member states.[21] Only in subsequent years did the EU budget move away from a model based on national transfers to a model based on the EU's own resources (section 6.4.1) and other revenues (6.4.2).

6.4.1 The EU's Own Resources

The current structure of the EU's own resources has been shaped by the Luxembourg Council of April 1970. This Council brought quite a dramatic change to the revenue side of the EU budget by establishing three types of resources and therefore granting financial autonomy to the EU budget. In particular the Council established as resources:[22] (a) agricultural and sugar levies (levied since 1971), (b) custom duties (progressively introduced during 1971–5), (c) the Value Added Tax (VAT) resource (fully implemented with the VAT sixth Directive of 1978).

This structure was left unchanged until 1984, when the Fontainebleau Council introduced the UK correction (or rebate), which is, formally speaking, a reduction of the contribution of the UK to the EU. Then, in 1988, the Delors I FP introduced a fourth resource, which is known as the GNP resource (now GNI resource, see note 1). The current structure is therefore the result of the three resources introduced by the 1975 Luxembourg Council, plus the 1984 UK rebate and the 1988 GNP/GNI resource. Below we shall analyse in turn the four EU resources as well as the UK rebate.

Agricultural levies and custom duties (the first and the second EU own resources) are commonly referred to as **traditional own resources** (TORs). They are the first and most complete expression of the financial autonomy of the EU. TORs are essentially represented by the revenues of the Common External Tariff imposed by the EU Customs Union on imported goods (see Chapter 2), with the exception of the sugar production and stocking levy (representing some 7–8 per cent of the total TORs, or only about 1.2 per cent of the total EU budget), which is levied on the EU sugar industry. In particular the custom duties are withheld by national customs authorities and transferred directly (after deduction of a collection fee for the member state of collection) to the EU coffers without any mediation of the national treasuries. Goods entering and paying duties in a country gain free circulation in all of the EU. The same logic of the import duties applies to the agricultural levies, which are duties levied on agricultural products for which no national mediation exists.

In the 1970s and 1980s, TORs used to represent about 50 per cent of the EU budget revenues; they have been steadily decreasing since then and by 2013 they will represent no more than 10 per cent of the EU budget revenues. Their decrease is due to two reasons: on the one hand, the increase in the absolute size of the EU budget; on the other hand, the reduction of

BOX 6.1 THE DISTRIBUTION OF THE CUSTOMS REVENUES ACROSS THE EU

The distribution across countries of TORs more accurately reflects the development of import–export facilities in each country than the economic weight of each country or its population. In other words, the internal market leads to a certain specialisation of countries, with some specialising in trade and others in manufacturing. For example, the custom duties paid at the ports of entry of Belgium and Netherlands (26 million people with a cumulated GDP of about 8 per cent of the EU total) are equal to the custom duties paid at the entry ports of Italy and France (120 million inhabitants with a cumulated GDP of about 30 per cent of the EU total). This is due to the fact of course that many of the goods entering Belgium and Netherlands find their final consumer in other EU countries. This effect, known as the 'Rotterdam effect' or 'Gateway effect', shows the extent of the production integration across EU countries and, as we shall explain in section 6.5, it makes it virtually impossible to allocate, across EU countries, the burden of the TORs.

the EU tariffs as the result of a number of trade liberalisation measures via general trade agreements such as GATT (General Agreement on Tariffs and Trade, see Chapter 10 for more details) and/or via agreements in given industries such as ITA.[23] Even if a lower tariff rate does increase the volume of imported products, in fact, the increase (via the elasticity of imported goods to custom rates) is not so great as to prevent a decrease in the total amount of duties collected.

The **VAT resource** was introduced progressively: it is computed by applying a common EU VAT rate to a VAT base commonly calculated across each EU country. If the calculated VAT base exceeds 50 per cent of the country's GNP, the common VAT rate is applied to 50 per cent of the GNP. The common VAT rate, applied to the common VAT base, is at present 0.5 per cent.[24] The VAT base is common across the EU since the implementation of the sixth and the ninth VAT Directives. However a few national exceptions still exist, which apply differently to different member states. In order to ensure that these exceptions are financially neutral (that is, that a given exception granted to one or more countries does not result in other countries having to finance the shortfall), the VAT rate is not applied to the VAT actually cashed, but to a VAT base recalculated by eliminating the financial impact of the exception. That means that what member states pay into the EU coffers as VAT resource is not the share of the VAT actually cashed, but rather a share of the VAT that would be cashed by a given country if the VAT base were totally harmonised and no exception were in place. On average, the variation in the VAT base accounting for these exceptions is in the order of 1 to 2 per cent. On the one hand, this procedure ensures fairness and budgetary neutrality; on the other hand, it breaks the link between the VAT paid by citizens and the VAT paid into the EU coffers. Given that the size of the difference between the 'cashed' VAT and the calculated VAT is relatively minute, the Commission has been arguing in recent years that the second argument could predominate and a transition towards a 'cashed' VAT resource (that is, without any correction) would be desirable. After the 1977 phasing out of the temporary and degressive national contributions previously discussed, the VAT resource played, during the period 1978–88, the role of the **marginal resource**, that is, the resource meant to ensure the budgetary balance, required by the principle of equilibrium discussed above. That means that the VAT rate could vary (albeit below a fixed ceiling of 1 per cent) so as to accommodate changes in total expenditure. Since 1988, with the introduction of the GNP resource, this role has been taken by the GNP resource itself.

The introduction of the **GNP resource** in 1988 is essentially due to the fact that expenditures started to outstrip revenues in the EU budget. During the 1980s, Europe was a victim of its own success and calls for more expenditure were widespread. Between 1981 and 1986, the EU was enlarged to admit 60 million new citizens from Greece, Portugal and Spain, whose per capita income was about 60 per cent of the EU's average, and who therefore immediately became large beneficiaries of EU expenditures. However, the Commission's ambitions of expanding the EU budget had to take into account the fact that revenues were growing much less than expenditures. To ease that constraint, the GNP resource, or 'fourth' resource, was introduced as a marginal resource: its amount is equal to the shortfall between the total expenditure and the revenues raised by the first three other resources. This shortfall is redistributed among member states according to their GNP (nowadays GNI) shares in the total EU GNP. This means that the taxpayers of the GNP resource are the governments and not the citizens directly, which considerably reduces the EU financial autonomy, or at least its perception.[25] In other words, the GNP resource is at the centre of a trade-off between financial sufficiency and financial autonomy.

The GNP resource has ensured financial sufficiency for the EU, by calling on national governments to meet the shortfall between expenditure and the other revenues, but at the cost of reducing the financial autonomy of the EU institutions. The EU has never been able to regain the financial autonomy lost with the introduction of the GNP resource and, through the simple fact of the expansion of the EU budget, the part of the budget financed by the GNP resource is bound to increase. In particular, as shown by Figure 6.1, from 0 per cent in 1988 it could reach some 90 per cent in 2013, therefore leaving the resources for the supranational EU policies entirely in the hands

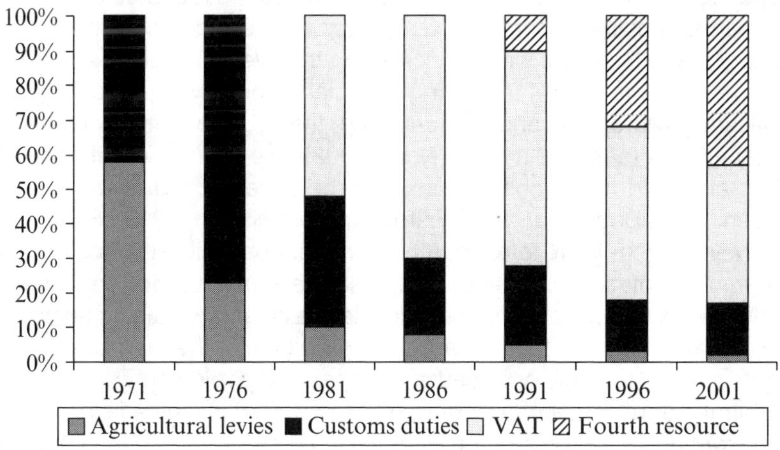

Source: Author's elaboration from European Commission (2004e).

Figure 6.1 Evolution of the EU budget resources

(and thus the willingness to contribute) of the EU governments. Because of the easily predictable, but almost irremediable, consequences of the loss of financial autonomy, we did not hesitate, in a previous work, to term the GNP resource as a 'Pact with the Devil' (see Nava, 2000).

The lack of financial autonomy of the EU can thus be corrected in two ways: either by linking the GNP/GNI contributions of member states to underlying taxes paid by citizens in each member state, therefore depriving this resource of its marginal character, or simply by introducing a new tax in (partial or total) replacement of the GNI contributions.[26] The first option was discussed within the Commission, but finally dismissed (European Commission, 2004e). The second option was retained by the Commission in its 2004 Communication, albeit not for the immediate future, but rather for the post-2013 period, as discussed in more detail in Box 6.2.

In particular, the Commission (European Commission, 2004e) has indicated three possible candidates for a tax-based resource: energy taxes, a genuine VAT (without the correction described above) and the corporate tax. The Commission sketched in July 2004 a sort of roadmap for introducing one or more of these three candidate tax-based resources, in partial

BOX 6.2 TOWARDS A TAX-BASED OWN RESOURCE?

The arguments in favour of introducing a tax-based resource in total or partial substitution for the GNI resource without increasing the EU budget, and therefore without increasing the overall fiscal pressure, hinge on the issues of improving financial autonomy, of increasing citizens' awareness and of rendering the EU Parliament more accountable (see Goulard and Nava, 2002). The economic literature has analysed many possible taxes to be levied at EU level (see Keen, 1995, Begg *et al.* 1997, European Commission, 1999). Some, however, seem likely to encounter more serious political difficulties or implementation problems while others are much more credible candidates. Furthermore some taxes have a clear rationale for being levied at EU level, either because the existence of their tax base is due to an EU policy, or because national reapportioning would be arbitrary, or because of a mixture of the two. That is the case for, as an example, the profits of the ECB (which exist only because EMU exists and whose reapportioning is difficult), of the corporate tax for trans-European firms, as well as the energy tax and many others.

substitution for the GNP/GNI resource so as to keep fiscal pressure unchanged, starting from 2013.

The **UK correction**, which, formally speaking, is an EU resource and an integral part of the own resources system, is, economically speaking, the most flagrant deviation from the rational financing rules of the EU budget. Its existence goes back to the beginning of the UK–EU relations. The UK joined the EU in 1973 and as early as 1974 it held a referendum to verify the popular support for its membership of the EU. The referendum was in favour of the UK remaining in the EU, but the argument over the financial position of Britain vis-à-vis the EU was singled out as one of the sourest incidents in the UK–EU relationship. Indeed, in 1975, the UK was the second poorest country in the Union and, because of the Community bias towards agricultural expenditure, the UK had a negative net balance vis-à-vis the Union: its contributions to the EU budget were higher than the share of EU expenditures it was receiving. After several years of negotiations, which invariably led to partial solutions giving little satisfaction to the UK, the UK decided from 1982 to oppose a systematic veto to any EU proposal, thus effectively blocking EU legislative activity.[27] Confronted with this stalemate, the 1984 Council of Fontainebleau agreed (by unanimity) to the UK correction mechanism, which, with some marginal modification introduced by the Delors packages and by Agenda 2000, is still implemented today. The Council decision of 1984 basically established that the UK budgetary position was excessively negative with respect to its relative prosperity and, on this ground, it granted a rebate to the UK contributions to the EU budget.

Clearly both the economic situation of the UK and its attitude towards the EU budget have changed dramatically since 1984: what could have been economically justifiable in the past, is not so today. In other words, the UK rebate, which was introduced to correct a distortion, today turns out to be the single largest distortion of the EU budget, and the very first blocking element of any budgetary negotiations aiming at modernising the EU budget. Since the UK correction is enshrined in the ORD, however, unanimity is required to make any changes to the mechanism, and obviously the UK opposes any change of this situation.

The EU Commission (see European Commission, 2004e) proposed a **Generalised Correction Mechanism** (GCM), open to all countries, to replace the UK correction. The logic of the GCM would be to grant a correction, not with respect to the whole net balance (as in the case of the UK), but only with respect to the part of the net balance that exceeds a commonly agreed threshold, or that is generated by a well identified type of expenditure. The overall amount of the GCM would not be much higher than the amount of the UK rebate. Since, financially speaking, this proposal would basically translate into more countries sharing a sum of money a bit larger than the UK rebate, it is easy to foresee that 24 countries will be immediately in favour of it and one (guess who) would need to be convinced.

In sum, maintaining the UK rebate in the EU-25 would amount to accepting a very unfair burden sharing across the EU countries, while the extension of the correction mechanism is justified by the new economic circumstances, namely by the fact that the UK is no longer the second-poorest EU country, since its per capita income is well above the EU average. In addition, the UK budgetary position vis-à-vis the EU is no longer unique. At any rate, it is extremely early at this stage to foresee what the chances are that the Council would actually accept the GCM by unanimity.[28]

The Generalised Correction Mechanism was not even discussed at the June 2005 European Council. On the contrary, the UK rebate was discussed at length, but no solution was found, in another proof that unanimity cannot be achieved. Clearly, either an alternative is devised for the UK rebate or some of the reasons that have generated the UK rebate (namely the CAP) are reduced: otherwise, there is no hope of seeing the UK rebate being written off. Just as for the expenditure side of the EU budget, at the moment of going to press it is very difficult to forecast how and when negotiations on resources will end. What is very clear, however, is that no pro-Community solution is currently envisaged. Rather, some *ad hoc* solutions have been voiced to accommodate this or that country. It would be a major defeat for Europe if the negotiations were to end in a further stratification of incoherent solutions of this kind.

6.4.2 Other Revenues

In addition to the own resources described in the previous section, other revenues of various sources and origin also finance the EU budget. It must be stressed that these other revenues, of an episodic and not foreseeable nature (with the exception of point 4 below), go to the benefit of the whole budget and have the function of reducing the GNI contributions of member states. In no case can they be used to increase the total expenditure. These other revenues are essentially made up of the following:

1. The budgetary surplus of the previous year.
2. Interests due from member states for late payments of own resources (TORs, VAT and GNI resource).
3. Fines and other sanctions, as foreseen, for example, by the competition policy (see Chapter 9).

4. Taxes levied on EU civil servants' wages and pensions. EU civil servants' wage taxes benefit the EU budget and therefore implicitly reduce the GNI payments of all countries.[29]

Finally, there are some other revenues, called 'allocated revenues', which do not go to the benefit of the whole budget, but to specific beneficiaries. The best-known example is the fines laid down by the Stability and Growth Pact which would be paid by the countries having an excessive deficit to the benefit only of those countries not having an excessive deficit.

6.4.3 An Assessment of the Revenue Side of the EU Budget

Back in 1998, the Commission published a long study on the EU financing system (European Commission, 1999). In that report, it proposed several criteria to evaluate the EU financing system. Of those criteria, we retain five for our discussion: (a) resource adequacy and sufficiency; (b) equity of gross contribution; (c) transparency and simplicity; (d) cost efficiency; (e) financial autonomy.

Even the most convinced Euro-sceptic would find it difficult to claim that the EU financing system has failed to give to the EU the resources the EU needed. Since the introduction of the FP in 1988, in conjunction with the introduction of the GNP resource, the EU budget has had an enviable track record of timely adoption and **resource adequacy**. Never since 1988 has a single Euro of expenditure had to be postponed to the following year because of a lack of resources. The GNP resource, therefore, has ensured, although at the cost of financial autonomy, a proper financing of the EU budget.

The **equity** of member states' gross contributions should be measured in respect to their contributive capacity, as discussed in Box 6.3. Since the contributive capacity is measured by the member states' GNI shares in the EU GNI, and since the GNI resource is more and more the dominant resource of the EU budget, there emerges a practically perfect proportionality of budget contributions to contributive capacity. The only element that makes member states' contributions move away from perfect proportionality with GNI is the UK rebate. As we have seen, the UK rebate reduces the UK gross contribution to a level far below its GNI share and it increases the other member states' contributions to a level above their GNI share, albeit in a non-linear manner. The equity of the TORs cannot be assessed against the income of the originating country, because of the very nature of the Traditional Own Resources. TORs are of a genuine EU nature, they exist because of the regional arbitrariness of their origin and therefore cannot be reattributed to member states.

BOX 6.3 IS THE EQUITY CONTENT OF THE GNI RESOURCE SATISFACTORY?

One may wonder whether the proportionality of member states contributions to income (the essence of the GNI contribution) is the right benchmark for equity of the EU budget, given that the vast majority of the national budget relies on the notion of tax progressivity. The rationale for enforcing proportionality of member states' contributions to income, instead of progressivity, is linked to the very target of EU solidarity. As will be explained at length in Chapter 8, EU solidarity does not aim at reducing interpersonal income differences by raising individual consumption (as most national policies do), but at reducing across-country inequalities by raising the level of investment. EU solidarity, therefore, aims at increasing investment in those regions having an income level which does not generate a rate of investment high enough to ensure rapid convergence towards the EU average. Given this link between solidarity and increased investment, progressivity of the revenues would, *ceteris paribus*, only weaken that link.

Let us assume that, for a given solidarity effort made by the rich EU countries, part of it is translated into structural expenditure in the poor EU countries while another part is translated into reduced contributions of the poor EU countries to the EU budget, because of a progressive revenue system. With respect to the present situation, where the whole of the solidarity effort is translated into structural expenditure, this would amount to transforming some of the money aimed at investment into money for any use. If money for any use was all spent on investment, nothing would change. However money for any use would only translate partly into increased investment and partly into increased consumption, given that, to any government, consumption and investment are normal goods (goods are termed 'normal goods' when the demand for a good increases with the consumer's income). With respect to the current situation, that would amount to a reduced convergence rate because of a reduced investment rate.

The system of EU financing is not more complicated or less **transparent** than a national system. We trust that most of our motivated readers have been able to read this section on EU financing in less than an hour. It is unlikely that the same could have been done had we dealt with the procedures of a national budget. However we also trust that most of our readers have realised the conceptual nightmare when reading, and eventually trying to understand, the part concerning the UK rebate (including the Appendix to the present chapter). In other words, if it were not for the UK rebate the budget would be of an absolute simplicity. The existence of the UK rebate makes it more complicated but still simpler and easier to understand than a national budget.

Within the EU budget, a trade-off certainly exists between **cost efficiency** and financial autonomy. Member states' direct contributions are very cost-efficient, but give no financial autonomy; tax-based resources are less cost-efficient, but give more financial autonomy.[30] The GNI resource gives no financial autonomy, but it is very simple to manage and extremely cost-efficient (there are only 25 taxpayers, and a handful of EU civil servants are enough to monitor and organise the system). The TORs as well as the VAT resource give financial autonomy to the EU, but they are very complicated to manage and require human intervention at many stages of the collection process. In view of this, a multilateral surveillance process exists at the EU level to monitor the way every country collects TORs and VAT and to combat frauds.

The mere existence of the EU Own Resources is one of the highest expressions of the political maturity of the EU and of its **financial autonomy**. Nevertheless the financial autonomy guaranteed by the EU Treaty is blurred by the use of the GNI resource that nullifies the perception that both citizens and governments may have of this EU financial autonomy. The growing importance (at least until 2013) of the GNI resource is worrisome, since it leads to a potential further reduction of the financial autonomy and risks of exacerbating the net balance discussions. It is however relatively clear that the Council has very little incentive today to give more financial autonomy to the EU. Direct contributions imply in fact less devolution of fiscal sovereignty, and a greater possibility of control.

To conclude, the EU financing system is performing relatively well under all criteria but financial autonomy. The lack of financial autonomy, essentially due to the ever-increasing part of financing ensured by the GNI resource, has implications also for the general development of EU policy. As argued by Sapir *et al.* (2004), direct member states' contributions are at the root of the net balance considerations dominating the EU budget negotiations, and hinder the development of a genuine debate on the EU added value of any expenditure. It would be in the collective interest of member states to move towards a tax-based EU resource, but individual countries' interests hamper the coordination of this collective move and no solution is in sight at least before 2013.

6.5 THE ISSUE OF BURDEN SHARING AND OF NET BALANCES

The issue of burden sharing of the **net financing** or **net balances** has become in the last few years an unavoidable stumbling block of nearly every EU negotiation. In plain and simple terms, burden sharing of the net financing looks at the difference between what each country pays into the EU budget and what it obtains from the EU budget either for any given policy or in total. It answers the question, 'What is my country's net financial position as a result of a given expenditure?' As we have seen, this issue was at the heart of the discussion on the UK rebate.

One must stress, on the one hand, that achieving a given distribution of the net balances is not an EU policy per se. Net balances are only and simply the arithmetical results of the difference between expenditures and revenues. Expenditures and revenues, on the other hand, are the result of EU policies and, as we discussed in section 6.2, their multi-annual planning is subject to unanimity. One may therefore wonder how it is possible that the EU governments can vote by unanimity in favour of expenditures and revenues but, at the same time, some of them are unhappy about the arithmetical difference. Common sense and logic dictate that, if one agrees with the two terms of a subtraction, one should also agree with the result of the subtraction. For as strange as it may seem, this is far from being the case in EU politics: although member states' governments do vote by unanimity on their revenues and expenditures, some of them do keep on complaining about the arithmetic difference.

Irony apart, it is clear that the notion of burden sharing exists only in an intergovernmental, non-solidaristic vision of Europe. In a communitarian approach, the notion of burden sharing across EU countries would be substantially irrelevant. Still, since the issue has been and is likely to be at the heart of every negotiation on future EU policies, it is worth looking at it in some detail.

6.5.1 Burden Sharing of a Given Policy or of the Whole Budget ?

The most obvious way of calculating EU burden sharing in accounting terms would be to look at any given policy (be it a 'spending' or a 'regulatory' policy), calculate its overall financial amount (including personnel, administration, and so on), see how this amount benefits different member states and then figure out the financing shares for that given policy. This, however, is not a clear-cut exercise for at least two reasons: (a) the financing shares depend on the total amount of the EU budget (which affects the amount of the fourth resource to be paid, whose financing base is different from that of the other resources); (b) the financing shares of any member state depend not only on their share of the EU GNI and VAT, but also on the total revenues and expenditures accruing from and to the UK (via the UK rebate). The UK rebate is very relevant given that it is sizeable and its financing, as we have seen, is very uneven across different groups of countries.

Given (a) and (b), there are at least two possible ways of calculating the financing share. The first option would be just to calculate the financing share of any country looking at the given policy as the 'marginal' policy (the very last policy to be financed). This would allow using only the GNI as a resource to calculate its 'marginal' impact on the UK rebate (by looking at the expenditure generated by that given policy) and finally obtaining the true financing shares. However this option is defendable only for 'small' policies. It is clearly inappropriate for the main policies because they cannot be considered as 'marginal', and therefore the use of the other budgetary resources has also to be considered in the calculations.

The only option left then is to calculate the net balance for the whole of the budget. However this also is not exempt from problems, as will be clarified in the next section. The result for any country will in fact depend on the possibility of objectively allocating expenditure and revenues and also on the distribution of spending between the UK and the other 24 member states, which affects the determination and the financing of the UK rebate. It is not clear, beyond the simple arithmetic, why one should take seriously a result which is so affected by the financial flows to and from the EU of a single country. And yet, from a political point of view, the exercise has received widespread consideration, and its main arguments are summarised in the next section. The uninterested reader can, however, skip the next two sub-sections and move directly to the conclusions of the chapter.

6.5.2 The Net Balance as a Positive Concept: Accounting Evidence versus Economic Significance

Here we look at the net balance as a positive concept. Our aim is therefore, first, to ascertain whether it is possible to calculate the net balances for all the EU countries and, second, whether the resulting figures carry any economic significance. If we were to prove that accounting figures carry no economic significance, one might want to verify whether it is possible to correct the crude 'accounting' figures to allow for an 'economic' interpretation.[31]

As for the **accounting exercise**, one must make sure that the 'accounting' attribution of expenditure and revenues to any country, in a given period of time, is from an accounting standpoint correct. The accounting calculation, however, is not always as straightforward as it might seem. This is the case for example in research expenditure: by definition research grants are given to transnational consortia of universities, firms and research centres. The share of each partner in each project is recorded only at the level of each contract, and not at the level of total EU budget expenditure, where each contract is attributed to the country of the largest receivers. Furthermore, according to the accounting evidence, Belgium and Luxembourg seem to receive a disproportionate amount of research funds. This is simply due to the fact that, to facilitate financial flows, many firms, universities and research centres dealing with the EU keep a bank account in Belgium or Luxembourg and ask to be paid there. The same happens for structural expenditure where not all of the payments destined to a given country or region are paid into a bank account that the receiving countries or regions own in their own countries. The very foundation of the single market allows member states or regions to hold bank accounts in other countries to facilitate, for example, financial relations with foreign suppliers or customers.

Not surprisingly, since 1992, there has not been a single year when the Commission (in the allocated expenditure report) and the Court of Auditors (in the annual Court report) published the same figures of per country expenditure and payments. Furthermore both the Court and the Commission publish net balance figures that do not add up to zero. The sum of the net balances across all EU countries is a negative figure equal to the external expenditure (which according to the accounting evidence does not benefit any country), plus the expenditure that the Commission or the Court were unable to allocate to one or the other country. This generates a negative bias in the net balances and makes the net balance appear smaller by a proportion equal to the part of this negative figure in the whole budget (normally well above 10 per cent). Recalling a famous master magician capable of making things disappear into thin air, this is called the **Houdini effect**.

A way to overcome the Houdini effect is to link directly the net balances only to the size of the allocated expenditure (for example, this is the way in which the UK correction is calculated). This is an effective solution in a given year. However, since the allocated amount varies considerably from one year to the next, the direct linkage amounts to inflating or deflating the net balance figures by different coefficients in different years. This would effectively render intertemporal comparisons virtually meaningless. This is called the '**scale effect**'.

Assuming that one has arrived at accounting evidence of the net balance divided by each member state and has been able to overcome the problems just highlighted, the issue is then how to interpret, from an economic standpoint, this accounting evidence. Actually accounting figures offer very little economic indication of the real burden sharing. The main reason is that EU expenditure has, by definition and by the legal requirement of subsidiarity,[32] a supranational character. That means that, even if the beneficiary is very clear in accounting and/or legal terms, it is much less clear who the beneficiary is in economic terms. As a result, in order to interpret the accounting evidence in economic terms, one needs to impose a certain set of assumptions concerning the probable economic impact of the different EU expenditures and revenues to and from different countries. At the end of this exercise one would have a net balance which would make economic sense, but which would certainly lack the simplicity of the accounting evidence. In the trade-off between 'simple, but meaningless' and 'complicated, but meaningful', many (especially among politicians) seem to have a crystal-clear preference for the former.

The set of assumptions necessary to translate the 'accounting net balances' into the 'economic net balances' is long and we recall here only the main ones. For the TORs, the accounting evidence of the country paying customs duties gives no indication of the country that ultimately bears the burden of them. It is enough to mention that, according to accounting evidence, 26 million Dutch and Belgians pay slightly more custom duties than 120 million Italians and French. Clearly this is due to the specialisation of economic activities and to natural comparative advantages. Thus Italian and French shores, blessed with blue and warm waters, focus on tourism, while Belgian and Dutch shores, blessed with grey and cold waters, focus on port activities. In technical terms this is called the 'Gateway effect' or the 'Rotterdam effect', and even Margaret Thatcher accepted the exclusion of the TORs from the calculation of the UK net balance for the UK rebate.

There is also no evidence that all the VAT paid in a country is paid by taxpayers of that country. This is particularly the case for small transit countries (VAT paid in Luxembourg is certainly not paid exclusively by tax residents in Luxembourg) and tourist locations (VAT paid in Italy, Spain and France in summer is certainly not paid only by residents in those countries). Not by chance is this effect called the '**Marbella effect**'.

As we will see, the Common Agricultural Policy (see Chapter 7) includes both income support and price support measures. Income support measures go straight to farmers, so its beneficiary is fairly evident. However price support includes measures such as exports subsidies, whereby the cost of implementing price support varies with places, even if its benefit is very similar (a unique and higher price). Furthermore money for exports subsidies goes to international trading houses often not located in the beneficiary country and sometimes outside the EU altogether. There are also spillover effects between the product policies of the CAP: a relaxation of milk policy would lead to a change in the beef policy,[33] with different geographic distribution of economic effects. Equally a relaxation of the set-aside policy would immediately benefit the few zones concerned by set-aside, but would negatively affect the whole of Europe. Even if prices are being supported by domestic intervention, the effect of such activity on the territory of one member state can be felt on the markets of its neighbours.

In terms of structural expenditures, the whole of these expenditure benefits go well beyond the country where that expenditure is first paid. Direct and indirect international feedbacks are huge in this area and are estimated to be of the order of 40 per cent. A simple example can clarify the situation. When any country receives, say, 100 Euros of EU funds to build up some large infrastructure projects it must (according to the principle of additionality – see Chapter 8) supplement this 100 Euros with 100 Euros of national investment. EU competition rules then oblige this country to follow a public tender procedure for assigning the 200 Euros of work. These days it is highly likely that the firm or the consortium of firms who finally obtain the contract to undertake the work is not tax-resident in the receiving country. In this case, the infrastructure will benefit the receiving country, but the added value generated in the construction of the infrastructure will return to the country where the winning firms are resident. This is substantial given that, for a large project, the added value may be as high as 40 per cent: 100 Euros from the EU budget together with 100 Euros from the national budget generate some 120 Euros in the receiving countries and 80 Euros for other countries. Any accounting evidence that would assign all 200 Euros to the receiving country would be economically erroneous.

By definition internal expenditure (research, education, internal market) are expenditures which try to internalise an externality,[34] and hence any national reallocation of that expenditure risks being arbitrary. Research expenditure is meant to make research 'more European' by encouraging transnational cooperation. Research expenditure represents only the cost of the research; the benefit of the research is represented by the results obtained. These results are the same for all participants in the research project, disregarding the share that every participant had in the research grants. Among the most successful EU programmes are the so-called Erasmus and Socrates programmes for the mobility of students and researchers, which have of course a non-negligible budgetary translation. Accounting evidence allocates the distribution of the Erasmus funds according to the university of residence of the benefiting students. But can we reasonably claim that a scholarship given to a German student to attend a UK university benefits only Germany, as the accounting evidence would suggest? Or that the scholarship of a Spanish student to attend a German university does not benefit Germany but only Spain? And, if it were so, why is Germany so interested in having foreign students on its campuses? The transeuropean networks represent another important part of the internal expenditure. This expenditure is accounted in favour of the countries where the networks are constructed, thus violating a basic principle of network economics which states that the value of a project is in the entire network, not in its individual pieces. Can we reasonably claim that the Brussels–Paris high-speed rail link benefits Belgium about one-quarter as much as it benefits France (there are 60km of line in Belgium and 240km of line in France), as the crude accounting evidence would suggest? Or, even, better, can we reasonably claim that the French bit of the London–Brussels high-speed rail link does not benefit either the UK or Belgium, but only France?

From an accounting standpoint, the administrative expenditure of the EU civil servants, as well as the cost of their business travels around the world, are accounted in favour of the country where civil servants are resident (mostly Belgium). That may be a convenient assumption, but is far from representing the economic reality. At the 1999 Berlin Council, Belgium and Luxembourg obtained the concession that this expenditure be not included when the net balances were calculated for 'illustrative purposes' (but included when the net balance is calculated for the UK rebate).

From an accounting standpoint, the benefit of external expenditure for the EU countries is zero, because it benefits only third countries. If this were the case, why were EU leaders so keen on expenditure for enlargement and why are they now so intent on expenditure benefiting third countries? Obviously there are large spillover effects, which are non-linear across EU countries and which are totally missed by any accounting evidence. For example, the EU expenditure made in Poland before the enlargement, was more likely to benefit Germany than Spain, just as the expenditures financing development programmes in Latin America are likely to benefit Spain more than Germany.

According to accounting evidence, any regulatory policy, such as EMU, competition policy, environmental policy, cultural policy or labour market policy, gives no benefits to any country in Europe. Who would agree with this? How is it possible not to account for the large benefits to EU citizens of, for example, telecom price reductions, travel costs reductions, the single currency and the like? Finally, and without rhetoric, can one honestly maintain that the benefit of 60 years of unprecedented peace in Europe, brought about by the mere power sharing implicit in the EU project, is really worth nothing, as the accounting evidence suggests?

The conclusion is that there is certainly more than one way to calculate the net balances. The whole net balance exercise is constructed on thin ice and no method can be logically defended as the best one. This means that the net balance lends itself to be used for political purposes, since its indefinite nature allows different people to use different results for different purposes. Indeed the net balance has a much greater political than economic significance.

The European Commission did not publish net balances until 1997, when so many and so wrong were the speculative figures floating around

Table 6.9 Net balances in the EU

'Operational' budgetary balance (after UK correction) based on the UK rebate definition (1), (2)

	1996		1997		1998		1999		2000		2001		2002	
	MECU	% GNP	MECU	% GNP	MECU	% GNP	Meuro	% GNP	Meuro	% GNP	Meuro	% GNP	Meuro	% GNI
BE	16.5	0.01	−395.7	−0.18	−406.5	−0.18	−314.6	−0.13	−214.1	−0.09	−629.5	−0.25	−256.4	−0.10
DK	273.4	0.20	131.0	0.09	7.1	0.00	122.6	0.08	240.5	0.15	−229.0	−0.14	−165.0	−0.09
DE	−10405.9	−0.56	−10552.9	−0.58	−8044.2	−0.43	−8494.0	−0.44	−8280.2	−0.42	−6953.3	−0.34	−5067.8	−0.24
EL	4039.0	4.13	4360.5	4.09	4735.7	4.36	3818.0	3.27	4433.3	3.66	4513.2	3.52	3387.9	2.39
ES	5970.2	1.28	5782.8	1.20	7141.1	1.40	7382.4	1.35	5346.8	0.91	7738.3	1.23	8870.8	1.29
FR	−822.2	−0.07	−1284.3	−0.11	−864.5	−0.07	30.0	0.00	−739.4	−0.05	−2035.4	−0.14	−2184.2	−0.14
IE	2421.8	4.61	2814.4	4.43	2379.2	3.38	1978.7	2.38	1720.8	1.77	1203.1	1.15	1576.7	1.50
IT	−1693.0	−0.18	−229.6	−0.02	−1410.6	−0.14	−753.9	−0.07	1210.1	0.11	−1977.9	−0.17	−2884.5	−0.23
LU	−45.8	−0.31	−54.3	−0.33	−76.6	−0.44	−85.0	−0.44	−56.6	−0.28	−144.1	−0.74	−48.9	−0.25
NL	−1295.0	−0.41	−1087.5	−0.34	−1539.8	−0.45	−1827.0	−0.50	−1540.3	−0.39	−2256.8	−0.54	−2187.7	−0.51
AT	−264.5	−0.15	−779.8	−0.43	−629.2	−0.34	−628.8	−0.32	−447.8	−0.22	−536.4	−0.26	−226.3	−0.11
PT	2839.1	3.28	2717.3	2.97	3018.9	3.09	2858.2	2.72	2168.5	1.95	1794.2	1.53	2692.3	2.14
FI	72.6	0.08	39.8	0.04	−102.4	−0.09	−194.8	−0.17	274.5	0.22	−150.4	−0.11	−5.7	0.00
SE	−587.9	−0.30	−1097.7	−0.54	−779.9	−0.38	−897.3	−0.41	−1059.5	−0.45	−973.3	−0.43	−746.6	−0.29
UK(3)	−518.3	−0.06	−242.6	−0.02	−3489.3	−0.28	−2826.7	−0.21	−2985.9	−0.19	707.5	0.04	−2902.8	−0.17
Total	**0.0**	**0.00**	**121.4**	**0.00**	**−60.9**	**0.00**	**167.8**	**0.00**	**70.8**	**0.00**	**70.3**	**0.00**	**−148.2**	**0.00**

Notes:
(1) The method was changed slightly in the report on the year 2001 as compared to the preceding years' reports in order to make the total EU-15 'operational' budgetary balance sum to zero before deduction of the UK rebate.
(2) The latest available GNP and GNI data have been used (GNI has replaced GNP in the area of the EU budget as from 2002: see also the preceding text).
(3) The positive budgetary balance in 2001 is due to the particularly high amount of the rebate budgeted in this year.

the issue that it finally took the political decision of publishing the net balances resulting from its own accounting evidence. Net balances now appear in a document called the '**Allocated Expenditure Report**' (see European Commission, 2003b) and are published normally between June and September of the year $N+1$ for the balances of the year N (see Table 6.9).

The Commission exercises a considerable degree of prudence in presenting these results, stating that 'constructing estimates of budgetary balances is merely an accounting exercise of the purely financial costs and benefits that each member state derives from the Union. This accounting allocation gives no indication of many of the other benefits gained from EU policies such as those relating to the internal market and economic integration, not to mention political stability and security'.

The net balances presented by the Commission in its report are based on the 'UK rebate definition', which is the only one that has a degree of formal recognition, being based on the Fontainebleau agreement and the method of calculating the correction of the UK budgetary imbalance. Furthermore, in accordance with the conclusions of the 1999 meeting of the European Council in Berlin, the balances are presented according to the 'operational' concept, that is, excluding administrative expenditure (EU expenditure on salaries, rental of offices and so on). Under this method, member states' total payments of the VAT and GNP/GNI-based resources are set to equal total allocated operating expenditure, which implies that the overall EU balance is, in principle, restricted to add up to zero (this prevents the Houdini effect, but it creates for intertemporal comparisons a misleading scale effect).

In particular the budgetary balances presented by the Commission show the relation between the share of a member state in total payments of the VAT and GNP/GNI-based resources and its share in total operating expenditure allocated to the member states. A positive figure means that the member state, according to this calculation method, is a 'net beneficiary' from the EU budget and a negative figure that it is a 'net contributor'. Ironically the most striking evidence is that net balances are very small. Countries having a total public spending well above 40 per cent of their GNP have negative net balances between −0.2 per cent and −0.5 per cent of the EU GNP.

6.5.3 The Net Balance as a Normative Concept: Does an Optimal Net Balance Exist?

All calculations of burden sharing seem to have an often implicit underlying notion of what the net balance should be. With some caveats and provisos, the vast majority of the studies seem to think that, to a greater or lesser extent, the EU should guarantee a certain inverse relationship between net balance and per capita income of a member state. In simple terms, the EU flow of funds should be organised so that rich countries pay and poor countries receive (**vertical equity**) and possibly that countries of similar wealth have a similar budgetary position (**horizontal equity**).

To be clear, we should say at the outset that the structure of the EU expenditure and EU revenues is such that to deliver this result is simply impossible. Indeed, from an economic standpoint, an inverse relationship between per capita income and net balance in the context of the EU budget could be obtained only under two conditions: first, that the whole expenditure has a redistributive aim across EU countries and, second, that this redistributive aim is pursued on a national (and not regional) scale.

Neither of the two conditions is at present realised in the EU context. Indeed more than half of the EU budget has an allocative rather than an explicit redistributive aim across EU countries (CAP, internal and external expenditure, administrative expenditure, and so on). This expenditure is obviously not inversely correlated to the GNI per capita of the EU countries. The part of the EU expenditure which is explicitly redistributive (structural expenditure) is spent in this way according to a regional (and not a national) key. The only type of expenditure that is explicitly redistributive across EU countries (and not regions) is the cohesion expenditure, but this currently represents less than €3 billion in a total budget of more than €120 billion (see Chapter 8).

Because of the joint effect of what is described above, it should therefore not come as surprise if, because of the importance of the allocative expenditure, some countries receive larger sums of money than other countries with similar or even lower levels of wealth (France and Denmark versus Germany). Equally it should not be surprising if two countries of similar wealth (in PPP terms) such as Sweden and Italy receive very different support from structural expenditure, owing to their largely different regional imbalances.

The existence of allocative expenditure, the regional focus for structural expenditure and the national contributions make it very difficult to have the net balances that distribute funds according to the intuitive notion of inverse relationship with per capita income. If one is really serious about obtaining this result, the whole structure of expenditure should be changed.

6.5.4 Conclusions on the Net Balances

The issue of net balances is far from being a simple and univocal one. At best it is meaningless, at worst it is completely biased. Indeed accounting evidence is not clear-cut because of the presence of many transnational projects and a mismatch of beneficiaries and place of payments. Furthermore the accounting evidence of the net balance is disconnected from the economic benefits, both in space and in time.

The implicit normative notion of net balance (there ought to exist an inverse relationship between per capita income and net balance) does not take into account two fundamental aspects of the EU budget: allocative expenditure (mainly CAP) counts for more than half of the total, and redistributive expenditure uses a regional, not national, key. The EU structure of expenditure is such that an inverse correlation of net balances with income cannot be delivered. The only element that is sure about the net balances is the relative dimension: when compared to the other public finance numbers net balances are, in financial terms, really very small.

In spite of all that, the concept of net balance is widely used and it has had a dramatic impact on EU policy making. With no fear of exaggeration one may say that the attempts to adjust net balances in a direction more favourable to the big payers have been the driving force behind the 1999 Berlin negotiations, and risk being the main force behind the next round of negotiations.

6.6 THE FUTURE OF THE EU BUDGET MECHANISM

In spite of the fact that the largest negative net balances hover between −0.3 and −0.5 per cent of the GNP (compared to a total public expenditure of some 40 to 50 per cent) of the concerned member state, the issue of the net balance has taken centre stage in the EU budget debate. To us, this is the clearest indication that the EU budget is in need of a complete overhaul. If EU expenditure were undertaken every time the 'double market failure' emerged and were aimed at EU added value maximisation, the net balance issue would be an extremely marginal one.

The two main policies (CAP and structural expenditures for cohesion), representing some 85 per cent of the current EU budget, still largely reflect a double deal: the EC-6's common market and the Single European Act of 1987. The first deal entailed a large share of Community expenditure devoted to the Common Agricultural Policy (CAP) as a price to be paid for allowing Germany's industrial products to enter the French market. The second deal saw the rise of spending on cohesion and regional policies in the context of the Iberian enlargement as the price to be paid for compensating the possible losers of the 1992 Single Market project.

It is increasingly evident that the current EU budget is inconsistent with the present state of affairs and future prospects of European integration. While its historical and political roots are deep, the EU budget does not stand up to economic and political scrutiny: no federation (mature or not) around the world has a budget whose dominant share is devoted to supporting a declining sector (agriculture), does not provide public goods typically featuring large economies of scale and is disconnected from the political objectives of the federation.

This situation has led to a confused perception that the current EU budget is a 'political equilibrium' whereby money is transferred across countries according to the logic of the net balances and, hence, any adjustment to the budget can only be at the margin. And yet we have shown that the net balance logic is extremely biased and, in any case, marginal with respect to the financial capacity of each member state. It is therefore paramount for the future growth of the EU, for its capacity to reach the Lisbon objectives and to make a success of the enlargement process, to dispel this perception and to use the budget again as an instrument for economic policy.

In order to do that, we have advocated three types of changes: expenditure should be refocused on growth and convergence (the Lisbon objectives), revenues should accrue more from tax-based resources and less from member state contribution and, finally, the multi-annual budget procedure should not be subject to Council unanimity. The 2004 Commission's proposal has gone a long way in these respects for the expenditure post-2007, and it has suggested more tax-based resources to be established from 2013. For the time being, however, nothing is foreseen to rid the multi-annual procedure of unanimity.

It is at present too early to judge what the Council will do following the Commission's proposal, but we consider that the Council, having set the Lisbon targets and having solemnly restated them several times, would make a very serious political error by departing from a budget proposal which finally cares more about increasing the EU added value than tilting with member states' net balances. Even if this consideration applies to both expenditure and revenues of the EU budget, the national forces in the Council are such that agreement on a new structure of expenditure is more likely than an agreement on new tax-based resources.

NOTES

1. Since the year 2000, the new ESA 95 (European System of Account approved in 1995) has been implemented in full. ESA 95 discontinues the calculation of the (familiar) concept of GNP (gross national product) in favour of the new concept of GNI (gross national income). The GNI is a more comprehensive measure of the economy and it takes better account of the unofficial economy. On average, the GNI is some three percentage points greater than what the GNP would have been, which explains why 1.27 per cent of GNP = 1.24 per cent of GNI. In this chapter we talk of GNP and GNP resource when referring to the past, and GNI and GNI resource when referring to the future, given the equivalence in the ceiling just discussed.

2. The whole EU budget is as large as the budget of a small country such as Denmark or Portugal and is about one-fifth that of a large country such as Italy or France.
3. Think for example of basic research and development: typically this is the case of a public good supplied also by the state, given the suboptimal quantities produced by the market. However this is also a public good where strong economies of scale are present, and thus it is optimal to have it produced at the centralised EU level, rather than at the single national levels, through the EU budget.
4. This standard view has been challenged by some authors. Indeed the answer to the question, 'Who is the EU government?' is not obvious. In many respects the Commission is the EU government, but in other respects the Council also has a governmental role, thus leading to what is called 'power fragmentation'. For a more detailed approach of political economy to the problem, see Collignon (2003) and Tabellini *et al.* (2003).
5. For a comparison between the 'pragmatic' and the official calendar for the EU budget, see European Commission (2002a).
6. We recall, as already explained in Chapter 1, that any European Treaty, and any modification of it, requires unanimity in the Council and ratification in all national parliaments.
7. For example, there is no EU involvement in the execution of regional expenditure, which is managed directly by the member states and their regions, or for research expenditures, which are managed by the research centres, universities and other entities to which the money is allocated. And yet R&D and regional expenditures constitute two of the major expenditure items of the EU budget.
8. See Chapter 1 for a definition of these categories.
9. In Brussels' jargon, this phase is often referred to as the European Parliament giving the 'discharge' to the Commission.
10. To be precise, in March 1999 the EP voted only the non-political clearing to the budget, but did not need to pass a vote of non-confidence against the Commission, since the Commission itself resigned a few hours before the vote would have taken place. This was the only case in 50 years in which the Brussels executive body had to resign.
11. The ORD is even subject to ratification in all national parliaments.
12. For more details on budgetary principles, see European Commission (2002a) and Nava (2000).
13. The European Development Fund (see section 6.3) as well as the activities of the European Investment Bank constitute an exception to this principle.
14. The best known (albeit probably only virtual) exceptions to the rule of universality are the (potential) proceedings of the sanctions for those countries breaching, according to a Council resolution, the budgetary limits imposed by the Stability and Growth Pact (see Chapter 4).
15. In addition to the external expenditure inserted in the budget, there exists the so-called European Development Fund (EDF), which lies outside the EU budget and finances EU expenditure in third countries.
16. As discussed in Chapters 1 and 3, the Copenhagen Council of December 2002 finally decided for a ten-country enlargement on 1 May 2004 and made the necessary financial adjustments to the Agenda 2000 FP. However these adjustments basically consisted in spreading the same amount of money foreseen for six countries for four years (2002–2006) to ten countries for two and a half years (from mid-2004 to 2006).
17. It is interesting to note that the absolute amounts of resources devoted to the CAP did not decrease over time. Simply the increase in the overall size of the budget went proportionally more to the other chapters of expenditure, which thus conquered a higher share of the EU budget.
18. This sentence is the incipit of Buti and Nava (2003), which was also a preparatory paper to the Sapir report.
19. To our mind, this is one of those clear cases where, as argued in section 6.2.2, unanimity in the Council amounts to the Council pre-empting the right of initiative of the Commission.

20. The Brussels Council of 25–6 March 2004 restated the political will to adopt the package during the first semester of 2005.
21. For a definition of the central concept of financial autonomy, see section 6.4.4 and European Commission (1999).
22. The Luxembourg council established as a fourth resource temporary and decreasing direct contributions from the National Treasuries of member states. These contributions were however due to expire by 1977.
23. The ITA (Information Technology Agreement) was signed in 1997 and it laid down that by 2000 the import of non-EU informatic products would be exempted from custom duties.
24. Formally speaking, the VAT rate applied is equal to 0.5 per cent minus the so-called 'frozen rate' (the part of the VAT that is 'occupied' by the UK rebate). However this detail is intellectually irrelevant and can be easily ignored by our readers. For details, see European Commission (2002a).
25. Formally speaking, the GNP also is an own resource. Its payment is guaranteed by the Treaty and by the Own Resources Decision, a juridical act adopted by unanimity and ratified in all the national parliaments. So, formally speaking, the GNP resource does not reduce the financial autonomy of the EU. However the GNP resource breaks any link between the taxes paid by citizens and the money received by the EU and therefore it dramatically reduces the perception of the financial autonomy of the EU.
26. Clearly, with a partial replacement, the GNI/GNP resource would maintain its marginal character (thus ensuring certainty in the size of the tax-based resource), but the political dependence on the EU by its member states would be attenuated.
27. We recall that, before the entry into force of the Single European Act in 1987, all EU decisions were taken by unanimity.
28. Many have argued that the EU Commission should not have proposed a GCM, but should have simply proposed a straight phasing out of the UK rebate. We believe that this position lacks any political realism. There is no chance that a UK prime minister, no matter how popular, would accept a simple writing off of a hardly won advantage vis-à-vis 'Brussels', conquered by Margaret Thatcher. On the contrary, the GCM does not amount to writing off the UK rebate, but rather to extending the principle of the UK rebate to all countries.
29. If EU civil servants were to pay their wage taxes to the national treasury of the country where they are posted, the advantage for Belgium and Luxembourg, which host some 80 per cent of the EU civil servants, would in fact be too great.
30. Within the tax base resources a trade-off could also exist between cost efficiency and equity. A poll tax (every citizen pays 100 Euros) is very cost-efficient, but maximally inequitable (that is, not correlated to the contributive capacity). An income tax taking into account family situation, debt repayments, health expenditure and whatever else is certainly more equitable, but also more costly to manage.
31. For example, one could obtain intra-EU trade data that would make it possible to see not only where custom duties are formally paid, but also in which goods these custom duties are embedded and where they are ultimately consumed.
32. TEC, art. 5 states that the EU intervention is justified only if the national intervention is suboptimal, as discussed in Chapter 1 of the book. That means that the EU expenditure must have a transnational character to be an improvement with respect to the national expenditure.
33. Owing to the biological link between milk production and the birth of cattle, the relaxation of milk quotas could cause an explosion of the birth rate and consequent beef surplus.
34. Research expenditures, because of the externality they generate, would be suboptimally produced at the national level. By moving some of them to the EU level, is possible to internalise this externality within the EU level, thus ensuring an optimal provision of it.

APPENDIX: THE DETAILS OF THE UK REBATE

1. An Intuitive Calculation of the UK Rebate and of its Financing

One of the most often heard criticisms of the UK abatement or rebate is that it is calculated using a system which is complex and incomprehensible for the politicians in the budgetary authority and they are unable therefore to judge whether it is sound or not. This appendix aims at explaining in mathematical terms how the UK abatement works and especially at understanding the impact of spending decisions on its size.

As a first intuition, the UK rebate consists of a two-thirds reduction of the UK net contribution to the EU budget. Formally speaking, the UK correction is calculated as follows. First the total of the EU allocated expenditure is calculated (that means the expenditure coming from the EU budget and benefiting all the EU countries). Then both the UK share of the total allocated expenditure and the UK share in the VAT contributions is calculated.[1] Finally the reduction in the UK contribution to the EU is calculated as 66 per cent of the difference between the two mentioned shares times the total allocated expenditure.

To fix the ideas, let us take an example by using the 2013 budget numbers of Table 6.7. The total EU budget is about 158 billion Euros and the total EU allocated expenditure is then 142 billion Euros (total expenditure minus the external expenditure). The UK share of VAT is assumed to be about 18 per cent (similar to the UK GNI share of the EU GNI). The UK share of the EU expenditure is assumed to be about 9 per cent (this is the average UK share of the EU expenditure following the 2004 enlargement). Following these assumptions the correction to the normal UK contribution to the EU budget would be equal to 66 per cent × (18 per cent – 9 per cent) × 142 = 8.5 billion Euros. That counts for a two-third reduction of the UK net balance towards the EU, that, in the absence of the UK correction, would have amounted to 12.8 billion Euros.

Obviously, to avoid shortfalls in the EU budget, the other 24 countries must contribute to the EU budget the 8.5 billion Euros which are not contributed by the UK. However, to add complication to complication, the sharing of this is not linear across countries. From the year 2000, the Berlin Council decided, by unanimity, that Germany, Austria, the Netherlands and Sweden should pay only one-quarter of their normal shares. That translates into saying that the other 20 countries' financing to the UK rebate is, as a percentage of their GNI, about six times as great as the financing of these four countries. In particular, France and Italy are financing together some 50 per cent of the UK rebate and the other 22 countries are financing the remaining 50 per cent.

2. A Mathematical Treatment of the UK Rebate

Though the mathematical developments may look a bit complicated in this section, the results are on the contrary quite simple and easy to interpret. Those readers who wish to skip the mathematics may jump straight to the rule of thumb derived in equation 6A.7 and applied in cases 1 and 4. On the other hand, those readers who find the simplification of equation 6A.1 to 6A.6 too easy may enjoy the full model with no simplifications which is developed in equations 6A.8 onwards.

As a general rule it should be remembered that the UK correction was introduced at the Fontainebleau Council, on the request of the UK, in order to reduce at the margin the UK net contribution by 0.66 per cent. The mechanism is such that *at the 'margin', the UK will not 'net contribute' more than 0.34 per cent of what it would have done, had the abatement not been in place.* The 'margin' is actually quite wide, being the part of resources not financed by the traditional own resources, which by 2013 will be about 90 per cent of the total EU budget.

The formula[2] for the calculation of the UK abatement, according to the new own resource system (that is, after the introduction of the GNP resource) is as follows:

$$A = 0.66\,((V_{uk} + G_{uk})/(V + G) - E_{UK}/E)) \times E + D_{88}, \qquad (6A.1)$$

where

V_{uk} = UK share of VAT payments,
G_{uk} = UK share of GNP payments,
V, G = total VAT, GNP payments,
E_{UK} = UK share of total expenditure,
E = total expenditure,
D_{88} = UK advantage from new system.

We want to show with this model how the abatement changes with a change in the total EU expenditure. In other words, we shall derive a general formula for the increase in the UK abatement for an increased additional expenditure of 100 Euros, of which the proportion x (where $0 \leq x \leq 1$) goes to the UK.

In general, an increase in the total EU expenditure has an impact on (1) a change in the UK share of the revenues, because, by TEC, art. 268, revenues must equal expenditure, (2) an increase in allocated expenditure, (3) a change in the UK share of the allocated expenditure, (4) a very small change in the UK 'advantage' (the difference between the old and the new system for the UK, that is D_{88} in the formula).

The standard way to measure the impact is to take the first derivative with respect to E_{UK} of the formula for A (eq. 6A.1 above). Note that as the formula (6A.1) is linear in E, the derivative is constant at any point and therefore, although we are doing marginal analysis (by definition of derivatives) it is valid also for non-marginal movements:

$$\frac{\partial A}{\partial E}=0.66\left\{\left[\frac{\dfrac{\partial(V_{uk}+G_{uk})}{(V+G)}}{\partial E}-\frac{\partial(E_{UK}/E)}{\partial E}\right]E+\frac{\partial E}{\partial E}\left[\frac{(V_{uk}+G_{uk})}{(V+G)}-\frac{E_{UK}}{E}\right]+\frac{\partial D_{88}}{\partial E}\right\}. \tag{6A.2}$$

Imposing $\dfrac{\partial D_{88}}{\partial E}=0$, the other three derivatives in eq. 6A.2 are as follows:

$$\partial\left(\frac{V_{uk}+G_{uk}}{V+G}\right)\Big/\partial E=\frac{1}{V+G}\times\left[\frac{G_{uk}}{G}-\frac{V_{uk}+G_{uk}}{V+G}\right], \tag{6A.3}$$

$$\partial\left(\frac{E_{UK}}{E}\right)\Big/\partial E=\frac{1}{E}\left(x-\frac{E_{UK}}{E}\right), \tag{6A.4}$$

$$\frac{\partial E}{\partial E}=1. \tag{6A.5}$$

Substituting (6A.3), (6A.4) and (6A.5) into eq. 6A.2 and making the necessary simplifications allows the formula to be reduced to

$$\frac{\partial A}{\partial E}=0.66\times\left[\frac{E}{V+G}\left(\frac{G_{uk}}{G}-\frac{V_{uk}+G_{uk}}{V+G}\right)-x-\frac{V_{uk}+G_{uk}}{V+G}\right], \tag{6A.6}$$

which can be used relatively quickly once the parameters E, V and G are known.

From eq. 6A.6 a rule of thumb, with an acceptable margin of error, could be constructed, just assuming $E/(V+G)=1$. This essentially amounts to arguing that the non-allocated part of the budget is also the part financed by resources other than VAT or GNP. A quick look at the budget of the last ten years shows that this is exactly the case, given that they both hover around 10–12 per cent. Once this simplification is accepted, formula (6A.6) becomes astonishingly simple, reducing to

$$\frac{\partial A}{\partial E}=0.66\times\left(\frac{G_{uk}}{G}-x\right). \tag{6A.7}$$

Various simulations for possible different values of x, using both eq. 6A.6 and eq. 6A.7, show that the error, using Eq. 6A.7, is limited.

As illustrated below, Eq. 6A.7 is of immediate and easy use and furthermore of crystalline interpretation. It says that for each additional 100 Euros of expenditure the UK abatement grows by 66 per cent of the difference between how much the UK pays for those 100 Euros and how much the UK derives from those 100 Euros. This reduces the UK *net* contribution for those *additional 100* Euros to only one-third.

Eq. 6A.7 may be used to answer quickly (and with a small error) the following question: 'If the EU budget spends 100 Euros more, of which x goes to the UK, by how much does the UK abatement change?' We will check its validity by substituting the four most interesting values of x into Eq. 6A.7. For the other parameters we will use a value of $G_{uk}/G = 0.15$ and a value of $E_{UK}/E = 0.10$. These are fictitious numbers, very close to the reality of the last few years.

Case 1: all 100 Euros to all countries other than the UK (UK share = 0)

The change in the UK abatement is maximally positive, being of $+0.66 \times (G_{uk}/G) = 0.1$. The UK gross contribution to those 100 Euros is 15, the increase in the abatement is 10, the increase in expenditure received is 0, the UK net contribution reduces by 5 (=15−10). This may be the most interesting case. Since it shows what happens to the UK net contribution, when some new expenditure, for example to eastern or southern countries, is decided.

Case 2: 100 Euros of which the UK receives a share equal to its standard share (UK share 0.1)

The change in the UK abatement is still positive being of $+3.33 = (0.66 \times (15-10))$. Thus the UK gross contribution to those 100 Euros is 15, the increase in the abatement is 3.3, the increase in expenditure received is 10, the UK net contribution reduces by 1.66 (=15−10−3.33).

Case 3: 100 Euros of which the UK receives a share equal to its standard budget contribution (GNP) share (UK share 0.15)

The change in the UK abatement is equal to zero $(0 = 0.66 \times (15-15))$. This is due to the fact that the UK is getting 15 Euros out of those 100 Euros, which is exactly what the UK pays for those additional 100 Euros. The claim, 'I want my money back' is therefore fully satisfied because the UK does get its money back and the abatement does not need to play any role. Thus the UK gross contribution to those 100 Euros is 15, the increase in the abatement is 0, the increase in expenditure received is 15, the UK net contribution reduces by 0 (=15−15).

Case 4: all 100 Euros to UK (UK share = 1)

The change in the UK abatement is negative = 0.66 × (15 − 100) = −56.66. This is because the UK more than 'has its money back'. The UK is getting 100 Euros, paying only 15. The change in the abatement is therefore negative. Thus the UK gross contribution to those 100 Euros is 15, the increase in the abatement is −56.66, the increase in expenditure received is 100, the UK net contribution increases by 28.33 (= 15 − (−56.66) − 100). In this case for each additional 100 Euros paid exclusively to the UK, only 28 are actually paid by the other 24 member states, 15 are paid by the UK as standard GNP contribution and 58 are paid by the UK as a reduction of its own abatement.

More generally, the correct formula for the calculation of the UK correction is as follows:[3]

$$A = 0.66\left(\frac{V_{uk}^{NE}}{V^{NE}} - \frac{E_{UK}}{E}\right) \times E + (G_{uk} + V_{uk}^{E} + S_{uk}^{E} - V_{uk}^{NE} - S_{uk}^{NE}), \qquad (6A.8)$$

where

V_{uk} = UK share of VAT payments,
G_{uk} = UK share of GNP payments,
V, G = total VAT, GNP payments,
E_{UK} = UK share of total expenditure,
E = total expenditure,
Suk = UK share of VAT and GNP adjustments for previous year's forecasting errors
NE: non-capped; E: capped.

The formula's first-order derivative is

$$\frac{\partial A}{\partial E} = 0.66\left\{\left[\frac{\partial\left(\frac{V_{uk}^{NE}}{V^{NE}}\right)}{\partial E} - \frac{\partial(E_{UK}/E)}{\partial E}\right]E + \frac{\partial E}{\partial E}\left[\left(\frac{V_{uk}^{NE}}{V^{NE}}\right) - \frac{E_{UK}}{E}\right]\right\}$$
$$+ \frac{\partial(G_{uk} + V_{uk}^{E} + S_{uk}^{E} - V_{uk}^{NE} - S_{uk}^{NE})}{\partial E}. \qquad (6A.9)$$

The four derivatives in eq. 6A.9 are as follows:

$$\partial(V_{uk}^{NE}/V^{NE})/\partial E = \left(\left[\frac{V_{uk}^{NE}}{V^{NE}} \times V^{NE} - V_{uk}^{NE}\right]\Big/(V^{NE})^2\right) = 0. \qquad (6A.10)$$

$$\partial(E_{UK}/E)/\partial E = \frac{1}{E} \times (x - \frac{E_{UK}}{E}). \tag{6A.11}$$

$$(\partial E/\partial E) = 1. \tag{6A.12}$$

$$\frac{\partial(G_{uk} + V_{uk}^{E} + S_{uk}^{E}\ V_{uk}^{NE} - S_{uk}^{NE})}{\partial E} = G_{uk}/G. \tag{6A.13}$$

Substituting (6A.10), (6A.11), (6A.12) and (6A.13) into equation 6A.9 and making the necessary simplifications allows the formula to be reduced to the following:

$$\frac{\partial A}{\partial E} = 0.66\left[0 - \left(\frac{x - E_{UK}/E}{E}\right) \times E + \left(\frac{V_{uk}^{NE}}{V^{NE}} - \frac{E_{uk}}{E}\right)\right] + \frac{G_{uk}}{G} - \frac{V_{uk}^{NE}}{V}$$

$$= 0.66\left[\frac{V_{uk}^{NE}}{V^{NE}} - x\right] + \left(\frac{G_{uk}}{G} - \frac{V_{uk}^{NE}}{V^{NE}}\right). \tag{6A.14}$$

This can be interpreted as follows: the first bracket accounts for the 'core' of the spirit of the correction (to avoid the UK net contribution at the margin – only the VAT resource under the old system – exceeding one-third) and the second bracket accounts for the difference between the old and the new system. The formula (6A.14) can also be rewritten in a less intuitive but easier to calculate form:

$$\frac{\partial A}{\partial E} = \left(\frac{G_{uk}}{G} - \frac{1}{3}\frac{V_{uk}^{NE}}{V^{NE}}\right) = -\,0.66x. \tag{6A.15}$$

Despite the fact that 6A.14 and/or 6A.15 look like accessible formulas they are harder to use than 6A.7 since data for V_{uk}^{NE}/V^{NE} are not so readily available.

The essence of this mathematical analysis of the UK rebate thus reveals that the UK rebate reduces the extent of the changes in the UK net balance due to increased EU expenditure. If additional EU expenditure goes predominantly to the UK, the rebate makes the UK pay more than it would otherwise; if additional EU expenditure goes predominantly to other countries, the UK would pay less than otherwise. We have derived a very simple equation (6A.7) that, however, is precise enough to be used for forecasting or simulation purposes (its inherent error would in any case be lower than the standard forecasting errors) and we believe it carries through the intuition rather well. We have also derived another formula (equation 6A.15), for very precise ex post calculations.

3. The Budgetary Treatment of the UK Rebate

The way used to insert the UK rebate into the EU budget is even more complicated, owing to the fact that the exact figures needed are available only with some delay. The UK rebate of the year N is first inserted in the preliminary budget of the year $N+1$, and then, on occasion, a first partial revision is budgeted in the supplementary and amended budget of the same year $N+1$. Finally the difference between the definitive calculation and the provisional estimate is inserted in the supplementary and amended budget of the year $N+4$,since the definitive data for GNP and VAT are available only with three years' delay. That means that in the supplementary and amended budget of any year, the amount referring to the UK correction is indeed the sum of a provisional estimate and the difference between a definitive and provisional calculation.

In other words, the whole mechanism is of an absolute opacity and impossible to understand for a normally informed citizen and thus it makes any form of democratic control difficult.

NOTES

1. Since the mechanism was agreed in 1984, before the introduction of the GNP resource, only the UK share of the VAT contributions is calculated so as to subtract implicitly from the mechanism the advantage that the UK derives from the introduction of the GNP resource. According to the same logic, since 2001 the advantage for the UK of the increase from 10 per cent to 25 per cent of the TOR's collection fees and the classification of pre-enlargement expenditure into EU expenditure from the 2004 enlargement is also subtracted from the UK rebate. It must be said, however, that these adjustments are very minor and account for less than 10 per cent of the UK rebate.
2. From a mathematical point of view the *exclusive* use of this formula is simply not possible. Indeed the term D_{88} has the function to equalise the correction calculated according to the new systems (post-1988 and post-1999 modifications), with the correction calculated according to the old system (that is, prior to the introduction of the GNP resource). Therefore D_{88} can be found only by equalising equation 6A.1 and equation 6A.8. The latter equation describes the old system, is much less intuitive and more complicated. However, since we show that the results are so similar using the 'simple' or the 'full' model, the additional complication of using the 'full' model may be easily spared.
3. To be excessively precise, the formula as of eq. 6A.8 was valid between 1988 to 2000. Since 2001, two terms, decided at the Berlin Council Meeting of March 1999 (see note 1 above), should also be added. We have decided to leave them out because they add nothing to the analysis and much to the complication of the issue.

7. The Common Agricultural Policy

7.1 INTRODUCTION

The Common Agricultural Policy (CAP henceforth) is the best-known and most debated common policy of the EU. Its origins, in the 1950s and 1960s, are linked to history and relate essentially to the transition of the post-war EU economy from an economy based on agriculture to an economy based on industry and services (see Chapter 1). Its continuation in the 1980s, 1990s and the first decade of the twenty-first century is a delicate balance between political and economic reasons.

The CAP is the only entirely communitarian policy in that, as we have seen in Chapter 6, its financing is entirely provided for by the EU budget. As we shall make clearer in what follows, its aims are sustaining the income of farmers, promoting technical progress in agriculture and ensuring self-sufficiency and stable food markets with reasonable prices for consumers in Europe.

Among policy makers, academics and practitioners, as well as ordinary citizens, the debate on the CAP is generally hot and often for the wrong reasons. The dividing line between those 'in favour' and those 'against' the CAP is however resilient to all possible classifications. Political, national or cultural categories are normally not a good indicator of one's preferences towards the CAP. Within a given political party of a given country, in fact, one may find opposite, often extreme, positions on the CAP. Similarly the change of political colour of a government of any given country does not necessarily translate into a change of that country's attitude towards the common agricultural policy.

Given that, the overall purpose of the present chapter is therefore neither to attack nor to defend the CAP, but only to explain it in terms of its economic and political rationale, by taking into account the constraints that history and society imposed and are still imposing on it. The structure of this chapter is the following: first we shall give a factual account of the reasons for the EU to set up and run a Common Agricultural Policy (section 7.2) and we shall look at both its tools (section 7.3) and its results (section 7.4). Then we shall look at the various attempts at reform of the CAP from the mid-1980s until today, in which various environmental, commercial, social, political and economic concerns were tackled, especially in light of the recent enlargement of the European Union (section 7.5). Finally we offer our views on the future prospects of the CAP within a global world (section 7.6) and then conclude (section 7.7).

7.2 HISTORY AND RATIONALE OF THE COMMON AGRICULTURAL POLICY

At the time when the Treaty of Rome was being negotiated, agriculture and its related issues sat very high on the agenda of European policy makers. On the one hand, the memory of post-war food shortages was still vivid, pushing policy makers to make sure that Europe was able to attain food self-sufficiency quickly and safely. On the other hand, policy makers were taken aback by the intensity and the rapidity of the transformations taking place in society. In many nations, in fact, the growing labour demand coming from the post-war booming industrial sector was creating increasing pressures for a potentially massive outflow of people from the rural areas towards the new urban industrial centres.[1]

Faced with this situation, the EU policy makers had two options: (a) to let the 'market' do the necessary adjustment, which would have translated into massive emigration out of the countryside and into the towns, or (b) to find ways to accompany this transformation of economy and society. The first solution was probably cheaper in budgetary terms (at least in the short run), but more expensive from the social point of view. The second solution was certainly more expensive in budgetary terms, since it required a policy specifically aimed at sustaining income levels of the rural population to prevent its urbanisation, but would have led to less serious social problems. In addition, it also became immediately clear to everybody that the transformation of the economy, and of the society alongside it, was so pervasive that any policy aimed at managing these processes clearly had a European rather than a national dimension. In other words, whatever the course of action taken by policy makers, it could have been successful only if it had been the result of a concerted effort of policy coordination across the member states.

The traditional European attention to the containment of social costs while fostering economic transformation and growth, already extensively discussed in the previous chapters, obviously made policy makers opt for the second solution, thus including the common agricultural policy as one of the main pillars of the Treaty on the European Economic Community signed in Rome in 1957.

The operational principles of the CAP were then set out at a Conference in Stresa (Italy) in 1958. In 1960, the CAP mechanisms were adopted by the six founding member states and, two years later, in 1962, the common agricultural policy came into force. The **objectives** of the CAP are clearly spelled out in TEC, art. 33:[2]

(a) to increase agricultural productivity by promoting technical progress and by ensuring the rational development of agricultural production and the optimum utilisation of the factors of production, in particular labour;
(b) thus to ensure a fair standard of living for the agricultural community, in particular by increasing the individual earnings of persons engaged in agriculture;
(c) to stabilise markets;
(d) to assure the availability of supplies;
(e) to ensure that supplies reach consumers at reasonable prices.

The objective under point (a) indicates an increase in the supply of agricultural production, to be achieved through technological progress and eventually some labour reallocation. Point (b) indicates point (a) as a means to increase the individual earnings of those employed in agriculture (note the 'thus' at the beginning of the text). The three remaining objectives seem to point to some market regulatory functions of the CAP. Point (c) simply says that demand and supply should possibly match: given the much greater rigidity of the demand for agricultural products with respect to the supply,[3] this translates into avoiding underproduction or overproduction, since most of the adjustment lies with the producers. Avoiding underproduction is also the concern of point (d) with memories of the post-war food crisis, while (e) seems to set a limit to the CAP in terms of prices: the common agricultural policy should not yield as a result prices of agricultural products that are not 'reasonable'.

To summarise, article 33 seems to pledge a policy fostering technological progress that increases production, thus guaranteeing EU food self-sufficiency, and ensuring equilibrium of demand and supply at a level which guarantees both a fair living standard for those engaged in agriculture and reasonable prices for consumers. It has been often pointed out that the simultaneous achievement of these five objectives is not an easy task, especially as some of these objectives might even be in contradiction. For example, a greater supply of agricultural products, made available via technological progress (such as better fertilisers), might certainly help in meeting the food self-sufficiency requirement, but, per se, may not be enough to stabilise markets (overproduction might arise) and/or to increase the individual earnings of the farmers (see below).

It is fair to say that some of the possible contradictions existing among these objectives are due to the fact that the CAP has been defined and established under the influence of different historical, social, economic, political and environmental dimensions, which we now analyse in turn.

First the **historical dimension**: when the CAP was set up, about 25 per cent of the work force of the six founding member states was engaged in agriculture. All six countries had their own national agricultural policy based on different tools: some policies attempted to modify prices charged by farmers, others to control quantities produced, and others again to support income without interfering with the market equilibrium. Different policies and different tools were obviously hardly compatible with the single market for agriculture advocated in the Treaty of Rome, and yet a compromise had to be found among the different needs, in order to reach a unanimous agreement and proceed with the integration process.

As regards the **economic and social dimension**, agricultural prices have shown a high degree of variability over time and generally, owing to technological progress, they have displayed a decreasing trend. Given the relative rigidity of the demand for agricultural products with respect to prices, a price reduction generated by a technological/climate shock, or by international market trends, normally translates into an income reduction for the producers.[4] If left to market forces, in order to make up for the lost income, producers would react by increasing their production, thus provoking an even greater reduction in agricultural prices and incomes, until the restructuring of the sector and the exit of the most inefficient firms takes place. Considering the opportunities offered by the growing industrial sectors, in terms of higher and more stable income, a massive exodus of producers from the countryside and the agricultural sector is thus very likely to happen, with the associated social problems. The common CAP has therefore been instrumental in controlling and/or accompanying such a change in the patterns of economic activity which took place in Europe after World War II.

Next, the **political dimension**: still today, in many member states, workers engaged in agriculture constitute a formidable lobby, because of their rooted allegiance to the territory and their links with many sectors of the economy. It has been argued by some observers (see Collignon, 2003) that the CAP was instrumental, at the moment Europe was being created, in reducing the inherent inward nationalistic attitude of agricultural workers. Essentially the CAP payments bought the consensus of agricultural workers to the common EU cause. Even today, in the enlarged Europe, the attitude of some of the new member states towards the integration process is heavily influenced by the opinions of their agricultural lobbies.

The **environmental concerns**, although not explicitly mentioned in article 33, are an integral part of the implementation of the CAP since article 6 of the Treaty reads: 'Environmental protection requirements must be integrated into the definition and implementation of the Community policies and activities referred to in Article 3 [among them agricultural policy], in particular with a view to promoting sustainable development.' It is clear that environmental concerns have become more and more prominent in the Union in recent years, because of both the change in attitudes of the EU citizens and the EU membership of the Nordic countries, who have a long tradition of environmental rigour.

The second paragraph of article 33 clarifies which elements should be taken into account in order to attain a 'reasonable' level of prices for agricultural products, a level which, presumably, is different from the market one (had market prices been acceptable, there would have been no need of a common policy). In particular, article 33 mentions the following:

> In working out the common agricultural policy and the special methods for its application, account shall be taken of:
> (a) the particular nature of agricultural activity, which results from the social structure of agriculture and from structural and natural disparities between the various agricultural regions;
> (b) the need to effect the appropriate adjustments by degrees;
> (c) the fact that in the Member States agriculture constitutes a sector closely linked with the economy as a whole.

The worries expressed in both (a) and (c) are linked to the inherent social relevance of agriculture and its interdependency with the rest of the economy, while (b) calls substantially for a gradual approach.

7.3 THE TOOLS OF CAP

The implementation of TEC, art. 33 and the achievement of its various goals required special instruments. To this end, TEC, art. 34 provides for the creation of the **common organisation of the agricultural markets** (COM or OCM[5]).

> This organisation shall take one of the following forms, depending on the product concerned:
> (a) common rules on competition;
> (b) compulsory coordination of the various national market organisations;
> (c) a European market organisation.

The OCM were introduced gradually, and now exist for most EU agricultural products (OCM beef, OCM rice and so on). Three main principles, defined in 1962, characterise them:

1. A **unified market** denoting the free movement of agricultural products within member states (disregarding whether they are of internal or external origin). Hence, for the organisation of the unified market, common means and mechanisms should be used throughout the EU.
2. **Community preference**, implying that EU agricultural products are given preference and a price advantage over imported products. The protection of the internal market from low-priced imports from third countries, which eventually translates into the imposition of import duties on agricultural products, is thus guaranteed, together with the isolation of the EU market from fluctuations in the world prices of agricultural products. Hence the price faced by the EU citizens on agricultural products is likely to be dissociated from the underlying market situation.
3. **Financial solidarity**, implying that all expenses and spending which result from the application of the CAP are borne by the Community budget. This amounts to saying that no national agricultural policy exists, and the CAP is not co-financed. As already discussed, such a set-up is a *unicum* in the EU budget, since all other financial interventions are co-financed by the receiving countries (to an extent going from 50 to 90 per cent) through their national budgets.

Within the above principles, which define the working of the OCMs and thus the CAP, there are essentially two radically different means of support for the agricultural sector: **price support** measures (section 7.3.1) and **income support** measure (section 7.3.2). The EU started by embracing the first, then progressively, and slowly, abandoned it in favour of the second, owing to mounting international pressures and the EU enlargement to Eastern Europe, as will be made clear in the remainder of the chapter. By 2013, the transition from price support measures to income support measures will probably be near to completion.

7.3.1 Price Support Measures

Price support has been for a long time the main instrument of the CAP. Figure 7.1 illustrates in brief how price support measures work. Let us assume that the market equilibrium price, before any political intervention, is P_0, with equilibrium quantities OQ, while the world market price is Pw. Recalling the standard results of Chapter 2, in the absence of a common protectionist policy intervening on market prices, the world price would

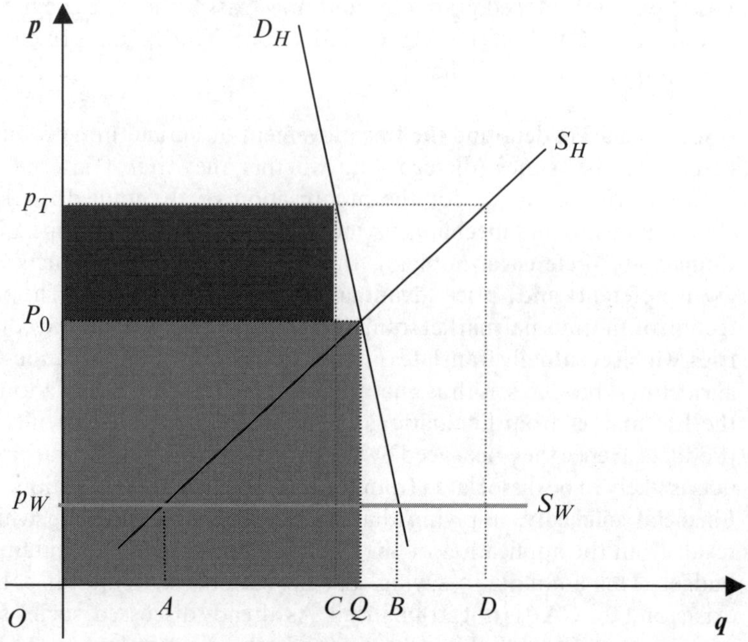

Figure 7.1 The working of the price support mechanism in the CAP

dominate and the gap existing at the world price between the domestic supply *OA* and the (higher) domestic demand *OB* would be covered by imports *AB*. Because of the rigidity of the demand curve, however, the demand does not benefit much from the access to lower world prices (*OB* and *OQ* are relatively similar), while the absence of an agricultural policy imposes a toll on EU production (the producers' surplus is reduced by an amount equal to area P_0QAP_w). This entails, in turn, a massive job relocation from agriculture to other sectors of the economy. Although such an outcome makes perfect economic sense (it is the good old law of Ricardian comparative advantages), for the reasons previously outlined the same outcome would be politically unacceptable. Therefore a community intervention is deemed necessary. In general, this can take the form of a price support mechanism, which consists of three elements.

1. A **tariff** on imported products. As in the standard theory of protectionism, the tariff serves the purpose of making imported products (priced at P_w) less competitive with respect to domestic products (whose market price is $P_0 > P_w$), and thus isolating the domestic market from international competition, at the expense of consumers' welfare.[6]

2. A politically determined domestic price (called **target price**, P_T) fixed at a level generally higher than the internal market price level.[7] As already discussed, the rigidity of the demand associated with a price increase translates into a fall in demand ($OC < OQ$) which is proportionally lower than the higher prices ($P_T > P_0$) obtained on each unit sold. Thus the imposition of the target price P_T translates into larger revenues for producers for the products sold on the market, as displayed comparing the $P_0 \times OQ$ and $P_T \times OC$ areas in Figure 7.1 (where $P_T \times OC > P_0 \times OQ$). Such an outcome allows reaching one of the objectives of the CAP, a fair standard of living for the agricultural community, but in partial contradiction to another objective of the CAP, ensuring reasonable prices for consumers.[8] In addition, given the shapes of supply and demand, the imposition of the intervention price $P_T > P_0$ also translates into larger production quantities and thus into sizeable market disequilibria, depicted by the excess of supply *CD*, contrary to another CAP objective: to stabilise markets.
3. Quota and/or export refunds. Because of the overproduction generated by the politically determined 'target price' (the quantity *CD* in Figure 7.1), some measures to cope with these excesses are necessary. Two categories of measures are possible and may eventually be deployed simultaneously: (a) quantity restrictions, such as a quota system, or a set-aside system (see *infra*); (b) export refunds, to allow domestic product to be exported at the world price on the world market. The export refunds (better known as **export subsidies**) call for the public authority to 'refund' to producers the difference between the world price P_w and the domestic (politically determined) target price P_T.

The price support mechanism applied into the CAP translates therefore into a policy which calls on three categories of actors to contribute to the increased welfare of the agricultural community: (1) consumers, who end up paying the target price $P_T > P_0 > P_w$; (2) taxpayers, via the financing of the export refunds operated through the EU budget; and (3) extra-EU producers, who suffer from the closure of the EU market.

The distributional and financial consequences of such a policy are very severe and transparency is hampered. The **burden on consumers** is equal to the difference between the smaller quantity actually consumed at the politically determined domestic target price (P_T) and the higher quantity eventually available for consumption without price intervention, at price P_0 or, without tariff protection, at price P_w. Due to the price support mechanism, the consumers' contribution to the CAP is thus sizeable and non-transparent, since consumers are clearly unaware of which part of the price they pay translates into a subsidy to producers, and which part does not.

Furthermore the consumers' contribution to the scheme is highly regressive, and hence socially undesirable, since in general poorer consumers spend a larger part of their income on food products than do richer consumers.

The overall **burden on taxpayers** is the difference between the cost of financing the export refunds and the revenues coming from the tariff revenues on those goods for which the various OCM eventually allow some imports. The cost of the export refunds is equal to the difference between the EU target price P_T guaranteed to the farmers and the world price P_w, multiplied by the excess supply (*CD*) so generated. The revenues on the duties received are instead equal to the size of the tariff times the quantity of the imported products.[9] In general imposing a burden on taxpayers is fairer than one on consumers from a distributional standpoint, since, in a progressive tax system, richer taxpayers tend to pay more than poorer ones. However export refunds have the potential to drive the EU budget out of control, since the world price is not under the control of the EU authorities and, therefore, should the gap between the target price and the world price increase too much, the total amount of export refunds to be granted may well be open-ended.

Finally the price support mechanism imposes a **burden on extra-EU producers**, in terms of forgone market opportunities and large negative externalities. In fact the price support mechanism largely prevents imports of commodities and other agricultural products originating from extra-EU countries to reach the protected markets of the Union, with sometimes dramatic consequences, since for some developing countries access to EU agricultural markets would be their only source of exports and international currency. In addition the mechanism also generates a dumping effect of agricultural world prices, caused by the European overproduction flooding the international markets thanks to the aid received by the farmer via the export subsidies. As a result developing countries not only are unable to sell their products to the EU, but also see the price of their agricultural exports fall on the international markets, always as a consequence of the price support mechanism of the EU common agricultural policy.

In other words, the price support mechanism, originally created to solve an internal European problem, turned out to generate highly regressive effects within the same EU, and to have a perverse effect vis-à-vis developing countries. As such, it was neither politically nor economically sustainable in the long run.

7.3.2 Direct Income Support

The direct income support mechanism of the CAP (often referred to as **direct aids**) works in a radically different way from price support. Direct income support does not intervene in the determination of the market price and therefore does not alter the demand and production decisions. It only supports directly, via financial subsidies paid by the EU budget, the income of those engaged in agriculture. These subsidies are meant to cover the difference between a politically determined 'fair' income, in the spirit of TEC, art. 33, and the income that each farmer generates in the market by selling his products. The attractiveness of this means of supporting income is at least threefold:

1. it does not entail market distortion either in terms of higher prices or in terms of excess supply;
2. it is fairer than price support from a distributive standpoint since, being financed by the EU budget, and hence by the EU taxpayers, it affects citizens progressively and not regressively;
3. it does not necessarily constitute a closure of the EU market to extra-EU imports, although the higher the protection through tariffs, the higher will be the initial income the farmers obtain on the market (because of higher internal prices) and thus the lower the amount of subsidies necessary to reach the 'fair' income level.

Clearly the greater is the distance between the politically determined 'fair' income and the income the producers initially make on the market, the higher is the burden for the EU finances. As a result the sensitive issues with this method lie in the determination of a 'fair' income, and in the degree of openness of the EU markets to world imports, since, as mentioned, the latter influences the initial income level of farmers.

In its purest form, the 'fair' income is linked to the **potential income** of the farmer (considering the dimension of his or her land and the number of the cattle, for instance), not to the actual production. In other words, the 'fair' income should be that resulting from a correct exploitation of the land/cattle available to the farmer, taking into account the need to preserve the environment and the guarantee of food quality and safety. However, for operational reasons, the amount of direct aid available to farmers in the EU has been calculated with reference to historical production records. This led to some agricultural producers trying to maximise their production output in order to get as many subsidies as possible, with the risk of overexploitation of the land or the cattle, at the expense of the environment or food safety.[10]

In order to tackle this and other distortions previously mentioned, historically the CAP has moved progressively, albeit slowly, from the untenable price support mechanism to income support, and, within income support, from direct aid linked to production records to aid linked to the concept of potential income previously outlined. The latter operation, in particular, is known as '**decoupling**'. Decoupling means that the amount of aid is less related to the historical production and more to the potential income. As such, the extent of decoupling of direct aid is one of the main controversial points in the current debate on the CAP reforms (see *infra*).

Our analysis has thus shown the superiority of the income support mechanism, when linked to the concept of potential income. However, having assessed this, what still needs to be demonstrated is that the optimal level at which one needs to take decisions on the amount of income support is the EU one. As a matter of fact, direct aid to farmers, especially if decoupled from production (that is, granted on the basis of the notion of potential income), amounts, plain and simple, to a policy of interpersonal income redistribution. Now we have extensively shown throughout the book how politicians and academics in the EU agree on the fact that interpersonal redistribution should be dealt with at the national rather than at the EU level (see Chapters 1, 5 and 6). This is essentially due to the application of the subsidiarity principle: a decision maker in Brussels has a very great information disadvantage as regards the individual income situation when compared with a national or a locally based one. As a result, the CAP having progressively become a system of interpersonal redistribution of wealth, the discussion on the need to maintain the decisions on income support for agriculture at the EU level was (and still is) possibly the hottest debate in recent reforms, and will be dealt with in section 7.5 of the chapter.

7.4 RESULTS OF THE COMMON AGRICULTURAL POLICY

The common agricultural policy managed to achieve some of its objectives pretty soon: a few years after the launch of the CAP, the EU reached self-sufficiency in agricultural consumption, no longer suffering from food shortage. The transition from an agricultural to an industrial economy was also successful and smooth, with the income of people engaged in agriculture increasing and becoming more stable. Many of the EU agricultural production units remained family-sized. Almost nowhere in the EU do we in fact witness the situation where very few people cultivate incredibly large domains, with the rest of the land being abandoned and having no market value. Quite to the contrary, the agricultural land in the EU (certainly also because of the CAP subsidies linked to it) has kept its market value.

However these results were initially achieved at the cost of some important distortions, which, as we have seen, were linked to the CAP price support mechanism, the very tool used to implement the CAP in its early years. We complete here the list of the most problematic aspects of the early CAP.

There is an effect of **market insulation.** In a free and competitive market every producer takes the price as given and maximises his or her profit by making his or her production decisions. The market price is determined by the sum of the individual supplies and demands. The political determination of the target price by the CAP instead breaks the link between demand and supply and makes individual decisions of consumption and production independent of the market signals. As a result, distortions of the types already mentioned, such as overproduction, pollution or poor food safety, arise. In addition, when market signals can be safely ignored by producers, **competitiveness** also will suffer in the medium to long run. This is all the more true if the EU market is closed to imports from extra-EU countries.

Moreover the early CAP had a negative impact on the **political economy of EU trade**. Both the tariffs imposed on imports in the EU market and the refunds on the EU exports generated a situation whereby our commercial partners (most of all the USA) started to feel damaged by the CAP. Furthermore, for the arguments previously developed, a diffused awareness emerged that the CAP price support was preventing developing countries from trading and growing richer, a situation which started to weaken the EU bargaining position within the World Trade Organisation (WTO).[11]

The price support mechanism was also particularly complicated and segmented across sectors and products. Complicated rules for different products are the perfect humus for **fraud** and make control and monitoring particularly complicated. The Court of Auditors in its annual report often highlighted potential and actual risks of fraud in the management of the CAP.

Finally, as analysed in Chapter 6, the CAP is the single most important element in the determination of what are (or are perceived to be) unfair **budgetary disequilibria**. Indeed this negative result of the CAP is independent of the chosen system of protection of farmers' income (price support or direct aid), since the effect essentially results from the allocation of CAP expenditure which, however undertaken, are totally independent of the income of the receiving country. On the one hand, relatively rich countries, such as Denmark and France, still receive very large chunks of EU money via the CAP; ultimately they have a budgetary position which is more favourable than what one would expect from a relatively rich country. On the other hand, relatively poor countries, such as the UK in the 1970s, were receiving very little from the EU budget, given that their agricultural sector was relatively small. As a result, the simultaneous enlargement in 1973 to admit the UK and Denmark (at that time respectively the second-poorest

Table 7.1 Farmer income by farm size, EU12, 1991/92

Income generated by the farm, by income class (Euros per year)	Number of holdings (millions)	Number of holdings as % share of all holdings	Average annual farm income per farmer, Euros	Average size (hectares)	Farm net value added per hectare, Euros
0–5 000	2.0	45	900	15.0	287
5 000–10 000	1.0	22	7 300	18.4	668
10 000–20 000	0.9	20	14 100	27.8	813
20 000–30 000	0.3	7	24 300	37.4	1 061
Over 30 000	0.3	6	51 800	55.4	1 527
All holding	4.4	100	9 300	22.3	762

Source: Table 3.2.4, *The agricultural situation in the Community*, 1993, European Commission; as retrieved from Baldwin and Wyplosz (2003).

and the second-richest EU country) at a time when the CAP was about 80 per cent of the EU budget, made their respective budgetary positions immediately very divergent (very negative for the UK and very positive for Denmark).[12] In addition the interpersonal income redistribution generated by the CAP often leads to a **regressive income redistribution**, with large, rich farmers and/or landowners receiving the greatest share of the transfers, as shown in Tables 7.1 and 7.2.

7.5 THE CAP REFORMS

The attempt to pursue multiple objectives with a single instrument is probably at the root of the many distortions ultimately generated by the early developments of the common agricultural policy. In a way the CAP originally tried to balance two quite distinct objectives: greater production via technological progress and efficiency, and social protection. A better, distinct achievement of these two objectives is the rationale for the series of reforms which started in the mid-1980s and which were also driven by the necessity of making the CAP compatible, on the one hand, with the global trading trends prevailing worldwide, and, on the other hand, with the 2004 enlargement of the Union to the east.

Actually, because of the distortions brought in by the price support mechanism, the first attempt at reforming the CAP came just ten years after its creation. In 1968, the Commission published a ‘Memorandum on the

Table 7.2 Inequity of direct payments, receipts per farm by farm size, 2000

Size of farm (hectares)	Payment per farm, Euros	% of EU15 farms in size class	Number of farms in size class	% of EU15 payments to size class	Cumulative % of budget (from largest to smallest)	Cumulative % of farms (from largest to smallest)
0–1.25	405	53.76	2 397 630	4.3	100.0	99.97
1.25–2	1 593	8.54	380 800	2.7	95.7	46.21
2–5	3 296	16.30	726 730	10.7	93.0	37.67
5–10	7 128	9.17	409 080	13.0	82.2	21.37
10–20	13 989	6.81	303 500	19.0	69.2	12.20
20–50	30 098	4.13	184 100	24.8	50.2	5.39
50–100	67 095	0.94	41 700	12.5	25.4	1.27
100–200	133 689	0.24	10 720	6.4	12.9	0.33
200–300	241 157	0.05	2 130	2.3	6.5	0.09
300–500	376 534	0.03	1 270	2.1	4.2	0.04
Over 500	768 333	0.01	610	2.1	2.1	0.01
Average, all farms	5 015					

Source: Table 3.6.1.10 in *Agriculture in the EU – Statistics and Economic Information*, 2002, European Commission; as retrieved from Baldwin and Wyplosz (2003).

reform of the CAP' (European Commission, 1968), commonly known as the **Mansholt Plan**. The Plan sought to reduce the number of people employed in agriculture and to promote the formation of larger and more efficient units of agricultural production, without however going to extremes similar to those of the USA.

In 1972, structural measures implementing the Mansholt Plan were introduced into the CAP, with the aim of restructuring EU farming into a mixture of commercial farmers and part-time farmers, helping viable farmers with selective investment aid and encouraging large numbers of non-viable farmers to leave the industry with retirement incentives. But, despite continued structural changes in the following years, the system of target prices kept driving the supply and demand of agricultural products out of balance, thus resulting in an ever-growing surplus. The EU Commission repeatedly proposed a prudent price policy to cut CAP prices. Agricultural ministers were reluctant to accept any serious cut, but eventually a 3 per cent annual cut was agreed in 1977 and this lasted until 1993. The 1973 enlargement, coupled with an economic slowdown, rendered the situation even more troublesome because of the financial problems previously cited, while the 1981 enlargement to Greece and the 1986 one to Portugal and Spain increased even further the number of people engaged in agriculture and entitled to receive support. The EU was no longer able to gain control of CAP expenditure in order to free financial resources and pursue other policies.

At the same time, in 1986, a new round of multilateral trade negotiations, known as the Uruguay Round, had opened under the GATT agreement (see Chapter 10): for the first time, countries were supposed to discuss also the issue of liberalising international trade in agricultural products. Clearly the original price support mechanism of the CAP was no longer sustainable internally, was not viable from an international perspective, and had to be replaced.

7.5.1 The 1988 Delors I Reform

As a result, in 1988, the European Council agreed on a package of reform measures, on the basis of a Commission Green Paper (European Commission, 1985b), which aimed at bringing supply and demand into balance, at introducing new ways of reducing production in some sensitive sectors and, generally, at analysing alternative solutions for the future of the CAP. The three main aspects of the 1988 reform were as follows.

1. The imposition of the EU 'agricultural guideline', which prevented the growth of CAP expenses to be greater than 74 per cent of the growth of the EU GNP. That amounts to saying that the share of CAP expenditures in the EU budget decreases with GNP growth, freeing resources for other EU policies, in particular structural expenditures for poorer regions (see Chapter 8).
2. The reduction of target prices, to allow a progressive reduction of overproduction, import tariffs and export refunds (thus contributing to the requests emerging within the GATT negotiations).
3. The imposition of **production quotas** to limit overproduction (in the graphical terms of Figure 7.1, it amounts to an arbitrarily imposed maximum of the production quantities). National quotas are imposed on countries and countries impose them, in turn, on producers. Quotas are certainly beneficial for the EU budget, but generate a sense of injustice. Box 7.1 shows that this is inevitable, since it is impossible to devise a fair system of quotas.

The 1988 reform obtained a very important result: for the first time the 'automatic' increase of the CAP was halted and the share of CAP in the EU budget was bound to decrease over time, even if the absolute level of CAP expenditures was not decreasing. The 1988 CAP reform therefore has been instrumental in making the EU able to pursue other policies.

BOX 7.1 A FAIR SYSTEM OF QUOTAS?

The imposition of production quotas is an exercise that inevitably generates some inequity. In this box we show that there are many ways to impose a system of quotas and, although one can be better than another, an optimal system (that is, one that could leave everybody equally satisfied or dissatisfied) does not exist.

Let us assume for example that there are three countries, called A, B and C (readers, if they wish, can think of real countries such as Italy, the Netherlands and Greece) among which quotas for, say, milk production should be imposed. At the target price, the market situation is such that the prevailing production and consumption in each of the three countries is as reported below.

	Production	Consumption	Domestic surplus/deficit
Country A	700	400	+300 (=+75% of consumption)
Country B	1100	300	+800 (=+266% of consumption)
Country C	200	300	−100 (=−33% of consumption)
Total	2000	1000	+1000 (+100% of consumption)

At the target prices there is an overall excess production capacity of 1000 litres (double the consumption). Production quotas should help to reduce this excess capacity and bring the market back to equilibrium, in spite of an above-the-market target price. There may be at least two ways to impose production quotas.

A ***near-autarchy system*** would amount to imposing on each country a production quota identical to its consumption capacity. Country A would then have imposed a quota of 400, country B 300 and country C 200. The 100 deficit left by country C would be filled with 39 litres from country A, that is the share of country A in the production of the exporting countries: 39=100 litres×700/(1100+700) and 61 litres from country B, that is the share of country B in the production of the exporting countries: $61=100\times 1100/(700+1100)$. Eventually country A would produce 439 litres, consume 400, and would have 261 litres of milk (its total potential production of 700 minus the 439 actually produced) 'unemployed'; that is 37 per cent of its total potential production. Country B would produce 361 litres, consume 300 and have 739 litres of milk (67 per cent) 'unemployed'. Country C would produce 200, consume 300 and have no unemployed milk.

A ***proportional reduction*** would amount to imposing on every country an identical restriction of the overall production: every country would curtail its production by, for example, 50 per cent. Country A would then produce 350, country B 550 and country C 100. Therefore country A produces 350, consumes 400 and imports 50 litres from abroad (in spite of being largely self-sufficient). Country B produces 550, consumes 300 and exports 250 litres to A and C. Country C produces 100, consumes 300 and then it imports 200 from country B. The three countries suffer an identical unemployment rate of 50 per cent.

The first solution generates vast differences in terms of unemployment and it is equivalent to a national segmentation of the single market. It is the negation of the very essence of the EU and the principles of an open market economy. Rationally country B should leave the EU and export its own surplus elsewhere. Solution 2 distributes unemployment evenly across countries, but it forces otherwise self-sufficient countries to import milk from other countries for their own domestic consumption.

Which is the fairer of the two solutions? If there were no restriction and the market was allowed to operate, overproduction would decrease the price, but also the largest producers would be able to profit from scale economies and gain a dominant position. It cannot be excluded that, via the price advantage induced by economies of scale, country B would be able to penetrate markets in countries A and C. That would amount to less unemployment in country B, and more in country A and C, given the demand rigidity of prices.

In this sense, the second solution can be read as a compromise solution between free goods circulation and equal distribution of the burden of unemployment. It is clear, however, that, under this solution, both country A and B will claim that there is a phenomenon of EU-generated unemployment, since their final unemployment is higher than what the domestic market would have generated had the prices been left free.

7.5.2 The 1992 MacSharry Reform

In 1991, the Uruguay Round negotiations got stuck precisely on the issue of the EU CAP: the 1988 reform was not enough to win support from other countries, and thus ensure for the EU the conclusion of the agreement on other important aspects of the trade negotiating issues (see Chapter 10 for a detailed discussion). The Commission, with Ray MacSharry as the Agriculture Commissioner, then put forward two discussion papers on the development and future of the CAP, which were the basis for a political agreement on the reform adopted by the Council on 21 May 1992. The **MacSharry reform** of 1992 built on the 1988 reform, allowed the Uruguay Round of GATT to be satisfactorily closed,[13] and marked a major change in the CAP. Its principal elements were (a) a drastic reduction of target prices (particularly in those sectors where competition was fierce and where no particular EU specificity was evident, as, for example, cereals), to render EU agricultural products more competitive in the world markets and to open up to imports the EU internal market; (b) an increase in the compensation of farmers for the subsequent loss of income through direct aids; (c) other measures relating to the market mechanism and the protection of the environment, such as the imposition of production quotas (already foreseen in the Delors' reform of 1988), and measures of agricultural land **set-aside**.[14]

Figure 7.2 shows the evolution of CAP over time, away from the price support mechanism and towards the income support one. As can be seen, the MacSharry reform constituted the first move away from a price support mechanism towards income support, with all the benefits described above. Even if the price reduction generated by the 1992 reform was not as spectacular as expected, the reform was generally regarded as successful, with positive and lasting effects on European agriculture, and the ability of the EU to win consensus at international fora. Most notably, the MacSharry reform was regarded as a turning point and successive reforms could be described as further and faster steps in the same direction.

Indeed, in the ensuing years, the enlargement towards the Central and Eastern European countries (CEECs), the international trend towards a more globalised economy, the preparation of the single currency and the resulting budgetary constraints, the increasing competitiveness of products from third countries and a new round of GATT negotiations within the newly created institution, the World Trade Organisation (WTO), were all elements that forced a further adaptation of the CAP, leading to a new series of reforms.

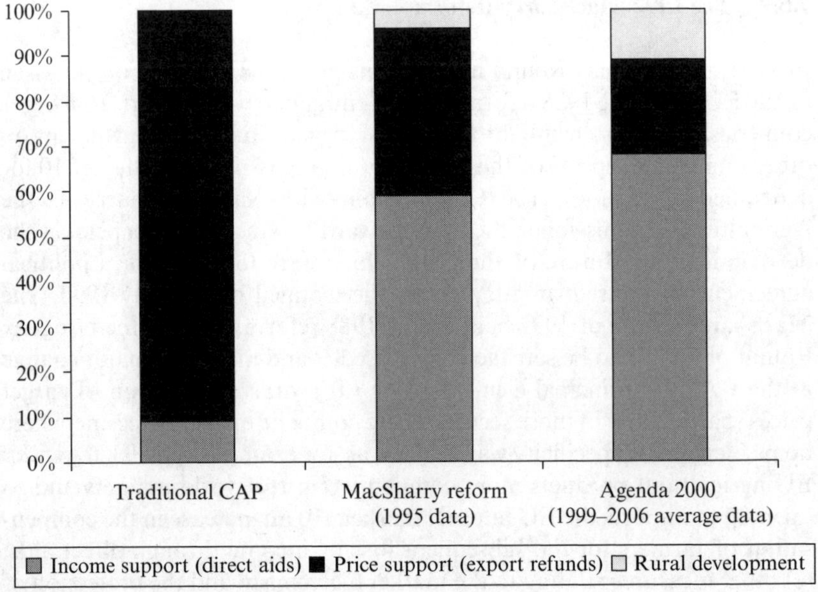

Source: Authors' elaboration on EU budget data.

Figure 7.2 The EU budget contributions to the different CAP mechanisms

7.5.3 Agenda 2000 and the Enlargement of the Union

In July 1997, the Commission started an overall reconsideration of European Union policies in view of the expected enlargement, producing a framework document known as **Agenda 2000** (European Commission, 1997), which contained specific initiatives on three key EU policies: the revision of the CAP, the revision of the EU regional policy (analysed in Chapter 8) and new policies to help the accession of the new member states of Central and Eastern Europe (already discussed at the end of Chapter 3). As explored in Chapter 6, the Agenda 2000 document then paved the way for the 2000–2006 Financial Perspectives.

The CAP chapter of the Agenda 2000 reform was mostly directed at moving the burden of the CAP further away from price support and towards income support (see Figure 7.2). Such a move was a precondition for making the CAP transposable to the new member states. In fact, as already recalled in Chapter 2, according to the GATT–WTO regulations, a regional integration agreement (such as the EU) can be accepted by international law only if non-members do not find trade with the group any more restrictive than before the group was set up (art. XXIV of the GATT regulation). As a result, enlarging to the new member states what still remained a quite protectionist CAP would have raised the overall degree of protectionism of the enlarged Union, violating WTO rules. Hence the price support mechanism, and the degree of protectionism of the agricultural sector, had to disappear before the enlargement could take place.

Clearly, since the price support was replaced by the income support mechanism, this meant, on the one hand, the shifting of the burden away from consumers and towards taxpayers. On the other hand, however, since the taxpayers' burden is visible (in the EU budget), while the consumers' burden is not, it seemed that the Agenda 2000 reform imposed higher, instead of lower, CAP costs. The fallacy of this argument, used by some conservative negotiators to dilute and delay the reform, was quickly uncovered and the argument dismissed. In other words, to have an in-depth reform which would have made the enlargement of the Union legally viable, the Council had to accept the increase in the absolute levels of EU budgetary resources directed to the CAP, with the benefit of lower prices for EU consumers.

Because of this dramatic switch, imposed by the needs of the enlargement, Agenda 2000 has been seen as the most radical and comprehensive reform of the CAP since 1962. Actually Agenda 2000 built on the logic of the 1992 MacSharry reform, and it provided a sound basis for the future development of agriculture in the Union, covering all functions of the CAP: economic, environmental and rural. In particular, apart from the general shift discussed above, the reform comprised the following measures:

1. the reinforcement of the competitiveness of agricultural commodities in domestic and world markets, by further reducing target prices and by fixing a mid-term review in 2002 to monitor the gap between target prices and market prices;
2. the creation of substitute jobs and other sources of income for farmers;
3. the formation of a new policy for **rural development**, which becomes the second pillar of the CAP;
4. the integration of more environmental and structural considerations into the CAP;
5. the improvement of food quality and safety;
6. the simplification of agricultural legislation and the decentralisation of its application, in order to make rules and regulations clearer, more transparent, easier to access and less conducive to fraud.

Hence it can be said that the clear will to (finally) approximate target prices to world market prices was the distinctive feature of the Agenda

2000, together with its attention to the environmental consequences of the CAP. With this reform, the common agricultural policy truly evolves towards an income policy, run through direct aid, where a 'fair' income is guaranteed to farmers and EU prices are progressively brought into line with world prices. As will be made clear in Chapter 10, the latter element constitutes one of the most important negotiating tools for the EU within the WTO, and has allowed the EU to extend its Customs Union legally to the new member states of Central and Eastern Europe without violating article XXIV of the GATT.

Beyond the creation of a suitable legal framework for the enlargement, Agenda 2000 had also to cater for the preparation of the extension of CAP to new member states by introducing some pre-accession instruments. In particular, Agenda 2000 introduced SAPARD (Special Accession Programme for Agriculture and Rural Development), a programme designed to assist the candidate CEECs with their agricultural development.[15]

However, no matter how radical the Agenda 2000 reform was, it lacked a central feature in its original design, the so-called '**CAP co-financing**'. Indeed, as already stated, the move away from price support towards income support amounts essentially to a move away from an allocative and towards a redistributive policy. Since interpersonal redistribution is not among the specific EU competences, the Commission had proposed that only the 'level' of the direct income had still to be centrally decided in Brussels; its financing had to be shared between the EU and the national budgets. This proposal, known as CAP co-financing, was instrumental in bringing the CAP policy into line with all the other EU policies which are already co-financed. One must underline that CAP co-financing would not have reduced the support to the agricultural sector of the Union, but it would have moved only part of its burden from the EU to the national taxpayers. Obviously the taxpayers of those countries receiving high CAP subsidies (for example, France and Denmark) would have been worse off and the others (such as Germany and the UK) better off. The Agricultural Council had first accepted, by unanimity, the proposal, but then the EU Council of the Heads of State and Government meeting in Berlin in March 1999 could not reach unanimity over it because of the French veto.

And yet, when one considers also the benefits of the externalities that agriculture generates in terms of better environment and better life quality, both in the countryside and in towns, an issue often referred to as the '**multifunctional character**' of agriculture (see the Appendix), it is clear that these externalities are very different across the EU and that a more localised approach could be defendable. Those regions or countries with a greater agricultural sector are better off from an environmental standpoint and may be able to make their citizens pay more for the right to stay in a more pleasant area. However, notwithstanding these arguments, the CAP still remains the only (redistributive) policy entirely financed through the central EU budget.

7.5.4 The CAP Reform up to 2013

Although a possible conflict with WTO agreements had been avoided thanks to the Agenda 2000 reform, there was another fundamental question regarding the extension of CAP to the new member states, namely that the provisions of an enlarged CAP would have increased the CEECs' prices and production, implying higher export subsidies in the unified EU, with mounting pressure on the EU budget. In fact, in 2001, the share of agriculture in the CEECs was around 3.1 per cent of GDP, while its share of employment was around 13 per cent. These figures are, respectively, about two and three times higher than for the EU-15 (see also Table 7.3).

Since the Council could not adopt in 1999 the co-financing of the CAP proposed in the Agenda 2000 reform, a further reform became necessary before the 2004 enlargement, to avoid a too high financial burden for the EU budget. To this purpose, the Brussels European Council in October 2002 defined the financial framework to be employed until 2013 for agricultural expenditure.

In particular, the Council decided on a progressive, rather than immediate, extension of the CAP to the new member states. Direct payments (that is, income support) in the accession countries have been set equal to 25 per cent of the level of such payments in the EU-15 in 2004, 30 per cent in 2005, 35 per cent in 2006, 40 per cent in 2007, 50 per cent in 2008 and

Table 7.3 Basic agricultural facts for the new member states, 2001

	Farmland (million hectares)	Number of farms (millions)	Average farm size (hectares)	Agricultural employment (millions)	Ag. share of employment (%)	Ag. share of GDP (%)
Poland	18.2	12.3	1.5	2.74	19.2	3.1
Other CEECs	20.1	11.6	1.6	1.16	7.2	3.1
EU15	128.3	6.8	18.7	6.7	4.2	1.7

Source: Table 2.0.1.2 in *Agriculture in the EU – Statistics and Economic Information*, 2002, European Commission; as retrieved from Baldwin and Wyplosz (2003).

thereafter 10 per cent annual increments so as to ensure that every member state attains by 2013 the same support level throughout the EU. To ensure the overall stability of the CAP financial envelope, the Council also provided that the total annual expenditure for CAP in a Union of 25 cannot (in the period 2007–13) exceed the amount agreed with the Agenda 2000 reform for the year 2006.[16]

In other words, the resources available for the CAP in the period 1999–2006 will be the same for the period 2007–13, with the difference that the number of countries benefiting from these resources will increase from 15 to 25, albeit the new members will have gradual access to the entire financial package. Once fully implemented, in per capita terms this may probably amount to the single largest reduction of CAP support ever agreed by the member states in the history of the Union.

To cope with this dramatic change in the overall financial framework agreed by the European Council, in January 2003 the European Commission adopted a series of proposals to reform the CAP, which constituted the follow-up to the so-called 'mid-term review' of summer 2002 foreseen in Agenda 2000 (European Commission, 2003e). The aim of this reform was to continue the trend towards a more competitive and market-oriented EU agriculture, to promote a substantial simplification in the CAP, to help to better defend the CAP in the WTO and, most particularly, to facilitate the integration of the new member states into the CAP. The key elements of the reform, finally adopted by the Council in June 2003, can be summarised as follows: (a) direct aid in the form of a single farm payment, progressively independent of production (decoupling); (b) a linking of those payments to the respect for environmental, food safety, animal welfare, health and occupational safety standards, as well as the requirement to keep all farmland in good condition (**cross-compliance**).

Thus, from June 2003, not only did the CAP entail internal prices in line with world prices (due to the progressive replacement of the price support mechanism with the income support mechanism already enforced by Agenda 2000) but it also entailed the income support mechanism becoming completely linked to the concept of potential income, with no reference to the historic production records. This allows a greater flexibility in the allocation of aid, and a better compliance with the objective of overall reduction of the individual financial support in the EU-15, in order to make room for the agricultural sector of the new member states. Still in line with these objectives, other characteristics of the June 2003 reform are (c) a stronger rural development policy with more money, new measures to promote quality and animal welfare, and to help farmers to meet EU production standards; (d) a reduction in direct payments (**degression**) for bigger farms, in order to minimise the existing distortions of the CAP harming small producers and to generate additional money for rural development and the financing of further reforms.

One might wonder why, after some 40 years of very marginal changes in the CAP, the same policy has been completely transformed within four years by two successive rounds of reforms. The answer is threefold. First of all, the last EU enlargement doubled the agricultural labour force as well as the arable area of the EU, adding as well over 100 million food consumers to the internal market. The CAP had to comply with such a dramatic change in its structure. Second, agriculture in the applicant countries has many deficiencies and requires substantial restructuring and modernisation. Only such a deeply reformed CAP will offer considerable opportunities to the candidate countries and help them to use their potential for efficient agriculture production, thus supporting the restructuring process in the new member states. Finally, only a CAP open to international markets is compatible with the behaviour of other countries within the world multilateral institutions, as will be clarified in the next section.

7.6 THE CAP WITHIN A GLOBAL WORLD

In the post-war scenario of the 1950s, the transformations of society were global and similar in different countries in different regional areas. Food shortages were also common to many areas of the world. All developed countries have therefore developed a more or less extensive agricultural policy based on different principles and different objectives.

In spite of what one often hears, protection and assistance of the agricultural sector is far from being a unique EU feature, although the EU has been accused in several instances of having an excessively generous CAP. The structure of the EU budget, in which the CAP has constituted about 50 per cent and has benefited about 4 per cent of the EU population, has contributed to reinforcing this impression. As already stated, the most compelling reason behind this apparent disproportion is that the CAP is still the only EU policy to be entirely financed by the EU budget, with no national intervention. If one takes this fact into account, the right benchmark for CAP is not the EU budget, but rather the sum of the national and EU public spending. Since 50 per cent of the EU budget corresponds to about 1.2 per cent of total public spending, the latter is the figure actually benefiting the 4 per cent of the EU population engaged in agriculture. Notwithstanding the 2002 Council agreement putting a threshold on future CAP expenditures, these proportions are not likely to change much in the years to come, since the CAP co-financing is now off the policy agenda, and not likely to be resurrected before 2014.

When looking at international comparisons across areas and countries of the developed world, one observes a great variety of results both in terms of the relation between the agricultural added-value and the agricultural subsidies (see OECD, 2003a), and in terms of the relation between farmers' income and all households' income (OECD, 2003b).

The data reported in Figure 7.3 reveal that, in the period 2000–2002, the amount of support received by each agricultural producer (as a percentage of the value of gross farm receipts) is slightly less than 40 per cent for the EU (it used to be much more before the last reforms), it is around 20 per cent for both Canada and the USA, and around 60 per cent for Iceland, Japan and Korea. Norway and Switzerland have the highest level of support, at around 70 per cent. And still, in the media, the USA and Canada can easily play the role of free-market defenders in the agricultural sector.

These figures also show one of the reasons why Norway finally chose not to enter the EU: with the EU support for the agricultural sector equal to less than 60 per cent of the Norwegian one, the country judged the protection offered by the CAP and the EU Fishery Policy to both farmers and fishermen inadequate. In particular, Norway underlined that the EU common agricultural policy was not able to fully compensate farmers for the positive externalities generated in terms of environmental protection and natural resources enhancement.[17]

As for the relationship between farmers' income and all households' income, the situation is less diversified across OECD countries, as reported by Figure 7.4. Outcomes of agricultural policies are in fact such that farmers' income in most countries is very comparable with other household incomes.

More generally, the agricultural sector is considered as very sensitive all over the world, because of its multifunctional character that some countries (such as the EU) recognise, or because of the pressures of lobbies which are particularly powerful in agriculture (as in the USA and, to a lesser extent, the EU). Environmental issues are also of paramount importance for the sector, especially in terms of the legality of the so-called 'Genetically-modified organisms' (GMO), whose use some countries would like to prohibit.

Thus agriculture is at the core of the new round of WTO negotiations that started in Doha in 2001, which meant to further reduce subsidies to agriculture, grant developing countries access to rich markets and regulate environmental issues. Hence the future development of agriculture clearly depends on the outcome of the current WTO negotiations, and therefore this and other issues will be analysed in detail in Chapter 10.

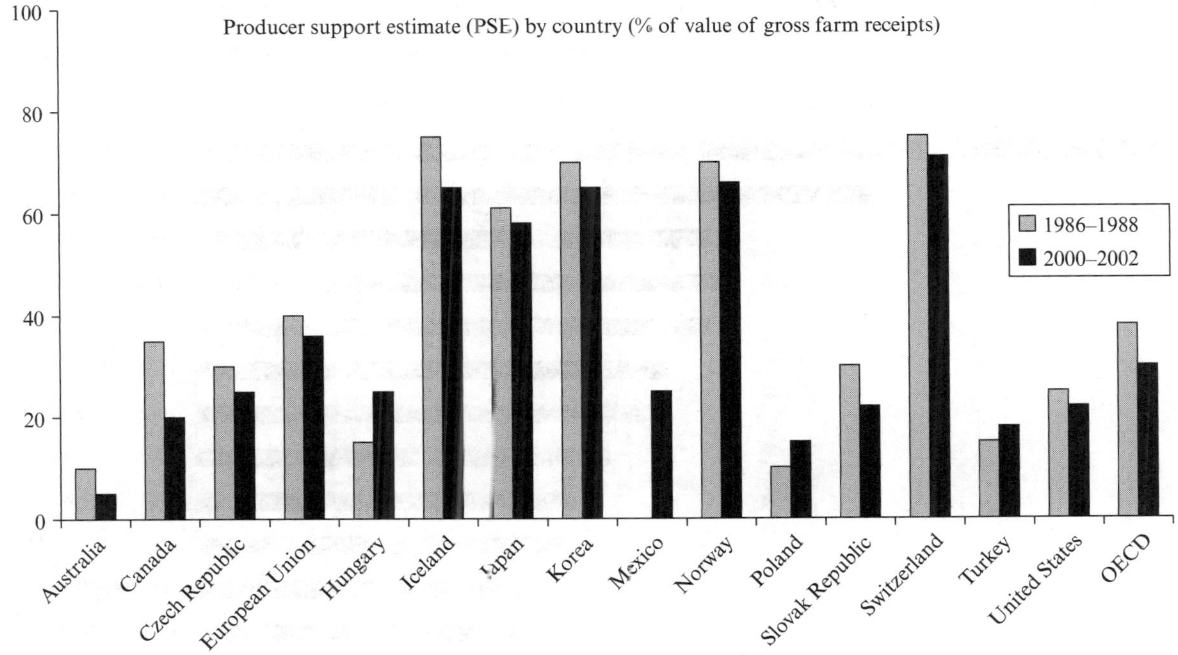

Source: PSE/CSE Support Estimate Database, OECD (2003a).

Figure 7.3 The support received by the agricultural sector in various OECD countries

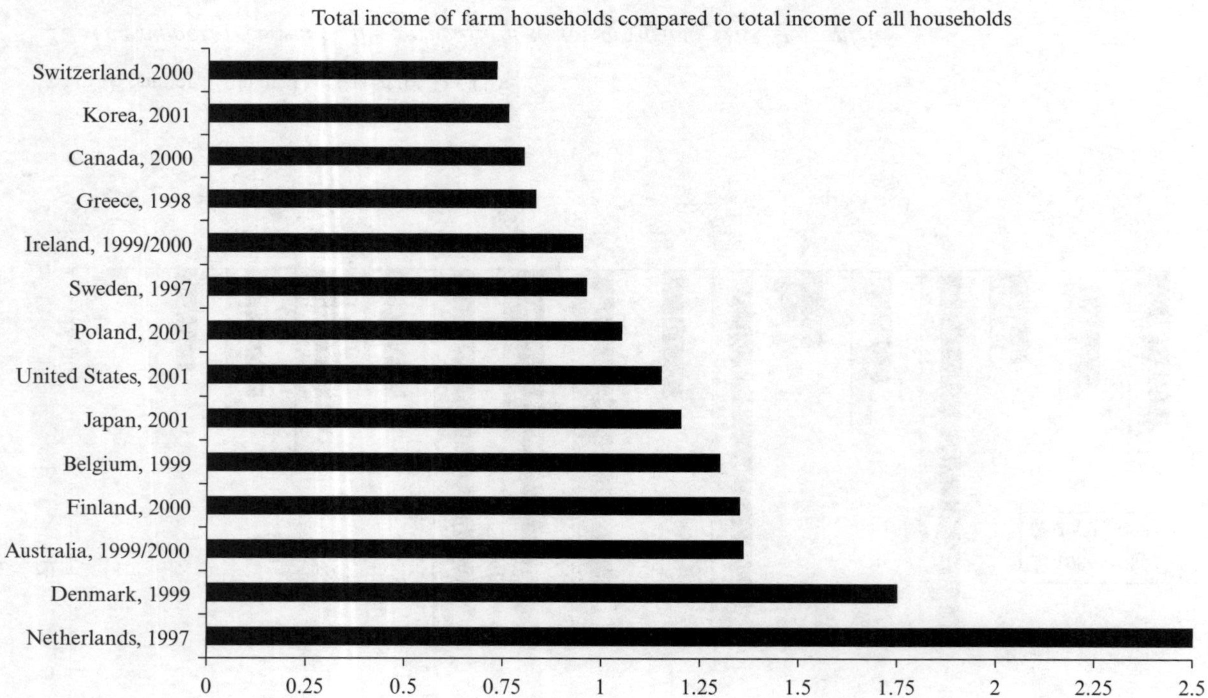

Source: OECD (2003a), Farm household incomes: issues and policy responses.

Figure 7.4 Income of farmers as a percentage of total income in OECD countries

7.7 WILL THERE STILL BE A 'COMMON' AGRICULTURAL POLICY?

The CAP has been the first community policy, instrumental to the whole EU project. Without the common agricultural policy the EU would probably not have been able to take off and to pursue the policies that came later.

Initially the CAP met its objectives and delivered the expected results. Especially in terms of food self-sufficiency and the support of farmers' incomes, both questions of great concern in the post-war period, the achievements were very relevant. However the CAP price support, the tool initially chosen for its implementation, proved rather problematic. In particular target prices higher than market prices caused recurrent excesses of supply and required high tariffs to protect the EU products against world imports, as well as high costs for the EU budget in terms of export subsidies. This type of instrument, which may be used in a closed economy, proved totally inadequate for an open economy such as the EU, which, furthermore, desired to play a crucial role in the global economy in many and different areas. As a result, the CAP was not only impoverishing third world countries, depriving them of an obvious exit market for their food products, but it was also seriously damaging EU credentials in international fora. From being a support and a pillar of the EU, the CAP as originally conceived thus risked becoming a burden.

A series of reforms then started. Initially most CAP reforms only tried to contain costs via different administrative measures (such as production quotas), but then they gradually changed the nature of the CAP. The common agricultural policy (progressively, albeit somewhat slowly) moved away from price support towards direct income support, thus evolving from an allocative to an (interpersonal) distributive policy. This move has opened up the EU markets for agricultural products, it has improved EU standing in international trade negotiations and it has allowed a smooth enlargement of the EU. In particular, the latest round of CAP reform, in 2003, focused essentially on making the CAP financially sustainable for the period 2007–2013 in an EU of 25 countries, maintaining its nature as a fully EU-financed policy, based essentially on direct aid, now linked to the concept of potential income, and thus decoupled from historical production records.

However, now that the CAP has become, essentially, an interpersonal income policy, financially viable in the years to come, it remains even more debatable why such a policy should remain the only one entirely dealt with at the EU level, not entailing national co-financing. The negotiations on the 2000–2006 Financial Perspectives had started to tackle the issue but, in spite of several counterarguments, member states finally resolved that the CAP has to retain this particularity, putting co-financing off the agenda.

Still we do feel that the important question in the enlarged EU should not be how to make the current CAP financially viable, but rather which type of CAP should be run at the EU level, a debate which we hope can start soon across member states.

NOTES

1. At the beginning of the 1950s, about 25 per cent of the workforce in the six founding members was still employed in agriculture.
2. The TEC articles dealing with agriculture are 32 to 38.
3. Given that the consumption of most agricultural goods (for example corn, beef, milk) satisfies basic needs, the demand for these products is in general less sensitive (relatively inelastic) to price changes with respect to the consumption of other 'standard' goods.
4. This is a standard result of microeconomic theory: a reduction of prices along a relatively inelastic demand implies that the increase in quantities demanded is proportionally smaller than the decrease in prices, and hence the total revenue for the producer (the market price times the quantity sold) decreases. The opposite is true for a price increase: the reduction in the quantity demanded is proportionally smaller than the price increase, and hence total revenues go up. The reverse result would be obtained for a relatively elastic demand curve.
5. For historical reasons the COMs are much better known with their original French acronym OCM *(Organisation Commune des Marchés)*. In what follows we shall use the French acronym because of its greater notoriety.
6. To be precise, the tariff is calculated so that the target price minus transport costs is equal to the lowest consignment price (that is, world price plus transport costs) plus the tariff. Since transport costs are not relevant here, we ignore them and assume for the sake of simplicity just a prohibitive tariff yielding no imports and a domestic price equal to P_0. For more details, see Nava (2000).
7. Essentially, P_T acts like a more than prohibitive tariff. Fixing the target price is arguably the greatest difficulty and the most important variable in the price support policy. The way traditionally used to fix it is to make reference to the historical income and/or to a notion of a fair income for that specific category of producers. Another possibility consists in determining the 'Pigouvian prices' for agricultural products: that is prices determined according to 'public' demand and cost function which integrates the positive and negative externalities that the production and the consumption of agricultural product generates (environmental protection, reduced urbanisation, health improvements and so on). It is clear that the determination of such a 'public' demand and cost function, sometimes referred to as the 'multi-functionality' characteristic of the CAP, is politically sensible. See in this regard the Appendix to this chapter.
8. Note that the new internal price for agricultural products P_T is now higher than the original equilibrium price P_0, and much higher than the price which would prevail in a free market, P_w.
9. As mentioned in Chapter 6, EU agricultural duties accrue to the EU budget but, due to the restrictions on EU agricultural imports, they contribute only about 1 per cent of its financing.
10. The so-called 'mad cow disease' affecting EU cattle in the 1990s, with serious risks also for citizens' health, should act as a reminder of the consequences of overexploitation of the agricultural sector.
11. These issues will be analysed in depth in Chapter 10.

12. The CAP had therefore a clear role in exacerbating the issue and the debate on the budgetary disequilibria, probably being the triggering cause of the British requests for budgetary compensations, which ended up in the creation of the UK rebate, the single greatest distortion of the EU budget rule (see Chapter 6).
13. Along with the CAP reform, an agreement, known as the 'Blair House Agreement', was concluded with the United States, closing all the pending trade issues in the Uruguay Round negotiations, and thus allowing the same round to be concluded in 1994, as discussed in Chapter 10.
14. Agricultural land set-aside consists in imposing a rotating period of 'biological stop' on the cultivation of given products across different land settlements. Such a constraint naturally reduces the supply of those products and improves their quality, thus sustaining their price.
15. In particular the objectives of the SAPARD programme were (1) to establish a Community framework for supporting sustainable agricultural and rural development in the applicant countries during the pre-accession period; (2) to solve problems affecting the long-term adjustment of the agricultural sector and rural areas; (3) to help implement the *acquis communautaire* in matters of agricultural policy and related policies.
16. More specifically the Council stated that 'The overall expenditure in nominal terms for market-related expenditure and direct payments for each year in the period 2007–2013 shall be kept below the 2006 figure, increased by 1 per cent per year.' We have already discussed in Chapter 6 the constraint that such a decision has imposed on the design of the 2007–13 Financial Perspectives.
17. In other words, Norway estimated that the EU prices were not close enough to 'Pigouvian prices' and therefore they failed to account for the complexity and the multifunctionality of agriculture, as discussed in detail in the Appendix of this chapter.

APPENDIX: AN ECONOMIC VIEW OF MULTIFUNCTIONALITY

1. What is Multifunctionality?

Multifunctionality is probably among the three most used words in the context of CAP reform (together with direct aid and decoupling), but its meaning differs widely across different actors. This appendix thus aims at giving a sort of theoretical framework to the understanding of multifunctionality, although we are aware that our understanding will probably not coincide with the notion of multifunctionality of other political (that is, member states) or academic observers.

Farmers, in addition to pursuing their core business (producing one or more agricultural goods), generate, as a by-product, some positive externalities,[1] which benefit the community as a whole. There are several examples of externalities generated by the agricultural sector. For example, the mere fact of living in the countryside, instead of being urbanised, generates some externalities, such as a decongestion of the market for housing and other services as well as the job market, a reduction of pollution, and the prevention of the phenomenon of land desertification.[2]

In addition farmers, by respecting higher than minimum environmental standards, might contribute both to the preservation of the rural environment (for example by maintaining an agricultural area larger than the one the market would require under intensive production, by reducing animal density, by reducing monoculture and by leaving free-flowing streams) and to rural employment (higher than minimum environmental standards call for higher employment). They might also improve landscape elements which they can eventually exploit (for example via so-called 'agri-tourism', although this is more a possibility for the largest farms).

Some of these externalities are generated almost 'automatically' (for example, those mentioned in the previous paragraph), while others might be generated or not by the farmers' behaviour in response to the economic incentives they face. Multifunctionality is linked to such a notion of positive externality. It aims at recognising the 'societal value' of these externalities by attaching remuneration to those which do not find a price in the private market.[3] Economics tells us that there is a clear need to remunerate externalities, because of the trade-off that might certainly arise between generating externalities or increasing business revenues via intensive farming which respects only minimum standards. Clearly, lacking a proper remuneration for the externality, farmers would resolve the trade-off in favour of their core business.

Obviously one may expect that society is not willing to accept payments for the fulfilling of certain minimal conditions, which can probably be best enforced through regulations. Payments for multifunctionality should thus be conceived so as to give an incentive to farmers to choose those options that bring a clearly defined added value in terms of, for example, environment promotion or rural employment, or landscape protection, or anything else that is positive which does not have an immediate price in the market.

2. How to Remunerate the Production of Externalities

Once we agree on the need to give financial incentives to farmers so that they can pursue 'multifunctionality' of agriculture and thereby produce the right 'societal' level of externalities, the big question is how to modulate these financial incentives for farmers. 'Pigouvian prices' for marketable goods are the classical way to remunerate externalities. However Pigouvian prices could work well if and only if there was a unique world agricultural market for any particular product. The current debate at the WTO suggests that this is definitely not the case.

So direct aid is the only solution. Direct aid is difficult to quantify because of the difficulty of assessing societies' demands, which vary significantly across regions and farmers, but are certainly more transparent and equitable than price subsidies, as argued in this chapter. In other words, direct aid for multifunctionality ought to be evaluated locally or regionally. Finally, the use of local/regional contracts for agri-environmental purposes could prove a useful instrument. The contract would involve the public actors (EU, national and local authorities) and the local/regional farmer association, defining the optimal level of externalities to be achieved in a given area. A contract between the public authorities and the local/regional farmer organisation would also give a strong signal of the public recognition of the territorial benefits that farmers are bringing to the local/regional community.

It would also show not only that agriculture involves producing agricultural goods, but that society is ready to pay for those farmers who choose to conduct agricultural business by adopting higher environmental standards.

Clearly these types of contracts are optimally set at the level where externalities are normally experienced, that is, at the local, or at the very most, the regional level. In other words, the impetus for multifunctionality can come from the EU level, but its implementation and translation into operative concepts has to be undertaken at the local level. As a result, for all these issues to be implemented in an efficient way, some form of co-financing of the CAP should be allowed.

NOTES

1. We assume throughout this appendix that farmers respect environmental standards, that is minimum standards defined by the EU and national legislation.
2. The comparison between Norway (where there exists a sort of Pigouvian price system for most goods which cross-finances positive environmental externalities) and Sweden is particularly telling: Norway has very few scarcely populated areas, while Sweden, despite broad similarities in environmental conditions, has many, which even led to the creation of Objective 6 in the Structural Funds (see Chapter 8).
3. Multifunctionality aims at correcting a market failure and hence, in theory, it should not comprise what the market itself is able to price efficiently. Quality of goods or food safety is a clear example of what has a value in the market, and thus does not need support via multifunctionality.

8. Policies for cohesion and sustainable growth

8.1 INTRODUCTION

In the first chapter of this book we stated that Europeans tend to reject growth as a single objective; rather they aim at a model of economic development which tries to achieve the highest possible **growth** compatible with its sustainability over time (**stability**) and its equalitarian distribution, a goal that we have referred to as **cohesion**.[1] By and large, the latter concept is associated with a low degree of inequality in the distribution of income across a society. In this regard, we have already shown in Chapter 1 that total inequality in the distribution of income can be decomposed into across countries inequality and within-country inequality. Moreover, in Chapter 5, we showed that, for the EU case, across-countries inequality decreased until the mid-1990s, and now it is only a fraction of within-country inequality, which alone drives around 90 per cent of the total inequality in the EU. We have however suggested that the latter inequality is very low if compared to the situation of other countries in the world. Hence prima facie evidence would indicate that the EU is a very cohesive society, a society characterised by a relatively low level of both across-country and within-country inequalities.

Still in Chapter 5, we also pointed out that the total degree of inequality in EU-25 is bound to increase, overtaking for the first time that of the USA, essentially on account of the relevant increase in the across-countries inequality brought in by the new, significantly poorer, member states. As a result, since within-country inequality is dealt with by the individual welfare state systems of each country in the EU, while the across-countries inequality is mainly managed at the EU level, the reduction of this type of inequality becomes a critical issue in EU policy making. Such a policy is known at the EU level as **cohesion**, **regional** or **structural policy**.

The key problem, then, is choosing the right policy to promote growth and cohesion simultaneously. We have already considered in Chapter 5 that a policy stimulating growth tends to reduce within-country inequalities, but not necessarily across-countries inequalities, with an ambiguous impact on total inequality. For example, a growth-stimulating policy like the completion of the Single Market Programme might in fact induce a polarisation of economic activities around the richest countries or regions, in order to allow the exploitation of economies of scale, thus eventually reducing within-country inequalities but exacerbating at the same time across-countries inequalities, with an overall negative effect on the total level of cohesion. At the same time, a policy stimulating cohesion might induce redistributive actions which interfere with the growth effects, reducing the benefits arising from integration.[2]

As a result, a policy strategy emerged which tends to look at cohesion and growth as two, mutually reinforcing, objectives. In this approach, cohesion policies towards the poor EU countries (or regions) are nothing more than policies which increase significantly the growth rate of the least prosperous areas, so as to ensure a faster pace of **convergence** of their (per capita) income levels to the EU average.[3] At the same time, if cohesion is enhanced, the heterogeneity of preferences across member states will be reduced, and hence a more efficient decision process regarding common growth-related targets (such as the previously discussed Lisbon Agenda) can be generated.[4]

The latter scenario is however much easier to theorise than to implement. Historically, in fact, the cohesion policy of the Union has tackled almost all member states, taking care of different needs not always strictly related to the reduction of across-countries inequalities. And yet, whatever the past focus of cohesion policies (more oriented to across-countries redistribution or more prone to foster growth in the poorest member states), some of the results achieved are indisputable, with across-countries inequalities decreasing over time since the start of these policies in the 1980s.

Nevertheless the new scenario of a Union with 25 member states is nowadays casting more than one shadow over the picture. On the one hand, there is a need to resurrect growth altogether, in order to maintain the viability of the economic and social model. On the other hand, for the first time in 20 years, cohesion in the Union is also regressing, as already discussed, because of the high levels of income disparity of the new member states. Finally we also have evidence that, while cohesion policies have managed to reduce across-countries inequalities, income levels have tended to diverge across EU **regions**, thus increasing inequalities measured at this level of disaggregation.[5] Clearly, if the average income levels of member states converge to the EU average, but the regions of the same member states fall apart, it is controversial whether the EU fails to fulfil its goal of cohesion.

Given this situation, the choice of the right policy approach where growth and cohesion, rather than substitutes, become complements, mutually reinforcing each other, becomes crucial. Hence we are back at our starting point: the EU needs growth both in those regions suffering from a gap in their level of development vis-à-vis the rest of Europe and in the EU as a whole. Indeed, to deliver growth, and thus convergence, the Lisbon Agenda rests on both a strategy of reforms and the promotion of some specific categories of expenditure. Chapter 5 dealt with reforms, while this chapter deals with expenditure aiming at fostering growth, both in the least prosperous EU areas and in the EU as a whole.

8.2 THE ECONOMIC RATIONALE OF THE EU COHESION POLICY

We have already considered that, when dealing with income inequality, a rather clear-cut distinction exists between the national and the EU role in this area: ensuring a proper income distribution within countries resides in the specific competence of national policies only, while ensuring a proper distribution of income across countries (cohesion) is also an EU competence and, ultimately, an EU goal. Indeed, in this respect, the current version of TEU, art. 2 is quite explicit: 'The Union shall set itself the following objectives: to promote economic and social progress and a high level of employment and to achieve balanced and sustainable development, in particular through the creation of an area without the internal frontiers, through the *strengthening of economic and social cohesion* [. . .]' (the emphasis is ours). Also TEC, art. 2 further clarifies that 'The Community [. . .] shall promote a harmonious balanced and sustainable development of economic activities, a high level of employment and of social protection [. . .] and *economic and social cohesion* and solidarity across member states' (our emphasis).

When looking at the original formulation of the treaties, however, the concept of a structural action by the EU institutions as a means to obtain economic and social cohesion was not explicitly stated. In fact, although some across-countries inequalities were present in the EC-6, they were exacerbated by the enlargement of 1973 (Ireland, the UK and Denmark) and, overall, by the two Mediterranean enlargements of the 1980s (Greece in 1981, Spain and Portugal in 1986). Thus it is only since 1975, when the European Fund for Regional Development was created, that regional policy has become a central policy in the EU. Then, in 1977, the extremely influential **MacDougall Report** (see European Commission, 1977) called for using the EU budget as a redistributive tool (and for increasing up to 7 per cent the size of the EU budget). In 1986, the equally influential **Padoa-Schioppa Report** (see Padoa-Schioppa *et al.*, 1987) contended that, in order to make sure that the Single Market Programme delivered the promised results, a sizeable structural policy was needed to compensate for the potential losses resulting in the poor countries from the increased process of economic integration. These concepts were then integrated in the current version of the treaties via the Single European Act; the Commission president of the time, Jacques Delors, started from there to give a fundamental impulse to the idea of an EU structural policy aimed at reducing across-countries inequalities, basically shaping it in the forms that we know today, and herein described (see also Chapter 6).

Thus, at the time of their creation, cohesion policies were seen essentially as a sort of monetary compensation for the poor countries for the single market policies benefiting the rich countries. The implicit bargain was that poor countries would open their markets to the goods of the rich countries and, in exchange, rich countries would support the growth of the poor ones.[6] On the one hand, the cohesion policy can therefore be seen as a **side payment** for the single market policy. On the other hand, rich members agree with these side payments, since they ultimately benefit from an increase in the wealth of the least prosperous members, via the so-called '**spillover effects**'. In fact, if the income and purchasing power of less prosperous countries, belonging to the same market, increases, there is a fair chance that consumers in these markets will then buy the goods produced in rich countries, eventually characterised by a better price–quality ratio. Understanding the possible economic benefit coming from the spillover effects, rich EU countries thus agree to invest money in supporting the growth of poor countries. In plain words, if Germany supports highway construction in Spain and thanks to it (and other factors) Spain becomes richer, there is a fair chance that Spaniards will buy Volkswagen and/or Mercedes cars to run on these highways.[7] Furthermore spillover effects are reinforced by the disparities in the level of prices across the EU countries. Rich countries have higher price levels than poor countries: a one million Euros in a rich country allows construction of fewer kilometres of highway than in a poor country. That means that the marginal cost of transferring one Deutschmark from Germany to Spain was much lower, in the 1980s and the 1990s, than the marginal benefit produced in Spain by that same Deutschmark. Thanks to this positive difference between the marginal benefit and the marginal cost, the transfer of some funds from a rich to a poor country is, on a EU-wide scale, welfare enhancing.

Such a vision of cohesion policies as monetary compensations started to be challenged in the mid-1990s, in parallel with the increase in the degree of economic integration in Europe. While neoclassical economic theories predict to different extents the natural convergence of factor returns and income levels of poorer regions as far as economic integration proceeds, the empirical evidence relative to the European Union started to reveal, on the contrary, a progressive reduction of disparities in national incomes (and thus of across-countries inequality), but a certain persistence of regional disparities. In this regard, the second intermediate report on economic and social cohesion of the European Commission (2003d) shows that, still in 2000, the top 10 per cent richer EU-15 regions had an average GDP per capita more than 60 per cent above the EU average, while the bottom 10 per cent poorer regions had a level almost 40 per cent lower. As a result, the per capita GDP of the richest EU-15 regions was 2.5 times higher than in the poorest ones, and this notwithstanding the 20 years of structural actions undertaken in the past.[8]

Should we then conclude, together with some authors (for example, Boldrin and Canova, 2001) that the entire set-up of the EU cohesion policy nowadays lies on wrong premises, given the new, highly integrated, economic scenario of the Union? And, if this is the case, how to promote both growth and cohesion in the enlarged EU?

In order to assess this question, it is useful to start from the consideration that, in the last 20 years, the policy actions dealing with regional disparities across the EU have been traditionally based upon neoclassical models of endogenous growth and comparative advantages, predicting a positive effect of economic integration on the convergence of incomes to a given average, once certain factor differentials among regions (such as the endowment of human and physical capital) were controlled for.[9] The concepts of absolute or conditional (to the initial endowments) convergence are often used to measure these effects. In particular, conditional convergence is also known as '**β-convergence**': the idea behind this concept is that, if convergence is in place, as integration proceeds initial (per capita) income levels of regions should be negatively correlated (through the beta coefficient of a linear regression) to their average growth rates. Hence initially poor regions will display higher growth rates than rich regions, and thus converge over time to their income levels.

However, using a sample of EU regions whose income is measured over the period 1984–99, one does not find strong support for the β-convergence hypothesis.[10] Figure 8.1 displays the average annual growth rate of each region's per capita GDP in PPS, plotted against its initial level at the beginning of the period considered. The horizontal and vertical axes represent, respectively, the EU-12 (15 where appropriate) levels and average growth rates of per capita GDP; this yields four quadrants displaying convergence or divergence of each region with respect to the European average, represented by the central axes. Convergence can be found in the second and fourth quadrants, where there is a negative correlation between the initial income level and the regional average growth rate, while diverging regions can be found in the first and third quadrants, where the correlation between income levels and average growth rates is positive.

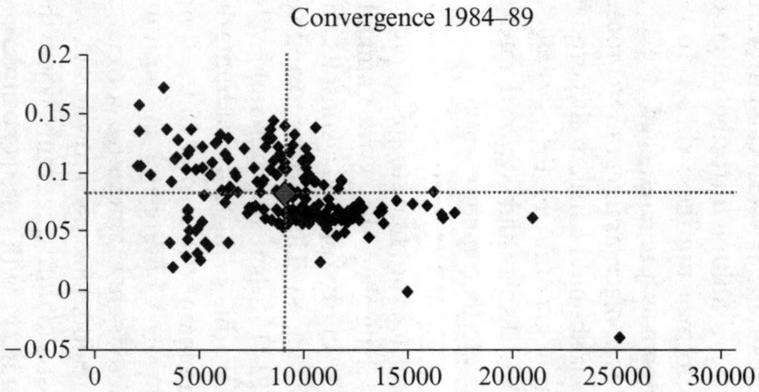
Convergence 1984–89
0.2
0.15
0.1
0.05
0
−0.05
0
5000
10000
15000
20000
25000
30000

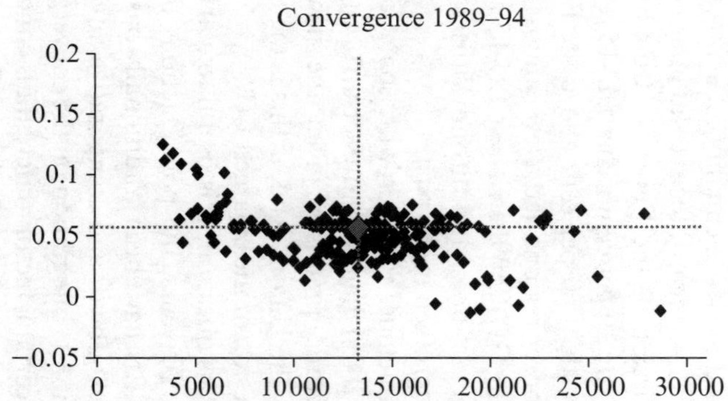
Convergence 1989–94
0.2
0.15
0.1
0.05
0
−0.05
0
5000
10000
15000
20000
25000
30000

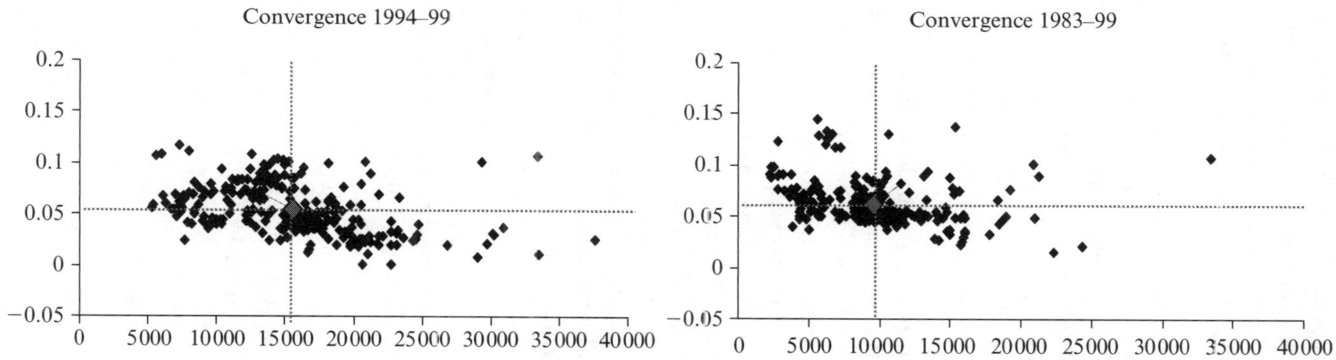

Source: Authors' elaboration on the basis of Eurostat data and Altomonte and Bonassi (2002).

Figure 8.1 Income β-convergence in a sample of EU-15 regions (NUTS2, 1983–99)

Considering the entire period 1983–99 and three subperiods, 1984–89, 1989–94 and 1994–99 (corresponding to the EU financial framework for regional policy, see below), there is a particular lack of convergence during the last period, from 1994 to 1999, that is, precisely when the integration process was strongest.

Even more worrisome, this lack of convergence of regional incomes is taking place notwithstanding the continuous expansion of the EU cohesion policy as a share of the EU budget since its establishment in the mid-1980s.[11] In particular, regional imbalances seem to display a geographical **core–periphery pattern**, with regions closer to the European 'centre' (the area ranging from North Italy to London, along the French–German border) performing better than regions at the periphery of the EU, as reported by Figure 8.2.

A first explanation for these quite puzzling findings has been recently provided by the so-called '**new economic geography**' (**NEG**) models of agglomeration and growth. According to this class of models, in the presence of positive trade costs and increasing returns to scale, firms tend to produce more efficiently and workers enjoy higher welfare by being close to large 'central' markets; but large markets are in turn those where more firms and workers locate. This creates a cumulative causation process that tends to open up regional differences as integration proceeds, since for lower transport costs it is more and more convenient for firms to serve 'peripheries' from the 'centre', and for workers to locate in these regions.[12] Thus, as economic integration proceeds, an even more pronounced role for cohesion policies should be advocated.

Understanding whether we live in a world of comparative advantages and convergence, or one of increasing returns and core–periphery patterns, is therefore crucial in order to assess the 'right' kind of policy to foster cohesion and growth in the presence of economic integration. Unfortunately, however, the theoretical discussion among economists has not yet reached a firm conclusion on the issue, and therefore the same 'optimal' set-up of the EU cohesion policy is still the object of a heated debate.[13]

Given the scope of the book, we limit ourselves to presenting in what follows the current set-up of the EU cohesion policy, together with the most recent Commission's proposals for its future evolution (European Commission, 2004e). We will also present an evaluation of the likely efficacy of these proposals in ensuring cohesion and growth for the enlarged Union. We leave to a more specialised forum of discussion the issue of the general theoretical premises on which the cohesion policy should be based.

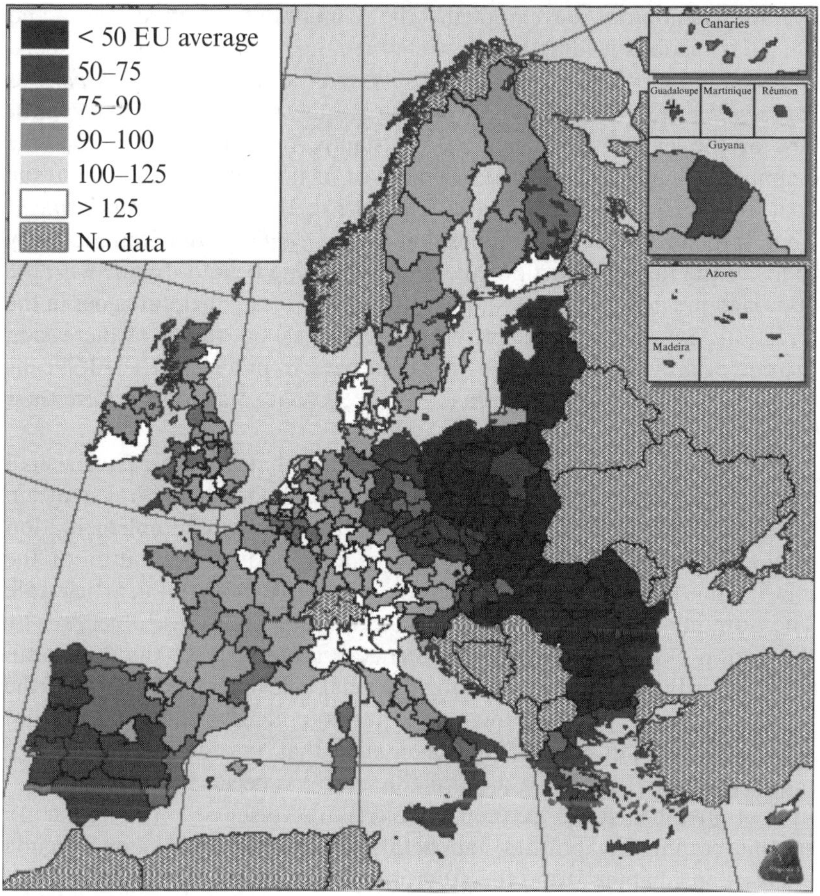

Source: European Commission (2003d).

Figure 8.2 Regional inequalities in EU-27, regional per capita GDP in PPS (NUTS2, 2001)

8.3 GOALS AND TOOLS OF THE EU COHESION POLICY

As previously mentioned, the notion of economic and social cohesion is already enshrined in article 2 of both TEC and TEU. But in order to have an operative definition of what exactly is intended by economic and social cohesion, one must turn to Title XVII of the TEC (articles 158 to 162).[14] The first article (TEC, art. 158) reads in particular: 'In order to promote its overall harmonious development, the Community shall develop and pursue its actions leading to the strengthening of its economic and social cohesion. In particular, the Community shall aim at *reducing disparities between the levels of development* of the various regions and the backwardness of the least favoured regions or islands, including rural areas' (the emphasis is ours). The italicised element of article 158 says it all about the goal of the EU intervention: the reference to the '*levels of development*' (that is, the income levels) implies that to '*reduce disparities*' it is necessary to foster the rate of growth of the regions lagging behind. In line with the approach previously discussed, the spirit of the Treaty therefore goes in the direction, not of simply redistributing resources, but rather of increasing the rate of growth of the beneficiary countries. In practice, article 158 calls for the EU funds to be earmarked for investment so as to maximise their impact on growth.

The second article (TEC, art. 159) specifies that 'Member States shall conduct their economic policies and shall coordinate them [. . .] to attain the objectives set out in article 158. The formulation and implementation of the Community's policies and actions and the implementation of the internal market shall take into account the objectives set out in article 158. The Community shall also support the achievement of these objectives by the action it takes through the Structural funds [. . .] the European Investment Bank and other existing financial instruments'. Because of the implicit emphasis put on growth as a means to achieve cohesion, it is not surprising that TEC, art. 159 makes it clear that, in order to achieve economic and social cohesion, a set of three tools is necessary: the coordination of member states' economic policies (as discussed in Chapter 4), specific community policies and actions (currently the Lisbon Agenda analysed in Chapter 5) and the provision of specific EU financial funds for cohesion-related expenditures.

These funds are however by no means the only element to support the achievement of economic and social cohesion. As we shall see in the following section, this is one of the reasons why it is difficult, if not impossible, to disentangle the contribution of the structural funds from the contribution of other Union's and member states' policies to economic cohesion within the EU.

8.3.1 The EU Funds for Regional Development

As already briefly analysed in Chapter 6, the EU funds for economic and social cohesion represent about 35 per cent of the EU budget until 2006, rising to more than 40 per cent in the 2007–13 Financial Perspectives, thus overtaking the share of the common agricultural policy. For the sake of the analysis, these funds can be broadly divided into three big groups: the **structural funds**, mentioned in TEC, art. 159, amounting to about 86 per cent of the total resources available for the period 2000–2006 (around €213 billion at 1999 prices); the **cohesion fund**, mentioned in TEC, art. 161, accounting for 8.5 per cent of the resources available and the **Community initiatives**, making up the difference.[15] The structural funds are themselves composed of three funds:

1. The guidance section of the **European Agricultural Guidance and Guarantee Fund** (**EAGGF** or FEOGA[16]) which aims at improving the production and marketing conditions of agricultural products. Until 2006 this expenditure is financed under the agricultural heading of the EU budget, while, after that, in consideration of its convergence aim, it is financed under the structural expenditure heading.
2. The **European Social Fund** (**ESF** or FSE), mainly devoted to improving the workforce conditions, including intra-EU mobility and lifelong training programmes.
3. The **European Regional Development Fund** (**ERDF** or FEDER), intended to help redress the main regional imbalances in the Union, through participation in the expenditures related to the structural adjustment of poor regions, and in the conversion of declining industrial regions (TEC, art. 160).

As previously mentioned, the predecessor of the ERDF was created in 1975, but essentially, until the introduction of the first Financial Perspectives in 1988, the structural policy lacked the necessary framework to develop properly. The Financial Perspectives brought about specific guidelines on the financial planning of resources, and seriously improved the coordination of the Union's policies with the ones developed within member states, organising the structural funds' disbursements around six objectives according to three priorities:[17] supporting regions significantly lagging behind the EU average income, supporting regions in industrial decline, and improving EU employment.

Since the year 2000, with the adoption of the 'Agenda 2000' Financial Perspectives (see Chapter 6), a major simplification of the structural funds took place and the six objectives were condensed into three objectives reflecting the above-mentioned priorities.[18] Each fund was then assigned to one or more of the three objectives, which thus became the focus of the EU structural policy.

Objective 1 supports the development and structural adjustment of **lagging behind regions**. This is the objective which channels most of the resources available via the structural funds (around 70 per cent, see Table 8.1), mostly

Table 8.1 Structural and cohesion funds in EU-15, 2000–06 (€ million at 2004 prices)

Member State	Objective 1 (*)	Objective 2	Objective 3	FIFG (**)	Cohesion	Community initiatives	**Total**	Population in Obj. 1 and 2 areas (million)	% of the national populations
Austria	288	740	585	0	0	395	**2 008**	2.270	28.20
Belgium	690	486	817	33	0	231	**2 257**	1.269	12.50
Denmark	0	199	397	221	0	92	**909**	0.538	10.20
Finland	1 008	541	442	33	0	280	**2 304**	2.650	51.70
France	4 201	6 569	5 013	254	0	1155	**17 192**	20.412	34.00
Germany	22 035	3 776	5 057	121	0	1 775	**32 765**	24.447	29.80
Greece	23 143	0	0	0	3 388	952	**27 483**	10.476	100.00
Ireland	3 409	0	0	0	584	183	**4 177**	0.965	26.60
Italy	24 424	2 749	4 129	110	0	1 294	**32 707**	26.704	46.50
Luxembourg	0	44	44	0	0	14	**103**	0.117	28.20
Netherlands	136	861	1 866	33	0	719	**3 615**	2.324	15.00
Portugal	21 010	0	0	0	3 388	741	**25 139**	6.616	66.60
Spain	42 061	2 904	2 363	221	12 357	2 162	**62 067**	32.027	80.70
Sweden	797	431	795	66	0	307	**2 396**	1.674	18.90
UK	6 902	5 068	5 046	132	0	1 061	**18 209**	18.909	32.20
EU-15	**150 104**	**24 367**	**26 553**	**1 226**	**19 717**	**11 361**	**233 328**	**149.13**	**40.30**

Notes: (*) Including phasing out; (**) Outside Objective 1.

Source: European Commission, Regional Policy website.

through the use of the ERDF. Regions lagging behind are defined as those whose per capita income, measured in terms of per capita GDP in PPS, is lower than 75 per cent of the EU average. These regions can be identified in Figure 8.2 for the EU-25.

Objective 2 promotes the development of border regions and the restructuring of regions in industrial decline through the ERDF and the EAGGF, as well as some Community initiatives. The resources allocated to this objective account for about 14 per cent of the total resources dedicated to the structural funds.

Objective 3 favours the adaptation and modernisation of education and training systems in order to promote employment in member states. The main instrument of expenditure is the ESF, with the objective covering about 16 per cent of the total structural expenditure. Table 8.1 reports the allocation of resources of structural expenditures for the EU-15 countries for the period 2000–2006.

Two of the three objectives previously analysed (Objectives 1 and 2) by their nature address EU regions (NUTS2) or even provinces (NUTS3), rather than national states, and are allocated accordingly to different regional eligibility criteria. The effective disbursement of the funds by the EU is however conditional on the presentation, by the benefiting regions, of a detailed regional programme of development and the respecting of some specific management criteria, discussed in the next section of the chapter. Some regions actually end up claiming and then using only a fraction of the funds that are assigned to them, and therefore the final distribution of the structural funds may be significantly different from the planned one, thus further complicating the analysis of the effectiveness of the regional policy.

The strict link between structural funds and regions (and not countries) is also at the root of two phenomena which are often discussed in both political and academic circles: (1) nearly all EU member states have at least one region officially labelled as 'poor', and thus entitled to receive Objective 1 funds;[19] and (2) countries of similar national wealth may receive extremely different support from the EU structural funds if they have different situations of regional income disparities, as seen in Table 8.1. This is the case, for example, of Italy and Sweden: since 1995 these two countries have had comparable national income levels (in per capita PPS), but the former receives incomparably greater support from the EU structural funds because it has a greater number of eligible regions than Sweden (in particular, six regions in southern Italy are entitled to receive funds under Objective 1 for the period 2000–2006, as compared with only one in Sweden). Some commentators have therefore argued that the structural funds, if not properly administered, might act as a premium to those countries that actually proved ineffective in reducing regional disparities.

Since 1993, TEC, art. 161 has also introduced the cohesion fund, as we have seen. Cohesion funds were established by the 'Delors II' Financial Perspectives in favour of the four poorest countries of the EU at the time (Greece, Ireland, Portugal and Spain), in a bid to compensate partially for the short-term effects of fiscal discipline imposed by the Maastricht Treaty, necessary to move to a single currency. These funds were subject to the presentation of a convergence programme (before the adoption of the Euro) and a programme of stability (after the adoption of the Euro) by the countries concerned. Today, the cohesion fund can be claimed by a country (not a region) which has a per capita GDP lower than 90 per cent of the EU average.[20] The cohesion fund provides in particular additional financial contributions (with respect to the resources eventually available through the structural funds) to projects in the field of environment and transport infrastructure.

8.3.2 The Operational Principles of the EU Funds

TEC art. 161 mentions that the Council (thus the member states), acting unanimously on a proposal from the Commission and after obtaining the mandatory and binding absent of the European Parliament, shall define the tasks, priority objectives and the organisation of the structural funds. The Council, acting by the same procedure, shall also define the general rules and the provisions necessary to ensure their effectiveness and their coordination with the other financial instruments.

In particular, structural funds are implemented following six principles: concentration, programming, partnership, co-financing and additionality, effectiveness and coordination and compatibility. We shall be discussing these in turn. The **concentration** principle calls for concentrating to a very significant extent (generally understood as around 70 per cent) structural funds in the least prosperous regions, and, within them, for concentrating on specific development projects, in order not to waste resources in micro-projects with limited impact on the territory.

The principle of **programming** specifies that the EU structural funds can be used only to finance specific and detailed programmes of development (known as '**Operative Regional Plans**') submitted by the beneficiary regions, and successively approved by the Community within a general framework of coordinated actions agreed with the concerned member state, known as the '**Community Support Framework**'.

The **partnership** principle requires a close consultation between the Community and the competent authorities (at state, regional or local levels) in the beneficiary areas at all stages of the support action. That translates into close consultation from the presentation, to the approval, to the implementation and finally to the monitoring of the projects financed by the EU funds. Partnership is crucial to identify the need for a project and ensure its successful integration in the member state economic and social environment.

The premise under which the EU budget grants regional aid is that these funds are dedicated to investment that otherwise would not have been undertaken and that they are useful for the goal of local development. The two requirements of **additionality** and **co-financing** are crucial in this respect. Additionality means that EU money should be added to national investments, and should not replace them. In other words, EU funds should not crowd out national investment: this requirement aims at ensuring that EU funds only finance new investments, not consumption. Co-financing means that all EU funds aimed at regions or countries cannot alone cover the entire costs of a project. Rather the EU funds can only accompany national funds, private or public, according to a co-financing rate that varies from 30 per cent to about 50 per cent.[21] The jargon tags the funds responding to the co-financing requirement as 'compulsory matching funds' and those meeting the additionality requirement as 'non-compulsory national matching funds'. National matching funds resulting from co-financing are usually much bigger than the EU funds, and thus add to the resources available for pursuing the different EU objectives. In 1999, for example, the total of national matching funds in Objective 1 regions amounted to almost 82 billion Euros (in comparison to about 30 billion of EU funds).

Since the year 2000 a **performance reserve**, equal to 4 per cent of the allocation of structural funds for each member state, has also been established in favour of those programmes implemented most effectively (accordingly to the objectives initially set), so to ensure the **effectiveness** of the expenditure. Finally, **coordination** and **compatibility** are the two principles of good management that should ensure coordination across the different structural funds and across the other instruments of regional intervention.

8.4 THE EFFECTIVENESS OF THE EU COHESION POLICY

So far, we have stumbled several times on various measures of convergence across the EU, both at the member states (see, for example, Table 5.4) and at the regional level (see, for example, Figure 8.1), and we have started to discuss the various implications of the results obtained in terms of the underlying economic theories. By and large, we can definitely conclude that a very considerable amount of economic convergence took place within the EU and it generated a clear reduction of income inequalities across the

EU countries.[22] Europe of the 1980s was in fact a totally different place from today's Europe. The GDP per capita of the poorest ten regions was equal to 41 per cent of the EU average in 1986, to 50 per cent in 1996 and to 56 per cent in 2000; and, as discussed in Chapter 5, the contribution to EU growth of the four poorest countries in the 1990s was equal to about 150 per cent of their economic weight. However it is also indisputable that, looking at the general picture of regional convergence, the results have been less clear-cut.

Figure 8.3 further confirms these findings for the EU-15 over a homogeneous measure of income disparities at both the national and the regional level for the period 1991–2000.[23] In particular, it can be seen how the standard deviation of member states' income clearly decreased in the period considered, while the same measure at the regional level within the different member states is much more heterogeneous; thus no clear trend can be detected when averaging these data across all the EU regions (compare the last two columns of Figure 8.3).

The rest of this section qualifies this statement along three directions: regional versus national convergence, automatic versus induced (by EU and national policies) convergence and the qualitative results generated by the EU cohesion and structural funds. The next subsection will look at the regional disparities when considering the enlarged EU-25 scenario.

8.4.1 National vs. Regional Convergence[24]

Given the contrasting messages obtained so far when assessing the results of cohesion policy, one might wonder what the proper level to assess the EU convergence is. To answer this question, one needs to define at least three parameters: the period of analysis, the indicators to use in order to ascertain convergence, and the definition of region.

As for the period of analysis, one must take into account that an institutional and proper cohesion policy started at the EU level only in 1988, with the Delors I financial perspectives (1988–92), then strengthened by Delors II (1993–9) and the Agenda 2000 Financial Perspectives (2000–2006). One therefore has to look at three points in time, representative of the three different programming phases, to gather a complete picture, as we have done in Figure 8.1.

As for the indicators of performance, the literature normally uses GDP-related indicators (usually in per capita terms and PPS) and unemployment-related indicators. As for the explanatory variables, the literature is extremely dispersed: however a consensus can be found around a few indicators, such as funds disbursed, administrative capacity, use of resources and macroeconomic environment. These are also the variables that we will discuss in what follows.

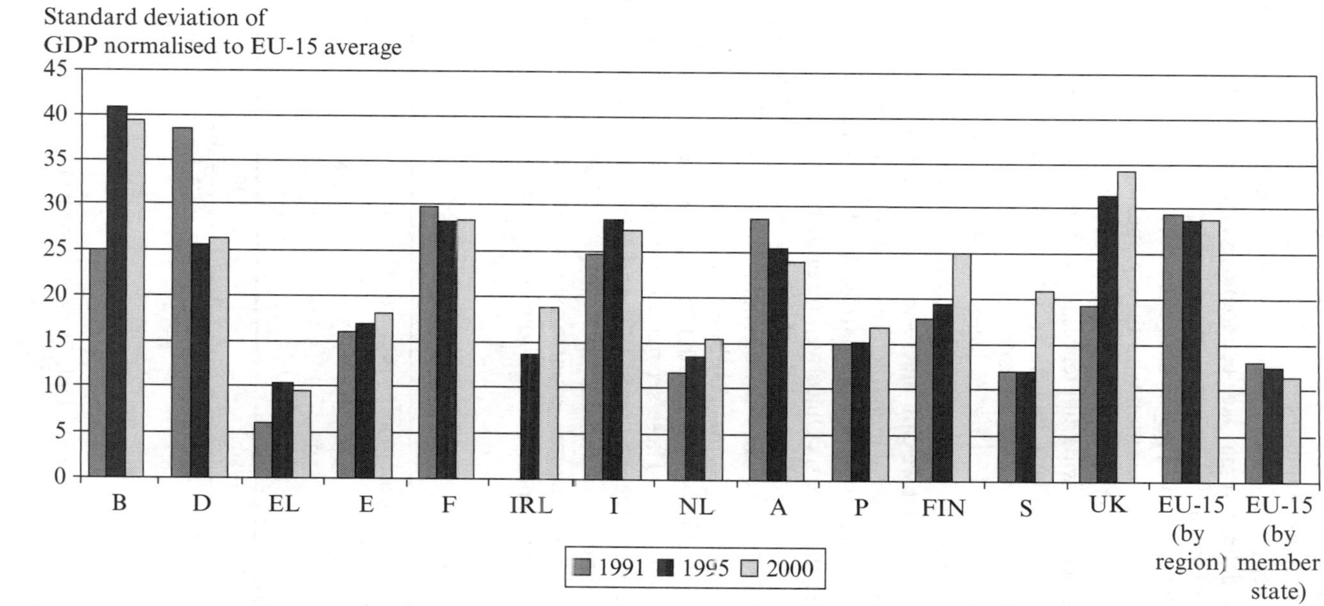

Source: Authors' calculations on Eurostat data; Luxembourg and Denmark are excluded from the regional calculations because of their territorial size.

Figure 8.3 *Income absolute convergence in EU-15 member states and NUTS2 region, 1991–2000 (per capita GDP in PPS)*

Finally, while the notion of nation is relatively clear and, in spite of greater economic integration, maintains a certain economic interest, the analysis of regional convergence presupposes a prior definition of what is a region, since the administrative definition may lack economic relevance. This is especially the case for some of the new member states of Central and Eastern Europe, where NUTS2 administrative regions have been only recently created, for a purpose of statistical harmonisation with the regional data computed at the European level. In addition, even disregarding the relevance of the level of aggregation, there exist very wide differences in size between units of the same statistical level. Hence similarly named 'regions' in different countries can induce very different economic effects, especially if the latter are scale-related.

As an example, let us look at the convergence process using an intermediate aggregation level between the state (NUTS1) and the administrative region level (NUTS2), that we call **'macro-regions'**; that is, an aggregate of administrative regions of similar characteristics, disregarding whether they formally constitute a country or only part of it. When studying convergence in the EU-15 there are six Objective 1 (lagging behind) macro-regions which are of immediate and intuitive relevance: they are Greece, Spain, Ireland and Portugal; the six eastern German Länder; and the six South Italian regions (the Mezzogiorno). As shown by Table 8.2, the income convergence of these six macro-regions with respect to the rest of the EU took place at a significant pace. These six macro-regions in fact displayed an annual growth of 3.3 per cent between 1991 and 2000, while the rest of the EU reported an annual growth of 1.9 per cent. As a result, these regions moved from an average income equal to about 70 per cent of the EU average to an average income equal to about 77 per cent of the EU average.

Table 8.2 Convergence in six EU lagging macro-regions

GDP growth rate	1980–1990	1991–2000	1991–1995	1995–2000
6 macro regions[a]	2.6	3.3	2.8	3.7
Rest of Europe	2.3	1.9	1.3	2.4
EU-15	2.4	2.1	1.5	2.6
Per capita GDP in PPS	**1980**	**1990**	**1995**	**2000**
6 macro regions[a]	69.3	70.7	73.5	76.8
Rest of Europe	109.5	109.1	109.9	108.7
EU-15	100	100	100	100

Note: [a]Greece, Ireland, Portugal, Spain, East Germany and South Italy.

Source: Sapir et al. (2004).

However, within this broad picture of convergence, there are wide and important differences across the six considered macro-regions. Three out of six (Spain, Portugal and Greece) have grown faster, albeit slightly, than the EU average, two (Ireland and East Germany) have grown significantly faster than the EU average[25] and one (the south of Italy) did not grow any faster than the EU average, thus displaying no convergence.

As a result, choosing either a 'large' (country, NUTS1) or a 'narrow' (region, NUTS2) definition of region amounts to ascertaining or refuting that any convergence has taken place in the last 15 years.[26] On the other hand, the problem might be solved when using an intermediate definition of macro-region. Box 8.1 looks in more detail at this debate. For assessing its convergence policies the EU uses two sets of aggregation: countries and regions. The cohesion fund, as we have seen, is currently granted to four countries (Greece, Spain, Ireland and Portugal), while the structural funds are distributed on the basis of a classification of the NUTS2 regions as administratively defined by the national administration, according to the various eligibility criteria previously considered. The bulk of the structural funds, however, flows into regions that lie close together, such as the six macro-regions previously discussed, which receive on average 70 per cent of the EU regional funds.

Hence, despite a less positive picture coming from the unemployment related figures (see Box 8.1), we tend to conclude with a positive assessment of the performance of regional convergence, at least at the macro-regional level. Despite many provisos, qualifications and methodology and data warnings,[27] when one looks at the big numbers, one cannot deny in fact that (macro-) regional convergence did take place for those macro-regions which are (or were) most in need of it, and which have received accordingly the bulk of the EU (financial and non-financial) support. The inequality figures shown in Chapter 5 support this positive assessment.

BOX 8.1 THE CONVERGENCE OF THE EU MACRO-REGIONS

In this box we look at eight macro-regions included in Objective 1 for the period 1999–2006: Greece, Ireland, Portugal, Spain, six Länder in East Germany, six regions in South Italy (Mezzogiorno) plus the UK regions receiving objective 1 funds (Northern Ireland, Highlands and Merseyside) and the Belgian Hainaut (the only Belgian region receiving Objective 1 funds). We do not look at Objective 1 regions of France (Corsica, Guadeloupe and Martinique), who receive sizeable funds, because of their geographical location: they are islands lying outside core Europe, whose economic performance might depend on too many other factors. All other Objective 1 regions are isolated points in the map of Europe, with their economic convergence likely to be more sensitive to other factors than EU structural funds.

Our data set for convergence in the EU at the level of macro-regions is thus divided into 19 regions: the eight Objective 1 macro-regions mentioned above, plus the four remaining countries mentioned not receiving Objective 1 funds (the rest of Germany, Italy, the UK and Belgium), plus the seven remaining member states. This breakdown is also compatible with data constraints, since several sources only offer data for the group of Objective 1 regions in a given country.

The following table shows that the average income of the lagging macro-regions has increased and is converging towards the EU average (set equal to 100). This result is also robust to the elimination of the two best performers. Within this globally positive picture, Ireland and the south of Italy stand out as those having the best and the worst performance.

GDP per capita in PPS (EU-15 = 100)	1980	1990	1995	2000	Average change 1980/2000
Obj. 1 – BE	82	77	82	73	−0.11
Rest of BE	111	109	117	112	0.01
DK	113	107	118	119	0.05
Obj. 1 – D	—	—	71	77	0.57
Rest of D	116	115	121	113	−0.03
Obj. 1 – EL	70	58	66	68	−0.03
Obj. 1 – E	73	76	78	82	0.12
F	110	107	104	101	−0.08
Obj. 1 – IRL	66	74	93	116	0.76
Obj. 1 – I	69	71	69	69	0.00
Rest of I	119	120	123	125	0.05
L	133	152	171	194	0.46
NL	108	103	109	113	0.05
A	106	106	110	113	0.07
Obj. 1 – P	56	62	71	73	0.30
Fin	97	103	97	104	0.07
S	113	110	103	101	−0.11
Obj. 1 – UK	—	—	76	78	0.16
Rest of UK	101	107	98	101	0.00
EU-15	100	100	100	100	0.00

In addition to the above evidence of convergence, we can also use, as already done for Figure 8.1, the notion of β-convergence to check the result of cohesion policies in the considered set of macro-regions. To this end, the figure below shows that, also using the latter measure of convergence, we obtain a positive picture of cohesion during the period considered (the broken lines indicate as usual the EU-15 average income in 1980 and average growth rate). The visual impression (discounting for the different sizes in initial GDP) is that, with the exception of three underperforming macro-regions (Hainaut, Greece and South Italy) convergence is taking place here to a larger extent than is obtained using NUTS2 regional level data (see the fourth quadrant of Figure 8.1).

In particular, the average growth rate through the period analysed for the eight macro-regions considered has been 17 per cent, against an average growth of the rest of the EU of 12 per cent. The total growth of the same macro-regions from 1980 to 2000 has been 68 per cent, against an average for the rest of the EU of 53 per cent.

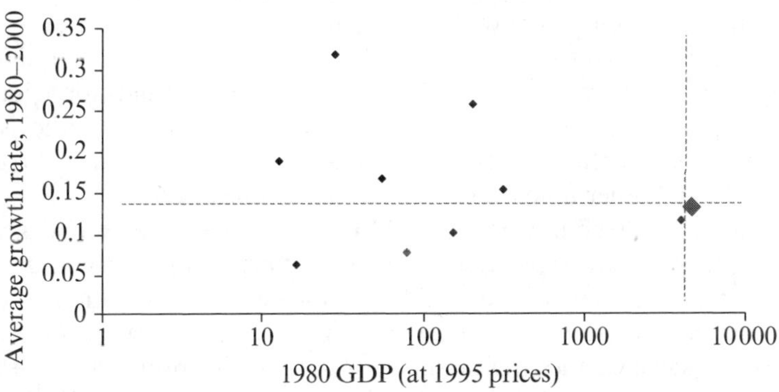

Such a positive assessment, nevertheless, cannot be confirmed if one looks at the unemployment figures, which show that unemployment in the macro-regions lies far above the EU average, and does not display any significant convergence towards the EU average (despite an overall reduction of unemployment in Europe). The same evidence of lack of convergence emerges from looking at the employment rate figures. Some extremely low employment rates, such as those in South Italy or in Hainaut (Belgium) are particularly striking. Considering what we argued in Chapter 5 on the importance of the employment rate for a successful implementation of the Lisbon strategy, this should be regarded as a cause for great concern.

8.4.2 EU vs. Nationally Supported Convergence

The amount of money channelled to the poor regions by the EU structural funds has certainly been very sizeable, reaching in peak years 11 per cent of GDP in Greece, 7 per cent in Ireland, and 8 per cent in Portugal. Despite this size, the EU structural funds are by no means the largest or the unique financial instrument for fostering convergence.

In fact convergence is not only related to the size of the EU financial disbursement (and some authors would even deny this statement), but it also depends on other factors: the national amount of expenditure, the administrative capacity of the receiving country or region to obtain the funds and put them to a good use, the national business environment in which this disbursement takes place and, in general, and probably most importantly, the economic policy of the receiving country/region and its ability to exploit its existing comparative advantage. The already quoted Sapir report (Sapir *et al.*, 2004), when it tried to disentangle the impact of the different factors that may induce convergence, in fact reached the conclusion that, to obtain convergence, one needs the joint combination of exactly the same factors that we have just quoted.

Looking at these factors in more detail, it is noteworthy that, in addition to the EU funds, there are at least three more sources of funds for lagging regions: regional and sectoral state aid that member states are authorised to pay in favour of their undertakings, matching national funds to structural funds, and other funds coming from the EU institutions.

As will be discussed in Chapter 9, TEC, art. 87, para. 3a and 3c allow member states to grant **regional state aid** for the purpose of economic development, provided that the same aids do not distort competition in the single market. Such state aid is in general smaller than the **national matching funds** available via the already analysed co-financing principle, since the latter tend to include projects related to infrastructure development. However state aid can play a significant role in affecting convergence. For example, in the year 2000 the regional state aid granted under TEC, art. 87, para. 3a and 3c amounted to €8.1 billion, half of which was spent in Objective 1 macro-regions. More notably, still in 2000, the member states granted an estimated €82.4 billion across the EU in general state aid granted to specific sectors (compared to less than €30 billion of EU structural funds), of which €14 billion was concentrated in activities located in the poorest macro-regions. As a result, given the size of the figures at stake, national intervention can significantly alter the convergence process measured on the basis of the obtained income levels.

For this reason, a growing body of recent literature addresses the question of regional convergence not only by looking at the structural funds, but also by looking at the total state aid,[28] or at a part of it ('localised state aid')[29] or at all the funds coming from the EU system.[30] In synthesis, there is a growing consensus that regional convergence cannot be explained only by looking at the structural funds; rather one needs to look at many other sources of funds and also at other variables to understand the causes of regional and national convergence. These issues are analysed thoroughly in the Appendix of this chapter.

In addition to the national matching funds and the state aid, national or local authorities across the EU also run various **redistribution schemes** that do not fall under TEC, art. 87, para. 3a and 3c, but are concentrated in, or even dedicated to, regions. Such schemes can be transparent, like the lump-sum transfer schemes between regional budgets in some federal member states. They can also be opaque, like overstaffing in public services in poor regions.[31] Since it is impossible to take full account of these schemes, and since they are beyond the legal reach of the EU system, they are not discussed further here.

Finally, in addition to the structural funds, the EU institutions contribute to cohesion through various other channels. In particular, **project loans** granted by the **European Investment Bank** (EIB) to the different regions represent another instrument of regional development. Though the increase of loans, over the period, was smaller than the increase of the Community Support Framework (in the period 1994–99 they were equal to about 50 per cent of the structural funds, down from about 70 per cent in the period 1988–93), they represent an important part of the community help. EIB loans are concentrated mainly on infrastructure and construction; however they must be reimbursed. The financial advantage of the EIB loans consists therefore in the difference between the EIB rate and the rate that the region would have obtained in the financial markets according to its own creditworthiness. Clearly the interest rate spread is very country- and region-specific. One may argue that some regions would simply not be able to go into the market and leverage funds, either because of their scant size or because of their non-existent creditworthiness; under these circumstances the EIB aid would be a crucial element. However, leaving aside this extreme hypothesis and assuming very roughly that the rate of spread ranges from two to eight percentage points, the financial advantage of the EIB loans then represents only 1 to 4 per cent of the Community Support Framework. The small size of the loans, summed up by the difficulty of choosing a benchmark and of assessing the creditworthiness of regions in the market, amounts to obliging us to leave this instrument out of the quantitative analysis. Qualitatively we are, however, convinced that, especially in the most difficult cases, EIB loans play a crucial role in endowing a region with funds on which to leverage growth.

8.4.3 Qualitative Results

Income convergence is not everything. Other results also matter. The EU structural and cohesion funds have brought about not only income convergence, to the extent previously described, but also a certain number of qualitative results, such as a general improvement of administrative capacity (especially at local level), a greater proximity of the Union to its citizens, a greater political visibility of the EU, a greater quality of the environment and an improved policy focus of EU policies.

The regional focus of the EU structural policy has forced several regional and local administrations, often of remote areas, to raise their own standards so as to be able to apply for EU funds, to link up with regions having similar characteristics in other countries, and to use EU funds to attract investors. Improved **administrative capacity** benefits, in the short and medium run, both citizens and firms, improve the business environment, reduce compliance costs, and increase both flexibility and certainty of law. Several authors (Mairate and Hall, 2000; Sapir *et al.*, 2004; European Commission, 2004a) have been able to show the contribution of administrative capacity to growth. It is not an accident if, in the run-up to the 2004 enlargement, about half of the funds benefiting the then candidate countries was earmarked for improving their national administrative capacity.

The EU structural policy has also been a powerful tool to enforce a **dialogue** between the Union and its citizens. The need for a region to prepare a programme, coupled with the pressure coming from the citizens to submit a programme and benefit from the opportunities offered by the EU funds, has increased the proximity between the EU institutions and the European citizens. Certainly, at the beginning of the process, not all regions proved able to profit from the available opportunities. Those countries with a more federal design (such as Spain or Germany, for example) have found the process more natural than have other countries with a more centralised design. For example, at the start of the cohesion policy, the difference between the Spanish and the Italian poorest regions in their capacity to relate to the EU institutions, to propose projects and to use the opportunities offered to them was rather noticeably in favour of the former. With time, these differences have tended to disappear.

The **political visibility** of the EU structural and cohesion funds is also extremely high. The signposts with the yellow and blue European flag indicating EU financing for a given infrastructure have in many countries become part of the landscape. As mentioned in Chapter 6, all countries ultimately benefit from EU cohesion and structural funds, and all countries (bar Luxembourg and Denmark) have at least one region labelled as an Objective 1 region. For example, even Austria, Sweden and Finland, the three rich countries that entered the EU with the 1995 enlargement, had insisted during the enlargement negotiations on having at least one region or a part of the population having the status of an Objective 1 region. The Burgerland (the region bordering the Slovak Republic) in Austria met the criteria to be included in the Objectve 1 list, but no region was found for Sweden and Finland. Therefore a new objective (Objective 6) in favour of the 'development of the scarcely populated regions' of both Sweden and Finland was established. The total endowment of this new Objective 6 (then absorbed into the current Objective 1) was extremely minute (some €30 million per annum, to be compared with a gross contribution of Sweden and Finland of nearly €4 billion per annum), but still the value attached to its political visibility was important.

The EU structural funds, in addition, entail a sizeable **leverage effect** in the benefiting countries. In the Objective 1 regions, one Euro of EU funds leverages one Euro of other public and private funds. Outside the Objective 1 regions the EU funds, thanks to the signalling effect they have vis-à-vis other investors, are estimated to be able to leverage 3 Euros for every Euro (see European Commission, 2004a).

Environment protection has also been one of the aims of structural expenditure. Not only is part of the expenditure explicitly aimed at improving the environment, but also the remaining expenditure is executed subject to relatively strict environmental requirements. Structural and cohesion funds thus contribute to the concept of sustainable growth elaborated in Chapter 5. Finally cohesion and structural expenditures have dramatically improved the **policy focus** and the **policy balance** of the Union. Until the 1980s, the EU was mostly engaged in the common agricultural policy and was not able to enter other policy areas. Today, structural expenditure, and in general growth-enhancing expenditure, is the core area of the EU intervention, accounting by 2013 for half of the EU budget.

8.5 THE COHESION POLICY IN AN ENLARGED UNION

As already discussed, the 2004 enlargement represents an unprecedented challenge for the internal cohesion of the Union. Overall, and for the first time in recent history, Europe will be a more unequal place than the USA (see Chapter 5), essentially because of the increase in its across-countries inequality.

In particular, with the new member states, the surface area of the Union has increased by 34 per cent, the population by 28 per cent but the GDP only by 5 per cent. Hence, by 1 May 2004, the average EU per capita GDP had decreased by 18 per cent, falling from €22 603 to €19 661 (if Bulgaria and Romania are included, this figure drops to €18 530). As a consequence, the gap in per capita GDP between the 10 per cent of the population living in the most prosperous regions (currently at 172 per cent of the EU average) and the same percentage living in the least prosperous ones (at 39 per cent of the EU average) has more than doubled when compared with the situation in EU-15 (where the figures were 155 per cent and 55 per cent, respectively). In short, the regions of the new member states, with very few exceptions, qualify for Objective 1 assistance, their per capita GDP being below 75 per cent of the EU-25 average. As a result, in EU-25 there are now 123 million citizens – some 25 per cent of the total population of the Union – who live in regions officially considered as poor, against 73 million people, or 18 per cent of the total EU population, in EU-15.

Faced with this challenge, the EU cohesion policy must not only increase its structural aid but, overall, it has to improve the efficacy of the expenditures it finances, making sure at the same time that the financed expenditure is in accordance with the Lisbon objectives. In this regard, the Copenhagen European Council in December 2002 essentially solved the problem up to 2006, since already in the 'Agenda 2000' Financial Perspectives the Union had set aside a specific heading for enlargement (see Chapter 6), endowed with enough resources (around €40 billion) to provide for the EU expenditure policies in the new member states for the period 2004–6.

In particular, as reported in Table 8.3, out of these resources, almost €22 billion are dedicated to structural expenditures and only €9.8 billion to CAP and rural development (4682 and 5110M€, respectively), essentially thanks to the 2002 agreement on agriculture which phases in over the next ten years the amount of agricultural aid to be granted to the new member states (see Chapter 7).[32]

When looking at the repartition of structural expenditures across the new member states, it is also interesting to observe for some countries the disproportional share allocated to the cohesion fund versus the structural funds, with respect to the same figure traditionally allocated in EU-15 (for example, 54 per cent of resources go to the cohesion fund in Poland, versus the current 8.5 per cent share of the cohesion fund in EU-15). Clearly this is related to the already mentioned problem of the economic relevance of administrative regions in the new member states. Owing to the novelty of the territorial classification, many new member states were felt to possess an inadequate administrative capacity in the newly created regions. As a

Table 8.3 Structural and cohesion funds in the new member states, 2004–6 (€ million at 2004 prices)

Country	Objective 1	Objective 2	Objective 3	Interreg	EQUAL	Cohesion Fund	**Total**	Population in Obj. 1 and 2 areas (millions)	% of the population
Cyprus(*)	0.00	28.02	21.95	4.30	1.81	53.94	**113.44**	0.212	30.90
Czech Republic	1 454.27	71.30	58.79	68.68	32.10	936.05	**2 621.19**	9.460	92.00
Estonia	371.36	0.00	0.00	10.60	4.07	309.03	**695.06**	1.379	100.00
Hungary	1 995.72	0.00	0.00	68.68	30.29	1 112.67	**3 207.36**	10.238	100.00
Latvia	625.57	0.00	0.00	15.26	8.03	515.43	**1 164.29**	2.391	100.00
Lithuania	895.17	0.00	0.00	22.49	11.87	608.17	**1 537.70**	3.531	100.00
Malta	63.19	0.00	0.00	2.37	1.24	21.94	**88.74**	0.387	100.00
Poland	8 275.81	0.00	0.00	221.36	133.93	4 178.60	**12 809.70**	38.654	100.00
Solvakia	1 041.04	37.17	44.94	41.47	22.27	570.50	**1 757.39**	4.957	91.90
Slovenia	237.51	0.00	0.00	23.65	6.44	188.71	**456.31**	1.986	100.00
Total	**14 959.64**	**136.49**	**125.68**	**478.86**	**252.05**	**8 495.04**	**24 451.18**	**73.195**	**97.70**

Note: (*) including Fisheries Fund.

Source: European Commission, Regional Policy website.

result, they preferred to manage at the central level a greater share of the structural expenditures (via the cohesion fund, which, as we recalled, is allocated to the country), rather than have the regions administer the EU resources via the structural funds (that, as also pointed out, are essentially dealt with directly by the NUTS2-eligible regions). The latter, however, is a provisional arrangement, which has to be discussed again in 2007, with the new programming period.

In this respect, we have already seen in Chapter 6 that the Commission proposal for the new 2007–13 programming period commits a total of €344.9 billion to the expenditures on **cohesion for growth and employment** (Item 1b of the 2007–13 proposed Financial Perspectives analysed in Chapter 6) versus €213 billion committed by Agenda 2000 for the period 2000–2006. Such an increase (by more than 60 per cent) in the resources devoted to cohesion reflects the magnitude of the challenges posed by the EU enlargement. In addition, the proposal envisages a more simplified and transparent priority framework. In particular, the allocation of the proposed funds should be channelled into three priorities, replacing the three current objectives (European Commission, 2004f).

A given percentage of funds (presumably close to 70 per cent) will be allocated for the priority of **convergence** and thus directed to the less developed member states and regions of the enlarged Union, thus replacing Objective 1. As for Objective 1, efforts under the new convergence programmes would be devoted to modernising and increasing physical and human capital, in order to increase long-term competitiveness, foster environmental sustainability and provide a greater contribution to the Union's overall economic performance, while developing best practices in governance and institutional capacities.

The allocation of these funds clearly implies a new list of eligible member states and regions. In particular, keeping the current Objective 1 eligibility criteria for the structural funds (NUTS2 regions whose per capita income, measured in terms of per capita GDP in PPS, is lower than 75 per cent of the EU average) amounts to excluding some regions in EU-15 that have not yet completed the process of convergence. The latter is the so-called '**statistical effect**', and essentially it takes place because, as we have seen, the average EU per capita GDP declined after the enlargement, from €22 603 in EU-15 to €19 661 in EU-25 (at year 2000 prices). As a result, the eligibility criterion for receiving structural funds (that is, a per capita GDP lower than 75 per cent of the latter figure) decreases, from €16 952 to €14 745. Hence an Objective 1 region of EU-15 that in 2006 would still have a per capita GDP of, say, €16 000, would not qualify for receiving the structural funds from 2007 in EU-25 (€16 000 > €14 745), while, without the effects due to the enlargement, it would have still matched the eligibility criterion in EU-15 (€16 000 < €16 952). The Commission estimates that, owing to the statistical effect, 19 million EU citizens in 17 regions of EU-15 will not qualify as recipients of the Objective 1 structural funds, starting with the new financial framework in 2007. Hence, in order to avoid political problems and suddenly depriving of the convergence funds those regions which, as a matter of fact, are still lagging behind, a **phasing out** period has been foreseen, during which these regions will receive, starting from 2007, a yearly diminishing amount of funds, initially similar to the 2000–2006 levels and then to be terminated by 2013.

Hence, out of the 50 NUTS2 regions of EU-15 receiving Objective 1 funds in the period 2000–2006, the Commission estimates that only 33 will remain eligible in 2007 because of the lower level of EU per capita GDP. However 36 NUTS2 regions in the new member states will have to be added to the picture, thus bringing the total of lagging regions entitled to receive structural funds in EU-25 to 69 (see European Commission, 2004).[33]To this list one should also add the financial disbursements foreseen for the 17 regions of EU-15 who will receive the phasing out funds in compensation for the statistical effect. In terms of eligibility of countries for the cohesion fund, it has already been decided that only Portugal and Greece will continue to benefit from this fund in EU-15, but all ten new member states will be added to the picture. Clearly, given the new number of regions and countries which have to receive structural and cohesion funds from 2007, plus the phasing out, it is evident that the money allocated for this purpose by the Commission in its 2004 proposal might be just adequate to the task.

The former Objective 2 and Objective 3 will instead be replaced, starting in 2007, by a new priority aimed at fostering **regional competitiveness and employment**. The regional competitiveness and employment programmes would cover the other regions and member states not eligible under the convergence priority, since significant needs will persist throughout the Union as a result of the economic and social restructuring that the internal market integration and the enlargement will bring about. In order to ensure the efficacy value of Community actions, interventions would need to concentrate on a limited number of policy priorities linked to the Lisbon Agenda, where they can provide added value and a multiplier effect on national or regional policies.

Finally some of the current Community initiatives will be incorporated in a new priority aimed at **European territorial cooperation** in the form of cross-border and transnational programmes. These programmes would seek to address the particular problems that exist in achieving a competitive and sustainable economy in areas of member states that are divided by national borders. The emphasis would be on the promotion of exchanges of experience and good practices, contributing to economic integration across the Union's territory and to more harmonious and balanced development.

However, notwithstanding this sustained effort by the EU to face the challenge of cohesion posed by the enlargement, the disparities in EU-25 are likely to persist in the following years. In particular, the same European Commission estimates that, if the new member states, thanks to the allocated funds and other related convergence policies, are able to grow on average by 1.5 per cent more per year than the EU-15, they will in any case qualify as behind areas until 2037. Even making the unrealistic assumption that all regions in the new member states will grow at 2.5 per cent more per year than the EU-15, structural funds will need to be granted, according to the current eligibility criteria, at least until 2023 (European Commission, 2004a). These estimates are also in line with Morrison and Murtin (2004), who forecast a reduction in the inequalities in the EU-25 to levels close to the ones achieved by the EU-15 in year 2000 not before the next 30 years.

8.6 POLICIES FOR SUSTAINABLE GROWTH

Consistently with the previously discussed goal of achieving simultaneously growth and cohesion in the Union, the European Commission, in addition to the funds allocated for structural expenditure, is also planning to strengthen significantly the amount of money to be used as allocative expenditure to finance growth.[34] In particular, if the Council accepts the Commission proposals on the new Financial Perspectives, some €132.7 billion will be devoted to this purpose in the 2007–13 programming period.

Indeed we have seen in Chapter 5 that, since the adoption of the Lisbon Agenda, a great deal of emphasis has been put on the necessary investment in education and training, network infrastructure and research, in order to raise EU overall productivity and hence growth. Now there is a sound economic rationale, given the potentially large-scale economies involved, to transfer part of this expenditure to the EU level. In the presence of economies of scale, since the expenditure undertaken at the EU level would substitute for the different national expenditure but at a lower cost, that would amount in fact to an overall decrease in total public expenditure, thus liberating extra resources to achieve the Lisbon targets.

As a result, the proposal of the Commission foresees the introduction of expenditures on **competitiveness for growth and employment** (Item 1a of the 2007–13 proposed Financial Perspectives analysed in Chapter 6), which include research expenditure, education and training expenditure and trans-European networks. Item 1a constitutes the single largest change to the structure of the EU budget for the next programming period. In monetary terms, the expenditure increases by about three times from 2006 to 2013 (from €48.5 billion in the period 2000–2006 to the already mentioned €132.7 billion), and as a share of the EU budget it increases from 8 per cent to 16 per cent. This reflects the Commission's strong will to transform the EU budget progressively into an instrument for achieving the Lisbon objectives. In particular, this expenditure is meant to be used to reach four mutually reinforcing objectives: (a) promoting the competitiveness of enterprises in a fully integrated single market, (b) strengthening the European effort in research and technological development, (c) connecting Europe through EU networks, and (d) improving the quality of education and training.

In order to **promote the competitiveness of enterprises**, it is necessary to complete and improve the single market, to improve the regulatory environment for business in the sense of less rigidity and more certainty and to foster entrepreneurship by facilitating access to finance. Some of these issues have already been discussed in Chapter 3, so we just recall here the provision of the resources allocated to this purpose. However, as already pointed out in Chapter 5, in order to achieve competitiveness it is of the utmost importance to create an environment where firms find the right incentives to innovate. Research shows (see Acemoglu *et al.*, 2002) that the closer a country is to the technology frontier, the more it needs to innovate to remain competitive, since it cannot rely any more only on imitation and scale economies. Certainly the Union can and should actively contribute to member states' efforts to gain competitiveness, but its action can only complement, and not replace, the ones to be undertaken by member states.

Research and technological development is another clear area where the EU budget can, and should, make a difference, although taking into account all the caveats already discussed in Chapter 5 on the efficacy of public versus private spending on R&D activities. However it is indisputable that, however rhetorical it might seem, the EU has pledged itself to become the most competitive economy in the world, based on knowledge, and to that end it has endeavoured to invest about 3 per cent of its GDP in public and private research. And yet the EU is still below target, devoting about 1.9 per cent of its GDP to research, compared with 2.7 per cent in the United States and more than 3 per cent in Japan. Hence an increase in public resources would in any case help in (partially) filling this gap, although, as already discussed, it is crucial that the private sector also finds the right set of incentives to contribute to this endeavour.

In particular, Europe should become able to attract researchers and investments from all over the world by fostering a programme that gives to excellence the right incentives. Currently the European research effort remains too fragmented, too nationally segmented and insufficiently connected to the rest of the world. To overcome this bottleneck to excellence, the EU should pursue the aim of creating a **European research area**, that is, an internal market for research and technology and a means to coordinate national and regional research activities. This translates into the EU adopting a more aggressive policy of research investment and allocating resources only on the basis of excellence, disregarding, for this particular type of fund, any other consideration. Too often the 'optimal' allocation of research funds has in fact been biased by considerations of national balance, or solidarity towards least favoured regions, or worse.

The construction, development and maintenance of the **Trans-European networks** is also essential to guarantee the mobility of people, goods and services in an enlarged EU market.[35] Trans-European networks in fact not only contribute to growth and competitiveness, but also offer a tangible symbol of European integration. In this respect, traffic on the EU networks of road, rail and energy infrastructures is continuing to grow. The Commission has estimated the cost of congestion to be about 1 per cent of the EU GDP (the whole EU budget!) in 2005, likely to rise to 2 per cent by 2020. The state of the infrastructure and the use of the networks are such that most of the increase in traffic will fall on roads, leading to very negative consequences in terms of congestion, the environment, safety and quality of life. Most of the EU axes, in addition, run north–south and few run east–west. Thus linking Europe through networks is, now, mainly a matter of reinforcing the transnational east–west axes. If nothing is done, Europe will not be thoroughly connected, and it will pay the price of a failing infrastructure on its potential for growth.

Education and training are among the main determinants of growth. Improvements in the Community's education and training systems is at the centre of the Lisbon Agenda. However a delicate balance must be achieved. On the one hand, education is one of those areas where the heterogeneity of preferences across the EU countries and the need to ensure proximity to citizens' choices call for a national, if not in many cases a regional, action. On the other hand, the continuing process of integration of the Union calls for at least a common part of the EU curricula and programmes. A way to strike this balance is thus to make sure that there exists a contribution to education also at the EU level, with adequate resources allocated for this purpose. In particular the financial contribution of the Union to the area of education has been mainly focused on improving and sustaining individual mobility (of students, teachers, academics, researchers and so on) and in promoting partnerships or networks between schools and universities in different countries. The most famous EU projects in this area (Erasmus and Leonardo) have had a striking success across Europe, and are generally regarded as an example of good policy.

8.7 THE FUTURE OF EU COHESION AND GROWTH POLICIES

Growth is the greatest European priority for the first decade of the new millennium but, according to the EU social model, it should not be achieved at the expense of stability and cohesion. Consistently with this goal, the EU has embarked on a rather audacious programme of radical reforms, trying to undertake policies able to deliver growth both in the areas lagging behind the EU average and in the rest of the Union.

As for the lagging regions, the results of the last 20 years are certainly positive, albeit not in all places or in every respect. Lagging macro-regions grew more than the rest of Europe in the 1980s and 1990s. The progress of some of them has been simply spectacular. Unfortunately, the stagnation of some others has been equally spectacular. The picture is even more fragmented at the regional (NUTS2) level. Evidence also reveals that, to cope with these needs, the EU funds are too small to matter unless they are used in combination both with other funds and with the right choice of policies in a conducive business environment. In fact, once controlling for the impact of the national contributions to convergence, the EU funds used with due respect for their operational principles have delivered a sizeable impulse to growth; those applied to vague projects not strictly linked to the comparative advantage of the beneficiary regions have not fostered convergence. The analysis reported in the Appendix also shows that the EU and national funds for convergence are correctly distributed across member states, that is, according to an inverse correlation with income. However the total of the EU budget does not. This is due to the fact that, even if the EU cohesion and structural funds benefit mostly the poorer countries, other funds (mainly CAP) bias this distribution.

In addition to the quantitative results, the cohesion policy has brought about some non-negligible qualitative results, such as a general improvement in the administrative capacity (especially at local level), a greater proximity of the EU to citizens, a greater political visibility of the EU, a better quality of the environment and an improved focus of the Union's policies.

The challenges ahead for the EU cohesion policy are immense, given the vast income inequalities brought into the EU by the 2004 enlargement. Focusing the funds on the least prosperous areas and linking the funds to the Lisbon targets is the recipe proposed by the Commission to the Council for the period 2007–13. Equally immense are the challenges ahead of the growth policies of the EU. The Commission's proposal, concerning EU-level contribution to the growth agenda, calls for focusing on improving education and training, completion of the trans-European networks and increasing the investment in research and development. Once more, these priorities are consistent with the Lisbon Agenda.

Member states should react consistently to these proposals. On the one hand, the Council should adopt the project of Financial Perspectives for the period 2007–13 without decreasing its overall amount. If instead member states have a different opinion, they should indicate in what areas the EU should not intervene. Given the challenges ahead in terms of cohesion and growth, in fact, the proposed resources are already stretched to the limit. A further reduction would therefore imply the abolition of one or more areas of intervention at the EU level, an input that the member states should provide, if they do not intend to carry on with the Commission's proposals.

On the other hand, member states should avoid pompous rhetoric at the EU meetings, especially if the latter are followed by inconsistent behaviour in the internal implementation of the proposed lines of action. In other words, the projects to be developed under the new structural and cohesion funds should be in line with each receiving region's competitive advantage, and the lines of action foreseen within the Lisbon strategy of economic reforms (innovation, research and development, education). The past examples of aid (both national and European) generously distributed to undertakings operating in mature manufacturing sectors, even if respecting formally all the operational principles of the structural funds and the provisions of the EU treaties, should be avoided. Rather, in every member state the entire programming of the policy actions for economic development, in both the lagging and the rich regions, should be rethought according to the lines along which the EU has committed itself to move.

NOTES

1. See Boeri *et al.* (2001) for a more detailed analysis. Using a survey of EU citizens' opinions, the authors found in particular that a majority of citizens do not want to change the present scale size of social expenditures, although some changes are advocated in the composition of transfers and the details of the programmes.
2. Empirical evidence of these effects is provided by Sapir *et al.* (2004, ch. 4).
3. For this reason, 'convergence' is often used as a synonym of cohesion, or regional, policy.
4. Although we agree with this approach, other authors have different views. Some put the emphasis primarily on growth, assuming that the market would then correct the imbalances in the distribution of income; others consider cohesion per se as a key policy objective.
5. Eurostat, the EU statistical office, provides economic statistics for different administrative territorial units in the EU, aggregated at the level of municipalities (NUTS4), provinces (NUTS3), regions (NUTS2) and states (NUTS1).
6. It is in fact a standard result of trade theory that, when two countries having two different levels of wealth and lying at different distances from the technology frontier join their

markets, the winner in the short run is the rich country, because of the better price–quality ratio of its goods. Rich countries find themselves closer to the technological frontier and their goods, thanks to a better price–quality ratio and greater innovation content, tend to win a greater and greater market share because of consumers' preferences

7. As we argued in Chapter 6, there is also a fair chance that the firms constructing the highways are also from the donor countries, given that they are likely to be more competitive.
8. Puga (2002) points out that regional disparities are much larger in Europe than in a country like the United States.
9. See De La Fuente (2002) for an extensive discussion.
10. Actually the question is still debated among economists. Using new econometric techniques of dynamic panels, which allow a correction for spatial correlation, Badinger *et al.* (2004) shed further light on the available measures of the speed of convergence.
11. In particular, regional policy accounts for over 30 per cent of total spending in the 1999–2006 Financial Perspectives, increasing its share from 0.29 per cent in 1988 to the current 0.46 per cent of the EU GNP.
12. See Ottaviano and Puga (1998) for a general survey, Fujita, *et al.* (1999) for a technical academic reference, Puga (2002) for an application to the EU-15 case; Resmini (2004) for an analysis of integration and regional disparities in the new member states of Central and Eastern Europe.
13. The most recent empirical studies combine the classic comparative advantage arguments with agglomeration variables derived within an NEG framework. In particular the studies of Davis and Weinstein (1999, 2003), Forslid and Wooton (1999), Midelfart-Knarvik and Overman (2002), Haaland *et al.* (1999), Altomonte and Bonassi (2002) all measure the local production or output according to a combination of comparative advantages and agglomeration forces, reaching, however, non-homogeneous conclusions. Sapir *et al.* (2004) claim therefore that, while the evidence is at least superficially consistent with the NEG-based concerns, thus justifying an interventionist EU cohesion policy, it is much harder to understand whether regional divergence would have been more pronounced in the absence of such a policy.
14. In addition to the treaties, five main regulations (the framework regulation n.2050/88, the horizontal regulation n.4253/88; the vertical regulation nn.4254/88, 4255/88, 4256/88) have been issued, initially for the period 1988–93, successively adapted and carried forward until 1999.
15. These are programmes managed directly by the EU Commission and aimed at addressing specific problems in border regions (Interreg), in rural areas (LEADER), in urban peripheries (URBAN) and in the fight against discrimination for less able workers (EQUAL). A specific, albeit small, fund is also allocated for the EU Fishery Policy (FIFG).
16. As in other chapters, we quote both the English and the French acronym, both used in Brussels jargon.
17. For a detailed description of the former six objectives, see Nava (2000) or European Commission (2001a).
18. There are five implementing regulations of the Agenda 2000 reforms related to the structural funds: the framework regulation n.1260/99 and four vertical regulations 1783/99, 1784/99, 1257/99 and 1263/99 implementing the framework one.
19. The exceptions are Denmark and Luxembourg until 2006, and Belgium, Denmark, Luxembourg and Netherlands thereafter.
20. As a result, Greece, Ireland, Portugal and Spain can claim the cohesion fund up to 2006, together with the structural funds addressed to their (eventually) eligible regions. Italy, for example, with a per capita GDP almost equal to the EU average, cannot claim the cohesion fund, notwithstanding the large amount of structural funds its regions can claim. After 2006, in EU-15 only Greece and Portugal will be eligible for the cohesion fund, which instead will cover all the new member states of Central and Eastern Europe.
21. Clearly, in order to avoid the opposite excess, that is, having businesses located in regions lagging behind essentially subsidised by public money, rules have been foreseen on the maximum intensity of aid (EU + national) allowed in a given region.

22. Hallet (2000), Leonardi (2003) and Mairate and Hall (2000) all agree with this result. Boldrin and Canova (2001) present the best-known critical view.
23. In particular, Figure 8.3 reports another widely used measure of income disparity, known as 'absolute convergence', that is, the standard deviation of the income of the considered country or region when measured over time with respect to the EU average. A decreasing standard deviation indicates convergence to the EU average.
24. This subsection builds on preparatory work for the Sapir report. We thank, without implicating, Peer Ritter for excellent research assistance.
25. In particular Ireland in only 15 years moved away from the group of the four poorest EU countries to enter the group of the four richest countries.
26. Davies and Hallet (2002).
27. See, for example, Bertola (1999): 'More complex and sophisticated theoretical approaches paying more attention to international interactions, will hopefully ascertain the structural causes of persisting inequality and indicate whether policy interventions are desirable'.
28. See, for example, Midelfart-Knarvik and Overman (2002).
29. European Commission (2002b), state aid scoreboard.
30. See European Commission (2001b).
31. Countries have different traditions in ways of approaching interregional transfers. Alesina *et al.* (2001b), for example, argue that public employment could be seen as a disguised mechanism of financial transfers between richer and poorer areas of the same country.
32. The pre-accession assistance funds (€3120 million per year), previously used for regional policy through the PHARE programme (see Chapter 3) will now be concentrated on Bulgaria and Romania.
33. The final list of eligible regions will be compiled in 2006, based on 2004 per capita GDP data.
34. Allocative expenditure responds rather well to the criterion of the 'double market failure' that we have elaborated in Chapter 6. In spite of that, EU involvement in this type of expenditure has always been rather marginal, reaching in the best of cases some 6 to 7 per cent of the total EU budget.
35. A group chaired by former Commissioner Van Miert estimated in 2003 the cost of the whole new rail and road trans-European network at some €600 billion (six times the EU budget). In this set of measures the Council has identified 26 priority measures for a total cost of about €250 billion, on which work should start as soon as possible.

APPENDIX: CONVERGENCE AND THE DISTRIBUTION OF REGIONAL SPENDING

Most of the literature on regional convergence quoted in this chapter tests whether regional investment (of any form) does have a positive effect on local development. As we have discussed extensively, the results tend to be influenced rather crucially by the definition of the territorial unit of analysis, and by how much one is able to take into account all the possible factors that contribute to convergence, including non-transparent national forms of aid. Given that, we look here at a slightly different question: does the distribution of the actual regional spending conform to the logic of fostering convergence? In other words, do poorer regions receive more regional funds than richer regions so as to make sure that their economic convergence is fostered?

If we were to find that there is no evidence that poor regions are privileged in terms of the total funds (EU and national) received with respect to rich regions, then the role that funds play in fostering convergence would necessarily be limited. Or, in other words, it would be hardly surprising if structural funds alone were found to have an insignificant impact on convergence. To carry on our analysis, we divide the EU and national expenditure into two categories: growth-enhancing expenditures aimed at poor regions and other transfers (thus including growth-enhancing expenditures not aimed at poor regions), at both the EU and the national level, as reported in Table A8.1.

Table A8.1 Categories of expenditures

	EU expenditure	National expenditure
Growth-enhancing expenditure	Cohesion and structural funds	RA + *a*SA + NMF
Other transfers	CAP + IP	(1−*a*)SA Other policies

Cohesion and structural funds are, as discussed, the EU funds aiming at enhancing growth in the least prosperous regions. On the member state side, the equivalents are the regional state aids (RA) granted under TEC, art. 87, para. 3a and 3c. In addition, we can include a share (*a*) of the total state aids (SA) which can be specifically localised in poor regions. We will refer to the sum of the two (RA + *a*SA) as 'localised state aid'. Finally the national matching funds (NMF) resulting from the principle of co-financing of the structural funds can be safely attributed to this category.

As argued in Chapter 7, the Common Agricultural Policy (CAP) has both an allocative and a (nowadays prevalent) redistributive purpose. Hence it appears as a 'transfer' under the EU column. Internal policies (IP) financed by the EU are aimed at the acceleration of the single market and often have the character of an investment, like the Research and Development Programme. However their allocation is, or should be, in principle independent of the convergence needs of the receiving country. In other words, they are a growth-enhancing expenditure, but not aimed at the poor regions and hence we consider them as other transfers. Finally national transfers $(1-a)$SA are state aid to industries in general with little growth potential, such as coal or steel, or to those industries that are not localised (like transport). The largest part of national transfers, in addition, are schemes aimed at the standard of living, without a growth presumption. Also other policies such as public sector overstaffing, or welfare schemes, constitute significant transfers for the beneficiary citizens. However these 'other policies' cannot be comprehensively measured for the whole EU, and thus they are left out in the subsequent quantitative analysis.

Having established this conceptual repartition of EU and national funds, we have estimated the amount of the different expenditures and run some correlations between the funds paid per head and the per capita GDP level across the 19 macro-regions classified in the chapter (that is, both poor and rich: see Box 8.1). First, we have used only the EU Cohesion and Structural Funds (CSF), calculated per head. Second, we have added the per head national spending on regional development (RA) under art. 87, para. 3a and 3c, in order to verify whether the correlation with the wealth of the receiving regions is respected. Third, we have regressed CSF plus the expenditure received by CAP and other EU internal policies on the per capita macro-regional income. The three regressions are run for three points in time: 1991 which falls into the five-year programming period of the 'Delors I' Financial Perspectives, 1995 ('Delors II') and 2000 ('Agenda 2000').

Table A8.2 Funds paid per head and per capita GDP, 1991, 1995, 2000

All regions, correlation with GDP/head (1991)		
	EU budget	National budgets in addition
Growth-enhancing at the local level	CSF: negative relation, $R^2 = 0.2$	CSF + RA + NMF: Negative rel., $R^2 = 0.34$
Other transfers	CSF + CAP + IP: very mild negative rel., $R^2 = 0.08$	No data

Table A8.2 (continued)

All regions, correlation with GDP/head (1995)		
	EU budget	National budgets in addition
Growth-enhancing at the local level	CSF: negative relation, $R^2 = 0.24$	CSF + RA + NMF: Negative rel., $R^2 = 0.32$
Other transfers	CSF + CAP + IP: almost no negative rel., $R^2 = 0.03$	No data

All regions, correlation with GDP/head (2000)		
	EU budget	National budgets in addition
Growth-enhancing at the local level	CSF: negative relation, $R^2 = 0.35$	CSF + RA + NMF: Negative rel., $R^2 = 0.35$
Other transfers	CSF + CAP + IP: almost no negative rel., $R^2 = 0.03$	No data

The results indicate that the cohesion and structural funds (CSF) flow mostly to poorer regions, always displaying a negative correlation with the regional per capita income. This pattern has been stable over the three points in time, and even strengthened, thus confirming a certain time consistence. National programmes for regional development purposes (RA + NMF) do not distort this picture, since when added to the CSF expenditure they do not alter the negative correlation with the regional per capita income. This result is reassuring, since the EU system has little power to ensure that national regional aid programmes do not dwarf the EU cohesion objectives but rather reinforce them.

Besides the regional development objective, state aid (SA) is also allowed for particular industries. Since we are interested only in whether the spending pattern is consistent with the purpose of convergence, we want to exclude state aid where the regional development purpose is not made legally explicit, $(1-a)$SA. This is essentially aid for coal and steel, transport and agriculture, and thus is excluded from the analysis. Hence our measure of 'localised state aid', RA$+a$SA, will be proxied by all state aid minus aid to the coal and steel sector, transport and agriculture. Taking the correlation between national localised state aid (instead of simply RA) and CSF together, the finding however is that the correlation does not change much from the previous pattern.

A totally different issue is whether the spending of the overall EU budget is consistent with the aim of convergence. As is known, the two largest items of EU expenditure are the structural funds and the agricultural policy (CAP). The agricultural spending allocation is largely based on personal criteria (being a farmer), but nonetheless it can be regionally attributed. However as explained in Chapter 7, the CAP does not carry the legal presumption that it should foster regional development and thus convergence. Also the EU internal policies (IP) are independent of the convergence needs of the receiving country. However they can be attributed to countries (and regions) on the basis of the annual Commission's 'Allocated Expenditure Report' discussed extensively in Chapter 6. Summing up CSF, CAP and IP expenditures over the 19 macro-regions, one finds that the EU expenditure is basically allocated independently of regional income per head. This is due to the fact that CSF are, as seen above, negatively correlated with regional income, but CAP funds per head tend to be positively correlated with GDP per head.[1] In other words, the distribution of resources of the CAP at the regional level seems such as to compensate the flow of the structural funds to poorer regions, thus making the total disbursement of the EU budget uncorrelated to the per capita income of the EU countries.

We now perform the same analysis only for the eight Objective 1 macro-regions (Greece, Spain, Ireland, Portugal, Southern Italy, East Germany, and the Belgium and UK Objective 1 regions) which are the main target of regional convergence programmes. Similarly to what we did for the EU as a whole, we run three regressions between funds paid per head and GDP per head for 1991, 1995 and 2000. Given that results are fairly similar across years, we present here only the year 2000.

Table A8.3 Eight Objective 1 macro-regions, correlation with GDP/head (2000)

	EU budget	National budgets in addition
Growth-enhancing at the local level	CSF: no correlation	CSF + RA + NMF: no correlation
Other transfers	CSF+CAP+IP: positive rel., $R^2 = 0.46$ (negative if IRL is excluded)	No data

Within the eight macro-regions that qualify for most of the Community funds, the funds per head do not depend on relative income. The latter is actually the result of the juridical design of the funds, which, as a general rule, tend to grant the same amount of resources per head once the 75 per cent threshold criterion is met. This seems to apply to both the EU funds and member states' funds. Clearly, an economist may wonder whether growth-enhancing funds unrelated to relative income of the receiving regions is the most supportive form of aid for achieving regional convergence. Furthermore, given the unrelated income character of CAP funds, the combined effect of CSF and CAP leads to a positive correlation between EU funds and GDP per head.

In sum, although the EU cohesion and structural funds are designed in a way consistent with the emergence of convergence, the whole of the EU budget alters this distribution. We have already found a similar result in Chapter 6: the design of the EU budget is not such as to be distributed across EU countries according to their relative wealth. However, within the realm of the expenditure explicitly dedicated to fostering convergence in the poorer areas, both the EU and national expenditure seem to show a certain degree of consistency.

NOTE

1. Clearly we do not imply any causality here, but only report statistical evidence, which nevertheless points to a certain regressivity of CAP, consistent with the findings of Chapter 7.

9. Competition policy*

9.1 INTRODUCTION

In Chapters 1 to 5 we saw how the European legislators set up the Customs Union, the Single Market and its latest developments (EMU and the Lisbon agenda). In earlier chapters we also saw how and to what extent the EU tries to take advantage of the benefits deriving from such a continuing process of economic integration, in order to pursue its joint goals of growth, stability and cohesion via a set of specific policies. However, from the very foundation of the Union, the EU legislators also recognised that the entire scope of integration could have been frustrated by business practices aiming at keeping markets partitioned and not exposed to competition forces. In particular, they recognised that the risk would have been possibly higher when not only trade, but also factors of production, through the process of completion of the internal market, started to be integrated across borders, significantly increasing the range of economic interests and sectors at stake. The same outcome could also have been generated as a consequence of unfair practices of member states, eventually led by the pressures of organised interest groups to support 'national' players.[1]

In brief, without an appropriate policy regulating competition on the European market, the entire process of economic integration would have been pointless. To this extent, as early as 1957 the Treaty of Rome (TEC, art. 3, para. 1g) stated among the objectives of the Union the setting up of 'a system ensuring that competition in the internal market is not distorted'. In order to achieve this objective, the original European legislators drafted an entire Title (currently TEC, Title VI) of the Treaty explicitly devoted to the setting up of common rules on competition policy. The Treaty lays down in particular rules related to the control of anticompetitive agreements and abusive behaviours by dominant firms in the internal market, as well as provisions restricting the granting of public aid to firms by member states. The general goal is to prevent the economic forces unleashed by the process of European integration to be distorted by interventions external to the working of the market, identifying in the European Commission the leading

* The chapter is a joint work of the authors together with Stefano Riela (Università Bocconi).

body responsible for the management of competition policy. Clearly this was (and to some extent it is still today) a big step forward in a continent where cartels and monopolies (both private and public) had always flourished.[2]

Even though the basic principles of competition policy did not change following their insertion in the Treaty, some refinements have been made over the years to the set of rules, in order to cope with the evolution of the economic system. In particular, in 1989, the European Union completed the legal framework dealing with business practices, adopting a Council regulation authorising some control, by the European Commission, of mergers and acquisitions activities (concentrations) of firms. The subsequent steps in the integration process, namely the single currency and the Lisbon agenda, which, as we have seen, need a thorough enforcement of competition rules to display their positive effects, together with the enlargement of the Union, stimulated further reforms of the EU competition policy framework. These took place starting on 1 May 2004, a date that will be remembered not only for the entry of ten new countries into the EU, but also for a turning point in applying competition principles in a more simplified and decentralised way.

In fact, from this date, the Commission began to devolve powers to national authorities and the business community, and new provisions related to the legal instruments used in managing competition policy entered into force, as will be discussed below. In particular, having provided a brief overview of the objectives and jurisdiction of the EU competition policy, this chapter analyses the various provisions currently in place, and the main problems related to their application. The chapter also touches upon the role of the EU as one of the main regulators of global merger operations and cartels, although its specific contributions to the definition of multilateral rules aimed at ensuring the effectiveness of competition policy worldwide will be more extensively discussed in Chapter 10.

As in the rest of the book, reference to specific historical episodes or cases will be made, but the focus is rather aimed at understanding the future implication of the policy in the new enlarged context of the Union.

9.2 THE OBJECTIVES OF THE EU COMPETITION POLICY

Competition is acknowledged by the EC Treaty as an instrument through which to achieve, via the market, the aims of the Union set out in TEC, art. 2 and already discussed in the first chapter of the book. These objectives, such as the 'harmonious balanced and sustainable development' of TEC, art. 2, can be interpreted in economic terms with an allocation of resources that maximises both welfare and efficiency. Now, according to the first fundamental theorem of welfare economics, perfectly competitive markets, through the interplay of demand and supply, can allocate resources achieving an 'optimal' equilibrium from a welfare point of view, that is, a distribution of resources such that any alternative allocation which would make anyone better off would make someone else worse off (the so-called 'Pareto-efficient equilibrium'). Perfectly competitive markets hence achieve **allocation effciency**, given that the prices of the products are equal to their marginal costs, with the competitive processes 'eliminating', through the free entry of new firms, any inefficiency of the incumbent players (that is, any price higher than the marginal cost) and ensuring the maximum level of surplus for consumers.[3]

However the requirements of perfect competition can seldom be found in real markets: for such a 'perfect' environment to work, in fact, apart from the maximising (profits or utility) behaviours of the economic agents, you would need a very large, tending to infinite, number of producers and consumers, homogeneity of the product, perfect information about market conditions, and free and costless entry of competitors. Still a clear understanding of the (theoretical) benefits of perfect competition may be used by the Commission as a benchmark, a reference point, in coping with market imperfections.

Another consideration to bear in mind is that, as clearly explained by Vickers (1995), allocative efficiency may not always lead to **productive efficiency**, since more competition, in the sense of more firms (or **undertakings**, to use the legal jargon) in the market, although letting prices equal marginal costs, can induce a lower exploitation of economies of scale.[4] Furthermore, in a dynamic view, the normal profitability of competitive markets might not guarantee both enough resources and the right incentive to undertake innovative processes, thus leading in the medium to long run to sluggish growth, to the detriment of consumers (Schumpeter, 1942; Littlechild, 1986). These trade-offs in terms of allocative versus productive efficiency thus have to be considered by the policy maker, taking into account welfare considerations and the time scale of decisions.

In this regard, there is a general opinion that the model of a 'social market economy' characterising the EU, analysed in Chapter 1, tends to lead the European competition authorities to care more about consumers' welfare than about producers, attaching greater weight to allocative efficiency than to productive efficiency, with a certain difference in attitude with respect to the behaviour of the US antitrust authorities. However, as will be made clear in the following paragraphs, some assessments in competition cases need to consider consumers' welfare in a dynamic perspective, where what maximises consumers' welfare today might cause damage tomorrow, owing to changes induced in the market structure (such as an increase in entry barriers). The key question, therefore, deals with the ease with which it is possible to intervene and change a given market structure, once it has evolved in a way that turns out to be detrimental for consumers. If an antitrust authority operates in an environment characterised by relatively high rigidities, where the market structures, once established, are difficult to change, as is the case of Europe when compared to the United States, then the same authority will tend to be more conservative: ex ante it will favour less drastic changes in market structures induced by considerations of productive efficiency, because, if these turn out to be detrimental to allocative efficiency, the authority knows that its ability to change them ex post will be limited.

To cope with all these issues, the EC Treaty specifically prohibits, as a general rule, agreements which restrict competition (art. 81), abusive behaviours of firms in a dominant position (art. 82), and state aid (art. 87). Merges and acquisitions started to be assessed at a European level in 1990, with Council Regulation EC/4064/89 on the control of concentrations between undertakings, then replaced by Council Regulation EC/139/2004, referred to as Merger Regulation in the following paragraphs. These are the main legal instruments used by the Commission to guarantee the effectiveness of competition in the single market. Finally it is worth recalling that the Treaty also assigns to competition policy a set of institutional objectives, related to market integration, such as technological and economic progress, discussed below.[5]

9.3 THE FRAMEWORK OF COMPETITION POLICY

The EU legislation not only identifies the instruments to be used in order to guarantee the effectiveness of competition in the single market, but it also defines its scope of application. The Treaty in fact states that EU rules apply only when a competition issue concerns practices which have the ability to 'affect trade between member states' (TEC, art. 81, 82 and 87, para. 1), where 'trade' covers all cross-border economic activities. The latter can be considered the criterion defining the so-called '**Community dimension**', marking the boundary between the European and the national competition legal frameworks.[6] In addition, it is stated in the legal texts that the EU competition policy applies to the behaviour of 'undertakings', where this word is not confined only to company or business; rather, the understanding is broader, covering any entity engaged in an economic activity regardless of its legal status.[7]

Given the broad scope of the European competition framework, more precise definitions of the community dimension have been elaborated by the Commission over time. According to the latter, there is no danger for the single market in the case of the following:

1. agreements or practices where undertakings concerned have an aggregate European market share lower then 5 per cent and a turnover lower than €40 million (para. 52 of guidelines on the effect on trade concept contained in Articles 81 and 82 of the Treaty, OJ C 101 of 27 April 2004);
2. mergers involving undertakings whose combined worldwide turnover is below certain thresholds and the aggregate turnover in the internal market of each undertaking involved is limited within national borders;[8]
3. State aid up to €100 000 granted to an undertaking over any period of three years (art. 2 of Regulation EC/69/2001 on the application of TEC, arts 87 and 88 to *de minimis* aid, published in OJ L 010 of 13 January 2001).

Above these thresholds, the competition authorities might intervene directly. The governments of member states (in the case of state aid) or the undertaking concerned (in the case of concentrations) have to notify their action to the Commission, which can then authorise it or not, according to its evaluation of the potential distortions generated in the single market. As far as agreements and practices are concerned, starting from 1 May 2004 there is a system of parallel competences, in which both the European Commission and the national competition authorities of the member states have the power to apply the provisions of arts 81 and 82.[9] This jurisdictional system is the result of a process of decentralisation of powers from the Commission (the only body that in 1962 seemed capable of ensuring sound competition in the single market), to national competition authorities and courts. Nowadays it is thought that decentralisation increases the overall efficiency of competition policy by letting the Commission concentrate its resources on 'big' cases, in particular on unveiling multinational cartels, while empowering national authorities to intervene where their expertise and knowledge is higher than that of the Commission, that is, their domestic markets. Nevertheless decentralisation requires a coherent application of Community competition rules. Therefore it is foreseen that national authorities and the Commission will have to work closely together in the framework of the European Competition Network.[10]

While concentrations, once they reach a community dimension, are subject in any case to the ex ante Commission's judgment via the notification procedure, fines are foreseen for conducts considered (ex post) prohibited by the provisions of art. 81 or art. 82, for amounts up to 10 per cent of the turnover of the firms concerned.[11] Specific provisions exist for state aid, as will be discussed below. If the undertakings sanctioned by the Commission do not agree on the decision of the Commission they have the right to appeal (TEC, art. 220) first to the Court of First Instance (CFI) and then, as a final appeal (TEC, art. 225) to the European Court of Justice (ECJ).

In addition to the powers explicitly foreseen by the Treaty, the EU competition policy is also being granted an extraterritorial competence, which is becoming more and more important in light of the increasing integration of economic activities worldwide. According to the so-called '**effect doctrine**', it is the economic effects of the actions of undertakings that matter, rather than their legal location. As a result, the prohibition of agreements or other practices under arts 81, 82 and the Merger Regulation remains in place if their effects concern the single market, even if the agreement is reached outside the single market, and even by non-European undertakings.[12]

The entire framework of the EU competition policy thus revolves around the concept of community dimension, and the ability of any given practice significantly to affect the single market. Above the thresholds previously discussed, which constitute a ***de minimis* rule**, an evaluation of the **market power** of each undertaking is then critical to assess whether it is likely that an agreement or practice is capable of significantly affecting trade between member states. In this regard, an often used proxy of market power is the market share of each undertaking: the higher the market share of an undertaking, the higher its ability potentially to bias the working of the single market. However, as we will see below, competition authorities, when assessing the community dimension, have also to take into account the position of other competitors, the presence and size of entry barriers, and other relevant variables influencing the market structure.

But, in order to define a market share, apart from information on the turnover or any other measure of the size of the undertaking, you also need a proper measure of the denominator, that is, the market in which the firm concerned operates. The competition authorities define the market by its 'relevant' boundaries, in terms of both products and geographic areas, based on the concept of **substitutability**.[13] The latter is defined through the so-called 'SSNIP test', the acronym of Small but Significant Non-transitory Increase in Price: the test assesses to what extent customers would switch to readily available substitutes or to suppliers of the same product located elsewhere if a hypothetical monopolist of the product in question raised the price permanently by 5–10 per cent. If the extent of substitution is such as to make the increase in price unprofitable for the hypothetical monopolist, because of the resulting loss of sales, then the product substitutes and/or additional geographic areas are included in the definition of relevant market. On the supply side, the relevant market may even include as substitutes those products to which suppliers can easily and immediately convert their production, once a given product is affected by the mentioned price increase. A proper definition of relevant market is also complicated by the fact that the EU is made up of different states, in which market conditions of competition might not be entirely homogeneous across the considered market. For these reasons, it is important to take into account the customers' geographic pattern of purchases and trade flows, eventual strong preferences for national brands, language and culture, and so on. For example, while oil, aircraft and operating systems for PCs are usually considered to have a relevant market defined all over the world, traditional banking services tend to be considered as part of national or even regional markets.

9.4 AGREEMENTS AND COLLUSIVE BEHAVIOURS RESTRICTING COMPETITION

Agreements, like any other conduct between two or more undertakings, are considered key commercial activities and they are helpful in developing business and in offering good deals to consumers. However some conducts are capable of restricting competition by decreasing the extent of independence and facilitating collusion rather than competition.

Thus, according to TEC, art. 81, para. 1 incompatible with the common market are 'all agreements between undertakings, decisions by associations of undertakings and concerted practices which may affect trade between member states and which have as their object or effect the prevention, restriction or distortion of competition within the common market'. According to TEC, art. 81, para. 2, any incompatible agreement is void of juridical effects,[14] even though not necessarily in its entirety, since, if the offending clauses can be separated from the agreement without stripping the essence of the agreement, this will be permitted. An agreement is considered to exist de facto, that is, it exists every time that there is the necessary consensus between the parties, therefore without the need for signatures on formal and written documents. For example, it is considered that undertakings might be capable of restricting competition even though they belong to the same industry associations. By supporting or promoting industry-wide campaigns, public education, market research and the setting of industry standards, these associations can in fact facilitate the collusive activity of members through decisions and recommendations.

According to art. 81, para. 1 agreements are capable of restricting competition if undertakings 'a) directly or indirectly fix purchase or selling prices or any other trading conditions; b) limit or control production, markets, technical development, or investment; c) share markets or sources of supply; or d) apply dissimilar conditions to equivalent transactions with other trading parties, thereby placing them at a competitive disadvantage'.

However, in line with the trade-off between allocative and productive efficiency, the competitive concerns of some agreements infringing art. 81, para. 1 might be outweighed by pro-competitive effects, and thus they can be exempted from the nullity foreseen under art. 81, para. 2 if specific conditions, laid down in art. 81, para. 3, are fulfilled. First, the agreement must contribute to improving the production or distribution of goods or contribute to promoting technical or economic progress, with the need to verify the efficiency claimed by undertakings in order to exempt their agreements. Second, consumers must receive a fair share of the benefits resulting from the agreement, in order to be compensated for any negative effect caused to them by the restriction of competition. Third, the restrictions must be strictly necessary to the attainment of the efficiencies claimed. Finally, notwithstanding the efficiency gains, the agreement cannot lead to the elimination of competition in a substantial part of the products in question.

In the application of the provisions of art. 81, **horizontal agreements**, made by firms that would otherwise compete with each other in the same industry market, are of more concern than agreements between firms at different levels of the production chain. The latter, called **vertical agreements**, are in fact more likely to generate outcomes in which each party will benefit from increased demand if the other supplies more, thus in stricter compliance with the exceptions foreseen by art. 81, para. 3, since these benefits lead to an increase in consumers' welfare.

Operationally the undertakings willing to subscribe an agreement potentially infringing competition rules are now required to assess by themselves whether they can benefit from an exemption under art. 81, para. 3.[15] To avoid fines raised by national or Community authorities in case of wrong assessments, undertakings are helped by a well developed body of legislation; in particular, apart from the jurisprudence developed from case law, **notices** are published by the Commission to 'codify' in a single text the previous case law on particular issues, basically to give indications about the way in which the Commission assesses the different situations. These notices, differently from regulations, are however not binding and are without prejudice to the interpretation of the CFI and the ECJ, and so are still subject to a certain degree of uncertainty. Specific regulations which explicitly exempt categories of agreements from the application of art. 81, para. 1 do exist, as a heritage of the past system of notification. They are known as **block exemptions** and will be discussed below.

9.4.1 Concerted Practices

The idea that an agreement may exist *de facto*, even without its formalisation, leads to the problem of defining the so-called '**concerted practices**'. By concerting their behaviours, undertakings can, in fact, coordinate their actions and pursue practices forbidden by art. 81, para. 1 in order to raise their profits. Such collusive behaviour does not always rely on explicit agreements but it can also result implicitly from situations where firms act individually, but, in recognition of their interdependence with competitors, they jointly exercise market power with the colluding competitors. For example, in a given market conditions might be such that a firm might optimally react to a price increase by its competitor (or even a move leading to such an increase, such as plans for new products to be launched) raising in turn its prices, thus generating implicit collusion. In fact, if a firm announces a price rise, competitors know that the rise is not sustainable unless most of them follow it. As a result, they have themselves an incentive to follow the price rise, in order to increase their profits.[16]

As a result, in oligopolistic markets it has proved very difficult to distinguish between an implicit collusion and independent firms' strategies. In the absence of explicit collusive agreements, the competition authorities can act against these practices by assessing market outcomes and evaluating some factors capable of fostering implicit collusion among undertakings such as concentration, transparency, entry barriers, product homogeneity and similar cost structures and preferences.

In particular the higher the number of firms operating in the market, the lower the chances of collusion, since the coordination process implicitly required to generate a collusive process will tend to be more complex. By trying to collude, in fact, undertakings decide to raise their prices to gain monopoly profits at the industry level. However, instead of sharing those profits with other colluding parties, an undertaking might find it more profitable to 'cheat' by pricing lower than its rivals and thus catch the entire market demand. Therefore a small number of firms fosters collusion since, with fewer firms, the probability of finding a 'cheater' is lower, and also because it is easier for firms to control one another's behaviour.

The transparency of information in the market can also foster, under certain conditions, collusion, since firms can better calculate the outcome, in terms of profits, of their potential collusive behaviour.[17] The erection of entry barriers is also a key feature of collusion, since it prevents potential competitors, attracted by the higher collusive profits, entering the market and thus lowering the price. Moreover it is easier to coordinate when the product is homogeneous (since fixing collusive prices requires a lower number of variables to evaluate) and when undertakings are similar in their cost structures and preferences (high-cost undertakings would in general agree on a collusive price higher than the one preferred by low-cost undertakings, and thus an implicit agreement would be more difficult to reach) as shown by Box 9.1.

Although some undertakings have been condemned on the basis of evidence of implicit collusion,[18] the difficulties associated with its evaluation have led the Commission to introduce a '**leniency programme**' (OJ C 45 of 19 February 2002), a notice with which the Commission encourages the undertakings to provide information on their unlawful collusive behaviours. In particular, under the leniency programme, the first undertaking which comes and denounces an undetected cartel will receive full immunity from fines.

BOX 9.1 A SIMPLE GAME-THEORETIC MODEL OF COLLUSION AND LENIENCY PROGRAMME

Collusion refers to a formal or informal agreement between two or more undertakings aimed at raising their profits, usually through higher than competitive prices. It is possible to model collusion as a version of a static prisoner's dilemma where π^P (profits of colluding undertakings as soon as someone cheats) $<\pi^N$ (normal profits of competition) $<\pi^*$ (collusive profits) $<\pi^C$ (profits from cheating). In this game the collusive behaviour is not a Nash equilibrium (a strategy such that every player's strategy is a best response to the strategies of the other players), because everyone has an incentive to cheat: if firm 1 colludes, firm 2 has an incentive to cheat, because in this case it will gain $\pi^C > \pi^*$ (the profit obtained had firm 2 colluded as well).

		Firm 2 Collude	Cheart
Firm 1	Collude	π^*, π^*	π^P, π^C
	Cheat	π^C, π^P	π^N, π^N

This implies that collusion is not sustainable: for everyone it is ex ante optimal to cheat and therefore the competitive outcome (π^N, π^N) will emerge. However, when interactions are repeated infinitely rather than prices being determined once and for ever, then there is the scope for the restoration of collusion as an equilibrium strategy. In this case, in fact, undertakings are seen as maximising the discounted stream of future profits: $\Sigma_{t=0}^{\infty}[\pi_t/(1+r)^t]$, where r is the subjective intertemporal discount rate ($0<r<1$, this is the higher, the more the undertaking cares about current profits relative to future profits). When the game is repeated, the cost of cheating at time t is magnified, since the cheating firm will gain $\pi^C>\pi^*$ at time t, but then it will induce a reaction by the other firm, thus losing all the future benefits of the collusion, getting from $t+1$ onwards only π^N. In particular, the gains from cheating are $(\pi^C-\pi^*)$, but the discounted value of future losses in terms of profits forgone is $(\pi^*-\pi^N)/r$, using the permanent discount rate formula $\lim_{t\to\infty}[(1/(1+r)^t)=(1/r)]$. Therefore, as long as $[\pi^c-\pi^*<((\pi^*-\pi^N)/r)]$ collusion will be optimal, and cheating will be deterred. In this setup, how can competition authorities (CA) reduce the incentive to collude? First of all, introducing a fine F for each colluding undertaking, subject to the probability α that the CA investigates an industry in each period ($0<\alpha<1$) and the probability λ that the CA successfully prosecutes cartel members after launching an investigation ($0<\lambda<1$). With the fine F, the payoffs of collusion are reduced and the incentive to cheat is relatively higher: $\pi^c-\pi^*-\alpha\lambda F<((\pi^*-\pi^N-\alpha\lambda F)/r)$ is thus less likely. Even an increase in the values of both α and λ tends to discourage collusion: this is why the European Commission has planned to devote more resources to cartel disclosure (thus raising α) and a more thorough economic assessment of the case presented before the ECJ (thus raising λ).

Motta (2004) shows that the CA can also find it useful to introduce a leniency programme by giving to a colluding undertaking the incentive to 'blow the whistle' and therefore to cheat. The CA can grant a reduced fine R to the first whistleblower (R is lower than F and it may equal zero in the USA and the EU), thus reducing the incentive to collude. In fact, with the leniency programme, α becomes equal to 1 (the investigation starts as soon as the whistle has been blown) and the value of λ increases (to get R rather than F, the whistleblower shall provide the CA with relevant information about the collusive agreement). As a result, the sustainability of collusion in the long run $\pi^c-\pi^*-R<((\pi^*-\pi^P-\lambda F)/r)$ is further reduced.

9.4.2 Vertical Restraints

In the case of most goods, and some services, there is a chain of production before the product reaches the consumer. In these cases, a supplier has in general no interest in protecting his dealers from competition between each other, since the lower the price they charge, the more will be sold and the greater the profit of the upstream firm. Hence vertical agreements are in general not considered prohibited by art. 81, para. 1. However, for complex products requiring assistance and after-sale services to customers, and for new and fashionable products for which promotion, quality and reputation are key drivers of the competitive process, the manufacturer may have an interest in protecting dealers from each other, thus reducing the so-called 'intra-brand' competition. The same dealer, who has to promote a new product or set up his shop in compliance with the manufacturer's requirements, does not want to fear competition from close, similar dealers. As a result, vertical restraints are concluded between the manufacturer and the dealer, with this concept including issues such as an attempt by an upstream manufacturer to control the price at which the product is resold (resale price maintenance), the divisions of downstream markets into a set of territorial monopolies, each assigned to one retailer (territorial restrictions) or contracts requiring that dealers sell only the manufacturer's brand within a defined market (exclusive dealings).

The assessment of these practices is quite delicate in terms of economic efficiency. On the one hand, by reducing transaction costs, improving methods of distribution and making it easier to bring products to the market, vertical restraints are often considered to have a pro-competitive effect. In addition, competition among similar dealers risks having an effect on those immaterial drivers, such as quality in the service, which would ultimately undermine both the manufacturer's interests and the consumers' welfare. On the other hand, however, vertical restraints might be able to impose some restrictions on competition and ultimately on consumers' choice, and thus the provisions of art. 81 might be applicable.

Looking at the behaviour of the Commission over time, as long as there is sufficient *inter*-brand competition in a relevant market, *intra*-brand restrictions tend to be tolerated, as stated in the guidelines on vertical restraints published by the European Commission (OJ 291 of 13 October 2000). The creation of the single market, leading to higher inter-brand competition by the undertakings of other member states, also induced a more lenient approach towards vertical restraints maintaining national divisions – that is, national or regional markets and territories assigned to particular distributors – practices which were condemned in the early 1960s.[19]

9.4.3 Block Exemptions

As already discussed, in the past, the Commission had to assess individual applications for exemption under art. 81, para. 3, in very numerous, but all basically, identical, cases for particular industries (for example, car distribution, insurance) or agreements (for example, franchising, specialisation, licensing) where exemptions were easy to obtain (see Box 9.2 and Box 9.3). In order to ease the administrative burden for the undertakings and the Commission, the so-called 'block exemption' regulations were created (according to art. 83, para. 2b), in order to define those kinds of agreements capable of being exempted. Those regulations, in fact, besides defining the relevant categories of agreements, identify all those clauses (the so-called 'black list') that prevent the agreement from being exempted according to art. 81, para. 3.

BOX 9.2 THE REFORM OF THE BLOCK EXEMPTION IN THE CAR SECTOR

Despite claimed efficiencies and welfare improvement for consumers, vertical restraints of exclusive dealership in the car sector have been block-exempted mainly thanks to the lobby pressures of car manufacturers. The 2002 reform[1] was therefore designed to create more competition in the industry. Consumers are now allowed to make cross-border purchases, while dealers are now able to sell more than one car brand within the same showroom, can actively sell to independent resellers within their exclusive territory and may also, if approached, sell to final consumers or resellers based outside their territory.[2] According to the new rules, dealers may also choose whether or not to carry out repairs themselves. Any repair shop that meets the quality standards set by a manufacturer is allowed to become an authorised repairer without being obliged to sell new cars.[3]

Apart from authorised repair shops, carmakers must also allow independent ones to compete. The independent repair sector – a valuable lower-cost alternative for the consumer – over the past few years has been increasingly squeezed out by a lack of access to the technical information and diagnostic equipment necessary to repair today's cars. Therefore carmakers must also allow independent repair shops to have access to all necessary information, tools, equipment, training and spare parts. The Commission recognised, in fact, the need to foster competition by developing new distribution channels for spare parts. Authorised repairers cannot be prevented from supplying original spare parts (or parts of matching quality) to independent repairers, and carmakers may no longer prevent authorised repairer shops from obtaining spare parts from other sources.[4] Compared to the regulations in force up to October 2002, the new regime thus ensures that the single market benefits consumers (carmakers could already move vehicles and components easily within the EU) in terms of lower prices[5] and availability of qualitative services.

Notes:

1. Commission Regulation (EC) 1400/2002 of 31 July 2002 on the application of Article 81(3) of the Treaty to categories of vertical agreements and concerted practices in the motor vehicle sector entered into force on 1 October 2002.
2. The so-called 'passive sale' restriction in place until October 2005. Since then, there has been no territorial protection for dealers in a selective distribution network thus allowing them to set up a secondary sales outlet or a delivery point in another part of the EU.
3. Before 1 October 2002 (when Regulation 1400/2002 entered into force), undertakings selling new cars were obliged to carry out repair services as well.
4. The commitment of the European Commission in opening up the market is furthermore showed by the directive proposed, on 14 September 2004, to allow independent part manufacturers to compete throughout the single market for visible replacement parts, such as bonnets, bumpers, doors, lamps, rear protection panels, windscreens and wings (Proposal for a directive amending Directive 98/71/EC - COM(2004)582).
5. The Commission's car price report has consistently revealed major differences in new car prices between EU member states (see http://www.europa.eu.int/comm/competition/car_sector/price_diffs).

BOX 9.3 FRANCHISING AS A PRO-COMPETITIVE VERTICAL RESTRAINT

An interesting case of vertical restraint 'block exempted' is the franchising agreement (Commission Regulation EC/2790/1999). The pro-competitive effects assessed under art. 81, para. 3 in fact are such as to enable the franchisor to establish, with limited investments, a uniform network for the distribution of his products, the franchisee to exploit a well-developed marketing and selling *formula*, for a royalty, and the consumers to reduce the information asymmetries in respect of price and quality of the product offered.

However, to be exempted, the restraints of the franchising contract must be proportional to the characteristics of the product involved. For example, the higher the importance of specific know-how, the more sunk and riskier is the investment for the franchisee, thus requiring territorial protection; the more important the service component, the more the franchisee needs a trained staff for its products, thus requiring exclusivity; the higher the reputation of the brand, the more selective the choice of franchisees, though according to objective criteria, in order to avoid forms of discrimination by the franchisor.

Combining the block exemption regulations with the requirement of the community dimension, in the case of vertical agreements there is a presumption of legality if the market share of the supplier or the buyer does not exceed the threshold of 30 per cent. For horizontal cooperation, although there are practices whose pro-competitive effects largely outweigh anticompetitive ones, the granting of an automatic block exemption is less obvious, because of the higher competition concerns raised by this kind of agreement. Therefore horizontal agreements are exempted when they favour research and development activities, specialisations and innovations in production, economies in purchasing and commercialisation, standard settings or improvement of environmental conditions,[20] or if market shares of the undertakings involved are low. In particular, in the case of horizontal agreements, the exemption holds if the cumulative market share of the undertakings involved is lower than 25 per cent for research and development agreements, but this threshold is lowered to 15 per cent for commercialisation agreements due to a cooperation very close to the final consumer, thus easing the scope for collusion.

Clearly the entire discipline of the block exemptions is nowadays being revised following the changes induced by the new Regulation 1/2003 (see, for example, the changes introduced in the car sector, discussed in Box 9.2). On the one hand, the possibility for the undertakings to assess by themselves whether they can benefit from an exemption under art. 81, para. 3 eliminates numerous bureaucratic burdens for both the firms and the Commission. However, at the same time, it introduces a greater degree of uncertainty, and therefore a requirement for more precise guidance notices from the Commission or, eventually, a revision of the block exemption regulations.

9.5 ABUSE OF DOMINANT POSITION

When undertakings, usually large companies, are unconstrained by market pressures, they can use their discretionary power to set prices and strategies capable of directly undermining consumers' welfare. For this reason, TEC, art. 82 accepts in principle the existence of dominant positions in the market, due to considerations linked to the minimum efficient scale of firms' operations, but it condemns any abuse of such a dominant position, leaving no scope for exemptions.

Clearly the critical issue in the application of art. 82 is related to the assessment of (a) what is an 'abuse', and (b) what is a 'dominant position'. In this regard, the definition of dominance, as elaborated over time by the jurisprudence,[21] relates to the ability of the undertaking, because of its economic and financial power, to act independently of competitors, customers and consumers, and thus to be capable of preventing effective competition in the relevant market. There is no fixed formula by which the dominance may be established. However, according to the ECJ, 'very large market shares are in themselves, and save in exceptional circumstances, evidence of the existence of a dominant position'.[22] According to Furse (2002), the general approach appears to be that a market share of 70 per cent and above will almost certainly constitute a dominant position; on the contrary, a market share below 40 per cent is highly unlikely to justify dominance unless other evidence is overwhelming. As in the case of application of art. 81, the evaluation of market structure is important in assessing dominance, with particular reference to the competitors' position, barriers to entry and scope for potential competition.

An 'abusive' behaviour is to be understood as the 'recourse to different methods from those arising in normal competition'.[23] Therefore the list of abuses explicitly set out in art. 82 merely gives examples of abusive exploitation: (a) directly or indirectly imposing unfair purchase or selling prices or other unfair trading conditions; (b) limiting production, markets or technical development to the prejudice of consumers; (c) applying dissimilar conditions to equivalent transactions with other trading parties, thereby placing them at a competitive disadvantage; (d) making the conclusion of contracts subject to acceptance by the other parties of supplementary obligations which, by their nature or according to commercial usage, have no connection with the subject of such contracts.

In the case of a monopolist, an undertaking operating by definition in a dominant position, the most popular abuse related to 'unfair trading conditions' refers to excessive prices. However the difficulty in measuring the marginal costs of undertakings (used as a benchmark for assessing the existence of unfair trading conditions) has led to very few excessive price cases being revealed. Price competition has also led to predatory behaviour, with dominant firms setting prices below marginal costs.[24] In this case, the dominant undertaking sells at a price below cost, but might avoid losses, for example, by selling its in-house assets, or by gaining profits in other markets where prices are higher than marginal cost (cross-subsidisation), or by liquidity coming from other firms belonging to the same group. The undertakings with limited financial resources are incapable of standing the losses deriving from being undercut on prices, and therefore are driven out of the market. This gives scope for the predatory undertaking to eliminate competition in the medium to long run, allowing it to recover the eventual losses incurred with its predatory strategy. Therefore what is good for consumers in the short run (price lower than marginal cost) is bad in the long run (price higher than marginal cost), with prices being higher the higher the barriers to entry in the resulting market structure. This is the case, for example, if the remaining firm on the market has a 'tough' reputation, that is, one of being capable of incurring losses for a relevant time period in order to eliminate competition, or in general if the resulting market is not contestable (in the sense of Baumol *et al.*, 1982). With higher barriers to entry, in fact, prices will tend to stay above the marginal costs for longer time periods. Except for the price levels, a pricing strategy can also lead to abuses when it is discriminatory; that is, differences in prices do not reflect objective conditions or differentials in cost factors.[25]

In addition, a dominant undertaking can use the leverage created by its position in one market to induce customers to purchase from it other goods and services that they might obtain from other suppliers on better conditions. Such a practice, known as 'tie-in' is prohibited under art. 82 if put in place by a dominant firm. The practice is often seen nowadays on the market, since it occurs when two products closely related by their nature or according to their commercial usage, do not necessarily have to be sourced from the same supplier, but are however sold together: for example, printers and their toner cartridges, or PC operating systems and software to play music and video files.[26]

Apart from prohibiting abusive behaviour, the field of application of art. 82 also allows the Commission to place positive obligations, rather than mere prohibitions, for example when a dominant undertaking refuses to deal with other undertakings. Notwithstanding the general presumption that economic agents are free to choose with whom to deal, an undertaking infringes art. 82 when, for example, being already dominant upstream, it wishes to exclude other undertakings from directly competing in downstream markets.[27] A dominant undertaking enjoying his economic freedom is therefore constrained by a special responsibility, since he 'may always take reasonable steps to protect its commercial interests, but such measures must be fair and proportional to the threat'.[28]

In following the principle according to which a refusal to deal is an abusive behaviour, the EU embraced the so-called 'essential facility doctrine', originally developed in the United States.[29] In the EU translation of the doctrine, art. 82 is infringed when (1) an essential facility or infrastructure is controlled by a dominant undertaking, (2) a competitor is unable practically or reasonably to duplicate the essential facility, (3) the undertaking denies the use of the facility to a competitor, and (4) the provision of the facility or access to the infrastructure is feasible.

The essential facility doctrine is today crucial in the programme of updating and completing the single market. In fact the doctrine is particularly relevant in the case of large infrastructures in transport, telecommunications and energy sectors, in which some facilities or infrastructures, such as airports, fixed telephone lines, electricity grids or pipelines for oil and gas transportation, are both indispensable for providing related services and characterised by high fixed and sunk costs (so that the minimum efficient scale is such as to leave no room for more than one efficient supplier). This market structure determines the so-called 'natural monopolies' which, in Europe, were mainly characterised by state-owned companies or strict public regulations. When these sectors started to be liberalised in the 1990s via the Single Market programme, ad hoc legal frameworks had to be designed in order to regulate the behaviour of the incumbent dominant undertakings holding the essential facilities (typically the ex-monopolists in each member state), as discussed in Chapter 3. The principles of the essential facility doctrine according to art. 82 were thus fundamental, since, had it not been possible to impose access to the essential facility (for example, fixed telephone lines) on the incumbent understanding, no competitors could have entered the market for related services (such as phone data transmission).

Such impositions are likely to persist until demand-side or supply-side substitutability will be such as to justify the shift from regulation to competition rules. For example, the current convergence between telephone and television is increasing the number of competing technologies once defining relevant markets, thus reducing the scope for dominant positions in essential facilities: fixed telephone lines can easily be bypassed today by mobile phones or by wireless and satellite communications, to supply voice, Internet and TV transmission.

9.6 CONTROL OVER CONCENTRATIONS

Unlike agreements and abuses of dominant position, concentrations among firms (mergers and acquisitions) are not explicitly disciplined under the EC treaty. As a result, until the entry into force of specific provisions, concentrations were controlled through the use of arts. 81 and 82 of the TEC.[30] However art. 82 was not opposable to any concentration, since it required the presence of a dominant position ex ante; in addition, the eventual anti-competitive effects of a merger were structural and clearly less reversible than the ones induced by agreements restricting competition disciplined under art. 81, and thus required a more stringent regulation.

This uncertainty about the legal basis paved the way for the first Council Regulation 4064/89 on concentrations between undertakings, recently replaced by Council Regulation 139/2004 (the Merger Regulation), which entered into force on 1 May 2004. The latter Regulation gives the Commission the power to prohibit 'a concentration which would significantly impede effective competition, in the common market or in a substantial part of it, in particular as a result of the creation or strengthening of a dominant position' (art. 2, para. 3 of the Merger Regulation). The concept of concentration thus covers any operation which, from an economic point of view, results in two or more previously independent undertakings being replaced by, or merged into, a single new undertaking. The latter has a broader scope with respect to the 1989 Merger Regulation, which was addressed exclusively to 'concentration which creates or strengthens a dominant position'. In sum, with the new Merger Regulation the Commission does not have to prove dominance any more, but only the extent to which competition is impeded in the common market.

To assess their impact on the internal market, mergers will be notified to the Commission prior to their implementation and following the conclusion of the agreement, the announcement of the public bid, or the acquisition of a controlling interest (art. 4, para. 1 of the Merger Regulation). Mergers might be horizontal, vertical or conglomerate. The former are important from the perspective of competition authorities since they tend to raise concentration in relevant markets, thus requiring ad hoc guidelines for their assessment.[31] Vertical mergers, instead, do not tend to increase market shares and may well increase productive efficiency by reducing transaction costs – the more so for conglomerate mergers, which refer to undertakings in unrelated industries.

In particular, horizontal mergers are able to affect competition via both non-coordinated and coordinated effects. As far as the former are concerned, the most direct effect of a horizontal merger will be the loss of competition between the merging firms. For example if, prior to the merger, one of the merging firms had raised its price, it would have lost some sales to the other merging firm. If instead two firms merge, there is no incentive for them to compete against one another, so this may reduce the extent of competition in the market.

Moreover, by changing the structure of markets, mergers also change the nature of competition, especially in concentrated markets characterised by the presence of firms with significant market shares. In those markets a merger may significantly impede effective competition, through the creation or the strengthening of a dominant position, since a smaller number of firms increases the likelihood of coordination among undertakings in order to raise profits, thus reducing consumers' welfare. Active collusive conduct is not a prerequisite for anticompetitive coordinated effects to occur, an adaptation to market conditions (typically in terms of prices or quantities) being sufficient, facilitated by those variables capable of leading to collusive behaviour under art. 81, para. 1.[32]

9.6.1 The Assessment

In assessing whether a merger would 'significantly impede effective competition', the Commission applies the so-called 'substantive test': whether, after the merger, sufficient competition remains in the market to provide consumers with sufficient choice. The assessment of the impediment of effective competition is thus undertaken ex ante by the Commission, based on the project of the merger, and takes into account the scope for potential competition, the characteristics of the demand, the efficiencies claimed by the merging undertakings and an evaluation of the social impact of the operation.

When assessing the scope for potential competition, after defining the relevant market (see section 9.3), the Commission takes into account the market position of the undertakings concerned. Although market shares in themselves are only a proxy of market power, they represent a starting point for the analysis and, according to the jurisprudence, only mergers between parties which have combined market shares greater than 40 per cent are likely to be subject to a serious scrutiny. In this regard, anti-competitive effects are considered to be non-coordinated, when competitors have low market shares, or coordinated, when the market is already concentrated.

The level of barriers to entry in the market is also considered,[33] as well as the demand and its volume relative to the minimum efficient scale, and the type of buyers operating on the market. If buyers are large and sophisticated, and the transaction is characterised by a certain degree of idiosyncrasy (see Box 9.4), any scope for the merger to result in an increase of market power may be offset by the countervailing power of customers, and thus the merger will be authorised.[34]

In addition the Commission will approve a concentration that delivers 'technical and economic progress that is to consumers' advantage and does not form an obstacle to competition' (art. 2, para. 1b of the Merger Regulation). Therefore there exists a so-called 'efficiency gain' accepted by the Commission as a pro-competitive effect resulting from a concentration. It is, however, quite a long shot to say that considerations of productive efficiency have overcome the allocative considerations in EU policy making. In fact, to get clearance, such an efficiency gain has to be non-achievable by less restrictive means other than the concentration, and the gain has to be reasonably passed on to consumers on a permanent basis in terms of lower prices or increased quality (see also Box 9.4).[35] Nevertheless the jurisprudence does not so far provide strong evidence on the assessment of efficiency gains by the Commission.

BOX 9.4 MARKET POWER VERSUS COST REDUCTION (WILLIAMSON'S TRADE-OFF)

The theory of mergers embodies a trade-off between a possible increase in market power (an impediment to effective competition, as stated in art. 2, para. 3 of the EC Merger Regulation) and possible cost reductions (according to art. 2, para. 1b of the same regulation) thus requiring a balance between allocative and productive efficiency. The latter argument can be made clear in a simple diagram initially presented by Williamson (1968). The basic model assumes two firms in the market, each producing at a constant marginal cost (c^A). They engage in Bertrand price competition so the market price is $p^A = c^A$ and a quantity q^A is sold. After the two

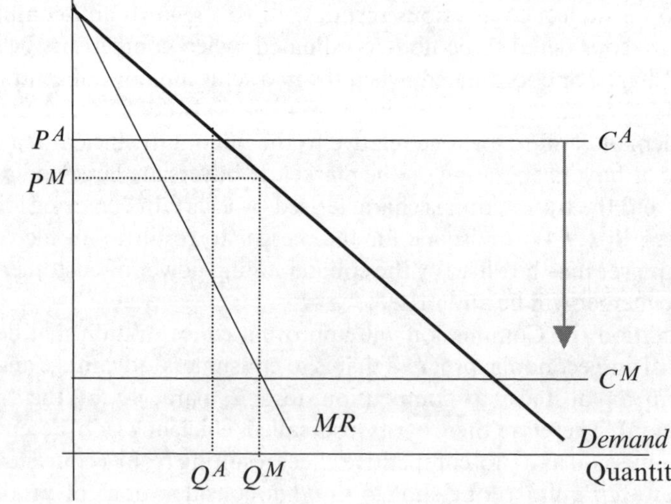

firms merge the unified firm acts monopolistically and sets marginal revenue (*MR*) equal to marginal cost (c^M). However the marginal cost has fallen ($c^M < c^A$) thanks to the efficiency gains achieved through the merger.

In this case, the cost reduction is so large that the post-merger monopoly price p^M is lower than the pre-merger competitive price p^A. Therefore consumers receive a greater surplus, obtaining larger quantities $Q^M > Q^A$ at lower prices. The producer also gains the monopolistic extra profits. Blocking this merger on the basis of impediments to effective competition would clearly be suboptimal from a welfare point of view.

Clearly this result holds given specific market conditions. However, the latter does not imply that contestability of the emerging monopoly should be ruled out as long as the market conditions evolve over time.

The European social market model also influences the clearance of a concentration, since the Commission sometimes applies the so-called 'failing firm defence' policy: the concentration tends to be cleared if the assets (and the workforce) of the merged firm would have otherwise exited the market, thus reducing the potential for increasing competition. Therefore concentrations, when leading to firm restructuring and the preservation of employment levels, tend to be judged positively, in line with the EU goal of jointly achieving its objectives of growth, stability and cohesion.

But what happens if the assessment of a merger by the Commission is such as to declare it incompatible with the common market? The merger might not be immediately stopped, rather the Commission starts a negotiation with the parties, officially identifying in a decision the remedies to be adopted in order to render the operation compliant with the competition principles. Remedies must be clear-cut and entirely remove competition concerns, and have to be implemented effectively and within a short period.[36] If the merging firms fail to comply with the remedies proposed by the Commission, the concentration is not cleared, and any eventual legal act related to the concentration is void.

Clearly the would-be merging firm can appeal to the CFI and then the ECJ if it considers itself unjustly damaged by the Commission's decision, asking for a reversion of the decision.[37] A debate has recently arisen, however, on the efficacy of such a procedure, especially in light of the rapidly changing market conditions which characterise today's businesses. If the concentration is blocked, then, by the time the appeal is processed, and eventually won, the market conditions may be changed and the merger may no longer be profitable for the firms considered. In order to react to this criticism, the EU allows since February 2001 a 'fast track procedure' to appeal to the Court of First Instance (art. 76a of the Rules of Procedure of the CFI), which guarantees decisions within one year of the Commission's decision. However even this shorter time span might not be enough to allow for a smooth working of the concentration operations. The debate is therefore open on whether the EU should move towards a US-type system of merger control, where the competition authority brings the case to court before the final decision on the prohibition of the concentration is taken.

9.7 STATE AID

Competition is not distorted if undertakings conduct their activities in a level playing field. Therefore, if public authorities devote favoured treatments to certain firms or products, they distort competition, since subsidised undertakings do not find the right incentive to strengthen or to create their competitive advantage in the market. State aid therefore delays inevitable restructuring processes, lowers the incentives for greater efficiency (and ultimately growth) and thus decreases the overall welfare of citizens, who in addition are also taxed in order to pay for the financing of the aid.

Recognising these detrimental effects, TEC, art. 87, para. 1 provides that state aid is, in principle, incompatible with the common market.[38] For an aid to fall under the provisions of art. 87, there has to be (a) a transfer of state resources (such as grants, interest or tax relief, loan guarantees); (b) an economic advantage that the undertaking would not have received in the normal course of business (such as rents from publicly owned land at less than the market price); and (c) a selection of beneficiaries of the aid undertaken without fair and objective criteria (for example, firms selected only on the basis of their nationality).

However particular categories of state aid can be exempted prior to a notification by the member state to the Commission. The same Commission has the power to decide whether the proposed aid measure qualifies for exemption or whether the state concerned shall abolish or alter such aid. State aid is exempted when it may have a beneficial impact in the EU as a whole, according to its objectives. Hence member states are allowed to grant aid having a social character to individual consumers and aid in case of damages caused by natural disasters such as earthquakes or floods, or exceptional occurrences.[39] Other categories of state aids may be exempted if they (1) promote the economic development of underdeveloped areas; (2) promote the execution of an important project of common European interest or remedy a serious disturbance in the economy of a member state; (3) facilitate the development of certain activities or areas; or (4) promote culture and heritage conservation. These exceptions are clearly important, since they make the discipline of state aid compatible with the framework for the regional policy (see Chapter 8), the development of the Trans-European Transport Networks (TEN-T) projects, the Research Framework Programmes as well as other EU policies. In particular, within the Lisbon strategy of structural reforms (analysed in Chapter 5), the Brussels European Council (March 2003) called for a further reduction in state aid and the redirection of aid to horizontal objectives, such as research and development, aid for small and medium-sized enterprises, environment, employment and training, which seldom distorts competition.

A typical category of state aid recipient is that of state-owned enterprises (SOEs), which have characterised the history of member states with very few exceptions. Still today, there are in Europe several cases of enterprises under the control of the state, although with various degrees of influence in the different countries. In this respect, the EC Treaty is neutral as far as the ownership is concerned, provided that the state behaves as a normal private investor without assuring any benefit to its undertakings. For this reason the Commission, the supranational controller, is in charge of guaranteeing a level playing field between SOEs and other private entities, punishing member states which might be tempted to favour the state-owned firms in order to gain short-term political benefits, to the prejudice of the EU interest (and, ultimately, of the overall interest of the state concerned).

Another general category of state aid is the one dealing with the so-called **services of general economic interest**. The term is used in TEC, art. 16 and 86, para. 2 and it refers to services which are subject to specific public service obligations by virtue of a general interest criterion. The typical case is an electricity provider, which is obliged to connect people to the network if they so request, even if the specific connection, owing for example to the remoteness of the site, is not economical at affordable prices (European Commission, 2004g). The concept of services of general economic interest thus covers in particular certain services provided by the big network industries, such as transport, postal services, energy and communications. The providers of these types of services receive compensation for the public service obligations they have (for example, universal service, quality, safety), normally payable as a fixed part of the bill. Such compensation, if not properly regulated, can, unconsciously or consciously, turn into a state aid. Therefore, to be sure that the compensation does not amount to a state aid, if there is no scope for competition *in* the market (because of the minimum efficient scale and the demand level), the public authority should create a competition *for* the market. Following this approach and the ECJ opinion,[40] the compensation granted to providers of services of general economic interest is not a state aid under a series of conditions: (1) the recipient undertaking must have public service obligations to discharge and the obligations must be clearly defined; (2) the parameters on the basis of which the compensation is calculated must be established in advance in an objective and transparent manner; (3) the compensation cannot exceed what is necessary to cover the costs incurred in the discharge of public service obligations (taking into account a reasonable profit).

Moreover, if the provider of the service is not chosen pursuant to a public procurement procedure, the level of compensation needed must be determined using as a benchmark the costs of a typical and well-run undertaking already operating in a similar market.

9.8 COMPETITION POLICY IN AN ENLARGED EUROPE

As it can be seen, 1 May 2004 brought about a radical change in the management of the EU competition policy. Two of the main policy areas (antitrust and concentration) saw the entry into force of new rules: the Council Regulation EC/1/2003, simplifying the framework of application of arts. 81 and 82 via the devolution of competences to the national authorities and the introduction of self-assessment in the foreseen antitrust exemptions; and the new Merger Regulation, which significantly broadened the scope of Commission actions in this area, and made it much more transparent.

It is not the case that these two major changes happened on the day that the European Union enlarged itself to accommodate ten new members. Given the characteristics of the new member states, in fact, competition policy faces a significant challenge in future years. The new members have certainly adapted to the macroeconomic criteria foreseen for accession, and have as well incorporated the Community *acquis*, but at the microeconomic level they still present some drawbacks in the working of the internal market. In particular, the same Commission pointed out how, in the new member states, administered prices is still pervasive, and the amount of state aid well above the European average (European Commission, 2003e). The phenomena of industrial restructuring still taking place in these countries also require close monitoring, in order to avoid the emergence of distortions to market conditions.

To this end, the simplification of procedures brought about by the recent legislative changes allows a greater focus of the Commission on major infringements of competition, thus ensuring that, with the same resources, the evolution of competition policy in the new member states can be adequately monitored. However some concerns remain, and will have to be addressed properly in the years ahead.

On the one hand, the devolution of significant powers to the national competition authorities can be risky in the new member states, given the limited experience of these (new) authorities in dealing with the complex competition issues emerging in the more and more sophisticated European marketplace. Adequate resources should be devoted by the EU, together with the concerned member state, to ensure a correct functioning of these authorities.

On the other hand, the real threat to competition posed by the situation in the new countries is likely to derive from state aid. This is due both to the heritage of SOEs in these countries, and to the enormous amount of resources these countries will receive in terms of structural funds (around 3–4 per cent of their GDP each year; see Chapter 8). Such an amount of money, if not properly monitored, can clearly lead to serious misallocation of resources, with serious consequences for competition in these countries. And yet the field of state aid is the one where member states seem most reluctant to change the rules, still those foreseen in 1957, thus preventing the Commission countering effectively any distorting practices.

If the enlargement of the Union is to prove a success in the future years, it is therefore of the utmost importance to solve quickly the remaining problems when applying competition rules to the new economic context.

NOTES

1. The reader might recall that, in Chapters 1 to 5, we discussed extensively the implications of various processes of economic integration, showing that higher levels of integration tend to be associated, via larger and more competitive markets, with lower prices and higher economic efficiency for consumers, and lower profits for producers.
2. See Motta (2004) for some examples.
3. Firms who set prices above the marginal costs would in fact be forced out of this market by the entry of new, cheaper competitors.
4. Apart from the extreme case of natural monopolies (see below), many markets, because of the demand level and the scope of fixed costs, can be considered as 'naturally' oligopolistic,that is, they require in equilibrium a limited number of firms, each one with a minimal size, or *minimum efficient scale*, of production.
5. Some authors (for example, Korah, 2004, p.14) claim that these objectives might be conflicting.
6. As stated by the European Court of Justice (ECJ) in *Hugin* v. *Commission* (case 22/78), any conduct whose effects are confined to the territory of a single member state has to be governed by the national jurisdiction (that is, the national laws, competition authorities and courts).
7. See the Commission's notice on the concept of undertakings concerned (published in OJ C 66 of 2 March 1998). In *Reuter/BASF* (case 743/76) the ECJ considered an inventor, thus a single individual, as an undertaking.
8. '2. A concentration has a Community dimension where: (a) the combined aggregate worldwide turnover of all the undertakings concerned is more than €5000 million; and (b) the aggregate Community-wide turnover of each of at least two of the undertakings

concerned is more than €250 million, unless each of the undertakings concerned achieves more than two-thirds of its aggregate Community-wide turnover within one and the same member state. 3. A concentration that does not meet the thresholds laid down in paragraph 2 has a Community dimension where: (a) the combined aggregate worldwide turnover of all the undertakings concerned is more than €2500 million; (b) in each of at least three member states, the combined aggregate turnover of all the undertakings concerned is more than €100 million; (c) in each of at least three member states included for the purpose of point (b), the aggregate turnover of each of at least two of the undertakings concerned is more than €25 million; and (d) the aggregate Community-wide turnover of each of at least two of the undertakings concerned is more than €100 million, unless each of the undertakings concerned achieves more than two-thirds of its aggregate Community-wide turnover within one and the same member state' (art. 1, paras 2 and 3 of the Merger Regulation).

9. On 1 May 2004 there entered into force the Council Regulation EC/1/2003 of 16 December 2002, on the implementation of the rules on competition laid down in Articles 81 and 82 of the Treaty (published in OJ L 1 of 4 January 2003), replacing the old Regulation 17/62 created by the provisions of the Treaty of Rome.
10. According to the European Commission, the European Competition Network is a forum for discussion and cooperation to maintain a common competition culture in Europe and to manage a system of parallel competences where cases can be dealt with by a single national competition authority, by a group of them or by the European Commission.
11. As stated by the ECJ in *Pioneer* (cases 100–103/80), the 10 per cent limit may be based on the turnover of the entire group of companies, worldwide and for all products.
12. See, for example, the cases of *Dyestuffs* for art. 81 (case 48/69), *Microsoft* for art. 82 (case Comp 37.924 – Commission decision of 18 April 2001) and *General Electrics/Honeywell* for merger regulation (case M 2220 – Commission decision of 3 July 2001).
13. Commission notice on the definition of the relevant market for the purpose of Community competition law (published in OJ C 372 of 9 December 1997).
14. Nullity under art. 81(2) does not need any formal decision and, as remembered by the ECJ in *Béguelin Import Co./GL Import Export SA* (case 22/71) an agreement that is void has no effect between the contracting parties and cannot be pleaded against third parties.
15. According to art. 2 of Regulation 1/2003, the burden of proof under Article 81(3) rests on the undertaking(s) invoking the benefit of the exemption rule.
16. Implicit collusion might arise in different situations. For example, Veugelers and Vandenbussche (1999) show how the European antidumping policy modifies the incentives for firms implicitly to collude domestically or internationally.
17. This ambiguous role of information availability and transparency has been considered a key issue in business-to-business electronic marketplaces by the Commission (for example, in the workshop, 'E-marketplaces: new challenges for enterprise policy, competition and standardisation', 2001), by the American FTC (for example, in the report, 'Entering the 21st Century: Competition Policy in the World of B2B electronic marketplaces', 2000) and by the OECD (report 'Competition Issues in Electronic Commerce', 2001).
18. In *Dyestuffs* (case 48/69), undertakings maintained that a simultaneous price increase in various national markets for dyestuffs was merely the result of parallel strategies. However the ECJ, in upholding the Commission's decision, confirmed that evidence of coordination, and thus collusion, could have been discerned by the simultaneity and similarity of price increases. However, in another instance a simple price announcement on the pulp market (*Wood Pulp*, cases 89, 104, 114, 116, 117 and 125–129/85) was not considered as an instrument of concerted practice by the ECJ, contrary to the Commission's decision, which instead detected in the announcement evidence of implicit collusion.
19. In *Consten-Grundig* (cases 56 and 58/64) the absolute territorial protection by which the exclusivity for France was guaranteed by the German manufacturer, Grundig, to the

French retailer, Consten, was considered illegitimate, as persistence of the segmentation of economic activities along national frontiers.

20. The Commission approved two regulations on the application of art. 81(3) to categories of specialisation, and research and development agreements (respectively Regulation n. 2658/2000 and n. 2659/2000 published in OJ L304 of 5 December 2000) complemented by Guidelines, covering a wider range of the most common types of horizontal agreements (Commission notice on guidelines on the applicability of Article 81 of the EC Treaty to horizontal cooperation agreements published in OJ C3 of 6 January 2001).
21. See the ECJ in *United Brands* (case 27/76) and in *Hoffman-La Roche* (case 85/76).
22. The ECJ in *Hoffman-La Roche* (para. 41).
23. The ECJ in *Hoffman-La Roche* (para. 91).
24. Areeda and Turner (1975) argue that predation occurs when prices are set below marginal cost; however, as marginal cost can be difficult to determine, a proxy measurement of average variable cost, which is more easy to ascertain by standard cost-account techniques, would produce an acceptably close result. In *Akzo* (case 62/86) the ECJ considered abusive the prices set below average total cost (though above the average variable costs) by the dominant firm, on the basis of the sole consideration that the goal of the pricing strategy was to eliminate a competitor.
25. In *United Brands* (case 27/76) the Commission had attacked UB for charging varying prices to its customers which were not attributable to any differences in customs duties or transport costs.
26. See respectively *Pelikan/Kyocera* (25th Report on Competition Policy, 1995, paras 86 and 87) and *Microsoft* 2000 (case Comp 37.792, Commission decision of 24 March 2004). In the latter case, the Commission found abusive the behaviour of Microsoft, which tied in its Windows Media Player (a product subject to widespread competition in its market) with its ubiquitous Windows operating system.
27. *Commercial Solvents*, for example, was the leading manufacturer of the raw material aminobutanol. In expanding into production of the final product, it decided to cease supplies of the raw material to other competitors, in order to limit competition in the downstream market. This practice having been recognised as abusive, the firm was required to resume supplies, following the complaints of *Zoja*, a firm which could not find a source of supply elsewhere.
28. Commission decision in *BBI/Boosey* (case Comp. 32.279, decision of 29 July 1987).
29. See case *MCI Communications Corp.* v. *AT&T* (case 708 F.2d 1081/83).
30. For example, the acquisition of a competitor by an already dominant firm was assessed under art. 82 in 1972 (judgment of the Court in *Europemballange Corporation and Continental Can Co.* v. *Commission*, case 6/72), while in 1987, the mere acquisition of shares in a competing and independent undertaking was assessed under art. 81 (judgment of the Court in *British-American Tobacco Company Ltd and R.J. Reynolds Industries Inc.* v. *Commission*, Joint cases 142/84 and 156/84).
31. Guidelines on the assessment of horizontal mergers under the Council Regulation on the control of concentrations between undertakings (published on OJ C 31 of 5 February 2004).
32. As set out by the Commission in *Gencor/Lonrho* (case M.619, decision of 24 April 1996). In the subsequent appeal case, the CFI in *Gencor Ltd* v. *Commission* (case T-102/96, judgment of 25 March 1999) upheld the Commission's negative decision, taking into account considerations related to the price transparency and homogeneity of the product in the market concerned, since in this case by means of the mere price a member of an oligopoly could immediately discern the decisions undertaken by the other members.
33. The Commission recognised as a barrier to entry the difficulty of gaining access to retailers in *Procter and Gamble/VP Schickedanz II* (case M.430, decision of 21 June 1994), overcapacity in the industry in *Friesland Coberco/Nutricia* (case M.2399, decision of 8 August 2001) and high sunk costs as in *Aérospatiale-Alenia/de Havilland* (case M.53, decision of 2 October 1991).

34. The evaluation of the power exercised by the customers of a dominant firm led the Commission to the clearance decision both in *Allied Lyons/HWE-Pedro Domeq* (case M.400, decision of 28 April 1994) and in *Friesland Coberco/Nutricia* (case M.2399, decision of 8 August 2001).
35. See para. 78 of the Guidelines on the assessment of horizontal mergers under the Council Regulation on the control of concentrations between undertakings, published in OJ L 31, 5 February 2004.
36. The most usual remedies advocated by the Commission in order to render a concentration compliant with the competition principles normally aim at creating the conditions for the emergence of a new competitive entity, or the strengthening of the other competitors in the market via the divestiture of assets by the merging firms: these assets were landing slots in *Alitalia/KLM* (case JV.19, decision of 11 August 1999), shareholdings in *Allianz/Dresdner* (case M.2431, decision of 19 July 2001), or the transformation of a major electricity producer jointly controlled by the duopolists into an independent competitor in *Veba/Viag* (case M.1673 in parallel with the Bundeskartellamt's investigation of *RWE/VEW*, decision of 13 June 2000).
37. In 2002, the CFI annulled within less than five months three merger prohibition decisions issued by the Commission (*Airtours/First Choice*, case M.1524, decision of 29 April 1999; *Schneider/Legrand*, case M.2283, decision of 10 October 2001 and *Tetra Laval/Sidel*, case M.2416, decision of 30 October 2001), on the grounds of an inadequate economic analysis by the Commission of the relevant market structure resulting from the merger.
38. The term 'State' includes national, regional or local authorities, and other institutions such as public banks.
39. According to art. 87, para. 3e, the Council has to decide by a qualified majority on a proposal from the Commission.
40. Judgment of 24 July 2003 in the case C-280/00 *Altmark Trans*.

10. The economic external dimension of the Union

10.1 INTRODUCTION

The **Common Commercial Policy** (CCP) of the European Union, together with the single currency and competition policy, is the only truly centralised policy of the Union. As such, it is also one of the most effective. The efficacy of the provisions of the CCP has in fact allowed the EU to speak with one voice in the global economic arena and, as a result, to exploit the combined bargaining power resulting from the economic weight of its members, which include some of the world's richest countries. And yet this is not the general feeling associated with the role of the Union in the world, a role often seen as politically inadequate, or simply not significant. The reasons behind such a perception, right or wrong as it may be, are likely to be twofold, formal and substantial.

From a formal point of view, the perceived limited role of the EU in the global scenario might lie in the scope of the Common Commercial Policy, which deals only with trade issues and thus, with respect to general issues of global governance, provides the Union with a limited (although relevant), set of tools. A significant political presence on the world stage would require in fact legal provisions leading to coordinated actions, not only in trade, but also in the fields of monetary governance (for the exchange rates system) and foreign policy (with the eventual support of a credible military capability). In terms of monetary governance, the legal provisions of the Maastricht Treaty deal also with the external aspects of the common monetary policy (TEC, art. 111).[1] Nevertheless these provisions have not been implemented so far, with the operational decisions still pending on the external representation of the Euro Zone (for example, an EU single seat in monetary international fora such as the IMF or the World Bank). Very limited progress, and many controversies, have instead been so far the dreadful score of the various attempts at creating a common European foreign policy, notwithstanding the various improvements in its juridical base contained in all the EU treaties approved in the last decade (Maastricht, Amsterdam, Nice). It remains to be seen whether the Constitutional Treaty, once ratified by the member

Table 10.1 The EU-25 external economic position (2002)

	Japan	USA	EU
Share in world trade in goods	7.6	19.7	19.1
Share in world trade in services	7.7	20.2	24.3
Share in foreign investment	3.0	29.1	32.2
Share in world GDP	7.3	21.3	19.8
Degree of openness[a]	17.1	16.6	19.9

Notes: [a] Exports + Imports/GDP; intra-EU trade and investment flows are excluded from calculations.

Source: European Commission DG Trade.

states, might improve the situation, as discussed in the last chapter of the book.

Looking at the picture from a substantial, rather than a formal point of view, we saw in Chapter 1 that on 1 July 1968, 18 months before the deadline foreseen in the Treaties of Rome, the EEC Customs Union entered into force; remaining customs duties in intra-Community trade were abolished and a Common External Tariff (CET) was introduced to replace national customs duties in trade with the rest of the world (RoW). Since then, the CCP and its main instrument, the CET, have evolved in parallel with the changing need of the Union, and have greatly contributed to making the Union the leading trading partner of the world: 20.5 per cent of total world exports in 2002 originated from the EU, against the USA's 14.7 per cent and Japan's 8.5 per cent.[2] The EU is also the leading world exporter of capital, in terms of foreign direct investment undertaken by its multinational corporations, and the world's most open economy, as shown by Table 10.1.

As a result of these figures, at least from an economic point of view, it would be unfair to undervalue the role of the Union in the global policy agenda: any change in European trade policy has in fact a substantial impact on the global economy.[3] However, it remains to be assessed how easily the EU trade policy can be changed to suit the political needs of the member states. Even when endowed with the bargaining power the CCP conferred on it, the EU is but one of the actors in the **multilateral trade system** organised around the **World Trade Organisation** (WTO). Hence the set of tools the EU can use in shaping its trade policy[4] is in any case limited by the rules agreed within the WTO. In addition, the trade policy of the Union has been traditionally biased in favour of the common agricultural policy (see Chapter 7) and hence, owing to this burden, the ability of EU negotiators in delivering a positive outcome in other sectors within the WTO rules tends to be structurally limited. These issues will be discussed in the remainder of the chapter.

We are thus confronted with a mixed picture when assessing the external role of the European Union: some lights (the common commercial policy, a powerful policy tool yet limited by the multilateral WTO regulations) and some shadows (the limited impact of the EU in global monetary governance and, overall, the non-existence of a truly common foreign policy). And yet it is clear that, in the complex scenario emerging after the end of the Cold War, no single European member state has enough bargaining power in the global arena to significantly steer in its direction the world's course of events. Challenges such as a correct redistribution of the gains of globalisation, the design of an appropriate immigration policy or the fight against global crime and terrorism can no longer be adequately met by measures taken at the national level only. The multinational character of the challenges requires an efficient multinational (European, in this case) reply. As a result, in order to preserve the welfare of their citizens, it is of paramount importance for member states to establish or strengthen appropriate common policies able to endow the Union with adequate political power.

The accession to the Union of the new member states, and the involvement of Turkey in the process, stress even more the importance of this process. The enlargement has in fact further changed the geopolitical space in which the Union will act in the coming decades, bringing the EU to the borders of strategically critical areas such as the former Soviet Union and the Middle East. As a result, two dimensions arise nowadays in EU external relations: the neighbourhood dimension, or 'proximity policy', which concerns the countries close to Europe, and the enhanced EU sphere of influence as a global partner. The former policy aims at strengthening the EU trade and political relations with the 'ring of friends', that is, the countries surrounding the EU, from Belarus to Morocco. The latter, more general, dimension aims at projecting the core values of peace, freedom and democracy around the globe, using them as a guide for the EU common foreign policy.

In this chapter, we will start by analysing the instruments of the EU Common Commercial Policy and the EU bilateral relations with different regions of the world, together with the changes brought in by the enlargement and the resulting 'proximity policy'. We will then discuss how the bilateral focus of the EU is affected by the evolution of multilateral trade rules within the WTO. Finally, we will dedicate the last part of the chapter to the issues related to monetary governance at the world level and the international role of the Euro. Given the economic focus of the chapter, we will not discuss here the EU foreign policy and its perspectives, which will be the object of some considerations in the concluding chapter of the book.

10.2 THE COMMON COMMERCIAL POLICY

10.2.1 Institutional Design

The Treaty of the European Communities (TEC) originally signed in Rome set the main instruments through which the CCP is implemented. In particular, TEC, art. 133, included in Part III-Title IX of the Treaty, specifically deals with the CCP, and states:

1. The common commercial policy shall be based on uniform principles, particularly in regard to changes in tariff rates, the conclusion of tariff and trade agreements, the achievement of uniformity in measures of liberalisation, export policy and measures to protect trade such as those to be taken in the event of dumping or subsidies.
2. The Commission shall submit proposals to the Council for implementing the common commercial policy.
3. Where agreements with one or more States or international organisations need to be negotiated, the Commission shall make recommendations to the Council, which shall authorise the Commission to open the necessary negotiations. [. . .]
4. In exercising the powers conferred upon it by this Article, the Council shall act by a qualified majority.
5. Paragraphs 1 to 4 shall also apply to the negotiation and conclusion of agreements in the fields of trade in services and the commercial aspects of intellectual property [. . .]

Hence the European Commission is responsible for the implementation of the CCP, both in terms of its original definition (it is the Commission that proposes eventual new trade initiatives to the Council) and as far as the practical implementation of the policy is concerned (the Commission conducts trade negotiations and manages the trade tariffs).[5] Most notably, art. 133 para. 4 calls for the decisions at the Council to be taken by qualified majority. Such a provision ensures efficiency in the EU decision making, and it is one of the main reasons behind the success of the CCP, contrary to the results of other policies, decided by unanimity by member states and analysed in other parts of this book. Equally interesting is para. 5 of art. 133, drafted in its current version since the entry into force of the Nice Treaty in 2003. In essence, this paragraph extends the competence of the EU common commercial policy to cover not only trade in goods, but also issues in services and intellectual property.[6] The amendment is consistent with the current trend in the negotiations at the World Trade Organisation (see *infra*) in which countries, in line with the evolution of economic activities from manufacturing to services, have progressively been regulating trade not only in goods but also in services and property rights.

An exception, known as **cultural exception**, is maintained, however, for the international negotiations related to 'cultural and audiovisual services, educational services, and social and human health services' (TEC, art. 133, para. 6). Since, by the subsidiarity principle, these issues are considered one of the areas in which the competence of the EU is complementary to that exerted by each member state (what the draft Constitutional Treaty refers to as 'shared competence'), it follows that any decision on common trade provisions related to this particular type of services has to be unanimously taken by the member states.[7]

Apart from the general provisions of the CCP laid down in art. 133, three other articles of the Treaty shape the external relations of the EU, disciplining the agreements that the European Union can sign with external countries. TEC, art. 300 lays down the general provisions for 'the conclusion of agreements between the Community and one or more States or international organisations'. Again the Commission makes a recommendation to the Council; the latter, deciding by qualified majority, authorises the Commission to open the necessary negotiations, and requests the opinion of the European Parliament before the eventual conclusion of the agreement.

More stringent provisions are set by TEC, art. 310, which establishes the so-called **association agreements**, stating that 'the Community may conclude with one or more states or international organisations agreements establishing an association involving reciprocal rights and obligations, common action and special procedure'.

The new Title XXI 'Economic, Financial and Technical Cooperation with Third Countries' of the TEC introduced by the Treaty of Nice disciplines and homogenises a series of agreements concluded in the past by the EU and its member states under different provisions,[8] and known as **cooperation agreements**. In particular, the new TEC, art. 181a states that 'the Community shall carry out, within its spheres of competence, economic, financial and technical cooperation measures with third countries. Such measures shall be complementary to those carried out by the member states and consistent with the development policy of the Community. Community policy in this area shall contribute to the general objective of developing and consolidating democracy and the rule of law, and to the objective of respecting human rights and fundamental freedoms'.

Both the association and the cooperation agreements commit the EU and an external partner country, or group of countries, to a series of reciprocal obligations. From an economic point of view, the two types of agreements are similar: they both aim at establishing free trade between the signatory parties. However the liberalisation does not necessarily concern all industries (in particular, agriculture tends to be treated differently by these agreements owing to the original protectionist nature of the EU CAP) nor does it necessarily involve a symmetrical obligation by the signatory parties, a principle known as **reciprocity**.[9]

The main difference between the association and the cooperation agreement, however, is related to the degree of political and financial involvement of the Union. In the association agreements, on top of the trade liberalisation provisions, specific policy areas are agreed upon, normally related to the goal of economic development of the partner country, and are jointly developed by the Union in association with the signatory party. A special institutional body is created for the running of these policies, known as the 'Association Council' where both the EU and the partner country are represented at the ministerial level. The actions to be developed are also granted a specific budget, provided for by the signatory parties, in order to endow the agreement with some autonomous financial capability for pursuing its statutory objectives. Because of the wider scope of the underlying political and financial obligations, the setting up of an association agreement requires a unanimous approval by the Council, and the mandatory assent of the European Parliament, in its capacity of budget co-authority of the Union (see Chapter 6).

The cooperation agreements, instead, are more limited in scope and, apart from the trade provisions, normally imply the commitment by the EU institutions to carry out technical cooperation programmes on specific issues, often complementing actions already undertaken by some member states.[10] Because of their less stringent degree of political and financial commitment, only a qualified majority in the Council is needed for the setting up of these agreements, while the European Parliament is required to express a non-binding opinion, as regards the general provisions on international agreements laid down in TEC, art. 300. Given their only partial community nature, in order to enter into force the cooperation agreements require the ratification of the member states as well as of the the EU institutions, and are thus also known as 'mixed' agreements.

Finally, apart from the previously described specific legal provisions, the Union can also use standard EU Regulations to derogate from the general provisions of its common commercial policy. This is the case with the so-called **Generalised System of Preferences** (GSP) that the Union has established since 1971 in favour of the developing countries (DC). Through this Regulation, the EU derogates from its standard CET offering tariff-free access, without demanding reciprocity, to the industrial and some agricultural exports of all DCs, although the same exports could be subject to a quantitative restriction, beyond which the CET applies as normal.[11] The GSP Regulation is updated every ten years and reviewed every two years. In particular, in addition to all DCs enjoying the benefit of the GSP, a special arrangement, known as the **Everything But Arms** (EBA) initiative, exists for least developed countries (LDCs). In particular, the EBA Regulation provides duty-free access to imports of all products from LDCs without any quantitative restrictions, except on arms and munitions.[12] Special arrangements are also in place to combat drug production and trafficking, for the protection of labour rights and for the protection of the environment. The product coverage varies for each arrangement and, depending on the sensitivity of the product, it may enter the EU market duty-free or enjoy a tariff reduction.

10.2.2 The EU 'Pyramid of Preferences' and the Structure of EU Trade

Historically, in order to attain its economic and political objectives, the EU has used the various types of trade instruments previously discussed in a variety of ways, concluding bilateral agreements and/or devising specific trading policies with third countries and regional areas. Currently more than 120 countries are potentially linked to the EU by regional trade agreements, many negotiated in the 1990s. This complex network of agreements has de facto created a ranking in the preferential relationships of the EU with the various signatory countries in the world. As a result, it is possible to visualise these countries according to a decreasing degree of preference, an exercise which yields the so-called EU '**pyramid of preferences**', shown in Figure 10.1.

The top of the pyramid expresses the maximum preferential treatment that the EU can grant to another country, that is, membership of the Union. Moving downwards we observe a lower and lower preferential treatment,

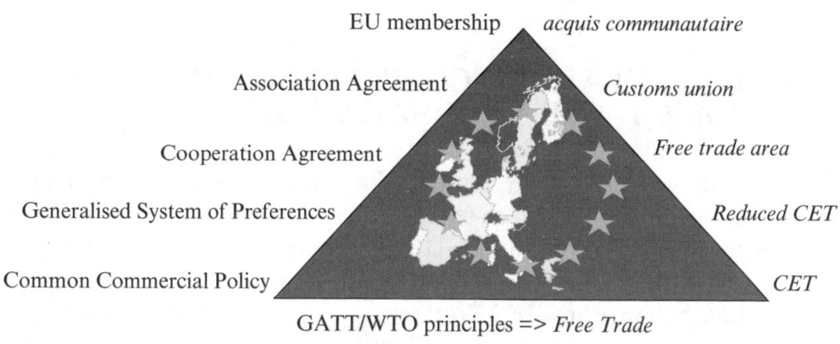

Figure 10.1 The EU 'pyramid of preferences'

until we reach countries positioned at the basis of the pyramid, which face the standard CET. On the left side of Figure 10.1 we have indicated the juridical instrument granting the preferential treatment, while on the right side we show the general content of the treatment. As a result, to the preferential treatment of EU membership, there corresponds the full incorporation in the legislation of the acceding country of the *acquis communautaire*, the EU body of legislation, as discussed in Chapter 3. The association agreements are the second-highest preferential form of treatment granted by the EU. They might involve the creation of a Customs Union or a Free Trade Area with the partner, together with agreements disciplining, for example, capital and people's mobility, industrial standards, non-tariff measures and some form of financial aid to development (thus requiring unanimous approval by the Council and the assent of the European Parliament). A step lower we find the cooperation agreements: as we have previously seen, they imply free trade provisions and some other forms of technical cooperation, without however reaching the scope and depth of the association agreements. One step above the bottom of the pyramid, we can place the Generalised System of Preferences, essentially involving a reduced common external tariff for specific products/countries.[13] Finally, at the bottom of the pyramid we have the standard CCP, where no specific preferences are granted but the ones agreed within the GATT/WTO rules (see *infra*).

Tables 10.2 and 10.3 provide some trade statistics for the 1997–2002 period, distinguishing between various sectors and countries. It can be seen how a growing component of the EU trade is related to developing countries. The impact of the CAP reforms discussed in Chapter 7 is also evident, with growing imports of agricultural products from the DCs, and stable or decreasing EU exports.

Table 10.4 translates the generic picture of the EU pyramid of preferences into the current system of agreements the Union has with the rest of the world.

10.3 THE ENLARGED COMMON COMMERCIAL POLICY: THE 'PROXIMITY POLICY'

The position of the EU in the world trading system has not changed much since its enlargement. As can be seen in Table 10.5, in fact, the EU acquires a larger share in terms of world GDP, becoming by far the largest market in the world, although its share in world trade flows decreases slightly (from 1.97 to 1.80 billion Euros in 2002), owing to the fact that the significant trade taking place between the EU-15 and the acceding countries has now become internal. In particular the intra-Community trade of EU-25 now

Table 10.2 The EU-25 external trade (Euros million)

	1997	1998	1999	2000	2001	2002
Imports from the world						
Total	672 568	710 538	779 825	1 033 436	1 028 238	987 196
Manuf. products	461 332	516 308	571 815	720 249	720 331	694 316
Agr. products	71 177	72 460	71 359	79 130	82 802	82 262
Energy	85 198	61 690	78 275	149 091	145 302	137 564
Of which: imports from developing countries						
Total	268 133	275 858	311 705	431 492	420 587	402 749
Manuf. products	165 528	182 394	206 000	270 493	268 588	264 253
Agr. products	41 811	42 748	42 075	46 447	48 717	48 207
Energy	48 761	35 639	46 088	88 297	81 392	72 346
Exports to the world						
Total	721 128	733 428	760 192	942 044	985 783	993 859
Manuf.Products	619 983	635 925	656 374	809 992	856 653	860 918
Agr. products	54 790	52 938	52 862	60 626	61 776	63 803
Energy	17 144	14 014	16 593	30 250	26 064	26 317
Of which: exports to developing countries						
Total	289 086	272 027	274 028	337 585	352 714	349 316
Manuf. products	252 523	236 599	234 761	290 258	310 455	305 062
Agr. products	22 200	21 381	21 789	25 364	24 429	23 953
Energy	6 891	5 476	5 830	9 420	6 186	6 440

Source: European Commission DG Trade.

accounts for 67.3 per cent of total Union exports and 65 per cent of total imports, up from the EU-15 percentages of 62 per cent and 60 per cent, respectively (2002 data). Also the ranking of the EU's trading partners as well as the composition of its trade flows remain virtually unchanged with the enlargement, as shown in Table 10.6. As a result, the negotiating position of the EU on both the bilateral and the multilateral trade fora should not be significantly affected by the trade orientation of the new member states, with the exception, of course, of the Common Agricultural Policy, already discussed in Chapter 7.

Table 10.3 The EU-25 external trade with selected regional groups (2002, Euros million)

Country	Exports	Imports	Net balance
NAFTA	277 186	207 015	70 171
Andean Pact	7 335	7 907	−572
MercoSur	19 105	25 851	−6 746
EFTA	97 598	107 259	−9 661
ACP	39 734	45 785	−6 051
MED countries	73 670	65 777	7 893
Middle East	35 722	18 333	17 389
Turkey	29 300	25 800	3 500
CIS	46 688	75 058	−28 370
India	16 412	21 287	−4 875
China	52 893	98 595	−45 702
Japan and Korea	58 560	96 844	−38 284
ASEAN	39 814	68 578	−28 764
Australia and New Zealand	18 792	11 283	7 509

Notes: NAFTA: USA, Canada, Mexico; Andean Pact: Venezuela, Colombia, Bolivia, Ecuador, Peru; MercoSur: Brazil, Argentina, Uruguay, Paraguay, Chile (associated); EFTA: Switzerland, Norway, Iceland, Liechtenstein; ACP: African, Caribbean and Pacific Countries; MED: Morocco, Algeria, Tunisia, Egypt, Israel, PNA, Syria, Lebanon, Jordan; ASEAN: Thailand, Taiwan, Indonesia, Malaysia, Singapore, Vietnam, Laos, Cambodia, Philippines, Myanmar, Brunei.

Source: European Commission DG Trade.

However the enlargement to the new ten members, and the forthcoming one to Bulgaria and Romania (and eventually Croatia and Turkey), brings about a change in the political, rather than economic, attitude of the EU towards its closest partners. In fact, for a Union that ranges from the Atlantic Ocean to the Black Sea, very close to Russia and the Middle East, it is crucial to prevent the emergence of new dividing lines with its new neighbours. The EU response to this challenge has been the opportunity granted to the new neighbours to participate in various EU activities, through greater political, security, economic and cultural cooperation. To this purpose, in 2003 the European Commission launched an initiative known as 'wider Europe', which then received its official name of **European Neighbourhood Policy** (ENP).[14]

Broadly put, the ENP's objective is to extend to the neighbouring countries (from the southern Mediterranean countries to the former Soviet Republics and Russia) an area of stability, security and economic development. Different from the enlargement policy, the ultimate goal of the

ENP is not the potential membership of these countries, since currently no participation in the EU institutions is foreseen for the neighbouring countries. Rather, a privileged relationship is offered, under the mutual commitment to some common values, such as respect for the rule of law, good governance, the respect for human rights, including minority rights, the principles of market economy and sustainable development, as well as the sharing of certain key foreign policy goals. The juridical tools on which the relationship will be established are, for the time being, the bilateral association or cooperation agreements previously discussed and already in place with the different partners. Within this legal framework, the countries participating in the ENP will define a set of priorities, incorporated in jointly agreed action plans, covering a number of key areas for specific action. The action plans will define the way ahead over the next three to five years. If successful, the next step could consist in offering a new privileged partnership to the countries concerned, in the form of special 'European Neighbourhood Agreements', a new generation of agreements which will replace the present association or cooperation agreements.

Essentially it can be stated that the ENP allows the EU to swap an increased access to its market, offered to the participating countries, for an extended political and foreign affairs influence in the area. As a result, the key areas in which the action plans will be developed are as follows:

(a) political dialogue, covering key issues including the fight against terrorism and the proliferation of weapons of mass destruction as well as cooperation to resolve regional conflicts;
(b) economic and social development, offering neighbouring countries participation in a number of EU programmes related to the single market (for example, education and training, research and innovation) and improved interconnection with the EU (for example, in the fields of energy, transport, environment and information society);
(c) trade, with greater access to the EU markets in accordance with the principles of the WTO and provided that a minimal approximation of rules and standards is agreed upon;
(d) justice and home affairs, foreseeing closer cooperation on issues like border management, migration, the fight against terrorism, trafficking in human beings, drugs and arms, organized crime and money laundering.

In order to minimise distortions for the participating countries, the action plans will be differentiated, that is, tailor-made to reflect the existing state of relations with each country, their needs and capacities as well as common interests. In organisational terms, the ENP is thus a replica of the

Table 10.4 The EU Pyramid of preferences in practice

Partner	Nature of agreement	Type of agreement
Central and Eastern Europe	Free Trade Area	Association Agreement 'Europe Agreements'
Turkey, Andorra	Customs Union	Association Agreement
EFTA (Iceland, Norway, Liechtenstein, Switzerland)	Free Trade Area	Association Agreement 'European Economic Space'
Mediterranean countries	Free Trade Area (to be fully established by 2010)	Association Agreements 'Euro-Med Agreements'
African, Caribbean and Pacific countries (ACP)	Regional Economic Cooperation Agreements	Association Agreements (Lomé-Cotonou Conventions)
Chile	Free Trade Area	Association Agreement
Mexico	Free Trade Area	Cooperation Agreement
South Africa	Free Trade Area	Cooperation Agreement
Latin America (MercoSur)	Free Trade Area	Cooperation Agreement
Other developing countries	Generalised system of preferences	EU Regulation

Source: Authors' elaboration based on the information available on the European Commission – DG Trade website. http://europa.eu.int/comm/trade/issues/bilateral/index_en.htm.

approach that the European Commission has had towards each of the acceding countries of Central and Eastern Europe, where bilateral, country-specific lines of action were agreed. In this sense, the ENP can be said to constitute an improvement with respect, for example, to the traditional Euro-Mediterranean partnership, originally conceived as relatively homogeneous across the participating countries.[15]

Status	Comments
In force 1994–9	Limited to Bulgaria and Romania after the 2004 EU enlargement. A Stabilisation and Association agreement was signed with Croatia in 2001, with membership as a goal
In force	The CU started in 1992 with Andorra and 1996 with Turkey
In force 1994	In addition to FTA provisions, the agreements call for the implementation of the four fundamental freedoms in the partner countries, with the exception of Switzerland, where specific provisions have been negotiated
Partly in force	Agreements with Israel, Morocco, PNA, Tunisia, Lebanon and Egypt in force. Algeria ready to enter into force. Negotiations going on with Syria
In force 1963–2000	Essentially FTA with non-reciprocal preferential access to the EU market. EU–ACP Joint Assembly
In force 2002	Free trade in goods plus common rules on investments, services, rule making, standards, non-tariff measures
In force 2000	Rules of origin negotiated in order to clear controversies with NAFTA; extended to services
In force 2000	Under an Exchange of Letters, the provisions establishing an FTA in goods are applied provisionally, pending entry into force of the full agreement
In force 1995	Seven rounds of negotiations since 1999 have already been undertaken in order to sign an association agreement
In force 1995–2004	Development-oriented reduced tariff rates on non-sensible products. EBA clause for the 45 least developed countries

The priorities set in the action plans will then be a reference for the financial support provided by the EU to the countries concerned. Assistance from existing sources – mainly the TACIS and MEDA programmes (concerning the former Soviet Republic and the southern Mediterranean countries, respectively) – will be complemented by a new financial instrument proposed for inclusion in the 2007–13 Financial Perspectives, the

Table 10.5 The external role of the EU before and after the enlargement (2002 data)

	EU-15	EU-25
Population, million (% world)	379 (6.1)	455 (7.3)
GDP, € billion (% world)	9275 (26.9)	9712 (28.7)
Total external trade, € million	1977	1999
Share in world trade, goods & services	20.1	19.8
Degree of openness	21.1	19.9

Source: European Commission DG Trade, COMEXT and AMECO databases.

Table 10.6 The structure of EU trade before and after the enlargement (2002 data)

EU-15 exports	EUR bn	%	EU-25 exports	EUR bn	%
Total	993.7	100.0	Total	900.3	100.0
USA	239.9	24.1	USA	244.7	27.2
Switzerland	70.6	7.1	Switzerland	72.6	8.1
Japan	42.3	4.3	Japan	43.0	4.8
China	34.1	3.4	China	34.8	3.9
Russia	30.4	3.1	Russia	34.2	3.8
Norway	26.5	2.7	Norway	27.9	3.1
Total for main partners	443.9	44.7	Total for main partners	457.2	50.8
EU-15 imports	**EUR bn**	**%**	**EU-25 imports**	**EUR bn**	**%**
Total	987.5	100.0	Total	940.7	100.0
USA	174.6	17.7	USA	181.0	19.2
China	81.8	8.3	China	89.6	9.5
Japan	68.5	6.9	Japan	73.3	7.8
Switzerland	58.8	6.0	Russia	61.9	6.6
Russia	47.7	4.8	Switzerland	61.5	6.5
Norway	45.8	4.6	Norway	47.3	5.0
Total for main partners	477.3	48.3	Total for main partners	514.5	54.7

Source: European Commission DG Trade, COMEXT database.

'European Neighbourhood Instrument'. Such a new budget item will explicitly focus on cross-border cooperation along the external border of the enlarged EU (see Chapter 6 for further details). If accepted, the Instrument will substantially increase the funding available for external assistance programmes, set at €255 million for the period 2004–6.

Finally, the ENP also strongly encourages regional and subregional cooperation, in order to create wider areas of shared peace and stability and larger local markets among the neighbouring countries. The issue of establishing regional integration networks among less developed countries is in fact of paramount importance to allow the same countries to grasp the full benefits of the continuing process of trade liberalisation, as will be made clear in the next section, where we analyse the role of the World Trade Organisation.

10.4 THE EU AND THE WORLD TRADE ORGANISATION

10.4.1 From GATT to WTO

The first attempts to create an international agency dedicated to the management of worldwide trade issues originated from the same post-World War II spirit that gave birth to such famous multilateral institutions as the International Monetary Fund (IMF) and the World Bank. In 1946, a project was also put forward to create an International Trade Organisation (ITO). During the negotiations on the ITO, 23 countries[16] reached an agreement to reduce some 45 000 different tariffs in place at the time, limited to manufacturing products (goods) but affecting $10 billion of trade, about one-fifth of the world's total. Pending the ratification of the ITO, the 23 countries agreed to start anticipating among themselves some of the trade rules contained in the draft ITO Charter, and thus wrote a provisional agreement in order to secure the tariff concessions they had negotiated. The combined package of trade rules and tariff concessions became known as the **General Agreement on Tariffs and Trade** (GATT) and entered into force in January 1948. The 23 countries became founding GATT members (officially, 'contracting parties'). In 1950, the United States government finally announced that it would not seek Congressional ratification of the ITO: the project was effectively dead. Even though it was provisional, the GATT thus remained the only multilateral instrument governing international trade from 1948, until the World Trade Organisation (WTO) was established in 1995.

Although provisional, the GATT was successful. In a series of trade negotiations known as rounds, the participating countries agreed to lower the average tariffs on traded goods from 50 per cent in 1946 to less than 4 per cent

Table 10.7 History of the GATT/WTO

Year	Place	Issues	No. of countries
1947	Geneva	Tariffs and duties on goods	23
1949	Annecy	Tariffs and duties on goods	13
1951	Torquay	Tariffs and duties on goods	38
1956	Geneva	Tariffs and duties on goods	26
1960–61 (Dillon Round)	Geneva	Tariffs and duties on goods	26
1964–67 (Kennedy Round)	Geneva	Tariffs and duties on goods Anti-dumping measures	62
1973–79 (Tokyo Round)	Geneva	Tariffs and duties on goods Non-tariff barriers	102
1986–94 (Uruguay Round)	Punta del Este Geneva Marrakesh	Tariffs and duties on goods Non-tariff barriers General Agreement on Services (GATS) Intellectual Property (TRIPS) MFA (textiles) Agreement on agriculture (AoA)	123
Creation of WTO (1 January 1995)			
1999 (Millennium Round)	Seattle	Tariffs and duties on goods Non-tariff barriers Agriculture	147[a]
2001–. . . (Development Round)	Doha Cancùn	Services Intellectual property Competition and investments Environment Development	

Note: [a] The WTO requires a formal membership procedure. In 2004, 147 countries were members, and 30 more observers. Observer countries are due to start negotiations for membership within five years of becoming observers.

in 1999. The number of GATT signatory parties also increased over time, from the original 23 to more than 120, as shown in Table 10.7. By the mid-1980s, however, the 40-years-old GATT started to be put under strain by the process of globalisation of economic activities and the ensuing change in the structure of trade flows across the world. More than 120 states, especially developing countries, were now participating in the GATT, and thus, apart from the liberalisation of trade in goods, new exigencies were emerging (the liberalisation of trade in agriculture and services, the guarantee of property rights, and so on) and had to be dealt with by the organisation. As a result, a new round of negotiations was launched in Punta de l'Este (Uruguay) in 1986, with the round becoming known as the **Uruguay Round**. Because of its complex agenda, the Uruguay Round went on for more than the originally foreseen five years, and only in December 1993, in Geneva, was a comprehensive agreement found on all the matters under discussion. The agreement was then signed in Marrakesh in 1994. The Round was, however, the most far-reaching and the most successful in the history of the organisation.

Among the main achievements of the Uruguay Round, alongside a series of decisions on the type of trade tools (tariffs, quotas, NTBs) that countries are allowed to use in international trade disputes, analysed later, we may mention the following:

- an overall reduction of tariffs and duties on manufactured goods by 38 per cent;
- the progressive abolition of quotas on trade in textiles and apparel by 2005, with the abolition of the **Multi-Fibre Arrangement**;[17]
- a **General Agreement on Trade in Services** (GATS), liberalising trade in crucial sectors such as telecommunications and financial services;[18]
- an **Agreement on Agriculture** (AoA), leading to an increase in access to the EU and US markets for developing countries' agricultural products (an issue already discussed in Chapter 7 when analysing the MacSharry reform of CAP).
- an **Agreement on Trade Related Intellectual Property rights** (TRIPs), establishing minimum levels of protection that each government has to give to the intellectual property of other countries (copyrights, patents, industrial design, geographical indications), as well as common rules on the enforcement of such protection.

Most importantly, the Uruguay Round saw the birth of the **World Trade Organisation**, which replaced from 1995 the GATT in handling all trade issues at the multilateral level. Contrary to the GATT, the WTO is not a provisional agreement, but has the status of an international organisation, sitting in Geneva. Therefore it is not composed of 'contracting parties', but of member countries, admitted through a formal procedure and after the agreement of all the other participating members. Also unlike the GATT, the WTO is not limited to trade in goods, but has a very broad competence, extended to services and all other general trade issues, for example related to issues like the environment, competition, investment, and so on. Last but not least, the WTO constitutes the most notable exception to the principle of national sovereignty codified by international law, since it is the only international (multilateral) organisation endowed with a binding system of dispute settlements, the so-called **Dispute Settlement Body**.[19] Member states are therefore obliged to follow the recommendations issued by the WTO if they want to avoid countersanctions by other members. Essentially a dispute arises when a country (*A*) adopts a trade policy measure or takes some action that one or more fellow-WTO members (*B*) consider to be breaking the WTO agreements, or when the same country *A* fails to live up to its obligations. The country (or group of countries) *B* can then appeal to the WTO for settling the dispute. A third group of countries can eventually declare that they also have an interest in the case and join.

Although a procedure for settling disputes existed under the old GATT, it had no fixed timetables, rulings were easier for countries to block and many cases dragged on for a long time inconclusively. The WTO procedure is instead binding, that is, countries are forced to comply, and it entails a limited length of time for a case to be settled (usually, no more than 15 months for the full procedure, including eventual appeals by the parties, with accelerated procedures if the case is considered urgent). Given its novelty and importance, the working of the dispute settlement mechanism is explained in greater detail in Box 10.1.

BOX 10.1 SANCTIONS AT THE WTO

If country *A* that is the target of the complaint loses its case before the Dispute Settlement Body, it must follow the recommendations set in the report produced by the panel of judges appointed to the case (or the appeal report, if it has presented an appeal during the process). If suddenly complying with the recommendations proves impractical, country *A* will be given a 'reasonable period of time' to do so. If it fails to act within this period, it has to enter into negotiations with the complaining country (or countries) *B*, in order to determine mutually acceptable compensation: for instance, tariff reductions in areas of particular interest to the complaining side. If no satisfactory compensation is agreed, country *B* may ask the Dispute Settlement Body for permission to impose limited trade sanctions ('suspend concessions or obligations') against country *A*. The Dispute Settlement Body must grant this authorization within 30 days. In principle, the sanctions should be imposed in the same sector in which the dispute has arisen. If this is not practical, or if it would not be effective given the trade pattern of the countries considered, the sanctions can be imposed in a different sector of the same agreement. In turn, if this is not effective or practicable and if the circumstances are serious enough, the action can be taken under another agreement. The objective is, however, to minimise the chances of actions spilling over into unrelated sectors while at the same time allowing the actions to be effective.

For example, on 23 January 1995, Venezuela complained to the Dispute Settlement Body that the United States was applying rules that discriminated against gasoline imports, imposing stricter rules on the chemical characteristics of imported gasoline than for domestically refined gasoline, and thus violating the 'national treatment' principle (see below). Just over a year later (on 29 January 1996) the dispute panel completed its final report. By then, Brazil had also joined the case, lodging its own complaint in April 1996, so the same panel considered both complaints. The United States appealed. The Appellate Body completed its report, and the Dispute Settlement Body adopted the report on 20 May 1996, one year and four months after the complaint was first lodged, condemning the United States. The agreed period for implementing a solution (the 'reasonable period of time') was 15 months from the date the appeal was concluded (20 May 1996 to 20 August 1997). Within this period, the United States, in agreement with Venezuela, amended its regulations and, on 26 August 1997, reported to the Dispute Settlement Body that a new regulation had been signed on 19 August.

10.4.2 Common Commercial Policy and Multilateral Rules

The previously analysed EU pyramid of preferences develops along its height the **bilateral level** of the EU trade relationships, that is the agreements autonomously decided by the Union with its partner countries. However, as already recalled, the tools employed by the EU in its bilateral relationships are not independent of the basis of the pyramid: the rules that are decided at the **multilateral level** (among all participating countries) within the World Trade Organisation.

The latter rules can be reduced to four basic principles: reciprocity, consensus, tariff binding and non-discrimination. The **reciprocity principle** establishes that WTO members have symmetric rights and obligations, and should obtain mutually beneficial reductions of trade barriers, therefore setting up a multilateral system of trade liberalisation. In practice, since every country starts from a different degree of openness to international trade, the principle ensures for the contracting parties balanced (that is, reciprocated) tariff reductions from the starting equilibrium, rather than an equal market access for everyone.

As we have seen in Chapter 2, such a principle is only partly consistent with standard theoretical predictions, which show that a unilateral (that is, not necessarily a reciprocal) tariff reduction is already optimal from a single country's point of view. However we have also shown that standard results change if we consider 'non-small' countries: in this case, countries can achieve an 'optimal' degree of protectionism, itself a function of the trade strategy of the other countries; thus large countries do not have incentives to cut tariffs unilaterally. The reciprocity principle corrects this imbalance, facilitating tariff reductions. In fact large countries can be assured that, once they reduce a tariff, thanks to reciprocity they can impose the same tariff reduction on their counterpart, essentially on a quid pro quo basis, thus offsetting the adverse terms of trade effects resulting for them from a unilateral trade liberalisation. As a result, a mutual agreement on a more liberal trade policy can be reached more easily (Bagwell and Staiger, 1999).

Under the **principle of consensus**, any decision taken within the WTO requires unanimity of all the participating countries. Although the need to reach a unanimous consensus might seem highly inefficient, given the high number of heterogeneous member countries belonging to the organisation, as a matter of fact countries often negotiate in **coalitions** centred on the main trading partners. Historically some of the most difficult negotiations have in fact been cleared with an initial breakthrough in talks among the four largest members, the United States, the European Union, Canada and Japan, known as the 'Quadrilaterals' or the **Quads**, with developing countries playing alongside one of the Quads. However, after the closure of the Uruguay Round, new coalitions of developing countries started to emerge, thanks to the pivotal role played by large DCs like India or Brazil. As will be discussed later, such a change in the political panorama of negotiations is dramatically shifting the traditional balance of powers at the WTO, with consequences yet to be understood, given also the still unclear attitude currently presented by China, the newest (2001) of the large WTO members..

In order to guarantee the enforcement of the decisions undertaken, the **tariff binding principle** ensures that, once a tariff reduction has been negotiated and accepted, it becomes 'bound' at the negotiated rate: a tariff cannot be subsequently increased above the bound rate without incurring sanctions. The tariff binding principle is important, since promising not to raise a trade barrier can be as important as lowering one: such a promise in fact gives businesses a clearer view of their future trade opportunities. Table 10.8 shows the contribution of the Uruguay Round to the tariff binding principle, showing how virtually all tariffs in developed countries and a large, increasing, number in developing countries are now bound.

Last but not least, the WTO negotiations are based on the **principle of non-discrimination**. The goal is to eliminate any form of discrimination in

Table 10.8 Percentages of tariffs bound before and after the Uruguay Round

	Before 1986	After 1994
Developed countries	78%	99%
Developing countries	21%	73%
Transition economies	73%	98%

Source: WTO Secretariat; percentages are calculated over the total number of tariff lines, hence not weighted by trade volumes.

international trade. In particular two clauses, enforced by the WTO regulations, rule out major forms of discrimination in international trade: the **national treatment** (NT) rule requires that, once foreign products enter an importing country, they should be accorded a treatment equal to that guaranteed to similar national products;[20] the **most-favoured-nation** (MFN) clause, on the other hand, states that all WTO members should receive from a given home country the same treatment as that accorded to the partner country that receives the best (most favoured) treatment. Therefore, if enforced, the MFN clause should guarantee that the tariff rate on any given product would be uniform across trading partners, at the lowest level.

The non-discrimination principle is therefore a key pillar of the WTO strategy, and hence it is not the case that the application of both the MFN and the NT rules are in general the main object of disputes among countries, as already seen from Box 10.1. The principle is also at the heart of a traditional debate among economists (starting from Keynes, during the GATT negotiations) between **multilateralism** and **regionalism**. It is worth recalling here our discussion in Chapter 2 about the setting up of regional integration agreements (RIAs). In fact, it is now clear that, when a WTO member signs a regional integration agreement such as an FTA or a CU, in principle it violates the MFN rule, since it grants more favourable conditions to its partners in the agreement than to other WTO members. Many economists therefore claim that regionalism (the tendency of countries to enter into preferential trade arrangements of a regional nature) leads to a less efficient trade system with respect to the multilateral reduction of trade barriers, guaranteed by the full application of the MFN clause.[21]

However, other arguments, often of a non-economic nature, are in favour of regionalism. In particular, they point to the fact that, if a group of countries completely abolishes internal trade restrictions, then such a group of countries can be considered as a single nation from the trade point of view: this translates, in political terms, into a step towards the multilateral goal of free trade for all. For example, services, intellectual property, environmental standards, investment and competition policies are all issues that were first raised within negotiations on RIAs, and only later developed into agreements or topics of discussion in the WTO. In a sense, therefore, regionalism offers a dynamic time path towards global free trade which seems to be more politically feasible than the multilateral negotiations, although at the cost of a loss in economic efficiency (Bhagwati, 1999).

Implicitly recognising the validity of the latter arguments, Paragraphs 4 to 10 of Article XXIV of GATT allow for regional integration agreements to be considered as an exception to the MFN rule. In particular it is stated that, if a free trade area or customs union is created (only these types of RIAs are allowed), duties and other trade barriers should be reduced or removed in substantially all sectors, in order to achieve the 'single nation' status. In any case, non-members should not find trade with the newly created group any more restrictive than before the group was set up, in order to ensure that regionalism acts as a complement to multilateralism.

As shown by the previously discussed data, the CCP of the European Union has undoubtedly contributed to international economic liberalisation, and hence in this case regionalism and multilateralism seem to have been mutually reinforcing. However, it is also true that the EU pyramid of preferences has generated some fragmentation of global markets (Panagariya, 2002), especially when the EU has favoured the so-called **hub and spoke** preferential trade agreements, negotiating bilateral concessions with each developing country or region individually (as with the southern Mediterranean countries or MercoSur). In this respect, nevertheless, we have seen that the new neighbourhood policy of the EU, strongly encouraging regional cooperation among all partners, is likely to change the situation.

But how have the principles at the root of the WTO trading system, just analysed, influenced or constrained the development of the EU common commercial policy? It is worth elaborating a scheme where we show the impact of the WTO rules on the various tools normally employed by the CCP. The exercise is presented in Table 10.9. As can be seen, WTO rules affect the definition of the EU commercial policy essentially in two ways. On the one hand, they constrain, through the negotiated tariff bounds, the level of the Common External Tariff applied by the EU Customs Union on the different products. On the other hand, on the basis of the non-discrimination principle, they limit the range of tools available for the CCP essentially to two: tariff rates and anti-dumping measures, the latter nowadays extensively used by the EU and therefore analysed in some detail in Box 10.2. Other tools, extensively employed by the EU in the past, such as quotas and the so-called 'voluntary export restraints' (VER) are now ruled

Table 10.9 The impact of WTO rules on the Common Commercial Policy

CCP tool before WTO	WTO rule	CCP tool after WTO
Average tariffs on manufactured goods at 6% of import values (1995)	Reduction of at least 38% by year 2000	Average tariffs on manufactured goods at 3.7% of import values in year 2000
Average tariffs on agricultural goods at 26% of import values (1995)	Reduction of at least 38% by year 2000	Average tariffs on agricultural goods at 18.4% of import values in year 2000
Quotas on textiles and other agricultural products	Banned under WTO	Multi-fibre arrangement dismantled in 2005. Other quotas progressively abolished
Voluntary Export Restraints	Banned under WTO	Abolished
Anti-dumping measures	Allowed	Extensively used by the EU also as a protectionist tool

Source: Authors' elaboration from European Commission and WTO official documents.

out.[22] The latter changes came as a consequence of the agreements undertaken within the Uruguay Round, according to which almost all import restrictions that did not take the form of tariffs, such as quotas, had to be converted to tariffs, a process known as **tariffication**.

Having assessed how the multilateral rules work, and how they affect the EU common commercial policy, we can now analyse the main current issues under negotiation at the WTO between the Union and its counterparts.

BOX 10.2 DUMPING AND ANTI-DUMPING MEASURES

Sometimes a company might decide to penetrate new markets by aggressively underpricing a product. When the company exports this product at what is considered to be an unfair price, that is, lower than the price it normally charges on its own home market or lower than its average cost of production, it is said to be *dumping* the product. The action distorts competition, since through dumping the exporter will harm domestic producers, acquire market shares and then eventually use its increased market power to the detriment of local consumers, raising the price once it has conquered the new market. As a result, many governments take action against dumping. The problem is, however, that, in order to pass protectionist policies, governments tend too often to declare that an imported product is 'dumped' on their market. To clear up the issue, an 'Anti-Dumping Agreement' has therefore been negotiated, disciplining the way governments can or cannot react to dumping. Broadly speaking the WTO agreement allows governments to act against dumping where there is genuine ('material') injury to the competing domestic industry. In order to do that, the government (or the European Commission, in the EU case) has to be able to show that dumping is taking place, calculate the extent or 'margin' of dumping (how much lower the export price is compared to the exporter's home market price) and show that the dumping is causing injury or threatening to do so on the domestic market (very small margins of dumping, lower than 2 per cent, or negligible volumes of dumped imports, less than 3 per cent of total imports, do not justify a government's action). If the dumping has been proved true and significant, countries are allowed to react in a way that would normally break the WTO principles of binding tariffs and not discrimination, that is, they can charge extra import duties on the particular product from the particular exporting country in order to bring its price closer to the 'normal value' (thus compensating the margin of dumping) and remove the injury to the domestic industry.

Since the calculation of dumping is the critical issue, the agreement narrows down the range of possible options, providing three methods to calculate a product's 'normal value' from which to derive the margin of dumping. The main one is based on the price in the exporter's domestic market. When this cannot be used, two alternatives are available: the price charged by the exporter in another country, or a calculation based on the combination of the exporter's production costs, other expenses and normal profit margins. Since the different methods yield different answers, countries have an incentive to use the method which maximises the dumping effect, in order to be able to impose more protectionist measures. In June 2004, for example, a dispute arose between the EU and China on whether China had the status of a 'market economy', which the EU was neglecting. The issue might seem of a political nature, but in reality it boiled down to whether the first method for the calculus of dumping (the price in the exporter's domestic market) or alternative ones had to be used. If China was not considered a market economy, then the first method for calculating dumping, not convenient for the EU in the case in question, could not be used; instead, using the alternative methods, a larger dumping could be proved to exist and therefore duties imposed on China imports.

10.5 THE DOHA ROUND OF TRADE NEGOTIATIONS AND THE ROLE OF THE EU

After the closure of the Uruguay Round, the newly established WTO started from 1995 to monitor the implementation of the agreements arising from the round. In particular, the WTO General Agreement on Trade in Services (GATS) committed member governments to undertake further negotiations on specific issues (public procurement, transport) and, no later than the year 2000, to enter into successive rounds of negotiations to progressively liberalise trade in services. Also the implementation of the TRIPS agreement on intellectual property was delicate, since a balance had to be found between the long-term benefits of intellectual property protection (increased incentives to invest in R&D) and possible short-term costs to society (such as the cost of using a particular drug).

Moreover, having the Uruguay Round solved several pending trade issues and with the globalisation of economic activities producing more and more interdependencies among countries, the ground was ready to start discussing new questions that were arising at the multilateral level, related to the interaction of trade with other policy areas such as competition, investment, environment, and so on. Ministers from WTO member countries therefore decided at the 1996 Singapore Ministerial Conference to set up three new working groups: on trade and investment, on competition policy and on transparency in government procurement.[23] These issues are known as the **Singapore issues**. A comprehensive work programme also started on **trade and environment**, with the creation of the Trade and Environment Committee, thus bringing environmental and sustainable development issues into the mainstream of WTO work. Last but not least, extensive discussions also started on **core labour standards**, essential standards applied to the way workers are treated.

In order to start formalising a comprehensive negotiation on all these issues, the member countries met in Seattle, in November 1999, to launch a new round of multilateral liberalisation, named the 'Millennium Round'. The meeting was a complete failure. For the first time, in fact, a compact, organised coalition of developing countries, led mainly by India, was opposing any further progress on the new Singapore issues, unless more flexibility was guaranteed on the implementation of the Uruguay Round agreements, less than five years old, together with a greater access to markets of developed countries, especially in agriculture. On the other side, the two largest Quads, the United States and the European Union, were in disagreement on several points of the agenda, starting from the way in which the works should proceed.[24] Also for the first time, a large and organised protest by non-governmental organisations was staged outside the meeting rooms of delegates, giving voice to the so-called 'Seattle' or 'no-global' movement, a complex mix of voices and often conflicting interests protesting against the ways in which the globalisation of economic activities is managed by governments worldwide.[25]

The failure of the Seattle meeting has however helped to clarify several issues. First of all, it is clear that, within the WTO, the political economy of negotiations (whereby the mechanism and equilibria behind the coalition formation of the organisation are defined) now needs to take into account also the coalitions of developing countries, who might take a political stance of their own. As a result, the developed countries, outnumbered by the developing ones in terms of votes, have now to find a common strategy if they want to retain some bargaining power. Even more relevant, the intensity of protests which surrounded the Seattle meeting revealed that moving from GATT to WTO had profoundly changed the organisation, not only in legal terms, but also, and especially, in its political dimension. The WTO is an international organisation with a very broad mandate and, for the first time, endowed with a binding mechanism for trade disputes. As such, it has a significant political influence on various issues related to the management of globalisation; therefore it has to be accountable to public opinion, guaranteeing the transparency of its work, a characteristic which was completely lacking before the Seattle meeting.

Member countries and the WTO took two years to learn from their mistakes.[26] at the Fourth Ministerial Conference in Doha, Qatar, in November 2001, WTO member governments finally agreed to launch new negotiations on all the issues originally on the agenda in Seattle. The entire package, called the **Doha Development Agenda** (DDA), is still under discussion, having already missed (like the early stage of the Uruguay Round) several previously set deadlines.

In what follows we present a broad overview of the different negotiations of the DDA, together with the position of the main counterparts, in particular of the European Union.[27] As a synthesis, the overview is neither exhaustive nor extremely detailed, in that other agreements on more specific topics are being negotiated, and several exceptions or particular procedures exist for specific aspects of the agreements herein presented. The interested reader should therefore refer to the WTO website (http://www.wto.org) for a complete and continuously updated status of the negotiations on each topic.

10.5.1 Agriculture

In Doha, member governments committed themselves to comprehensive negotiations on agriculture, with a three-pillar approach: an increase in the **access to markets** of developed countries; reductions of **domestic support** measures that distort trade flows; and reduction, with a view to phasing out, of all **export subsidies**. The negotiations explicitly state a special and differential treatment for developing countries, which should be able to meet their needs in food security and rural development issues. The ministers, under pressure from the European Union, decided to take into account in the negotiations also the so-called '**non-trade concerns**' (such as environmental protection, food security and rural development) thus recovering also within the WTO the concept of multifunctionality currently at the root of the EU common agricultural policy (see Chapter 7).

In terms of market access, the new rule in agricultural products is 'tariffs only'. As we have seen, before the Uruguay Round some agricultural imports were restricted by quotas and other non-tariff measures, trade tools that are not allowed any more. As a result, these tools have now been replaced by tariffs that provide more or less equivalent levels of protection,[28] that is, the exercise of tariffication previously mentioned. Quite obviously, countries disagree on the modalities and the rates at which tariffication has to be implemented, and hence negotiations are taking place on this issue, as well as on special safeguards that governments might want to introduce in order to prevent swiftly falling prices or surges in imports from harming their farmers.

As far as domestic support is concerned, the main complaint about these kinds of policies is that they encourage overproduction, resulting in the squeezing out of imports or the emergence of export subsidies and low-priced dumping on world markets, as we have seen when studying the EU common agricultural policy. The Agriculture Agreement in particular distinguishes between support programmes that stimulate production directly and those that are considered to have no direct effect. Domestic policies that do have a direct effect on production and trade enter the so-called

amber box (a reference to the amber colour of traffic lights, which means 'slow down') and should be cut back.[29] Therefore, as we have seen in Chapter 7, if direct aid granted by the European Union to farmers is linked to production, this violates the WTO agreements, and should be reformed, an undertaking the Union has started to tackle with the June 2003 reform of the CAP. On the contrary, measures with minimal impact on trade can be used freely (they are listed in a **green box**, indicating road clear as with traffic lights). They include payments made directly to farmers that do not stimulate production, such as direct aid linked to the concept of potential income (see Chapter 7), help to farmers for restructuring agriculture, and direct payments under environmental and regional assistance programmes (the rural development chapter of the CAP, for example). Also permitted are certain direct payments to farmers where the farmers are required to limit production called '**blue box**' measures (such as the set-aside measures under the CAP), certain government assistance programmes to encourage agricultural and rural development in developing countries, and other support which takes place on a small scale (***de minimis*** rule), when compared with the total value of the product or products supported (5 per cent or less in the case of developed countries, and 10 per cent or less for developing countries). The latter exception, however, is currently under discussion, because of the distortions it is creating in some sectors (such as cotton, whose production is heavily subsidised by the United States under this rule).

As regards export subsidies, the Agriculture Agreement simply prohibits them, unless the subsidies are specified in a member's list of commitments. If listed, the agreement requires WTO members to cut both the amount of money they spend on export subsidies and the quantities of exports that receive subsidies. Taking averages for 1986–90 as the base level, developed countries agreed to cut the value of export subsidies by 36 per cent over six years, starting in 1995 (24 per cent over ten years for developing countries). Developed countries also agreed to reduce the quantities of subsidised exports by 21 per cent over the six years (14 per cent over ten years for developing countries). Least-developed countries do not need to make any cuts.

Apart from the dividing line between developed and developing countries, agriculture negotiations are also complicated because of the diverging goals within developed countries. Large countries practising intensive industrial-style agriculture, such as Canada, the USA or Australia, are broadly in favour of more free trade for agricultural products, which basically amounts to denying any specificity of agriculture, although still retaining some distortive measures in specific sectors. The EU, on the contrary, is attached to the multifunctional character of agriculture (see

Chapter 7) and therefore tends to ensure some protection for the agricultural markets, based on regulations for non-trade concerns.

The EU broadly agrees with the three-pillar agenda set in Doha. In particular, it agrees to: (1) open markets for farm imports by slashing tariffs; (2) to cut trade-distorting farm support measures under the amber box; (3) to scale back all forms of export subsidies, on the condition that all forms of export subsidisation and distorting domestic support measures from other countries (especially the USA) are treated on an equal footing. The EU also agrees on granting special treatment for developing countries, to ensure that they fully benefit from the expansion of world trade. The special treatment means increased market access for them, while accepting the need for the most fragile developing countries to maintain protection in order to have adequate time for adaptation.

Owing to their technical difficulty, and the contrasting desiderata of countries, the negotiations on agriculture are one of the main stumbling blocks on the road to a successful outcome of the Doha Round. The most recent progress in negotiations achieved at the July 2004 WTO General Council,[30] however, allows a certain degree of optimism in their positive conclusions.

10.5.2 Services

Negotiations on services were already almost two years old when they were incorporated into the new Doha agenda, since they officially started in early 2000, while in March 2001 the negotiating guidelines and procedures were agreed upon. The Doha Declaration thus endorses the work already done, reaffirms the negotiating guidelines and procedures, and establishes some key elements of the timetable including, most importantly, an agreement for concluding the negotiations as part of a **single undertaking**, that is, with a comprehensive agreement on the different issues currently under discussion.

The contents of the talks include some of the disciplines not yet included in GATS: rules on emergency safeguard measures,[31] government procurement, electronic commerce and, possibly, air transport services. Work also started in 1995 to establish discipline on domestic regulations, the requirements that foreign service suppliers have to meet in order to operate in a local market. The focus is on qualification requirements and procedures, technical standards and licensing requirements. By December 1998, members had, for example, agreed disciplinary measures on domestic regulations for the accountancy sector. Since then, members have been engaging in developing general discipline for all professional services and, where necessary, additional sectoral discipline. As already stated, all the agreed disciplinary measures will be integrated into GATS and become legally binding once the comprehensive package is signed at the end of the current services negotiations.

As far as **government procurement** is concerned, the issue arises because in most countries the government, and the agencies it controls, are the biggest purchasers of goods of all kinds, ranging from basic commodities to high-technology equipment. As a result, the political pressure to favour domestic suppliers over their foreign competitors can be very strong. To prevent distortions, an Agreement on Government Procurement had already entered into force on 1 January 1981, with the purpose of opening up as much as possible this sector to international competition as well as making laws, regulations, procedures (especially tendering procedures) and practices regarding government procurement more transparent, avoiding discrimination against foreign products or suppliers. The agreement is, however, plurilateral: only 28 WTO members signed it, among them the European Union and the United States. In the Uruguay Round the coverage of the agreement was extended to services (including construction services), procurement at the subcentral level (for example, states, provinces, departments and prefectures) and procurement by public utilities. The new agreement took effect on 1 January 1996. Among the Singapore issues, as we have seen, talks have also started on whether it is possible to extend this agreement from the plurilateral level to the multilateral level (for all WTO members).

The Doha Declaration also endorses the work already done on **electronic commerce**. In particular, the declaration on electronic commerce from the Second Ministerial Conference in Geneva, 1998, said that WTO members will continue their practice of not imposing customs duties on electronic transmissions. The Doha Declaration states that members will continue this practice until the closure of the round, where possibly new arrangements could be undertaken.

Finally, at present, most of the **air transport sector** – traffic rights and services directly related to traffic rights – is excluded from the GATS coverage. However GATS mandates a review by members of this situation. The purpose of the review, which started in early 2000, is to decide whether additional air transport services should be covered by GATS. The review could develop into a negotiation in its own right, resulting in an amendment of GATS itself by adding new services to its coverage, and by adding specific commitments on these new services to national schedules.

10.5.3 TRIPS and Public Health

An issue that has arisen recently within the implementation of the TRIPS agreement is how to avoid the risk that patent protection for **pharmaceutical**

products prevents people in poor countries from having access to medicines, while at the same time maintaining the patent system's role in providing incentives for research and development into new medicines. Although flexibilities are foreseen in the TRIPS Agreement, some governments were unsure how these would be interpreted, and how far their right to use them would be respected. In this regard, a special declaration was issued at the Doha Ministerial Conference in November 2001. On that occasion countries agreed that the TRIPS Agreement does not and should not prevent members from taking measures to protect public health. In addition countries also agreed to extend exemptions on pharmaceutical patent protection for least-developed countries until 2016. Extra flexibility was also granted in August 2003, so that countries unable to produce pharmaceuticals domestically can now import patented drugs made under compulsory licensing in other developing countries, thus benefiting from the patent exception.

Another issue related to the TRIPS agreement of particular interest for the EU is related to the protection of **geographical indication**: a brand or label such as 'Champagne', 'Scotch', 'Roquefort', 'Parmigiano' or 'Chianti' does not only say where the product was made but also, and more importantly, identifies the product's special characteristics, which are the result of the product's origins. Clearly wines and spirits makers are particularly concerned about the use of place names to identify products, and the TRIPS Agreement contains special provisions for these products. However the issue is also important for other types of goods, since misusing the geographical indication, as in the controversy over 'parmesan' cheese, can mislead consumers, and it can lead to unfair competition. Countries are therefore obliged to prevent this misuse of place names, although some exceptions are allowed, for example if the name is already protected as a trademark or if it has become a generic term.[32] However, any country wanting to make an exception under these reasons must be willing to negotiate with the country which wants to protect the geographical indication in question.

As a result, further negotiations are necessary in order to establish a multilateral, more automatic and transparent system of notification and registration of geographical indications. The issue is particularly important for the EU, given the increased focus of its agricultural policy on quality goods highlighting particular, location-specific characteristics, a strategy that risks failing if inadequate protection for these products is not guaranteed at the multilateral level.

10.5.4 Trade, Competition and Investment: the 'Singapore' Issues

The close relationships between trade, investment and competition policy have long been recognised. As a result, over the years both GATT and the

WTO have increasingly dealt with specific aspects of these relationships. For example, one type of trade covered by the General Agreement on Trade in Services (GATS) is the supply of services by a foreign company setting up operations in a host country, through foreign investment. The **Trade-Related Investment Measures Agreement** (TRIM) negotiated within the Uruguay Round also says that investors' right to use imported goods as inputs should not depend on their export performance, therefore constraining the imposition of specific rules on multinational companies by host governments.

The same goes for competition policy. The agreements on both goods and services at the WTO contain rules on monopolies and exclusive service suppliers. The principles have been elaborated thoroughly in the rules and commitments on telecommunications within GATS. Also the agreements on intellectual property and services recognise both governments' rights to act against anti-competitive practices, and their rights to work together to limit these practices.

As a result, in search of a comprehensive agreement, these subjects, together with transparency in government procurement, were originally on the Doha Development Agenda. However, for all these issues, the 2001 Doha declaration did not launch negotiations immediately, postponing them until the Fifth Ministerial Conference in Cancùn in 2003. The failure of the latter meeting then led the WTO in 2004 finally to remove these issues from the Doha agenda.

10.5.5 Trade and Environment

Currently there are about 200 international agreements in force (outside the WTO) dealing with various environmental issues, in general called **multilateral environmental agreements** (MEAs). About 20 of these include provisions that can affect trade: for example they ban trade in certain products, or allow countries to restrict trade in certain circumstances. Disputes often arise, given the increased environmental sensibility of developed countries (especially the European Union) and the suspicious attitude of developing countries, which tend to consider trade restrictions for environmental purposes as hidden forms of protectionism.

Hence negotiations on trade and environment are currently going on within the Doha Development Round, and are essentially based on two important principles: (a) the WTO is only competent to deal with trade-related aspects of environmental issues, that is, its only task is to study questions that arise when environmental policies and trade rules affect one another, leaving the definition of national or international environmental policies or standards to other specialised agencies; b) the solution to any controversy arising in the field must continue to uphold the principles of the WTO trading system of non-discrimination, consensus, tariff binding and reciprocity.

Clearly the relationship between trade rules and environmental policies is multifaceted: environmental rules can affect trade flows; specific actions taken on trade flows can play a positive, important role in some environmental agreements (for example, lower tariffs for environmentally friendly products or services such as catalytic converters, air filters or consultancy services on wastewater management); trade facilitation in certain products can be a direct cause of the environmental problems, as with the controversy reported in Box 10.3.

As a result of these complex interactions, however, it is clear that, when studying the relationship between trade and environment, trade restrictions are not the only actions that can be undertaken, and they are not necessarily the most effective. Alternatives include helping countries acquire environmentally friendly technology, giving them financial assistance and providing training. Negotiations are thus focusing also on these issues. Finally another area of negotiation is related to the issue of **eco-labelling**, the requirement to indicate (or not) on a product some of its components (such as genetically modified organisms) that might be considered dangerous for the environment.[33]

10.5.6 Labour Standards

The discussion on labour standards, or the **social clause**, as it is sometimes called, relates to the definition worldwide of essential standards applied to the way workers are treated. The term clearly covers a wide range of issues: from the use of child labour and forced labour, to the right to organise trade unions and to strike. The subject has been discussed extensively within the WTO, because of its potential impact on trade, although never in a formalised forum. In particular, three broad questions emerge: whether trade actions should be permitted as a means of putting pressure on countries considered to be severely violating core labour rights; whether a country which applies lower standards for labour rights gains an unfair advantage; and whether the WTO is the proper place to discuss labour. Clearly all three questions have a political angle: developed countries (the USA and the EU in particular) agree in principle to use trade actions to impose labour standards, while for developing countries these are simply excuses for hidden forms of protectionism.[34]

Lacking a consensus on the issue, however, at the 1996 Singapore Ministerial Conference members identified the International Labour Organization (ILO) as the competent body to deal with labour standards.

BOX 10.3 THE SHRIMP–TURTLE CASE

In early 1997, India, Malaysia, Pakistan and Thailand jointly complained to the WTO against a ban imposed by the USA on the importation of certain shrimp and shrimp products. In order to prevent sea turtles being killed by fishing nets, in fact, the US Endangered Species Act of 1973 required US shrimp trawlers to use 'turtle excluder devices' (TEDs) in their nets when fishing for shrimps in areas where there is a significant likelihood of encountering sea turtles. As a consequence, US laws declared that shrimp harvested with a technology that may adversely affect sea turtles may not be imported into the USA, unless the harvesting nation was certified as having a regulatory programme and an incidental take-rate comparable to that of the USA, or the particular fishing environment of the harvesting nation did not pose a threat to sea turtles. In practice, countries that had sea turtles within their waters and harvested shrimp with mechanical means had to impose on their fishermen requirements comparable to those borne by US shrimpers if they wanted to be certified to export shrimp products to the USA. In its report, the WTO made clear that under its rules countries have the right to take trade actions to protect the environment (in particular, human, animal or plant life and health), provided certain criteria such as non-discrimination were met. However the USA lost the case: not because it sought to protect the environment but because it discriminated between WTO members. In fact it provided countries in the western hemisphere – mainly in the Caribbean – with technical and financial assistance and longer transition periods for their fishermen to start using turtle excluder devices. It did not give the same advantages, however, to the four Asian countries (India, Malaysia, Pakistan and Thailand) that filed the complaint to the WTO.

To expand the scope of the discussion, suppose instead that this trade dispute had arisen among member countries also signatories of an environmental agreement outside the WTO. Should the dispute be handled under the WTO or under the other agreement? The WTO says that, if a dispute arises over a trade action taken under an environmental agreement, and if both sides to the dispute have signed that agreement, then they should try to use the environmental agreement to settle the dispute. But if one side in the dispute has not signed the environment agreement, then the WTO will provide the only possible forum for settling the dispute.

As a result, there is currently no formal work on the subject in the WTO, although the countries concerned may continue their pressure for more work to be done in this forum.

10.5.7 The Political Economy of Negotiations from the EU Perspective

The Doha Development Round, once concluded, will push even further the liberalisation of trade flows worldwide and, as we have seen, will be the first comprehensive attempt to manage some of the more controversial issues arising from the globalisation of economic activity. The EU, as the largest world trading partner, has therefore a strong interest in the closure of the round, since this will entail, on average, a broader market access for EU products (especially services) and more transparent and generally agreed rules on sensitive issues like the environment. In addition, the focus of the round on the needs of developing countries is in principle entirely shared by the EU, which is already the largest donor of development aid in the world.

However, given the centrality of agriculture in the political economy of negotiations, the EU had to concede even more on its agricultural policy than the proposals put forward for the Fifth Ministerial Meeting in Cancùn, in 2003 (and analysed in Chapter 7). These proposals were in fact judged insufficient and essentially led to the failure of the conference. In May 2004, the Commission agreed on a proposal to abolish export subsidies completely, provided that other developed countries eliminate other trade-distorting measures. The resulting combined proposals were accepted in principle by the WTO members within the so-called **July 2004 package** on the Doha Agenda work programme, together with the decision of aborting any further negotiations on the Singapore issues, as we have seen.

It remains to be seen whether, after these concessions on agriculture and on the Singapore issues, the gains that the EU figures to make in other sectors (services, environment) will be enough to generate, within the single undertaking summarising all the negotiations, the agreement of the EU member states, and thus the final closure of the Doha Round.

10.6 THE INTERNATIONAL DIMENSION OF THE EU MONETARY POLICY

So far we have seen in what respect the Common Commercial Policy adds to the role of the EU within the issues of global governance, and to what extent the same policy is constrained by the multilateral agenda of trade liberalisation negotiated at the WTO. Although providing a substantial contribution, the CCP alone is not able to guarantee to the Union a political presence on the world stage comparable to that of the USA, since common actions are also needed in the field of monetary governance.

As already discussed in the introduction to this chapter, the operational decisions are still pending on the external representation of the Euro zone: whether the EU should speak with a single voice in multilateral fora such as the IMF or the World Bank, or enter a system of exchange rates. Therefore significant room for improvement exists in this area, given also the fact that, should the EU member states vote together at, say, the IMF, they would overcome the voting power of the USA, currently the largest member in the multilateral financial institutions. Nevertheless, even in this situation, the launch of the Euro, per se, has endowed the EU with a currency that is increasingly being used in international financial transactions, therefore contributing to the external role of the EU.

To look at this issue in more detail, we have first to assess what is in general the role of a currency. In particular, the economic literature traditionally identifies three main functions of a currency:

1. **means of exchange**: a currency can be used to conclude transactions, being the currency of denomination of exports or imports (for example, oil is traded in US dollars);
2. **unit of account**: a currency can be used as the unit of denomination of prices of financial assets (that is, the currency in which stocks or corporate bonds are denominated);
3. **store of value**: a currency can be used as the preferential tool to transfer purchasing power to the future, through the constitution of foreign exchange reserves of central banks, or being used as the vehicle currency[35] of exchange rate systems (for example, the US dollar in the Bretton Woods system analysed in Chapter 3).

The use of the Euro as a currency of settlement or invoicing for international trade transactions in selected Euro area countries has continued to increase. In 2002, for most Euro area countries the share of the Euro used for exports with non-Euro area residents was above 50 per cent for both goods and services, reaching levels close to 60 per cent in a few cases. Data on the currency breakdown of international trade of two of the Euro area's largest trade partners, namely Japan and the United Kingdom, broadly confirm this picture. It is worth noting, however, that the share of the Euro – relatively high when only bilateral transactions within the

European Union are considered – decreases substantially when trade with the rest of the world is examined. For instance, the Euro is the first currency used by Japan to export to the European Union, yet the Euro's share falls to below 10 per cent when all Japanese exports are considered. This is due to the still predominant role of the US dollar in the market of the main commodities (oil, metals, cereals and so on), a situation which is difficult to reverse for the EU since trade invoicing tends to be very strongly related to the political (and military) power of the country whose currency is used as a vehicle.

As unit of account, Figure 10.2 shows how the use of the Euro as a currency of emission of debt securities has increased by ten percentage points over the 1994–2003 period, significantly reducing its gap with respect to the US dollar.[36] The ECB (2003) reports that similar trends can be found when looking at non-securitised financial instruments, that is, the use of the Euro by non-Euro area residents in international loan markets. Figure 10.3 shows that the role of the Euro in the foreign exchange (FX) markets was broadly similar to that of the Deutschmark in the past. The Euro is the second currency (25 per cent of total) in FX trading, although the US dollar remains the preferred (50 per cent) vehicle currency, without any indication of changes in this allocation of portfolios.

Finally, as a store of value, around 40 non-EU countries use the Euro either as the sole anchor or reference currency for their exchange rates, or as part of the currency basket including the Euro as the anchor, with many of these countries being close to the Euro area and/or having established special institutional arrangements with the European Union (accession countries, as well as countries of the western Balkans, northern Africa and the CFA Franc Zone). In the rest of the world, however, the Euro only plays a very limited role as an anchor currency.

The situation is slightly better in terms of reserves. Since 2000, the share of the Euro in global foreign exchange reserves has been growing gradually, from 15.9 per cent to 18.7 per cent with both industrial and developing countries having increased their holdings of Euro-denominated reserve assets. Symmetrically the share of reserve holdings in US dollars decreased in 2002, in spite of an increase, in absolute terms, of central banks' reserves worldwide. The gradual increase in the share of the Euro can be partly explained by historical evidence, suggesting that the currency composition of reserves changes only gradually. Moreover there is a strong regional pattern in the recent build-up of foreign exchange reserves, as revealed in Table 10.10. This reflects a general trend whereby the currency composition of foreign exchange reserves is closely linked to the choice of an anchor currency as well as to trade invoicing (Eichengreen and Mathieson, 2000). Since the latter is a component in which the EU, as we have seen, is still

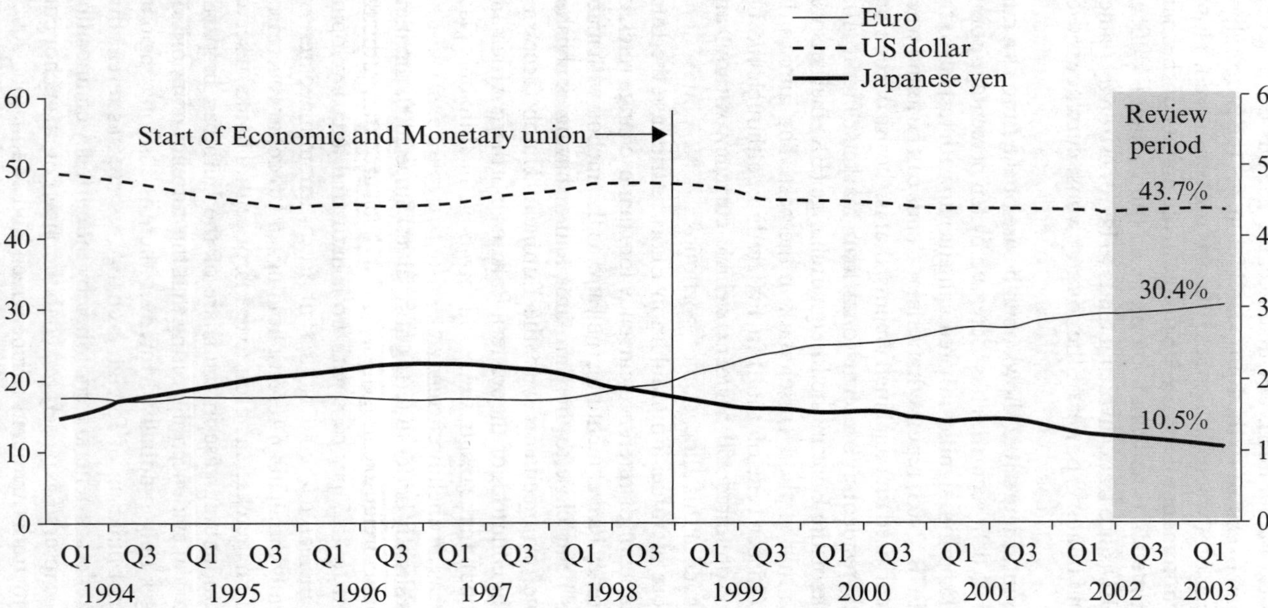

Note: International debt securities stock: currency shares (bonds and notes and money market instruments, excluding home currency issuance, as a percentage of the total amount outstanding and at 1994 QI exchange rates).

Source: ECB (2003).

Figure 10.2 The role of the Euro in international financial markets

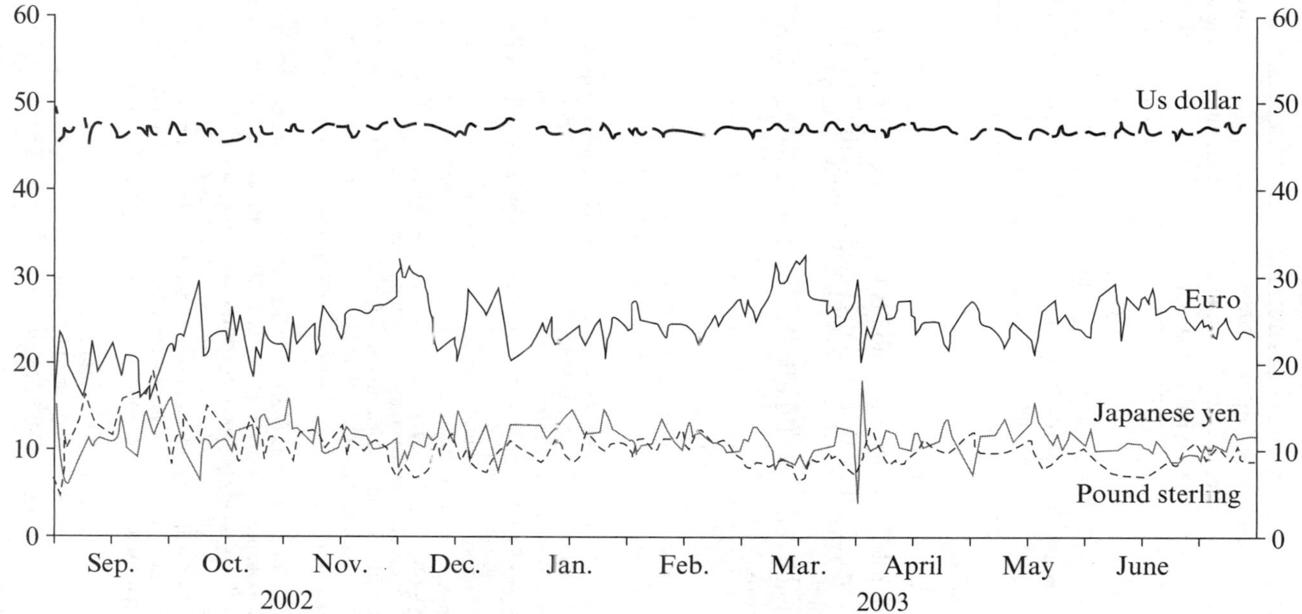

Source: ECB (2003).

Figure 10.3 The role of the Euro in foreign exchange markets

Table 10.10 The role of the Euro in Central Bank reserves

Region	Range of holdings of US dollars	Average holdings of US dollars	Range of holdings of Euro	Average holdings of Euro
Africa	40–100	62	0–30	18
Emerging Asia	24–85	60	0–16	6
Emerging Europe	1–80	39	11–98	50
Western Hemisphere	0–100	77	0–50	14
Total	**0–100**	**57**	**0–98**	**29**

Source: ECB (2003).

playing a minor role, because of its inability to construct a serious and credible common foreign policy, that prevents a major growth of the Euro as a reserve currency.

In the concluding chapter of the book, these latter considerations will be analysed in more detail.

NOTES

1. In particular, TEC, art. 111, para. 4 states that 'the Council, acting by a qualified majority on a proposal from the Commission and after consulting the ECB, shall decide on the position of the Community at international level as regards issues of particular relevance to economic and monetary union and on its representation'. The same TEC art. 111, paras 1 and 2, lays down the provisions relative to the management of the exchange rate of the Euro (including eventually the setting up of a system of exchange rates).
2. Yet the combined share of the exports of the three regions – the so-called Triad – declined from 56.1 per cent to 43.7 per cent between 1965 and 2002, indicating the growing role assumed by the emerging economies. Note also that the EU reported figures exclude intra-EU15 trade, which accounts for almost two-thirds of its total trade. Adding to this amount the trade with the new member states of Central and Eastern Europe, the intra-European trade would account for almost 80 per cent of the EU-25 trade.
3. See OECD (2000) or Messerlin (2001) for a detailed analysis of the effects of the CCP.
4. As recalled in Chapter 2, various tools can be used to influence the trade flows of a given country: tariffs (*ad valorem* or specific), quotas, non-tariff barriers (NTBs).
5. More specifically, the Commission conducts trade negotiations, the European Parliament eventually gives its endorsement and the Council finally approves them, according to the procedure set out in TEC, art. 300. We also recall that the tariffs' provisions constitute one of the sources of revenues for the EU budget, as analysed in Chapter 6.
6. In the pre-Nice version, the article also conferred powers on the EU institutions for dealing with trade issues in services and property rights, but required a unanimous decision by member states, rather than the more efficient qualified majority voting procedure.

7. Such an amendment to the new version of art. 133 agreed in Nice was strongly requested by France, where the protection of the cultural and linguistic heritage is a very sensitive political issue. For example, foreign movie advertising is forbidden on French TV.
8. In general exploiting to various extents the juridical base of art. 300 of the Treaty, previously discussed.
9. In particular, in the trade agreements the EU might grant free access to imports of manufactured goods and services from its trade partners, especially developing countries, without requesting a similar treatment for its exports, owing to the concerns for the competitiveness of the same developing countries. Similar provisions, albeit more limited in scope, exist for trade in some agricultural products.
10. Such as, for example, the definition of common standards in pythosanitary measures, or stricter cooperation in the field of the fight against fraud and the protection of property rights, and so on.
11. As will be made clear, the preferences offered by the GSP were violating the non-discrimination principle of the GATT/WTO, and hence they required a waiver which was granted in 1971 with the 'Enabling Clause' for a ten-year period, then renewed in 1979 for an indefinite period. More detailed information on the Generalised System of Preferences can be found at http://europa.eu.int/comm/trade/issues/global/gsp/index_en.htm.
12. Regulation (EC) 416/2001 was then incorporated into the GSP (Regulation 2501/2001). Only imports of fresh bananas, rice and sugar were not fully liberalised immediately. Duties on those products will be gradually reduced until duty-free access will be granted for bananas in January 2006, for sugar in July 2009 and for rice in September 2009.
13. We could place the EBA initiative somewhere in between the cooperation agreements and the GSP, since it is disciplined by a standard EU regulation, but it offers free trade access (not just a reduced CET) to the EU market.
14. For more updated information and the legal texts produced so far by the European Commission on the subject, see the ENP website: http://europa.eu.int/comm/world/enp/index_en.htm.
15. The so-called 'Barcelona process' originated in 1995 with all the Southern Mediterranean countries (Morocco, Algeria, Tunisia, Egypt, Israel, PNA, Syria, Lebanon, Jordan, Cyprus, Malta and Turkey) except Libya, and was centred on the three pillars of political, social and economic partnership. More information is available on the Commission's dedicated website: http://europa.eu.int/comm/external_relations/ euromed/index.htm.
16. The list is available at www.wto.org/english/thewto_e/gattmem_e.htm.
17. From 1974 until the end of the Uruguay Round, trade in textiles was governed by the Multi-Fibre Arrangement (MFA). This was a framework for bilateral agreements or unilateral actions that established quotas limiting imports into countries whose domestic industries were facing serious damage from rapidly increasing imports. Quotas were the most visible feature of the system, since they conflicted with GATT's general preference for customs tariffs instead of measures that restrict quantities. They were also exceptions to the GATT principle of treating all trading partners equally because they specified how much the importing country was going to accept from individual exporting countries. The MFA was dismantled on 1 January 2005, with trade in textiles finally homogenised to trade in standard goods.
18. The GATS is possibly the widest agreement negotiated at the Uruguay Round, and the one that has set the most significant future agenda in terms of subjects to be progressively liberalised. More information can be found at the WTO Services Gateway: http://www.wto.org/english/tratop_e/serv_e/serv_e.htm.
19. The European Court of Justice within the European Union is also endowed with binding powers with respect to national member states, but it is a regional, not a multilateral, institution.
20 Note that the NT rule ensures equal competitive opportunities to the imported products (for example, same tax rates, same sales or transport opportunities, same content requirements) only once they have entered the domestic market. It does not imply equal opportunities for the foreign products in the sense of zero tariff rates.

21. In particular, efficiency breaks down when FTA or CU are set up among countries that are not 'natural' partners, that is, countries that have similar income levels and governments that maximise similar welfare functions (Rivera-Batiz and Oliva, 2003, p. 598). The debate between regionalism and multilateralism has produced a great body of literature. Recent contributions in favour of multilateralism are Rivera-Batiz and Oliva (2003) and Tharakan (2002). Bhagwati (1999) provides a detailed analysis of this discussion, from both an economic and an historic perspective. Rose (2004) claims that multilateral rules negotiated at the GATT/WTO have been much less relevant in increasing trade flows among countries than regional integration agreements or other standard determinants of trade.
22. VER are arrangements between countries, usually negotiated bilateral agreements, in which suppliers in an exporting country (or their government) agree to limit to predetermined levels their exports of a particular product to an importing country. The WTO agreement states that members must not seek, take or maintain any voluntary export restraints, orderly marketing arrangements or any other similar measures on the export or the import side. The bilateral measures that were not modified to conform to the agreement were phased out at the end of 1998. Countries were allowed to keep one of these measures an extra year (until the end of 1999), but only the European Union – for its restrictions on imports of cars from Japan – made use of this provision, now dismantled.
23. They also instructed the WTO Goods Council to look at possible ways of simplifying trade procedures, an issue sometimes known as 'trade facilitation'.
24. The USA, having to face an electoral year in 2000, pressed for the closure of specific deals as soon as an agreement could be found, leaving more controversial issues for future negotiations. The EU, which had to compromise on agriculture in order to gain in other sectors, insisted instead on a comprehensive approach, in which no deal could be closed unless every deal was closed.
25. See Deutsch and Speyer (2001) for a detailed discussion of the Millennium Round failure.
26. The USA and the EU agreed on a common initial position to be presented at the negotiations, while the WTO significantly improved the transparency of its work through its website. A nice example of this improved transparency, quoting the WTO position on 'ten common misunderstandings' about trade talks, can be found at http://www.wto.org/english/thewto_e/whatis_e/10mis_e/10m00_e.htm.
27. We have used various sources for the elaboration of the overview, mostly through websites. The main reference, however, has been WTO (2003).
28. For example, if the previous policy generated domestic prices 75 per cent higher than world prices, then the new *ad valorem* tariff could be set at around 75 per cent.
29. WTO members calculated how much support of this kind they were providing per year for the agricultural sector (using calculations known as 'total aggregate measurement of support' or 'Total AMS') in the base years of 1986–88. Developed countries agreed to reduce these figures by 20 per cent over six years, starting in 1995. Developing countries agreed to make 13 per cent cuts over ten years. Least-developed countries do not need to make any cuts.
30. The latest developments on agriculture, together with updates on the negotiating positions of countries, can be monitored on the WTO dedicated website: www.wto.org/english/tratop_e/agric_e/agric_e.htm.
31. Safeguards are temporary limitations on market access to deal with market disruption, and the negotiations aim to set up procedures and discipline for governments using these.
32. For example, 'cheddar' now refers to a particular type of cheese not necessarily made in Cheddar, in the UK.
33. The controversy on genetically modified organisms (GMO) is a good example of the problems arising when dealing with trade and environment. Products containing GMOs could be denied access to domestic markets if considered dangerous by the importing state (the WTO has already ruled against this procedure), or could be requested to have a specific label explicitly indicating that they contain GMOs, thus leaving the choice to

the consumers. The latter seems to be the general orientation of the WTO, and hence specific rules have to be agreed on labelling.

34. Many officials in developing countries believe that the campaign to bring labour issues into the WTO is actually an attempt by industrial nations to undermine the comparative advantage of lower-wage trading partners.
35. A vehicle currency (let us call it *B*) is defined as a currency that is used in the foreign exchange markets as a means to exchange two other currencies, *A* and *C*, so that currencies *A* and *C* are not exchanged directly (*AC*) but via *B* in two transactions (*AB* and *BC*). In the foreign exchange markets, most transactions between relatively illiquid currencies are effected via vehicle currencies because of lower transaction costs, and in order to avoid excess intra-day volatility (ECB, 2003).
36. Debt securities comprise both instruments with long-term maturities (bonds and notes) and short-term maturities (money market instruments).

11. Conclusions

Writing the conclusions to a book that discusses a continuing process of integration is never easy, since there is no actual conclusion. To ease the task, we have decided to split the issue into two sections: the first section recalls the main themes and subjects tackled by the book, while the second looks at what has been left out of the book, and yet it may constitute an important challenge for the future of the EU. The first section may thus be read as a summary of the risks and opportunities that lie ahead of the enlarged Europe, and which were dealt with in detail in the book, while the second section may be read as a sketchy account of those risks and opportunities that lie ahead of the enlarged Europe and which were not dealt with in detail in the book.

11.1 THE LOGIC AND THE OBJECTIVES OF THE ENLARGED EU

Far too often, in our professional and academic life, we have experienced discussions and analyses of the EU and its policies undertaken in a way which is, to say the least, piecemeal and centred on details, thus leading to a major confusion between the trees and the forest. In other words, we believe that a credible and informed discussion on, say, the EU agricultural policy or the EU competition policy, can only take place if the logic, the values and the objectives of the EU have been made explicit at the outset. Understanding, explaining and discussing the logic, the values and the objectives of the EU is the major objective of this book. The first chapter is entirely dedicated to this purpose, presenting the **European social model** as a policy framework that tries to achieve simultaneously the three objectives of **growth**, **stability** and **cohesion**. We are confident that our willingness to keep this general logic of integration in the background of any detailed explanation is apparent throughout the book.

After the introductory chapter, the book falls into two parts. Chapters 2 to 5 are dedicated to the economic framework of Europe, that is to the microeconomic and macroeconomic fundamentals of the Union, their theoretical underpinning and the policies aiming at ensuring a sound EU economic policy. Chapters 6 to 10 are dedicated to five of the most important

EU policies. We have selected these five policies because of their importance and economic impact, and because, in their governance, the EU plays a larger role than the national level.

Chapters 2 and 3 look at the EU **Customs Union** and **Single Market**, while Chapter 4 deals with the **Economic and Monetary Union**. The theoretical foundations of these steps in the integration process are analysed in depth, as well as the current open issues and the implications of the EU enlargement. These chapters support one of the main theses of our book: sustained and sustainable growth for Europe can only come from a dynamic, competitive and non-secluded (neither sectorially nor nationally) single market, provided macroeconomic discipline and stability is achieved. In other words, we consider the EU tension towards macroeconomic stability as a necessary (but not sufficient) condition for growth. In addition to that, Europe needs an open and dynamic microeconomic policy for its single market in order to reach the sustainable growth that it wants to achieve. This interaction between macro and micro measures to achieve sustainable growth in Europe is the objective of the so-called **Lisbon Agenda**, which constitutes the subject of the fifth chapter. The Lisbon Agenda is also the framework within which 'sustainable' growth is defined: that is, growth with a high level of social cohesion, respecting natural resources and the environment. Chapter 5 dips into the question of cohesion within the EU, showing the originality of the EU together with its ability, even in periods of slow growth, to ensure and defend, over the last 35 years, the highest world level of social cohesion. To preserve these results in a Union of 25, soon to be 27 (if not more) countries, will probably be the single greatest challenge of the coming years for the EU.

Chapter 6 looks at the **EU budget** and its evolution in the period 2007–13, while Chapters 7 and 8 look at two main policies pursued by the EU, the **Common Agricultural Policy** and the **Cohesion Policy**. Consistent with the earlier chapters, these policies are analysed against the objectives they are supposed to attain (namely growth and cohesion), in comparison with the possible alternatives and having regard to the governance of these instruments in the enlarged Europe. The conclusion of these three chapters is that the EU budget and its policies have solid roots in the past, but are now certainly in dire need of a major overhaul if they are to play a major role in helping the Union to achieve sustainable growth with social cohesion.

Chapters 9 and 10, finally, deal with **competition policy** and the **EU external policy** (that is essentially the EU commercial policy and the deriving EU position in the world). The conclusion of these two chapters is that these policies, whose governance is such that the EU level largely dominates the national level, have been, to our mind not by chance, instrumental in allowing the Union to become the success story that it represents today.

11.2 THE FUTURE OF THE ENLARGED EU IN THE GLOBAL WORLD

This book has also argued that, historically, the European Union has always been the equilibrium result of two forces: one aimed at **widening** its geographical scale, enlarging the European institutions to accept new member states; the other directed at **deepening** the scope and pervasiveness of its actions within national and local policy making. The deepening versus widening tension has in fact characterised several moments of the integration process. To recall but a few examples, mentioned throughout the book, the widening of the EU to Spain and Portugal in the 1980s induced the deepening of EU policies in the new field of economic and social cohesion; to the contrary, the deepening of the 1990s in the field of monetary policy prevented the member states from successfully enlarging the EU institutions at the time of drafting the Amsterdam Treaty (1997), paving the way for the reforms then agreed in Nice in 2000, when the process of monetary unification was (at least from an institutional point of view) already completed.

In the early years of the twenty-first century, the EU successfully, and quite remarkably, managed to propose jointly its widening to ten new states, who became official EU members in May 2004, and a further deepening of its institutions and policies, with a Constitutional Treaty politically agreed by the (now) 25 member states on 18 June 2004, and then signed in Rome on 29 October of the same year. The two forces, however, have not yet reached an equilibrium: in terms of widening the Union, Romania and Bulgaria are expected to become EU members by 2007, Croatia possibly by 2009, and a timetable for the start of negotiations on the future membership of Turkey has been agreed; in terms of deepening, the Constitutional Treaty has started a very uncertain process of ratification by the 25 member states (see *infra*).

Not surprisingly, the outstanding pace at which such a new, still changing and uncertain institutional framework was established has left clear traces in the attitude of the citizens and member states towards the integration process. On the one hand, the tremendous deepening in the scope and extent of the EU policies has brought 'Brussels' into the day-to-day activities of national policy making. In fact, as we have shown throughout the book, member states have realised that in the current world state of affairs the effectiveness of their policies is heavily dependent on joint, commonly agreed actions, and hence they have attributed greater and greater competences to the EU institutions. However this process has made the same institutions vulnerable to the twists and turns of the daily political process. In other words, even in the most enthusiastic and convinced member state, there is no longer a sacred or fideistic concept of Europe, whose ultimate goals and ideals have to be shared and proclaimed; rather the process of European unification is finally leaving the politically correct vacuity of formal declarations of intents, to become more and more a very substantial and very actual constraint on the national (and local) policy making at almost a daily level. European policies are consequently subject to the standard, brutal mechanisms shaping the national political process.

On the other hand, the recent enlargement of the Union to new members, and the controversial Turkey question, has left many people with a sense of confusion about the general shape and scope of the entire project. Borders and bounds have in fact always helped in the definition of identities, while the European process, if successful, aims at removing them at an increasingly rapid rate. As a result, there is a risk that the success of integration might translate into a dilution of its ultimate sense.

The question, then, is whether, after 50 years, the concept of European unity is rooted enough in citizens and policy makers to survive its success without a backlash. The outcome of the 2004 European elections is quite revealing in this regard: by and large, a rising turnout rate in the old member states, but characterised by a vote of protest against the ruling governments, and a very low turnout rate (below 40 per cent) in the new member states. Clearly this is a sign that the joint process of substantial deepening and widening into which the Union plunged in these years has yet to find an equilibrium among EU citizens.

As a result it is legitimate to speculate on the type of actions that, in the next few years, might be able to rebalance the current status of development of the EU integration process, bringing it to a full and definitive maturity. In our opinion, two types of actions will be needed in this regard. On the one hand, it is necessary to fill the gaps inevitably left by the sudden acceleration of the integration process: to guarantee a better working of the single market induced by structural, supply-side reforms (the Lisbon agenda), in order to generate proper growth rates for the EU economies; to implement a better governance of the non-monetary side of the Economic and Monetary Union, in order not to jeopardize the stability of the process; to achieve results quickly in the fight against rising regional inequalities, which are undermining the social and economic cohesion of the enlarged Union. Not surprisingly, the most important remaining loopholes are related to the key joint objectives of the European economic and social model: growth, stability and cohesion. Consequently we have extensively discussed their origin, rationale and possible future throughout the previous chapters of the book.

On the other hand, it is of the utmost importance for the future of the Union to quickly stabilise the dynamics of deepening and widening that are still currently and substantially modifying its underlying framework. More detailed, precise and stable guidelines have to be defined in at least three key policy areas: the Common Foreign and Security Policy (CFSP), the process of ratification of the Constitutional Treaty and the future enlargements of the Union.

11.2.1 The Future of the Common Foreign and Security Policy

As far as the CFSP is concerned, we have already discussed at several points in the book the importance, given the complex worldwide situation, of an efficient multinational (European) reply to global challenges, even from a military perspective. Such a scenario is not only perfectly rational from an analytical point of view,[1] but it is also highly desirable to the vast majority of EU citizens, as revealed by a series of polls repeated over the years by the EU statistical office. Moving on from these considerations, and actually without stirring up too much public opinion, the EU has started, for the first time, to find serious answers in its quest of becoming a global player.

During the December 2003 European Council in Brussels, the heads of state and government approved the so-called **European Security Strategy**, the basic charter identifying the principles under which the EU will use its political (and possibly military) power to act as a global player.[2] Under this strategy, the EU commits itself to addressing threats to its security, making a wide use of two key principles: (a) the concept of **preventive engagement**, that is, the predisposition to act directly abroad, intervening before a crisis occurs;[3] (b) the principle of **effective multilateralism**, that is, the promotion and development of stronger, well-functioning international institutions, the only ones seen as able to guarantee a rule-based order worldwide.

Surprisingly these political statements did not remain void declarations, but had an operational follow-up: the heads of state and government endorsed in June 2004 the so-called **Headline Goal 2010**, the document defining in detail the main parameters for the development of EU military capabilities with a 2010 horizon, notably the definition of the minimum force packages, based on the battlegroup concept, to be provided by the various member states. The goal is to be able to take the decision to launch an operation within five days of the acknowledgement of a crisis by the Council, and to deploy the forces and start to implement the mission on the ground no later than ten days after the EU decision to launch the operation. Specific milestones have been set with respect to these targets in the various fields of military operations, and progress has been surprisingly rapid.[4]

More generally, after the drawbacks of the Iraqi crisis, there seem to be signs of an increased political will by the EU member states to project their power onto global scenarios, an issue far more important, and more effective, that the mere preparation and display of military hardware. The next few years will reveal how committed the member states are to implementing this key policy area for the future of the Union.

11.2.2 The Ratification of the Constitutional Treaty

In terms of the internal institutional developments, there is still a strong degree of uncertainty in relation to the process of approval and ratification of the EU Constitutional Treaty, which is an entirely new treaty, not simply an amendment to an old one. The same draft treaty signed in Rome foresees that, in case of problems in the ratification by some members, the European Council can decide on how to proceed if at least four-fifths of the member states have already ratified it. At the time of going to press the Treaty has been ratified by 13 member states (Austria, Belgium, Cyprus, Germany, Greece, Hungary, Italy, Latvia, Lithuania, Luxembourg, Malta, Slovakia and Slovenia) with a total of around 200 million people, which is already more than 50 per cent of the citizens of the EU, while its ratification has been rejected in two member states (France and The Netherlands, with a total of 72 million citizens).

In spite of the numbers just quoted, the French 'Non' and the Dutch 'Nee' have provoked a shock wave in the EU, essentially because this pronouncement came from two EU founding member states, and because it came from popular referenda.[5] However, the complexity of the Constitutional Treaty is such that, in our opinion, a popular referendum very easily risks becoming a hostage of national politics, with people voting on issues only remotely connected to the European project. In fact, opinion polls taken in both countries after the two rejections seem to suggest that among the main reasons behind the results are: the depressed economic situation, the fear of globalisation and its impact on the labour market, some nostalgia for the national currencies existing before the Euro, and the fears generated by the 2004 enlargement and even more by the foreseen 2007 enlargements to include Bulgaria and Romania, not to mention the more distant and hypothetical, but very controversial, possible enlargement to Turkey.

Following the French and Dutch rejections, the June 2005 European Council decided to postpone the deadline for national ratifications, initially foreseen for November 2006. Some of the remaining 13 member states have declared their will to go forward with the ratification process, while others seem more inclined to take a 'reflection pause' and to better explain to their citizens the rationale and the purpose behind the EU Constitutional Treaty. In the words of the European Council: 'this period of reflection will be used to enable a broad debate to take place in each of our countries, involving citizens, civil society, social partners, national parliaments and political parties. This debate, designed to generate interest, which is already under way in many member states, must be intensified and broadened. The European institutions will also have to make their contribution, with the Commission playing a special role in this regard'. The European Council of June 2006, under Austrian Presidency, is due to take stock of the progress undertaken, and to decide on the way forward.

At the time of going to press, it is impossible to forecast the overall mood of European citizens in mid-2006. Certainly the future prospects of the institutional dimension of the EU integration process will depend on the economic situation, on the ability of Europe to reach a convincing agreement on EU financial perspectives, on the state of ratifications in the remaining countries in Europe and on many other issues. We are convinced, however, that excessive pessimism is out of proportion and that, while the current difficulties experienced by the EU institutions in the link with its citizens should not be underestimated, the political and economic rationale for 'an ever closer' integration remain as strong as ever.

11.2.3 The Borders of the European Union

A final, but equally fundamental, question to be decided by the EU in the next few years is related to the definition of its own borders. Even if we do not necessarily find this consistent with the current, globalised world, borders have historically been functional to the definition of social and political identities, and identities define by and large the interplay of geopolitics on a global scale.[6] The European Union, therefore, needs to deliver to its citizens a clear view of what its geopolitical space is going to look like. No serious discussion has started yet on this issue, but nowadays, especially at the time when Turkey is negotiating its membership with the European Union, it is time for the debate to emerge. Hence it is of the utmost importance for these issues to be considered extensively in the definition of our new European Neighbourhood Policy (see Chapter 10).

Failing to do so would be internally very dangerous, since this lack of clarity risks increasing the sense of confusion and anxiety among EU citizens, with the risk of a powerful backlash in the integration process when that process goes back to the people for its final approval. The outcome of the recent European elections or the outcome of the referenda on the Constitutional Treaty should serve as a warning in this respect.

A lack of clarity on the geopolitical borders of Europe is also dangerous from an external point of view. The 2004 political crisis in Ukraine probably would not have emerged with such force, had the EU attitude with respcct to this and other neighbouring countries been delivered with clarity in the past. In other words, the success of the EU integration process in terms of peace and prosperity, and the ability displayed by the Union to actually enlarge this process to other countries, act as a powerful catalyst, not only for the legitimate aspirations of many citizens living in neighbouring countries, but also for the (equally legitimate) preoccupations of other countries, traditionally occupying a well-determined area of strategic geopolitical influence.

Paradoxically, therefore, it is the success of the European Union, this outstanding and unprecedented construction in the relations of states, that is condemning the Union to keep on acting, without drawing back from its forward momentum. We hope that our policy makers and all of us, the EU citizens, will be able meet the challenge.

NOTES

1. All the models of political economy (see, for example, Alesina *et al.*, 2001a) point to the fact that joint actions are optimal when the economies of scale of a given policy are high and the heterogeneity in the degree of preferences is low; by and large, and notwithstanding the divisions on the Iraqi crisis, all analysts agree that this is the situation faced by the EU member states as far as the CFSP is concerned.
2. 'The increasing convergence of European interests and the strengthening of mutual solidarity of the EU makes us a more credible and effective actor. Europe should be ready to share in the responsibility for global security and in building a better world', *European Security Strategy*, p. 1.
3. 'With the new threats, the first line of defence will often be abroad. The new threats are dynamic . . . This implics that we should be ready to act before a crisis occurs. Conflict prevention and threat prevention cannot start too early', *European Security Strategy*, p. 7.
4. The evolution of the EU Common Foreign and Security Policy, together with the relevant documents and an update on the EU peace-keeping and peace-enforcing missions worldwide, are available at http://ue.eu.int, under the Secretary General home page.
5. The ratification process is subject to nation-specific procedures: some member states approve the EU treaties via parliamentary ratifications (for example, Italy or Germany), others via a popular referendum (for example, Denmark and Ireland). France decided to change its Constitution to allow for a popular referendum. An updated situation of the ratification status in the various member states can be found at: http://europa.eu.int/futurum/ratification_en.htm.
6. Still today, a large part of international trade flows among non-protectionist countries are characterised by the so-called 'home-bias puzzle', with trade within borders being of several orders of magnitude larger than trade across borders (Obstfeld and Rogoff, 2000).

References

Acemoglu, D., P. Aghion and F. Zilibotti (2002), 'Distance to frontier, selection and economic growth', NBER Working Paper no. 9066, Washington, DC.

Akerlof, G., W.T. Dickens and G.L. Perry (2000), 'Near-rational wage and price setting and the optimal rates of inflation and unemployment', *Brookings Papers on Economic Activity*, **1**, 1–45.

Alesina, A. and R. Perotti (1995), 'The political economy of budget deficits', *IMF Staff Papers*, **42**, 1–31.

Alesina, A. and R. Perotti (2004), 'The European Union: a politically incorrect view', *Journal of Economic Perspectives*, **18**(4), 27–48.

Alesina, A., I. Angeloni and F. Etro (2001a), 'The political economy of international unions', NBER Working Paper no. 8645, Washington, DC.

Alesina, A., O. Blanchard, J. Gali, F. Giavazzi and H. Uhlig (2001b), 'Defining a macroeconomic framework for the Euro area', MECB Report no. 3, CEPR, London.

Alesina, A., S. Danninger and M. Rostagno (2001c), 'Redistribution through public employment: the case of Italy', IMF Staff Paper, **48**(3), Washington, DC.

Alesina, A., S. Ardagna, R. Perotti and F. Schiantarelli (2002), 'Fiscal policy, profits, and investment', *American Economic Review*, **92**, 571–89.

Alessandrini, S. (ed.) (2000), *The EU Foreign Direct Investment in Central and Eastern Europe*, Milan: Giuffrè Editore.

Altomonte, C. and C. Bonassi (2002), 'Regional disparities and the location of economic activities. An empirical test on a sample of EU regions', IEP-Bocconi Working Paper no. 3–2002, Applied Economics Series.

Altomonte, C. and P. Depace (2003), 'An enlarged Economic and Monetary Union: effects and policy implications', in F. Praussello (ed.), *The Economics of EU Enlargement*, Milan: Franco Angeli.

Altomonte, C. and C. Guagliano (2003), 'The location of FDI in Central and Eastern Europe vs. the Mediterranean countries', *Economic Systems*, **27**, 223–46.

Andrés, J., I. Hernando and D. López-Salido (2000), 'Assessing the benefits of price stability', Banco de España, *Estudios Económicos*, **69**, Madrid.

Areeda, P.E. and D. Turner (1975), 'Predatory pricing and related practices under section 2 of the Sherman Act', *Harvard Law Review*, **88**, 697–733.

Badinger, H., G.W. Muller and G. Tondl (2004), 'Regional convergence in the European Union, 1985–1999: a spatial dynamic panel analysis', *Regional Studies*, **38**(3), 241–53.

Bagwell, K. and R.W. Staiger (1999), 'An economic theory of GATT', *American Economic Review*, **89**(1), 215–48.

Balassa, B. (1975), *European Economic Integration*, Amsterdam: North Holland.

Baldwin, R.E. (1989), 'On the growth effects of 1992', *Economic Policy*, **9**, 248–81.

Baldwin, R.E. (1992), 'Measurable dynamic gains from trade', *Journal of Political Economy*, **100**, 162–74.

Baldwin, R.E. and C. Wyplosz (2003), *The Economics of European Integration*, New York: McGraw Hill.

Baldwin, R.E., J.F. Francois and R. Portes (1997), 'The costs and benefits of eastern enlargement: the impact on the EU and Central Europe', *Economic Policy*, **12**, 127–70.

Baldwin, R.E., E. Berglof, F. Giavazzi and M. Widgrén (2001), '*Nice* try: should the Treaty of Nice be ratified?', MEI Report no. 11, CEPR, London.

Barr, J. and F. Passarelli (2004), 'Who has the power in the EU?', Working Papers, Rutgers University, no. 2004–005, Newark.

Barro, R. (1996), 'Inflation and growth', *Federal Reserve Bank of St. Louis Review*, **78**, 153–69.

Barro, R. and R. Gordon (1983), 'Rules, discretion and reputation in a model of monetary policy', *Journal of Monetary Economics,* **12**, 101–21.

Baumol, W.J., J.C. Panzar and R.D. Willig (1982), *Contestable Markets and the Theory of Industry Structure*, New York: Harcourt Brace Jovanovich.

Beetsma, R. (2001), 'Does EMU need a stability pact?', in A. Brunila, M. Buti and D. Franco (eds), *The Stability and Growth Pact*, Hundsmills: Palgrave.

Begg, I., N. Grimwade and P. Price (1997), 'The own resources of the European Union: analysis and possible developments', Report prepared for the Directorate-General for Research of the European Parliament, draft 19 August.

Bertola, G. (1999), 'Convergence . . . an overview', in R. Baldwin, D. Cohen, A. Sapir and A. Venables (eds), *Market Integration, Regionalism and the Global Economy,* Cambridge: Cambridge University Press.

Bhagwati, J. (1999), 'Regionalism and multilateralism: an overview', in J. Bhagwati, P. Krishna and A. Panagariya (eds), *Trading Blocs*, Cambridge, MA: MIT Press.

Blanchard, O. (2004), 'The economic future of Europe', *Journal of Economic Perspectives,* **18**(4), 3–26.

Boeri, T., A. Borsch-Supan and G. Tabellini (2001), 'Would you like to shrink the welfare state? The opinions of European citizens', *Economic Policy*, **16**, 7–50.

Boeri, T., G. Bertola, H. Brücker, F. Coricelli, A. de la Fuente, J. Dolado, J. Fitzgerald, P. Garibaldi, G. Hanson, J. Jimeno, R. Portes, G. Saint-Paul and A. Spilimbergo (2002), 'Who's afraid of the big enlargement?', CEPR Policy Paper no. 7, London.

Boldrin, M. and F. Canova (2001), 'Inequality and convergence: reconsidering European regional policies', *Economic Policy*, **16**, 205–53.

Bordo, M.D. and L. Jonung (1999), 'The future of EMU: what does the history of monetary unions tell us?', NBER Discussion Paper no. 7365, Washington, DC.

Bourguignon, F. and C. Morrisson (2002), 'Inequality among world citizens: 1820–1992', *American Economic Review*, **92**(3), 727–44.

Breuss, F. (2001), 'Macroeconomic effects of EU enlargement for the old and the new members', WIFO Working Paper no. 143/2001, Vienna.

Buti, M. and G. Giudice (2002), 'Maastricht's fiscal rules at ten: an assessment', *Journal of Common Market Studies*, **40**, 823–48.

Buti M. and M. Nava (2003), 'Towards a European budgetary system', EUI Working Papers, no. RSC 2003/8, Florence.

Buti, M. and A. Sapir (1998), *Economic Policy in EMU*, Oxford: Oxford University Press.

Buti, M., S. Eijffinger and D. Franco (2003), 'Revisiting the stability and growth pact: grand design or internal adjustment?', CEPR Discussion Paper no. 3692, London.

Canzoneri, M.B. and B. Diba (1996), 'Fiscal constraints on central bank independence and price stability', CEPR Discussion Paper no. 1463, London.

Chisik, R. (2003), 'Gradualism in free trade agreements: a theoretical justification', *Journal of International Economics*, **59**, 367–97.

Collignon, S. (2003), *The European Republic: Reflections on the Political Economy of a Future Constitution*, Washington, DC: The Federal Trust.

Conceição, P. and P. Ferreira (2000), 'The young person's guide to the Theil index: suggesting intuitive interpretations and exploring analytical applications', UTIP Working Paper no. 14, University of Texas, Austin.

Corden, W.M. (1971), *The Theory of Protection*, Oxford: Clarendon Press.

Corden, W.M. (1997), *Trade Policy and Economic Welfare*, 2nd edn, Oxford: Clarendon Press.

Crafts, N. (2004), 'Globalisation and economic growth: a historical perspective', *The World Economy*, **27**(1), 45–58.

Crockett, A., A. Fatàs, A. Siebert, R. Strauch and J. von Hagen (2003), 'Stability and growth in Europe: towards a better pact', MEI Report no. 13, CEPR, London.

Davis, D. and D. Weinstein (1999), 'Economic geography and regional production structure: an empirical investigation', *European Economic Review*, **43**, 379–407.

Davis, D. and D. Weinstein (2003), 'Market access, economic geography and comparative advantage: an empirical test', *Journal of International Economics*, **59**, 1–23.

Davies, S. and M. Hallet, (2002), 'Interactions between national and regional development', HWWA Discussion Paper no. 207, Hamburg.

De Grauwe, P. (2000), 'Monetary policies in the presence of asymmetries', *Journal of Common Market Studies*, **38**(4), 593–612.

De Grauwe, P. and M. Polan (2003), 'Globalisation and social spending', CESIfo Working Paper no. 885, Munich.

De la Fuente, A. (2002), 'On the sources of convergence: a close look at the Spanish regions', *European Economic Review*, **46**, 569–99.

Deardorff, A. (ed.) (2004), *The Past, Present and Future of the European Union*, London: Palgrave.

Denis, C., K. McMorrow, W. Röger and R. Veugelers (2005), 'The Lisbon Strategy and the EU's structural productivity problem', *European Economy*, Economic Papers Series no. 221, Brussels.

Deutsch, K.G. and B. Speyer (eds) (2001), *The World Trade Organization Millennium Round*, London: Routledge.

Eichengreen, B. and F. Ghironi (2002), 'EMU and enlargement', in M. Buti and A. Sapir (eds), *EMU and Economic Policy in Europe: the Challenge of the Early Years*, Cheltenham, UK and Northampton, MA, USA: Edward Elgar.

Eichengreen, B. and D.J. Mathieson (2000), 'The currency composition of foreign exchange reserves: retrospect and prospect', IMF Working Paper no. WP/00/131, Washington, DC.

EU Council (2000), 'Presidency conclusions of the Lisbon European Council', 23 and 24 March 2000 (available at http://ue.eu.int).

European Central Bank (2003), 'Review of the international role of the Euro', December.

European Commission (1968), 'Memorandum on agriculture reform in the European Community', COM(68) 1000, Brussels.

European Commission (1977), *Report of the Study Group on the Role of Public Finance in European Integration* [better known as the 'MacDougall Report'], Brussels.

European Commission (1985a), 'Completing the internal market', White

Paper from the Commission to the European Council (Milan, 28–29 June 1985), COM(85) 314, Brussels.
European Commission (1985b), 'Perspectives for the common agricultural policy', COM(85) 333, Brussels.
European Commission (1987), 'The Single Act: a new frontier for Europe', COM(87) 100 [better known as 'Delors I package'], Brussels.
European Commission (1988), 'The economics of 1992', *European Economy*, **35**, Brussels.
European Commission (1990), 'One market, one money', *European Economy*, **44**, Brussels.
European Commission (1992), 'From the Single Act to Maastricht and beyond: the means to match our ambitions', COM(92) 2000 [better known as 'Delors II package'], Brussels.
European Commission (1996a), *The Single Market and Tomorrow's Europe*, Brussels.
European Commission (1996b), 'Taxation in the European Union', SEC(1996) 487 final, paper presented at the Verona Informal Ecofin Council of April 1996.
European Commission (1997), *Agenda 2000: For a stronger and wider EU* (vol. 1), and *Agenda 2000: The challenge of enlargement* (vol. 2), Luxembourg: Office for Official Publications of the European Communities.
European Commission (1999), 'Agenda 2000, financing the European Union, Commission report on the operation of the own resources system', bulletin, Supplement 2/99.
European Commission (2001a), 'The economic impact of enlargement', *Enlargement Papers*, **4**, June.
European Commission (2001b), *Unity, Solidarity, Diversity for Europe, its People and its Territory: Second Report on Economic and Social Cohesion*, Luxembourg: Office for Official Publications of the European Communities.
European Commission (2002a), *European Union Public Finance*, Luxembourg: Office for Official Publications of the European Communities.
European Commission (2002b), 'State aid scoreboard', COM(2002) 242 final, Brussels.
European Commission (2002c), 'Strengthening the coordination of budgetary policies', COM(2002) 668, Brussels.
European Commission (2002d), 'A project for the European Union', Communication from the Commission', COM(2002) 247, Brussels.
European Commission (2003a), 'Public finances in EMU', *European Economy*, 3/2003, Brussels.

European Commission (2003b), 'European competitiveness report 2003', SEC(2003) 1299, Brussels.
European Commission (2003c), 'Allocated expenditure report', July (available yearly at http://europa.eu.int/comm/budget/agenda2000/reports en.htm).
European Commission (2003d), 'Second progress report on economic and social cohesion', COM(2003) 34 final, Brussels.
European Commission (2003e), 'Proposals for a CAP reform', COM(2003) 23 final, Brussels.
European Commission (2003f), 'Key structural challenges in the acceding countries: the integration of the acceding countries into the Community's economic policy co-ordination processes', *European Economy*, Occasional Paper no. 4, Brussels.
European Commission (2004a), *A New Partnership for Cohesion. Third Report on Economic and Social Cohesion*, Luxembourg: Office for Official Publications of the European Communities.
European Commission (2004b), 'Progress report on the Financial Services Action Plan' (available at http://europa.eu.int/comm/internal_market /en/finances/ actionplan/index.htm).
European Commission (2004c), 'Strengthening economic governance and clarifying the implementation of the Stability and Growth Pact', COM(2004) 581 final, Brussels.
European Commission (2004d), 'Economic forecasts, Spring 2004', *European Economy*, 2/2004, Brussels.
European Commission (2004e), 'Building our common future. Policy challenges and budgetary means of the enlarged Union 2007–2013', COM(2004) 101, Brussels.
European Commission (2004f), 'Proposal for the new structural funds regulations', COM(2004) 492 final, Brussels.
European Commission (2004g), 'White paper on Services of General Interest', COM(2004) 374 final, Brussels.
Feldstein, M. (ed.) (1999), *The Costs and Benefits of Price Stability*, Chicago: University of Chicago Press and NBER.
Forslid, R. and I. Wooton (1999), 'Comparative advantage and the location of production', CEPR Discussion Paper no. 2118, London.
Fujita, M., P. Krugman and A. Venables (1999), *The Spatial Economy: Cities, Regions and International Trade*, Cambridge, MA: MIT Press.
Furse, M. (2002), *Competition Law of the UK and EC*, Oxford: Oxford University Press.
Galì, J. (2002), 'Monetary policy in the early years of EMU', in M. Buti and A. Sapir (eds), *EMU and Economic Policy in Europe: the Challenge*

of the Early Years, Cheltenham, UK and Northampton, MA, USA: Edward Elgar.

Galì, J., S. Gerlach, J. Rotemberg, H. Uhlig and M. Woodford (2004), 'The monetary policy strategy of the ECB reconsidered', MECB Report no. 3, CEPR, London.

Giavazzi, F. and M. Pagano (1990), 'Can severe fiscal contractions be expansionary? Tales of two small European countries', *NBER Macroeconomics Annual*, **5**, 75–111.

Giavazzi, F., T. Jappelli and M. Pagano (2000), 'Searching for non-linear effects of fiscal policy: evidence for industrial and developing countries', NBER Working Paper no. 7460, Washington, DC.

Giudice, G., A. Turrini and J. in t'Veld (2003), 'Can fiscal consolidations be expansionary in the EU? Ex-post evidence and ex-ante analysis', *European Economy*, Economic Papers Series no. 195, Brussels.

Goulard, S. and M. Nava (2002), 'Vers un financement plus démocratique de l'Union européenne', *Revue Française des Finances Publiques*, **80**, December.

Gros, D. and N. Thygesen (1998), *European Monetary Integration*, 2nd edn, London: Addison-Wesley.

Gros, D., J.F. Jimeno, T. Mayer and N. Thygesen (2003), *Adjusting to Leaner Times*, 5th Annual Report of the CEPS Macro-Economic Group, Brussels: CEPS.

Grubel, H. (1967), 'Intra-industry specialization and the pattern of trade', *Canadian Journal of Economics and Political Science*, **22**, 374–88.

Haaland, J., H. Kind, K. Midelfart-Knarvik and J. Torstensson (1999), 'What determines the economic geography of Europe?', CEPR Discussion Paper no. 2072, London.

Hallet, M. (2000), 'Regional specialisation and concentration in the EU', *European Economy*, Economic Papers Series no. 141, Brussels.

Hubbard, R.G. (2002), 'An agenda for global growth', Council of Economic Advisers, Washington, DC.

Jonung, L. (2002), 'EMU and the euro – the first 10 years', *European Economy*, Economic Papers Series no. 165, Brussels.

Keen, M. (1995), 'Objectives and criteria of the community's fifth own resource', study prepared for the Commission of the European Economy DG-XIX, Final Report, December.

Keller, W. (2004), 'International technology diffusion', *Journal of Economic Literature*, **43**(3), 752–82.

Kok, W. (chair) (2004), 'Facing the challenge. The Lisbon strategy for growth and employment', Report from the High Level Group, November.

Korah, V. (2004), *An Introductory Guide to EC Competition Law and Practice*, 8th edn, Oxford: Hart Publishing.

Krueger, A. (1997), 'Free trade agreements versus customs unions', *Journal of Development Economics*, **54**(1), 169–87.

Krugman, P. and M. Obstfeld (2003), *International Economics – Theory and Policy*, 6th edn, Boston, MA: Addison-Wesley.

Kydland, F. and E. Prescott (1977), 'Rules rather than discretion: the inconsistency of optimal plans', *Journal of Political Economy*, **85**(3), 473–92.

Leonardi, R. (2003), *Regional Policy in the European Union: The Role of Cohesion in the Building of a United Europe*, Basingstoke: Palgrave.

Littlechild, S. (1986), 'Three types of market process', in R.N. Langlois, (ed.), *Economics as a Process*, Cambridge: Cambridge University Press.

London Economics (2002), 'Quantification of the macro-economic impact of integration of EU financial markets' (joint with Price Waterhouse Coopers and Oxford Economic Forecasting), Final Report to the European Commission–DG Internal Market, November.

Mairate, A. and R. Hall (2000), 'Structural policies', in L. Tsoukalis (ed.), *Competitiveness and Cohesion*, Oxford: Oxford University Press.

Messerlin, P.A. (2001), *Measuring the Costs of Protection in Europe*, Washington, DC: Institute for International Economics.

Micossi, S. (2002), 'Economic policy co-ordination and policy regimes in the European Union', XIV Villa Mondragone International Economic Seminar, June, Rome.

Midelfart-Knarvik, K.H. and H.G. Overman (2002), 'Delocation and European integration: is structural spending justified?', *Economic Policy*, **17**, 321–60.

Mishkin, F.S. and A. Posen (1997), 'Inflation targeting: lessons from four countries', *Federal Reserve Bank of New York Economic Policy Review*, **3**, 9–110.

Moesen, W. and M. Nava (2004), 'A note on a SMART stability and growth pact', IIPF Conference 2004, Milan, August.

Morrisson, C. and F. Murtin (2004), 'Inequality among Europeans (1970–2000)', report for the European Commission, mimeo.

Motta, M. (2004), *Competition Policy: Theory and Practice*, Cambridge: Cambridge University Press.

Mundell, R. (1961), 'A theory of optimal currency areas', *American Economic Review,* **53**, 657–64.

Nava, M. (2000), *La Finanza Europea,* Rome: Carocci Editore.

Nava, M. (2004), 'L'allargamento dell'Unione Europea: questioni finanziarie, di competitività e di crescita', *L'Industria*, 2/2004, 219–40.

Obstfeld, M. and K. Rogoff (2000), 'The six major puzzles in international macroeconomics: is there a common cause?', *NBER Macroeconomics Annual*, **15**, 339–90.

OECD (2000), *The European Union's Trade Policies and their Economic Effects*, Paris: OECD.

OECD (2003a), *OECD Agricultural Outlook 2003–2008*, Paris.

OECD (2003b), *Farm Household Income, Issues and Policy Responses*, Paris.

Ottaviano, G. and D. Puga (1998), 'Agglomeration in the global economy: a survey of the "New Economic Geography"', *The World Economy*, **21**(6), 707–32.

Padoa-Schioppa, T., M. Emerson, M. King, J.C. Milleron, J.H.P. Paelinck, L.D. Papademos, A. Pastor and F.W. Scharpf (1987), *Efficiency, Stability and Equity: A Strategy for the Evolution of the Economic System of the European Community*, [better known as the 'Padoa-Schioppa Report'], Oxford: Oxford University Press.

Panagariya, A. (2002), 'EU preferential trade arrangements and developing countries', *The World Economy*, **25**(10), 1415–32.

Perotti, R. (1999), 'Fiscal policy in good times and bad', *Quarterly Journal of Economics*, **114**, 1399–436.

Persson, T. and G. Tabellini (2004), 'Constitutional rules and fiscal policy outcomes', *American Economic Review*, **94**(1), 25–45.

Puga, D. (2002), 'European regional policy in light of recent location theories', *Journal of Economic Geography*, **2**(4), 372–406.

Radaelli, C. (2003), 'The open method of coordination, a new governance architecture for the European Union?', SIEPS Working Paper no. 1, Bradford.

Resmini, L. (2004), 'Economic integration and industry location in transition countries', 31st EARIE Conference, Berlin, August.

Rivera-Batiz, L.A. and M.A. Oliva (2003), *International Trade: Theory, Strategies and Evidence*, Oxford: Oxford University Press.

Robson, P. (1998), *The Economics of International Integration*, 4th edn, London: Routledge.

Rodrik, D. (2002), 'Feasible globalisations', NBER Working Paper no. 9129, Washington, DC.

Roland, G. (2001), *Transition and Economics – Politics, Markets and Firms*, Cambridge, MA: MIT Press.

Rose, A.K. (2004), 'Do we really know that the WTO increases trade?', *American Economic Review*, **94**(1), 98–114.

Saint-Paul, G. (1996), *The Political Economy of Labour Markets Reform*, Oxford: Oxford University Press.

Saint-Paul, G. (2004), 'Why are European countries diverging in their unemployment experience?', *Journal of Economic Perspectives*, **18**(4), 49–68.

Salvatore, D. (2003), *International Economics*, 8th edn, New York: Wiley.

Sapir A., P. Aghion, G. Bertola, M. Hellwig, J. Pisani-Ferry, D. Rosati, J. Viñals, H. Wallace, M. Buti, M. Nava and P.M. Smith (2004), *An Agenda for a Growing Europe: The Sapir Report* [better known as the 'Sapir Report'], Oxford: Oxford University Press.

Sargent, T. and N. Wallace (1981), 'Some unpleasant monetarist arithmetic', *Federal Reserve Bank of Minneapolis Quarterly Review*, **5**, 1–17.

Schumpeter, J.A. (1942), *Capitalism, Socialism, and Democracy*, London: Allen & Unwin.

Secchi, C. and C. Altomonte (2002), *L'euro, una moneta, una Europa*, Venice: Marsilio.

Smith, A., A.J. Venables and M. Gasoriek (1992), '1992: trade and welfare – a general equilibrium model', in A. Winters (ed.), *Trade Flows and Trade Policy after 1992*, Cambridge: Cambridge University Press.

Tabellini, G., E. Berglof, B. Eichengreen, G. Roland and C. Wyplosz (2003), 'Built to last: a political architecture for Europe', MEI Report no. 12, CEPR, London.

Taylor, J. (1998), *Inflation, Unemployment, and Monetary Policy*, Boston, MA: MIT Press.

Tharakan, P. (2002), 'European Union and preferential arrangements', The World Economy, **25**(10), 1387–98.

Theil, H. (1967), *Economic and Information Theory*, Amsterdam: North-Holland.

Thisse, J., S. Anderson and A. de Palma (1992), *Discrete Choice Theory of Product Differentiation*, Cambridge, MA: MIT Press.

Venables, A. (2000), 'Regional economic integration', *International Encyclopedia of the Social and Behavioral Sciences*, Amsterdam: Elsevier Science.

Veugelers, R. and H. Vandenbussche (1999), 'European anti-dumping policy and the profitability of national and international collusion', *European Economic Review*, **43**, 1–28.

Vickers, J. (1995), 'Concepts of competition', *Oxford Economic Papers*, **47**(1), 1–23.

Viner, J. (1950), *The Customs Union Issue*, London: Stevens & Sons.

Williamson, O.E. (1968), 'Economies as an antitrust defence: the welfare trade-offs,' *American Economic Review*, **58**, 18–36.

World Bank (2002), *Transition. The First Ten Years*, Washington, DC: World Bank.

WTO (2003), *Understanding the WTO*, September, Geneva.

Index

Abbreviations used in the index include:
CAP: Common Agricultural Policy
CCP: Common Commercial Policy
CEECs: Central and Eastern European Countries
DDA: Doha Development Agenda
ECB: European Central Bank
EMU: Economic and Monetary Union
EU: European Union
GATS: General Agreement on Trade in Services
OECD: Organisation for Economic Cooperation and Development
SGP: Stability and Growth Pact
WTO: World Trade Organisation